UNIX AND SHELL PROGRAMMING

B.M. HARWANI

Founder & Owner
Microchip Computer Education (MCE)
Ajmer

OXFORD

UNIVERSITY PRESS

OXFORD
UNIVERSITY PRESS

Oxford University Press is a department of the University of Oxford.
It furthers the University's objective of excellence in research, scholarship,
and education by publishing worldwide. Oxford is a registered trade mark of
Oxford University Press in the UK and in certain other countries.

Published in India by
Oxford University Press
YMCA Library Building, 1 Jai Singh Road, New Delhi 110001, India

ISBN-13: 978-0-19-808216-3
ISBN-10: 0-19-808216-9

Typeset in Times
by Quick Sort (India) Private Limited, Chennai
Printed in India by Raj Kamal Electric Press, Kundli, Haryana

Dedicated to my mother,
Nita Harwani
Mom, whatever I am today is
because of the moral values taught by you.

I also pay tribute to the officers,
men and women of all ranks,
of the Indian Armed Forces.
I salute these brave, patriotic, and disciplined people
for serving our country.

Features of the Book

AWK Script
Interprocess Communication
Unix System Administration and Networking

Comprehensive Coverage

The book provides comprehensive coverage of all aspects of the Unix operating system, its associated shells, and the scripting language. Dedicated chapters on AWK scripting, tools and debuggers, and system administration and networking are also provided.

Exclusive Coverage of Shells

Dedicated chapters on all the three shells—C, Bourne, and Korn—are provided in the book.

Bourne Shell Programming
Korn Shell Programming
C Shell Programming

4.2.5 groups: Displaying Group Membership

The groups command is used for finding the group to which

Syntax   groups username1 [username2 [username3 …]]

Example

(a) % groups chirag
    mba
    This example asks the group name of the user, chirag.

Lucid Representation of Commands

Each command in the book is represented by its syntax, followed by one or more examples with all possible options, and a description of the examples for ease of understanding.

Complete Scripts with their Outputs

The book gives the complete scripts along with their outputs. This will help students implement the concepts learnt in an easy manner.

The following script prints that particular day's date only.
```
printdate
#!/bin/bash
m=`date +%d/%m/%Y`
echo "Current system date is $m"
```
Output
```
Current system date is 26/02/2012
```

Table 4.3 Brief description of modes used with the chmod command

Mode	Description
r or 4	Represents read permission
w or 2	
x or 1	

■ FUNCTION SPECIFICATION ■

Command	Function
chmod	It changes file/directory permissions.
umask	It stands for user file creation mask and sets the default permissions of the files that will be created in the future.
chown	It transfers ownership of a file to another user. Once the ownership of a file is transferred to another user, one cannot change its permissions until they become the owner again.

Tabular Representation of Extensive Information

Several tables are provided in the book in support of the text for representing several command options and descriptions.

Notes

Numerous notes are interspersed with the text for providing extra, yet relevant, information.

Note: If a directory does not have an execute permission we will never be able to enter data into it.

Note: The output from dd can be a new file or another storage device.

Objective Type Questions

State True or False

5.1 All devices are considered as files in Unix.
5.2 All device files are stored in /etc or in its subdirectories.

Multiple-choice Questions

5.1 The fdisk command is used to
(a) format a disk
(b) remove bad sectors from a disk
(c) create partitions
(d) repair a file system
5.2 The gzip command compresses the file with the extension

Fill in the Blanks

14.1 The IPC mechanisms that are used in Unix are _____, _____, and _____.

14.2 A pipe is a buffer that implements communication between two processes, one of which is considered a _____ and the other, a _____.

Objective-type Questions

Objective-type questions put to test a reader's theoretical knowledge gained after reading the chapter. These include State True or False, Fill in the Blanks, and Multiple-choice Questions. Answers to these questions are provided at the end of every chapter.

Brain Teasers

Apart from various review questions and programming exercises, several brain teasers have been provided at the end of each chapter to promote analytical thinking of the readers. This will also help them think outside the box.

Brain Teasers

5.1 In long listing command ls -l, if you find a file with mode field set to 1, what does it mean?
5.2 Correct the following command to backup a hard disk to a file.

```
$ dd if=/file.dd of=/dev/hda
```

Preface

Unix operating system, developed in the 1960s, is regarded as one of the most powerful operating systems, due to its portability and usage in almost all kinds of environments. It is the result of the combined efforts of many people—students, professors, researchers, and commercial companies. It is a multitasking and multi-user operating system that is portable on several hardware platforms and is very secure. It provides a rich set of tools and utilities that help administrators, programmers, and users, to a great extent, in executing their tasks. Besides this, Unix offers the flexibility of controlling individual jobs executed by a user.

Since its inception, Unix has been evolving constantly and has given rise to various products such as Linux, Ubuntu, FreeBSD, SunOS, Solaris, SCO, and AIX. In order to understand and learn these products that are widely in use, it is imperative for users to have a clear understanding of the root, that is, the actual Unix operating system—its features, management of devices and files, implementation of security, scheduling of CPU, and memory management.

Nowadays, Unix and its by-products are used as servers and in developing mobile applications. Unix has also served as a model for the development of the Internet, thus shifting the focus of computers towards the creation of networks.

ABOUT THE BOOK

The book has been designed to cater to students, teachers, professionals, and developers to help them learn the fundamental concepts of the Unix operating system. It follows a bottom-up approach, that is, it explains basic commands and gradually moves towards advanced commands. Similarly, it begins with small and easy scripts and makes the reader acquainted with the fundamental statements, loops, and conditional statements in a systematic manner. Gradually, it moves on to explain large, complex, and critical scripts. The book focuses on advanced Unix commands that perform critical functions such as setting access permissions, changing ownerships of the files, sharing files among groups, performing input/output (I/O) redirections, cutting or slicing the file vertically, pasting content, comparing files, and printing documents. It explains in detail the manipulation of processes and signals and the role of system calls. All the major editors in Unix, namely, stream editor (sed), visual editor (vi), and modeless editor (emacs) are explained in detail.

The book describes Bourne, Korn, and C shell programming and covers all important topics and commands associated with these shells. It also includes numerous programming scripts for better understanding of the three types of shells. The later part of the book includes dedicated chapters on language development tools (Yacc, Lex, and M4), text-formatting tools (troff and nroff), and Unix networking and administration.

KEY FEATURES

The book is packed with numerous student-friendly features that are described here.
- Complete scripts along with their outputs are provided for easy implementation of the concepts learnt.
- Each command is explained with its syntax with the help of multiple examples.

- Several options of a single command have been provided in a tabular format along with their function, description, and examples for quick understanding and usage.
- Numerous notes are interspersed with the text for providing additional relevant information.
- Around 1000 solved examples and over 900 end-chapter exercises (with answers to objective-type questions) are provided.
- Specially designed brain teasers are provided at the end of most chapters for the readers to develop an analytical approach to problem-solving.
- A variety of objective-type questions—state true or false, fill in the blanks, and multiple-choice questions—are provided at the end of every chapter for testing the understanding of the concepts learnt.
- Several review questions and programming exercises are provided for the reader to practise the commands and scripts explained in the chapters.

ONLINE RESOURCES

The companion website of the book, http://oupinheonline.com/book/harwani-unix-shell-programming/9780198082163, provides the following additional resources:

For faculty
- Chapter-wise PowerPoint Slides
- Answers to select programming exercises given in the book

For students
- Chapter-wise executable and complete shell scripts and codes for all the programs given in the book
- Mail Organizer—a small project that sends mail to the desired recipient on a given date
- Inventory Management System—a small project that explains maintenance of inventory using MySQL database server
- Debugging exercises with solutions
- Flashcards—for active recall of all important Unix commands

ORGANIZATION OF THE BOOK

The book is organized into 15 chapters.

Chapter 1, Unix: An Introduction, focuses on the fundamentals of operating systems, history of Unix, structure of the Unix operating system, Unix environment, and different types of shells.

Chapter 2, Unix File System, explains the different types of regular and device files, organization of a file system, accessing, mounting, and unmounting a file system, different blocks of a file system, and structure of inode blocks.

Chapter 3, Basic Unix Commands, describes basic commands such as logging into the system, changing the password, checking who is logged in, displaying date and time of the system, and dealing with file operations such as creating files, displaying their contents, deleting files, creating links to files, renaming files, and moving files. The chapter also explains commands for maintaining directories, creating a directory, changing the current directory, removing a directory, displaying calendars, using basic calculators, displaying information about current systems, deleting symbolic links, and exiting from a Unix system.

Chapter 4, Advanced Unix Commands, discusses advanced commands such as setting access permissions for the existing files and directories, setting default permissions for the newly created files and directories, creating groups, changing ownerships of the files, and sharing files among groups. The chapter covers commands for sorting content, performing I/O redirections, cutting the file vertically, pasting content, splitting files, counting characters, words, and lines in files, using the pipe operator, comparing files, eliminating and displaying duplicate lines, among others.

Chapter 5, File Management and Compression Techniques, explains the types of devices, role of device drivers, and the way in which devices are represented in the Unix operating system. It details different disk-related commands required for copying, formatting, finding usage, finding free space, and making partitions. It also covers compression and decompression of files.

Chapter 6, Manipulating Processes and Signals, focuses on processes and their address space, structure, data structures describing the processes and process states, commands related to scheduling processes at the desired time, handling jobs, and switching jobs from the foreground to the background and vice versa. It explains suspending, resuming, and terminating jobs, executing commands in a batch, ensuring process execution even when a user logs out, increasing and decreasing the priority of processes, and killing processes. The chapter also discusses signals, their types, and the methods of signal generation, virtual memory and its role in executing large applications in a limited physical memory, and mapping of a virtual address to the physical memory.

Chapter 7, System Calls, is devoted to the role of system calls in performing different tasks. The chapter explains system calls that are used in file handling operations such as opening, creating, reading from and writing to files, closing, deleting, and linking to files, changing file access permissions, accessing file information, and relocating and duplicating file descriptors. The chapter covers the system calls that perform different tasks related to directory handling such as changing, opening, and reading directories. The chapter throws light on the system calls involved in process handling operations such as the exec(), fork, and wait system calls and those that deal with memory management—allocating memory, freeing memory, changing the size of the allocated memory, file locking, and record locking .

Chapter 8, Editors in Unix, explains the usage of the stream editor (sed) in filtering out the desired data from the specified file, inserting lines, deleting lines, saving filtered content into another file, loading the content of another file into the current file, and searching for content that matches specific patterns. The chapter also explains the visual editor (vi) and the modeless editor (emacs).

Chapter 9, AWK Script, discusses the role of the AWK scripts in filtering and processing content. It explains the different functions used in AWK for printing results, formatting output, and searching for desired patterns. The chapter also details different operators (comparison, logical, arithmetic), functions (string, arithmetic, and search and substitute), and built-in variables to perform the desired operations quickly and with the least effort. It also discusses different loops to perform repetitive tasks, taking input from the user to perform operations on the desired content.

Chapter 10, Bourne Shell Programming, explains different command line parameters used in Bourne shell scripts, conditional statements, loops, reading input, displaying output, testing data, translating content, and searching for patterns in files. The chapter also covers displaying the exit status of the commands, applying command substitution, sending and receiving messages between users, creating and using functions, setting and displaying terminal configurations, managing positional parameters, and using fetch options in the command line.

Chapter 11, Korn Shell Programming, helps us in understanding different features of the Korn shell, command line editing, file name completion, command name aliasing, command history substitution, and meta characters. It explains different operators, shell variables, basic I/O commands, command line arguments, if else and case statements, strings, files, loops, arrays, functions, and I/O redirection.

Chapter 12, C Shell Programming, describes the C shell and its different features. The chapter explains command history, command substitution, filename substitution (globbing), filename completion, and aliases. It also covers job control, running jobs in the background, and suspending, resuming, and killing jobs. It aids in the understanding of environment variables, shell variables, built-in shell variables, and customizing the shell and C shell operators. The chapter also discusses different flow control statements, loops, arrays, and errors.

Chapter 13, Different Tools and Debuggers, describes language development tools Yacc, Lex, and M4 and text-formatting tools, troff and nroff. The chapter covers different preprocessors for nroff and troff such as tbl, eqn, and pic. The chapter also discusses debugger tools, dbx, adb, and sdb.

Chapter 14, Interprocess Communication, covers pipes and messages as also accessing, attaching, reading, writing, and detaching the shared memory segment. It helps the readers in getting acquainted with initializing, managing, and performing operations on sockets (stream and datagram), I/O multiplexing, filters, and semaphores.

Chapter 15, Unix System Administration and Networking, discusses the Unix booting procedure, mounting and unmounting file systems, managing user accounts, network security, and backup and restore.

ACKNOWLEDGEMENTS

I thank my family, my small world: my wife, Anushka and my wonderful children, Chirag and Naman for inspiring and motivating me and forgiving me for spending long hours on the computer during the course of development of this book.

Speaking of encouragement, I must thank my students who, with their innumerable queries, helped me understand the essential expectations of a reader. This in turn made me add numerous examples and exercises, thus giving a practical approach to the book.

My acknowledgements would remain incomplete if I did not thank the editorial team at Oxford University Press, India, who supported me throughout the development of this book. My special thanks are due to the reviewers for their constructive comments and valuable suggestions.

I have tried to cover the necessary topics and explain them in a simple and user-friendly manner. Any comments or suggestions that can be incorporated in future editions of this book may be sent to me at bmharwani@yahoo.com.

B.M. Harwani

Brief Contents

Detailed Contents

Unix: An Introduction

> After studying this chapter, the reader will be conversant with the following:
>
> - Fundamentals of operating systems
> - History of Unix
> - Structure of the Unix operating system
> - Various types of shells and their responsibilities
> - Numerous features of the Unix operating system
> - The Unix environment

Even after four decades of use, Unix is regarded as one of the most powerful operating systems, due to its portability and usage in almost all kinds of environments, ranging from micro to supercomputers.

We cannot even think of using a computer system without an operating system. An operating system is an interface that enables the use of a computer system's resources; without an operating system, the computer will be a dead piece of electronic device.

In this chapter, before delving into the history and structure of Unix, we will attempt to understand the following: what an operating system is; why it is essential in running a computer system; and in what manner Unix is different from the other operating systems used earlier and in recent times.

1.1 OPERATING SYSTEM

An operating system is the main software component of a computer system. It provides users with an environment that makes it possible to use the hardware devices of a computer. Without an operating system, we cannot access any of the resources of the computer system, including its hardware and software. Examples of popular operating systems available nowadays include Android, BSD, iOS, LINUX, Microsoft Windows, Mac OS X, and z/OS. Apart from Microsoft Windows and z/OS, all the other operating systems in this list are Unix-based.

Let us understand how an operating system is related to hardware, software, and the users (see Fig. 1.1).

As depicted in Fig. 1.1, it is evident that users are able to interact with hardware through the operating system. The operating system as well as the software creates an environment for the user that enables easy access and use of hardware. Basically, the operating system creates an interface between the user and the hardware.

The following section discusses the functions that an operating system performs, which enable easy operation of a computer system.

1.1.1 Functions of Operating Systems

An operating system performs the following functions:

Memory and data management All operating systems provide methods for controlling data in the memory. When a job has to be performed, the operating system should allocate the memory for loading that job into the memory.

Communication An operating system should support methods in such a manner that the various computer systems can communicate with one another for exchange of data.

Time sharing Time sharing enables several people to use the same computer simultaneously. A few operating systems support time-sharing features.

Security In a multi-user environment, security should be provided by the operating system. This security prevents one user from interfering with the work done or being done by another user. It also prevents unauthorized personnel from using the computer system.

User-command interpretation This is a function of the operating system using which the commands that are typed in by the user are read and interpreted by the operating system. Through interpretation, the operating system understands what the user wants.

Accounting Through this function, the operating system keeps an account of all the resources used by different processes. *Resources*, here, means memory, CPU, disk space requirement, and so on.

Program development tools All operating systems provide program development tools, which assist users in writing and maintaining programs. Software development is one of the important features provided by the operating system.

Scheduling A scheduler is the heart of all multi-user operating systems. This program enables many people to use the computer simultaneously. The scheduler assigns the CPU time slice to the ready process. After that time slice, the process is stored in the wait queue, the next process in the ready queue is picked, and the CPU pays attention to it.

Swapping When several users are working simultaneously, their processes are stored in the memory. When the memory is full and a new process has to be activated, the scheduler takes the current process in the memory and copies it to the hard disk. Next, the scheduler starts a new process in the space freed in the memory. This process is known as *swapping*. After returning to the time slice, the process that was swapped out of the memory is brought in (swapped in), and some other process is swapped out. This feature is available in a virtual memory environment.

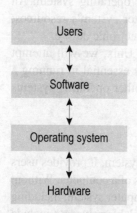

Fig. 1.1 Operating system in relation to hardware, software, and users

1.2 HISTORY OF UNIX

The development of the Unix operating system began in 1957 and had its roots in Bell Labs. The growth of this wonderful, multitasking, highly powerful, affordable, and secure operating system was not an accident, but the result of the joint efforts of many people, including students, professors, researches, and commercial companies. A short date-wise history of the evolution of Unix is given here.

In 1957, Bell Labs required an operating system for their in-house computer centre. They created BESYS to sequence their jobs and to control the system resources. However, they wanted a more efficient operating system.

In 1964, the researchers from General Electric, MIT, and Bell Labs came together and created a new general-purpose, multi-user, time-sharing operating system known as Multiplexed Information and Computing System (Multics).

In 1969, the Multics project was withdrawn because of the high cost of development and due to differences among its members. When this happened, Ken Thompson, Dennis Ritchie, Douglas Ritchie, and Douglas Mcllroy, along with a few others, began working on Uniplexed Information and Computing System (UNICS) by using an old PDP-7 computer. The name *Unics* was then shortened to *Unix*. While working on the early assembly versions of Unix, Thompson worked on a FORTRAN compiler that evolved to support the language B, which was a smaller version of BCPL.

In 1971, the first edition of Unix appeared along with the B compiler. It introduced several well-known Unix commands including cat, chdir, chmod, chown, and cp. Together it included more than 60 commands. However, it did not have the pipe feature. Some of the utilities in this first edition were written in the B compiler. In the next few years, Dennis Ritchie rewrote the B compiler and developed the C compiler.

In 1972, the second edition of Unix was released.

In 1973, the third edition of Unix appeared along with the Unix C compiler (cc). The kernel was still written in assembly language. The pipe feature was also introduced in this version.

In 1973, the fourth edition of Unix was released. The kernel was rewritten in the C compiler.

In 1974, the fifth edition of Unix was released. The source code was made freely available to universities for educational purposes. Unix also spread outside AT&T and Bell Labs and was provided to academic institutions at a very small charge. It became very popular, as it was inexpensive, could run on the available hardware, was provided along with the source code, and was written in a programming language that was easier to understand. In 1974, Thompson taught Unix for a year at the University of California, Berkeley. When Thompson returned to Bell Labs, students and professors at Berkeley continued to enhance Unix. This led to the formation of the Berkeley Software Distribution, which was commonly known as BSD.

In 1975, the sixth edition of Unix was released. This edition, also known as V6 UNIX, was the first edition that was available outside Bell Labs.

In 1977, 1BSD, the first edition, was released; in 1978, 2BSD, the second edition, was released.

In 1979, the seventh edition of Unix was released. This edition was released along with Steve Bourne's shell (sh). The kernel was rewritten to make it more portable to other types of architecture. At this point, the Unix systems group (USG) was created, and it was focused on enhancing the seventh edition. Three groups were working in all and the original versions of Unix were developed by the computer research group (CRSG) of Bell Labs. The support for internal releases was provided by the USG. The task of developing and writing tools was done by another group at Bell Labs, the programmer's workbench (PWB).

The development of Unix split into two main branches: System 5 (SYSV) and Berkeley software distribution (BSD). BSD was developed by students and professors at the University of California, Berkeley. SYSV was developed by AT&T and other commercial companies. In 1979, 3BSD, the third edition, was released.

In 1980, 4.0BSD, the fourth version of the BSD Unix variant, was released.

In 1982, AT&T transferred its Unix development to Western Electric, which developed the System III version of Unix.

In 1983, Western Electric released System V, whereas System IV was reserved for only AT&T's use.

In 1984, the USG group, which was renamed the UNIX system development laboratory (USDL) group, released System V Release 2 (SVR2), which was the first version of Unix that supported paging, shared memory, and other associated features.

In 1985, the eighth edition of Unix was released on the basis of the 4.1BSD version.

In 1987, the USDL group, which was renamed AT&T Information Systems (ATTIS) group, released System V Release 3 (SVR3).

In 1988, the ninth version of Unix was developed, and it was based on the 4.3BSD version.

In 1989, the tenth version of Unix was developed.

Unix is one of the most popular operating systems, which was developed step by step, as evident from the aforementioned timeline.

Let us now have a broad overview of the Unix system.

1.3 OVERVIEW AND FEATURES OF UNIX SYSTEM

The Unix system is a multitasking, multi-user operating system that is portable on several hardware platforms and which is quite secure. It also provides a rich set of tools and utilities that help administrators, programmers, and users, to a great extent, in executing their tasks. Besides this, the system provides the flexibility of controlling individual jobs executed by the user.

Some of the important features of the Unix operating system are as follows:

1. Multitasking
2. Multi-user
3. Portability
4. Job Control
5. Tools and Utilities
6. Security

1.3.1 Multitasking

Unix is a multitasking operating system, that is, it can execute multiple tasks simultaneously. In a multitasking environment, the CPU processes a task and when the process waits for an input/output (I/O) operation to be completed, the CPU switches to another task. The switching between tasks is so fast that it appears that the operating system is executing all the tasks simultaneously. Due to multitasking, we can carry out several tasks simultaneously.

For instance, commands for printing a file, editing text, and managing files can be given simultaneously; all tasks are thus performed simultaneously. With the help of this feature, Unix maximizes the computer resource utilization and hence, the computer's efficiency.

1.3.2 Multi-user

The multi-user feature of Unix enables several users to work simultaneously and access system resources concurrently. The operating system not only receives commands from all the users, but also carries out the desired processing and responds accordingly. The operating system manages the consumption of system resources among the users and implements the locking mechanism to maintain the integrity and consistency of applications and data that are accessed simultaneously. The multi-user approach maximizes the computer resource utilization and hence reduces the cost per user. Since the system resources are shared, resource management is done so as to avoid any deadlock.

Note: *Deadlock* is a situation wherein two or more competing actions wait for each other to finish and, as a result, neither reaches completion.

1.3.3 Portability

Unix is portable, that is, it is available on a wide range of hardware. Since the Unix operating system is coded in a high-level language, C programming language, it is less hardware dependent and, hence, can be easily moved from one brand of computer to another without a major code rewrite. It is also the kernel that provides an interface between the hardware and other application modules. The application modules interface with the kernel and not the hardware, and hence, when Unix is ported to another hardware platform, only the kernel and not the application modules requires modification. This makes the operating system almost hardware independent and does not require much modification.

1.3.4 Job Control

Unix enables us to control the execution of jobs. For example, we can suspend or resume any job, switch a job from the background to the foreground, and kill a job. The jobs that require user interaction frequently need I/O operation, have specific time constraints, and are executed in the foreground. In foreground jobs, the shell waits for a job to be completed and only then displays a prompt to execute another job. Background jobs are those that are executed behind the scenes. Jobs of a lower priority do not require user interaction and are executed in the background. Suspended jobs are paused for a while and can be moved to either the background or the foreground. The job control feature of Unix enables users to execute several jobs and control them on the basis of their priority.

1.3.5 Tools and Utilities

Unix supports a number of tools and utilities that make the users' job easier. Tasks such as splitting files, merging files, searching for content in files, arranging files, and sending mail can be simply done by issuing certain commands. Unix not only has a vast library of system tools, but also has programming tools that provide a flexible platform for programmers and developers to create portable and efficient applications.

1.3.6 Security

Unix is considered a comparatively more secure operating system. Each user has an identity through a unique user ID and group ID. In order to avoid any unauthorized access, each file and directory has an owner and a group that are associated with it. Three permissions are attached to each file and directory—read, write, and execute. The set of permissions, r, w, and x, are associated with the three types of users—owners, groups, and others. Hence, we can individually assign the desired permissions to these three types of users. Next let us explore the structure of the Unix system.

1.4 STRUCTURE OF UNIX SYSTEM

The structure of the Unix operating system consists of four parts (as shown in Fig. 1.2): hardware, kernel, shell, and tools and applications. The various parts of the Unix system are discussed in detail in the following sections.

1.4.1 Hardware

Hardware refers to the physical components that collectively form a computer machine. The following three primary components constitute the hardware of a computer system:

I/O devices   Data is supplied or entered into the computer for processing through input devices such as keyboard, mouse, track ball, magnetic ink character recognition (MICR), optical character recognition (OCR), and optical mark recognition (OMR). Output devices display processed data. The two most common output devices are screen and printer.

Central processing unit   The central processing unit (CPU) is the heart of the computer. It obtains the data from the user through input devices, processes the entered data into information, and displays the information through output devices. The processed data can be saved in the memory for future use.

Memory   It is used for storing data and is of two types: primary and secondary. The primary memory includes RAM and ROM, out of which RAM is volatile in nature. While the data is being processed by the CPU, it is temporarily stored in the RAM. After processing, it is removed and replaced by new data, which has to be processed further. 'Volatile' means that the data stored in the RAM is temporary in nature, (i.e., it is overwritten by the new data and the whole data is lost on switching off the computer). The secondary memory includes hard disk drives, pen drives, CDs/DVDs, and so on. These devices are of a permanent nature, that is, once data is written in them, it will be stored until deleted by the user.

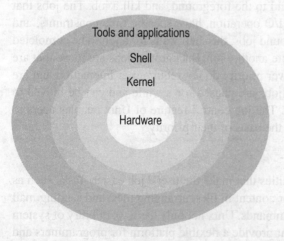

Tools and applications

Shell

Kernel

Hardware

Fig. 1.2   Structure of the Unix system

Note: Networking components such as LAN cards, cables, routers, and switches are also considered part of the hardware.

1.4.2 Kernel

The kernel is the heart of any operating system. Its main purpose is to ensure that the jobs of the operating system are performed properly. These jobs mainly include the scheduling of tasks, resource management, process management, and file management. *Resource management* refers to the allotment of CPU time, disk space, memory space, and so on to different processes. *Process management* includes the allocation of resources such as CPU, memory, and other devices. *File management* includes the management of files and their permissions, among others.

The kernel hides all the complexities of accessing hardware and provides a user-friendly interface by doing all the tasks behind the scene.

A brief view of the different tasks performed by the kernel is provided in Fig. 1.3.

Let us take a quick look at the operations that a kernel can perform:

1. It controls the execution of processes by enabling their creation, termination or suspension, and communication.
2. It schedules processes fairly for execution on the CPU. The processes share the CPU in a time-shared manner. The CPU executes a process; the kernel suspends it when its time quantum elapses and schedules another process to be executed. Later, the kernel reschedules the suspended process.
3. It allocates the main memory for an executing process. The kernel enables processes to share portions of their address space under certain conditions, but protects the private address space of a process from outside tampering. If the system runs low on free memory, the kernel frees the memory by writing a process temporarily to the secondary memory, which is called a *swap device*. If the kernel writes entire processes to a swap device, the implementation of the Unix system is called a *swapping system*, whereas if it writes pages of memory to a swap device, it is called a *paging system*.
4. It allocates secondary memory for efficient storage and retrieval of user data. This service constitutes the file system. The kernel allocates secondary storage for user files, reclaims unused storage, structures the file system in a well-understood manner, and protects unauthorized users from illegal access.

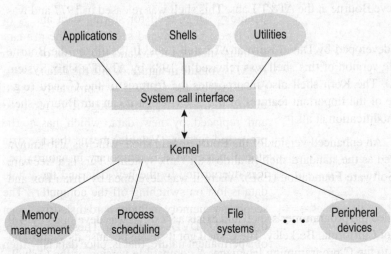

Fig. 1.3 Different tasks performed by the kernel

5. It allows processes-controlled access to peripheral devices such as terminals, tape drives, disk drives, and network devices.
6. It provides the necessary functionality to applications, shells, and utilities through the system call interface. The applications of all the respective systems are called in order to get certain tasks performed by the kernel.

After having understood the kernel and the tasks that it performs, we are ready to understand the next part of the Unix structure—the shell.

1.4.3 Shell

The shell is an interface between the user and the kernel. The kernel does not know human language; hence the shell accepts the commands from the user and converts them into a language that the kernel can understand. It is a program that interprets user requests, calls programs from the memory, and executes them one at a time. Several shells such as Bourne, Korn, Bourne-again, and C Shell are available.

The shell also provides the facility of chaining or *pipelining* commands. This means the output of one command is sent to the input of another command for further processing. In this manner, one input data can be processed by several commands.

There are two major parts of a shell. The first is the interpreter. The interpreter reads out commands and works with the kernel to execute them. The second part of the shell is a programming capability that enables us to write a shell (command) script. A shell script is a file that contains a collection of shell commands to perform a specified task. It is also known as a shell program.

Types of shells

Shells are independent of the underlying Unix kernel. This fact has enabled the development of several shells for Unix systems. Each type of shell has its own special features.

Bourne shell   It is the most common shell in Unix systems and was the first major shell. It was developed by Steve Bourne at the AT&T Labs. This shell was released in 1977 and was called 'sh'.

Korn shell   It was developed by David Korn at AT&Bell Labs. It is built on the Bourne shell. The most stable version of this shell was released in 1988 by AT&T's Unix System Laboratories as 'ksh'. The Korn shell also incorporates the features of the C shell (e.g., process control). One of the important features of this shell is that it can run Bourne shell scripts without any modification at all.

Bourne-again shell   An enhanced version of the Bourne-again shell, which is also known as 'bash', is distributed as the standard shell in almost all Unix systems. This is a freeware shell from the Free Software Foundation (FSF), where it was developed by Brian Fox and Chet Raney.

C shell   It is also called the programmer's shell and exists as 'csh.' It was developed by Bill Joy at the University of California, Berkeley. The C shell got its name because its syntax and usage is very similar to the C programming language. A compatible version of the C shell, 'tcsh' is used in Linux.

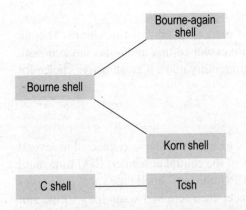

Fig. 1.4 Different shells in Unix operating system

The C shell is not always available on all machines. In addition, shell scripts written in the C shell are not compatible with the Bourne shell. Such scripts should be modified for working with the Bourne shell. One of the major advantages of the C shell (compared with the Bourne shell), however, is its ability to execute processes in the background.

The four shells are shown in Fig. 1.4. Tcsh is a compatible version of the C shell that is used in LINUX.

Both the Korn shell (ksh) and the Bourne-again shell (bash) are extensions of, and compatible with, the basic Bourne shell (sh). The original C Shell (csh) is only partially based on the Bourne shell and has been extended into a shell called the 'TC shell' (tcsh), which is a C Shell with some additional features. Since the TC shell is completely compatible with the C shell, it is also frequently referred to as the 'C shell'.

Until now, we have seen the functions that are generally performed by an operating system; we should also know the additional features of the Unix operating system.

1.4.4 Tools and Applications

Tools and applications are built-in modules that are used by the operating system to perform the tasks assigned by the user. These are available in the form of libraries that add special capabilities to the operating system. Irrespective of whether the task is to display date and time, find files, copy files, list files, or translate characters, among others, all tasks are performed through Unix utilities. The tools and utilites are categorized on the basis of the kind of tasks they perform. For example, file utilites do the tasks related to files: breaking text files into pieces, combining text files together, and sorting their contents. Other utilities such as grep, sed, and awk help in filtering or searching the desired content from the files.

Some of the most commonly used file-related Unix utilities are as follows:

1. `cp`: Copying files
2. `ln`: Linking one file to another
3. `ls`: Listing files or directory contents
4. `mv`: Moving or renaming files
5. `rm`: Removing files
6. `pr`: Printing files
7. `tr`: Translating characters

Usually an operating system is used in a single environment, but Unix is an operating system that can be used in several environments. Let us now have a brief discussion of the Unix environment.

1.5 UNIX ENVIRONMENT

Unix is a multi-user and multiprocessing operating system that can be used in three environments: stand-alone personal environment, time-sharing environment, and client–server environment.

1.5.1 Stand-alone Personal Environment

Unix can be installed on personal computers and used as stand-alone machines. Though the major features of the Unix operating system are exploited in a multi-user environment, its security features, multitasking capability, and portability make it an attractive choice for installation on personal computers.

1.5.2 Time-sharing Environment

A time-sharing environment is an environment in which a computer is connected to several terminals and all the terminals share the resources of the central computer: CPU time, hard disk, and printer. The central computer divides its CPU time into small time slices and serves each terminal in the time slot assigned to it. Hence, each terminal waits for its time slot to get its jobs processed by the central computer. Though this environment is economical, the total dependency on the central computer is its major drawback. If the central machine fails, all the terminals connected to it stop working, and hence, this environment is not very popular nowadays. Since all the tasks of the terminals are performed by the central CPU, it is overloaded and hence its response is very poor.

1.5.3 Client–Server Environment

The client–server environment is better than the time-sharing environment, as here, the central computer is not connected to dumb terminals but to workstations or PCs that have their individual processing power. As a result, all the processing tasks are not assigned to the central computer but are divided among the central computer and the connected workstations so that the local and small tasks can be processed at the workstation level (without bothering the central computer), and the main tasks (that require more resources) are transferred to the central computer. The workstations in this environment are known as clients, and the central computer (that serves the requests sent by the clients) is known as server. In this environment, dependency on the central computer is decreased and since the local tasks are performed at the client's level, the server is not overloaded, hence increasing its response time.

Note: We can customize the Unix shell environment by also making use of system variables known as environment variables, which will be discussed in Chapter 10.

■ **SUMMARY** ■

1. Operating systems provide an environment that makes it possible for us to use the resources of a computer, namely hardware and software. A few examples of modern-day operating systems include Android, BSD, iOS, LINUX, Microsoft Windows, Mac OS X, and z/OS.

2. The various functions that an operating system performs include memory and data management, interprocess communication, time sharing, security, user-command interpretation, accounting, program development, scheduling, and swapping.

3. In 1960, Multics started the development of the now well-known Unix operating system. Unix became commercially viable in 1973 when it was entirely recoded in C, thereby facilitating portability in other hardware. A typical structure of the Unix operating

system consists of hardware, a kernel, a shell, and various tools and applications.

4. The kernel is the heart of the operating system. It is defined as a nucleus of the operating system that manages all the resources and gets the task performed by the desired hardware.

5. A shell acts as an interface between a user and a kernel. Mainly four types of shells are available in the Unix operating system, namely Bourne shell (sh), C shell (csh), Korn shell (ksh), and Bourne-again shell (bash).

6. The main features of the Unix operating system are portability, multitasking, and multi-user capability.

7. Since Unix is a multiprocessing and multitasking operating system, it can be used in three different types of environments: stand-alone personal environment, time-sharing environment, and client–server environment.

8. Currently, Unix is also portable on mobile devices. Almost all mobile operating systems, including iOS, Android, and webOS, run on Unix or LINUX kernels.

■ EXERCISES ■

Objective-type Questions

State True or False

1.1 The Unics operating system was further developed to Unix.

1.2 An operating system creates an environment that enables us to use different resources of a computer system.

1.3 The Korn shell is the oldest of all shells.

1.4 The Korn shell and Bourne-again shell are not compatible with the Bourne shell.

1.5 Unix is a multi-user and multitasking operating system.

1.6 The Bourne-again shell (bash) was developed by David Korn.

1.7 The Korn shell was developed by Brian Fox and Chet Raney.

1.8 The Bourne shell derives its name from Stephen Bourne.

1.9 The shell manages all the resources and gets the tasks performed by the desired hardware.

1.10 Unix enables a user to run only one process at a time.

Fill in the Blanks

1.1 Unix operating system is written in _____ language.

1.2 BSD stands for _____.

1.3 The operating system creates an _____ between the user and the hardware.

1.4 C shell was developed by _____.

1.5 When a job has to be performed, the _____ should allocate the memory for loading that job into the memory.

1.6 In a _____ environment, the central

computer is connected to the workstations or PCs.

1.7 Unix treats each job or task as a _____.

1.8 Both the Korn shell (ksh) and the Bourne-again shell (bash) are extensions of, and compatible with, the _____ shell.

1.9 _____ prevents unauthorized personnel from using the computer system.

1.10 _____ schedules processes for execution on the CPU.

Multiple-choice Questions

1.1 Which of the following is the heart of any operating system?
   (a) Hardware (c) Software
   (b) Kernel   (d) Users

1.2 Korn Shell was developed by
   (a) David Korn   (c) Bill Joy
   (b) Steve Bourne (d) Ken Thompson

1.3 The default prompt of the C shell is
   (a) $ (b) % (c) cs (d) >
1.4 The three environments in which the Unix operating system can be used are stand-alone personal environment, time-sharing environment, and _____
   (a) client–server environment
   (b) LAN environment

   (c) WAN environment
   (d) isolated environment
1.5 The shell that is completely compatible with the C shell is
   (a) Korn shell
   (b) Bourne-again shell
   (c) TC shell
   (d) Bourne shell

Review Questions

1.1 Write short notes on the following:
   (a) Different tasks performed by the kernel
   (b) Role of shell in the Unix operating system
   (c) Structure of the Unix system
1.2 Explain the functions performed by an operating system.

1.3 How did the Unix operating system come into the picture? Briefly explain its history.
1.4 How many different types of shells are there? Explain in detail.
1.5 Explain the time-sharing and client–server environment of the Unix operating system.

■ ANSWERS TO OBJECTIVE-TYPE QUESTIONS ■

State True or False

1.1 True
1.2 True
1.3 False
1.4 False
1.5 True
1.6 False
1.7 False
1.8 True
1.9 True
1.10 False

Fill in the Blanks

1.1 'C'
1.2 Berkeley Software Distribution
1.3 interface
1.4 Bill Joy
1.5 operating system
1.6 client–server
1.7 process
1.8 Bourne
1.9 Security
1.10 Scheduler

Multiple-choice Questions

1.1 (b)
1.2 (a)
1.3 (b)
1.4 (a)
1.5 (c)

Unix File System

After studying this chapter, the reader will be conversant with the following:

- Unix files and their types
- Different types of device files
- Organization of a file system
- Accessing, mounting, and unmounting a file system
- Different blocks of a file system
- Structure of inode blocks

2.1 INTRODUCTION TO FILES

A file is a container of text, images, codes, and so on. Everything is a file on a Unix system. Not only the data, programs, and applications, but also the directories and input/output (I/O) devices are considered special kinds of files.

Generally, files are ordered in a hierarchical tree-like fashion with a root represented by the character, '/'. The directories are the internal nodes of the tree structure, while the files are considered to be the leaves. Let us learn about the different types of files in Unix.

2.1.1 Types of Files

The files are divided into the following three categories in the Unix operating system:

Ordinary files   These files contain only data.
Directory files   These files act as a container and can contain ordinary files and device files along with directory files.
Device files   These files represent all the hardware devices.

Ordinary files

We can store anything we want in these files. These files include data, source programs, objects, executable codes, Unix commands, and any file created by the user. Commands such as cat and ls are treated as ordinary files. An ordinary file is also referred to as a *regular file*.

The most common type of ordinary file is the text file. This is just a regular file that contains printable characters. For example, the programs that we write are text files. However, the Unix commands that we use or the C programs that we execute do not fall into the category of text files.

The characteristic feature of text files is that the data stored inside them is divided into groups of lines, with each line terminated by the newline character. This character is not visible, and it does not appear in the hard copy output. It is generated by the system when we press the <Enter> key.

Examples   letter.txt, bank.sh, payment

The files in Unix may or may not have any extension. The first two examples depict files with extensions .txt and .sh, respectively. The third example depicts a file without any extension. In most Unix systems, a filename can have approximately 255 characters. If we enter more than 255 characters while specifying a filename, only the first 255 characters are effectively interpreted by the system.

Note: We have to assign extensions for the AWK files or other programming files (e.g., C).

Directory files

A directory contains no external data, but it stores some details of the files and sub-directories it contains. The Unix file system is organized into a number of such directories and sub-directories, which can also be created as and when needed. We often need to group a set of files pertaining to a specific application. This enables two or more files in separate directories to have the same filename.

If a directory contains, for example, 10 files, there will be 10 entries in the directory file displaying information such as size of the file, date and time of creation, or last modification. When an ordinary file is created or removed, its entry in the corresponding directory file is automatically updated by the kernel with the relevant information about the file.

Note: The directory file contains the names of all resident files in the directory.

Examples   projects, shell_scripts

These examples show two directories named projects and shell_scripts.

Device files

In the Unix operating system, peripheral devices, terminals, printers, CD-ROMs, modems, disks, and tapes are treated as special files that are termed *device files*. The representation of devices in the form of device files simplifies the task of using them. For example, printing content on a printer is as simple as copying that content to the printer device file. A device file interacts with the device driver, making it possible for the user to directly interact with the device driver using standard I/O system calls, hence controlling the device more precisely.

There are two types of device files based on how data is read or written into them: character devices and block devices.

Character devices   Character devices are those in which the read and write operations are performed character by character, that is, one byte at a time. These devices are also known as *raw devices*. The read and write operations in these device files are performed in the actual transfer units of the device, that is, single characters at a time without collecting or combining them into a block. It is quite obvious that character devices are comparatively slow and have a large access time.

Examples include virtual terminals, terminals, and serial modems.

Block devices Block devices are those in which the read and write operations are performed one block at a time, where the size of one block can range from 512 bytes to 32 KB. When compared with character devices in which transactions are performed one character at a time, block devices are quite fast. Moreover, block devices use caching to reduce the access time. By caching, we mean that when a block device is accessed, the kernel reads the whole block into a buffer in the memory, so that future read and write operations are performed to the cached version in the memory, hence reducing the access time to a great extent. Finally, the modified buffer contents are written to block devices. The only drawback in using memory buffers is that if the system crashes before modified buffers are written into the block device, the data will be inconsistent. Hence, we need to periodically flush out the modified buffers to the block device.

Examples include hard disk, DVD/CD ROM, and memory regions.

Note: All device files are stored in the /dev directory.

2.1.2 Symbolic Links

A symbolic link is a special file that points to another existing file on the system. This link contains the path name of the file it is pointing to. We can create several names for the same file through symbolic links. In order to create symbolic links, the ln command is used, and for listing them, the long-listing command ls -l is used. These commands will be discussed in detail in Chapter 3. A brief introduction to these commands is as follows.

For example, let us assume we have a file letter.txt. Through the ln command, we can create its symbolic link in the file memo.txt as shown here:

Syntax `ln -s source destination`

Here, source is the absolute or relative path of the file whose link we want to create, and destination is the name of the link.

Example `ln -s letter.txt memo.txt`

The two filenames, letter.txt and memo.txt, refer to the same file, and changes made in either file will be reflected in the other file.

2.1.3 Pipes

Pipes are used for sending the output of a command as the input to another command. Pipes are created through the vertical bar character '|', which contains commands on either side. The output of the command on the left-hand side is sent as input to the command on the right-hand side. The syntax for creating a pipe is as follows:

Syntax `command1 | command2`

Example `ls | sort`

We will discuss two commands, ls and sort, in Chapter 3, but for the time being, it is enough to understand that the output of the ls command is sent to the sort command before outputting the result on the screen.

The pipe created through this syntax is known as *anonymous pipe*, because it is created and later destroyed when the process is over. command1 and command2 on either side of the pipe have their own file descriptors that are automatically closed when the process is over.

Apart from anonymous pipes, we can also create named pipes. As the name suggests, named pipes have specific names that are assigned to them, and exist as special files within the file system. Named pipes are known as first in first out (FIFO) because of two reasons. First, once the data is read from the pipe, it cannot be read again. Second, the order in which the data is read cannot be deviated. The named pipes are not automatically deleted as in the case of anonymous pipes but have to be explicitly deleted using the rm or unlink command. The command used for creating named pipes is mknod. The three commands, mknod, rm, and unlink, will be discussed in detail in Chapter 3.

2.1.4 Sockets

Socket files are used for transferring information between two processes that are running on different machines. Socket files are basically used as an interface between our Unix process and the networking protocol. For example, while accessing the Internet through a web browser, sockets are used to establish communication between the Unix process and the browser. The creation of socket files is explained in detail in Chapter 14.

2.2 ORGANIZATION OF FILE SYSTEMS

The file system is organized as a tree with a single root node called *root* (written as '/'); every non-leaf node of the file system structure is a directory of files, and files at the leaf nodes of the tree are directories, regular files, or special device files. The name of a file is indicated by a path name that describes how to locate the file in the file system hierarchy.

A path name is a sequence of component names that are separated by slash characters. A component is an arrangement of characters that designates a filename that is uniquely contained in the previous (directory) component. A full path name starts with a slash character and specifies a file that can be found by starting at the file system root and traversing the file tree, following the branches, which lead to successive component names of the path name.

Unix is an operating system that is divided into directories and sub-directories. The system programs and libraries are categorized according to their functions and placed in their respective directories. The forward slash (/) at the top of the tree is the root of the tree. All other directories are the sub-directories of the root directory as shown in Fig. 2.1.

The following is the list of directories and their contents:

bin Executable files are kept in this directory and these files can be run by users. After compilation, a program is converted into an executable binary and is usually kept in the /bin directory.

dev All the special files in the Unix file system, such as the keyboard or terminal device drivers, are kept in this directory.

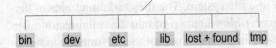

Fig. 2.1 List of files and directories in the Unix operating system

etc All administrative files of Unix are kept in this directory.

lib This is the central library storage for files that are commonly used by other programs. A library is a collection of files (usually binary) that can be shared among many processes. The advantage of having a library is that it is a single source of data and each program can use it without needing a unique copy of these executable functions for itself.

lost + found This is the most likely place where files can be found after the system crashes.

tmp Programs usually need extra space to store data on a disk. The /tmp directory is a directory used by programs that need extra buffer area in order to be executed.

Since the memory of a computer is limited in nature, we need to swap in the desired process and swap out the process whose task is done. This swapping is handled by a special file system known as the *swap file system*, which is discussed here.

Swap file system

Swapping is a useful technique that enables us to execute programs and manage files that are larger than the computer's primary memory. The program or file that we wish to execute or manage is logically split into small blocks that are known as *pages* or *segments*. One of the blocks is loaded into the primary memory where it can be worked on, whereas the remaining blocks of the program or file are stored in the physical disk drive. When a part of the program or file that is not in the primary memory is required, swapping takes place.

Swapping is an operation by which the block of the program or file in the primary memory is swapped out to the physical disk drive and the next block from the physical disk drive is loaded into the primary memory. Swapping continues until the desired block is loaded in the primary memory. The concept by which a system appears to have more memory than what it actually has is known as *virtual memory*.

In the Unix operating system, a partitition of hard disk can be treated as virtual memory. Thus, a separate partition known as swap partition is created on the disk that is meant to hold the swapped pages of the program or file. Every system should have a swap file system that is used by the kernel to control the movement of processes. When the system memory is heavily loaded, the kernel has to move processes out of the memory to this file system. When these swapped processes are ready to run, they are loaded back to the memory. Users cannot access this file system directly.

2.3 ACCESSING FILE SYSTEMS

Let us assume we have a device such as a floppy or CD containing a few files, and we want to view and access those files. The files on these devices make up an individual file system with its root as '/'. The file system on these devices will not be accessible by the Unix system unless it is mounted.

Mounting a file system means assigning the root directory of the new file system to a subdirectory of the root directory of our Unix system. The subdirectory on which the new file system is mounted is called the *mount point* of a file system. The files and directories in the new file system or mounted file system are accessible when we go into that subdirectory. By mounting a file system, it will become a non-distinguishable part of the existing file system. Basically, mounting is a procedure of making the main existing file system aware of the new file system.

2.3.1 Mounting File Systems

By mounting a file system of any device, we make its file and directories accessible through the existing Unix file system. The format of mounting a file system is as follows:

Syntax   `mount filesystem/devicename directory`

The device name or file system is mounted on the given directory. The directory, also known as *mount point*, is the name of the directory that the newly mounted file system will be assigned to.

Note: For the file system to be mounted on a particular directory, the directory should already exist on the current file system.

In order to mount a file system that has the special device name /dev/fd00 (for floppy disk 0) onto the existing /mnt directory, the following command is used:

```
#mount   /dev/fd00   /mnt
```

The new file system is simply an extension of the /mnt directory. We can view and access the files and directories of the mounted file system by changing the directory to the /mnt directory. We can also create directories and files in the /mnt directory sub-tree.

The mount point (/mnt) should usually be an empty directory, as we will not be able to access its original files and subdirectories once a file system is mounted on it. The files of the /mnt directory will be accessible only when the file system is unmounted.

The file system that is mounted to the main file system should be unmounted after its job is done. Before shutting down the Unix system, all the mounted file systems need to be unmounted; otherwise this may result in corruption of the content.

2.3.2 Unmounting File Systems

Unmounting a file system means detaching the mounted file system from the directory of the Unix system on which it was mounted. Once a file system is unmounted, we will not be able to access its files or directories.

A file system cannot be unmounted if any of its files or directories are still active, that is, if they are currently in use. If we try unmounting a file system whose file or directory is currently open, we get an error message, 'device busy'.

To unmount a file system that is mounted on any directory, first of all, we need to close all the open files and directories and then proceed to unmount it. We use the following command without any arguments, in order to know the file systems mounted within a file system:

```
mount
```

It gives a list of the mounted file systems. We might obtain the following output:

```
mounted        mounted over
/dev/fd00      /mnt
```

This output shows that the file system /dev/fd00 is mounted on the /mnt directory.

The command that is used for unmounting the mounted file system is umount. The following format is adopted for using the umount command:

Syntax   umount filesystem name/mount point

Example   The command to unmount the file system, /dev/fd00 that we mounted on the /mnt directory will be as follows:

umount /mnt

We cannot unmount the file system even if we are sitting in the same file system. Thus, unmounting the /dev/fd00 file system while sitting in the /mnt directory is not possible. We have to come out of the /mnt directory before giving the umount command.

Note: A file system cannot be dismounted if it is busy, that is, when a file or directory on that file system is being accessed.

Nowadays, floppy disk drives are no longer manufactured or used. Only for the sake of explaining mount and umount commands, the concept of floppy disk drives is used. In the currently available Unix operating systems (like Oracle Solaris 10, which we are using in this book) and Linux systems, CD ROMs, DVDs, and USB storage devices are automatically mounted without using the mount command. Thus, mount and umount commands are no longer needed in the currently available Unix operating systems or equivalents. The USB storage device is automatically mounted and is available under the /rmdisk directory, whereas the CD ROM/DVD is automatically mounted and available under the /cdrom directory. This also means that the following commands will navigate us to the CD ROM/DVD drive and will depict its contents:

```
$ cd /cdrom
$ ls
```

Table 2.1 gives a brief comparison of the file systems of Windows and Unix operating systems.

Table 2.1   Comparison between file systems of Windows and Unix operating systems

Unix	Windows
In Unix, the / (forward slash) represents a separator while defining the path to indicate a new directory level. The following command represents two directory levels, usr and projects: cd /usr/projects	In Windows, the \ (backslash) is used for defining the path. For example, the directory levels, usr and projects, in Windows are represented as follows: cd \usr\projects
In Unix, the forward slash (/) indicates the root directory, that is, the directory from where all other directories begin. All other hard disk drives, pen drives, CD ROM/DVD drives, etc., are accessed via the root (/) directory. For example, /cdrom represents the CD ROM drive.	In Windows (and in DOS), C:\ indicates the top-level directory of the file system. Other hard disk drives, floppy disk drives, and CD ROM/DVD drives are indicated by various top-level directory equivalents such as D:\ and E:\.
In Unix, the root account acts as the Unix administrator.	In Windows, there is an administrator account that performs the administrative tasks.

2.4 STRUCTURE OF FILE SYSTEMS

A file system is a group of files and directories that exists in the form of a tree-like structure with its root in the form of a root directory. A hard disk can be partitioned into several parts with each part having its own file system; there can be several file systems in a hard disk. A file system cannot be split on two different disks; it has to be entirely on a single disk.

A file system has the following four sections that are known as *blocks*: boot, super, inode, and data.

The first block of a file system is called the boot block, and it is followed by super, inode, and data blocks, as shown in Fig. 2.2.

| Boot block | Super block | Inode block | Data blocks |

Fig. 2.2   File system of Unix

2.4.1 Boot Block

The boot block is the first block of the file system that contains a small bootstrap program. The bootstrap program is a short program that is loaded by the basic input/output system (BIOS) on starting any computer. It checks and initializes the I/O devices and also loads the operating system. During bootstrapping, which is also known as *booting*, the master boot record (MBR) is loaded into the memory, which in turn, loads the kernel into the memory.

2.4.2 Super Block

The boot block is followed by the super block. This block contains global file information about disk usage and availability of data blocks and inodes. It also contains a pointer to the head of the free list of data blocks.

The super block consists of the following information:

1. Size of the file system
2. Number of free data blocks available in the file system
3. List of free data blocks available in the file system
4. The index of the next free data block in the free data block list
5. Size of the inode list
6. Number of free inodes available in the file system
7. List of free inodes in the file system
8. The index of the next free inode in the free inode list

Figure 2.3 shows a super block containing an array of free data block numbers and a pointer to the head of the free list of data blocks.

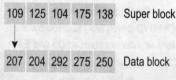

Fig. 2.3   List of free data blocks in super block

The values 109, 125, 104, 175, and 138 in this figure refer to the free data block numbers. The entry 109 is a data block that contains a pointer to an array of free data blocks. We assume that the index, which points to the next free data block in the free data block list, is pointing to the last data block number, which is 138.

When a process requests for a data block, it searches the free data blocks in the super block and returns the available data block

| 207 | 204 | 292 | 275 | 250 | Super block |

Fig. 2.4 List of free data blocks copied from data block to super block

pointed to by the index, that is, the data block number 138 will be returned and the index will shift to another data block in the list. Thus, after having assigned data block 138 to the requesting process, the index will shift to the point at the data block numbered 175, and the procedure will continue. If the super block contains only one entry, which is a pointer to the array of free data blocks, all the entries from that block will be copied to the super block free list as shown in Fig. 2.4.

As usual, the requesting process will continue to get block numbers from the ones listed in the super block.

2.4.3 Inode Block

Every file or directory has an inode number—a unique number that recognizes the file or directory in the file system. All inodes are stored in inode blocks.

We know that a hard disk is organized into blocks (or sectors) and a file stored in a hard disk may be scattered in different blocks. The addresses of these blocks (containing file parts) are stored in the form of a linked list in an inode block, that is, a table of blocks is maintained for each file. Each Unix file system has its own inode table in which inode blocks are stored. Each inode is referenced by a device + inode number pair. There are three reserved inode numbers—0, 1, and 2—defined as follows:

0 refers to the deleted files and directories.
1 refers to file system creation time, bad blocks count, and so on.
2 refers to the root directory of the file system.

The inode block contains information on each file in the data block. The information comprises owner of the file, file type, permissions, address of the file, and so on. Each inode block usually contains the following entries:

1. Owner: Indicates the owner of the inode
2. Group: Indicates the group to which the inode belongs
3. File type: Indicates the type of file, that is, whether the inode represents a file, a directory, a FIFO, a character device, or a block device (The type value is set to 0 to indicate that the inode is free).
4. Permissions: Indicates the read, write, and execute permissions of the owner (user), group, and other members, for the file
5. Access time: Indicates the time at which the file was last accessed
6. Modification time: Indicates the time at which the file was last modified
7. Inode modification time: Indicates the time at which the inode was last modified. (The inode is modified when the contents of the file are changed, the permission of the file is changed, link for the file is created, and so on.)
8. Number of links to the file: Indicates the number of links of the file
9. Physical addresses: Indicates the blocks containing the file parts
10. Size: Indicates the actual size of the file

A file's inode number can be found using the `ls -i` command.

Example   `$ ls -i letter.txt`
              `45267 letter.txt`

Here, 45267 is the inode number.

The Unix system also maintains an inode table in the memory for a file that it uses. When the file is opened, its inode is copied from the hard disk to the system's inode table.

Note: The inode contains all the attributes of a file except the filename. The filename is stored in the directory in which the file is kept. The i number is also not stored in the inode, but is used to locate the position of the inode in the inode blocks.

Directory

The directory contains only two file attributes: inode number and filename. When we create a link for a file, no separate inode is allocated for it, but the link count in the inode is incremented by one. A directory entry is also created with the new filename. When we remove a linked file with the `rm` command, the link count in the inode is decremented, and the directory entry for that link is also removed. A file is removed when its link count becomes zero. The associated disk blocks are also freed in order to make them available for new files.

A file is internally identified by Unix through a unique inode number that is associated with it. A directory file contains the names of the files and the subdirectories present in that directory along with an inode number for each. The inode number is nothing but an index to the inode table in which information about the file is stored. For example, if the inode number of the file `letter.txt` is 45267, it means that the slot number 45267 in the inode table contains information about the file `letter.txt`.

Suppose the file `letter.txt` is present in a directory called `India`. If we attempt to `cat` the `letter.txt` file, Unix will first check if the user has the read permission for the directory `India`. If so, it will find out whether this directory has an entry with `letter.txt`. If such an entry is found, its inode number is fetched from `India`. This inode number is an index to the inode table. The contents of the file `letter.txt` are read from the disk addresses mentioned in the inode entry of `letter.txt` and then displayed on the screen.

The file contents are placed in the form of data blocks dispersed throughout the disk. In each inode, an array is maintained to keep track of the data blocks. The first 10 elements of the array indicate direct indexing, that is, they directly point to the data blocks that contain the file content. Thus, a file that needs less than or equal to 10 data blocks is accessible via the direct index entries. After direct indexing comes single indirect indexing, which in turn, is followed by double indirect indexing and triple indirect indexing, as shown in Fig. 2.5.

If the file needs more than 10 blocks, it uses single indirect indexing. It contains a pointer that points to a block, which in turn, contains an array of pointers pointing to the file's data blocks.

Double indirect indexing is used for larger files where a pointer points to a block of pointers that point to other blocks of pointers, which in turn, point to the file's data blocks.

Triple indirect indexing is used for extremely large files where a pointer points to a block of pointers that point to other blocks of pointers, which in turn, point to other blocks of pointers, which finally point to the file's data blocks.

A question arises with regard to the maximum size of a file that can be pointed to by an inode.

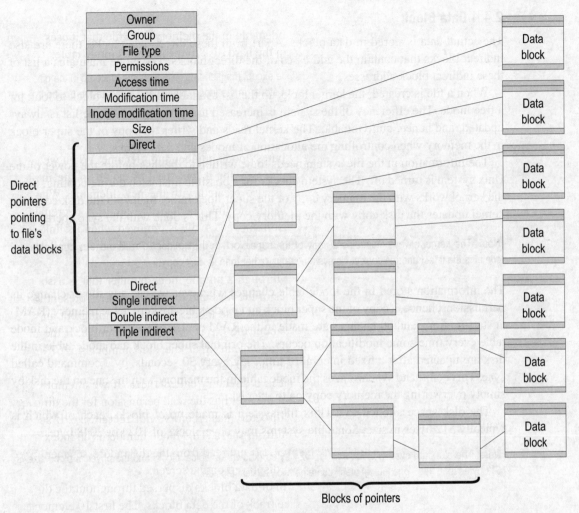

Owner
Group
File type
Permissions
Access time
Modification time
Inode modification time
Size
Direct

Direct pointers pointing to file's data blocks

Direct
Single indirect
Double indirect
Triple indirect

Data block

Blocks of pointers

Fig. 2.5 Single, double, and triple indirect addressing for large files

Assuming a data block is of size 4KB and there are 10 direct pointers in an inode, the directly addressable data block size is $10 \times 4KB = 40KB$.

In case of single indirect indexing, a pointer points to an entire block of pointers. If a block is of size 4KB, and each pointer is of 4 bytes, there will be 4 KB/4 pointers, that is, 1024 pointers in a block, where each pointer points to a 4KB block. This means that a single indirect addressing can address a file that is $1024 \times 4KB$ in size.

Similarly, in double indirect indexing, a pointer points to a block of pointers, which in turn, point to a block of pointers. Hence, a double indirect addressing can address a file that is $1024 \times 1024 \times 4KB$ in size. By following the same pattern, a triple indirect addressing can address a file of $1024 \times 1024 \times 1024 \times 4KB$ size.

Note: The maximum file size that Unix supports is the sum of sizes accessible by the direct, single indirect, double indirect, and triple indirect addressing.

2.4.4 Data Block

The actual data is stored in data blocks. Apart from these direct data blocks, there are also indirect blocks that contain the addresses of the direct blocks. The inode maintains a list of these indirect block addresses.

When a file is created, the kernel looks up the list available in the super block to look for a free inode. The efficiency of the system is increased to a great extent, as the list is always updated, and hence, quite reliable. The kernel reads and writes the copy of the super block in the memory when controlling the allocation of inodes and data blocks.

The information in the file system needs to be written to the disk before the power of the Unix system is turned off. The system checks for a possible mismatch during booting. Since the kernel works with the memory copy of the superblock rather than with the disk copy, the kernel updates the disk copy with the memory copy. This is done with the sync operation.

Note: The kernel always maintains a copy of the superblock in the memory. The in-memory copy actually contains the latest and the correct file system status rather than its disk copy.

The information stored in the inode table changes whenever we use any file or change its permissions; hence, a copy of the super block and inode table are kept in the memory (RAM) at start-up time, and all changes are made in the RAM copies of the super block and inode table every time some modification occurs. The original super block and inode table in the disk are updated after a fixed interval of time, say every 30 seconds, by a command called sync. This command synchronizes the inode table in the memory with the one on the disk by simply overwriting the memory copy on to the disk.

The disk space allotted to a Unix file system is made up of blocks, each of which is typically 512 bytes in size. Some file systems may have blocks of 1024 or 2048 bytes.

Note: The standard system block size is 1024 bytes (known as logical block) and the physical block size is 512 bytes long (i.e., one logical block contains two physical blocks).

■ SUMMARY ■

1. In the Unix operating system, there are three types of files: ordinary files, directory files, and device files. Ordinary files are also referred to as *regular files,* and they may contain printable characters.

2. The device files are of two types—character device files and block device files. In character devices, read and write operations are performed character by character, that is, 1 byte at a time, whereas in block devices, read and write operations are performed one block at a time.

3. Caching is a process in which the block of the disk accessed is kept in buffer in the memory so that in future, read and write operations are performed in the cached block of the memory.

4. All device files are stored in the /dev directory.

5. A symbolic link is a special file that points to another existing file on the system. These links are used to create several names for the same file. Through the ln command, we can create the symbolic link of a file.

6. A pipe is represented as a vertical bar character (|) and is used for sending the output of a command as an input to another command. Pipes are of two types: anonymous pipes and named pipes. Named pipes are known as FIFO, as once the data is read from the pipe, it cannot be read again.

7. Socket files are used for transferring information between two processes that are running on different machines.
8. The file system is organized as a tree with a single root node called *root* that is represented as '/'.
9. The concept by which a system appears to have more memory than what it actually has is known as *virtual memory*.
10. Mounting a file system means assigning the root directory of the new file system to a subdirectory of the root directory of our Unix system. The subdirectory on which the new file system is mounted is called the *mount point* of a file system.
11. Unmounting a file system means detaching the mounted file system from the directory of the Unix system on which it was mounted.
12. A Unix file system typically consists of four blocks: boot, super, inode, and data.
13. Every file or directory has an inode number—a unique number that recognizes the file or directory in the file system.
14. A file's inode number can be found using the `ls -i` command.

■ EXERCISES ■

Objective-type Questions

State True or False

2.1 The first block of the Unix file system is known as super block.
2.2 Every file or directory has a unique inode number.
2.3 Unix also treats the physical devices as files.
2.4 `tmp` is the folder in which all administrative files are kept.
2.5 Double indirection is used for smaller files.
2.6 We can create several names for the same file through symbolic links.
2.7 Named pipes are also known as last in first out (LIFO).
2.8 In order to see the files or directories of any device, its file system needs to be mounted.
2.9 In block devices, read and write operations are performed one byte at a time.
2.10 Pipes are of two types: anonymous and named.

Fill in the Blanks

2.1 In the Unix system, a filename may approximately be _____ characters long.
2.2 Every Unix system has a _____ file system in it.
2.3 The _____ command is used to unmount a file system.
2.4 There are three types of files in Unix: _____, _____, and _____.
2.5 Every file or directory is represented by a unique number known as _____.
2.6 The concept by which our system appears to have more memory than what it actually has is known as _____.
2.7 Character devices are also known as _____.
2.8 The boot block is the first block of the file system that contains a _____ program.
2.9 Inodes are maintained in an array form and are accessed through their indices known as _____.
2.10 Ordinary files are also referred to as _____, and they contain printable characters.

Multiple-choice Questions

2.1 The first block of a file system is
(a) super block (c) inode block
(b) data block   (d) boot block

2.2 If a directory has 10 files, the number of entries in the directory file will be
(a) 10 (b) 11 (c) 9 (d) 0

2.3 In the Unix operating system, the files are divided into three categories—ordinary, directory, and
   (a) special files   (c) device files
   (b) hidden files   (d) inode files

2.4 The directory in which executable files of the Unix operating system are kept is
   (a) lib   (c) dev
   (b) etc   (d) bin

2.5 The Unix file system is organized as a tree with a single node at the top known as
   (a) foundation   (c) seed
   (b) root   (d) stem

2.6 The indexing by which a pointer points to a block of pointers that point to other blocks of pointers, which in turn, point to the file's data blocks is known as
   (a) direct addressing
   (b) single indirect addressing
   (c) double indirect addressing

(d) triple indirect addressing

2.7 The command that synchronizes the inode table in the memory with the one on the disk is
   (a) sync
   (b) synchronizer
   (c) tally
   (d) matcher

2.8 The reserved inode number 0 refers to the
   (a) linked files
   (b) deleted files and directories
   (c) directories
   (d) device files

2.9 The bootstrap program is a short program loaded by
   (a) data block   (c) BIOS
   (b) hard disk   (d) named pipe

2.10 The number of sections or blocks that a file system has is
   (a) 1   (b) 2   (c) 3   (d) 4

Review Questions

2.1 Write short notes on the following:
   (a) Inode block
   (b) Ordinary files
   (c) Pipes
   (d) Symbolic link
   (e) Inode table

2.2 What are the different blocks that constitute a Unix file system?

2.3 Explain the procedure of mounting and unmounting a file in a Unix operating system. What is the significance of this process?

2.4 Differentiate the following:
   (a) Character and block devices
   (b) Boot block and data block
   (c) Single and double indirect addressing

2.5 Explain the role of default files and directories in the Unix operating system.

■ ANSWERS TO OBJECTIVE-TYPE QUESTIONS ■

State True or False

2.1 False
2.2 True
2.3 True
2.4 False
2.5 False
2.6 True
2.7 False
2.8 True
2.9 False
2.10 True

Fill in the Blanks

2.1 255
2.2 swap
2.3 umount
2.4 ordinary files, directory files, device files
2.5 inode number
2.6 virtual memory
2.7 raw devices
2.8 bootstrap
2.9 i number
2.10 regular file

Multiple-choice Questions

2.1 (d)
2.2 (a)
2.3 (c)
2.4 (d)
2.5 (b)
2.6 (c)
2.7 (a)
2.8 (b)
2.9 (c)
2.10 (d)

Basic Unix Commands

After studying this chapter, the reader will be conversant with the following:

- Some basic commands that are frequently used
- Logging in to the system, changing password, checking who is logged in, and displaying date and time of the system
- Dealing with file operations such as creating files, displaying their contents, deleting files, creating links to files, renaming files, and moving files
- Maintaining directories, creating a directory, changing the current directory, and removing a directory
- Displaying calendars, using basic calculators, displaying information about current systems, deleting symbolic links, and exiting from a Unix system

Unix has a large family of commands. However, even before we discuss how to perform a task with the help of these commands, we need to first log in to the system. Let us see how this is done.

3.1 LOGIN: LOGGING IN TO SYSTEMS

The first step involved while working on the Unix system is to log in or identify ourselves with the system. We should be assigned a user ID and password by the administrator, which would enable us to log in to the system. The user ID and password (along with other information) are assigned while adding a new user to the system. As soon as we switch on the Unix system, we are prompted to log in. The login prompt appears as Login.

At the login prompt, we type the user ID (a unique login name provided by the administrator).

After having typed the user ID, we are prompted for a password. The password entered here is encrypted and appears in the form of a string of asterisk symbols in the following manner.

Example   login: chirag
          password: *****

Note: One of the main security features of the Unix operating system is the displaying of asterisks while typing the password and storing the actual password in an encrypted format (also known as the *hash of the password*) in the /etc/shadow file that can be accessed only by the root.

In case the user ID or password is wrongly entered, we get the following error message:

Login incorrect
login:

This message informs the user that either the user ID or the password has been entered incorrectly, and a new login prompt is displayed to try again.

If the user ID and password are correct, we will be allowed to log in to the Unix system and will be navigated to our home directory, that is, the directory in which our personal files and settings are stored. In addition, a message indicating when we last logged in, along with the shell prompt, is displayed:

Last login: Fri Dec 15 10:30:05 on ttys17
$

This message indicates the date, time, and terminal from which we last logged in. The message is followed by the default Unix shell prompt by which we can write and execute Unix commands. The default Unix prompt for the Bourne, Bash, and Korn shells is the dollar sign ($). For C and tcsh shells, the prompt is the percentage sign (%).

You must be wondering who the administrator refers to. Let us understand this term.

System administrator   A system administrator is a person who is responsible for setting up and maintaining the Unix operating system. He/She is responsible for the proper functioning of the Unix system and also ensures that the system resources are optimally utilized. The following are a few of the tasks performed by the system administrator:

1. Set up and maintain user accounts
2. Monitor access and privileges and set up security policies
3. Monitor system performance and ensure proper utilization of resources
4. Install and upgrade software whenever desired
5. Take backup at regular intervals and restore systems in case of a crash
6. Perform proper starting and shutting down of systems

3.2 OVERVIEW OF COMMANDS

Commands refer to one-line statements that operate on the supplied operands to perform some action. Each command is supported with certain options that add extra features to the command. These options enable the user in driving the command to carry out the desired action. The options are mostly prefixed with a hyphen (-) and more than one option can be used in a command.

We are going to look at very basic internal and external commands that users execute while working on the Unix operating system. These command functions include listing of files and directories, making new directories, changing directories, removing directories, creating files, looking at the content of the files, copying, renaming, and deleting files, viewing system date and time, and knowing the list of users who are logged in, among others.

The user performs very general operations while working with the Unix operating system.

3.2.1 Structure

As mentioned in Section 3.2, a traditional Unix command consists of options and operands, where options are generally in the form of a character prefixed by a hypen (-), which is used for exploiting a particular feature of the command. The *argument* refers to the content or data to which the command has to be applied. An argument can be a file, directory, terminal, device, etc.

The syntax of a Unix command is as follows:

```
Unix_Comannd [-option1][-option2]...[Argument]
```

Let us understand the different types of commands in Unix.

3.2.2 Types of Commands in Unix

The basic commands in Unix are divided into two broad categories:

Internal commands   The shell has a number of built-in commands that are known as *internal commands*. Some of these, such as `cd` and `echo`, do not generate a process, and are directly executed by the shell. These commands are built into the shell and do not exist as separate files.

External commands   External commands are Unix utilities and programs such as `cat` and `ls`. These commands exist in the form of individual files and are distributed in different directories. The commonly used user commands are placed in the `/bin` directory, and the commands that are usually used only by system administrators are placed in the `/etc` directory.

In the subsequent sections, we will be learning about the usage of the basic commands in Unix, namely `passwd`, `ls`, `mkdir`, `cd`, `rmdir`, `pwd`, `uname`, `touch`, `cat`, `cp`, `rm`, `mv`, `ln`, `unlink`, `tput`, `who`, `finger`, `date`, `cal`, `echo`, `bc`, `globbing`, and `exit`, and some line-continuation characters.

➤ passwd: Changing password

It is considered good practice to change the login passwords at regular intervals so as to avoid any possibility of illegal access of the files by any unauthorized person. The command for changing the password is `passwd`.

Syntax   `$passwd`

On executing the `passwd` command, we will be prompted to enter the old password before giving the new password (to confirm that only authorized people are changing the password). In addition, the new password should be significantly different from the older one. It should be at least six characters long, and have at least two alphabets, one numeric, and one special character. On executing the command, we may get the output shown in the following example.

Example

```
$passwd
Changing password for chirag
Old password: *********
New password:  **********
Re-enter new password:  **********
```

If the new password and the old password are not very different from each other, we may get the following error:

`Passwords must differ by at least 3 positions`

The two passwords entered in `New password` and `Re-enter new password` should be the same; else we will get the following error:

`They don't match`

`Try again`

In case the two passwords entered in `New password` and `Re-enter new password` are exactly the same, the password of the user will be changed and we will get a confirming message:

`Password updated successfully.`

➤ `ls`: Listing files and directories

This command shows the files and directories on the disk. By default, the files and directories are displayed in alphabetical order. If the name of the directory is not specified, it will display the list of files and directories of the current working directory.

| Syntax | `$ ls -[options]` |

There is a list of options available with the `ls` command, as shown in Table 3.1.

Table 3.1 List of options available with the `ls` command

Options	Syntax	Description
-x	`ls -x`	Shows files in multiple columns (default)
-F	`ls -F`	Shows files and directories, files have / as suffix
-r	`ls -r`	Shows files sorted in reverse alphabetical order
-R	`ls -R`	Shows the recursive listing, that is, files of directories as well as subdirectories are also displayed
-a	`ls -a`	Shows all the hidden and visible files; hidden files start with a dot (.)
-d	`ls -d directory_name`	Shows only the directory name instead of listing its content; used with –l option to know the status of the directory
-l	`ls -l`	Shows files in the long-listing format (shows seven attributes of a file, that is, file permissions, number of links, owner, group, size, date and time, and file/directory name)
-t	`ls -t`	Sorts files by modification time; the latest file is on the top
-u	`ls -u`	Sorts files according to the last access time, starting with the most recent file
-i	`ls -i`	Shows inode number of all the files

While listing and searching for files and directories, we can also make use of wild-card characters. These characters help in finding files and directories that begin with specific character(s), contain specific character(s) or a range of characters in their names, consist of names of a specific length, and so on. They provide a quick and convenient way of searching for the desired files and directories.

Wild card matching A string is a wild-card pattern if it contains one of the following characters: '?', '*', or '['.

1. '?' matches any single character.
2. '*' matches 0 or more instances of any character, that is, it also matches the empty string.
3. [c1-c2] matches a single instance of any character within the range c1 and c2. For example, [a-d] is equivalent to ['abcd']. Similarly, [0–9] represents a value from 0 to 9. [a-zA-Z] represents all lower-case and upper-case letters.

We will learn more about wild cards and filename substitution (globbing) at the end of this chapter. In order to understand these options, let us for a while assume that on giving the ls command in the current directory, we get a list of the following files and directories:

```
$ls
courses
notes.txt
programs.doc
university
..
```

To get all the files beginning with a specific character, we can give a command using the following syntax:

Syntax $ ls charactername*

Here, * represents 0 or more occurrences of any character.

Example   In order to obtain all the files beginning with character n, we can give the following command.

```
$ ls n*
notes.txt
```

In order to get all the files beginning with a character in a given range, we give the command in the following syntax.

Syntax $ ls [c1-c2]*

Here, c1 and c2 represent the beginning and ending character of the range, respectively.

Example   In order to get all the files beginning with characters a to d, we can give the following command.

```
$ ls [a-d]*
courses
```

Similarly, we can use the wild-card character, ?, which represents a single character, to get the desired files. For example, to get all the files that consist of three characters and begin with character a, we can give the following command:

```
$ ls a??
```

However, since none of the files meet these criteria (assuming no filename exists that is three characters long and begins with character a), we will not get anything as the output.

In order to get all the files that begin with character a followed by any digit, we can give the following command:

```
$ ls a[0-9]*
```

Again, as we can see, no file that begins with character a is followed by a digit in our list of directories and thus no output is generated.

If we use the –1 option for long listing, we may get the following output:

```
$ls -l
-rwxr--r--   2        chirag  it    48      Nov    11:31   courses
-rw-rwxr--   1        chirag  it    669     Dec    09:15   notes.txt
-rwxrwxrwx   1        chirag  it    1560    Nov    11:21   programs.doc
-rwxr-xrw-   2        chirag  it    65      Dec    05:10   university
```

Seven attributes are displayed: file permissions, number of links, owner, group, size, date and time, and file/directory name.

In order to see all the files, including the hidden files, we use the –a option. The output is as follows:

```
$ls -al
-rwxr--r--        2        chirag  it    80      Nov    11:31   .
-rwxr--r--        2        chirag  it    72      Nov    11:31   ..
-rwxr--r--        1        chirag  it    210     Nov    11:31   .profile
-rwxr--r--        2        chirag  it    48      Nov    11:31   courses
-rw-rwxr--        1        chirag  it    669     Dec    09:15   notes.txt
-rwxrwxrwx        1        chirag  it    1560    Nov    11:21   programs.doc
-rwxr-xrw-        2        chirag  it    65      Dec    05:10   university
```

Note: Filenames that begin with the dot (.) are considered hidden files in Unix.

By default, the file and directory names are sorted alphabetically. We can use the –t option to sort them according to the modification time; the file that is created last is displayed at the top.

```
$ls -lt
-rwxrwxrwx   1        chirag  it    1560    Nov    11:21   programs.doc
-rwxr--r--   2        chirag  it    48      Nov    11:31   courses
-rwxr-xrw-   2        chirag  it    65      Dec    05:10   university
-rw-rwxr--   1        chirag  it    669     Dec    09:15   notes.txt
```

In order to get the inode number of the specified file, we can use the –i option, as shown here:

```
$ ls -li  programs.doc
39984 -rwxrwxrwx   1        chirag  it    1560    Nov    11:21   programs.doc
```

The digit 39984 is the inode number of the file programs.doc. Let us recall a concept from Chapter 1: each file or directory in the Unix operating system has a unique number known as *inode number*, which recognizes the file or directory in the file system.

➤ mkdir: Making directories

The mkdir command enables us to create one or more new directories.

Syntax	$ mkdir -[mp] dirname

The option –m stands for mode and is used for creating the directory with certain specific permissions.

The option -p stands for parent and is first used for creating all the non-existing parent directories that are mentioned in the given path.

dirname is the directory name that may be either an absolute path name or a relative path name. We may specify more than one directory name on a single command line.

> **Note:** *Absolute and relative paths*—A *path* refers to the exact location of a given file or directory. Basically, directories exists in a tree hierarchy, one inside another, and a directory or file is referred through a path, where the path components are delimited by the forward slash (/).
>
> A path can be an absolute path or a relative path. The absolute path points to the given file or directory regardless of the current working directory and is written in reference to the root directory, whereas the relative path is a path for a given file or directory in relation to the current working directory. Remember, the absolute path always starts with a forward slash, which represents the root directory. Moreover, the absolute path of the given file or directory is always the same, whereas the relative path changes according to the current directory location. The following are the examples:
>
> (a) Assuming a directory projects exists inside another directory usr, exists on the root and that the current working directory is usr, the following are the two paths to the projects directory:
> Absolute path: /usr/projects
> Relative path: projects
> (b) Similarly, if there is another directory experiment inside the directory /usr, and the current working directory is projects, then the following are the two paths to the experiments directory:
> Absolute path: /usr/experiments
> Relative path: ../experiments

Consider the following example.

```
$ mkdir courses
```

This command creates a directory by the name courses under the current directory.

```
$ mkdir courses faculty placement
```

This command will create three directories by the names courses, faculty, and placement.

> **Note:** If dirname already exists, the mkdir command aborts and does not overwrite the existing directory.

```
$ mkdir courses
```

Since a directory with the name courses already exists, this command generates the following error:

```
mkdir: can't make directory courses
```

By default, the directories are created with read, write, and execute permissions for owners and with read and execute permissions for groups and others, respectively. However, in order to create a directory with a particular set of permissions of our choice, we can use the following command:

```
$ mkdir -m 746 country
```

This command creates a directory country with read, write, and execute permissions for the owner; only read permission for the group; and read and write permissions for others.

The option -p stands for parent and is used for creating a parent directory in the given path.

Example $ mkdir -p university/colleges/professors

This command creates a directory university; within the university, a subdirectory colleges gets created, and under that, a sub-subdirectory professors is created.

There are several situations in which the directory is not created and the mkdir command is aborted while displaying the following error:

```
mkdir: Failed to make directory
```

The reasons for this error can be any of the following:

1. A directory with the same name already exists.
2. An ordinary file by the same name exists in the current directory.
3. The user does not have the read and write permissions to create files and directories in the current directory.

Line-continuation characters   Sometimes, we come across commands that are too long to be accommodated in a single line. Such commands are continued in the next consecutive line by making use of the line-continuation character. The line-continuation character is \ (backslash). Hence while writing a long command, when we come to the end of a line, we have to type \ (backslash) and press the Enter key without any space or character following it. The shell displays the '>' symbol to indicate that the current line is in continuation of the previous line. We can continue typing the remaining part of the command to the right of the '>' symbol and press the Enter key when the command is over in order to get its output. We can use the line-continuation character, that is, \ (backslash) any number of times for a single command.

Figure 3.1 demonstrates this by using the mkdir command for creating three directories, courses, faculty, and placement, while using the line-continuation character (i.e., backslash).

➤ **cd: Changing directories**

We use the cd command to change to any directory in the file system.

Syntax $ cd pathname

Here, path name is either an absolute or a relative path name for the desired target directory.

Example $ cd ajmer

This command changes our current directory to ajmer (that is assumed to exist in the current directory). When we directly give the directory name (without using '/' as prefix), it means that it is a relative path (i.e., a path related to the current directory).

```
$ mkdir courses \
> faculty \
> placement
$
```

Fig. 3.1   Line-continuation character used in the mkdir command

$ cd /home/chirag/ajmer

This command takes us to the sub-subdirectory ajmer, which is in the chirag subdirectory of the home directory. The path used in the aforementioned example is an absolute path.

$ cd ..

This command takes us to the parent directory.

Note: .. refers to the parent directory.

We can return to our home directory from any other directory by simply typing the cd command without an argument. We do not need to specify our home directory as an argument, because our shell always knows the name of our home directory.

➤ rmdir: Removing directories

This command is used to remove a directory.

Syntax $ rmdir [-p] pathname

Here, the -p option is used for deleting the parent directory if it is empty.

Note: The rmdir command cannot remove a directory until it is empty.

Examples

(a) In order to remove a single directory, consider the following example.

    $ rmdir ajmer

This removes the directory ajmer if it is empty; else, we will get the following error:

    rmdir: ajmer: Directory not empty

(b) We can delete more than one directory using the following single command.

    $ rmdir courses placement

The directories that are empty will be deleted with this command.

    $ rmdir university/colleges/professors university/colleges university

This command deletes the professors sub-subdirectory from the colleges subdirectory; then it deletes the colleges subdirectory from the university directory and finally, from the university directory.

    We can get the same result using the -p option as follows:

    $ rmdir -p university/colleges/professors

Remember, we cannot use rmdir to remove our current working directory. If we wish to remove our working directory, we have to first come out of it.

➤ pwd: Print working directory

pwd stands for print working directory. It displays the absolute path name of our working directory.

Syntax $ pwd

Example $ pwd
          /home/chirag

This output indicates that we are in the home directory of the user ID chirag. We can see that the pwd command displays the full path name of the current directory.

The `pwd` command is a valuable utility when we are moving around in the file system hierarchy. If we change our directory, `pwd` confirms the change of our location, as shown in the following sequence of commands:

```
$ pwd
/home/chirag
$ cd ajmer
$ pwd
/home/chirag/ajmer
```

We can see that when we change our directory to the `ajmer` subdirectory, the output displayed by the `pwd` command confirms the same.

➤ uname: Displaying information about current system

The `uname` command displays information about the current system: hardware platform, name of the operating system, and release level.

Syntax	`uname [-a] [-i] [-n] [-r] [-v] [-s] [-S system_name]`

The options and arguments shown in the aforementioned syntax are briefly explained in Table 3.2.

Table 3.2 Brief description of the options in the `uname` command

Options	Description
-a	Displays basic information currently available in the system
-i	Displays the name of the hardware platform
-n	Displays the node name, the name by which it is connected to the communication network
-r	Displays the operating system release level
-v	Displays the operating system version
-s	Displays the name of the operating system (default)
-S	Used to get basic information of the specified system name (Only the super user can use this option.)

Note: *Super user* and *root user* refer to the Unix administrator.

Examples

(a) `$ uname -a`

`SunOS station1 5.10 Generic_147441-01 i86pc i386 i86pc`

This output shows the basic information of the system, including the hardware platform, the operating system, its version, and so on.

(b) `$uname -n`

`station1`

This output shows that our machine is connected in the network by name, station1.

(c) `$uname -i`

`i86pc`

This output indicates that our machine is using a 64-bit processor.

(d) `$uname -r`

   `5.10`

   This output shows the operating system release level.

(e) `$uname -s`

   `SunOS`

   This output indicates that our machine has a Linux operating system installed.

➤ touch: Creating files and changing time stamps

The `touch` command is used for creating files and changing time stamps. Here, *time stamps* means both the times, that is, the time the file was last accessed and the time the file was last modified.

> Syntax   `touch -[ma] time_expression filename`

Here, the `-m` option is used for changing the modification time, and the `-a` option is used for changing the access time. The `time_expression` that we would provide should be in the following format: MMDDhhmm, where M: month, D: day, h: hour, and m: minute.

When the `touch` command is given without any option and time expression, it simply creates a file of zero bytes.

> Examples

(a) `$ touch chirag.txt`

   This creates a file called `chirag.txt` of zero byte.

   We can create several empty files quickly with the `touch` command.

(b) `$ touch chirag1 chirag2 chirag3 chirag4`

   This command creates four new files with the following names: `chirag1`, `chirag2`, `chirag3`, and `chirag4` (without any contents in them).

(c) `$ touch 09211520 chirag.txt`

   This sets the modification and access time of the file `chirag.txt` to Sep 21 15:20.

(d) `$ touch -m 11071015 chirag.txt`

   This command sets the modification time of the file `chirag.txt` to Nov 07 10:15.

(e) `$ touch -a 07120820 chirag.txt`

   This will set the access time of the file `chirag.txt` to Jul 12 08:20.

> *Note*: The commands `ls -l` and `ls -lu` can also be used to set the modification time and access time, respectively, of any file.

➤ cat: Showing, creating, and concatenating files

The `cat` command is basically a short form of concatenate, which means 'combine'. With the `cat` command, we can not only create files and see their contents but also combine their contents. The operator > can be used with the cat command to combine multiple files into a single one. The operator >> can be used to append to an existing file.

> Syntax   `cat [-n] [-s] [-v] files`

The options and arguments shown in the aforementioned syntax are briefly explained in Table 3.3.

Table 3.3   Brief description of options available with the cat command

Options	Description
-n	It precedes each line output with its line number.
-s	It suppresses messages when non-existent files are used in the command.
-v	It displays non-printing characters, except tabs, new lines, forms, and feeds, that exist in a file. To display new lines, the -e option is used along with the –v option. To display tabs and form feeds, the -t option is used along with the –v option. The new lines are represented by '$', tabs are represented by '^I', and form feeds are represented by '^L'.

Showing content   To display the contents of any file, we just need to specify the filename after the cat command

```
$ cat chirag
```

This command shows the contents of the file chirag.

If more than one filename is specified, cat will display the contents of all the files one after the other, that is, the contents of the first file followed by the contents of the second file, and so on.

```
$ cat chirag  notes.txt
```

This command displays the contents of the file chirag followed by the contents of the file notes.txt.

To get the line numbering along with the file contents, we use the –n option with the cat command:

```
$cat –n chirag
1 Today      it      might      rain
2 Thanks so much
3 This is supposed   to be a leap year
```

Note: We assume that the file chirag contains a couple of tabs that are deliberately added to the file.

Creating files   For creating files through the cat command, we redirect the standard output to a file instead of the monitor, as shown in the following example:

```
$ cat >chirag
```

If we press the Enter key, we would find the cursor positioned in the next line, waiting to type the matter that we want to store in the file chirag. After typing a few lines, press Ctrl-d.

Note: Ctrl-d keys indicate the end of file character (EOF).

Example
```
$ cat >chirag
Today      it      might      rain
Thanks so much
This is supposed   to be a leap year
Ctrl-d
```

Showing hidden characters in files   The following command shows the hidden characters and new lines in the form of $ (refer to Fig. 3.2):

```
Today  it  might                rain$
Thanks so much$
This is supposed        to be a leap year$
```

```
Today^Iit^Imight^I^Irain
Thanks so much
This is^Isupposed^Ito be a leap year
```

Fig. 3.2 New lines displayed in the form of $

Fig. 3.3 Tabs and form feeds displayed as ^I and ^L

```
$ cat -ve chirag
```

The following command shows the hidden characters and tabs in the form of '^I' and form feeds as '^L' as shown in Fig. 3.3.

```
$ cat -vt chirag
```

The cat command, apart from displaying the contents of the file, also helps concatenate the contents file.

Concatenating files   To concatenate the contents of two files and store them in the third file, we can use the following command:

```
$ cat chirag1 chirag2 >chirag3
```

This command stores the contents of the file chirag1 followed by the contents of the file chirag2 into the file chirag3. If chirag3 already contains something, it would be overwritten. If we want it to remain intact and the contents of chirag1 and chirag2 to be appended, we should use the following command:

```
$ cat chirag1 chirag2 >>chirag3
```

➤ **cp: Copying files**

The cp command is used to create a duplicate copy of ordinary file(s) in another name.

| Syntax | `$ cp -[ir] srcfile  destfile` |

Here, srcfile is the original or source filename, and destfile stands for destination filename. If a file by the destination filename already exists, it will be overwritten with the contents of the source file without any warning.

The option -i is used for interactive copying, that is, if a file by the destination filename already exists, then cp will prompt us before overwriting the file.

The option -r is used for recursive copying and especially when we want to make a copy of an entire directory (along with its subdirectories and files) using another directory name.

| Example | `$ cp chirag chirag1` |

This example makes a copy of the file chirag in the name chirag1. We can confirm this by looking at the content of both the files. If the contents of both the files are found to be the same, it indicates that the chirag file is successfully copied in the name chirag1. With the help of the cat commands, we can look at the contents of the files chirag and chirag1.

```
$ cat chirag
Microchip Computer Education
Sri Nagar Road, Ajmer
Gone time never returns
```

```
$cat chirag1
Microchip Computer Education
Sri Nagar Road, Ajmer
Gone time never returns
```

The contents of chirag and chirag1 are found to be the same and hence, this confirms that the file chirag is copied in the filename chirag1.

```
$ cp /home/chirag/ajmer/a.bat .
```

This command copies the file a.bat from the directory ajmer (subdirectory of chirag) into the current directory. The period (.) at the end of the cp command denotes the current directory.

For interactive copying, we use the following command:

```
$ cp -i chirag chirag1
```

If a file by the name chirag1 already exists, then, before overwriting it, we will be notified with the following message:

```
cp: overwrite chirag1 (yes/no)?
```

Here, we need to enter y followed by the Enter key if we want to overwrite the file.

For copying an entire directory along with its subdirectories, we use the following command:

```
$ cp -r courses latestcourses
```

It will make a copy of the courses directory (along with its files and subdirectories) with the name latestcourses.

➤ mv: Renaming files

The mv (move) command changes the name of a file. Basically, using the mv command, the file is removed from its current location and is copied to another location. In the directory entry, the link to the old filename is removed, and it is replaced by a link to the new filename.

Syntax   `$ mv oldname newname`

This command in the syntax will change the filename from oldname to newname.

Example   `$mv chirag chirag2`

This command moves or renames the file chirag to chirag2. When we look at the contents of the file chirag2, we get the same contents that were in the file chirag, which is shown here.

```
$ cat chirag2
Microchip Computer Education
Sri Nagar Road, Ajmer
Gone time never returns
```

It indicates that the file chirag2 is nothing but the same file that existed earlier with the name chirag.

```
$ mv chirag2 ajmer
```
or
```
$ mv chirag2 /home/chirag/ajmer
```

This moves the file chirag2 into the ajmer subdirectory. Now, the file chirag2 is no longer available in the current directory.

For moving more than one file, we use the following command:

```
$ mv notes.txt programs.doc /home/chirag/ajmer
```

The files notes.txt and programs.doc are removed from the current location and moved to the ajmer subdirectory.

➤ **rm: Removing files**

This command removes one or more ordinary files from a directory. The file is removed by deleting its pointer in the appropriate directory. In this way, the link between that filename and the physical file is broken, hence, the file can no longer be accessed.

| Syntax | `$ rm -[irf] filename` |

Here, each filename is separated by white space. The options and arguments shown in the aforementioned syntax are briefly explained in Table 3.4.

Table 3.4 Brief description of options available with the rm command

Options	Description
-i	It is used for interactive file deletion, i.e., we will be prompted for confirmation before the file is deleted.
-r	It is used for recursive deletion, i.e., it is used for removing an entire directory along with its files and subdirectories.
-f	It is used to forcibly remove a file for which we do not have the write permission.

We will learn about file permissions shortly.

Examples

(a) `$rm notes.txt`

This command deletes the files notes.txt.

(b) `$rm -i programs.doc`

This command prompts us for confirmation before removing the file. The prompt may be as follows:

```
rm: remove programs.doc (yes/no)?
```

To delete the file, we type y followed by the Enter key (or type character n in case we do not want to delete the file).

(c) We can delete more than one file using a single rm command.

```
$ rm syllabus notes.txt programs.doc
```

This command deletes all the three files syllabus, notes.txt, and programs.doc.

(d) `$ rm -r courses`

This command removes all the files and subdirectories of the courses directory and, finally, the courses directory itself.

(e) To remove a file that is write protected (for which we do not have the write permission), we can use the following command.

```
$ rm -f results
```

This command deletes the `results` file even if we do not have the write permission for doing so.

➤ ln: Linking files

The Unix file system allows the creation of more than one filename for the same physical file. In other words, it is possible to have aliases (links) for any given file.

The `ln` command may be used for establishing additional links. There are two types of links—hard as well as symbolic links—and both can be created with this command.

Syntax   `$ ln -[sf] oldname newname`

After the `ln` linking, both `newname` and `oldname` refer to the same file.

The default link type is hard. In order to create a symbolic link, the symbolic option (-s) is used.

Example   `$ln chirag1 mce1`

`$ls`

Through this command, a hard link will be created for the file `chirag1` by the name `mce1`.

Note: When the -s option is not used with the `ln` command, a hard link is created.

We get several filenames and directories in the current directory along with the two filenames `mce1` and `chirag1`, and when we write the following command,

```
$ ls -l chirag1
```

we get the following output:

```
-rwxrwxrwx   2 chirag      it      7669   Nov      11:21   chirag1
```

The group of `rwx` is the permissions for owners, groups, and others; 2 is the number of links (also known as *link count*) of the file; and `chirag` is the owner. The group name is `it`. The size of the file is 7669 bytes. Next comes the date and time the file was last modified. The output ends with the filename `chirag1`.

If another link was to be created, the link count would change to 3.

Note: A link count is an integer value that is maintained for each file or directory and indicates the total number of links pointing to it. When a new link is created, the link count value is increased by one. Similarly, when a link is removed, the value is decreased by one. When a link count becomes zero, it means the file or directory has no links, and hence, the disk space allocated to it is deallocated.

Both `mce1` and `chirag1` point to the same file. When we look at the contents of the file `mce1`, we get the same contents as in `chirag1`.

```
$cat mce1
Microchip Computer Education
Sri Nagar Road, Ajmer
Gone time never returns
```

Note: If we change the contents of the file mce1, the contents of chirag1 will also change, because although the names mce1 and chirag1 are different, both of them refer to the same file.

To see the inode numbers of the linked files, we give the following command:

```
$ls -li ichirag1 mce1
20985 -rwxrwxrwx    2        chirag  it    320    Nov    11:21   chirag1
20985 -rwxrwxrwx    2        chirag  it    320    Nov    11:21   mce1
```

The -li option with the ls command displays the inode number along with the long listing of the specified files. We can see that both the files have the same inode number, 20985, which confirms that both point to the same file.

In order to remove a file with more than one link from the file system, we should delete all the links with the rm command. For example, let us delete the link mce1 using the following command:

```
$ rm mce1
```

The file still exists under the name chirag1 as confirmed by the following command:

```
$cat chirag1
Microchip Computer Education
Sri Nagar Road, Ajmer
Gone time never returns
```

Let us remove the file chirag1.

```
$ rm chirag1
```

The file is now completely inaccessible.

If the destination file already exists, the link will not be created. Assume we want to make xyz.txt as the link of the file abc.txt and xyz.txt is already an existing file that has some contents. Let us give the following command:

```
$ ln abc.txt xyz.txt
```

The link will not be created and the following error will be displayed:

```
ln: xyz.txt: File exists
```

The -f option stands for force option and is used when we want to overwrite an existing file (while creating a link) without getting any message.

```
$ ln -f abc.txt xyz.txt
```

Hard links The default link that is created is a hard link (which we have been using until now). The following are the characteristics of hard links:

1. Unix hard links can point to programs and files, but not to directories.
2. If the original program or file is renamed, moved, or deleted, the hard link is not broken.
3. Hard links in Unix cannot span different file systems, that is, we cannot have a hard link on the /usr file system that refers to a program or file on the /tmp file system. The reason is that hard links share an inode number, whereas each file system has its own set of inode numbers.

Symbolic links   Hard links cannot be created for different file systems. that is, they can be made within the current directory structure. Symbolic links (symlinks) are used to link to a different file system. The symbolic link, also referred to as *soft link*, is a special type of file that references another file or directory. It simply contains the name of the file that it references and contains no actual data. It gives us power and flexibility to manage files. We can change the symlink to point to the desired files. Soft links also inherit the permission of the folder they are pointing at. To create a symbolic link in Unix, let us use the following syntax:

Syntax   `ln -s target_file symbolic_link`

Here, `target_file` is the name of the existing file for which we want to create the symbolic link, and the `symbolic_link` is the symbolic link for the `target_file`.

Example   Consider a file named `chirag1`. Let us create a symlink called `mce1`, which points to the original file, `inventory.txt`.

```
$ ln -s chirag1 mce1
```

We first specify the target file, the file that we want our symlink to point to, and then specify the name of our symbolic link. On executing the `ls -al` command, we will find that the `mce1` file will have an '1' in the long format of the `ls` command, which confirms that it is a symbolic link.

> **Note:** An orphan symlink is a symbolic link that points nowhere, that is, the original target file it used to point to earlier is either deleted or renamed.

```
20985 -rwxrwxrwx    2     chirag it     320    Nov    11:21   chirag1
20985 lrwxrwxrwx    2     chirag it     320    Nov    11:21   mce1->chirag1
```

The difference between symbolic link and hard link is that the symbolic link has the ability to link to directories or files on remote computers. In addition, when you delete a target file, the symbolic links to that file become unusable, whereas the hard links preserve the contents of the file.

➤ unlink: Deleting symbolic links

The unlink command removes the specified file, including symbolic links.

Syntax   `unlink filename`

Example   `unlink accounts.txt`

If this file `accounts.txt` exists as a linked file, it will be deleted.

➤ tput: Exploiting terminal capabilities

The `tput` command is used for exploiting terminal capabilities through the terminfo database. Hence, we can use the `tput` command to clear the screen, move the cursor, and underline text. The `tput` command uses the terminfo database to know the different features that are supported by a terminal, and converts the commands given by the user through the `tput` command into the code that the terminal understands.

Terminfo is a database that defines terminal and printer attributes and capabilities. It contains information such as the number of rows and columns in a terminal and the attributes of text displayed on the terminal.

Syntax   `tput [clear][cup col row] [cols][lines][sc][rc][civis][cnorm][dl n][setb]`
`[setf][bold][sgr0][smul[rmul]`

Table 3.5 gives a list of options available with the `tput` command.

Table 3.5   Brief description of the options available with the `tput` command

Options	Description
clear	It clears the whole screen.
cup col row	It moves the cursor position to the given row and col position.
cols	It displays the number of columns on the terminal screen.
lines	It displays the number of lines on the terminal screen.
sc	It saves the current cursor location.
rc	It restores the cursor position, i.e., it returns the cursor to its last saved location.
dl n	It deletes n number of lines below, including the current row, i.e., the row in which the cursor is positioned.
bold	It makes the text appear in bold.
sgr0	It turns off bold.
Smul	It begins underlining text.
Rmul	It stops underlining text.

Examples

(a) `$ tput cup 10 5`

This statement moves the cursor to the fifth row and the tenth column.

(b) `$ tput cols`

This statement displays a value 80, which represents the number of columns of the terminal screen.

(c) `$ tput dl 4`

This statement deletes four lines below, including the current row.

(d) `$ tput bold`

This statement will make the text appear in bold until the `srg0` command is invoked.

(e) `$ tput clear`

It clears the whole screen.

Note: We know that the `tput` command is mostly used in scripts but is deliberately provided here, as its option `clear` is frequently used for clearing the screen while running commands at the command prompt.

➤ who: Who is online

The `who` command displays all users who are currently logged in to the system. It returns the user's name (ID), terminal, and the time at which he or she logged in.

Table 3.6 Brief description of options in the who command

Options	Description
-u	It displays information regarding users who are logged in. Their login name, name of the terminal through which they are logged in, and the date and time of login are displayed.
-H	It displays information pertaining to the users who are logged in along with the column headings.
am I	It displays information of the users who are logged in.

Syntax who [-u] [-H] [am i]

These options are briefly explained in Table 3.6.

Examples

(a) $ who

```
anil        tty1      Oct      15      10:56
chirag      tty2      Oct      10      11:25
ravi        tty5      Oct      15      13:07
```

To know whether the user is active, we use the -u option, which also indicates how long it has been since there was any activity. This is known as *idle time*. It also returns the process ID for the user.

```
$ who -u
anil        tty1      Feb      10      14.25      0:45      1103
chirag      tty2      Feb      08      11:25      old       1568
ravi        tty5      Feb      10      15:10      .         1456
```

If we look at this example carefully, we will see three different formats for idle time. The first user has had no activity for 0 hours and 45 minutes. The second user has had no activity for more than 24-hours. Since there is only enough room for 24 hours in the idle time format, when a user is inactive for more than 24 hours, the system simply says 'old'. The third user's idle time is a period (.), that is, he/she has carried out an activiy in the last minute.

(b) If we use the H option, Unix displays a header that explains each column.

```
$ who -uH

NAME         LINE      TIME                           IDLE      PID       COMMENTS
anil         tty1      Feb      10      14.25         0:45      1103      (:0)
chirag       tty2      Feb      08      11:25         old       1568      (:0.0)
ravi         tty5      Feb      10      15:10         .         1456      (:0.0)
```

(c) If we want to view information about ourselves, we can use the argument am I along with the who command.

```
$who am I
chirag      tty2      Feb      08      11:25
```

> **finger: Online user's details**

The finger command displays information of users who are logged in. Compared to the who command, the finger command displays more elaborate information pertaining to these

Table 3.7   Brief description of the options in the `finger` command

Options	Description
`-1`	Displays information of the user in a long format comprising login name, real name, terminal name, write status, idle time, login time, office location, office phone number, user's home directory, home phone number, login shell, mail status, and the contents of the files, `.plan`, `.project`, and so on, from the user's home directory
`-s`	Displays information of the user in a short format comprising login name, real name, terminal name, write status, idle time, login time, office location, and office phone number
`-b`	Suppresses printing the user's home directory and shell in a long format display
`-w`	Suppresses printing the full name in a short format display

users. Apart from the login name, terminal name, date, and time of the logged-in users, the command also displays other information such as the user's home directory, phone number, login shell, and mail status, among others.

Syntax   `finger [-b] [-1] [-s] [-w] [username]`

These options are briefly explained in Table 3.7.

If no options are specified, the finger defaults to the `-1` option output if `username` is provided; else, the `-s` option output is chosen. In the case of fields whose information (such as office location and phone number) is not available, the information will not be displayed in the output.

To find out who is logged in to which terminal, we use the finger command without an argument, as in the following example.

Example
```
$ finger
Login    Name     TTY    Idle   When       Where
chirag   chirag   tty2   3:10   Sat 08:15  :0
ravi     ravi     tty3          Sat 11:33  :0.0
root     root     tty1   10d    Sat 08:15  :0.0
```

This list shows three active logins. The actual time at which each user logged in and the time the terminal has been idle are also listed. The idle time is the time that has elapsed since the last keystroke. From the idle time, we can usually tell whether someone is at the terminal. For example, we can say that there is no root user at the `tty1` terminal, because there has been no keystroke for 10 days. The user on the `tty2` terminal has not used the terminal for more than three hours.

The finger command can also be used to get the details of a single user, as shown in the following example.

```
$ finger chirag
Login: chirag                         In real life: (null)
Directory: /home/chirag              Shell: /bin/bash
On since Mon Dec 26 02:15 on tty2 from :0.0
No mail.
No Plan.
```

This output shows the login name, real name (null), home directory, login shell, login time, terminal name, mail status, and so on.

➤ date: Displaying system date and time

This command displays the system date and time.

```
$ date
```

If no argument is given, the current date and time are displayed:

```
Sunday 12 February 2012 05:32:20 AM IST
```

The command can also be used with suitable format specifiers as arguments. Each format is preceded by a + symbol followed by the % operator, and a single character describing the format.

Syntax   `date [arguments]`

The arguments are used for displaying the date in the desired format. The list of available arguments is given in Table 3.8.

Table 3.8   Brief description of the arguments used in the `date` command

Arguments	Description
%d	For displaying day (01–31)
%m	For displaying month (01–12)
%b	For displaying abbreviated month name (Jan, Feb, etc.)
%y	For displaying the year—last two digits (00,..., 99)
%Y	For displaying the year with century—four digits
%H	For displaying hours—military format (00,01,..., 23)
%I	For displaying hours (0,1,..., 12)
%p	For displaying a.m./p.m.
%M	For displaying minutes (0,1, ..., 59)
%S	For displaying seconds (0,1,..., 59)
%x	For displaying only date (07/15/12)
%X	For displaying only time (17:15:30)
%a	For displaying abbreviated weekday (Fri)

Examples

(a) `$ date + %m`
    It prints only the month, that is, 07.
(b) `$ date +%b`
    It prints the month name, that is, Jul.
(c) `$ date +%Y`
    It prints the year with century, that is, 2012.
(d) `$date + "%I %p"`
    It displays the hour with a.m./p.m.
    05 PM

➤ cal: Displaying calendar

The `cal` command is used to display the calendar of a specified month and year.

Syntax   `cal {month [1-12]} {year[1-9999]}`

Here, values 1–12 represent the month, and values 1–9999 represent the year.

Examples

(a) To display the current month's calendar, just use the `cal` command without any arguments (refer to Fig. 3.4).

`$cal`

(b) To display the calendar of March 2012, write the following command (refer to Fig. 3.4).

`$ cal 3 2012`

(c) To display the calendar for a whole year, specify the year in the `cal` command as shown in Fig. 3.5.

`$ cal 2012`

➤ echo: Displaying messages and results

The `echo` command is used to display messages and the results of computation on the screen.

Syntax   `echo [-n] message/variables`

These options are briefly explained in Table 3.9.

Table 3.9   Brief description of an option in the echo command

Option	Description
-n	It suppresses a new line after the echoed message or variables. The output of the next echo statement will appear on the current line. This option is usually used while scripting.

The `echo` command recognizes the following `Escape` characters:

\\ represents backslash.

\a rings a bell.

\b represents the backspace key.

\f represents the form feed.

\n represents a new line character.

\r represents carriage return.

\t represents a horizontal tab character.

\v represents a vertical tab character.

Example   `echo "Hello World"`

This example displays the message, `Hello World` on the screen.

Figure 3.6 shows how `Escape` sequences can be used with the `echo` command. We can see that the \n results in a new line character, displaying the following word, `World` that appears on the next line. Similarly, \t results in a horizontal tab between the words `Hello` and `World`. The third example displays backslash (\) between `Hello` and `World`. The fourth example shows how \b takes the cursor one character back, hence overwriting the character 'o' of `Hello` and displaying the word, `HellWorld`. The fifth example inserts a vertical tab between the words `Hello` and `World`.

➤ bc: Basic calculator

The `bc` command activates a basic calculator that is meant for doing simple calculations. The command is executed in the interactive mode, that is, we enter the expression we wish to compute

```
# cal
      April 2012
  S   M  Tu   W  Th   F   S
  1   2   3   4   5   6   7
  8   9  10  11  12  13  14
 15  16  17  18  19  20  21
 22  23  24  25  26  27  28
 29  30
```

```
# cal 3 2012
      March 2012
  S   M  Tu   W  Th   F   S
                      1   2   3
  4   5   6   7   8   9  10
 11  12  13  14  15  16  17
 18  19  20  21  22  23  24
 25  26  27  28  29  30  31
```

Fig. 3.4 Calendar of current month and specified month

```
$ echo "Hello\nWorld"
Hello
World

$ echo "Hello\tWorld"
Hello World

$ echo "Hello\\World"
Hello\World

$ echo "Hello\bWorld"
HellWorld

$ echo "Hello\vWorld"
Hello
     World
```

Fig. 3.6 Echo command output

```
      Jan
  S   M  Tu   W  Th   F   S
  1   2   3   4   5   6   7
  8   9  10  11  12  13  14
 15  16  17  18  19  20  21
 22  23  24  25  26  27  28
 29  30  31
```

```
      Feb
  S   M  Tu   W  Th   F   S
              1   2   3   4
  5   6   7   8   9  10  11
 12  13  14  15  16  17  18
 19  20  21  22  23  24  25
 26  27  28  29
```

```
      Mar
  S   M  Tu   W  Th   F   S
                      1   2   3
  4   5   6   7   8   9  10
 11  12  13  14  15  16  17
 18  19  20  21  22  23  24
 25  26  27  28  29  30  31
```

```
      Apr
  S   M  Tu   W  Th   F   S
  1   2   3   4   5   6   7
  8   9  10  11  12  13  14
 15  16  17  18  19  20  21
 22  23  24  25  26  27  28
 29  30
```

```
      May
  S   M  Tu   W  Th   F   S
              1   2   3   4   5
  6   7   8   9  10  11  12
 13  14  15  16  17  18  19
 20  21  22  23  24  25  26
 27  28  29  30  31
```

```
      Jun
  S   M  Tu   W  Th   F   S
                          1   2
  3   4   5   6   7   8   9
 10  11  12  13  14  15  16
 17  18  19  20  21  22  23
 24  25  26  27  28  29  30
```

```
      Jul
  S   M  Tu   W  Th   F   S
  1   2   3   4   5   6   7
  8   9  10  11  12  13  14
 15  16  17  18  19  20  21
 22  23  24  25  26  27  28
 29  30  31
```

```
      Aug
  S   M  Tu   W  Th   F   S
              1   2   3   4
  5   6   7   8   9  10  11
 12  13  14  15  16  17  18
 19  20  21  22  23  24  25
 26  27  28  29  30  31
```

```
      Sep
  S   M  Tu   W  Th   F   S
                              1
  2   3   4   5   6   7   8
  9  10  11  12  13  14  15
 23  24  25  26  27  28  29
 30
```

```
      Oct
  S   M  Tu   W  Th   F   S
      1   2   3   4   5   6
  7   8   9  10  11  12  13
 14  15  16  17  18  19  20
 21  22  23  24  25  26  27
 28  29  30  37
```

```
      Nov
  S   M  Tu   W  Th   F   S
                      1   2   3
  4   5   6   7   8   9  10
 11  12  13  14  15  16  17
 18  19  20  21  22  23  24
 25  26  27  28  29  30
```

```
      Dec
  S   M  Tu   W  Th   F   S
                              1
  2   3   4   5   6   7   8
  9  10  11  12  13  14  15
 16  17  18  19  20  21  22
 23  24  25  26  27  28  29
 30  31
```

Fig. 3.5 Calendar of the entire year

on the command line, and the command immediately displays the result on pressing the Enter key. To quit the interactive mode, we either press Ctrl-d or type quit followed by the Enter key.

Syntax   bc [-l]

-l defines the math functions and initializes the scale to 20, instead of the default zero.

The functions that can be used with the bc command are given in Table 3.10.

Table 3.10   List of functions available with the bc command

Function	Description
sqrt()	It calculates the square root of the supplied number.
s()	It calculates the sine value. The argument should be in radians.
c()	It calculates the cosine value. The argument should be in radians.
a()	It calculates the arctangent. The result of the function is displayed in radians.
l()	It calculates the natural logarithm of the supplied number.
e()	It calculates the exponential of the supplied number.

We can use all operators including +, -, *, /, %, ^, where % represents the mod operator, that is, it returns the remainder and ^ represents 'to the power'.

Apart from the -l option, we can also use the scale to specify the number of digits to the right of the decimal point.

Examples   bc

```
$bc
5/3
1
quit
$ bc -l
5/3
1.66666666666666666666
quit
$ bc
2 + 2
4
5/3
1
scale = 2
5/3
1.66
3^2
9
sqrt(81)
9.00
quit
```

```
$ x='echo "5/3" | bc -l'
$ echo $x
1.66666666666666666666
```

Table 3.11 Brief description of the wild cards used in filename substitution

Wild card	Description
!	Used with [] to negate the meaning
~	Substitutes the user's home directory
{characters}	Matches the given set of characters

Filename substitution—Globbing

Filename substitution is the process by which the shell expands a string containing wild cards into a list of filenames. The process of filename substitutions is also known as *globbing*. Apart from the wild cards, *, ?, and [c1-c2], which we discussed while learning the ls command, Table 3.11 shows the wild cards that are used in filename substitution.

Examples

(a) `$ ls *`

It displays all the names of the files and directories in the current directory.

(b) `$ ls a*`

It displays all the names of the files and directories that begin with the character a.

(c) `$ ls *a`

It displays all the names of the files and directories that end with the character a.

(d) `$ ls *ab*`

It displays all the names of the files and directories that contain ab.

(e) `$ ls a*/*`

It displays all the names of the files and directories that begin with the character a in all the directories that are one level under the current directory.

The filename substitution applies to the files in the current directory. To match filenames in the subdirectories, we need to use the / character.

(f) `$ ls a*/*/*`

It displays all the names of files and directories that begin with the character a in all the directories that are two levels under the current directory.

(g) `$ ls ???`

It displays all the names of the files and directories that consist of three characters.

(h) `$ ls ???*`

It displays all the names of the files and directories that consist of at least three characters.

(i) `$ ls student?.txt`

It displays all the names of the files and directories that begin with the word student followed by one character followed by extension .txt such as stduent1.txt, student2.txt, and studenta.txt.

(j) `$ ls [ab]*`

It displays all the names of the files and directories that begin with either character a or character b followed by zero or more occurrences of any character.

(k) `$ ls [ab]*[12]`

It displays all the names of the files and directories that begin with either character a or character b followed by zero or more occurrences of any character and which end with either the digit 1 or 2.

(l) `$ ls [ab]*[1-5]`

It displays all the names of the files and directories that begin with either character a or character b followed by zero or more occurrences of any character and which end with any digit from 1 to 5.

(m) `$ ls [a-d]*`

It displays all the names of the files and directories that begin with any character from a through d followed by zero or more occurrences of any character.

(n) `$ ls [a-d]??`

It displays all the names of the files and directories that begin with any character from a through d followed by exactly two characters.

(o) `$ ls [!a-d]*`

It displays all the names of the files and directories that begin with any character except a through d followed by any number of characters.

(p) `$ ls [A-Za-z]*`

It displays all the names of the files and directories that begin with any character from a through z in either upper case or lower case followed by any number of characters.

(q) `$ ls [A-Za-z][a-z]*`

It displays all the names of the files and directories that begin with any character from a through z in either upper case or lower case, followed by any character from a through z in lower case, followed by any number of characters.

(r) `$ ls [A-Za-z][a-z][12]`

It displays all the names of the files and directories that begin with any character from a through z in either upper case or lower case, followed by any character from a through z in lower case, followed by either digit 1 or 2.

(s) `$ ls {aa,bb,cc}*`

It displays all the names of the files and directories that begin with the characters aa, bb, or cc followed by any number of characters.

(t) `$ ls a*{d,1,z}`

It displays all the names of the files and directories that begin with the character a followed by any number of characters and, which end with d, 1, or z.

(u) `$ ls a*{d,[1-3],[ab]}`

It displays all the names of the files and directories that begin with the character a followed by any number of characters and which end with d, a number from 1 through 3, or by either character a or b.

(v) The tilde (~) character by itself expands to the full path name of the user's home directory. The following echo command confirms this:

```
$ echo ~
/home/bintu
```

(w) When the tilde is appended before a path, it expands to the home directory and the rest of the path name. Consider the following command.

```
$ cd ~/data
```

(x) We will be taken into the directory, data that is present within the user's home directory. The following `pwd` command confirms this.

```
$ pwd
/home/bintu/data
```

(y) When the tilde is appended before a username, it expands to the full path name of that user's home directory. Consider the following command.

```
$ cd ~john
```

We will be taken to the user john's home directory. The following command confirms this:

```
$ pwd
/home/john
```

➤ exit: Exiting

The `exit` command is used to log out of the Unix system, exit from a shell, and exit from a shell script.

> **Syntax**   `exit`

> **Example**   `exit`

To log out of the Unix shell, Ctrl-d is a short cut that is used. Before exiting from the Unix system, we should make sure that all the files that were open are saved and closed; else they might get corrupted. Usually, when we exit from the shell, the currently running process or command is automatically killed. In order to run the task in the background even after exiting from the shell, we should use the `nohup` command (discussed in Chapter 6).

■ SUMMARY ■

1. When compared with the `who` command, the `finger` command displays more elaborate information pertaining to users who are logged in.
2. The `finger` command not only displays the login name, terminal, date, and time of the logged-in users, but also displays other information such as the user's home directory, phone number, login shell, mail status, and much more.
3. *Filename substitution or globbing* is the process by which the shell expands a string containing wild cards into a list of filenames.

■ FUNCTION SPECIFICATION ■

Command	Function
ls	To see a list of files and directories, including hidden files
mkdir	To create directories. We can also create directories with specific permissions with this command.
cd	For changing a directory. We can use both relative and absolute paths for changing the directory.
pwd	To know the current working directory
touch	To create empty files and also change the modification and access time of a file

Command	Function
mv	For moving files from one directory to another as well as for renaming files
passwd	For changing the password
ln	For creating links of files. There are two types of links—hard links and symbolic links.
who	To know how many users are currently online
finger	To know the current working directory
touch	To know who is online, when the user is logged in, and for how long his/her terminal has been idle.
date	For displaying system date and time

Command	Function
cat	For displaying contents of files, creating files, and concatenating files
rmdir	For removing a directory provided it is empty
cp	For copying files as well as an entire directory
rm	For deleting files as well as an entire directory
cal	To display the calendar of the specified month and year. By default, it displays the calendar of the current month.
mv	For moving files from one directory to another as well as for renaming files
cal-y	To display the calendar of the current year

Command	Function
uname	For displaying information of the current system such as its hardware platform, name of the operating system, and its release level.
unlink	To remove the specified file, including symbolic links
bc	To activate a basic calculator that is meant for doing simple calculations. It can also be used to compute square root, sine value, cosine value, natural logarithms, and exponential values.
exit	To log out from the Unix system, a shell, or a shell script

■ EXERCISES ■

Objective-type Questions

State True or False

3.1 The ls command shows the list of files and directories that are sorted alphabetically by default.

3.2 The option used with the ls command to see the names of the files and directories in reverse order is -R.

3.3 We can create only one directory at a time using the mkdir command.

3.4 The cd command, if given without any arguments, will take us to our home directory.

3.5 With the touch command, we can only change the timestamps of the files but cannot create files.

3.6 While creating a file with the cat command, we need to use Ctrl-d to specify the end of the file.

3.7 With the rmdir command, we can remove the non-empty directory as well.

3.8 If we use the -i option with the cp command, it will prompt us before overwriting the destination file if it already exists.

3.9 The cp command is used for making a copy of the files; we cannot use it for copying an entire directory with its files and subdirectories.

3.10 We can delete more than one file with a single rm command.

3.11 With the rm command, we can forcibly delete a file even if we do not have its write permission.

3.12 With the mv command, we can move a file from one directory to another but cannot rename it.

3.13 The hard link should be created within the current directory structure.

3.14 We can log out of the Unix system using Ctrl-d.

3.15 Through the cal command, we cannot see the calendar of the previous month.

3.16 The mail status of the user can be seen through the finger command.

3.17 The uname command can be used to know the version and release of the operating system.

3.18 The wild-card character '?' represents a single character.

3.19 The bc or the basic calculator command can be used to find the square root of a number.

3.20 The unlink command cannot delete symbolic links.

Fill in the Blanks

3.1 The option used with the ls command to see hidden files is _____.

3.2 The option used with mkdir for creating directories with specified permission is _____.

3.3 With the cd command, we can give absolute as well as _____ path names.

3.4 The command used to know our current working directory is _____.

3.5 The format of time expression used to change modification or access time in the touch command is _____.

3.6 The option used with the rmdir command to

delete an empty parent directory is _____.

3.7 The _____ option is used with the rm command to recursively delete all the files and subdirectories of the specified directory.

3.8 The command used to create a link for a file is known as _____.

3.9 There are two types of links to a file: _____ and _____.

3.10 The option used with the date command to display only the time is _____.

3.11 The function used to find the natural logarithm in the bc command is _____.

3.12 The command used to display the calendar of the current year is _____.

3.13 The command used to display information of the logged-in user, including home directory, login shell, mail status, and phone number is _____.

3.14 The option used with the ls command to display the inode number of files is _____.

3.15 The option used with the cat command that displays non-printing characters in the file is _____.

Multiple-choice Questions

3.1 The command bc -l sets the scale to
(a) 20   (c) 10
(b) 5   (d) 6

3.2 The tput cup 7 5 command moves the cursor to the
(a) seventh row and fifth column
(b) fifth row and seventh column
(c) top left corner of the screen
(d) right bottom corner of the screen

3.3 The command date +%M will display
(a) month in character form
(b) month in numerical form
(c) minutes
(d) a.m./p.m.

3.4 The option used in the cp command for interactive copying is
(a) -i   (b) -r   (c) -c   (d) -d

3.5 The following option is used in the cat command to suppress messages when a non-existent file is used in the command:
(a) -o   (b) -v   (c) -n   (d) -s

3.6 Apart from displaying contents of the files, the command used for concatenating files is
(a) concat   (c) merge
(b) cat   (d) add_files

3.7 There are two types of links of files—hard and
(a) tough   (c) volatile
(b) robust   (d) symbolic

3.8 The echo command ~ will display
(a) error
(b) list of files and directories
(c) home directory of the user
(d) profile file

3.9 The following command is used to display the names of the files and directories that consist of at least two characters:
(a) ls??*   (c) ls *
(b) ls   (d) ls ?*

3.10 The option used in the ls command to show files and directories that are sorted on their modification time is
(a) -m   (b) -a   (c) -t   (d) -u

Programming Exercises

3.1 What will the following commands do?
(a) $ls [a-d]??
(b) $ls [a-z][0-9]*
(c) $ls -Rt
(d) $mkdir -m 740 apple
(e) $mkdir -p fruits/delicious/apple
(f) $touch 07151000 mbacourse.txt
(g) $ cat mbacourse.txt lawcourse.txt
(h) $rmdir -p fruits/delicious/apple
(i) $ cp /fruits/delicious/apple/juice.

txt/college/students
(j) $ rm -r college
(k) $ mv mbacourse.txt management.txt
(l) $ ln -f juice.txt energy.txt
(m) $ finger Charles
(n) $ bc
    scale = 2
    17/3
(o) $cal 10 2012

3.2 Write the command for the following tasks:

(a) To display the list of files and directories that begin with a vowel

(b) To change the access time of the file mbacourse.txt to Feb 10 09:15

(c) To show the contents of the file mbacourse.txt along with line numberings

(d) To concatenate the contents of the two files mbacourse.txt and lawcourse.txt and store them in a third file career.txt

(e) To remove the empty subdirectories, students and teachers, from the college directory

(f) To copy the entire directory teachers along with its subdirectories in the name *faculty*

(g) To forcibly remove the file mbacourse.txt from the college directory

(h) To move the file mbacourse.txt from the current directory to the professional sub-directory of the college directory

(i) To change the password

(j) To create a link of the file mbacourse.txt in the name management.txt (If a file by the name management.txt already exists, we should be asked for a confirmation before overwriting its contents.)

(k) To get the list of all online users with their activity and column headers

(l) To display day, month, and year in the format 17 Nov 2012

(m) To log out from the Unix system

(n) To show all the names of the files and directories that begin with any character from a through z followed by exactly three characters

(o) To find the square root of number 17 (The result should be displayed up to five places of decimals.)

Review Questions

3.1 Explain the following commands with their syntax and examples.
  (a) ls (d) rmdir
  (b) who (e) cp
  (c) touch

3.2 Explain the differences between the following:
  (a) Hard and symbolic links
  (b) who and finger commands
  (c) cat and touch commands
  (d) rm and rmdir commands

3.3 What is the use of the bc command? Explain a few functions that are associated with it.

3.4 What do you mean by *escape characters*? Explain their usage through the echo command.

3.5 Explain the term *globbing* with examples.

3.6 What is the use of the date command? Name the options that are used with the date command to display only the year, hour in military format, and only the day.

3.7 Explain the command used to exploit terminal capabilities.

3.8 Explain with examples the command that is used to display the calendar of the desired month and year.

Brain Teasers

3.1 In the long-listing command ls -li, if you find two or more files having the same inode number, what does it mean?

3.2 Identify the error in the following command and correct it to display all the files that consist of exactly four characters.
  $ ls ****

3.3 Identify the error in the following command and correct it to display the hardware platform of the current machine.
  $ uname -v

3.4 Can you display the node name, that is, the name by which your machine is connected in the communication network? If yes, mention the command.

3.5 Consider the following cat command:
  $ cat chirag notes.txt
  It displays an error indicating that the file notes.txt does not exist. How can you avoid this error message?

3.6 If on using s() function in the bc command for finding sine value, a wrong answer was obtained, identify the error.

3.7 You want to change your password but the following command is not working. Where is the error?
  $password

3.8 Is there any way to copy the content of the files `a.txt` and `b.txt` to a file `c.txt` without deleting the earlier content of file `c.txt`? If yes, what is that?

3.9 What should the command given to display the hardware platform and name of the operating system on a machine be?

3.10 You wish that a confirmation prompt appears before deleting the files. However, by using the following command, the confirmation message is not prompted. Where and what is the error?
```
$ rm -f a*.*
```

3.11 The following command creates a hard link of the file `a.txt` in the name `b.txt`. What changes are required to be made to this command in order to create a symbolic link instead of a hard link?
```
$ ln a.txt b.txt
```

3.12 The following `bc` command displays the result to 0 places of decimal. What change is required to be made in order to get the result up to 20 decimal places ?
```
$ bc
17/3
```

3.13 What is the mistake in the following command for changing the modification time of the file? `a.txt` to `Oct 15 04:15`?
```
$ touch -a 10150415 a.txt
```

3.14 The following command to recursively copy the content of the directory projects to experiments is not working. Identify the error and correct it.
```
$ cp projects experiments
```

3.15 The following date command is not displaying century in four digits. Identify the error and correct it.
```
$ date +%y
```

■ ANSWERS TO OBJECTIVE-TYPE QUESTIONS ■

State True or False

3.1	True
3.2	False
3.3	False
3.4	True
3.5	False
3.6	True
3.7	False
3.8	True
3.9	False
3.10	True
3.11	True
3.12	False
3.13	True
3.14	True
3.15	False
3.16	True
3.17	True
3.18	True
3.19	True
3.20	False

Fill in the Blanks

3.1	-a
3.2	-m
3.3	relative
3.4	pwd
3.5	MMDDhhmm
3.6	-p
3.7	-r
3.8	ln
3.9	hard, symbolic
3.10	%x
3.11	l()
3.12	cal -y
3.13	finger
3.14	-i
3.15	-v

Multiple-choice Questions

3.1	(a)
3.2	(b)
3.3	(c)
3.4	(a)
3.5	(d)
3.6	(b)
3.7	(d)
3.8	(c)
3.9	(a)
3.10	(c)

Advanced Unix Commands

After studying this chapter, the reader will be conversant with the following:

- Advanced commands used in the Unix operating system such as setting access permissions for the existing files and directories, setting default permissions for the newly created files and directories, creating groups, changing ownerships of the files, and sharing files among groups
- Sorting content and performing input/output (I/O) redirections, that is, diverting the output of a command to a file or providing input to a command from a file
- Cutting or slicing the file vertically, pasting content, splitting files, counting characters, words, and lines in files or other content, and using a pipe operator, that is, sending the output of a command as input to another command
- Displaying the top and bottom contents of a file, presenting content page-wise, and displaying the manual of any command
- Comparing files, eliminating and displaying duplicate lines in two files, and displaying and suppressing the unique and common content in two files
- Printing documents, setting reminders of appointments, carrying out conversions between DOS and Unix files, and measuring time usage in the execution of commands

4.1 OVERVIEW

The advanced Unix commands help us perform several tasks such as setting access permissions for the existing files and directories, setting default permissions for the newly created files and directories, changing ownership of the files, and sharing files among groups. These commands also include sorting file content, performing input/output (I/O) redirections, and piping the output of a command as input to another command. Unix also offers commands for operations such as cutting or slicing the file vertically, pasting content, splitting files, counting characters, words, and lines in files, extracting the top and bottom contents of files, presenting content page-wise, and displaying manual commands. These commands also include comparing files, eliminating and displaying duplicate lines in two files, suppressing the unique and common content in two files, printing documents, setting reminders of appointments, carrying out conversions between DOS and Unix files, and measuring the time usage in the execution of commands.

The list of advanced commands that will be covered in this chapter is as follows:

chmod, umask, chown, chgrp, groups, input/output redirection in Unix, pipe operator, cut, paste, split, wc, sort, head, tail, diff, cmp, uniq, comm, time, pg, lp, .profile, calendar, script, dos2unix, and man.

4.2 FILE ACCESS PERMISSIONS

The data in the Unix system is contained in files. We may restrict or permit access to this data by restricting or permitting access to the files containing the data. There are three types of Unix files: ordinary, directory, and special files.

We may use file permissions to avoid any accidental modifications. We can retain the ability to read the file while restricting the ability to write in them. Similarly, we can also restrict other users in a multi-user environment from reading our files.

There are three classes of system users. The first is the *user*. The user is usually the system user who created the file. The user has full control over restricting or permitting access to the file at any time. In addition to individual file ownership, it is possible for one or more system users to own the file collectively in a kind of *group* ownership. A system user who is not the file owner may access the file if this user belongs to the group of system users who are allowed to access the file. The last category of system users is the one who is neither the owner nor part of the group and is known as the *other* user. Hence, there are three classes of system users:

1. *User* refers to the system user who created the file and is also sometimes called owner.
2. *Group* refers to one or more users who may access the file as a group.
3. *Other* refers to any other users of the system.

There are several permissions for system usage. System users with a *read* permission may read the contents of an ordinary file while users with a *write* permission may write in a file and change its contents. Write permission is also required to delete the file using the rm command (Table 4.1).

Table 4.1 Access modes and permissions

Access mode	Ordinary file	Directory file
Read	Allows examination of file contents	Allows listing of files within the directory
Write	Allows changing of contents of the file	Allows creation of new files and removal of old ones
Execute	Allows execution of the file as a command	Allows searching of the directory

We can view the permissions of a file or directory through the *long listing* command. The following example shows the long listing of file mce1.

Example   `$ ls -l mce1`

This statement requests the long directory listing for the ordinary file called mce1. We might get the output shown in Fig. 4.1.

The *dash* (-) in the file type field indicates that it is an ordinary file. The access permissions field tells us what kinds of access permissions are granted. The number, 1, indicates that there is *only one link* for this file from the directory, which means that this file only has one

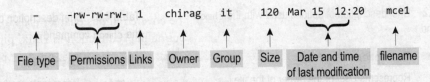

Fig. 4.1 Output of the long listing command for the file mce1

name associated with it. The word chirag is the owner's name; it is the group name that has access to this file; 120 refers to the file size; Mar 15 12:20 is the date and time the file was last modified; and mce1 is the filename.

We have seen that long listing shows the permissions for all the three system users—*User, Group,* and *Other*—besides other information such as name of the file (or directory), size, date, and time of last access. Assume that the permissions for the file mce1 are as follows:

```
r w x r - x r - -     1 chirag     it   120 Mar 15 12:20 mce1
```

The first three characters, r, w, and x, are the permissions for the *User*. This is followed by the permissions for the *Group* members. The last three characters represent the permissions for the *Other* member. The aforementioned output indicates that the *User* has all the three permissions, r w x (read, write, and execute), for the file mce1. The permissions r - x indicate that the *Group* members have read and execute permissions for the file mce1. The missing permission is represented by a hyphen (-). The *Other* users have only r, that is, read permission for the file mce1.

Suppose the permissions for the file mce1 are as follows:

```
r - x - - x - - -     1 chirag     it   120 Mar 15 12:20 mce1
```

The permissions indicate that the *User* has r - x, that is, read and execute permissions for the file mce1. The *Group* members have - - x, that is, only execute permission for the file, and the *Other* members have no permission (- - -), that is, the *Other* members cannot read, write, or execute the file mce1.

Let us take a look at how we can assign and remove permissions from a file or directory.

4.2.1 chmod: Changing File Access Permissions

chmod stands for change mode and the command is used for changing the access permission for files and directories. Only the owner or super user can change the access permission for files.

Syntax chmod [option] mode files

Here, option refers to the following elements given in Table 4.2.

The keyword mode refers to the three access permissions given in Table 4.3.

Examples

(a) $chmod 751 a.txt

This command assigns permission 7 to user (i.e., owner), 5 to group, and 1 to other. Permission 7 means 4(r) + 2(w) + 1(x), that is, the user has all the three permissions, read, write, and execute for the file a.txt. Similarly, the group members have 4(r) + 1(x), that is, read and execute, but no write permission for the file a.txt. However, the other users can only execute th e file. Refer to Fig. 4.2 to view the output of the command.

(b) $chmod 760 a.txt

Table 4.2   Brief description of options used with the `chmod` command

Option	Description
u	Represents *User* or the owner of the file
g	Represents *Group*
o	Represents *Other*
A	Represents all (*User*, *Group*, and *Other*). It is the default option
+	Adds access permission
-	Removes access permission
=	Assigns permission to u, g, o, or a

Table 4.3   Brief description of modes used with the `chmod` command

Mode	Description
r or 4	Represents read permission
w or 2	Represents write permission
x or 1	Represents execute permission

This command assigns permission 7, $4(r) + 2(w) + 1(x)$, that is, read, write, and execute permissions for the file `a.txt` to the user (or owner) of the file. Permission 6, $4(r) + 2(w)$, that is, read and write permission is assigned to the group members of the file, and 0 or no permission to other users. The other users cannot read, write, or execute the file `a.txt`. Refer to Fig. 4.2 to view the output of the command.

(c) `$chmod o+r a.txt`

This command adds the read permission to the other members for the file `a.txt`. Other existing permissions are left undisturbed. Refer to Fig. 4.2 to view the output of the command.

(d) `$chmod u-x,g-w+x,o+wx a.txt`

It removes the execute permission of the user (i.e., owner), removes the write permission of the group members, adds execute permission to the group members, and adds write and execute permissions to the other users. The existing permissions are left undisturbed. Refer to Fig. 4.2 to view the output of the command.

Note: There should not be any space after the comma (,) or while specifying permissions of the user, group, and others in the command.

(e) `$ chmod u=rwx,g=rx, o=x a.txt`

This command assigns permission, rwx, that is, read, write, and execute permission to u, that is, the user or owner of the file. It also assigns, rx, that is, read and execute permission to the group members of the file and x, that is, execute permission to the other users. Previous permissions assigned to user, group, and other members will be removed. Refer to Fig. 4.2 to view the output of the command.

(f) `$ chmod u=w a.txt`

This command assigns write permission to the user, that is, owner of the file `a.txt`. Previous permissions assigned to the user will be removed. Existing permissions to the group and other users will be undisturbed. Refer to Fig. 4.2 to view the output of the command.

4.2.2 umask: Setting Default Permissions

The `umask` command sets the default permissions for the files that will be created in the future.

```
$ chmod 751 a.txt

$ ls -al a.txt
-rwxr-x--x 1 bintu None 21 Dec 30 19:10 a.txt

$ chmod 760 a.txt

$ ls -al a.txt
-rwxrw---- 1 bintu None 21 Dec 30 19:10 a.txt

$ chmod o+r a.txt

$ ls -al a.txt
-rwxrw-r-- 1 bintu None 21 Dec 30 19:10 a.txt

$ chmod u-x,g-w+x,o+wx a.txt

$ ls -al a.txt
-rw-r-xrwx 1 bintu None 21 Dec 30 19:10 a.txt

$ chmod u=rwx,g=rx,o=x a.txt

$ ls -al a.txt
-rwxrw-x--1 bintu None 21 Dec 30 19:10 a.txt

$ chmod u=w a.txt

$ ls -al a.txt
--w-r-x--x 1 bintu None 21 Dec 30 19:10 a.txt
```

Fig. 4.2   Output of application of the chmod command on file a.txt

Syntax   umask ugo

Here, u, g, and o refer to the permissions that we do not want the user, group, and others to have for the new files. Yes, you have read correctly, umask is not for assigning but for removing permissions of the three categories of system users—*user* (owner), *group*, and *other*—for the future files.

To understand this better, let us first create an empty file called chirag using the touch command and then try to list it.

Example
```
$ touch chirag
$ ls -l chirag
-rw-r--r--   1    mce   it 26 Oct 27
10:12    chirag
```

The permission of this file is 644. Whenever we create a file, Unix uses the value stored in a variable called umask to *decide the default permissions.* umask stands for *user file creation mask,* and is used for defining the permissions to mask or hide, that is, the permissions that we want to deny. The current value of umask can be easily determined by typing umask followed by the Enter key.

```
$ umask
0022
```

The first 0 indicates that what follows is an octal number. The three digits that follow the first zero refer to the permissions to be denied to the owner, group, and others. This means that for the owner no permission is denied, whereas for both the group and others, write permission (2) is denied.

Whenever a file is created, Unix assumes that the permissions for this file should be 666. However, since our unmask value is 022, Unix subtracts this value from the default system-wide permissions (666) resulting in a value 644. This value is then used as the permissions for the file that we create.

This is the reason why the permissions turned out to be 644 or rw-r--r-- for the file chirag that we created.

Similarly, the system-wide default permissions for a directory are 777. This implies that when we create a directory its permission would be 777 – 022, that is, 755.

Note: If a directory does not have an execute permission we will never be able to enter data into it.

To change umask value:
```
$ umask 342
```

This would ensure that from this point onwards, any new file that we create would have the permissions 324 (666 − 342) and any directory that we create would have the permissions 435 (777 − 342).

4.2.3 chown: Changing File Ownership

The chown command is used for changing the owner and group owner of a file.

Syntax   chown [-R] new_owner[:[new_group]] filenames

The options and arguments of this command are briefly explained in Table 4.4.

Table 4.4   Brief description of options used in the chown command

Option	Description
-R	The command applies recursively to the files and subdirectories of the current directory.
new_owner	It is the new owner of the files, that is, new_owner will become the new owner of the files and hence gets all the permissions to access the file and modify its access permissions.
new_group	It is the group name to which we want to assign the files.
filenames	These are the files whose ownership we wish to change.

To change both the owner and the group of the file, new_owner must be followed by a colon and a new_group with no space in between.

Note: If no new_group is specified after the new_owner and colon, the owner and group of the file is changed to new_owner and group of new_owner, respectively.

If the new_owner is missing but colon and new_group are specified then only the group of the files is changed, that is, the command will act as the chgrp command. We will learn about the chgrp command next.

Examples   By default, when we create or copy a file, we become its owner. For example, suppose we have a file named notes.txt and we want to change its ownership to another person named Ravi.

Let us first view the current owner of the file by giving the following command:

(a) $ ls −l notes.txt

    -rwxrwxr-x 1 chirag it 120 Mar 15 12:20 notes.txt

    We can see that chirag is the current owner of the file. Now chirag can give the following command to give the ownership of the file notes.txt to Ravi.

(b) $ chown ravi notes.txt

    To see whether the ownership is changed, let us again give the ls −l command.

(c) $ ls −l notes.txt

    -rwxrwxr-x 1 ravi it 120 Mar 15 12:20

    notes.txt

We can see that the owner of the file notes.txt is changed from chirag to ravi.

Now, chirag will no longer be able to change the permissions of the file notes.txt and only ravi can do so.

Note: This process is one way because we must either be the owner of the file or the super user to change its ownership. After we give the file to ravi, we cannot get its ownership back until and unless ravi issues the chown command to return the ownership to us.

Examples   The following are a few more examples.

(a) $ chown chirag:mba notes.txt

This command will change the owner and group of the file notes.txt to chirag and mba, respectively.

Note: The user chirag, and group mba must exist before giving the command. The commands to add a new user and group to the system are useradd and groupadd, respectively (discussed in Chapter 15).

(b) $ chown chirag: notes.txt

This command will change the owner of the file notes.txt to chirag and the group of the file is changed to the one to which chirag belongs.

(c) $ chown :mba notes.txt

This command will change the group of the file notes.txt to mba.

(d) $ chown -R chirag projects

This command will change the ownership of the files and subdirectories of the directory projects to chirag.

4.2.4 chgrp: Changing Group Command

The chgrp command is used for changing the group of the specified number of files. The files will thereby be made accessible to the specified group.

Syntax   chgrp [-R] [-h] new_group filenames

The options and arguments of this command are briefly explained in Table 4.5.

Table 4.5   Brief description of the options used in the chgrp command

Option	Description
-R	It recursively changes the group of the files and subdirectories of the specified directory.
-h	If the specified file is a symbolic link, its group is changed. In the absence of a -h option, the group of the file referenced by the symbolic link is changed and not the symbolic link.
new_group	It is the group name we want to assign the files to.
filenames	Specifies the files whose group we want to change.

By default the file we create gets group ownership in the group we belong to, that is, the group to which the owner belongs becomes the default group ownership of the file.

For example, if we belong to the group *it*, our file will also have the same group ownership, as can be seen by the following command:

```
$ ls -l notes.txt
-rwxrwxr-x    1 chirag      it        120 Mar 15 12:20 notes.txt
```

The following command is used to change the group ownership of a file named notes.txt from group it to group hospital:

```
$ chgrp hospital notes.txt
```

Note: The group `hospital` must exist before giving this command.

Now, the group ownership may appear as follows:

```
$ ls -l notes.txt
-rwxrwxr-x    1 chirag        hospital        120 Mar 15 12:20 notes.txt
```

Note: Since we are still the owner of the file, we can again change its group ownership any time.

Examples

(a) `$chgrp -R hospital projects`

This command changes the group of all the files and subdirectories present in the projects directory to `hospital`.

(b) `$chgrp -h hospital finance.txt`

This changes the group of the symbolic file `finance.txt` to `hospital`.

4.2.5 groups: Displaying Group Membership

The `groups` command is used for finding the group to which a user belongs.

Syntax   `groups username1 [ username2 [username3 …]]`

Example

(a) `% groups chirag`

`mba`

This example asks the group name of the user, `chirag`. The output `mba` signifies that the user `chirag` belongs to the group named `mba`.

We can also find the group membership of more than one user simultaneously as follows:

(b) `% groups chirag ravi`

`chirag : mba`

`ravi : other`

This command asks the group names of the two users, `chirag` and `ravi`. The output indicates that the user `chirag` belongs to the `mba` group and the user `ravi` belongs to the `other` group.

4.2.6 groups: Sharing Files Among Groups

Files can be shared with a group of users so that they can simultaneously read, work, and operate the files(s). For this to happen, a group needs to be created by the system administrator.

To create a group, we give the command with the following syntax:

Syntax   `groupadd group_name`

Example   `% groupadd bankproject`

This will create a group by the name `bankproject`. After creating a group, the next step is to set the group ownership of the file(s) to the given group using the `chgrp` command.

Syntax   `$ chgrp groupname filename`

Example

(a) $ `chgrp bankproject accounts.txt`

This will set the group owner of the file `accounts.txt` to our newly created group `bankproject`. Similarly, we need to change the group ownership of all the files that we wish to share with the users of our group *bankproject*. Thereafter, we need to set the file permissions so that everybody in the group can read and write the file through the following syntax:

Syntax $ `chmod g+rw filename`

We can also assign access permissions to the group in the following way:

Syntax $ `chmod 770 filename`

This example assigns read, write, and execute permissions to the *owner* and *group* members of the file and no permission to the *other* users.

4.3 INPUT/OUTPUT REDIRECTION IN UNIX

The input to a command or a shell is usually provided through the standard input, that is, the keyboard, while the output of the command is displayed on the standard output, that is, on the terminal screen. By default, each command takes its input from the standard input and sends the results to the standard output.

By making use of the I/O redirection operators, we can change the location of providing input to a command and displaying the output of the command. Let us first understand the output redirection operator.

4.3.1 Output Redirection Operator

The output redirection operator is used to redirect the output (from a command) that is supposed to go to a terminal by default, to a file instead. This process of diverting the output from its default destination is known as *output redirection*. For redirecting the output, the operator that we have to use is the '>' operator in shell command. The '>' symbol is known as the output redirection operator and we can use it to divert the output of any command to a file instead of the terminal screen.

Syntax   `command [> | >>] output_file`

Here, `output_file` is the name of the file where we wish to direct and save the output of the command.

Example $ `ls > kk`

On using this command, nothing will appear on the output screen and all output, that is, the list of files and directories from the `ls` command is redirected to the file `kk`.

On viewing the contents of the file `kk`, we get the list of files and directories in it.

Note: If the file `kk` does not exist, the redirection operator will first create it, and if it already exists, its contents will be overwritten.

In order to append output to the file, the append operator, >> is used as shown in the following command:

$ `ls >> kk`

4.3.2 Input Redirection Operator

In order to redirect the standard input, we use the input redirection operator, the < (less than) symbol.

Syntax   `command < input_file`

Here, `input_file` is the name of the file from where the data will be supplied to the command for the purpose of computation.

Examples

(a) `$ sort < kk`

The `sort` command in the example receives the input stream of bytes from the file `kk`. We can also combine input and output redirection operators.

(b) `$ sort < kk > mm`

On using the command, nothing will appear on the terminal screen; instead the content of the file `kk` will be sorted and sent directly to the file `mm`.

4.4 PIPE OPERATOR

The pipe operator, represented by the symbol 'I', is used on the command line for the purpose of sending the output of a command as an input to another command. The pipe operator is different from the output redirection operator, '>' in a way that the output indirection operator '>' is mostly used for sending the output of a command to a file, whereas the pipe operator is used for sending output of a command to some other command for further processing.

Syntax   `command1 | command2 [| command3...]`

Example   `$ cat notes.txt | wc`
```
         4       20       75
```

Here, the output of the `cat` command is sent as input to another command, `wc`. The `wc` command counts the lines, words, and characters in the file `notes.txt` whose content is passed to it.

We can combine several commands with pipes on a single command line as follows:

`$ cat notes.txt | sort| lp`

This command sorts the content of the file `notes.txt` and sends the sorted content to the printer for printing.

Note: The pipe operator provides a one-way flow of data that is from left to right, whereas the redirection operator enables two-way flow of data.

4.5 cut: CUTTING DATA FROM FILES

The `cut` command is used for slicing (cutting) a file vertically.

Syntax   `cut [-c -f] file_name`

Here, `-c` refers to columns or characters and `-f` refers to the fields, that is, words delimited by whitespace or tab.

Examples

(a) `cut -c 6-22,30-35 bank.lst`

This command retrieves 6-22 characters and 30-35 columns (characters) from the file `bank.lst` and displays them on the screen.

Let us look at another example.

(b) `$ cut -f2 bank.lst`

We get the content of the second field of the file `bank.lst` displayed on the screen.

Let us assume the file `bank.lst` has the following content.

```
101     Anil
102     Ravi
103     Sunil
104     Chirag
105     Raju
```

Note: The fields in the file `bank.lst` are separated by a tab space.

Here, the `cut` command will display the second field of the file `bank.lst`, that is, we will get the output shown in Fig. 4.3.

```
$ cut -f2 bank.lst

Anil
Ravi
Sunil
Chirag
Raju
```

Fig. 4.3 Output displaying second field of the file `bank.lst`

The fields in the file `bank.lst` are delimited by a tab. If they are separated by a delimiter other than tab or white space, then the output of the `cut` command will be different.

Let us assume the file `bank.lst` has the following content.

```
101,Anil
102,Ravi
103,Sunil
104,Chirag
105,Raju
```

We can see that the fields of the file `bank.lst` are delimited by a comma (,) and not by a tab or white space. The following command will not display anything on the screen as the default delimiter for identifying fields is either white space or tab.

`$ cut -f2 bank.lst`

Hence, the file `bank.lst` will be considered to be consisting of a single field on each line.

To specify the delimiter when the fields are delimited by some other character other than tab or white space as in the aforementioned file, we use `-d` (delimiter) to specify the field delimiter as shown in the following example:

`cut -f2  -d "," bank.lst`

This statement will show the second field of the file `bank.lst` where the fields are delimited by commas (,).

Assume that the fields are delimited by a comma (,). The following statement cuts the fields, starting from the first, from the file `bank.lst`:

`$ cut -d"," -f1- bank.lst`

Assuming that the fields are delimited by commas (,), the following statement cuts the first field, fourth field, and so on, from the file `bank.lst`:

```
$ cut -d"|" -f1,4- bank.lst
```

Can we cut the fields of two separate files and paste them to make a third file? Yes, of course. Let us see how.

Assume there are two files, *Names* and *Telephone*, with the following contents.

The *Names* file consists of employee codes and names as follows:

```
101          Anil
102          Ravi
103          Sunil
104          Chirag
105          Raju
```

The *Telephone* file consists of employee codes and telephone numbers as follows:

```
101          2429193
102          3334444
103          7777888
104          9990000
105          5555111
```

Let us cut the second field from both the files and paste them to make a third file, that is, cut the employee names from the *Names* file and telephone numbers from the *Telephone* file and paste them to create a third file.

To cut out the second word (field) from the file *Names,* we give the following command:

```
$ cut -f2  Names
```

We get the output as shown in Fig. 4.4.

Similarly, to cut the telephone numbers, that is, the second field from the *Telephone* file, we give the following command:

```
Anil
Ravi
Sunil
Chirag
Raju
```

Fig. 4.4 Output showing second field of file `Names`

```
$ cut -f2  Telephone
2429193
3334444
7777888
9990000
5555111
```

We can save the output by redirecting the standard output to a file.

```
$ cut -f2 Name > names.txt
$ cut -f2 Telephone > numbers.txt
```

The names and telephone numbers will be saved in two files, `names.txt` and `numbers.txt`, respectively. To paste the content of the two files, we need to understand the `paste` command. Let us now study this command.

4.6 paste: PASTING DATA IN FILES

It is used to join textual data together and is very useful if we want to put together textual information located in various files.

Syntax   paste [-s] [-d "delimiter"] files

These options are briefly explained in Table 4.6.

Table 4.6   Brief description of the options used in the paste command

Option	Description
-s	The paste command usually displays the corresponding lines of each specified file. The -s option refers to a serial option and is used to combine all the lines of each file into one line and display them one below the other.
-d	This option is for specifying the delimiter to be used for pasting lines from the specified files. The default delimiter used to separate the lines from the files is the *Tab* character.

```
Anil      2429193
Ravi      3334444
Sunil     7777888
Chirag    9990000
Raju      5555111
```

Fig. 4.5   Pasting of two files names. txt and numbers.txt with the default tab character in between

```
Anil:2429193
Ravi:3334444
Sunil:7777888
Chirag:9990000
Raju:5555111
```

Fig. 4.6   Two files names.txt and numbers.txt pasted with the '|' symbol in between

```
$ paste -s names.txt numbers.txt
Anil      Ravi      Sunil     Chirag    Raju
2429193   3334444   7777888   9990000   5555111
```

Fig. 4.7   Two files names.txt and numbers.txt pasted one below the other

Example   Consider the file names.txt mentioned in Section 4.5.

```
$ paste names.txt numbers.txt
```

The output will be as shown in Fig. 4.5.

We can see that the corresponding lines of the files names.txt and numbers.txt are pasted with a tab character in between. By default, the paste command uses the tab character for pasting lines; however, we can specify a delimiter of our choice with the -d command as shown in the following example.

```
$ paste -d"|" names.txt numbers.txt
```

This joins the two files with the help of the | delimiter and not tab (i.e., between names and telephone numbers, there will be a '|' symbol instead of the tab character, as shown in Fig. 4.6).

The example shown in Fig. 4.7 serially pastes the contents from the files. It combines all the lines of each file into one line and displays them one below the other.

4.7 split: SPLITTING FILES INTO LINES OR BYTES

The split command is used to split a file into pieces.

Syntax   split [-b n [K | M]] [-l n] [-n] file_name dest_file

The options and arguments are briefly explained in Table 4.7.

Table 4.7 Brief description of the options and arguments used in the `split` command

Option	Description
`-b n`	It splits the specified file into pieces that are *n* bytes in size.
`-b nK`	It splits the specified file into pieces that are *n* kilo bytes in size.
`-b nM`	It splits the specified file into pieces that are *n* mega bytes in size.
`-l n`	It splits the specified file into *n* number of lines (default option). The default value of *n* is 1000.
`-n`	It is the same as `-l n`.
`File_name`	It is the name of the file to be split.
`dest_file`	It is the name of the file in which the split pieces will be stored. If the `dest_file` is, say, demo, the split pieces will be stored in the files demoaa, demoab, demoac, and so on.

```
$ split numbers.txt trial

$ ls trial*
trialaa

$ cat trialaa

2429193
3334444
7777888
9990000
5555111
```

Fig. 4.8 File `numbers.txt` split into the file `trialaa`

```
$ split -b 20 numbers.txt temp

$ ls temp*
tempaa tempab

$ cat tempaa
2429193
3334444
7777

$ cat tempab
888
9990000
5555111
```

Fig. 4.9 File `numbers.txt` split into two 20-byte files, `tempaa` and `tempab`

```
$ split -l 2 numbers.txt temp

$ ls de*
tempaa demoab demoac

$ cat demoaa

2429193
3334444

$ cat tempab
777888
9990000

$ cat demoac
5555111
```

Fig. 4.10 File `numbers.txt` split into three files, `demoaa`, `demoab`, and `demoac`, which are two lines each

Example When the `split` command is given without any option, the file is split into pieces that are 1000 lines each, that is, the default option is –l as shown in Fig. 4.8.

We can see that the file numbers.txt is split into a single file trialaa consisting of the complete content of the file numbers.txt (because the size of the file numbers.txt is lesser than 1000 lines).

The example in Fig. 4.9 splits the file numbers.txt into files that are 20 bytes each.

The file numbers.txt is split into two pieces, tempaa and tempab, where tempaa contains the first 20 bytes of the file numbers.txt while the file tempab contains the remaining number of bytes.

The example in Fig. 4.10 splits the file numbers.txt into pieces, each of which consists of two lines.

The file numbers.txt is split into three files with the following names: demoaa, demoab, and demoac. Each of these files contains two lines (as shown in Fig. 4.10).

4.8 wc: COUNTING CHARACTERS, WORDS, AND LINES IN FILES

The wc (word count) command is usually used to find the number of lines in any file. By default, it displays all the three counts—characters, words, and lines—of any given file.

Syntax   wc [-l -w -c] [filename]

Here, -l counts the number of lines.

-w counts the number of words delimited by white space or a tab.

-c counts the number of characters.

Example $ wc phone.lst

           12 124 650 phone.lst

This command displays the count of lines, words, and characters in the file phone.lst, that is, the numerical values 12, 124, and 650 represent the count of lines, words, and characters, respectively in the file phone.lst.

If we wish to view only the number of lines in the file, we need to only use the –l option, as in the following example:

$ wc -l phone.lst

12 phone.lst

As we can see, the command displays the count of the number of lines in the file phone.lst. Similarly, the -w option will give the total number of words in a file, and the -c option gives the total number of characters in a file.

4.9 sort: SORTING FILES

It is used for sorting files either line-wise or on the basis of certain fields, where the fields refer to the words that are separated by one of the following: white space, tab, or special symbol.

Syntax   sort [-n][-r][-f][-u] filename

The options and arguments shown here are briefly explained in Table 4.8.

Table 4.8   Brief description of the options used in the sort command

Option	Description
-n	Sorts numerical values instead of ASCII, ignoring blanks and tabs
-r	Sorts in reverse order
-f	Sorts upper and lower case together, that is, ignores the difference in upper and lower case
-u	Displays unique lines, that is, it eliminates duplicate lines in the output
filename	Represents the file to be sorted

All lines in the filename will be arranged in alphabetical order on the basis of the first character of the line.

The other syntax for using the sort command is as follows:

Syntax   sort +p1 - p2 filename

This limits the sort to be applied on the basis of the characters beginning from field p1 and ending at field p2. If p2 is omitted, then sorting will be done on the basis of the characters beginning from field p1 till the end of the line.

Examples

(a) $ sort +2 -4 bnk.lst

This command skips the first two fields and uses the third and fourth fields for sorting the file bnk.1st.

(b) `$ sort +3 -4 bnk.1st`

This command skips the first three fields and uses the fourth field for sorting the file bnk.1st.

(c) `$ sort +2 bnk.1st`

This command skips the first two fields and uses the third and the rest of the fields up till the end of the line for sorting the file bnk.1st.

(d) `$ sort bnk.1st -o bank.1st`

This command sorts the file bnk.1st and stores the result in bank.1st.

(e) `$ sort +0 -1 bnk.1st`

This command sorts the file bnk.1st on the basis of the first field.

(f) `$ sort +1 -4 bnk.1st`

This command sorts the file bnk.1st from the second to the fourth fields.

(g) `$ sort +2b bnk.1st`

This command sorts the file bnk.1st on the third field after ignoring leading blank spaces. The -f option is used to ignore the upper and lower case distinction.

(h) `$ sort +2bf bnk.1st`

The command will sort the third field after ignoring leading blank spaces and sort the upper and lower case data together.

The -n option is used for sorting the file on the basis of numerical values rather than ASCII values.

(i) `$ sort -n +2 -3 a.bat`

The command sorts the file a.bat on the third field, on the assumption that it is a numerical field.

The -r option is used for sorting a given file in reverse order.

(j) `$ sort -r link.1st`

The command will sort the file link.1st in the reverse order. The -u option will eliminate duplicate lines in the sorted output.

(k) `$ sort -nu +2 -3 a.bat`

The command sorts the file a.bat on the third field after eliminating duplicate lines.

4.10 head: DISPLAYING TOP CONTENTS OF FILES

The head command is used for selecting the specified number of lines from the beginning of the file and displaying them on the screen.

Syntax   `head –[n] file name`

Here, n is the number of lines that we want to select.

Example   `head bnk.1st`

When used without an option, this displays the *first ten records* (*lines*) of the specified file.

`head -3 bnk.1st`

It displays the first three lines of the file bnk.1st.

We can also specify more than one file.

```
head -3 bnk.lst notes.txt
```

It will display the first three lines of both the files, bnk.lst and notes.txt, one after the other.

4.11 tail: DISPLAYING BOTTOM CONTENTS OF FILES

The tail command is used for selecting the specified number of lines from the end of the file and displaying them on the screen.

Syntax   tail -[ncbr] filename

The options of the command are briefly explained in Table 4.9.

Table 4.9   Brief description of the options used in the tail command

Option	Description
-n	Selects the last n lines
-c	Selects the last c number of characters
-b	Selects a specified number of disk blocks
-r	Sorts the selected lines in reverse order

Note: There is one more option that is used with the tail command. +n gives an instruction to skip $n-1$ lines and select the rest until the end of the file.

Examples

(a) $ tail -3 bnk.lst
It will display the last three lines.

(b) $ tail -10 bnk.lst
It will display the last 10 lines.

(c) $ tail +10 bnk.lst
It will start extracting from the tenth line (it will skip nine lines) up to the end of the file.

(d) $ tail -50c bnk.lst
It will display the last 50 characters of the file bnk.lst.

(e) $ tail -2b bnk.lst
It will display the last two disk blocks of the file bnk.lst. A disk block is usually 512 bytes big.

(f) $ tail -2r bnk.lst
It will display the last two lines of the file bnk.lst in reverse order, that is, the last line will appear first followed by the second last line.

(g) $ head -25 a.txt | tail +20 > b.txt
It extracts lines numbering from 20 to 25 from the file a.txt.
The head utility extracts the first 25 lines from the file a.txt and pipes them to the tail utility, which skips the first 19 lines and extracts lines 20 to 25. The results are then stored in file b.txt.

4.12 diff: FINDING DIFFERENCES BETWEEN TWO FILES

The diff command is used for comparing two files. If there are no differences between the two files being compared, the command does not display any output. Otherwise it displays the output indicating the changes that need to be made to the first file to make it same as the second file.

Syntax   diff file1 file2

All the differences found in the two files are displayed in a format consisting of two numbers and a character in between. The number to the left of the character represents the line number in the first file, and the number to the right of the character represents the line number in the second file. The character can be any of the following:

1. d: delete
2. c: change
3. a: add

Example Assume we have two files, `users.txt` and `customers.txt`, with the following content.

```
users.txt       customers.txt
John            John
Peter           Charles
Troy            Troy
```

Now on comparing the two files, we get the following output.

```
$ diff users.txt customers.txt
2c2
< Peter
--
> Charles
```

Note: The < character precedes the lines from the first file and > precedes the lines from the second file.

This output indicates that the two files differ by only one line. It indicates that if the second line, `Peter`, in the first file (`users.txt`) is changed to the second line, `Charles`, of the second file (`customers.txt`), both files will be exactly the same.

To better understand the `diff` command, let us twist the content of the first file `users.txt` as follows:

```
users.txt
John
Peter
Charles
```

Keeping the content of the file `customers.txt` same as before, when we compare the two files, we get the following output.

```
$ diff users.txt customers.txt
2d1
< Peter
3a3
> Troy
```

The output indicates that to make the file `users.txt` the same as `customers.txt`, we have to delete the second line, `Peter`, and add the third line, `Troy`, from `customers.txt` after the third line in `users.txt`.

4.13 cmp: COMPARING FILES

The cmp command compares two files and indicates the line number where the first difference in the files occurs. The cmp command does not display anything if the files being compared are exactly the same.

Syntax   cmp [[-l][-s]] file1 file2 [skip1] [skip2]

The related options and arguments are briefly explained in Table 4.10.

Table 4.10   Brief description of the options and arguments used in the cmp command

Option	Description
-l	It prints the byte number and the differing byte values in octal for each difference.
-s	It displays nothing but the return exit status on the screen. The status returned can be any of the following:
	0: If the two files are identical
	1: If the two files are different
	>1: If an error occurs while reading the files
file1 and file2	These are the files to be compared.
skip1 and skip2	These are the optional byte offsets from the beginning of *file1* and *file2* respectively, where we wish to begin the comparison of files. The offset can be specified in decimal, octal, and hexadecimal. The offsets in hexadecimal and octal formats have to be preceded by '0x' and '0', respectively.

Example   Consider we have two files, users.txt and customers.txt, with the following content.

users.txt	customers.txt
John	John
Peter	Charles
Troy	Troy

The following are examples of commands that are used to compare the two files.

```
$cmp users.txt customers.txt
```

The cmp command compares the files users.txt and customers.txt and displays the following output.

```
users.txt customers.txt differ: byte 6, line 2
```

The output indicates that the byte location where the first difference between the two files (users.txt and customers.txt) occurs is 6.

The following example shows the list of byte locations and the differing byte values in octal format for every difference found in the two files:

```
$cmp -l users.txt customers.txt
```

```
$ cmp -1 users.txt customers.txt
  6  120  103
  7  145  150
  8  164  141
  9  145  162
 10  162  154
 11   12  145
 12  124  163
 13  162   12
 14  157  124
 15  171  162
 16   12  157
cmp: EOF on users.txt
```

Fig. 4.11 List of byte locations and the differing bytes in the two files users.txt and customers.txt

```
$ cmp -s users.txt customers.txt
$ echo $?
1
$ cmp -s users.txt customers.txt 12 14
$ echo $?
0
```

Fig. 4.12 Comparison between files and display of status

We get the output shown in Fig. 4.11.

The output displays the byte locations of the difference between the two files and also shows that the users.txt file is smaller than the customers.txt file as it encounters its end of file (EOF) marker while being compared with the content of customers.txt.

The following example shows the status returned on comparing the two files.

```
$ cmp -s users.txt customers.txt
```

This example returns the exit status. On displaying the exit status value (Fig. 4.12), we get a value one, confirming that the two files are not the same but different.

The following example compares the two files after skipping the offset of 12 and 14 bytes from the two files respectively.

```
$ cmp -s users.txt customers.txt 12 14
```

On displaying the return status (Fig. 4.12), we get an output 0, which confirms that the two files are exactly the same after giving the offset values.

4.14 uniq: ELIMINATING AND DISPLAYING DUPLICATE LINES

The uniq command is used to find and display duplicate lines in a file. In addition, we can use it to eliminate duplicate lines and display only unique lines.

Syntax　uniq [-c | -d | -u] [-f fields] [-s char] [input_file [output_file]]

The related options and arguments are briefly explained in Table 4.11.

Table 4.11 Brief description of the options and arguments used in the uniq command

Option	Description
-c	It precedes each line with a count of the number of occurrences.
-d	It displays only repeated lines (duplicate) in the input.
-u	It displays only unique lines in the input.
-f fields	It ignores the first given number of fields on each input line.
-s char	It ignores the first given number of characters of each input line. If this option is used along with the -f option, the first given number of characters after the first fields will be ignored.
input_file	It is the name of the file whose content we need to compare.
output_file	It is the name of the file where the output of the command will be stored. If no output file is specified, the output will appear on the standard output.

Example   `$ uniq a.txt > b.txt`

This command removes duplicate lines in the file `a.txt` and saves it in another file `b.txt`.

Let us assume the file `a.txt` contains the following content:

```
a.txt
It may rain today
I am leaving now
It may rain today
Lovely weather
I am leaving now
```

The following is the command for removing all duplicate lines from a file.

`$ sort a.txt | uniq`

This command sorts and removes all the duplicate lines in the file `a.txt` and displays only the unique lines on the screen. We get the following output.

```
I am leaving now
It may rain today
Lovely weather
```

The following command is used to display only the unique lines.

`$ sort a.txt | uniq -u`

The command sorts and displays only the unique lines in the file `a.txt` on the screen. We get the following output.

```
Lovely weather
```

The following command is used to display all the duplicate lines in a file.

`$ sort a.txt | uniq -d`

We get the following output.

```
I am leaving now
It may rain today
```

The following command is used to display the count of duplicate occurrences in a file.

`$ sort a.txt | uniq -c`

We get the following output.

```
2 I am leaving now
2 It may rain today
1 Lovely weather
```

4.15 comm: DISPLAYING AND SUPPRESSING UNIQUE OR COMMON CONTENT IN TWO FILES

The `comm` command displays or suppresses the content common to two files. The output is displayed in a column format, where the first column represents the output related to the first file and the second column displays the output related to the second file.

Syntax `comm [-1] [-2] [-3 ] file1 file2`

The options and arguments are briefly explained in Table 4.12.

Table 4.12 Brief description of the options and arguments used in the `comm` command

Option	Description
`-1`	It suppresses the display of the content that is unique to `file1`. It also displays the unique content in `file2`.
`-2`	It suppresses the display of the content that is unique to `file2`. It also displays the unique content in `file1`.
`-3`	It suppresses the display of the content that is common to both `file1` and `file2`, that is, it displays the unique content in `file1` and `file2`.
`file1` and `file2`	These are the two files being compared.

Note: When the `comm` command is executed without any options, the output will comprise three columns, where the first column displays content unique to the first file, the second column displays content unique to the second file, and the third column displays content common to both the files.

Examples Suppose we have two files, `users.txt` and `customers.txt`, with the following content.

```
users.txt       customers.txt
John            John
Peter           Charles
Troy            Troy
```

```
$ comm users.txt customers.txt
                John
        Charles
Peter
                Troy
$ comm -1 users.txt customer.txt
        John
Charles
        Troy
$ comm -2 users.txt customers.txt
        John
Peter
        Troy
$ comm -3 users.txt customers.txt
        Charles
Peter
```

Fig. 4.13 Output of the `comm` command on comparing two files

(a) This example compares the two files (`users.txt` and `customers.txt`) and displays the output in three columns. The first column displays content unique to the first file, the second column displays content unique to the second file, and the third column displays content common to both the files (Fig. 4.13).

`$comm users.txt customers.txt`

(b) This example compares the two files, `users.txt` and `customers.txt`, suppresses the content that is unique in `users.txt`, and also displays the unique content in `customers.txt` (Fig. 4.13).

`$comm -1 users.txt customers.txt`

(c) This example compares the two files, `users.txt` and `customers.txt` and suppresses the content that is unique in `customers.txt` and also displays the unique content in `users.txt` (refer to Fig. 4.13).

`$comm -2 users.txt customers.txt`

(d) This example compares the aforementioned two files and suppresses the content that is common in customers.txt and users.txt (Fig. 4.13).

```
$comm -3 users.txt customers.txt
```

4.16 time: FINDING CONSUMED TIME

The time command executes a specified command and also displays the time consumed in its execution. The time usage of the specified command is displayed on the screen.

Syntax   time command [arguments]

In the aforementioned syntax, command is the command whose time usage is to be determined.

Examples   We can determine the time taken to perform the sorting operation by preceding the sort command with the time command.

(a) $ time   sort -o newlist invoice.lst
```
real  0m1.18s
user 0m0.73s
sys  0m0.38s
```

The *real* time refers to the time elapsed from the invocation of the command till its termination. The *user* time shows the time spent by the command in executing itself while *sys* indicates the time used by the Unix system in invoking the command.

(b) Let us see how much time it takes to store the recursive long listing of files and directories sorted on modification time in a file.
```
$ time ls -ltR >k.out
real 0m0.04s
user 0m0.01s
sys  0m0.01s
```

Real time   The real time represents the time taken by the command (from its initiation to termination) to execute.

User time   The user time represents the time taken by the command to execute its own code, that is, the code run in user mode. It represents the actual CPU time used in executing the command. For small programs that take milliseconds to execute, this time is often reported as 0.0.

Sys time   The sys time is the amount of CPU time spent in the kernel for running the command. It represents the CPU time spent in executing the system calls that are invoked by the command within the kernel.

The time command can be used to isolate the commands that are time consuming so that they can be run in the background. We will learn the process of executing the commands in the background in Chapter 6.

Note: The combination of user and sys time is known as CPU time.

4.17 pg: SHOWING CONTENT PAGE-WISE

This command displays the specified long file page-wise, that is, one screen page at a time. It also enables us to navigate to the previous or following screen. In addition, we can search for the desired pattern in the given file. On giving this command, it shows the first screen page of the given file and shows the colon (:) at the bottom of the screen where we can use the following character(s) to view the desired content in the given file.

Syntax   `pg [-number] [+ linenumber] [+/pattern/] [filename]`

Here, `-number` specifies the screen size in lines. The default screen size is 23 lines. `+line_number` shows the file from the given line number. `+/pattern/` shows the file where the given pattern begins. `filename` specifies the filename that we wish to view page-wise along with its path.

Table 4.13   Brief description of the list of commands given on execution of the `pg` command

Command	Description
h	Displays help information
q or Q	Quits the `pg` command
`<blank>` or `<newline>`	Moves to the next page
$	Moves to the previous page
f	Skips the next page
/pattern	Searches forward for the given pattern and displays it
?pattern	Searches backward for the given pattern and displays it

The list of commands that can be given on execution of the `pg` command are briefly explained in Table 4.13.

Examples

(a) `$ pg letter.txt`
This command displays the file `letter.txt` one screen page at a time.

(b) `$pg letter.txt -10`
This command displays the content of the file `letter.txt` one screen page at a time where a page consists of 10 lines.

(c) `$pg letter.txt +25`
This command displays the content of the file `letter.txt` page-wise from the 25th line.

(d) `$pg letter.txt +/happy/`
This command displays the content of the file `letter.txt` from the location where the word `happy` occurs in the file.

4.18 lp: PRINTING DOCUMENTS

The term `lp` stands for line printer and the command is used for printing files.

Syntax   `lp [ -d printer_destination ] [ -n number_of_copies] [ -q priority ]`
`[ -H ] [ -P page_list ] file(s)`

The options used in this command are briefly explained in Table 4.14.

Table 4.14   Brief description of the options used in the `lp` command

Option	Description
-d	It is used for defining the printer destination, that is, the name of the printer we wish to print the file(s) with.
-n	It is used to define the number of copies to print. The valid range is from 1 to 100.
-P	It is used to define the pages of a selected file that we wish to print. The page list contains the page numbers and page range separated by commas (,). Examples: 1, 5, 9–11, 20.
-i	It is used to identify the job ID assigned to the `print` command. On giving the `lp` command, it notifies the job ID assigned to the task.
-H	It is used to control the printing job. The values used with this option are as follows: 1. Hold: Holds the printing job 2. Resume: Resumes the printing job 3. HH:MM: Holds the job till the specified time 4. Immediate: Prints the job immediately
-q -	It is used to set the priority of the print job. The valid values are from 1 (indicates lowest priority) till 100 (indicates highest priority). The default priority value is 50.

Examples   The following are the examples of the `lp` commmand.

(a) `$lp notes.txt`
This command prints the file `notes.txt` on the default printer.

(b) `$lp -d Deskjet1001 notes.txt`
This command prints the file `notes.txt` on the printer named `Deskjet1001`.

(c) `$lp -d Deskjet1001 -n 2 notes.txt`
This command prints two copies of the file `notes.txt` on the printer named `Deskjet1001`.

(d) `$lp -d Deskjet1001 -P 2, 5-7, 10, 15- notes.txt`
This command prints pages 2, 5, 6, 7, 10, and from 15 till the end of the file `notes.txt` on the printer `Deskjet1001`.

Note: The hyphen after 15 suggests from page 15 onwards.

(e) `$lp -d Deskjet1001 notes.txt accounts.txt`
This command prints the file `notes.txt` and `accounts.txt` on the printer `Deskjet1001`.

(f) `$lp -i 1207 -H hold`
The print job number 1207 is held for a while.

(g) `$lp -i 1207 -H resume`
The print job number 1207 is resumed for printing.

(h) `$lp -i 1207 -q 100`
The print job number 1207 is given the highest priority.
A command that goes along with the `lp` command is the `cancel` command. Let us now discuss this briefly.

4.19 cancel: CANCELLING PRINT COMMAND

The cancel command cancels existing print jobs.

Syntax cancel [id] [printer_destination]

The options and arguments used in this command are briefly explained in Table 4.15.

Table 4.15 Brief description of the options used in the cancel command

Option	Description
id	It indicates the print job ID that we wish to cancel.
printer_ destination	It removes all jobs from the specified printer destination.

Examples

(a) $cancel Deskjet1001

This command cancels all print jobs sent for printing at the Deskjet1001 printer.

(b) $cancel 1207

This command cancels the print job with ID 1207.

4.20 UNDERSTANDING .profile FILES

The .profile file exists in our home directory and is the start-up file that is automatically executed when we log in to the Unix system. The file can be used to customize our environment, setting PATH variable and terminal type, and also to write the commands and scripts that we wish to automatically execute when we log in.

Note: The Unix operating system executes several system files including the .profile file before returning the command prompt to the user.

The most basic variables used in the .profile file to set up an environment for us are as follows:

1. The PATH variable defines the search path to find the commands and applications that we execute. Through the PATH variable, the commands and scripts can be executed in directories other than their source directories (directories where the command or script exists).
2. $HOME is the name of the directory from where we begin our Unix session.
3. ENV refers to the environment variables.

We will learn about these variables in detail in Chapter 5.

Using any editor, we can add commands to the .profile file, which we wish to execute automatically when we log in. Chapter 8 will help you use different editors. A new command added to .profile will come into effect either when we log out and log in again or when we run the .profile file at the command prompt through the following command:

$.$HOME/.profile

4.21 calendar: GETTING REMINDERS

The calendar command reads the calendar file and displays appointments and reminders for the current day.

Syntax   calendar

Example   For this command to work, we need to create a file named calendar at the root of our home directory and write our appointments or reminders in the following format.

```
10/7/2012  Today is Board Meeting
10/8/2012  Visiting Doctor
```

Now, if today is 7 October 2012, and we execute the calendar command, the line Today is Board Meeting will appear on the screen.

Note: To avoid executing the calendar command every day, add it at the end of our .profile file that we just discussed.

4.22 script: RECORDING SESSIONS

The script command is used for recording our interaction with the Unix system. It runs in the background recording everything that is displayed on our screen.

Syntax   script [-a] filename

The options and arguments used in the command are briefly explained in Table 4.16.

Table 4.16   Brief description of the options used in the script command

Option	Description
-a	It appends the session into the filename. If this option is not specified, the filename will be overwritten with the new data.
filename	This gives the name of the file where our session will be recorded. If we do not provide a filename to the script command, it places its output in a default file named transcript.

Example   The following example will begin recording the session in the file transact.txt:

```
$ script transact.txt
```

To exit from the scripting session, either press Ctrl-d or write exit on the command prompt followed by the Enter key.

Figure 4.14(a) shows how the session is recorded in the file transact.txt. The commands executed, cat, sort, mkdir, rmdir, etc., are recorded into the file transact.txt. To stop recording, Ctrl-d keys are pressed. To confirm if the session is properly recorded in the file, we execute the cat command to view the contents of the file transact.txt. Figure 4.14(b) confirms that the session is correctly recorded in the file transact.txt.

```
$ script transact.txt                    $ cat transact.txt
Script started, file is transact.txt     Script started on 21 February 2012
                                         10:24:40 PM IST
$ cat bank.lst
101  Aditya    0      14/11/2012  current   $ cat bank.lst
102  Anil      10000  20/05/2011  saving    101  Aditya    0      14/11/2012  current
103  Naman     0      20/08/2009  current   102  Anil      10000  20/05/2011  saving
104  Rama      10000  15/08/2010  saving    103  Naman     0      20/08/2009  current
105  Jyotsna   5000   16/06/2012  saving    104  Rama      10000  15/08/2010  saving
106  Mukesh    14000  20/12/2009  current   105  Jyotsna   5000   16/06/2012  saving
107  Yashasvi  14500  30/11/2011  saving    106  Mukesh    14000  20/12/2009  current
108  Chirag    0      15/12/2012  current   107  Yashasvi  14500  30/11/2011  saving
109  Arya      16000  14/12/2010  current   108  Chirag    0      15/12/2012  current
110  Puneet    130    16/11/2009  saving    109  Arya      16000  14/12/2010  current
                                            110  Puneet    130    16/11/2009  saving
$ sort -r bank.lst
110  Puneet    130    16/11/2009  saving    $ sort -r bank.lst
109  Arya      16000  14/12/2010  current   110  Puneet    130    16/11/2009  saving
108  Chirag    0      15/12/2012  current   109  Arya      16000  14/12/2010  current
107  Yashasvj  14500  30/11/2011  saving    108  Chirag    0      15/12/2012  current
106  Mukesh    14000  20/12/2009  current   107  Yashasvj  14500  30/11/2011  saving
105  Jyotsna   5000   16/06/2012  saving    106  Mukesh    14000  20/12/2009  current
104  Rama      10000  15/08/2010  saving    105  Jyotsna   5000   16/06/2012  saving
103  Naman     0      20/08/2009  current   104  Rama      10000  15/08/2010  saving
102  Anil      10000  20/05/2011  saving    103  Naman     0      20/08/2009  current
101  Aditya    0      14/11/2012  current   102  Anil      10000  20/05/2011  saving
                                            101  Aditya    0      14/11/2012  current
$ mkdir projects
                                            $ mkdir projects
$ rmdir projects
                                            $ rmdir projects
$ Script done, file is transact.txt
                                            $ ^d

                                            $ Script done on 21 February 2012
                                            10:25:19 PM IST
```

(a)   (b)

Fig. 4.14   Recording a session (a) Recording in the file `transact.txt` (b) Recorded session

4.23 CONVERSIONS BETWEEN DOS AND UNIX

There is a difference in format between Unix and DOS files. DOS (or Windows) files end with both the line feed and carriage return, whereas Unix files end only with the line feed character. It also means that in DOS files the new line character comprises carriage return and line feed, whereas in Unix files, the new line character comprises only the line feed character. The following are the two commands used in conversions between DOS and Unix files:

1. `dos2unix`: Converts text files from DOS to Unix format
2. `unix2dos`: Converts text files from Unix format to DOS format

The syntax for the `dos2unix` command is as follows:

> Syntax   `dos2unix [-b] file1 [file2]`

The options and arguments used in this command are briefly explained in Table 4.17.

Table 4.17 Brief description of the options used in the `dos2unix` command

Option	Description
-b	It creates a backup of file1 with the name file1.bak before converting it into Unix format.
File1	It is the file in DOS format.
File2	It is the file in which we wish to store the Unix format of the file. If file2 is not used, the original file file1, will be converted into the Unix format.

Table 4.18 Brief description of the options and arguments used in the `unix2dos` command

Option	Description
-b	It creates a backup of file1 by name file1.bak before converting it into DOS format.
file1	It is a file in the Unix format.
file2	It is the file in which we wish to store the DOS format of the file. If file2 is not used then the original file, file1 will be converted into the DOS format.

Examples

(a) `$ dos2unix a.txt b.txt`

This converts the DOS file `a.txt` into `b.txt`. The new line characters consisting of the carriage return and line feed character in `a.txt` will be converted to line feed character and stored in file `b.txt`, which is a file in Unix format.

(b) `$ dos2unix -b a.txt`

The command converts the DOS file `a.txt` into the Unix format. The original DOS format will be backed up and stored as `a.txt.bak`.

The syntax for the `unix2dos` command is as follows:

Syntax   `unix2dos [-b] file1 [file2]`

The options and arguments used in this command are briefly explained in Table 4.18.

Examples

(a) `$ unix2dos a.txt b.txt`

The command converts the Unix file `a.txt` into `b.txt`. The new line characters consisting of line feed character in `a.txt` will therefore be converted to a combination of carriage return and line feed character and stored in file `b.txt`, which is a file in DOS format.

(b) `$ unix2dos -b a.txt`

The command converts the Unix file `a.txt` into DOS format. The original Unix format will be backed up and stored as `a.txt.bak`.

4.24 man: DISPLAYING MANUAL

The term `man` stands for manual and displays the online documentation of the given Unix command. This command is meant for helping the user by providing usage, syntax, and examples of using the given command.

Syntax   `man [-] [-k pattern] command`

Here, - (hyphen)displays the information without stopping; `-k pattern` searches all the commands documented in the `man` pages that contain the specified pattern, and displays the list of matching commands.

Example   `$ man cp`

This example displays the manual of the `cp` command. If the manual consists of several pages, the first page will be displayed and we can press the spacebar to move on to the next page.

`$ man -k backup`

```
$ man -k backup
/usr/dt/man/windex: No such file or directory
/usr/man/windex: No such file or directory
/usr/oenwin/share/man/windex: No such file or directory

$ catman -w
/usr/lib/getNAME: gnome-session-save.1 - repeated date

$ man - k backup
asadmin-backup-domain                    asadmin-backup-domain (las) - performs a backup
on the domain
asadmin-list-backups                     asadmin-list-backup (las)   - lists all backups
and restores
asadmin -restore-domain                  asadmin-restore-domain (las) - restores files
 from backup
backup-domain     asadmin-backup-domain (las) - performs a backup on the domain
list-backups      asadmin-list-backups (las) - lists all backups and restores
nisbackup         nisbackup (lm) - backup NIS+ directories
nistrestore       nisrestore (lm) - restore NIS+ directory backup
restore-domain    asadmin-restore-domain (las)  - restores files form backup
tdbackup          tdbbackup(lm) - tool for backing up and for validating the in
egbrity of samba \&. tdb files
```

Fig. 4.15   Manual containing the specified pattern

This example searches the documentation in the man pages and displays the list of commands that contain the pattern backup. In case we get an error—windex directory not found—as shown in Fig. 4.15, we need to create the windex directory by giving the catman -w command. The windex directory once created will show the manual entry of the desired pattern. Figure 4.15 shows the manual entry having the pattern backup.

4.25 CORRECTING TYPING MISTAKES

While typing commands on the terminal screen, it is inevitable that we might commit typing mistakes. To correct the typing mistakes, the default key combinations listed in Table 4.19 are used.

Table 4.19   Default key combinations

Keys	Description
Ctrl-h	It erases text.
Ctrl-c	The Interrupt key terminates any currently running process and returns to the prompt.
Ctrl-d	It represents the exit or end of a transaction. The keys are used to indicate that the entering of text is complete.
Ctrl-j	It represents the Enter key.
Ctrl-s	It suspends the output temporarily and is usually used to stop the scrolling of screen output.
Ctrl-q	Its function is opposite to that of Ctrl-s. It resumes the scrolling of output.
Ctrl-z	It temporarily suspends a program and provides another shell prompt. In order to resume, it uses the jobs command to find the program's name and restarts it with the fg command.
Ctrl-u	It kills the command line, that is, clears the complete line.
Ctrl-\	It terminates the running command and creates a core file containing the memory image of the command.

We can change these default keys for erasing characters and killing a line through the stty command. The stty command is discussed in detail in Chapter 10.

This chapter dealt with numerous advanced Unix commands. It covered the essential commands for changing the permissions of files and directories, changing ownership and groups, sharing files among groups, pipe operators, etc. In addition, the chapter covered commands such as cut, paste, head, and tail that are used to extract desired regions from given files. For comparing files, diff, cmp, uniq, and comm commands were discussed. Commands for printing, measuring the time consumed in running certain commands, showing calendar, recording sessions, and configuring the environment through .profile have also been explained in detail.

■ SUMMARY ■

1. There are three classes of system users in Unix: Owner, Group, and Other. The read permission has a value = 4, the write permission has a value = 2, and the execute permission has a value = 1.

2. Unix assumes the default permissions of a directory to be 777 and that of a file as 666 and subtracts the permissions specified in the umask command to define their permissions at the time of their creation.

3. By default, each command takes its input from the standard input and sends the results to the standard output; however, through I/O redirection, we can change the default location of input and output.

4. The '>' (greater than) symbol is known as the output redirection operator and we can use it to divert the output of any command to a file instead of the terminal screen.

The append operator, '>>' is used for appending the output of a command to a file, that is, without overwriting its older content. To redirect the standard input, we use the input redirection operator, that is, the '<' (less than) symbol.

5. The pipe operator '|' is used for sending the output of one command as the input to another command.

6. The difference between the pipe operator and the output indirection operator '>' is that the output indirection operator '>' is mostly used for sending the output of a command to a file, whereas the pipe operator is used for sending output of a command to another command for further processing.

7. DOS (or Windows) files end with both the line feed and carriage return, whereas Unix files end only with the line feed character.

■ FUNCTION SPECIFICATION ■

Command	Function
chmod	It changes file/directory permissions.
umask	It stands for user file creation mask and sets the default permissions of the files that will be created in the future.
chown	It transfers ownership of a file to another user. Once the ownership of a file is transferred to another user, one cannot change its permissions until they become the owner again.
chgrp	It changes the group ownership of the file.
groups	It creates a group.
sort	It sorts files either line-wise or on the basis of certain fields.

Command	Function
cut	It slices (cuts) a file vertically. Files can be cut on the basis of characters and fields too.
paste	It joins content from different files.
wc (word count)	It calculates the number of characters, words, and lines in a file.
head	It selects the specified number of lines and characters from the beginning of the given file; the default number of lines selected is 10.
tail	It selects a specified number of lines and characters from the bottom of the specified file; the default number of lines selected is 10.
pg	It displays a long file page-wise, that is, one screen page at a time.

Command	Function
man	It displays the online documentation or manual of the given Unix command.
diff	It displays the difference between two files in a format that consists of two numbers and a character in between. The number to the left of the character represents the line number in the first file, and the number to the right of the character represents the line number in the second file.
uniq	It finds and displays duplicate lines in a file. In addition, it can be used to display only the unique lines in a file. The -u option of the uniq command removes all duplicate lines from a file. The -d option of the uniq command is used to display all duplicate lines in a file.
split	It splits a file into a specified number of lines or bytes.
cmp	It compares two files and indicates the line number where the first difference in the files occurs. It does not display anything if the files being compared are exactly the same.
comm	It displays or suppresses the content common to two files.
time	It displays the time usage by a specific command. The real time is the elapsed time from the invocation of the command till its termination. The user time represents the

Command	Function
	amount of time that the command takes to execute its own code. The sys time represents the time taken by Unix to invoke the command.
lp	It stands for line printer and prints files. Using the lp command, we can define the printer we wish to use through the -d option, the number of copies through the -n option, the pages to print through the -p option, and priority through the -q option.
cancel	It cancels existing print jobs.
profile file	It exists in the home directory and is the start-up file that automatically executes when we log in to the Unix system. It can be used to customize our environment. It can also be used to write the commands and scripts that we wish to execute automatically when we log in.
calendar	It reads the calendar file and displays appointments and reminders for the current day.
script	It records our interaction with the Unix system. It runs in the background recording everything that shows up on the screen.
dos2unix	It converts text files from a DOS to a Unix format.
unix2dos	It converts text files from a Unix format to a DOS format.

■ EXERCISES ■

Objective-type Questions

State True or False

4.1 The three classes of system users that are used in assigning permissions to the files and directories are Owner, Group, and Family.

4.2 To delete a file, a write permission is not required but an execute permission is required.

4.3 By using the umask command, we can specify the permissions that we want to deny.

4.4 The system-wide default permission for a directory is 666.

4.5 If we transfer the ownership of our file to another person, we can no longer change its file permissions.

4.6 Either the owner or the super user can change the ownership of a file.

4.7 We can make a group of users share permissions on a given set of files.

4.8 The sort command can sort the file on the basis of a given field in the file.

4.9 We cannot sort a file in the reverse order through the sort command.

4.10 The '<' symbol is the output redirection operator and the '>' symbol is the input redirection operator.

4.11 The '>>' symbol redirects the output of a command to a file after overwriting its earlier content.

4.12 Several commands can be attached using the pipe operator.

4.13 The default number of lines into which the split command splits a file is 100 lines.

4.14 The cmp command compares two files and indicates the line number where the first difference

in the file occurs.

4.15 The cmp command displays a message 'exactly same' if the files compared are exactly the same.

4.16 The comm command either displays or hides the content common to two files.

4.17 The time command displays the system time and even allows it to be modified.

4.18 The real time is the elapsed time from the invocation of the command till its termination.

4.19 The calendar command displays the calendar of a specified month and year.

Fill in the Blanks

4.1 There are three types of system users: owner, group, and _____.

4.2 The command used to change the permission of the file or directory is _____.

4.3 The symbol x in the chmod command represents _____ permission.

4.4 The command used to get the specified number of lines from the beginning of a file is _____.

4.5 The option used with the tail command to skip the specified number of lines is _____.

4.6 The option used with the tail command to get the specified number of characters from the end of file is _____.

4.7 Unix assumes the default permissions for a file to be _____.

4.8 The input redirection operator is represented as _____.

4.9 To display content one screen page at a time, _____ command is used.

4.10 The _____ command is used for displaying the documentation of a command.

4.11 The diff command displays the differences between two files that are being compared in a format that consists of two _____ and a _____ in between.

4.12 The _____ command is used for identifying and displaying duplicate lines in a file.

4.13 The _____ option of the uniq command removes all duplicate lines from a file.

4.14 The _____ file can be used to customize our environment.

4.15 For recording our interaction with the Unix system, _____ command is used.

4.16 The _____ option of the lp command is used for defining the destination printer while the _____ option is used for defining the number of copies to be printed.

4.17 The _____ command is used to display appointments and reminders for the current day.

4.18 The _____ command converts text files from the DOS format to the Unix format.

4.19 The _____ command is used for cancelling a print job.

Multiple-choice Questions

4.1 The command used for setting default permissions of files and directories is
(a) chmod　　　　(c) default
(b) umask　　　　(d) chstat

4.2 The three types of system users are User, Group, and
(a) Other　　　　(c) Community
(b) Society　　　(d) Everyone

4.3 The option used with the chgrp command to change the group of a symbolic link is
(a) -s　　(b) -l　　(c) -g　　(d) -h

4.4 The command used for comparing two files is
(a) comp　　　　(c) uniq
(b) compare　　 (d) diff

4.5 The option of the uniq command that removes all duplicate lines is
(a) -d　　　　(c) -r
(b) -u　　　　(d) -m

4.6 The command used to change the group of a file is
(a) groups　　　(c) chgrp
(b) chmod　　　 (d) ls -g

4.7 The statement $chown :accounts a.txt will change
   (a) group of the file
   (b) owner of the file
   (c) nothing
   (d) owner and group of the file

4.8 The option used with the sort command to remove duplicate lines in a sorted output is
   (a) -d   (b) -q   (c) -u   (d) -n

4.9 The option used with the tail command that

selects and displays lines in reverse order from the bottom to the top is
   (a) -t   (c) -b
   (b) -r   (d) -c

4.10 The statement $ head -c 10 a.txt b.txt displays
   (a) the first 10 lines of a.txt file only
   (b) the first 10 lines of a.txt and b.txt files
   (c) the first 10 characters of a.txt file only
   (d) the first 10 characters of a.txt and b.txt files

Programming Exercises

4.1 What will the following commands do?
   (a) $chmod 410 management.txt
   (b) $umask 233
   (c) $chgrp jobs mbacourse.txt
   (d) $head -c 100 mbacourse.txt management.txt
   (e) $tail -2 management.txt
   (f) $man -K disk
   (g) $cut -d"," -f3 bank.lst
   (h) $paste -d"<>" names.txt numbers.txt
   (i) $sort a.txt > b.txt
   (j) $ split -5 numbers.txt temp
   (k) $ cmp -s a.txt b.txt 3 5
   (l) $ time ls | sort | lp
   (m) $ lp -d Epson100 -P 10-15, 20 a.txt
   (n) $ comm a.txt b.txt

4.2 Write the command for the following tasks:
   (a) To assign read, write, and execute permissions to the owner; read and write permission to the group; and only read permission to others for the file mbacourse.txt
   (b) To set permissions for the directories to be created in the future as read, write, and execute for the owner; read and write for the group; and only read for others
   (c) To change the ownership of the file mbcourse.txt to charles

   (d) To display the first two lines of the files mbacourse.txt and management.txt
   (e) To display lines starting from the fifth till the end of the file in mbacourse.txt
   (f) To show the content of the file finance.txt located in accounts directory page-wise
   (g) To sort the file a.txt in reverse order and store it in file b.txt
   (h) To cut the first and third fields of the file letter.txt that is delimited by a tab space
   (i) To create a group by the following name: latestprojects
   (j) To compare two files, accounts.txt and finance.txt, and show the changes that need to be made in the file accounts.txt to make it similar to finance.txt
   (k) To display all duplicate lines in the file accounts.txt
   (l) To remove all duplicate lines in the file accounts.txt and save it in another file correct.txt
   (m) To split a file accounts.txt into the files accountaa, accountab, accountac, and so on, each consisting of 20 bytes
   (n) To compare two files, a.txt and b.txt, and display the first character that is different in the two files

Review Questions

4.1 Explain the following commands with syntax and examples.
   (a) pg   (c) dos2unix
   (b) wc   (d) tail
4.2 (a) What is the difference between the chown and chgrp commands?

   (b) What is the difference between the cmp and diff commands?
4.3 (a) Explain the different options used in the lp command while printing a file.
   (b) Explain how a file is sorted.
4.4 What is the difference between the following pairs

of commands that are used for extracting content from the files?

(a) `cut` and `split` commands

(b) `head` and `tail` commands

4.5 Briefly explain how the file access permissions are handled in the Unix operating system.

Brain Teasers

4.1 Suppose you want to assign read, write, and execute permissions to the user, that is, the owner of the file a.txt using the following command. What is wrong with the following command? Correct the mistake.

`$ chmod o=rwx a.txt`

4.2 Correct the following command to change the owner and group of the file a.txt to user chirag and accounts respectively.

`$ chown accounts:chirag a.txt`

4.3 Correct the mistake in the following command in order to change the group of the symbolic file b.txt to accounts.

`$ chgrp accounts b.txt`

4.4 Can you sort the file a.txt on the second and third field skipping the first field? How?

4.5 The following command overwrites the content of the file a.txt. What command will you use to avoid the accidental overwriting of an existing file?

`$ ls > a.txt`

4.6 Correct the mistake in the following command to cut the first and third fields of the file a.txt delimited by the '|' symbol

`$ cut -f1,3 a.txt`

4.7 Is there a way to split a file a.txt into pieces that are 10 kB each? If yes, what is that?

4.8 When you compare two files, a.txt and b.txt with the cmp command, no output appears on the screen. What does this mean?

4.9 Correct the mistake in the following command to suppress the display of the content, that is, commands in the files a.txt and b.txt.

`$ comm -1 a.txt b.txt`

4.10 Correct the mistake in the following command in order to print two copies of the file a.txt.`$ lp a.txt -q 2`

4.11 What will happen if you add the `calendar` command in the .profile file?

4.12 Correct the mistake in the following command to extract line numbers 10 to 15 from the file a.txt.

`$ head -10 a.txt | tail +15`

■ ANSWERS TO OBJECTIVE-TYPE QUESTIONS ■

State True or False

4.1	False
4.2	False
4.3	True
4.4	False
4.5	True
4.6	True
4.7	True
4.8	True
4.9	False
4.10	Teasers
4.11	False
4.12	True
4.13	False

4.14	True
4.15	False
4.16	True
4.17	False
4.18	True
4.19	False

Fill in the Blanks

4.1	Other
4.2	chmod
4.3	execute
4.4	head
4.5	+n
4.6	-c

4.7	666
4.8	<
4.9	pg
4.10	man
4.11	numbers, character
4.12	uniq
4.13	-u
4.14	.profile
4.15	script
4.16	-d, -n
4.17	calendar
4.18	dos2unix
4.19	cancel

Multiple-choice Questions

4.1	(b)
4.2	(a)
4.3	(d)
4.4	(d)
4.5	(b)
4.6	(c)
4.7	(a)
4.8	(c)
4.9	(b)
4.10	(d)

File Management and Compression Techniques

After studying this chapter, the reader will be conversant with the following:

- The types of devices, role of device drivers, and the way in which devices are represented in the Unix operating system
- Using disk-related commands for copying disks, formatting disks, finding disk usage, finding free disk space, and dividing the disk into partitions
- Compressing and uncompressing files using different commands such as gzip, gunzip, zip, compress, uncompress, pack, unpack, bzip2, bunzip2, and 7-zip
- The types of files, locating files, searching for files with a specific string, and finding utility on a disk
- Checking a file system for corruption
- Important files of the Unix system, where and how passwords are kept, where the list of hosts is kept, and how to allow or deny any user from accessing certain resources

5.1 MANAGING AND COMPRESSING FILES

File management deals with the different types of files that are managed in the Unix system. It helps one understand the various ways of searching for the desired files, repairing the file system, and the important files of the Unix system that manage user passwords, store addresses of hosts, and the list of users that are allowed or denied access to the system. Since files are stored on disks, different disk-related commands have also been referred to. Compression techniques encompass the various methods of compressing and uncompressing files. Compressing files is the best way to optimize the disk usage. Moreover, it is quite easy to manage compressed files, that is, we can backup and restore the compressed files easily. We will see the pros and cons of different commands and the extent of compression they carry out. In this chapter, we will learn the following types of commands:

1. Dealing with devices
2. Device drivers

3. Block and character devices
4. Major and minor numbers
5. Disk-related commands: dd, du, df, dfspace, and fdisk
6. Compressing and uncompressing files: gzip, gunzip, zip, unzip, compress, uncompress, pack, unpack, bzip2, bunzip2, and 7-zip
7. Dealing with files: file, find, which, locate, and fsck (file system check utility)
8. Important files of the Unix system: etc/passwd, /etc/shadow, /etc/hosts, etc/hosts.allow, and /etc/hosts.deny
9. Shell variables:
   (a) User-created shell variables
   (b) System shell variables: CDPATH, HOME, PATH, Primary Prompt (PSI Prompt), and TERM
   (c) Local and global shell variables: export

Disks are considered to be the essential devices of a computer. Let us first understand what the different devices are and how they are dealt with in the Unix system before discussing the different disks and file management commands.

5.2 COMPUTER DEVICES

While working on a computer, we deal with various peripherals such as hard drives, floppy and CD-ROM drives, audio and video cards, and serial and parallel ports. These peripherals are also known as devices. These devices combine to make the computer the system it is. In Unix, all devices are considered to be files, which are also known as device files. We learnt in Chapter 1 that there are several categories of files, namely ordinary files, directory files, device files, symbolic links, pipes, and sockets. The question that arises here is how the different categories of files can be differentiated. The answer lies in the *long listing command*.

On executing the long listing command, ls -al, the list of files and directories that is displayed as a result helps us distinguish the different categories of files. The mode field, the first character in the listing, indicates what type of file it represents. The first character in the listing may be either a hyphen (-) or one of the following letters: l, c, b, p, s, or d. Table 5.1 explains the different characters that may be displayed in the mode field (of the long listing) and the type of file represented by it.

Table 5.1 Characters used in the long listing command

Character	File type
-	Regular file
l	Symbolic link
c	Character special
b	Block special
p	Named pipe
s	Socket
d	Directory file

Let us observe the output of the long listing command, which is as follows:

```
$ls -al
-rwxrwxrwx  1  chirag  it    344 Dec  2  09:20  letter.txt
drwxrwxrwx  1  chirag  it     10 Oct 12  10:45  projects
lrwxrwxrwx  2  chirag  it    669 Feb  8  03:15  xyz.txt
prw-r--r--  1  root    root    0 Apr 15  05:20  pipe
srwx—       1  root    root    0 May 12  12:30  log
crw--------12  bin     6,      0 Dec  5  09:11  lp0
brw-rw-rw-  1  root    51,     0 Jul 31  07:28  cd0
```

The output of this long listing command shows different types of files and directories, which are as follows:

Regular file   The file letter.txt that is represented by a hyphen (-) in the mode field is a regular file. This is the simplest and most common type of file in the Unix system. It is just a collection of bytes.

Directory   The file projects that is represented by character d in the mode field is a directory—a container of several file directories.

Symbolic link   The file xyz.txt that is represented by character l in the mode field is a symbolic link that refers to other file(s) of the file system.

Named pipe   The file pipe that is represented by character p in the mode field is a named pipe and is used in interprocess communication, that is, sending the output of one process as input to another process.

Socket   The file log that is represented by character s in the mode field is a socket and is a special file used for advanced interprocess communication.

Special device file   The files lp0 and cd0 represented by the characters c and b in the mode field are special device files. They may be either characters or block device files.

Now we can understand how the device files can be recognized through the long listing of files and directories.

Next, we will see how the Unix operating system manages and deals with all the devices of a computer system.

5.2.1 Dealing with Devices

As mentioned in Section 5.2, all devices are represented as files in the Unix operating system. Like files, we can open and read a device, write into it, and then close it. The functions for opening, reading, and writing into a device are built into the kernel for each/every device of the system. These functions or routines for specific devices are known as the *device drivers*.

Although the terms device driver and device files appear to be similar, they are totally different. A device file is the representation of a device on the file system hierarchy. It is basically a special type of file that points to an *inode* that contains information about the device that it actually represents. The information in the inode includes major and minor device numbers where the major device number defines the type of device and the minor device number identifies a particular device in that type.

On the other hand, a device driver is a program that establishes communication between the computer and the device by translating the calls given by the user into calls that the device understands. It hides the inner complexities of how a device works. The commands given by the user to operate a device are passed to the device driver in the form of calls. The device driver then maps those calls to device-specific operations.

In order to access a particular device, the kernel calls its device driver. The kernel must not only know the type of device but also certain details about that device such as the density of a floppy or the partition of the disk for using the device efficiently.

All device files are stored in /dev or in its subdirectories and can be listed by executing the following command:

```
$ ls -l /dev
brw-rw-rw-    1    root    51,    0    Jul    31    07:28    cd0
brw-rw-rw-    1    bin     2,     48   Oct    22    12:10    fd0135ds18
```

brw-rw-Hv-	1	bin	2,	42	Nov	30	19:44	fd196ds15
crw--------	1	bin	6,	0	Dec	5	09:11	lp0
cr—r—rp-	1	root	50,	0	Mar	31	06:15	rcdt0
crw-rw-rw-	1	bin	2,	48	Jun	22	11:25	rfd0135ds15
...	...	...	...	...	...	...	...
...	...	...	...	...	...	...	...

The files that we see in this listing are not device drivers but are just pointers to where the driver code can be found in the kernel. In the mode field of the file permissions, we can see that there is a character c or b. The character c represents a character device whereas the character b represents a block device. Following the mode field are the permissions, the links count, and finally the owner of the file. After the owner, we see two numbers that are separated by a comma (,). These two numbers refer to the major and minor device numbers respectively. The major device number refers to the device type and the minor number refers to different instances of the device. For example, two floppy disk drives (second and third rows in the aforementioned listing) can have the same major number (2), but different minor numbers as one represents the 1.2 MB and the other represents the 1.44 MB floppy disk drive. Following the major and minor numbers are the date and time of last modification. The last column displays the device filenames.

When we provide commands to operate a device, the system uses the major and minor numbers of the device file to identify the device and henceforth, determines the device driver that will be used to communicate with the device.

The device driver simplifies the input/output (I/O) tasks performed with the respective devices. Hardware devices such as printers, disk controllers, network devices, and serial ports are attached with a device driver that enables the kernel to communicate with them, and hence get the desired task performed. Device drivers drive the device to perform according to the requests received by the kernel, as shown in Fig. 5.1.

A device driver has the following uses:

1. It connects and communicates with the hardware device.
2. It is the software that operates the device controller.
3. It resides within the Unix kernel and provides an interface to hardware devices.

The two general kinds of device files in the Unix-like operating systems are character special files and block special files. The difference between them lies in how data is written into them and read from them, and how it is processed by the operating system and hardware. These together can be called device special files, in contrast to named pipes, which are not connected to a device but are not ordinary files either. A brief introduction of block and character devices is given in Section 5.2.2.

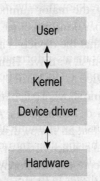

Fig. 5.1 Interactions between user, kernel, device driver, and hardware

5.2.2 Block device

Block special files represent the devices that move data in the form of blocks. When such a device file is accessed for reading or writing data, the kernel provides the address of a kernel buffer (i.e., buffer cache) that can be used for data transmission to the device driver. Hence, while reading a block device, the data is first read in the block and then written into the buffer cache, so that when the same data is again required, it is read from the buffer cache instead of being read from the device. Similarly, while writing on a block device, the data is first stored in the buffer cache before writing on the device. The block devices enable random access. In other words, the data can be accessed from these devices in a random order. Examples of block devices include hard disks, CD-ROM drives, and flash drives.

The character devices (or raw devices) are those that can be accessed directly bypassing the operating system's buffer caches. This means that the data is read or written into these devices directly without being stored in the buffer cache. In addition, the name 'character device' itself signifies that the data from such a device is accessed one character at a time. Data is accessed from a character device sequentially (not randomly) in the form of a stream of characters. Examples of character devices include serial port, mouse, keyboard, virtual terminal, and printer.

In the long listing, the first character in the mode field is c or b. Refer to the long listing shown in Section 5.2.1, where the floppy drive, CD-ROM, and the hard disk have b prefixed to their permissions confirming that they are block devices. Similarly, printers, raw floppy drives, and tape drives have c prefixed to their permissions, which confirms that they are raw devices.

5.2.3 Major and Minor Numbers

Devices are divided into sets called major device numbers. For instance, all small computer system interface (SCSI) disks have major number 8, floppy disks have major number 2, and so on. Further, each individual device has a minor device number too. For example, the device /dev/sda has minor device number 0 and /dev/fd135ds18 has minor number 48. It also means that the major number helps the kernel in recognizing the device category and the minor number makes the recognition more precise. Similarly, the major number 8 informs the kernel that the device is a SCSI disk, and the minor number 0 informs that it is the first disk drive. Similarly, the major number 2 informs the kernel that the device is a floppy disk drive and the minor number 48 informs that the device is the first, A: drive. Hence, both the major and minor device numbers collectively identify the device to the kernel.

In the output of the long listing command, ls -al, the fifth column shows a pair of two numbers, separated by a comma. These numbers are the major and minor device numbers. As the major number represents the type of device, we can see in the output that all floppy disk drives have the same major number 2. The minor number indicates the special characteristics of the device to recognize it precisely. For example, fd0135ds18 and fd196ds15 represent two floppy disk drives, hence both of them have the same major number (2), but different minor numbers (48 and 42) to distinguish that one is floppy disk drive A: and the other is floppy disk drive B: respectively.

Note: Taking backup is an essential task in an operating system. A backup helps in restoring the data in case of any disk failure or system crash. The commands that we are going to learn in Section 5.3 are concerned with formatting disks, backing up data, restoring, etc.

5.3 DISK-RELATED COMMANDS

In this section, we will focus on different disk-related commands. We will learn about the commands that are used for copying data from one disk to another, formatting disks, displaying usage of disk space, that is, the space used by different files and directories of the disk, the amount of free disk space in all the file systems in our machines, the amount of free disk space in terms of megabytes (MB) and percentage, and dividing the disk drive into different partitions. Let us see how disks are copied.

5.3.1 dd: Copying Disks

The dd (data dump) command is used for copying data from one medium to another. It reads and writes data in block-sized chunks, where the default size of the block is 512 bytes.

Syntax   `dd if=INPUT-FILE-NAME of=OUTPUT-FILE-NAME [options]`

Here, if represents input and of represents output.

Examples

(a) To backup a hard disk to a file, type the following command.
    `dd if=/dev/hda of=/file.dd`
    It copies the entire disk, hda, to another file, file.dd.
(b) To backup a hard disk to another disk, type the following command.
    `dd if=/dev/hda of=/dev/hdb`
    It copies the entire disk, hda, to another disk, hdb.

Note: The output from dd can be a new file or another storage device.

Table 5.2 shows the common options used with the dd command.

Table 5.2   Options used with the dd command

Options	Description
bs = n	Sets the block size to n bytes
count = n	Copies n blocks and then stops
skip = n	Copies after skipping n blocks
conv = noerror	Prevents dd from stopping on encountering an error
sync	Pads the input block with null bytes to make it equal to the block size

Examples

(a) `dd if=/dev/hda of=/dev/hdb conv= noerror,sync`
Here, hda is the source disk, hdb is the destination disk, sync is for synchronized I/O, and noerror is for continuing the copy operation even if there are read errors.
(b) `dd if=/dev/.hda count=1 of=file.dd`
It copies just one sector of the disk hda.

(c) `dd if=/dev/hda skip=1 count=1 of=file.dd`
    It skips the first sector and copies just the second sector of the disk hda.

Note: dd uses only raw devices.

5.3.2 du: Disk Usage

This utility is used to get complete information about the usage of disk space by each file and directory of the system. If we specify a directory name along with the du utility, we get the list of disk space consumed by the directory and all of its subdirectories.

Syntax   `du [options] directories`

Table 5.3 shows the common options used with the du command.

Table 5.3 Options used with the du command

Options	Description
-k	Displays the block size in units of 1024 bytes, rather than the default 512 bytes
-a	Displays the blocks used by each file
-s	Displays the summary (total) for each of the specified files

Examples

(a) By default, the du command without any options displays the directories (in the current directory). The following are the blocks consumed by each of those directories.

```
$ du .
2 ./.snap
31068 ./bin
96 ./include/altq
68 ./include/arpa
128 ./include/bsm
```

Here, du reports the number of blocks used by the current directory (denoted by .) and those used by subdirectories within the current directory.

(b) The number of blocks used by the etc directory and its subdirectories are displayed using the following command.

```
$ du /etc
54 /etc/defaults
2 /etc/X11
8 /etc/bluetooth
4 /dev/devd
```

These blocks (to the left of each directory) are 512 bytes in size.

(c) To ascertain the blocks (that are 1024 bytes in size) that are used by the subdirectories in the etc directory, we will use the following command.

```
$ du –k /etc
27 /etc/defaults
1 /etc/X11
4 /etc/bluetooth
2 /dev/devd
```

The blocks shown in this output are 1024 bytes in size.

(d) To find the usage of every file, we can use the following command.

```
$ du -a
```

(e) The option -a displays all the files and the blocks used by each file.

```
2 ./.snap
82 ./bin/ctfconvert
20 ./bin/ctfdump
56 ./bin/ctfmerge
18 ./bin/sgsmsg
```

(f) If we want to view only the total number of blocks occupied by the specific directory, we have to use the summary (-s) option. The following example displays the total number of blocks used by the current directory.

```
$ du -s
3616480
```

(g) To ascertain the number of blocks used by a specific file(s), we can use the following command.

```
$ du -s *.txt
10 abc.txt
7 pqr.txt
11 xyz.txt
```

This output shows the number of blocks used by the different files with extension .txt.

Note: The du command displays information in terms of 512-byte blocks independent of the actual disk block size.

5.3.3 df: Reporting Free and Available Space on File Systems

This command reports the free disk space for all the file systems installed on our machines in terms of disk blocks. The command displays the capacity of each file system, the space in use, the free space, and the number of free files.

Syntax df [-options][filesystem]

Table 5.4. shows the common options used with the df command.

Table 5.4 Options used with the df command

Options	Description
h	Displays the size in human readable formats (KB, MB, and GB)
e	Displays only the number of files free
k	Displays the size in terms of blocks where a block is of 1 KB

Examples

(a) If we want to have information regarding the free and available disk space of a particular file system, we can mention it in the df command. Furthermore, we can use the df command without any option or file system (as shown here) in order to obtain information about all the file systems installed on our machines.

```
$ df
Filesystem    1K-blocks   Used      Avail     Capacity   Mounted on
/dev/ad0s1a   507630      165380    301640    35%        /
devfs         1           1         0         100%       /dev
/dev/ad0s1e   507630      12        467008    0%         /tmp
/dev/ad0s1f   73138272    3616480   63670732  5%         /usr
/dev/ad0s1d   1185230     2050      1088362   0%         /var
```

The first column displays the different partitions on the disk of our system. The second column displays the size of the partitions in terms of blocks of size 1 KB. Similarly, the size of the first partition represented by ad0s1a is of size 507630 KB (507 MB). Out of the 507630 KB, 165380 KB is used up and 301640 KB is free, as represented by the third and fourth columns respectively. The fifth column shows the used (consumed) percentage of the disk. The last column indicates where the partition is connected to the Unix file system. For example, the partition ad0s1a (shown in the first row) is the root partition and hence is represented to be mounted on.

(b) To know the amount of free space in a particular partition, we can specify that while giving the df command. For example, in order to know the amount of free disk space in the *root* partition, we need to give the following command.

```
$ df /
Filesystem  1K-blocks Used      Avail     Capacity   Mounted on
/dev/ad0s1a 507630    165380    301640    35%        /
```

This output shows the total size of the root partition in terms of KB, the amount of used space, free space, and percentage of disk space used.

(c) In order to easily remember the size of the partitions, we make use of the -h option to display the size of the partitions in human readable forms.

```
$ df -h
Filesystem   Size    Used    Avail   Capacity   Mounted on
/dev/ad0s1a  506MB   164MB   300MB   35%        /
devfs        1KB     1KB     0       100%       /dev
/dev/ad0s1e  506MB   0       506MB   0%         /tmp
/dev/ad0s1f  71GB    5.4GB   62GB    5%         /usr
/dev/ad0s1d  1GB     1.8MB   1GB     0%         /var
```

In this output, the size of the partitions is displayed in megabytes, which is computed by dividing the block sizes in KB by a value 1024.

(d) The option -k of the df command displays the size of the file systems in kilo bytes as shown in the following example.

```
$ df -k
Filesystem   KBytes     Used      Avail     Capacity   Mounted on
/dev/ad0s1a  518144     167936    307200    35%        /
devfs        1          1         0         100%       /dev
/dev/ad0s1e  518144     0         518144    0%         /tmp
/dev/ad0s1f  74448896   5662310   65011712  5%         /usr
/dev/ad0s1d  1048576    18432     1030144   0%         /var
```

(e) The option -e of the df command displays the number of files that are free on the file systems as shown in the following example.

```
$ df -e
Filesystem   ifree
/dev/ad0s1a  34596
devfs        0
/dev/ad0s1e  7483620
/dev/ad0s1f  8402
/dev/ad0s1d  56129
```

This output shows the numbers of files free on each of the file systems.

5.3.4 `dfspace`: Reporting Free Space on File Systems

The `dfspace` command is specific to the SCO Unix system. It works in a manner similar to the `df` command and presents information regarding free space on file systems on our disks in a more readable format, that is, it reports the free disk space in terms of megabytes and percentage of the total disk space.

Note: This command will work with SCO Unix and not on Oracle Solaris 10, which this book focuses on.

Syntax   `dfspace [file system]`

Here, the file system is used to find out the free disk space available on it. If the file system is not specified, all file systems on the disk are displayed along with the information on available disk space on each of them.

Example   `$/etc/dfspace`

```
: Disk Space: 6.32MB of 137.74MB available (4.59 %)
Total disk Space: 10.50MB of 200MB available (3.89%)
```

In the aforementioned example, we have written `/etc/dfspace` instead of `dfspace`, because the `dfspace` command exists in the `etc` directory. The output reports free disk space for the root file system. If there had been other file systems installed, their free space would have also been reported. It also reports the total disk space available.

It is to be noted that the `df` and `dfspace` commands report the disk space available in the file system as a whole, whereas `du` reports the disk space used by specified files and directories.

5.3.5 `fdisk`: Dividing Disks into Partitions

Dividing the hard disk into one or more logical disks is called partitions. The partitions, the divisions of the disk, are described in the partition table found in sector 0 of the disk. However, *fdisk* in Linux creates both partitions as well as file systems.

A large disk drive is partitioned into smaller segments to increase system performance. It is quite obvious that searching or interacting with a file in a smaller disk drive segment will be quite faster when compared to a larger disk drive. There are two types of partitions: *primary partition* and *extended partition*. A hard drive can contain up to four primary partitions. A primary partition is necessary to make the drive bootable—an operating system is installed in it. It is not used for data storage. Multiple primary partitions are created to make a multiboot system. For a single boot system, one primary partition is sufficient. In order to overcome the limitation of having a maximum of four primary partitions on a drive, we make use of the extended partition. An extended partition is the only kind of partition that can have multiple partitions inside. The partitions created inside the extended partition are known as logical drives. An extended partition acts as a container for the logical drives. It cannot hold any data without first installing a logical drive. We can create as many logical drives as we want on an extended partition.

Note: On an IDE drive, the first drive is called `hda`, and the partitions are shown as `hda1`, `hda2`, etc. The second drive is called `hdb`, and the partitions are shown as `hdb1`, `hdb2`, etc. On an SCSI drive, the first drive is called `sda`, and the partitions are `sda1`, `sda2`, and so on. The second drive is called `sdb` and the partitions are `sdb1`, `sdb2`, etc.

The fdisk command is used to create, delete, and activate partitions.

Syntax   fdisk [-l] [-u] [-b sector_size] [-v] [device] [-s partition]

Table 5.5 shows the aforementioned options.

Table 5.5   Options used with the fdisk command

Option	Description
-l	It lists the partition tables for the specified device. The device is usually one of the following: /dev/hda /dev/hdb /dev/sda /dev/sdb
-u	It displays the sizes in terms of sections instead of cylinders while listing partition tables.
-b sector_size	It specifies sector size of the disk (valid values are 512, 1024, or 2048).
-s partition	It displays the size of the specified partition in blocks.
-v	It prints the version number of the fdisk command.

Table 5.6   Menu options of the fdisk command

Option	Description
d	Deletes a partition
l	Lists the partitions
m	Displays this menu
n	Creates a new partition
p	Prints the partition table
q	Quits without saving changes
w	Writes the partition table to the disk and exits

When the fdisk command is active, it displays a menu of options that we can use to create, list, display, and delete partitions. Table 5.6 gives the menu options of the fdisk command.

We can create a primary partition with one file system on it, or an extended partition with multiple logical drives in the partition.

Example $ fdisk -l

This command lists the partition information of the disk drive on our computer system as given here:

```
Disk /dev/hda1: 64 heads, 63 sectors, 1023 cylinders
Units = cylinders of 4032 * 512 bytes

Device Boot    Begin    Start    End    Blocks    Id    System
/dev/hda1      636      636      902    538272    64    Linux native
/dev/hda2      903      903      1024   245952    8     Extended
/dev/hda3      229      229      635    819189    5     Linux
/dev/hda4      903      903      1024   245920+   4     Linux swap
```

The first hard disk as a whole is represented as /dev/hda, while individual partitions in this disk take on names hda1, hda2, and so forth. hda1 here is a primary partition, hda2 is an extended partition containing a logical partition hda4. The active partition is indicated by an * in the second column. The second hard disk will have the name /dev/hdb with similar numeric extensions.

5.4 COMPRESSING AND UNCOMPRESSING FILES

In this section, we will learn about the different ways of compressing and uncompressing files using commands such as gzip, zip, compress, pack, and bzip2, and gunzip, unzip, uncompress, unpack, and bunzip2, respectively, along with their syntax and examples. The implementation of these commands is discussed in Section 5.4.1.

5.4.1 gzip Command

The gzip command compresses the specified file and replaces it with the .gz extension file, that is, the original file is deleted and is replaced by the compressed version having the same primary name (as that of the original file) and the secondary name as .gz.

Syntax   gzip [-d][-l][-f][-c] file_name

Table 5.7 shows the aforementioned options.

Table 5.7 Options used with the gzip command

Option	Description
-d	It decompresses the specified file.
-l	It lists the information of each compressed file. The information includes compressed size, uncompressed size, compression ratio, and name of the uncompressed file.
-f	It means force compression or decompression. This option performs the operation without giving a confirmation message and overwrites the existing file, if the corresponding file already exists.
-c	It displays the compressed output on the screen, keeping the original file unchanged. The command provides several compressed files in the output if there are several input files—one for each input file.
file_name	It refers to the filename that we wish to compress.

Figure 5.2 shows two files names.txt and numbers.txt with the initial content that we wish to compress.

Examples

(a) $ gzip -c names.txt
   This command does not compress the file names.txt, but displays the compressed output on the screen (refer to Fig. 5.2).

(b) $ gzip names.txt
   The file names.txt is compressed and renamed names.txt.gz and is confirmed using the ls command (refer to Fig. 5.2).

(c) $ cat names.txt.gz
   The command shows the compressed content of the file names.txt. We can see (refer to Fig. 5.2) that the output displayed using the -c option matches the output of this example.

(d) $ gzip numbers.txt
   The file numbers.txt is also compressed into the file numbers.txt.gz and is confirmed using the ls command, which is shown in Fig. 5.2.

(e) $ gzip -l *.gz
   It lists the information of compressed files, names.txt and numbers.txt. This is evident from the list of commands shown in Fig. 5.2. This figure shows the compressed size, uncompressed size, compression ratio, and the name of the uncompressed file.

```
$ ls n*
names.txt numbers.txt

$ cat names.txt
Anil
Ravi
Sunil
Chirag
Raju

$ cat numbers.txt
2429193
3334444
7777888
9990000
5555111

$ gzip -c names.txt
?█N ♥names.txt s█████
J,
.✦1█32█?''Y█\█xA█

$ gzip names.txt

$ ls n*
names.txt.gz numbers.txt

$ cat names.txt.gz
?█N ♥names.txt s█████
J,
-✦1█32█?''Y█\█xA█

$ gzip numbers.txt

$ ls n*
names.txt.gz numbers.txt.gz

$ gzip -1 *.gz
        copmressed      uncompressed    ratio   uncompressed_name
              54              28         7.1%    names.txt
              63              40        17.5%    numbers.txt
             117              68       -27.9%    <totals>

$ gzip -d names.txt.gz

$ ls n*
names.txt numbers.txt.gz

$ cat >numbers.txt
12345

$ ls n*
names.txt numbers.txt numbers.txt.gz

$ gzip -d numbers.txt.gz
gzip: numbers.txt already exists; do you wish to overwrite <y or n>? n
        not overwritten

$ gzip -df numbers.txt.gz

$ ls n*
names.txt numbers.txt
```

Fig. 5.2 Compression and uncompression of files `names.txt` and `numbers.txt` using the `gzip` command

(f) `$ gzip -d names.txt.gz`

The compressed file `names.txt.gz` is uncompressed or decompressed to `names.txt` and is confirmed using the `ls` command, which is shown in Fig. 5.2.

(g) `$ gzip -d numbers.txt.gz`

The compressed file `numbers.txt.gz` is supposed to be uncompressed to `numbers.txt`. However, since a file `numbers.txt` already exists, a warning message—gzip: numbers. txt already exists; do you wish to overwrite (y or n)?—is displayed.

(h) `$ gzip -df numbers.txt.gz`

The option `-f` results in force decompression and overwrites the existing file `numbers.txt` without displaying any warning message. Figure 5.2 shows both the uncompressed files `names.txt` and `numbers.txt`.

5.4.2 gunzip Command

This command is used to uncompress the compressed file using the commands `gzip`, `compress`, or `pack`.

Syntax `gunzip [-l][-f][-c] file_name`

Table 5.8 shows the aforementioned options.

Table 5.8 Options used with the `gunzip` command

Option	Description
-l	It lists the information of each compressed file. This includes compressed size, uncompressed size, compression ratio, and name of the uncompressed file.
-f	This means force decompression. It overwrites the existing file without confirmation, if the corresponding uncompressed file already exists
-c	It displays the content of the compressed file in an uncompressed format on the screen keeping it in the compressed form. This option uncompresses the input files and arranges the uncompressed content of each file one below the other without any blank line in between.
file_name	It refers to the filename that we wish to uncompress.

Examples We compressed files `names.txt.gz` and `numbers.txt.gz`. Let us look at the examples to uncompress them using the `gunzip` command.

(a) `$ gunzip -l *.gz`

It lists the information of compressed files `names.txt` and `numbers.txt`. Figure 5.3 shows that the output is the same as `gzip -l *.gz`. The listing shows the compressed size, uncompressed size, compression ratio, and the name of the uncompressed file.

(b) `$ gunzip -c names.txt.gz`

This command does not uncompress the file `names.txt.gz`, but displays its uncompressed content on the screen (refer to Fig. 5.3).

(c) `$ gunzip -c names.txt.gz numbers.txt.gz`

When more than one compressed file is used with the `-c` option, their uncompressed contents will be displayed on the screen one below the other without any blank line in between (refer to Fig. 5.3). The files remain unchanged.

```
$ ls n*
names.txt.gz numbers.txt.gz

$ gunzip -1 *.gz
        compressed     uncompressed    ratio uncompressed_name
                54               28    7.1% names.txt
                63               40   17.5% numbers.txt
               117               68  -27.9% <totals>

$ gunzip -c names.txt.gz
Anil
Ravi
Sunil
Chirag
Raju

$ gunzip -c names.txt.gz numbers.txt.gz
Anil
Ravi
Sunil
Chirag
Raju
2429193
3334444
7777888
9990000
5555111

$ gunzip  names.txt.gz

$ ls n*
names.txt numbers.txt.gz

$ cat >numbers.txt
12345

$ ls n*
names.txt  numbers.txt numbers.txt.gz

$ gunzip numbers.txt.gz
gzip: numbers.txt already exists; do you wish ot overwrite <y or n>? n
        not overwritten

$ gunzip -f numbers.txt.gz

$ ls n*
names.txt  numbers.txt
```

Fig. 5.3 Uncompression of files `names.txt` and `numbers.txt` using the `gunzip` command

(d) `$ gunzip names.txt.gz`

The file `names.txt.gz` is uncompressed and renamed `names.txt`. This is confirmed using the `ls` command (refer to Fig. 5.3).

(e) `$ gunzip numbers.txt.gz`

The compressed file `numbers.txt.gz` is supposed to be uncompressed to `numbers.txt`. However, as the file `numbers.txt` already exists, the following warning message—gzip: `numbers.txt already exists; do you wish to overwrite ( y or n)?`—is displayed.

(f) `$ gunzip -f numbers.txt.gz`

The option `-f` results in force decompression and hence overwrites the existing file `numbers.txt` without displaying any warning message. We can see the uncompressed files `names.txt` and `numbers.txt` in Fig. 5.3.

Note: When we uncompress a file, the compressed file is automatically deleted from the system.

5.4.3 `zip` Command

The `zip` command compresses a set of files into a single archive. The syntax for zipping a set of files into a compressed form is as follows:

Syntax   `zip [-g][-F][-q][-r] file_name files`

Table 5.9 shows the aforementioned options.

Table 5.9   Options used with the `zip` command

Option	Description
`-g`	Adds files to an existing zip file
`-F`	Fixes any zip file, if damaged
`-q`	Makes the `zip` command run in the quiet mode, so that the files are compressed without displaying any response on the screen
`-r`	Compresses the files in the current directory as well as subdirectories
`file_name`	Refers to the archive in which compressed files are stored (an extension .zip will be automatically appended to `file_name`)
`files`	Refers to the files that we wish to compress

Examples

(a) `$ zip abc *`

All the files in the current directory are compressed into a single file `abc.zip`.

Note: The `gzip` command can only compress a single file whereas the `zip` command can compress multiple files.

A range of filenames can be given using wild cards. As the `zip` command compresses the files, the progress will be reported on the screen. When we compress these files, the original files remain unchanged.

(b) If we wish to add a file(s) that we forgot to add in the `zip` file, the following statement will solve the purpose.

`$ zip -g abc a.txt`

This example adds the file `a.txt` to an existing `zip` file `abc.zip`.

(c) The following is the option to correct the damaged zip file.

`$ zip -F abc -out pqr`

This example fixes the `zip` file `abc.zip` if damaged, and copies the fixed version into another `zip` file `pqr.zip`.

(d) The following example compresses the files with extension `.dat` from the current directory in the quiet mode, that is, without displaying any response on the screen.

`$ zip -q abc *.txt`

(e) In order to compress the files of subdirectories, we use the `-r` option.

`$ zip -r abc projects`

This example compresses all the files in the projects directory as well as in its subdirectories and saves them in the `abc.zip` file.

The execution of the aforementioned commands is shown in Fig. 5.4.

```
$ ls -l
total 12
-rw-r--r--     1 root  root      18 Feb 22 14:51 customers.txt
--w-r-x--x     1 root  root       6 Feb 22 14:51 letter.txt
-r-----r--     1 root  root     113 Feb 22 14:51 matter.txt
drwxr-xr-x     2 root  root     512 Feb 22 14:53 projects
-rw-r--r--     1 root  root     892 Feb 22 14:51 transact.txt
-rw-r--r--     1 root  root      16 Feb 22 14:51 users.txt

$ zip abc *
  adding: customers.txt (stored 0%)
  adding: letter.txt (stored 0%)
  adding: matter.txt (deflated 21%)
  adding: projects/ (stored 0%)
  adding: transact.txt (deflated 64%)
  adding: users.txt (stored 0%)

$ ls -l
total 16
-rw-r--r--     1 root  root    1370 Feb 22 14:55 abc.zip
-rw-r--r--     1 root  root      18 Feb 22 14:51 customers.txt
--w-r-x--x     1 root  root       6 Feb 22 14:51 letter.txt
-r-----r--     1 root  root     113 Feb 22 14:51 matter.txt
drwxr-xr-x     2 root  root     512 Feb 22 14:53 projects
-rw-r--r--     1 root  root     892 Feb 22 14:51 transact.txt
-rw-r--r--     1 root  root      16 Feb 22 14:51 users.txt

$ cat > a.txt
Testing
^D

$ zip -g abc a.txt
  adding: a.txt (stored 0%)

$ zip -F abc --Out pqr
Fix archive (-F) - assume mostly intact archive
Zip entry offsets do not need adjusting
  copying: customers.txt
  copying: letter.txt
  copying: matter.txt
  copying: projects/
  copying: transact.txt
  copying: users.txt
  copying: a.txt

$ ls -l
total 158
-rw-r--r--     1 root  root       8 Feb 22 14:56 a.txt
-rw-r--r--     1 root  root    1516 Feb 22 14:56 abc.zip
-rw-r--r--     1 root  root      18 Feb 22 14:51 customers.txt
--w-r-x--x     1 root  root       6 Feb 22 14:51 letter.txt
-r-----r--     1 root  root     113 Feb 22 14:51 matter.txt
-rw-r--r--     1 root  root    1516 Feb 22 14:58 pqr.zip
drwxr-xr-x     2 root  root     512 Feb 22 14:53 projects
-rw-r--r--     1 root  root     892 Feb 22 14:51 transact.txt
-rw-r--r--     1 root  root      16 Feb 22 14:51 users.txt

$ zip -q abc *.txt

$ zip -r abc projects
updating: projects/ (stored 0%)
  adding: projects/bank.lst (deflated 45%)
```

Fig. 5.4 Compression of files using the `zip` command

5.4.4 `unzip` Command

The `unzip` command is used to unzip the archive and extract all the files that were compressed in it.

Table 5.10 Options used with the `unzip` command

Option	Description
-p	Extracts files in the archive (`zip` file) to the screen (i.e., the files' content is displayed on the screen)
-t	Tests the archive file and determines if it is consistent and prints only the summary message to indicate whether the archive is OK or not
-l	Lists the archive file, which shows the names of the compressed files, their size, modification date, etc
-d directory_name	Extracts the compressed files from the zip file into the specified directory
-f	Updates only the existing files, that is, only the files that exist in the current directory and are newer than the current disk copies are uncompressed from the archive

Syntax `unzip [-p][-t][-l][-d directory_name][-f] file_name`

Table 5.10 shows the aforementioned options.

Examples

(a) To unzip a zipped archive, we use the following `unzip` command.
$ unzip abc
This example extracts all the files stored in the zip file `abc.zip` into the current directory.

(b) $ unzip –d temp abc
This command extracts the files in the archive `abc.zip` into the temporary directory.

(c) $ unzip –p abc
This command extracts the files in the archive `abc.zip` on the screen. The file content is displayed on the screen.

(d) $ unzip –t abc
This command tests the archive `abc.zip` and displays a summary message informing us if the archive is OK or not.

(e) $ unzip –l abc
This command lists the archive `abc.zip` and shows the names of the compressed files, their size, modification date, etc.

(f) $ unzip –f abc
This command extracts and updates only those files from the archive `abc.zip` that exists in the current directory.

Figure 5.5 demonstrates the execution of the aforementioned commands.

5.4.5 compress Command

The `compress` command compresses the specified file. It replaces the original file with its compressed version that has the same filename with a `.z` extension added to it.

Syntax `compress [-c] [-f] [-v] file`

Table 5.11 shows the aforementioned options.

Table 5.11 Options used with the `compress` command

Option	Description
-c	Compresses the file and displays the compressed version on the screen; retains the original file, that is, no `.z` file is created
-f	Applies force compression of the files and overwrites the corresponding `.z` file if it exists without verification
-v	Displays the size of the compressed files
file	Represents the files that have to be compressed

```
$ ls -l
total 4
-rw-r--r-- 1 root        root      1869 Feb 22 15:01 abc.zip

$ unzip abc
Archive:   abc.zip
 extracting: customers.txt                        $
 extracting: letter.txt
  inflating: matter.txt
   creating: projects/
  inflating: transact.txt
 extracting: users.txt
 extracting: a.txt
  inflating: projects/bank.lst

$  ls -l
total 18
-rw-r--r--       1 root  root         8 Feb 22 14:56 a.txt
-rw-r--r--       1 root  root      1869 Feb 22 15:01 abc.zip
-rw-r--r--       1 root  root        18 Feb 22 14:51 customers.txt
--w-r-x--x       1 root  root         6 Feb 22 14:51 letter.txt
-r-----r--       1 root  root       113 Feb 22 14:51 matter.txt
drwxr-xr-x       2 root  root       512 Feb 22 14:53 projects
-rw-r--r--       1 root  root       892 Feb 22 14:51 transact.txt
-rw-r--r--       1 root  root        16 Feb 22 14:51 users.txt

$ ls projects
bank.lst

$ unzip -d temp abc
Archive: abc.zip
 extracting: temp/customers.txt
 extracting: temp/letter.txt
  inflating: temp/matter.txt
   creating: temp/projects/
  inflating: temp/transact.txt
 extracting: temp/users.txt
 extracting: temp/a.txt
  inflating: temp/projects/bank.lst

$ ls -l
total 152
-rw-r--r--       1 root  root         8 Feb 22 14:56 a.txt
-rw-r--r--       1 root  root      1869 Feb 22 15:01 abc.zip
-rw-r--r--       1 root  root        18 Feb 22 14:51 customers.txt
--w-r-x--x       1 root  root         6 Feb 22 14:51 letter.txt
-r-----r--       1 root  root       113 Feb 22 14:51 matter.txt
drwxr-xr-x       2 root  root       512 Feb 22 14:53 projects
drwxr-xr-x       3 root  root       512 Feb 22 15:50 temp
-rw-r--r--       1 root  root       892 Feb 22 14:51 transact.txt
-rw-r--r--       1 root  root        16 Feb 22 14:51 users.txt

$ unzip -p abc
John
Charles
Troy
hello
Hello this is testing of cut command
I think it is working as per the expected
result. it is going to rain today

$ unzip -t abc
Archive:   abc.zip
    testing: customers.txt              OK
    testing: letter.txt                 OK
    testing: matter.txt                 OK
    testing: projects/                  OK
    testing: transact.txt               OK
    testing: users.txt                  OK
```

Fig. 5.5 Screenshots of the `unzip` command   (Contd)

```
        testing: a.txt                        OK
        testing: projects/bank.lst            Ok
No errors detected in compressed data of abc.zip.

$ unzip -l abc
Archive: abc.zip
  Length      Date      Time      Name
-----------  --------  -----     -----
       18    02-22-2006  14:51    customers.txt
        6    02-22-2006  14:51    letter.txt
      113    02-22-2006  14:51    matter.txt
        0    02-22-2006  14:53    projects/
      892    02-22-2006  14:51    transact.txt
       16    02-22-2006  14:51    users.txt
        8    02-22-2006  14:56    a.txt
      347    02-22-2006  14:53    projects/bank.lst
--------                         --------
     1400                         8 files

$ ls -l
total 360
-rw-r--r--     1 root     root         8 Feb 22 14:56 a.txt
-rw-r--r--     1 root     root      1869 Feb 22 15:01 abc.zip
-rw-r--r--     1 root     root        18 Feb 22 14:51 Customers.txt
--w-r-x--x     1 root     root         6 Feb 22 14:51 letter.txt
-r------r--    1 root     root       113 Feb 22 14:51 matter.txt
drwxr-xr-x     2 root     root       512 Feb 22 14:53 projects
drwxr-xr-x     3 root     root       512 Feb 22 15:50 temp
-rw-r--r--     1 root     root       892 Feb 22 14:51 transact.txt
-rw-r--r--     1 root     root        16 Feb 22 14:51 users.txt

$ rm a.txt

$ rm matter.txt

$ unzip -f abc
Archive: abc.zip

$ ls-l
total 356
-rw-r--r--     1 root     root      1869 Feb 22 15:01 abc.zip
-rw-r--r--     1 root     root        18 Feb 22 14:51 Customers.txt
--w-r-x--x     1 root     root         6 Feb 22 14:51 letter.txt
drwxr-xr-x     2 root     root       512 Feb 22 14:53 projects
drwxr-xr-x     3 root     root       512 Feb 22 15:50 temp
-rw-r--r--     1 root     root       892 Feb 22 14:51 transact.txt
-rw-r--r--     1 root     root        16 Feb 22 14:51 users.txt
```

Fig. 5.5 (Contd)

Examples

(a) $ `compress transact.txt`

This example compresses the file `transact.txt` and renames it `transact.txt.Z`.

Note: The original file is replaced by another file, which has the same name with a `.z` extension added to it (i.e., `transact.txt` is replaced by the file `transact.txt.Z`).

(b) $ `compress -c customers.txt`

It displays the compressed format of the file `customers.txt` on the screen, but does not compress it.

(c) $ `compress -f transact.txt`

If a file `transact.txt.Z` already exists, this command overwrites it with the compressed

```
$ ls -l transact*
-rw-r--r--    1 root root          892 Feb 22 14:51 transact.txt

$ compress transact.txt

$ ls -l transact*
-rw-r--r--    1 root root          551 Feb 22 14:51 transact.txt.Z

$ compress -c customers.txt
.□□J,q□□0r□□□□□□□7y_#

$ cat > transact.txt
testing
^D

$ compress transact.txt
transact.txt.Z already exists; do you wish to overwrite transact.txt.Z (yes or no)? n

not overwritten

$ compress -f transact.txt

$ ls -l transact*
-rw-r--r--    1 root root           12 Feb 22 16:51 transact.txt.Z

$ compress -v matter.txt
matter.txt: Compression: 12.38% -- replaced with matter.txt.Z
```

Fig. 5.6 Compression of files using the `compress` command

version of the earlier file `transact.txt` without confirmation. If `-f` option is not used, the `compress` command asks for confirmation before overwriting any existing file.

(d) `$ compress -v matter.txt`

This example displays how much compression was carried out by showing the output given here.

`matter.txt: Compression: 12.38% -- replaced with matter.txt.Z`

The output of these commands is given as a screenshot in Fig. 5.6.

5.4.6 uncompress Command

This command is used to get the compressed file back to its original form. The uncompressed file will have the same filename with the extension `.Z` removed.

Syntax `uncompress [-c] [-f] file`

Table 5.12 Options used with the `uncompress` command

Option	Description
`-c`	It displays the content of the compressed file without uncompressing it.
`-f`	It applies force uncompression to the file, that is, it overwrites the corresponding file if it exists without verification.
file	It represents the file that we wish to uncompress.

Table 5.12 shows the aforementioned options.

Examples

(a) `$ uncompress transact.txt.Z`

Using this command, the compressed file `transact.txt.Z` is uncompressed into the file `transact.txt`, that is, the file `transact.txt.Z` is deleted and the original file `transact.txt` is recreated in its original size.

(b) `$ uncompress -c matter.txt.Z`

It displays the uncompressed version of the file `matter.txt.Z` on the screen, keeping the compressed file intact.

(c) $ uncompress -f matter.txt.Z

Using this command, the compressed file matter.txt.Z is uncompressed into the file matter.txt. The -f option performs force uncompression. In other words, if a file matter.txt already exists, it is overwritten by the uncompressed version of the file matter.txt.Z without confirmation.

To see the contents of the compressed files, we use the zcat command.

Syntax zcat file_name.Z

Here, file_name.Z represents the compressed file.

Example

$ zcat matter.txt.Z

This example will display the content of the compressed file matter.txt.Z without uncompressing it. Figure 5.7 shows the output of the aforementioned commands.

5.4.7 pack Command

It compresses or shrinks files. The original file is replaced with a packed version. The original filename will have the .z extension appended to it.

Syntax pack [-f] file_name

-f It applies force to pack the file. Sometimes if not much compression is possible, the pack command refuses to pack the file. The -f option forcefully packs the file into the .z extension even if there is not much saving.

file It represents the file we wish to pack.

Examples

(a) $ pack a.png

pack: a.png: 0.3% compression

The compressed file will be stored in the name a.png.z and the original file will be deleted. In the pack command, the degree of compression is low.

(b) $ pack -f matter.txt

It packs the file matter.txt in the name matter.txt.z forcefully, that is, even when not much compression is possible, the files will still be compressed into matter.txt.z.

To view the contents of a packed file, we use the pcat command.

Syntax pcat file_name.z

Here, file_name.z represents the packed file whose content we wish to see.

Example $ pcat matter.txt.z

This example will display the content of the packed file matter.txt.z without unpacking it. Figure 5.8 shows the output of the aforementioned commands.

5.4.8 unpack Command

This command is used to get back the original file from the packed file.

Syntax unpack file_name

```
$ ls -l transact*
-rw-r--r--      1 root  root     551 Feb 22 17:04 transact.txt.z

$ uncompress transactl.txt.Z

$ ls - l transact*
-rw-r--r--      1 root  root     892 Feb 22 17:04 transact.txt

$ ls -l matter*
-r------r--     1 root  root      99 Feb 22 17:08 matter.txt.Z

$ uncompress -c matter.txt.Z
Hello this is testing of cut command
I think it is working as per the expected
result. it is going to rain today

$ cat > matter.txt
Hello
^D

$ uncompress matter.txt.Z
matter.txt already exists; do you wish to overwrite matter.txt (yes or no)? n
not overwritten

$ uncompress -f matter.txt.Z

$ ls -l matter*
-r------r--     1 root  root     113 Feb 22 17:08 matter.txt

$ compress matter.txt

$ ls -l matter*
-r------r--     1 root  root      99 Feb 22 17:08 matter.txt.Z

$ zcat matter.txt.Z
Hello this is testing of cut command
I think it is working as per the expected
result.it is going to rain today
```

Fig. 5.7 Uncompression of files using the `uncompress` command

```
$ ls -l a*
-rw-r--r--      1  root   root 34878 Feb 22 17:28 a.png

$ pack a.png
pack: a.png: 0.3% Compression

$ ls -l a*
-rw-r--r--      1  root   root 34779 Feb 22 17:28 a.png.z

$ ls -l matter*
-r------r--     1  root   root    113 Feb 22 17:08 matter.txt

$ pack matter.txt
pack: matter.txt: no saving - file unchanged

$ pack -f matter.txt
pack: matter.txt: 11.5% Compression

$ ls -l matter*
-r------r--     1  root   root    100 Feb 22 17:08 matter.txt.z

$ pcat matter.txt.z
Hello this is testing of cut command
I think it is working as per the expected
result. it is going to rain today
```

Fig. 5.8 Compression of files using the `pack` command

Here, file_name unpacks or uncompresses the packed file by removing its extension .z.

Example $ unpack matter.txt.z

The packed file matter.txt.z will be unpacked to the file matter.txt as shown in Fig. 5.9.

```
$ ls - l matter*
-r-----r--        1 root  root        100 Feb 22 17:08 matter.txt.z

$ unpack matter.txt.z
unpack: matter.txt: unpacked

$ ls - l matter*
-r-----r--        1 root  root        113 Feb 22 17:08 matter.txt
```

Fig. 5.9   Uncompression of files using the unpack command

5.4.9 bzip2 and bunzip2 Commands

bzip2 and bunzip2 are the compression commands similar to gzip/gunzip, but with a different compression method. As far as the technique is concerned, these methods are considered better than gzip/gunzip. However, they comparatively take a longer time to compress and uncompress the files. The bzip2 command compresses the specified file by replacing it with its compressed version having a .bz2 extension.

Syntax   bzip2 [-d][-f][-k][-v] filenames

Table 5.13 shows the aforementioned options.

Table 5.13   Options used with the bzip2 command

Option	Description
-d	It decompresses the file.
-f	It performs force operation, that is, it overwrites the corresponding file without warning.
-k	It keeps the original file and creates another compressed file with an extension .bz2.
-v	Verbose mode shows the compression ratio for each compressed file .
Filenames	It represents the files that have to be compressed.

Assume that we have two files, names.txt and numbers.txt, with the initial content shown in Fig. 5.10, which we wish to compress.

Examples

(a) $ bzip2 names.txt
The file names.txt is compressed and is renamed names.txt.bz2, which is confirmed by the ls command (refer to Fig. 5.10).

(b) $ cat names.txt.bz2
The command shows the compressed content of the file names.txt.bz2 (refer to Fig. 5.10).

(c) $ bzip2 -v numbers.txt
The file numbers.txt is compressed into the file numbers.txt.bz2, but this time in verbose mode. This means that it displays the information regarding compression ratio, number of bits per byte, and other related information, as shown in Fig. 5.10.

(d) `$ bzip2 -d names.txt.bz2 numbers.txt.bz2`

The compressed files `names.txt.bz2` and `numbers.txt.bz2` are uncompressed or decompressed to `names.txt` and `numbers.txt`, respectively, which is confirmed by the ls command shown in Fig. 5.10.

(e) `$ bzip2 -k names.txt`

The file `names.txt` is compressed and its compressed version is stored in another file `names.txt.bz2`, keeping the original file intact. Hence, the original file `names.txt` will not be overwritten by its compression version, but a separate file is made to keep the compressed format.

(f) `$ bzip2 -d names.txt.bz2`

The `names.txt.bz2` file is supposed to be uncompressed into the file `names.txt`. However, as the file `names.txt` already exists, uncompression does not take place and the following warning message is displayed: `bzip2: Output file names.txt already exists`.

(g) `$ bzip2 -df names.txt.bz2`

The option -f results in force decompression. The file `names.txt.bz2` is uncompressed, overwriting the existing file `names.txt`, without displaying any warning message. We can see both the uncompressed files, `names.txt` and `numbers.txt`, in Fig. 5.10.

In addition to the `bzip2 -d` command, we can also uncompress files using the `bunzip2` command.

```
$ ls n*
names.txt numbers.txt

$ cat names.txt
Anil
Ravi
Sunil
Raju

$ cat numbers.txt
2429193
3334444
7777888
9990000
5555111

$ bzip2 names.txt

$ ls n*
names.txt.bz2 numbers.txt

$ cat names.txt.bz2
███H█AY&SY={█  : ►< ↑  █  !█4=L█P█Q█l'′z█PE{
█W█

$ bzip2 -v numbers.txt
  numbers.txt:  0.635:1, 12.600 bits/byte, -57.50% saved, 40 in, 63 out.

$ ls n*
name.txt.bz2 numbers.txt.bz2
```

Fig. 5.10 Compression and uncompression of files `names.txt` and `numbers.txt` using the `bzip2` command

(Contd)

```
$ bzip2 -d names.txt.bz2 numbers.txt.bz2

$ ls n*
names.txt numbers.txt

$ bzip2 -k names.txt

$ ls n*
names.txt names.txt.bz2 numbers.txt

$ bzip2 -d names.txt.bz2
bzip2: Output file names.txt already exists.

$ bzip2 -fd names.txt.bz2

$ ls n*
names.txt numbers.txt
```

Fig. 5.10   (*Contd*)

5.4.10 `bunzip2` Command

This command uncompresses the file that is compressed by the `bzip2` command.

Syntax   `bunzip2 filename`

Example   `$ bunzip2 numbers.txt.bz2`

The file `numbers.txt.bz2` is uncompressed into the file `numbers.txt` (i.e., the file `numbers.txt.bz2` will be deleted).

5.4.11 `7-zip`—Implementing Maximum Compression

Besides `zip`, `bzip`, `gzip`, and other similar commands, Unix also supports the `7-zip` command. The `7-zip` command is the file archiver command that compresses files at the highest compression ratio (around 30–50% more than the other zip formats). This is because it uses the Lempel–Ziv–Markov chain algorithm (LZMA) compression algorithm, which enables it to have the highest compression ratio. The syntax for this command is as follows:

Syntax   `7z[a][d][e][x][l][t]compressed_file [files_to_compress]`

Table 5.14 shows the aforementioned options.

Examples

(a) The following example compresses all the files with extension `.txt` in the current directory into the file `data.7z`.

`$ 7z a data.7z *.txt`

Table 5.14   Options used with the `7-zip` command

Option	Description
a	It adds file(s) to the compressed_file.
d	It deletes file(s) from the compressed_file.
e	It extracts the content from the compressed_file in the current directory, that is, extracts the files of the directories (if in the compressed form) into the current directory
x	It extracts the content from the compressed_file along with the full paths, that is, the files of the directories (if in the compressed form) will be extracted into their respective directories. These directories will be created if they do not exist and the files will be extracted into them.
l	It lists the content in the compressed_file.
t	It tests whether the compressed file is OK or not (i.e., corrupted).

(b) The following example displays the list of files compressed in the file data.7z.

```
$ 7z l data.7z
```

(c) The following example tests whether the files in the compressed file data.7z are OK or not. If the files are found to be OK, the filenames are displayed along with a of information about the compressed files: size and number of files and folders compressed in it.

```
$ 7z t data.7z
```

(d) The following example adds the files of the directory projects to an existing compressed file data.7z.

```
$ 7z a data.7z projects
```

(e) The following example extracts the files found in the compressed file data.7z into the current directory.

```
$ 7z e data.7z projects
```

Note: The compressed files of subdirectories will also be uncompressed into the current directory, that is, the respective subdirectories will not be created.

To create subdirectories and uncompress files into the respective subdirectories, option x is used instead of e.

(f) The following example deletes the directory projects and its files from the compressed file data.7z.

```
$7z d data.7z projects
```

The screenshot of the aforementioned examples is shown in Fig. 5.11.

```
$ ls - l
total 10
-rw-r--r--      1 root  root       18 Feb 22 14:51 customers.txt
-rwx--xr-x      1 root  root        6 Feb 22 14:51 letter.txt
-rwx--xr-x      1 root  root      113 Feb 22 17:08 matter.txt
drwxr-xr-x      2 root  root      512 Feb 27 20:30 projects
-rw-r--r--      1 root  mba       892 Feb 22 17:21 transact.txt

$ ls -l projects
total 4
-rwxr-xr-x      1 root  root      347 Feb 22 14:53 bank.lst
-rw-r--r--      1 root  root        6 Feb 27 20:30 hello.txt

$ 7z a data.7z *.txt

7-Zip 4.55 beta Copyright (c) 1999-2007 Igor Pavlov 2007-09-05
p7zip Version 4.55 (locale=en_IN.UTF-8,Utf16=on,HugeFiles=on,1 CPU)
Scanning
Creating archive data.7z

Compressing customers.txt
Compressing letter.txt
Compressing matter.txt
Compressing transact.txt
```

Fig. 5.11 Compression and uncompression of files using the 7-zip command   *(Contd)*

```
Everything is ok

$ ls - l
total 102
-rw-r--r--     1 root  root       18 Feb 22 14:51 customers.txt
-rw-------     1 root  root      639 Feb 27 20:31 data.7z
-rwx--xr-x     1 root  root        6 Feb 22 14:51 letter.txt
-rwx--xr-x     1 root  root      113 Feb 22 17:08 matter.txt
drwxr-xr-x     2 root  root      512 Feb 27 20:30 projects
-rw-r--r--     1 root  mba       892 Feb 22 17:21 transact.txt


$ 7z l data.7z


7-Zip 4.55 beta Copyright (c) 1999-2007 Igor Pavlov 2007-09-05
p7zip Version 4.55 (locale=en_IN.UTF-8,Utf16=on,HugeFiles=on,1 CPU)

Listing archive: data.7z


Method = LZMA
Solod = +
Block = 1

   Date      Time    Attr        Size  Compressed   Name
------------------- ----- ----------- ------------  --------------------
--------
2006-02-22 14:51:18....A          18          423   customers.txt
2006-02-22 14:51:18....A           6                letter.txt
2006-02-22 17:08:46....A         113                matter.txt
2006-02-22 17:21:48....A         892                transact.txt
------------------- ----- ----------- ------------  --------------------
                                1029          423 4 files, 0 folders
$ 7z t data.7z


7-Zip 4.55 beta Copyright (c) 1999-2007 Igor Pavlov 2007-09-05
p7zip Version 4.55 (locale=en_IN.UTF-8,Utf16=on,HugeFiles=on,1 CPU)

Processing archive: data.7z

Testing          customers.txt
Testing          letter.txt
Testing          matter.txt
Testing          transact.txt

Everything is ok

Total:
Folders: 0
Files: 4
Size: 1029
Compressed: 639


$ 7z a data.7z projects

7-Zip 4.55 beta Copyright (c) 1999-2007 Igor Pavlov 2007-09-05
p7zip Version 4.55 (locale=en_IN.UTF-8,Utf16=on,HugeFiles=on,1 CPU)

Scanning
```

Fig. 5.11 (Contd)

```
Updating archive data.7z

Compressing projects/hello.txt
Compressing projects/bank.lst

Everything is ok

$ 7z l data.7z

7-Zip 4.55 beta Copyright (c) 1999-2007 Igor Pavlov 2007-09-05
p7zip Version 4.55 (locale=en_IN.UTF-8,Utf16=on,HugeFiles=on,1 CPU)

Listing archive: data.7z

Method = LZMA
Solid  = +
Blocks + 1


   Date      Time    Attr      Size  Compressed  Name
------------------- ----- ----------- ----------- --------------------
--------
2006-02-22 14:51:18 ....A       18          423  customers.txt
2006-02-22 14:51:18 ....A        6               letter.txt
2006-02-22 17:08:46 ....A      113               matter.txt
2006-02-22 17:21:48 ....A      892               transact.txt
2006-02-27 20:30:21 ....A        6          198  projects/hello.txt
2006-02-22 14:53:14 ....A      347               projects/dank.lst
2006-02-27 20:30:19 D....        0            0  projects
------------------- ----- ----------- ----------- --------------------
                              1382          621 6 files, 1 folders
$ rm *.txt

$ rm -r projects

$ ls -l
totla 276
-rw-------    1 root   root            909 Feb 27 20:36 data.7z

$ 7z e data.7z

7-Zip 4.55 beta Copyright (c) 1999-2007 Igor Pavlov 2007-09-05
p7zip Version 4.55 (locale=en_IN/UTF-8,Utf16+on,HugeFiles=on,1 CPU)

Processing archive: data.7z

Extracting customers.txt
Extracting letter.txt
Extracting matter.txt
Extracting transact.txt
Extracting projects/hello.txt
Extracting projects/bank.lst
Extracting projects

Everything is ok
```

Fig. 5.11 *(Contd)*

```
Total:
Folders: 1
Files: 6
Size: 1382
Compressed: 909


$ ls - l
total 462
-rwxr-xr-x    1 root  root       347 Feb 22 14:53 bank.lst
-rw-r--r--    1 root  root        18 Feb 22 14:51 customers.txt
-rw-------    1 root  root       909 Feb 27 20:36 data.7z
-rw-r--r--    1 root  root         6 Feb 27 20:30 hello.txt
-rwx--xr-x    1 root  root         6 Feb 22 14:51 letter.txt
-rwx--xr-x    1 root  root       113 Feb 22 17:08 matter.txt
drwxr-xr-x    2 root  root       512 Feb 27 20:30 projects
-rw-r--r--    1 root  root       892 Feb 22 17:21 transact.txt


$ 7z d data.7z projects

7-Zip 4.55 beta Copyright (c) 1999-2007 Igor Pavlov 2007-09-05
p7zip Version 4.55 (locale=en_IN.UTF-8,Utf16=on,HugeFiles=on,1 CPU)


Updating archive data.7z

Everything is ok

$ 7z l data.7z

7-Zip 4.55 beta Copyright (c) 1999-2007 Igor Pavlov 2007-09-05
p7zip Version 4.55 (locale=en_IN.UTF-8,Utf16=on,HugeFiles=on,1 CPU)


Listing archive: data.7z

Method = LZMA
Solid = +
Blocks = 1

   Date      Time    Attr      Size  Compressed  Name
------------------- ----- ------------ ------------ ------------------------
--------
2006-02-22 14:51:18 ....A        18          423  customers.txt
2006-02-22 14:51:18 ....A         6               letter.txt
2006-02-22 17:08:46 ....A       113               matter.txt
2006-02-22 17:21:48 ....A       892               transact.txt
------------------- ----- ------------ ------------ ------------------------
                              1029          423 4 files, 0 folders
```

Fig. 5.11 *(Contd)*

5.5 DEALING WITH FILES

In this section, we will learn the different commands that deal with files such as finding the file type (finding whether the specified file is a regular file, directory, device file, or something else), locating or searching for files with the given criteria, confirming the presence of a specified application program or system utility on the disk drive, and checking the file system. Let us see how we can find the file type.

5.5.1 file: Determining File Type

This command determines the file type, that is, whether the specified name belongs to a file or a directory. The command does certain checks or tests on the specified file to determine its type.

Syntax   file [-f filelist]files

-f filelist   Determines the type of files contained in the file filelist.
Files   Filenames whose file type we wish to determine.

Examples

(a) $ file matter.txt

matter.txt: English text

This command determines if the file matter.txt is a directory, a special device file, or an ordinary file. If matter.txt is an ordinary file, it checks to see whether it is empty and displays the message 'empty'.

If the file command finds that the file matter.txt is not empty, it checks to see if it begins with a *magic number*, that is, a numeric or string constant used to indicate the type of file if it is not suitable for human reading. It is to be remembered that files that are not ASCII text files, such as executable files, archive, and library files, contain a magic number at the beginning of the file.

If the file matter.txt does not have a magic number, the file command examines its first block comprising 512 bytes and finds its language (i.e., whether its language is English, a programming language, or some other special data). On the basis of all these analyses, the file command displays the type of the specified file.

(b) The following example displays the file type of all the files and directories in the current directory.

$ file *

(c) The following example displays the file type of all the files that are mentioned in the file, filenames.

$ file -f filenames

The output of these commands is shown in Fig. 5.12.

In this output of the file command, the file letter.txt is declared as the command text because the execute permission is assigned to this file.

Note: For the file that does not have the read permission, the file command displays the output 'cannot open for reading'.

5.5.2 find: Locating Files

It is used to locate one or more files that satisfy the given criteria. We can also perform certain operations or actions that we want to perform on the searched files.

```
$ ls - l
total 148
-rw-r--r--   1 root  root    34878 Feb 22 17:30 a.png
-rw-r--r--   1 root  root    34779 Feb 22 17:28 a.png.z
-rw-r--r--   1 root  root       18 Feb 22 14:51 customers.txt
--w-r-x--x   1 root  root        6 Feb 22 14:51 letter.txt
-r-----r--   1 root  root      113 Feb 22 17:08 matter.txt
drwxr-xr-x   2 root  root      512 Feb 22 16:39 projects
-rw-r--r--   1 root  root      892 Feb 22 17:21 transact.txt

$ file matter.txt
matter.txt:    English text

$ file customers.txt
customers.txt: ascii text

$ file a.png
a.png:         PNG image data

$ file a.png.z
a.png.z:       packed data

$ file projects
projects:      directory

$ file *
a.png:         PNG image data
a.png.z:       packed data
customers.txt: ascii text
letter.txt:    commands text
matter.txt:    English text
projects:      directory
transact.txt:  ascii text

$ cat filenames
letter.txt
a.png
transact.txt

$ file -f filenames
letter.txt:    commands text
a.png:         PNG image data
transact.txt:  ascii text
```

Fig. 5.12 File types using the file command

Syntax   # find path criteria action_list

Here, path refers to the directory or location of the disk in which we want the find command to search for the desired files. The path may include more than one directory separated by a space. The find command searches all the subdirectories specified in the path to find the file(s) that meets the given criteria. Table 5.15 shows the options for writing criteria.

The *action-list* in the syntax indicates that we can apply several actions on the files that are searched through the find command. Table 5.16 lists the most frequent actions that are applied to the found files.

Table 5.15 Options used with the find command

Options	Description
-atime n	It finds files that were accessed n days ago.
-ctime n	It finds files that were created n days ago.
-mtime n	It finds files that were modified more than +n days, less than −n days, or exactly n days ago.
-size n[c]	It finds files that are n blocks or c bytes in size. One block is equal to 512 bytes.
-name pattern	It finds files where the filename matches the pattern.
-perm octal_num	It finds files that have given permissions.
-type	It finds files of the specified type. The type is represented through the following characters:
	b: Block file
	c: Character file
	d: Directory
	l: Symbolic ink
	f: Regular file
	p: Named pipe
	s: Socket
-user name	It finds files that are owned by the given user_name. We can also use the user ID instead of the username.
-group group_name	It finds files that belong to a given group_name. We can also use the group ID instead of the group name.

Table 5.16 Actions applied to the found files

Action	Description
-print	Default action that displays the path name of the files that meet the given criteria
-exec command	Executes the Unix system command on the files that meet the given criteria
-ok command	Same as the exec command, it prompts the user for confirmation, that is, the user has to press 'y' for executing the command

In case of the -exec or ok command, a pair of braces {} is used to represent the files that are found by the find command. In other words, the files located by find will replace the braces and the specified command will be applied on each found file one by one. In order to distinguish between the command being executed and the arguments used by the find command, a semicolon (;) is used. Since the shell also uses the semicolon, we use the 'escape' character (a backslash or quotes) to differentiate it. A format of the find command when a command is executed on the found files is as follows:

```
$ find pathname-list condition-list -exec command {} \;
```

While using complex expressions for finding files, we can use the operators explained in the next sub-section.

Using find operators

While writing expressions for finding files in the find command, we can use the following find operators (see Table 5.17).

Table 5.17   List of find operators used to connect expressions

Operator	Description
! (Negation operator)	This performs reverse action, that is, it finds the files that do not satisfy the specified expression.
-o (OR operator)	This is used to connect one or more expressions. On using an operator, the files that satisfy even a single expression will also be displayed.
-a (AND operator)	This is the default operator. Only the files that satisfy all the expressions connected with the −a operator are displayed.

Note: While using –a or –o operators, we may use parentheses ( ) for separation, but they must be 'escaped' as they are used by the shell. This means that the parentheses must be prefixed with a backslash, '\(', '\)'

Examples

(a) The following command displays the files and their path names that have not been accessed for over a month (+30).

```
$ find / -atime +30 -print
```

(b) To find files that are of a size larger than 20 blocks and which have not been accessed for over a month (+30), use the following command.

```
$ find / -atime +30 -size +20 -print
```

(c) To search for files that are of a size between 1000 and 2000 bytes, use the following command.

```
$ find . -size +1000c -size -2000c -print
```

We can see in this command that a minus sign designates 'less than,' and the plus sign designates 'greater than'.

(d) To remove files that are of a size larger than 20 blocks with the interactive action command ok, enter the following.

```
$ find / -atime +30 -size +20 -ok rm -f { } \;
```

(e) To list all files and directories under the current directory, use the following command.

```
$ find . -print
```

(f) To search for the file a.txt in the current directory and its subdirectories, use the following command.

```
$ find -name 'a.txt' -print
```

(g) To search for the file a.txt on the root and all its subdirectories, use the following command.

```
$ find / -name 'a.txt' -print
```

(h) To display all .c files under the current directory, use the following command.

```
$ find . -name '*.c' -print
```

(i) To print all files beginning with the word *test* in the current directory and its subdirectories, use the following command.

```
$ find . -name 'test*' -print
```

(j) To print all filenames comprising three characters that begin with an upper-case or a lower-case character in the current directory and its subdirectories, use the following command.

```
$ find . -name '[a-zA-Z]??' -print
```

(k) To display the list of the directories, use the following command.

```
$ find . -type d -print
```

(l) To find all those .c files that were last modified less than three days ago, use the following command.

```
$ find . -mtime -3 -name "*.c" -print
```

Note: We can use single quotes as well as double quotes for defining the pattern.

(m) To find all those .c files that were last modified more than three days ago, use the following command.

```
$ find . -mtime +3 -name "*.c" -print
```

(n) To find all those .c files that were modified exactly three days ago, use the following command.

```
$ find . -mtime 3 -name "*.c" -print
```

(o) To find the .txt files that have the 755 permission, use the following command.

```
$ find . -name '*.txt' -perm 755 -print
```

We can see that 755 is an octal number representing read, write, and execute permissions for the owner, and read and execute permission for the group and other members.

We can also use the and operator, that is, the -a operator in the aforementioned command. The and operator shows only those files that satisfy both the specified expressions. With the and operator, this command can be written as follows.

```
$ find . -name '*.txt' -a -perm 755 -print
```

Remember, -a is the default operator, so we can optionally omit it.

(p) To find the subdirectories under the current directory having the 755 permission, use the following command.

```
$ find . -type d -perm 755 -print
```

(q) To find all the files that have the User (owner) as root, use the following command.

```
$ find . -user root -print
```

Instead of the username, we can use the user ID. The following command is used.

```
$ find . -user 0 -print
```

(r) To find all the files that belong to the group projects, use the following command.

```
$ find . -group projects -print
```

As with the username, instead of the group name, we can use the group ID. The following command is used.

```
$ find . -group 15 -print
```

(s) To find all the files except the a.txt file, use the following command.

```
$ find . ! -name 'a.txt' -print
```

In this command, ! is the negation operator and it reverses the meaning of the expression.

(t) To find all the files except the ones with the extension .txt, use the following command.

```
$ find . ! -name '*.txt' -print
```

(u) To find .txt files or files that have the 755 permission, use the following command.

```
$ find . \( -name '*.txt' -o -perm 755 \) -print
```

The -o operator is the 'OR' operator and hence the files that satisfy either expression will be displayed. We have used the 'escaped' parentheses in this expression, that is, they are prefixed by a backslash to avoid them from being interpreted by the shell.

(v) To find .txt as well as .doc files, use the following command.

```
$ find . \( -name '*.txt' -o -name '*.doc' \) -print
```

We can also execute commands on the files that we find. The following is an example.

```
$ find . -name "*.txt" -exec wc -l '{}' ';'
```

This command counts the number of lines in every .txt file in and under the current directory. The count of the lines is displayed before the name of the respective file. Basically in this command, all the .txt files that are found replace the '{ }' braces, that is, the wc -l command is applied to each of the files that is found. The ';' ends the -exec clause.

(w) To display the names of the files and subdirectories in the current directory, use the following command.

```
$ find . -exec echo {} ';'
```

We can see that the semicolon is quoted.

(x) The following example finds the .txt files that have the 755 permission. From the files that are found, the group read permission is removed, as shown here.

```
$ find . -name '*.txt' -perm 755 -exec chmod g-r '{}' ';';
```

The find command has several significances, which are as follows:

1. Searching for files with a specific pattern
2. Searching for files that are accessed a specific number of days ago
3. Searching for files of a specific size
4. Searching for files with specific permissions
5. Searching for files belonging to a specified user or group
6. Applying commands on the found files

5.5.3 locate: Searching for Files with Specific Strings

This command is used for searching for files whose name or path matches a particular search string and for which, the user has access permissions.

Syntax   `locate [-q][-n] [-i] pattern_to_search`

Table 5.18 explains these options.

Examples

(a) `$ locate ".txt"`
This command will find all filenames in the file system that contain .txt anywhere in their full paths and for which the user has access permissions. It may display error messages when it comes across the .txt files for which the user does not have access permissions.

(b) `$ locate -q -n 10 ".txt"`

Table 5.18 Options used with the `locate` command

Options	Description
-q	It suppresses error messages that are displayed for files for which the user does not have access permissions.
-n	It limits the result to a specified number.
-i	It ignores the case while searching, that is, it returns the result that matches the pattern in upper case or lower case.
pattern_to_search	It represents the string that we wish to search for in the path names or in the filenames. All the files that contain the *pattern_to_search* string in their path or filename will be listed on the screen.

This command will find the first 10 files that contain .txt anywhere in their full paths and for which the user has access permissions. It will not display any error messages on finding the files for which the user does not have access permissions.

(c) `$ locate -i "project.txt"`

This command will find all `project.txt` files, be it in the upper case or lower case, for which the user has access permissions.

One disadvantage of `locate` is that it stores all filenames on the system in an index that is usually updated only once a day. This means `locate` will not find files that have been created very recently. It may also report filenames as being present even though the file has just been deleted. Unlike `find`, `locate` cannot track down files on the basis of their permissions, size, and so on.

5.5.4 which/whence: Finding Locations of Programs or Utilities on Disks

This command is used to find out where the specified application program or system utility is stored on the disk.

> **Note:** The command `whence` works only in the Korn shell. The syntax for using `whence` is the same as that of the `which` command.

Syntax `which program_name/utility`

Here, `program_name/utility` represents the command or programs whose location we wish to find out.

Example `$ which ls`

Output `/usr/bin/ls`

5.5.5 fsck: Utility for Checking File Systems

The Unix file system can easily be corrupted if it is not properly shut down. Therefore, we need to periodically check the file system and repair it. If the errors in the file system are not repaired then and there, the whole system may crash. The `fsck` command checks our file system, reports the errors that it may come across, and interactively prompts us for 'Yes' or 'No' decisions to correct those error conditions. It operates in two modes: interactive and non-interactive. In the interactive mode, this command examines the file system and stops at each error found in the file system. It displays the error description and asks for the user's response. On the basis of the user action, either the error is removed or `fsck` will continue checking without making any changes to the file system. In the non-interactive mode, `fsck` tries to repair all the errors found in the file system without waiting for the user response. Although this mode is faster, it may delete some important files that have become corrupted.

Syntax   `# fsck [-y] [-n] [ filesystem ]`

Note: The option –y or –n, if used, runs the `fsck` command in the non-interactive mode.

Here, `filesystem` is the name of the file system to be checked. If we do not specify the file system, `fsck` will use the files `/etc/checklist` or `/etc/fstab` to know the names of the file systems to be checked.

The options –y and –n are used to automatically provide answers *Yes* and *No*, respectively, to all the queries that appear when using the `fsck` command.

Examples

(a) `# fsck -y`
This command checks all the file systems installed in our machines and displays the answer 'Yes' (meaning granted) for all the queries that come up.

(b) `# fsck -n`
This command checks all the file systems installed in our machines and displays the answer 'No' for all the queries that come up.

The `fsck` command runs in several phases as follows:

```
# fsck /dev/root
** Currently Mounted on /
** Phase 1  – Check Blocks and Sizes
** Phase 2  – Check Pathnames
** Phase 3  – Check Connectivity
** Phase 3b – Verify Shadows/ACLs
** Phase 4  – Check Reference Counts
** Phase 5  – Check Cylinder Groups
7899 files, 406203 used, 279169 free (257 frags, 34864 blocks, 0.0% fragmentation)
```

Let us have a quick view of all the phases of the `fsck` command.

In phase 1, each inode in the file system is checked and then the disk blocks pointed to by the inode are checked. Error messages may appear at this stage if the block address in the inode is invalid, a block is already being used by another inode, the expected number of blocks for an ordinary file does not match with the actual number of blocks used by the inode, and there are other similar errors. In short, phase 1 performs the following tasks:

1. Checks the inodes, looks for valid inode types, and corrects the inode size and format.
2. Checks for bad or duplicate blocks.

In phase 2, `fsck` checks all directory inodes in the file system. First, the inode for the root directory is examined. In case the root inode is corrupted, the `fsck` will abort. If the inode number of the directory entry is invalid, the inode field of the directory entry is set to zero. It is ensured that none of the directory entries points to an unallocated inode. In short, this phase is focused on removing the directory entries that are invalid or pointing to invalid inode(s). Thus, this phase reports errors that result from root inode mode and status, directory inode pointers in a range, directory entries pointing to bad inodes, etc.

Note: This phase removes directory entries pointing to bad inodes used in phase 1.

In phase 3, all the allocated inodes are scanned for unreferenced directories, that is, directories where the inodes corresponding to the parent directory entry do not exist. In this case, we will be prompted to reconnect to any orphaned directories. If our answer is yes, then a link between the orphan directory and the special directory /lost+found will be made. When the fsck command is over, we can examine the entries in /lost+ found and can move them to their respective directories.

Phase 4 deals with the inode count or reference count information, which was accumulated in phases 2 and 3. In phase 1, the reference count is first set to the link count value stored in the inode. The link count is the number of links to a physical file. Then, in phases 2 and 3, the reference count is decremented each time a valid link is found while scanning the file system. Therefore, the reference count value should be zero when phase 4 begins.

Phase 5 checks the free block list. Any bad or duplicate blocks in this list are flagged, which are later salvaged. On salvaging the free list, phase 6 is initiated that reconstructs the free block list.

If a file system was corrupted and then fixed, the system is rebooted without a sync operation (to prevent the 'file system fixing' from being undone). The reboot process modifies the file system to repair it.

Note: Unless fsck is used in the single-user mode, the file system corruption will spread to other mounted file systems.

The fsck command checks the integrity of the file systems, especially the superblock, which stores summary information of the volume. Whenever data is added or changed on a disk, it is the superblock that is frequently modified to reflect the changes. There are many chances of the superblock getting corrupted. Hence, the fsck checks the superblock for any errors. The following two checks are essentially done:

1. The size of the file system must be greater than the size of the number of blocks identified in the superblock.
2. The total number of inodes must be less than the maximum number of inodes.

Besides checking the superblock, the fsck command also checks the number and status of the cylinder group blocks, inodes, indirect blocks, and data blocks. This command checks if all the blocks that are marked as free are not being used by any files. If they are being used, it means the files may be corrupted. In addition, fsck confirms if the number of free blocks plus the number of used blocks equals the total number of blocks in the file system. In case of any ambiguity, the maps of unallocated blocks are rebuilt.

When inodes are examined, fsck searches for any inconsistency in the format and type, link count, duplicate blocks, bad block numbers, and inode size. Inodes should always be in one of the three states: allocated (being used by a file), unallocated (not being used by a file), and partially allocated (the procedure of allocation and unallocation is performed, but the data that was supposed to be deleted is still there). The fsck command will clear the inode if inconsistency of any type is detected.

The link count is the number of directory entries that are linked to a particular inode. The entire directory structure is examined to find the number of links for every inode. If the stored link count and the actual link count do not match, it confirms that the disk was not synchronized before the shutdown, that is, while saving the changes in the file system, the link count was not updated. In case the stored count is not zero but the actual count is zero, then disconnected files are placed in the lost+found directory. In other cases, the actual count replaces the stored count.

The output of the fsck command is shown in Fig. 5.13.

```
# fsck -y
/dev/dsk/c0d0s0 IS CURRENTLY MOUNTED READ/WRITE.
CONTINUE? yes

** /dev/dsk/c0d0s0
** Currently Mounted on /
** Phase 1 - Check Blocks and Sizes
** Phase 2 - Check Pathnames
** Phase 3a - Check Connectivity
** Phase 3b - Verify Shadows/ACLs
** Phase 4 - Check Reference Counts
** Phase 5 - Check Cylinder Groups
FILESYSTEM MAY STILL BE INCONSISTENT.
7899 files, 406203 user, 279169 free (257 frags, 34864 blocks,
0.0% fragmentation)

***** PLEASE RERUN FSCK ON UNMOUNTED FILE SYSTEM *****
/dev/dsk/c0d0s6 IS CURRENTLY MOUNTED READ/WRITE.
CONTINUE? yes

** /dev/dsk/c0d0s6
** Currently Mounted on /usr
** Phase 1 - Check Blocks and Sizes
** Phase 2 - Check Pathnames
** Phase 3a - Check Connectivity
** Phase 3b - Verify Shadows/ACLs
** Phase 4 - Check Reference Counts
** Phase 5 - Check Cylinder Groups
FILESYSTEM MAY STILL BE INCONSISTENT.
150119 files, 3244347 used, 1892040 free (5304 frags, 235842 blocks,
0.1% fragmentation)

***** PLEASE RERUN FSCK ON UNMOUNTED FILE SYSTEM *****
/dev/dsk/c0d0s3 IS CURRENTLY MOUNTED READ/WRITE.
CONTINUE? yes

** /dev/dsk/c0d0s3
** Currently Mounted on /var
** Phase 1 - Check Blocks and Sizes
** Phase 2 - Check Pathnames
** Phase 3a - Check Connectivity
** Phase 3b - Verify Shadows/ACLs
```

Fig. 5.13 Output displayed while running the fsck command (*Contd*)

```
** Phase 4 - Check Reference Counts
** Phase 5 - Check Cylinder Groups
FILESYSTEM MAY STILL BE INCONSISTENT.
19560 files, 83088 used, 156495 free (455 frags, 19505 blocks,
0.2% fragmentation)

***** PLEASE RERUN FSCK ON UNMOUNTED FILE SYSTEM *****
/dev/dsk/c0d0s7 IS CURRENTLY MOUNTED READ/WRITE.
CONTINUE? yes

** /dev/dsk/c0d0s7
** Currently Mounted on /export/home
** Phase 1 - Check Blocks and Sizes
** Phase 2 - Check Pathnames
** Phase 3a - Check Connectivity
** Phase 3b - Verify Shadows/ACLs
** Phase 4 - Check Reference Counts
** Phase 5 - Check Cylinder Groups
FILESYSTEM MAY STILL BE INCONSISTENT.
2 files, 9 user, 31295480 free (16 frags, 3911933 blocks,
0.0% fragmentation)

***** PLEASE RERUN FSCK ON UNMOUNTED FILE SYSTEM *****
/dev/dsk/c0d0s5 IS CURRENTLY MOUNTED READ/WRITE.
CONTINUE? yes

** /dev/dsk/c0d0s5
** Currently Mounted on /opt
** Phase 1 - Check Blocks and Sizes
** Phase 2 - Check Pathnames
** Phase 3a - Check Connectivity
** Phase 3b - Verify Shadows/ACLs
** Phase 4 - Check Reference Counts
** Phase 5 - Check Cylinder Groups
FILESYSTEM MAY STILL BE INCONSISTENT.
98 files, 25985 used, 24505 free (9 frags, 3062 blocks,
0.0% fragmentation)

***** PLEASE RERUN FSCK ON UNMOUNTED FILE SYSTEM *****
/dev/dsk/c0d0s1 IS CURRENTLY MOUNTED READ/WRITE.
CONTINUE? yes

** /dev/dsk/c0d0s1
** Currently Mounted on /usr/openwin
** Phase 1 - Check Blocks and Sizes
** Phase 2 - Check Pathnames
** Phase 3a - Check Connectivity
** Phase 3b - Verify Shadows/ACLs
** Phase 4 - Check Reference Counts
** Phase 5 - Check Cylinder Groups
FILESYSTEM MAY STILL BE INCONSISTENT.
8305 files, 206932 used, 116320 free (400 frags, 14490 blocks,
0.1% fragmentation)

***** PLEASE RERUN FSCK ON UNMOUNTED FILE SYSTEM *****
```

Fig. 5.13   (Contd)

5.6 IMPORTANT UNIX SYSTEM FILES

In this section, we will learn about the important files of the Unix system such as /etc/passwd, /etc/shadow, /etc/hosts file, /etc/hosts.allow, and /etc/hosts.deny. These are the files where important information is kept as passwords of the users, IP addresses of the computers on our network, and permissions to access different services, among others. Let us begin with the /etc/passwd file. These files are very critical and can hinder the performance of the Unix system if modified.

5.6.1 /etc/passwd

passwd is a file found in the /etc directory. It contains login names, passwords, home directories, and other information about users. Each line of the file contains a series of fields, which defines a login account. The fields in each line of the /etc/passwd file are separated by colons. Table 5.19 shows the aforementioned fields.

Table 5.19   Fields found in the /etc/passwd file

Field	Description
user name	The username is the string entered in response to the login prompt. It is a unique identifier for the user throughout the session. The program that prompts for the login name reads this file to get information pertaining to the user
encrypted password	This program prompts for the login name, reads the information found in this field, and uses the information to validate the password entered by the user
user ID number	Each user has an ID number that can be used as a synonym for the username. Both the ID number and the username are unique within the system.
group ID number	Each user has one group ID number. Any number of users can be assigned to the same group. The group ID number is used to assign group access permissions to files, directories, and devices.
real name	This is a sort of comment or complete name of the user (login names are usually unique identifiers only)
home directory	It is the directory that the user reaches after entering the correct logon name and password. This is the name that gets stored in the HOME environment variable
shell program	This is a shell program that is run once the user logs in. If nothing is specified, /bin/sh is assumed

Example $ grep ravi /etc/passwd

    ravi:x:235:614:ravi sharma:/home/ravi:/bin/sh

Note: The grep command is used to search for a given pattern in a file and displays all the lines where the pattern is found. We will learn about the grep command in detail in Chapter 10.

We can always find a root login in the /etc/passwd file, which is as follows:

root:x:0:0:root:/root:/bin/sh

The root user has a user ID of 0 and a group ID of 0. For security reasons, some systems move the list of usernames into the shadow file.

5.6.2 /etc/shadow

Passwords are encrypted for security. We only need to use the same algorithm to encrypt a newly entered password and then compare the result against the encrypted version stored in the file; if they match, the password is correct.

The /etc/passwd file must be readable by everyone because it is used by so many programs to find the user ID number, group membership, and home directory. This allows one to get a copy of the /etc/passwd file, and thus get a copy of all the password encryptions. It may result in security problems.

The solution is to hide the passwords in another file. The file holding the passwords is known as the shadow file and is normally named /etc/shadow. The shadow file is only readable by its owner, which is the root. This means that no one can read the passwords unless they have the root access.

We can tell by looking at the data in the /etc/passwd file whether the actual password is in a shadow file, because the password field displays an x rather than an encrypted password. The shadow file is a text file, and each line displays the password information of a user. The fields in each line of the /etc/shadow file are separated by colons. Table 5.20 gives a brief description of the fields found in this file.

Table 5.20 Fields found in the /etc/shadow file

Field	Description
user name	The same name found in the /etc/passwd file
encrypted password	The encrypted form of the password
password last changed	The day the password was last changed (The date is a count of the number of days since 1 January 1970.)
password may be changed	The number of days before the user has permission to change the password (A value of -1 means that it can be changed any time.)
password must be changed	The number of days from the time the password is set until the password expires and must be changed
password expire warning	The number of days prior to the password expiry date that the user has to be warned
disable after expires	The number of days after the password expires that the account is to be automatically disabled
disabled	The date that the account was disabled (The date is a count of the number of days since 1 January 1970.)

The shadow file also contains dates and day counters, which can be used to force the users to change their passwords from time to time, under the threat of their account getting disabled.

5.6.3 /etc/hosts

The hosts file contains static address information for computers on our local network. Whenever we refer to a computer by its name, the commands that we use must have some way to translate that name into an IP address. Our Internet service provider (ISP) should provide us with the address of one or more name servers that we can use. If we use a dial-up connection, the address of a name server is normally returned to our computer as part of the initial connection sequence. However, in some cases, we must configure the address of the name server into the routing table.

If we have a local network, we will need to provide each member of our network with the address of all the other members. If there are many computers on our local network, it is easier to use one of them as a name server by configuring a daemon to respond to address requests and then configuring other computers to send address queries to our local name server.

The contents of /etc/hosts file may be as follows:

```
127.0.0.1      localhost    localhost.localdomain
192.168.0.1    mce1         mce1.localdomain
192.168.0.2    mce2         mce2.localdomain
192.168.0.3    mce3         mce3.localdomain
```

The same list of addresses is required for every computer on the network, and a computer's address can be included in the file, so that the file can be duplicated everywhere on the network by simply copying it from one computer to another. Each line in the file contains an IP address, followed by a list of alias names for the computer. In this example, each computer can be located by its simple name or domain name.

The first line of the file is always named the local host and always has the address 127.0.0.1. This special *loopback address* is used by programs on the local computer to address its own services.

5.6.4 /etc/hosts.allow and /etc/hosts.deny

When an Internet packet arrives, the contents of the hosts.allow file are scanned, and if a specific permission is found for the requested action, access is granted and no further checking is made. If the hosts.allow file did not specifically grant permission, the hosts.deny file is scanned, and if access is not specifically denied, it is granted.

Each line specifies a service followed by a colon, which separates it from the list of hosts being granted or denied that particular service. The keyword ALL can be used to specify all services or all hosts.

```
$ cat /etc/hosts.deny .
ALL: ALL
```

If the content of hosts.deny file is as given, it means that every service is denied to every host. The following example of hosts.allow begins by granting all permissions to every host in the local domain and every host in the domain philips.com. All permissions are also granted to the computer with the IP address 234.51.135.18. Finally, HTTP web service (specified by naming the daemon to receive the message) is granted to every host except the ones in the domain .godrej.com

```
$ cat /etc/hosts.allow
ALL: LOCAL.philips.com
ALL: 234.51.135.18
httpd: ALL EXCEPT .godrej.com
```

5.7 SHELL VARIABLES

A variable is a medium to store the value to be used for manipulation or storage in a programming language. It offers a symbolic way to represent and manipulate data. The shell also has variables to serve the same purpose. Shell variables are of two types: those created and maintained by the Unix system itself, and those created by the user.

5.7.1 User-created Shell Variables

To create a shell variable, we can simply use the following syntax:

Syntax   `name=value`

Examples

(a) `radius=5`
    Creates a shell variable having the name `radius`.
    Similarly, `name="ravi"`
    `name` is the variable with the value `ravi`.

(b) Null string is a string with no characters.
    `area=" "`
    We can use letters, digits, and the underscore character in variable names.
    `area_circle=56`

(c) To find out the value of a shell variable, we can use the `echo` command. Ordinarily, `echo` merely echoes its arguments on the screen.

    ```
    $ echo radius
    radius
    ```

    However, if we use a variable name preceded by a $ as an argument to `echo`, the value of the variable is echoed.

    ```
    $ echo $radius
    5
    $ echo The radius of circle is $radius
    The radius of circle is 5
    ```

5.7.2 System Shell Variables

The shell maintains its own set of shell variables. To find what your system is using, just type `set`.

```
$ set
```

You may get the following output:

```
EXINIT='set ai nu'
HOME=/usr/ravi
IFS=
MAIL=/usr/mail/ravi
PATH=.:/bin:/usr/bin
```

```
PS1=$
PS2=>
TERM=adm5
```

Table 5.21 shows the description of these shell variables.

Table 5.21 Shell variables

Shell variable	Description
EXINIT	This refers to the initialization instructions for the ex and vi editors.
HOME	This is set to the path name of our home directory.
IFS (Internal field separator)	This is set to a list of the characters that are used to separate words in a command line. Normally, this list consists of the space character, the tab character, and the newline character.
LOGNAME	This gives the user's login name.
MAIL	This variable's value is the name of the directory in which an electronic mail addressed to us is placed. The shell checks the contents of this directory very often, and when a new content shows up, we are informed about it.
PATH	This names the directories that the shell will search in to find the commands that we execute. A colon is used to separate the directory names without spaces.
PS1 (Prompt string 1)	This symbol is used as our prompt. Normally, it is set to $, but we can redefine it by merely assigning a new value. For example, the command PS1=# resets the prompt to a # symbol.
PS2 (Prompt string 2)	This prompt is used when a new line is started without finishing a command (command continuation symbol).
TERM	This identifies the kind of terminal we use (it helps the shell understand what to interpret as erase key, kill line, etc.)

Note: Some variables like PS1 are defined by default. Others like PATH are defined in our .profile file.

A description of these terms is provided in the following sections.

CDPATH variable

The CDPATH variable contains a list of path names separated by colon (:) as shown.

```
:$HOME: /bin/usr/files
```

There are three paths in this example. Since the path starts with a colon, the first directory is the current working directory. The second directory is our home directory. The third directory is an absolute path name to a directory of files.

The contents of CDPATH are used by the cd command using the following rules:

1. If CDPATH is not defined, the cd command searches the working directory to locate the requested directory. If the requested directory is found, cd moves to it. If it is not found, cd displays an error message.
2. If CDPATH is defined as shown in the previous example, the actions listed are taken when the following command is executed.

```
$ cd ajmer
```

(a) The `cd` command searches the current directory for the `ajmer` directory. If it is found, the *current directory* is changed to `ajmer`.

(b) If the `ajmer` directory is not found in the current directory, the `cd` command searches in the *home directory*, which is the second entry in CDPATH. If the `ajmer` directory is found in the home directory, it becomes the current directory.

(c) If the `ajmer` directory is not found in the home directory, `cd` tries to find it in `/bin/usr/files`, which is the third directory in CDPATH. If the `ajmer` directory is found in `/bin/usr/files`, it becomes the current directory.

(d) If the `ajmer` directory is not found in `/bin/usr/files`, the `cd` command displays an error message and terminates.

```
$ echo $CDPATH
$ CDPATH= : $HOME: /bin/usr/files
```

HOME variable

The HOME variable contains the PATH to our home directory. The default is our login directory. Some commands use the value of this variable when they need the PATH to our home directory. For example, when we use the `cd` command without any argument, the command uses the value of the HOME variable as the argument.

```
$ echo $HOME
/mnt/disk1/usr/chirag

$ oldHOME=$HOME
$ echo $oldHOME
/mnt/disk1/usr/chirag

$HOME=$(pwd)
/mnt/disk1/usr/chirag/ajmer

$ HOME =$oldHOME
$ echo $ HOME
/mnt/disk1/usr/chirag
```

PATH variable

The PATH variable is used for a command directory. The entries in the path variable must be separated by colons. It works just like CDPATH. When the SHELL encounters a command, it uses the entries in the PATH variable to search for the command under each directory in the PATH variable. The major difference is that the current directory, which will be searched for by the command, is mentioned at the end in this variable.

If we set the PATH variable as follows,

```
$ PATH =/bin:/usr/bin::
```

then, the shell will look for the commands that we execute in this sequence—shell will first search the `/bin` directory, followed by the `/usr/bin` directory, and finally the current working directory.

Primary prompt variable

The primary prompt (PSI prompt) is set in the variable PS1 for the Korn and Bash shells and `prompt` for the C shell. The shell uses the primary prompt when it accepts a command. The default is the dollar sign($) for the Korn and Bash shells and the percent sign (%) for the C shell.

We begin by changing the primary prompt to reflect the shell we are working in, the Korn shell. Since we have a blank at the end of the prompt, we must use quotes to set it. As soon as it is set, a new prompt is displayed. At the end, we change it back to the default.

```
$ PS1="mce>"
mce > echo $PS1
mce>
mce > PS1="$"
$
```

SHELL variable

The SHELL variable holds the path of our login shell.

TERM variable

It holds the description for the computer terminal or terminal emulator we are using. The value of this variable determines the keys that we can use for the purpose of editing. The default value of TERM variable is vt100 (a terminal type).

Setting/Unsetting system shell variables

The following are the ways by which we can set or unset system shell variables:

An assignment operator is used to set the value for a system shell variable.

Syntax	variable=value

Example	$ TERM=vt100

The unset command is used to unset a system shell variable. The syntax for using the unset command is as follows:

Syntax	unset shell_variable

Example	unset TERM

We can look at the value assigned to a system shell variable through the echo command.

```
$ echo $TERM
```

We can use the set command with no arguments to display the variables that are currently set.

```
$ set
```

5.8 EXPORT OF LOCAL AND GLOBAL SHELL VARIABLES

When a process is created by the shell, it makes available certain features of its own environment to the child processes. The created process (i.e., the command) can also make use of these inherited parameters for it to operate.

These parameters include the following:

1. The PID of the parent process
2. The user and group owner of the process

3. The current working directory
4. The three standard files
5. Other open files used by the parent process
6. Some environment variables available in the parent process

By default, the values stored in shell variables are local to the shell, that is, they are available only in the shell in which they are defined. They are not passed on to a child shell. However, the shell can also export these variables recursively to all child processes so that, once defined, they are available globally. This is done using the export command.

> **Note:** A variable defined in a process is only local to the process in which it is defined and is not available in a child process. However, when it is exported, it is available recursively to all child processes.

The syntax for the export command is as follows:

Syntax   `export variable[=value]`

Examples

(a) `$ export welcomemsg`
This example exports an earlier defined shell variable `welcomemsg` to make it available to child processes.

(b) `$ export welcomemsg='Good Morning'`
This example defines a shell variable `welcomemsg` as well as exports it to be available to child processes.

> **Note:** While defining a shell variable, there should not be any space on either side of the '=' sign.

(c) The following example creates a new shell variable `radius`.

```
$ radius=5
$ echo $radius
5
$ sh  - Create new shell
$ echo $radius
$
```

We can see that the value of the shell variable `radius` is not seen in the new shell as it does not know about this.

If we want the new shell to know about the shell variables created by us, we use the export command. By using the export command, the shell variables are exported to child processes, making it a global variable. The following example demonstrates this implementation.

Example   `$ radius=5`

```
$ echo $radius
5
$ export radius
$ sh - Create new shell
```

```
$ echo $radius
5 - The new shell has a copy of radius

$ radius=30 - The copy gets a new value
$ echo $radius
30
$ Ctrl-d - Return to old shell
$ echo $radius
5 - We get the original value of radius
```

The export command causes a new shell to be given a copy of the original variable. This copy has the same name and value as the original. Subsequently, the value of the copy can be changed but when the subshell dies, the copy is gone though the original variable remains.

To erase or remove a global variable, we use the unset command.

Syntax   unset variable_name

Example $ unset radius

Note: To find out the list of variables exported, just type the set command followed by the enter key: $ set

In this chapter, we understood the different types of files, the role of device drivers while operating the devices, differences between block and character devices, usage of disk space, amount of free disk space in all file systems, and partition in a disk drive. We learnt how commands such as gzip, gunzip, zip, unzip, compress, uncompress, pack, unpack, bzip2, and bunzip2 can be used for compressing and uncompressing files. We also discussed how desired files can be found and executed specific commands on them. In addition, we learnt how a corrupted file system can be repaired. We have also seen the role of important files of the Unix system, shell variables, and system shell variables. In Chapter 6, we will learn about handling processes, jobs, and signals in detail.

■ SUMMARY ■

1. All devices are considered to be files in Unix. Devices such as floppy drive, CD-ROM, and hard disk are known as block devices as data is read from and written into these devices in terms of blocks. Character devices, on the other hand, are also known as raw devices as the read/write operations in these devices are done directly, that is, 'raw' without using the buffer cache.

2. A disk can be divided into several partitions. It can have a primary partition and an extended partition. There can be multiple logical drives in an extended partition.

3. The hosts file contains static address information for computers on our local network.

4. The hosts.allow file defines the list of hosts for whom the services are allowed; the hosts.deny file defines the list of hosts for whom the services are denied.

5. By default, the values stored in shell variables are local to the shell, that is they are available only in the shell in which they are defined.

6. The export statement exports the local variables recursively to all child processes so that they are available globally.

■ FUNCTION SPECIFICATION ■

Command	Function
dd (disk data)	Used for copying data from one medium to another.
format	Used for formatting disks.
du (disk usage)	Used to display information about the usage of disk space by each file and directory of the system.
dfspace	Used to report the free disk space in terms of megabytes and percentage of the total disk space.
fdisk	Used to create, delete, and activate partitions.
gzip	Used to compress the specified file and replace it with the compressed file having the extension .gz. The -l option is used with gzip to know the extent to which a file is compressed.
gunzip	Used to uncompress a compressed file.
zip	Used to compress a set of files into a single file.
unzip	Used to unzip a zipped archive.
compress	Used to compress a specified file. It replaces the original file with its compressed version that has the same filename with a .Z extension added to it.
uncompress	Used to uncompress the compressed file back to its original form.
zcat	Used to see the contents of the compressed files.
pack	Used to compress the given file and replace the original file with the same filename having a .z extension added to it.

Command	Function
	The degree of compression in the pack command is less than the compress command.
pcat	Used to view the contents of a packed file.
unpack	Used to uncompress the packed file into the original file.
bzip2	Used to compress a specified file by replacing it with its compressed version having a .bz2 extension.
7-zip	Used to compress files at the highest compression ratio (around 30–50% more than the other zip formats).
file	Used to determine the file type, that is, if it is a regular file, directory, device file, etc.
find	Used to locate one or more files that satisfy the given criteria.
which/ whence	Used to find out the location of a specified application program or system utility on the disk.
locate	Used to search for files whose names match a particular search string.
fsck	Used to check and repair a file system if corrupted.
passwd	A file found in the /etc directory containing login names, passwords, home directories, and other information about users.
set	Used to see the list of shell variables.

■ EXERCISES ■

Objective-type Questions

State True or False

5.1 All devices are considered as files in Unix.

5.2 All device files are stored in /etc or in its subdirectories.

5.3 CD-ROM is a character device.

5.4 Printer is a character device.

5.5 The minor number represents the type of device.

5.6 The dd command is used for copying data from one medium to another.

5.7 The term bs in the dd command stands for block size.

5.8 The du utility displays complete information about the usage of disk space by each file and directory.

5.9 By default, the du command displays information in terms of 1024-byte blocks.

5.10 The df command reports only the free disk space of the file system installed on our machines.

5.11 The `dfspace` command reports the used disk space of the file system.

5.12 The `-q` option of the `zip` command makes it run in quiet mode.

5.13 The extension added to the file that is compressed by the `compress` command is `.C`.

5.14 The `find` command is used for searching for files.

5.15 The `file` command is used for displaying filenames.

5.16 The `gunzip` command is used to uncompress a compressed file that is compressed by the `gzip`, `compress`, or `pack` commands.

5.17 The `fdisk` command can be used to create and delete partitions on a disk, but cannot activate partitions.

5.18 A disk can have several primary partitions.

5.19 The `gzip` command compresses the specified file and replaces it with the compressed file having the extension `.gz`.

5.20 By default, the values stored in shell variables are local to the shell, that is, they are available only in the shell in which they are defined.

Fill in the Blanks

5.1 Devices are of two types: _____ and _____.

5.2 The term 'if' in the `dd` command refers to _____.

5.3 The option used with the `du` command to see the usage of every file is _____.

5.4 The _____ command compresses the specified file and replaces it with the extension `.gz`.

5.5 The command used to uncompress any compressed file is _____.

5.6 The command used to compress a set of files into a single, compact archive is _____.

5.7 The option used with the `zip` command to fix any damaged zip file is _____.

5.8 The option of the `compress` command that displays the amount of compression is _____.

5.9 The command used to repair the file system is _____.

5.10 The option used with the `find` command to search for files that have not been accessed for a given time length is _____.

5.11 The option used with the `find` command to search for files of the specific owner is _____.

5.12 The _____ option in the `compress` command stands for verbose and displays how much compression has been done.

5.13 To see the contents of the compressed files, _____ command is used.

5.14 The `pack` command compresses the given file and replaces the original file with the same filename having _____ extension added to it.

5.15 The _____ compresses the specified file by replacing it with its compressed version having a `.bz2` extension.

5.16 The _____ option of the `bzip2` command can be used to uncompress a file.

5.17 The _____ command is used to convert a local shell variable into a global variable.

5.18 The system shell variable _____ stores the information of the terminal that we are using.

5.19 The system shell variable _____ indicates the location where emails of a user are stored.

5.20 The path name of the home directory of the user is stored in the _____ variable.

Multiple-choice Questions

5.1 The `fdisk` command is used to
   (a) format a disk
   (b) remove bad sectors from a disk
   (c) create partitions
   (d) repair a file system

5.2 The `gzip` command compresses the file with the extension
   (a) `.gzip`
   (b) `.gz`
   (c) `.gp`
   (d) `.g`

5.3 The command used to view the contents of a packed file is
   (a) `pcat`   (c) `show`
   (b) `cat`   (d) `catpack`

5.4 The user's log name is stored in
   (a) LOGNAME   (c) OWNER
   (b) USER   (d) LOGIN

5.5 The command to see the list of shell variables is
   (a) `showvar`   (c) `disp`
   (b) `showshell`   (d) `set`

5.6 The command that is used to find out where an application program or system utility is stored on a disk is
    (a) search
    (b) findapp
    (c) whence
    (d) util

5.7 The fsck command is used for
    (a) finding a file
    (b) compressing a file
    (c) uncompressing a file
    (d) repairing a file system

5.8 The list of hosts for whom the services are allowed is stored in the file
    (a) hosts.allow   (c) hosts
    (b) services.txt   (d) allowed

5.9 The shell variable that sets the symbol for the primary shell prompt is
    (a) PS2   (c) shellpr
    (b) sprompt   (d) PS1

5.10 The TERM shell variable stores
    (a) shell duration
    (b) terminal description
    (c) logged-in time
    (d) booting time

Programming Exercises

5.1 Write the command for the following tasks:
    (a) To copy the entire disk, hdb, to a file called back.dd
    (b) To find the disk usage of every file in /project directory
    (c) To find the total number of blocks occupied by the /project directory
    (d) To display a report of the free disk space for all the file systems installed on our machines
    (e) To display the free disk space in terms of megabytes and percentage of total disk space
    (f) To compress a file a.txt to a.txt.gz
    (g) To add a file account.txt to a zipped file finance.zip
    (h) To fix a zipped file finance.zip
    (i) To compress a file a.txt and also show how much compression was done
    (j) To uncompress a file a.txt.bz2 file
    (k) To set the secondary prompt, the prompt that is displayed when a command is continued to the second line to '>>>'
    (l) To display the list of path names
    (m) To determine the type of the file, accounts.txt
    (n) To display the files and their path names that have not been accessed for over 10 days
    (o) To check the file system

5.2 What will the following commands do?
    (a) $ export project_name
    (b) $ PS1="UnixPrompt>"
    (c) $ passwd
    (d) $ grep john /etc/passwd
    (e) $ which cat
    (f) $ find . - mtime - 10 -name "*.txt" - print
    (g) $ bunzip2 accounts.txt.bz2
    (h) $ pack accounts.txt
    (i) $ zip -q accounts.zip *.txt
    (j) $ df -h
    (k) $ du -s *.txt
    (l) $du /projects
    (m) $ locate "projects"
    (n) $ find / -size +15 -print
    (o) $ echo $HOME

Review Questions

5.1 Explain the following commands with syntax and examples:
    (a) dd   (c) uncompress
    (b) format   (d) unpack

5.2 (a) What are the points of comparison between the following commands: gzip, zip, compress, and pack?
    (b) What is the difference among the following commands: du, df, and dfspace?

5.3 (a) Explain the different options used in the find command to search for a desired file.
    (b) How is the file system repaired in Unix? Explain.

5.4 What is the difference between the following files?
    (a) /etc/passwd and /etc/shadow
    (b) /etc/hosts.allow and /etc/hosts.deny

5.5 How is a shell variable created and how can a local shell variable be made a global variable?

5.6 Explain the usage of the following system shell variables:

(a) HOME   (c) PS2   (e) TERM
(b) MAIL   (d) PATH

Brain Teasers

5.1 In long listing command `ls  -l`, if you find a file with mode field set to 1, what does it mean?

5.2 Correct the following command to backup a hard disk to a file.

```
$ dd if=/file.dd of=/dev/hda
```

5.3 Correct the mistake in the following command for compressing few `.txt` files in the name `abc.zip` in quiet mode.

```
$ zip *.txt abc.zip
```

5.4 Can you uncompress a `.bz2` file to the standard output? If yes, how?

5.5 How will you know whether a particular file in the `/dev` directory represents a character device or block device?

5.6 If a device has a major number 8 and minor number 0, what does it represent?

5.7 Is there any way to uncompress a `.bz2` file without

using the `bunzip2` command? If yes, what is that?

5.8 If we provide the command `file a.txt`, we get the output, 'cannot open for reading'. What does it mean?

5.9 What command must be given to delete all the files that have not been accessed for the last six months?

5.10 Correct the following command to display all `.txt` files in the current directory.

```
$ find . - name "*.txt" - ls
```

5.11 What will happen if answer *Yes* is provided to the question "CLEAR?", which appears while running `fsck` command?

5.12 Is the following command to set the primary prompt correct? If not, identify the mistake.

```
PS2='UnixPrompt>'
```

■ ANSWERS TO OBJECTIVE-TYPE QUESTIONS ■

State True or False

5.1	True
5.2	False
5.3	False
5.4	True
5.5	False
5.6	True
5.7	True
5.8	True
5.9	False
5.10	True
5.11	False
5.12	True
5.13	False
5.14	True
5.15	False
5.16	True
5.17	False
5.18	False
5.19	True
5.20	True

Fill in the Blanks

5.1	character, block
5.2	input
5.3	-a
5.4	gzip
5.5	gunzip
5.6	zip
5.7	-F
5.8	-v
5.9	fsck
5.10	-atime n
5.11	-user name
5.12	-v
5.13	zcat
5.14	.Z
5.15	bzip2
5.16	-d
5.17	export
5.18	TERM
5.19	MAIL
5.20	HOME

Multiple-choice Questions

5.1	(c)
5.2	(b)
5.3	(a)
5.4	(a)
5.5	(d)
5.6	(c)
5.7	(d)
5.8	(a)
5.9	(d)
5.10	(b)

Manipulating Processes and Signals

After studying this chapter, the reader will be conversant with the following:

- Processes and their address space, structure, data structures describing the processes, and process states
- Difference between a process and a thread
- Commands related to scheduling processes at the desired time, handling jobs, switching jobs from the foreground to the background and vice versa, etc.
- Suspending, resuming, and terminating jobs, executing commands in a batch, ensuring process execution even when a user logs out, increasing and decreasing priority of processes, and killing processes
- Signals, their types, and the methods of signal generation
- Virtual memory and its role in executing large applications in a limited physical memory and mapping of a virtual address to the physical memory

6.1 PROCESS BASICS

All processes in the Unix system are created when an existing process executes a process creation system call known as fork. The first process in the Unix system, also known as process 0, is related to bootstrapping. The process of starting a computer is known as bootstrapping or booting. During bootstrapping, a computer runs a self test, and loads a boot program into the memory from the boot device. The boot program loads the kernel and passes the control to the kernel, which in turn, configures the devices, performs hardware status verification, detects new hardware, and initializes the existing devices and system processes. After performing these initial activities, the kernel creates an init process with process identification 1 (PID 1). The process 0 is a part of the kernel itself and basically functions as a sched (or swapper). It also does the job of swapping, that is, moving in and out of the processes.

The init process always remains in the background while the system is running. It is the ancestor of all further processes. It is the init process that forks the getty process, which enables users to log in to the Unix system. When a user logs in, the command shell runs as the first process from where other processes are forked in response to the commands, programs, utilities, etc., executed by the user.

Note: The process that calls fork is known as the parent process and the process that is created through fork is known as the child process. The child process is an exact clone of the parent process. Both these processes share the same memory, registers, environment, open files, etc. In addition, the parent and child processes have separate address spaces enabling them to execute independently.

A process operates in either user mode or kernel mode:

User mode   User mode is the mode in which processes related to user activities get executed. Commands, programs, utilities, etc., executed by the user are run in this mode. These processes being trivial in nature, the code in the user mode runs in a non-privileged protection mode. Switching from user to kernel mode takes place either when a user's process requests services from the operating system by making a system call or when some interrupt occurs during the events such as timers, keyboard, and hard disk input/output (I/O).

Kernel mode   In kernel mode, the system processes, that is, the processes related to managing a computer system and its resources get executed. The processes used to allocate memory to access hardware peripherals such as printer and disk drive run in this mode. These processes are critical in nature, that is, they can make an operating system inconsistent if they are not handled properly. Hence for security reasons, these processes are run in a privileged protection mode.

The user and kernel modes can be better understood with the help of a block diagram (Fig. 6.1) of the kernel architecture.

In Fig. 6.1, the users initially execute their processes in the user mode. When the user process needs some kernel service (such as accessing memory, disk file, printer, or other hardware peripherals), it interacts with the kernel through the system call. System calls are functions that run in the kernel mode. Hence while executing system calls, the user process switches from the user mode to the kernel mode.

Figure 6.1 shows the following two main components that make up the kernel:

File subsystem

The file subsystem manages the files of the Unix system. In the previous chapters, we learnt that everything in Unix is in the form of files, that is, all devices and peripherals are considered files. Communication between the hardware and their respective device drivers are managed by the file subsystem. Even the buffers that are used for storing the data that is either fetched from the devices or is to be written to the devices are managed by the file subsystem.

Process control subsystem

The process control subsystem manages all the tasks required for successful execution of processes. It allocates memory to the processes and schedules, synchronizes, and even

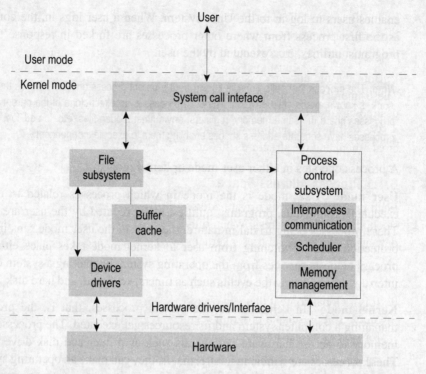

User mode

Kernel mode

System call inteface

File subsystem

Buffer cache

Device drivers

Process control subsystem

Interprocess communication

Scheduler

Memory management

Hardware drivers/Interface

Hardware

Fig. 6.1 Block diagram of kernel architecture

implements communication between them. The processes are basically executable files that are designated for certain tasks. For loading the executable file into the memory, the process control system interacts with the file subsystem and thereafter executes it to perform the required action. The process control subsystem comprises the following three modules:

Interprocess communication An application usually consists of several processes that undergo execution simultaneously. In addition, the data processed by one process has to be input into another process for further processing. This module performs all the tasks required to establish communication among the different processes and also synchronizes them. By process synchronization, we imply that the module manages the locks when two processes update a particular type of content, that is, it ensures that no two processes update the same data simultaneously.

Memory management This module manages memory allocation. It allocates memory to the required process. If the memory is not enough, it transfers certain selected pages of the current process to the secondary storage, hence creating space for the required process. In addition, it frees the memory assigned to the process when it is terminated so that memory can be assigned to some other process.

Scheduler The task of this module is to pick up the ready-to-run processes from the memory and assign the CPU to it. When the current process suspends for some I/O operation, its job is to seek the next process and schedule it for execution. In addition, when some higher priority process comes in, the scheduler pre-empts the current process and brings in the higher priority process and assigns the CPU to it.

Both the file and process subsystems are used for managing the hardware of a system. These interact with the drivers and hardware interface (part of the kernel) for getting the desired task performed by the hardware.

We will now be dealing with the processes in more detail, including the segments that create them and the structures that are involved in handling them.

6.1.1 Process Address Space

Each process runs in its private address space. A process running in user mode refers to a stack, data, and code areas. When running in kernel mode, the process addresses the kernel data and code areas and uses a kernel stack. In short, a process includes three segments:

1. *Text*: It represents the program code, that is, the executable instructions.
2. *Data*: It represents the program variables and other data processed by the program code. It is a global content that can be accessed by the program and its subroutines (if any).
3. *Stack*: It represents a program segment that is used while implementing procedure calls for storing information pertaining to parameters, return addresses, etc.

Besides these three segments, the process also uses a memory heap to store the dynamic structures. These dynamic structures are those that are created during the execution of the process and are successfully removed when their task is completed, that is, the resources allocated to the dynamic structures are immediately freed when their purpose is finished so that those resources can be reused by other structures.

6.1.2 Process Structure

A process structure comprises a complex set of data structures that provide the operating system with all the information necessary to manage and dispatch processes. It consists of an address space and a set of data structures in the kernel to keep track of that process. The address space is a section of the memory that contains the execution code, data, signal handlers, open files, etc. The information about processes is described in the following data structures:

Process table

The process table (also known as kernel process table) is an array of structures that contains an entry per process. Every process entry contains process control information required by the kernel to manage the process and is hence maintained in the main memory. The process entry is also known as process control block (PCB) and contains the following information:

Process state   It represents the process state, that is, whether it is in ready, running, waiting, sleeping, or zombie mode.

Process identification information   It uniquely identifies a process and consists of the following three elements:

1. *Process identifier* (*PID*): This refers to a unique number assigned to identify a process.
2. *User identifier* (*UID*): This refers to the ID of the user who created the process. The process identification also includes the group ID of the user (GID), the effective user ID (EUID), set user ID (SUID), file system user ID (FSUID), the effective group ID (EGID), set group ID (SGID), and file system group ID (FSGID) of the user who also starts the process.
3. *Parent process identifier* (*PPID*): This refers to the identifier of the parent process that created the process.

Program counter   It stores the address of the next instruction to be executed by this process.

CPU registers   It helps in initiation of the process using general-purpose and other registers.

CPU scheduling information   It includes an algorithm on the basis of which the scheduling of the process is determined.

Memory-management information   It stores information of the memory used and released by the process.

Accounting information   It stores information such as process numbers, job numbers, and CPU time consumed.

I/O status information   It stores information such as the list of I/O devices and the status of open files allocated to the process.

User area

The Unix kernel executes in the context of certain processes. The user area (U area) refers to private information in the context of a process. The U area of a process contains the following:

1. User IDs that determine user privileges
2. Current working directory
3. Timer fields that store the time the process spent in the user and kernel modes
4. Information for signal handling
5. Identification of any associated control terminal
6. Identification of data areas relevant to I/O activity
7. Return values and error conditions from system calls
8. Information on the file system environment of the process
9. User file descriptor table that stores the file descriptors of the files that the process has opened

Note: The process entry also contains certain pointers such as pointers to the user and shared text areas.

You may recall that all the information of a file, such as file data, access permissions, and access times, is stored in an inode. Inodes are maintained in the inode table. Besides inode table, the kernel has two other file structures known as the file table and the user file descriptor table.

File table   It is a global kernel structure that contains information such as storing the byte offset in the file and indicating the location from where the next write/read operation will start, mode of opening, and reference count of all the currently opened files. The file table also contains the permissions that are assigned to the process.

User file descriptor table   An individual file descriptor is allocated per process. It keeps track of the files that are opened by the process.

When a process opens or creates a file, a file descriptor for it is returned by the kernel, which is stored as a new entry created in the user file descriptor table. For reading and writing into a file, the file descriptor in the user file descriptor table is located and the pointers from it to the *file table* and *inode table* are used to access or write the file data (refer to Fig. 6.2).

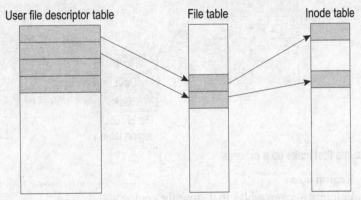

Fig. 6.2   Relation between user file descriptor table, file table, and inode table

After understanding the process table, let us discuss the next structure that stores information that is private to the process.

Per process region table

The kernel process table points to per process region table as each process has a per process region (*pregion*) table associated with it. The per process region table in turn points to the region table to indicate the regions that are private to it and the regions that are shared with other processes. This is to say that an entry in the region table may be shared with other processes too. The per process region table is used to keep the following information of a *pregion*:

1. A pointer to an inode of the source file that contains a copy of the region, if any exists
2. The virtual address of the region
3. Permissions of the regions, that is, whether the region is read-only, read–write, or read–execute
4. The region types (e.g., text, data, and stack)

Region table

A region is a continuous area of a process's address space such as text, data, and stack. Region table entries indicate whether the region is shared or private. They also point to the location of the region in the memory (refer to Fig. 6.3). A region table stores the following information:

1. Pointers to inodes of files in the region
2. The type of region

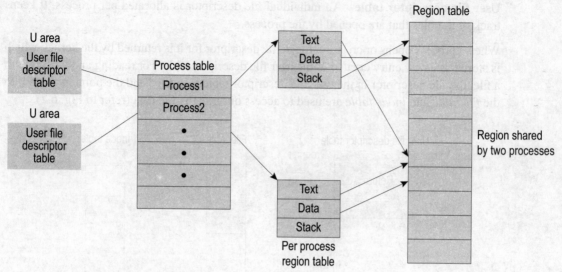

Fig. 6.3 Structures that make up a process

3. Region size
4. Pointers to page tables that store the region
5. Bit indicating if the region is locked
6. The process numbers currently accessing the region

6.1.3 Creation and Termination of Processes

Besides the built-in processes that are auto created on booting the Unix system, we can also create our own processes. In addition, the processes can be terminated after their tasks are completed in order to release the resources acquired by them. In Chapter 7, we will learn about the system calls that are required to create, suspend, and terminate a process.

A process consumes system resources, such as memory, disk space, and CPU time. If there is more than one process running at a time, the kernel allocates system resources to one process, while keeping other processes waiting.

Let us see how the processes change their states and undergo transitions.

6.2 PROCESS STATES AND TRANSITIONS

A process is created through the fork command, and depending on the availability of the primary memory, it is either kept in the memory in *ready to run* state or is swapped out to the secondary memory in *ready to run swapped out* state, as shown in Fig. 6.4. The kernel monitors the processes that are in *ready to run* state in the memory and schedules the process depending on the algorithm used by the operating system. When scheduled, the process executes in the *kernel* mode, that is, it switches to the *kernel running* state. From the *kernel running* state, the process can be moved to the *pre-empted* state if a process of a higher priority is scheduled. As a result, process switching takes place, wherein the current process is switched to the *pre-empted* state and another process is scheduled to switch to the *kernel running* state. In addition, the process running in kernel mode can return to the user mode,

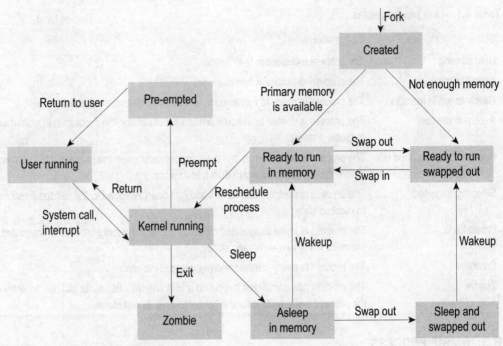

Fig. 6.4   Different states of a process

that is, to the *user running* state. Besides this, a process in the *kernel running* state can also switch to the *sleep* state, waiting for the occurrence of an event (like waiting for the user to enter some data). This stage is known as *asleep in memory* state. The process in the *kernel running* state can also terminate switching itself to the *zombie* state. A *zombie process* is a dead child process that has completed its execution and has sent a SIGCHLD signal to its parent allowing it to read its exit status. Until and unless the parent reads the exit status of the child process, its entry remains in the process table. The process sleeping in the memory can either be swapped out to the secondary storage to *sleep and swapped out* state or woken up to move to the *ready to run* in memory state, if the event that it was waiting for occurs. The process in *sleep and swapped out* state will be moved to the *ready to run swapped out* state where it waits for the swapper to move it to the *ready to run in memory* state whenever it is required.

Note: When a process is required, the space for it is created in the primary memory and is swapped into the primary memory by the swapper switching it to the *ready to run* state.

The process in the *preempted* state returns to the user mode, that is, the *user running* state when it is required by the user. The process running in the user mode switches to the kernel mode when an interrupt occurs, a system call is made to access operating system services, or when some fault or exception occurs.

Note: The scheduler decides the process that has to be submitted next to the CPU for action.

The different states of a process are briefly described in Table 6.1.

Almost all the process states discussed are self-explanatory, except one, the zombie process. We will elaborate on this in Section 6.3.

Table 6.1 Unix process states

State	Description
User running	The process executes in user mode.
Kernel running	The process executes in kernel mode.
Ready to run in memory	The process is ready to run as soon as the scheduler schedules it.
Asleep in memory	The process is unable to execute until an event occurs; the process is in main memory (a blocked state).
Ready to run, swapped out	The process is ready to run, but the swapper must swap the process into the main memory before the scheduler can schedule it to execute.
Sleeping, swapped	The process is waiting for an event and has been swapped to the secondary storage (a blocked state).
Pre-empted	The process is in the suspended mode as the higher priority process is scheduled and switched to the kernel running state.
Created	The process is newly created and not yet ready to run.
Zombie	The process has completed execution and is currently dead, but still has an entry occupied in the process table, waiting for the parent to read its exit status.

6.3 ZOMBIE PROCESS

A zombie process is a process that has completed execution and is currently dead, but still has an entry occupied in the process table, waiting for the process that started it to read its exit status. The zombie process does not consume any memory or other resources. Zombie processes are usually created when a child process is spawned, but dies before the parent process reads its exit status. Since the parent process has not received its return value, the process becomes a zombie.

We can identify a zombie process by executing the ps command. Zombie processes contain a character Z in their state field (S), as shown in the following output:

```
$ ps -el

F   S   UID   PID   PPID   C   PRI   NI   ADDR       SZ     WCHAN      TTY
1   Z   0     146   0      0   0     20   fec20000   0      d6dd12f2   tty01
0   S   1     6     0      0   40    15   d0b5c488   635    d08f8bfc   tty01
1   R   0     3     1      0   0     12   dob5aad8   1175   d29bb8f2   tty01
```

The description of the output is as follows:

1. F represents flags associated with the process.
2. S represents the state of the process.
3. UID represents the user ID.
4. PID represent the process ID.
5. PPID represents the parent process ID.
6. C represents the utilization of the processor.
7. PRI represents the scheduling parameters for a process.
8. NI represents the nice value (discussed in Section 6.8.6) assigned to the process.

Table 6.2 Brief description of the characters that may appear in the s column

Process	States
D	Indicates a process in disk
I	Indicates an idle process
R	Indicates a runnable process
S	Indicates a sleeping process
T	Indicates a stopped process
Z	Indicates a zombie process

9. ADDR represents the memory address of the process.
10. SZ represents the total number of pages in the process.
11. WCHAN represents the address of an event where the process is switched to sleep mode.
12. TTY represents the terminal from where the process is created.

The character Z in the S column confirms that it is a zombie process. We can see in this output that the process with PID 146 is zombie. The other characters that may appear in the S column to show the current state of the process are shown in Table 6.2.

To remove or delete a zombie process, the kill command is used. To kill, the zombie process with PID 146, shown in the output, can be deleted using the following statement:

```
$ kill -9 146
```

Conventionally, to remove a zombie process, its parent is informed that the child has died by sending a SIGCHLD signal manually using the kill command. Thereafter, the signal handler executes the wait system call that reads its exit status and removes the zombie. In case a parent fails to call the wait system call, the zombie will be left in the process table. On reading the exit status of the zombie process, it is removed. Once removed from the process table, the zombie's process ID and entry in this table can be reused. In case the parent process refuses to remove the zombie, we can forcefully remove a zombie by removing the parent process.

Note: A zombie process is not the same as an orphan process. An orphan process is a process that is still executing, but whose parent has died. Orphan processes do not become zombie processes, because when a process loses its parent, the init process becomes its new parent.

What is the name of the task that suspends the execution of one process on the CPU while resuming execution of some other process? It is called context switching. We will now discuss this in detail.

6.4 CONTEXT SWITCHING

Depending on the priority, a current running process can be switched from the running state to the blocked state (pre-empted, sleeping, etc.) at any time, and higher priority processes can be scheduled to run. The state of the blocked process is saved so that in the future, it can run further from the state at which it was held. The tasks conducted during process switching, that is, saving the state of the current process and loading the saved state of the new process is known as context switching. While context switching, the information of the program counter and other registers of the blocked process is saved. In addition, its PCB is updated to change its state from the running state to a pre-empted, sleeping, or other state. The PCB of the process that is scheduled to run is updated to indicate its running state.

We usually get confused while differentiating between processes and threads, as both are meant for processing. Then what is the difference between the two? Let us clarify this confusion.

6.5 THREADS

A thread is the smallest unit of processing. A process can have one or more threads. This is shown in Fig. 6.5. Multiple threads within a process share memory resources whereas different processes do not share these resources. In multithreading, a processor switches between different threads. A thread has its own independent flow of control as long as its parent process exists and dies if the parent process dies.

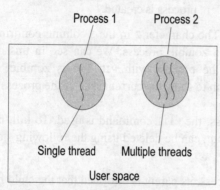

Fig. 6.5 Threads within processes

Figure 6.5 shows two processes, Process 1 and Process 2, in the user space. Process 1 consists of a single thread whereas Process 2 is multi-threaded.

Threads have some properties of processes. Like processes, a thread consists of the following:

1. A program counter to indicate which instruction to execute next
2. Registers to store data in the variables
3. A stack to store information related to the procedure called

Having properties similar to processes, threads are also known as lightweight processes.

6.5.1 Comparison Between Threads and Processes

Table 6.3 shows the differences between processes and threads.

Table 6.3 Differences between processes and threads

Process	Thread
Processes are individual entities. It takes quite a long time to create and terminate a process.	Threads are part of processes. It comparatively takes lesser time to create a new thread than a process, because the newly created thread uses the current process address space. Similarly, it takes lesser time to terminate a thread than a process.
It takes longer to switch between two processes as they have their individual address spaces.	It takes lesser time to switch between two threads within the same process as they use the same address space.
Communication of data among processes is quite sophisticated as it requires an inter process communication mechanism.	Communication of data among threads is quite easy as they share a common address space.

Similar to a traditional process, a thread can be in any one of the following states: running, blocked, ready, or terminated. A running thread is the one to which the CPU is assigned and is currently active. A blocked thread is the one that is waiting for some event to occur. On occurrence of the event, the blocked thread turns into a ready state. A ready thread is a thread that has all the resources except the CPU, and hence waits for the CPU's attention. The thread that has completed its work is said to be in a terminated state. A thread can also be terminated in between, if desired by the process.

When a process is created, it is assigned a unique identification number known as the *process identifier (PID)* by the kernel. The PID value can be any value from 0 to 32767. However, this range depends on a particular Unix variant. It is typed as `pid_t`, whose size may vary from system to system. The name of the process remains same as the name of the program being executed. Every process is created from a parent process. The process that is created is known as the child process and the process from which it is created is known as its parent process. Unix creates the first process with PID as 0 when the system is booted.

Let us take a look at the commands that give us information of the processes running in our system.

6.6 ps: STATUS OF PROCESSES

This command is used to display the list of processes that are running at the moment. The list of the processes along with their PID number, terminal from where the process is executed, the elapsed time (time consumed by the process since it started), and the name of the process will be displayed.

Syntax `ps [-a] [-e] [-f] [-l] [-L] [ -u user_name ] [ -g group_IDs ]`
`[ -t terminal] [ -p process_IDs ]`

The options of the `ps` command are briefly described in Table 6.4.

Table 6.4   Brief description of the options used in the `ps` command

Options	Description
-a	It displays information regarding all the processes.
-e	It displays information regarding every running process.
-f	It displays full information regarding each process.
-l	It displays a long listing.
-L	It displays threads with lightweight processes (LWP) and number of lightweight process (NLWP) columns.
-u user_name	It displays the list of processes of the specified user. We can also specify the user ID instead of the login name. In addition, we can specify more than one username or user IDs separated by a space or comma (,).
-g group_IDs	It displays the list of processes of the specified group_ID. We can specify more than one group ID, separated by a space or comma (,).
-t terminal	It displays the list of processes associated with the specified terminal.
-p process_IDs	It displays information regarding specified process ID numbers.

Examples

(a) $ ps

```
PID    TTY      TIME      CMD
739    tty01    00:00:03  sh
894    tty01    00:00:12  ps
```

By default, the ps command displays only the processes that are running at the user's terminal.

(b) To get the list of processes of the other users logged in to the system, we use the following command.

```
$ ps -a
PID        TTY              TIME        CMD
739        tty01            00:00:03    sh
894        tty01            00:00:12    ps -a
224        tty02            00:00:10    sh
901        tty02            00:00:07    cat
724        tty03            00:00:08    sh
```

The option –a is used for displaying the processes of all the users.

(c) To get the list of processes of a particular user, we give the following command.

```
$ ps –u ravi
```

Here, the option –u is used for displaying a list of processes of only the specified user and ravi is the login ID of the user whose process list we want to see. We may get the following output.

```
PID        TTY              TIME        CMD
224        tty02            00:00:10    sh
901        tty02            00:00:07    cat
```

(d) To get complete (full) information of the processes, including the login ID of the user, ID of the parent process, CPU time consumed, etc., we give the following command.

```
$ ps -f
```

Here, the option –f stands for full information. We may get the following output.

UID	PID	PPID	C	STIME	TTY	TIME	CMD
ravi	423	341	3	13:01:39	tty01	00:00:01	-sh
ravi	661	423	9	13:05:78	tty01	00:00:01	ps -f

The first column (UID) displays the login ID of the user. PID stands for the *process identifier* and is used for the identification of the process. PPID is the identification of the parent process from where the current process was born (or created). C is the amount of CPU time consumed by the process. STIME is the time when the process started. The login shell has PID 423 and PPID 341, which implies that the shell is the child process that was created by a system process with PID 341. The parent PID (i.e., PPID) of the ps -f command is 423 as this command was launched by the shell (hence the shell is the parent process of the ps -f command).

(e) To get the list of processes that are created by the user from a particular terminal, we give the following command.

```
$ ps –t tty02
PID        TTY              TIME        CMD
224        tty02            00:00:10    sh
901        tty02            00:00:07    cat
```

The option –t is used for specifying the terminal number.

Besides the processes that we create, there are several processes that are automatically created by the Unix operating system at the time of booting and are used for managing different tasks that include handling memory and other resources.

(f) To see the list of the processes that are system-generated and the ones that are running at the current instant, we give the following command.

```
$ ps -e
PID    TTY     TIME      CMD
0      ?       00:00:00  sched
1      ?       00:00:01  init
2      ?       00:00:00  vhand
3      ?       00:01:01  bdflush
970    ?       00:00:00  getty
975    ?       00:01:00  getty
```

Most of the processes that we see in this listing are very important for the functioning of the Unix operating system and hence keep running continuously in the background until the system shuts down. These processes are known as *daemons* as they run automatically without any request generated from the user. Since these system processes or daemons are not executed from any terminal, we see a ? in the column TTY in the listing provided. We also see in the aforementioned listing that the first process is the sched (scheduler) that schedules the next process from the ready queue and submits it to the CPU for necessary action. The init is the parent process of a daemon and its PID is 1. The vhand is a sort of *page stealing daemon* that releases pages of the memory for use by other processes. The rest of the processes (found in the list) also help in some way or the other in the proper functioning of the Unix system and do different tasks such as initializing the processes, swapping in and out the active processes, and flushing the buffer for different I/O operations, among others.

(g) To see the threads of the currently running processes, we use the following command.

```
$ ps -L
PID    LWP    TTY      LTIME   CMD
739    1      tty01    0:00    sh
894    1      tty01    0:00    ps
```

This command shows threads with LWP and NLWP columns. As said in Section 6.6, LWP and NLWP represent lightweight processes and number of lightweight process, respectively.

6.7 HANDLING JOBS

A job refers to a command or program executed by the user to perform some task. As discussed in Section 6.6, a process is nothing but a program in execution mode. In other words, we can call our jobs as processes. The jobs or processes are controlled by the shell. For example, the following command is a job or process.

Example $cat letter.txt

There are two types of jobs—foreground and background. Foreground jobs are those that appear active on the terminal and need continuous interaction with the user for their execution. In other words, a foreground job might require input from the user and until and unless it is completed or suspended, no other job or command can be executed, whereas background jobs are those, which on execution, immediately display the shell prompt allowing the user to execute other jobs. This means that the background job does not lock the input and output terminals and instead allows the user to execute more processes.

6.7.1 fg: Foreground Jobs

Jobs that require a high level of user interaction are executed as foreground jobs. In addition, the most preferred jobs, whose results we want to see immediately, are executed in the foreground. The foreground job locks the standard input and output terminals and does not allow any other job to begin until and unless it is either suspended or complete. To start a foreground job, just type in a command followed by the Enter key.

Syntax   `fg [%job]`

Here, %job represents the job we wish to run in the foreground.

Examples

(a) `$ fg`
    When fg command is used without any arguments, it resumes the first job.
(b) `$ fg %1`
    This statement resumes the job whose ID is 1.
(c) Any command that is issued initially runs the job in the foreground. The following sort command executes in the foreground.
    `$ sort letter.txt`

Suspending, resuming, and terminating foreground jobs

We can suspend any running foreground job and resume it any time we want. To suspend a running foreground job, we press the Ctrl-z keys and to resume the suspended job, we use the fg command.

Example

```
$ sort a.lst > b.lst          Foreground job
Ctrl-z                        Suspended job
```

On suspending a foreground job, we immediately get the shell prompt. We can then give any other command that we want to execute. For example,

```
$ date
Tuesday 10 Sep 2012 12:43:44 AM IST
```

To resume the suspended job, we use the fg command in the following way.

`$    fg`: It resumes the same suspended job, sort a.lst > b.lst (i.e., sort command).

To terminate (kill) a running foreground job, we use Ctrl-c. After terminating the job, we press the Enter key for getting the command prompt.

6.7.2 bg: Background Jobs

The jobs whose results are not urgent, that is, jobs that have no time constraint and usually take a longer time to complete are executed in the background. As mentioned in the beginning of this section, the background jobs do not lock the standard input and output terminals and immediately display the shell prompt, allowing us to execute jobs of a higher preference. To execute any job in the background, simply add the ampersand symbol (&) after the command.

Syntax   `bg [%job]`

Here, `%job` represents the job we want to run in the background.

Examples

(a) `$ bg`

This command displays the list of currently running jobs in the background.

(b) `$ bg %1`

This statement resumes or restarts the stopped background job with job ID 1.

Assuming we have a file `letter.txt`, we use the following command to sort the file `letter.txt` in the background and save the sorted rows in the file `better.txt`.

`$ sort letter.txt > better.txt &`

`[1] 53702`

Since several jobs (commands) can be executed in the background, the kernel issues and displays a unique job number and PID number of the executed background jobs for our reference. Hence, the number `[1]` (1 within square brackets) is the job number and `53702` is the PID number of the job (sorting of file `letter.txt`). We can use the job number to stop, restart, or kill the desired background job.

Suspending, resuming, and terminating background jobs

To suspend a background job, we use the `stop` command. To restart it, we use the `bg` command. To terminate it, we use the `kill` command. For all the three commands, (`stop`, `bg`, and `kill`), we need to specify the job number of the desired background job prefixed by the percent (%) sign.

Syntax   `stop pid`

Here, `pid` represents the process ID that we wish to suspend.

Examples

To understand how the background jobs are stopped, resumed, or killed, let us look at the following steps:

(a) To execute a job in the background, we give the following command.

`$ sort letter.txt > better.txt &`

`[1]  53702`

Here, `[1]` is the job number of the given background job.

(b) To stop the job of sorting the file `letter.txt`, we specify its job number in the stop command.

`$ stop %1`

`[1] + 53702 stopped  (SIGSTOP} sort letter.txt > better.txt &`

(c) To resume or restart the stopped background job (of sorting the file `letter.txt`), we specify its job number in the `bg` command.

```
$ bg %1
[1]  sort letter.txt > better.txt &
```

(d) If we do not want to sort the file letter.txt and wish to terminate the background job, we kill the job by specifying its job number by using the following command.

```
$ kill %1
[1] + Terminated          sort letter.txt > better.txt &
```

We can see that all the three commands—stop, bg, and kill—display the program name on the right.

6.7.3 Switching Jobs from Background to Foreground and Vice Versa

Sometimes, we might want a task (running in the background) to finish a little faster or we may expect a background job to request for user input. In such cases, we switch the background job to the foreground job. Similarly, we may also need to switch a task running in the foreground to the background so as to execute other jobs that are of a higher priority. We can switch a job from the background to the foreground and vice versa when the job is in the suspended mode. A foreground job (in suspended mode) can be switched to the background with the bg command. Similarly, to switch a background job to the foreground, we use the fg command.

Since the background jobs run in the background, we might forget their job numbers and hence would also like to see their status (i.e., if they are in the stopped or running mode). To get a list of all the jobs running in the background along with their statuses, we use the jobs command.

6.7.4 jobs: Showing Job Status

The jobs command displays all the jobs with their job number and the current status (running or stopped mode).

Table 6.5 Brief description of the options of the jobs command

Options	Description
-1	Displays the process ID along with the job ID for each job
-p	Displays only the process ID for each job, without the job ID
%job_id	Represents the identification number of the job whose status we wish to find out
%str	Represents the job whose command begins with the string, str
%?str	Represents the job whose command contains the string, str
%%	Represents the current job
%+	Represents the current job (same as %%)
%-	Represents the previous job

Syntax   jobs [-1][-p] [%job_id][%str][%?str][%%][%+][%-]

The options of the jobs command are briefly described in Table 6.5.

All the jobs running in the foreground or background will be displayed. The output of the jobs command displays the job number, currency flag, and the status of the job.

Examples

```
(a) $jobs
    [3]  + Stopped(SIGTSTP)    sort letter.txt
                               > better.txt &
    [2]  - Running             cat abc.txt | lp
    [1]  + Running             chirag1.sh&
```

In this listing, we see that job 3 has a plus (+) and job 2 has a minus (−) in the second column. These +

and – signs are known as the *currency flags*. The plus sign (+) indicates the default job. The default job is the job that will be considered when any of the commands, namely `stop`, `bg`, `fg`, and `kill`, is given without specifying the job number. For example, if we issue the `kill` command (without specifying the job number of the job that we want to kill), job number 3 will be killed as it is the default job. The currency flag minus sign indicates the default job that follows the first job. In other words, when the first default job is terminated or is complete, the job with minus sign will become the default job, that is, its sign currency flag will be changed from – sign to + sign.

When any job is suspended (by issuing Ctrl-z command), it automatically becomes the default job and is assigned a + currency flag. When another job is also suspended, that one becomes the default job (getting the + currency flag) and the earlier suspended job gets the – currency flag, and so on.

(b) To display the process ID along with the job ID use the `-l` option in the following way.

```
$jobs –l
[3]   +   30178      Stopped(SIGTSTP)     sort letter.txt > better.txt &
[2]   –   30189      Running              cat abc.txt | lp
[1]       30190      Running              chirag1.sh&
```

(c) To display the status of the job with ID 2, we give the following command.

```
$jobs %2
[2]    - Running  cat abc.txt | lp
```

(d) To display the status of the job that contains the `lp` command, we give the following command.

```
$jobs %?lp
[2]    - Running  cat abc.txt | lp
```

Note: Process synchronization—When more than one process runs simultaneously, it is quite possible that they try to access and modify the same content (of a file or its region) simultaneously. This situation may result in inconsistency and ambiguity, that is, modifications made by one process may be lost or overwritten by the modifications performed by another. Synchronization among the processes is implemented to maintain consistency and avoid ambiguity. Process synchronization sets up a mechanism where only one process is able to modify the content and other processes that wish to modify the same content are compelled to wait until the first process is complete. Enabling only a single process to modify the content ensures the integrity of the content. We will discuss process synchronization through semaphore in detail in Chapter 14.

6.8 SCHEDULING OF PROCESSES

Scheduling of a process is a mechanism of defining a timetable for different processes to auto execute at a prescribed date and time. The tasks that are to be executed at the defined period or time can be scheduled. For example, tasks such as sending reminders to save files, taking a backup of data, or mailing important information can all be scheduled to run at a specific date or time.

Unix provides several commands for scheduling a process to execute within a desired period.

The first topic we will discuss in this section is `cron`, a time-based job scheduler.

6.8.1 cron: Chronograph—Time-based Job Scheduler

cron is a daemon that keeps running and ticks (fires) every minute, that is, it gets activated every minute and opens its special file to check if there are any processes waiting to be executed in that particular minute. If none of the processes is found waiting, it goes to sleep again (to fire in the next minute). If there are any processes to be executed in that minute, it executes them and again goes to sleep. This daemon continues to execute until the Unix system shuts down.

The cron automatically starts when the Unix system boots. During booting, Unix executes the file /etc/cron (to execute cron) and displays the message 'cron started' on the terminal. The special file that is opened by the cron to view the list of processes that are required to be executed is stored in the /usr/spool/cron/crontabs directory. We can also create our own crontab file containing the list of processes along with their schedule and place it in the /usr/spool/cron/crontabs directory. Let us see how a crontab file is created.

6.8.2 crontab: Creating Crontab Files

The crontab command creates a crontab file (containing the list of processes and their schedule time) and places it in the /usr/spool/cron/crontabs directory with our login name. For example, if your name is Ravi, then the crontab file made for you will be created with the name Ravi in the /usr/spool/cron/crontabs directory. The crontab file is made on behalf of the local file that we create in our home directory. The local file can be given any name, say, a.bat, and it must contain a list of the processes that we want to execute along with the schedule (date and time at which we want them to be executed) in a specific format.

Syntax crontab [-l | -r | -e] [filename]

The options of the crontab command are briefly described in Table 6.6.

The format in which the command and schedule is specified in the local file is as follows:

Minute Hour Day Month Day of week Command

Example

Let us assume that we want the following task to be executed at the specified date and time.

```
$ cat a.bat
15 12 10,20   *  *    echo "Keep smiling and
                      work hard"
0  10 1       1  *    date > /dev/console
```

The first command will echo the message at 12:15 on the 10th and 20th day of every month. The second command will display the time at 10 a.m. on January 1, every year. The asterisk in any field designates a wild card that matches any value. For specifying more than one value we can

Table 6.6 Brief description of the options of the crontab command

Options	Description
-l	It displays the crontab file.
-r	It removes the crontab file.
-e	It edits the crontab file using the editor defined through the VISUAL or EDITOR environment variables. The modified crontab file is taken into consideration when saved.
filename	It refers to the optional file where the list of commands and their schedules are defined. The crontab file has five fields for specifying day, date, and time followed by the command that we wish to run at that time. The five fields are given here: *Minute*: The valid value is from 0–59. *Hour*: The valid value is from 1–23. *Day of month*: The valid value is from 1–31. *Month*: The valid value is from 1–12. *Day of week*: The valid value is from 0–6. Sunday is represented by 0.

use a comma (,). In this example we have used a comma to specify both the 10th and 20th day of every month.

Each field in a.bat is separated by either a space or a tab. The first day of the week, Sunday, is represented by 0.

When we execute the crontab command, the following occurs:

```
$ crontab a.bat
```

The contents of a.bat are automatically transferred to the /usr/spool/cron/crontabs directory where they are stored in a file with our login name. From there onwards, the cron daemon will read this file (crontab file) and execute the commands (processes) specified in it regularly.

If we want to make some changes in the scheduling of the processes, we need to edit our local file a.bat (in our home directory) and after saving the changes, again execute the crontab command to re-transfer it in the /usr/spool/cron/crontabs directory using our login name (the earlier crontab file will be replaced by the new one).

To view the commands that we have supplied to our crontab file, we use the -l option with the crontab command:

```
$crontab -l
```

To remove the crontab file, we use the following command:

```
$ crontab -r
```

Another command that allows the scheduling of processes is the at command. We will now study this.

6.8.3 at: Scheduling Commands at Specific Dates and Times

The at command is used for executing Unix commands at a specific date and time. Tasks such as taking backup of the disk at regular intervals or sending mail messages at odd hours can be easily accomplished using the at command. We can specify the Unix commands (to be executed) at the command prompt or save them in a file and use the file to execute the commands.

> Syntax   at [-f filename] [-m] [-l] [-r] time

The options of the at command are briefly described in Table 6.7.

Table 6.7   Brief description of the options of the at command

Option	Description
-f filename	It reads the commands to be executed from the specified filename instead of the standard input.
-m	It mails the user when the commands are executed.
-l	It lists the commands that are scheduled to run.
-r	It cancels the scheduled command.
time	It indicates the time at which we wish to execute command(s). We can define the time either specifically or relatively. The specific time can be given in the following format: hh:mm a.m./p.m

(Contd)

Table 6.7 (*Contd*)

Option	Description
	Here, a.m./p.m. indicates that time is in the 12-hour format. Without a.m./p.m., the time is assumed to follow a 24-hour clock. We can also specify optional time zone such as EST and GMT after the time. The time can be relatively specified in any of the following ways: *now*: This indicates the current day and time. *today*: This indicates the current day. *tomorrow*: This indicates the day following the current day. *midnight*: This indicates the time 12:00 a.m., that is, 00:00. *noon*: This indicates the time 12:00 p.m.

We can also specify a future time by adding a plus sign (+) followed by the minute, hours, days, weeks, months, or years.

Examples

(a) `$at 18:00`

```
echo "Office time over. Time to log out"> /dev/tty02
Ctrl-d
Job 3434443 at Sun Nov 16 18:00:00 IST 2012
```

On pressing Ctrl-d, the `at` command displays the job number and the date and time of the scheduled execution of the echo command. The job number terminates with 'a' indicating that this job has been submitted using the `at` command.

Now, the following message will be echoed on the `tty02` terminal at 6:00 p.m.

`Office time over. Time to log out.`

Note: When the output is redirected to a terminal, as is done in the aforementioned command (`/dev/tty02`), the message will be echoed on the screen and when redirection is not specified, the message is received by the target through mail command.

(b) We can also execute the commands stored in a file as shown in the following example.

```
$at 18:00
jobstodo.sh
Ctrl-d
Job 3434443.a at Sun Nov 16 18:00:00 IST 2010
```

By executing this command, all the commands stored in the script file `jobstodo.sh` will be executed at 6:00 p.m. and their outputs will be mailed to us. You may recall that if the redirection is not specified for any command, its output is sent to the user through mail.

(c) It can be noted that we can also add a.m. or p.m. with the time. For example, in the aforementioned command, we can write `$at` 18:00 as `$ at 6pm`

On executing this `at` command, we will see a message on our screen displaying 'you have `mail`' at 6 p.m.

(d) To view the output of the aforementioned command, we use the following `mail` command.

```
$mail
message 1:
To: ravi
```

```
Date: Sun Nov 16 18:00:00 IST 2010
Office time over. Time to logout
$
```

(e) To schedule jobs from the given file, we give the following command.

```
$ at -f jobs.txt 11:00 today
```

All the commands specified in the file jobs.txt will be executed at 11 o'clock on that particular day.

Note: The commands specified in jobs.txt will still run even if we exit from the system.

(f) To view the list of jobs submitted using the at command, we give the following command.

```
$at -l
```

(g) To remove scheduled jobs from the job queue, we use the following command.

```
$ at -r 3434443
```

This command will remove job 3434443 from the job queue.

(h) We can use a lot of keywords when specifying the time for scheduling jobs such as now, today, tomorrow, noon, day, year, month, hours, and minutes. The following are some examples.

   (i)   `$ at now + 2 hours`

   (ii) `$ at now +1 week`

  (iii) `$ at 6pm today`

  (iv) `$ at 6pm next month`

   (v) `$ at 6pm Fri`

  (vi) `$ at 0915 am Nov 16`

 (vii) `$ at 9:15 am Nov 16`

The two commands that are often discussed along with the at command are atq and atrm.

atq   This command lists the jobs that are scheduled to run, similar to the at -l command. The jobs are displayed along with their job number, date, hour, etc.

Syntax   atq

Example

```
$ atq
324556      2012-10-15 10:30 a sort a.txt
324557      2012-10-16 07:00 a date
```

atrm   This command deletes the specified job number, similar to the at -r command.

Syntax   atrm job_no

Example   `$ atrm 3434443`

This command will remove job 3434443 from the job queue.

Note: The difference between the at and crontab commands is that the jobs scheduled by the at command have to be rescheduled after their execution (if we want to execute them again). On the other hand, crontab carries out the submitted job every day for years without the need for rescheduling.

6.8.4 batch: Executing Commands Collectively

As the name implies, the batch command is used for issuing a set of commands that we want to execute collectively (in a batch). The commands given in the batch will be executed later when the system load permits, that is, when the CPU is free, it will execute the commands specified by the batch command.

Syntax   batch [-f filename] [-m] [-l] [-r] time

The options of the batch command are briefly described in Table 6.8.

Table 6.8   Brief description of the options of the batch command

Option	Description
-f filename	It reads the commands to be executed from the specified filename instead of the standard input.
-m	It sends mails to the user when the commands are executed.
-l	It lists the commands that are collected to run in a batch.
-r	It cancels the scheduled command.
time	It indicates the time at which we wish to execute commands. Its options are similar to what was discussed in the at command.

Examples

(a) `$batch`

```
echo "Keep smiling and work hard"
date > /dev/console
sort letter.txt > better.txt
Ctrl d
job 6646566.b at Sun Nov 16 18:00:00 IST 2010
```

On pressing Ctrl-d, we will get a job number that terminates with b indicating that this job is submitted by the batch command. The aforementioned jobs consisting of displaying of the echo message and date, and sorting of letter.txt will be performed when the load of the system allows the execution of these tasks.

(b) We can also collect the commands in a file and execute it using the batch command as follows:

```
$ batch < jobstodo.sh
job 6646566.b at Sun Nov 16  18:00:00 IST 2010
```

(c) The following command can also be given.

```
$ batch -f jobstodo.sh
```

6.8.5 nohup: No Hangups

Traditionally, when we log in to the Unix system, a default login shell is started with which we interact. When we log out of the system, the current shell terminates. If the current shell is a child process, the execution returns to the parent process when it exits. If the current shell is the login shell, it terminates when we log out of the system. When the login shell terminates, it kills all the background jobs. To ensure that the processes we have executed do not die even when we log out, we use the nohup command. nohup stands for 'no hangups'.

Syntax   nohup command_name &

Here, `command_name` represents the command name, shell script, or command name and `&` ensures that the command is run in the background.

Examples

(a) `$ nohup sort letter.txt > better.txt &`

`1296`

We can see that we get the PID of the command (sorting of the file) that we wanted to execute in the background. The sorting of the file will now continue to run even if we log out of the system and we will find the sorted rows in the file `better.txt` when we log in to the system again.

In the preceding example, the sorted rows of the file `letter.txt` are redirected to another file `better.txt`. In case we do not specify the file that the output has to be redirected to, the output of the command will be saved in a file called `nohup.out`. As in the following example, the sorted rows of the file `letter.txt` will be saved in the `nohup.out` file.

(b) `$ nohup sort letter.txt &`

`sending output to nohup.out`

`1296`

The `nohup.out` file will be created in the current directory.

6.8.6 `nice`: Modifying Priority

We are aware that Unix, being a multitasking operating system, executes several processes together, that is, there may be several processes running in the memory at a time. Each process is assigned a time slot in which it gets the CPU's attention. If the process is not completed in that time slot, it is added back to the queue to wait for another time slot.

The `nice` command is used for modifying the priority of the processes. It is obvious that we would like to complete tasks of a higher priority before tasks that are of a lower priority. Using the `nice` command, we can modify the priority of the processes. The higher priority process will get an earlier time slot and hence will be executed before the other processes in the queue. The priority of a process is decided by a number associated with it. This number is called the 'nice' value of the process. *Higher the nice value of a process, lower is its priority*. The nice value of a process can range from −20 to 19, with 0 being the default nice value.

Syntax `nice [-increment | -n increment ] command [argument ... ]`

The options of the `nice` command are briefly described in Table 6.9.

Table 6.9 Brief description of the options of the `nice` command

Options	Description
Increment	It represents a value in the range 1–19 by which we wish to increase the nice value. A default increment value of 10 is assumed. If a value greater than 19 is entered, the highest increment value (19) will be assumed.
-n increment	It is used to decrement the priority of the specified command. Only a super user can decrease the nice value of a command, it is otherwise ignored.
command	It represents the command whose priority we wish to change and argument refers to the arguments (if any) of the specified command.

Examples

(a) The following is the command to increase the nice value of one of the processes.

```
$ nice sort letter.txt
```

This would increase the nice value of our sort from 0 to 10, that is, the priority of the sort command is reduced by 10 units. Since we did not specify the increment value, an increment of 10 is taken as the default.

(b) If we want to increase the nice value by a specific value, we give the following command.

```
$ nice -5 sort letter.txt
```

This statement will increase the nice value of the sort command by 5, and hence, the nice value of the sort command will now become 15. This happens because we had already changed the nice value of the sort command to 10 by implementing the aforementioned statement. You may recall that the value given by us for the increment should be in the range 0 to 19.

(c) To decrease the nice value by a specific value, we use the -n option in the following example (assuming the command is given by the super user).

```
$ nice -n 7 sort letter.txt
```

This command, will decrease the nice value of the sort command by 7 (assuming its previous nice value is 15) making its current nice value 8, hence increasing its priority by 8 units.

Note: Only the super user can increase the priority of a process (by reducing its nice value).

6.8.7 kill: Killing Processes

Killing a process means canceling the ongoing execution of a command. Consider a situation where a command is taking a long time to complete or where we do not want to execute a background job any more, or where a program has gone into an infinite loop. In such a situation, we are left with no other option but to kill (terminate) the job. For killing a job, we only need to find the PID of the job or process that we want to kill (terminate) and pass it to the kill command.

Syntax kill [-s signal_name][-l] PID

The options of the kill command are briefly described in Table 6.10.

Table 6.10 Brief description of the options of the kill command

Options	Description
-s signal_name	It specifies the signal that we wish to send to the process. We will be learning about signals in detail in Section 6.9. However for the time being, we can assume signals as symbolic constants each meant for performing a specific task.
-l	It displays the list of signal names.
PID	It represents the process identifier to which we wish to send the signal. If a value 0 is entered for the PID, the signal will be sent to all the processes in the current process group.

Examples

(a) Assuming the PID of the job that we want to kill is 2098, the following command is given.

```
$ kill 2098
```

```
2098 terminated
```
This command will immediately kill (terminate) the process with PID 2098.

(b) Consider the following example of sorting a file, letter.txt in the background.
```
$ sort letter.txt > better.txt &
53702
```
Here, 53702 is the PID of this sorting command.

(c) If we do not want this sorting to happen, we can kill it by giving the following command.
```
$ kill 53702
53702 terminated
```

(d) We can kill more than one background job with a single kill command by specifying all the PIDs together.
```
$kill 53702 48901 56005
```
When a kill command is executed, a termination signal is sent to the process being killed, that is, the process reacts on the basis of the signal sent to them. Some processes do not get killed by this termination signal. For killing such processes, we specify an option, 9, with the kill command.

(e) For sending the SIGSTOP signal to the process with identifier 53701, we give the following command.
```
$kill -s SIGSTOP 53701
```

(f) To kill a process with certainty, we send a SIGKILL signal to the process. SIGKILL is a signal that cannot be caught or ignored, and hence, forcefully kills the specified process, as shown in the following statement.
```
$kill -s SIGKILL 53701
```

We have seen that the term *signal* has appeared enough number of times in our discussion. Let us now talk about this term in detail.

6.9 SIGNALS

A signal is a technique of informing or sending notifications to a process about a particular event that requires immediate action. It is considered a software interrupt that can be used to stop the current process and get the desired task performed in between. Each signal has a default action associated with it, which can be changed, so that different signals can take different actions.

All signals have a unique signal name that begins with SIG (for signal) and a number (or integer). A few important signals for shell scripts are given in Table 6.11.

Table 6.11   Brief description of a few important signals

Name	Value	Description	Default action
SIGHUP	1	The signal is generated either when a hangup is detected on the terminal or when the controlling process is terminated.	Exit
SIGINT	2	The signal is generated when the user interrupts using the keyboard by pressing Ctrl-c.	Exit
SIGQUIT	3	The signal is generated when the user wishes to quit by pressing Ctrl-\ from the keyboard.	Dump core

(Contd)

Table 6.11 (*Contd*)

Name	Value	Description	Default action
SIGSTP	25	The signal is generated to suspend a running process. The process can opt to ignore the signal, register a signal handler, or suspend the process.	Stop
SIGCHLD	18	The signal is generated when the process status of the child process changes.	Ignore
SIGABRT	6	This signal is generated to terminate the execution of the program.	Dump core
SIGKILL	9	This signal cannot be caught or ignored and is used to terminate a process with certainty.	Exit
SIGALRM	14	It is an alarm clock signal (used in timers).	Exit
SIGTERM	15	It is a termination signal that is generated when a particular software is terminated.	Exit
SIGCONT	19	This signal is generated to continue a stopped process.	Ignore
SIGSTOP	20	It is a stop signal that temporarily suspends the process. The signal cannot be ignored. The suspended process resumes on receiving the SIGCONT signal.	Stop
SIGPIPE	13	This signal is generated when a process attempts to write to a pipe when no process is present on the other end to read it.	Exit
SIGILL	4	This signal is generated on illegal instruction.	Dump core
SIGFPE	8	The signal is generated on floating point exception	Dump core

The signals are numbered from 0 to 31. *Value* in this table represents the positive integer by which these signals are defined in the header file, <signal.h>.

In Table 6.11, the SIGSTP and SIGSTOP signals appear to be similar. Further details about the two signals are given here:

SIGTSTP is a signal that tells a program to stop temporarily. The signal is sent to a process by its controlling terminal when the user requests to suspend the process by pressing special Ctrl-z keys. By default, SIGTSTP causes the process receiving it to stop until a SIGCONT signal is received.

The same is the case with the SIGSTOP signal. When SIGSTOP is sent to a process, the process is suspended in its current state and will resume execution when the SIGCONT signal is sent.

The difference between the SIGSTP and SIGSTOP signals lies in the flexibility of handling them. When a process receives the SIGSTOP signal, it has no option but to suspend the process, that is, 'suspending' is the required action in the case of the SIGSTOP signal. On the other hand, when a process receives the SIGSTP signal, it has several options to choose from. It can suspend the process (default action), register a signal handler, or ignore it.

Note: SIGSTOP and SIGCONT are generally used for job control in the Unix shell.

Furthermore, the signals are treated as either synchronous or asynchronous signals:

Synchronous signals These signals are also known as *traps* and usually occur when an unrecoverable error such as an illegal instruction (say, division by zero) or an invalid address reference occurs. The occurrence of a trap is handled by the kernel trap handler to be delivered to the thread that caused the error.

Asynchronous signals These occur when an external event happens, for example, when a process or thread sends a signal via kill(), and then the user puts the process to sleep. On the occurrence of such a signal, it is delivered to the desired process.

Though signals are synchronously generated by errors in a program, they are mostly asynchronous events that can occur at any random time. The following are a few of the conditions that generate signals:

1. Termination or cancellation of a program by the user by pressing key pairs such as Ctrl-c or Ctrl-z
2. Execution of illegal instructions (e.g., dividing by 0 and using invalid memory reference.)
3. Processes that send signals using kill() system call
4. Kernels that need to inform processes when some event occurs

When a signal occurs, it is said to be generated. On generation of the signal, it is disposed or handled by any of the following default actions:

1. *Ignore*: It ignores the signal; no action is taken.
2. *Exit*: It forces the process to exit.
3. *Dump core*: It terminates the process with dumping of the core. The core file will then be examined by debuggers to understand the reasons for termination.
4. *Stop*: It stops or suspends the process.
5. *Continue*: It continues the stopped process.

> **Note:** The two signals that cannot be ignored are SIGKILL and SIGSTOP as the kernel and the superuser use them to kill or stop any process.

After a signal is delivered, its handling starts. Till the time a signal is generated and delivered or accepted, it is said to be in a *pending state*. It is also possible for a process to block the signal from being delivered. The blocked signals remain in the *pending* state until they are either *ignored* or *unblocked*. The kernel can deliver the signal once or more than once. If the signal has to be delivered more than once, it is *queued*. Each process has a *signal mask*, that is, an array of bits that define blocked signals for a process. The signal mask contains a bit for each signal. If the bit is *On*, it means that the corresponding signal will be blocked.

SIGINT (signal 2) is sent when the user interrupts a process by pressing the Ctrl-c keys. The SIGHUP signal is generated either when hangup is detected on the terminal or when the controlling process is terminated. The program that catches SIGHUP performs a clean shutdown. The signal SIGTERM (software terminate—signal 15) is used to terminate a software. On pressing Ctrl-\, the SIGQUIT signal is generated.

6.9.1 Classes of Signals

The signals are basically divided into two classes, which are described as follows:

Reliable signals

Old Unix system signals were unreliable. A frequent problem was race condition (i.e., receiving another signal while the current signal was still being handled). The recent method available for signal implementation is quite reliable and more functional. The signals are not lost and hence, are properly handled. Besides this, the state of the signals can also be controlled—they can be blocked, kept in pending state, or can be unblocked to deliver them whenever needed.

Unreliable signals

Unreliable signals are those that are lost or cannot work properly in the absence of their signal handlers. For a signal to work properly, it is required that its signal handler exists or is installed before the signal is generated. In the absence of the signal handler, the default action is taken, that is, the signal is lost or killed.

In unreliable signals, the signal handler does not remain installed once called; hence the signal handler needs to be re-installed immediately after the signal is called. An easy way to do so is to write the instruction to install the signal handler within the signal handler itself. However, this may result in a problem when the signal may arrive before the handler is reinstalled, which can cause the signal to be lost.

Before we learn how signals are handled, let us take a quick look at the functions that generate signals.

6.9.2 Sending Signals Using `kill()` and `raise()`

The two functions used to send signals are `kill()` and `raise()`.

The syntax for `kill()` is as follows:

Syntax   `int kill(int pid, int signal)`

Here, `pid` is the non-zero (positive) process identifier to which the signal is sent. If `pid` is equal to 0, the signal is sent to all processes whose group ID matches with the group ID of the sender process. If the value of the `pid` is set to −1, the signal will be sent to all the processes for which the sender process has permission. The signal parameter is either the number or name of the signal to deliver. The `kill()` function returns a value 0 when successful and −1 otherwise, and sets an *errno* variable to describe the error.

Example   `kill(getpid(),SIGINT);`

This example sends the interrupt signal to the ID of the calling process.

The second function used to send signals is `raise()`. Its syntax is as follows:

Syntax   `int raise(int signal)`

Here, `signal` represents the integer value or symbolic constant of the signal that we wish to send to the executing program.

Example   `int return_flag = raise(SIGINT);`

This statement sends an interrupt signal to the executing program.

Usually, when a signal is generated and delivered to a process, the kernel saves the current state on the stack and calls a signal handler for the respective signal. The signal handler performs the necessary actions and returns to the kernel. Once the signal handler finishes its actions, the kernel restores the process state from the stack and resumes execution. The `signal()` function is used to define signal handlers for signals.

Let us look at the process for handling signals that help in obtaining the desired task on the occurrence of a signal.

6.9.3 Signal Handling Using `signal()`

In order to perform a desired task on the occurrence of a signal, a program defines a function called a signal handler. The signal handler function carries the code that we wish to execute on the occurrence of the specific signal. On the occurrence of a signal, a process can let the default action take place, block the signal, or catch the signal with a handler.

If the process executes the signal handler (on the occurrence of a signal), it makes use of the stack to store the return address so as to continue the program from the place where the signal was generated.

The `signal()` function is used to define the signal and the signal handler in the following syntax:

Syntax	`int (*signal(int sig, void (*sig_handler)()))()`

Here, `sig_handler` is the function that is called on the occurrence or receiving of the signal, `sig`. The `signal()` function, when successful, returns a pointer to the function `sig_handler`. When it fails, the `signal()` function returns –1 and also sets the value to the *errno* variable.

The `sig_handler()` can have any of following three values:

SIG_DFL   It is a pointer to the default function. The default function depends on the kind of signal. For example, the default action for the interrupt signal is to terminate the process.

SIG_IGN   It is a pointer to the system ignore function, `SIG_IGN()`, which will ignore all the signals except `SIGKILL` and `SIGSTOP`.

Address of the signal handler function   It is the function that contains the code we wish to execute on receiving the signal.

Examples

(a) `signal(SIGINT, SIG_IGN);`
     This statement will ignore the interrupt signal that occurs on pressing the Ctrl-c keys.
(b) `signal(SIGINT, SIG_DFL);`
     This statement will execute the default function, that is, it will terminate the program on the occurrence of the interrupt signal (on pressing the Ctrl-c keys).

The following program demonstrates the handling of different signals. `SIGINT`, `SIGQUIT`, and `SIGSTOP` are generated when the user presses the designated keys. The `SIGINT` and `SIGQUIT` signals are caught by the custom signal handlers, whereas the `SIGSTOP` signal will terminate the program.

```
signalhandling.c
#include <stdio.h>
#include <signal.h>

void inthandler(int sig_no);
void quithandler(int sig_no);
```

```
main()
{
    signal(SIGINT, inthandler);
    signal(SIGQUIT, quithandler);
    printf("Press Ctrl-c to generate the interrupt signal\n");
    printf("Press Ctrl-\\ to generate the quit signal\n");
    for(;;); /* infinite loop */
}

void inthandler(int sig_no)
{
    signal(SIGINT, inthandler);
    /* resetting signal. Some versions of UNIX reset the signal to the
    default when called*/
    printf("\nCtrl-c keys are pressed\n");
}

void quithandler(int sig_no)
{
    signal(SIGQUIT, quithandler);
    printf("\nCtrl-\\ keys are pressed. Quitting from the program\n");
    exit(0);
}
```

Output

```
$ ./signalhandling
Press Ctrl-c to generate the interrupt signal
Press Ctrl-\ to generate the quit signal
^C
Ctrl-c keys are pressed
^\
Ctrl-\ keys are pressed. Quitting from the program
```

In the output of the program, we can see that a menu is displayed prompting the user to either press Ctrl-c or Ctrl-\ to generate *interrupt* (SIGINT) or *quit* (SIGQUIT) signals, respectively. When we press a key combination for generating a signal, the respective signal handler function is invoked. For example, on pressing the Ctrl-c keys, the SIGINT signal will be generated and its handler function, inthandler will be executed displaying the following message: Ctrl-c keys are pressed.

Compiling C programs

To compile a C program, we use the gcc command in the following format:

Syntax $ gcc program.c -o executable_name

Here, program.c represents the C program that we wish to compile and executable_name is the name by which we wish to create the executable file.

Examples

(a) `$ gcc signalhandling.c  -o signalhandling`

This command compiles the C program, `signalhandling.c`, and creates its executable version with the name, `signalhandling`. The executable file is run by giving the following command.

`$./signalhandling`

Here, dot (.) represents the current directory where the executable file is kept.

This example only explains how the signals are handled but does not address how they are generated.

(b) The following program demonstrates both: how the signals are generated as well as how they are handled. Here we create a child process through the `fork()` system call and the parent process generates signals that are handled by the child process.

```
signalgenerating.c
#include <stdio.h>
#include <signal.h>

void inthandler(int sig_no);
void quithandler(int sig_no);
void huphandler(int sig_no);

main()
{
  int pid;
    if ((pid = fork()) < 0) {
          perror("Child process could not be created");
          exit(1);
    }
  if (pid == 0)
  {
          /* Code executed by the child process */
          signal(SIGINT, inthandler);
          signal(SIGQUIT, quithandler);
          signal(SIGHUP, huphandler);
          for(;;); /* infinite loop */
  }
  else
  {
          printf("pid is %d\n",pid);
          /* Code executed by the parent process */
          printf("Sending SIGINT signal \n");
          kill(pid,SIGINT);
          sleep(5);
          printf("Sending SIGQUIT signal \n");
          kill(pid,SIGQUIT);
```

```
            sleep(5);
            printf("Sending SIGHUP signal\n");
            kill(pid,SIGHUP);
            sleep(5);
            printf("Sending SIGSTOP signal - terminating program \n");
            kill(pid,SIGSTOP);
    }
}

void inthandler(int sig_no)
{
  signal(SIGINT, inthandler); /* reset signal */
    printf("The interrupt signal handled by the child process\n");
}

void quithandler(int sig_no)
{
  signal(SIGQUIT, quithandler); /* reset signal */
    printf("The quit signal handled by the child process\n");
}

void huphandler(int sig_no)
{
  signal(SIGHUP, huphandler); /* reset signal */
    printf("The hangup signal handled by the child process\n");
}
```

Output

```
$ ./signalgenerating
pid is 1358
Sending SIGINT signal
The interrupt signal handled by the child process
Sending SIGQUIT signal
The quit signal handled by the child process
Sending SIGHUP signal
The hangup signal handled by the child process
Sending SIGSTOP signal - terminating program
```

In the output of the program, we can see that a child process is created using the fork() system call. The pid of the newly created process, 1358, is displayed. Four signals, SIGINT, SIGQUIT, SIGHUP, and SIGSTOP are generated through the kill() system call with a time gap of five seconds in between. On the generation of a signal, the respective handler function is invoked automatically. Each signal handler displays the respective message to inform that the respective signal is handled by the child process.

We will now discuss some functions that generate certain specific signals.

alarm() and pause() functions

The alarm function is used for generating the SIGALRM signal. The function actually sets a timer. When the time set through the timer expires, the function generates the SIGALRM signal.

Syntax   `unsigned int alarm(unsigned int seconds);`

Here, seconds refers to the time in seconds, which when expired generates the SIGALRM signal. If the generated SIGALRM signal is ignored or is not handled, the default action, that is, termination of the process will take place. The function returns 0 when the alarm signal is called. The function may also return the number of seconds left to the expiry of the previously set timer, which is still active and has not yet expired.

Example   `alarm(60);`

By executing this statement, the SIGALRM signal will be generated after 60 seconds.

Note: If the SIGALRM signal is generated without defining its signal handler, the process will terminate.

The pause function suspends the calling process until a signal is caught.

Syntax   `int pause(void);`

The pause function returns when a signal is caught and its signal handler is executed. On returning from the signal handler, the pause function returns a −1 value and sets an *errno* variable to the EINTR value.

Example   `pause();`

This statement suspends the calling process until the signal is caught.

abort function

The abort function causes abnormal program termination.

Syntax   `void abort(void);`

This function sends the SIGABRT signal to the caller process informing us about an abnormal program termination. The signal handler to the SIGABRT signal performs the desired clean-up, release of resources, etc., before the process terminates.

Example   `abort();`

Using this statement, the program is abnormally terminated.

sleep function

The sleep function suspends the execution of a process for the specified interval of time.

Syntax   `unsigned sleep(unsigned seconds);`

Here, the parameter, seconds, represents the time at which we wish the process to temporarily be suspended. The suspended process will resume after the specified time duration is over. On successful execution, the sleep() function returns a 0 value. If sleep() returns due to the delivery of a signal, the return value will be equal to the seconds that were left.

Example   `sleep(60);`

Using this statement, the execution of the process will suspend for 60 seconds.

The following program demonstrates the usage of the `alarm()`, `pause()`, `sleep()`, and `abort()` functions.

usagefunc.c

```
#include <stdio.h>
#include <signal.h>
V
void inthandler(int sig_no);
void alarmhandler(int sig_no);
void huphandler(int sig_no);
main()
{
    signal(SIGINT, inthandler);
    signal(SIGALRM, alarmhandler);
    printf("Alarm set to go off in 10 seconds \n");
    alarm(10);  /* alarm set to go off in 10 seconds */
    printf("The process paused for a while \n");
    pause();
    printf("The process is going to sleep for 20 seconds \n");
    sleep(20);
    abort();
}
void inthandler(int sig_no)
{
    signal(SIGINT, inthandler); /* reset signal */
    printf("The interrupt signal handled by the process\n");
}
void alarmhandler(int sig_no)
{
    signal(SIGALRM, alarmhandler); /* reset signal */
    printf("The alarm signal handled by the process\n");
}
```

Output

```
$ ./usagefunc
Alarm set to go off in 10 seconds
The process paused for a while
The alarm signal handled by the process
The process is going to sleep for 20 seconds
Abort - core dumped

$ ./usagefunc
Alarm set to go off in 10 seconds
The process paused for a while
^CThe interrupt signal handled by the process
```

```
The process is going to sleep for 20 seconds
The alarm signal handled by the process
Abort - core dumped
```

In the output of the program, we can see that if the process is not interrupted, all the scheduled tasks will occur sequentially one after the other. The alarm is set to go off in 10 seconds, the process is paused, the alarm signal is handled, the process is suspended (is set to sleep) for 20 seconds, and finally, the process is aborted and the core is dumped. In the second run of the program, we see that besides the scheduled tasks sequence, if the process is interrupted by pressing ^C keys, the function, `inthandler`, meant to handle the interrupt, is invoked displaying the following message: `The interrupt signal handled by the process`.

6.10 VIRTUAL MEMORY

The primary physical memory on a computer is limited and situations arise when we need to run applications that are larger than the size of the physical memory. Such large applications certainly cannot be entirely accommodated in the physical memory at one go. To execute large applications, a small part of the application is kept in the memory, and the rest of the application, in a special area of the disk known as *swap area*. The application runs through its part, which is present in the memory. When the part of the application that is not present in the memory is required, swapping takes place, *swapping out* the part in the memory to the *swap area* and *swapping in* the required part of the application to the memory. With this swapping procedure, an application that is quite larger than the size of the primary memory can be run giving us the illusion of a large physical memory, hence named virtual memory.

Virtual memory refers to the concept of running applications whose size is larger than that of the primary memory. This is achieved by logically splitting the application into small parts and keeping only the parts currently focused by the user in the memory and the rest on the *swap area* of the disk.

Note: Swap area is a part of the hard disk that is meant for holding swapped pages. Pages, here, refer to the parts or logical pieces of the application.

In the virtual memory technique, an application is assigned a virtual address space, which is a block of memory addresses. When a part of the application is supposed to run, its virtual memory space is mapped to the physical address space (swapping in from the swap area to the physical memory). The process of mapping is performed for each part of the application that is swapped in. The task of mapping virtual memory space into the physical address space is done through the memory management unit (MMU), a part of the CPU. All memory calls between the CPU and the main memory go through the MMU where they are translated from virtual addresses to physical addresses and vice versa.

Virtual memory is implemented in one of the following two ways:

1. Paging
2. Segmentation

6.10.1 Paging

Each application is assigned a virtual address space. Since the entire application cannot be accommodated in the physical memory at one go, the virtual address space assigned to the application is divided into small chunks known as pages. To accommodate the pages, the physical memory is also divided into sizes equal to the size of the pages. The corresponding range of consecutive addresses in the physical memory is called page frame (refer to Fig. 6.6). In Fig. 6.6, we have assumed that the size of pages and page frames is 4K.

A *page map table* is maintained by the MMU to map the pages in the virtual memory to page frames in the physical memory. Depending on the size of the primary memory, more than one page can be kept in the corresponding page frames of the memory.

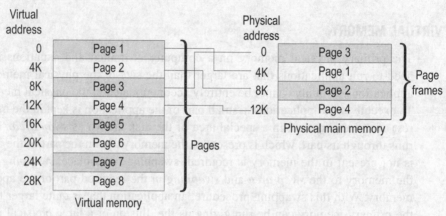

Fig. 6.6　Demonstration of pages and page frames in the virtual and physical main memory

6.10.2 Demand Paging

While executing the application, if a part of the application that is not present in the memory is required, an exception called a page fault is thrown. A page fault represents the specific page (part of the application) demanded by the application. The process of swapping only the demanded page of the application into the physical memory is known as demand paging. In fact, when a page fault occurs, the page in memory is swapped out to the swap area and the required page is swapped into the memory. The page that has to be swapped out is determined on the basis of the algorithm being used (LRU, LFU, FIFO, etc.) by the operating system. Contrary to demand paging is anticipatory paging, in which the operating system anticipates the pages that might be required next by the application, and hence copies them to the physical memory before they are actually required.

Since the application is assigned a virtual address space, the addresses that the application generates are known as virtual addresses. The virtual addresses used by the application are mapped to the physical addresses using the *page map table*. The virtual address space assigned to the application is divided into pages, hence the virtual addresses generated by the application comprises a page number and an offset shown in Fig. 6.7.

In Fig. 6.7, 'p' represents the page number and 'd' represents the offset, that is, 'p' represents the sequence number of the page and 'd' represents the relative address in the page

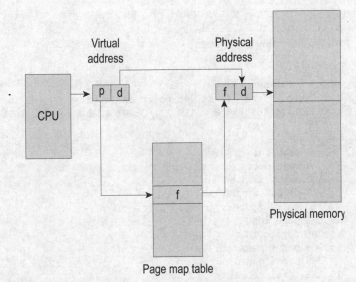

Fig. 6.7 Mapping virtual address to physical address using page map table.

from the base of that page. The page map table of the memory management unit (MMU) translates the page number to the corresponding frame number.

Now let us look at the command to view the virtual memory of our computer system.

vmstat: Fetching virtual memory information

vmstat displays the virtual memory activity since the computer system was booted.

Syntax   vmstat [-c] [-i] [-s] [-S] [interval]

The explanation of the syntax is as follows:
-c displays the number of cache flushed since booting.
-i displays the number of interrupts per device.
-s displays the total number of system events since booting.
-S displays swapping information.
Interval displays the virtual memory information after every interval second.

When used without options, the vmstat command displays a summary of the virtual memory activity since booting. The output of the vmstat command is shown in Fig. 6.8.

```
$ vmstat
 kthr        memory          page          disk        faults      cpu
 r b w   swap    free  re mf pi po fr de sr cd -- -- --   in   sy   cs us sy id
 0 0 0 1926992 1634216 106 321 112 1 1 0 211 13 0 0    0  372 1678 722    4  3 93

$ vmstat -c
vmstat: This machine does not have a virtual address cache

$ vmstat -i
interrupt    total    rate
------------------------
clock        153429    100
```

Fig. 6.8 vmstat command run with different options   *(Contd)*

```
SUNW,aud          7      0
--------------------------
Total         153436    100

$ vmstat
 kthr      memory            page            disk          faults      cpu
 r b w   swap    free  si so pi po fr de sr cd -- -- --   in   sy   cs us sy id
 0 0 0 1926136 1633396 0 0 110 1 1 0 207 13 0 0  0 372 1651  713   4  3 93

$ vmstat -s
        0 swap ins
        0 swap outs
        0 pages swapped in
        0 pages swapped out
   495765 total address trans. faults taken
    15021 page ins
      149 page outs
    43369 pages paged in
      288 pages paged out
   162152 total reclaims
   162150 reclaims from free list
        0 micro (hat) faults
   495765 minor (as) faults

$ vmstat 3
 kthr      memory            page            disk          faults      cpu
 r b w   swap    free  re  mf  pl po fr de sr cd -- -- --   in   sy   cs us sy id
 0 0 0 1922736 1630140  96 295 103 1 1 0 191 12 0 0  0 371 1550   676  4  3 93
 0 0 0 1882356 1591560   3   9   0 0 0 0   0  0 0 0  0 350  218   228  0  0 99
 0 0 0 1882356 1591600   0   0   0 0 0 0   0  0 0 0  0 347  185   223  0  0 99
 0 0 0 1882356 1591600   0   0   0 0 0 0   0  0 0 0  0 348  218   222  0  1 99
 0 0 0 1882356 1591600   0   3   0 0 0 0   0  0 0 0  0 360  401   315  1  1 99
 0 0 0 1882028 1591448   0  29   1 0 0 0   0  0 0 0  0 396 1010   515  2  1 98
 2 0 0 1879640 1589884   0 186   0 0 0 0   0  9 0 0  0 397 1226   528  3  1 96
 0 0 0 1879636 1589148   0   0   8 0 0 0   0  1 0 0  0 426 1518   697  3  1 96
 0 0 0 1879636 1589148   0   0   0 0 0 0   0  0 0 0  0 364  370   305  0  5 95
 0 0 0 1879200 1588688 112 540   1 0 0 0   0  1 0 0  0 415 4065  1003 26  4 70
```

Fig. 6.8 *(Contd)*

6.10.3 Segmentation

The concept of virtual memory in a computer system is applied in two ways, paging and segmentation. Paging, as discussed in Section 6.10.1 is implemented by dividing the memory into pages of equal size. On the other hand, segmentation is implemented by assigning segments or blocks of memory of variable size to the desired process with gaps between the segments. A process may have one or more segments. In fact, the process address space consists of different segments such as the main code segment, the functions segment, the library code segment, the table segment, and the stack segment.

In segmentation, memory blocks can be of variable sizes. For example, if one segment is of 1024 bytes, then the others can be of 2048 bytes, 512 bytes, etc. In addition, their addresses are not contiguous because they are referenced through the following formula:

```
virtual_address = (s_no, addr)
```

Here, s_no is the segment number and addr is the address within the segment.

Hence, in segmentation, address spaces are not contiguous enabling segments to expand or compress without any fear of overwriting the content of the next segment in sequence.

6.10.4 Memory-mapped Input/Output

Memory-mapped I/O is a method used to perform an I/O operation between the CPU and I/O devices (i.e., peripheral devices). Basically, a computer has two buses: memory bus and I/O bus. The memory bus is used for implementing communication with the memory (physical RAM) and the I/O bus for accessing and managing operations with the I/O devices. In memory mapped I/O, both the I/O devices and memory use the same address bus. In other words, the address in the address bus can refer to a region that can belong to both the RAM as well as the I/O device. The benefit of using the memory mapped I/O is that the same CPU instruction for accessing physical memory can also be used to access I/O devices. The drawback of using this approach is that the address space meant for accessing physical memory is reduced as a region of address space is reserved for I/O devices.

Thus, a process that is created by a system call, fork, undergoes different transition states during its life cycle. It can be scheduled to run at a specific date and time through different commands. The execution of a process can be controlled, suspended, and killed as desired. Different notifications can be passed to a process in the form of signals. In order to run larger processes in the small primary memory, the concept of virtual memory has been implemented in the operating system.

■ SUMMARY ■

1. An executing program is known as a process. In a time-sharing system, every process gets a time slot in which it undergoes execution. Every process is assigned a unique identification number known as process identifier (PID).

2. The system processes are also known as daemons and they keep running continuously in the background.

3. The crontab file used to schedule processes is stored in the /usr/spool/cron/crontabs directory. Using the crontab command, a crontab file is created with our login name in the /usr/spool/cron/crontabs directory. To remove the crontab file, we use the crontab -r command.

4. The first process in the Unix system, also known as process 0, is created during bootstrapping. The init process has PID 1 and is the ancestor of all other processes.

5. The getty process enables users to log in to the Unix system.

6. A process includes three segments: text, data, and stack.

7. The process state indicates if the process is in ready, running, waiting, sleeping, or zombie mode.

8. Parent process identifier (PPID) represents the identifier of the parent process that created the process.

9. Files are internally represented by inodes that are maintained in the inode table.

10. When a process opens or creates a file, a corresponding file descriptor is returned by the kernel.

11. The *ready to run swapped out state* represents the state when the process is ready to run and is kept on secondary storage. In such a state, the process waits for the swapper to swap it into the main memory before the scheduler can schedule it to execute.

12. The pre-empted state refers to the state when the kernel suspends or pre-empts the current process to schedule a higher priority process.

13. The zombie state represents a state when a process

is terminated, but keeps the resources allocated to it and does not declare its termination status to its parent process.

14. The tasks conducted while process switching, that is, saving the state of the current process and loading the saved state of the new process is known as context switching.

15. A thread is the smallest unit of processing. A process can have one or more threads. A thread has its own independent flow of control as long as its parent process exists and dies if the parent process dies.

16. The zombie process is a process that has completed execution and is currently dead but still occupies an entry in the process table, waiting for the process that started it to read its exit status.

17. A signal is a technique of informing or sending notifications to a process or thread of a particular event that requires immediate action. Each signal has a default action associated with it. The default action can be changed for certain signals to take different actions.

18. Virtual memory refers to the concept of running applications larger than the size of the primary memory. In the virtual memory technique, an application is assigned a virtual address space, which is a block of memory addresses.

19. To accommodate the pages of the application, the physical memory is split into chunks known as page frames.

20. The process of swapping only the demanded page of the application into physical memory is known as demand paging.

21. In paging, the pages are of fixed sizes and are contiguous too, that is, one page follows the other without any gap in the virtual address space. In segmentation, on the other hand, blocks of memory of variable size are assigned to the process with gaps of empty memory blocks between the segments.

22. Memory-mapped I/O is a method that is used to perform the I/O operation between the CPU and the I/O devices, that is, peripheral devices.

■ FUNCTION SPECIFICATION ■

Command	Function
ps	It is used to know the process status. The command also gives information on system processes, and processes generated by a user and from a particular terminal.
fg	It is used for switching a background job to the foreground.
bg	It is used for switching a foreground job to the background.
kill	It is used for terminating a job or a process.
jobs	It is used to know the status of the background jobs.

Command	Function
cron	It is a daemon that gets activated every minute.
at	It is used for executing Unix commands at a specific date and time.
batch	It is used for specifying the collection of commands we want to execute when the system load permits.
nohup	It is used for ensuring that the background jobs keep running even if we log out of the system.
nice	It is used for increasing and decreasing the priority of a process.

■ EXERCISES ■

Objective-type Questions

State True or False

6.1 In the Unix system, there may be several processes running in the memory at a time.

6.2 Every process in the Unix operating system gets a time slice in which it undergoes execution.

6.3 Unix creates the first process with a PID of 1.

6.4 We cannot know about the processes created

from a particular terminal.

6.5 We can switch a background job to the foreground but the vice versa is not possible.

6.6 We can execute a process in the background by adding ampersand symbol (&) after the command.

6.7 The job number should be prefixed by the percent sign (%) while specifying it in suspending, resuming, and terminating background jobs.

6.8 The daemon `cron` gets activated every hour.

6.9 The `crontab` command creates a crontab file with our login name.

6.10 The jobs scheduled using the `at` command have to be rescheduled after their execution.

6.11 The jobs executed through the `batch` command run when the system load permits.

6.12 By decreasing the *nice* value of a command, we

decrease its priority.

6.13 Processes are only created while bootstrapping and cannot be created later.

6.14 The boot program loads the kernel.

6.15 The `init` process is the ancestor of all other processes.

6.16 The process that calls the `fork` is known as a child process and the process that is created is known as a parent process.

6.17 A process includes three segments: text, data, and stack.

6.18 The process table holds information that is private to the process.

6.19 Per process region table defines the mapping from the virtual to the physical addresses.

6.20 A region is a continuous area of a process's address space.

Fill in the Blanks

6.1 It is the job of _____ to decide which process has to be submitted to the CPU for action.

6.2 Every process is assigned a unique identification number known as _____.

6.3 The command to know the status of the processes running in a Unix system is_____.

6.4 The command used to see the list of system processes running in a Unix system is_____.

6.5 To suspend a running foreground job, we press _____.

6.6 To resume a suspended foreground job, we give the _____ command.

6.7 The command _____ is used to know the job status.

6.8 The crontab file is stored in the _____ directory.

6.9 The command used to remove the crontab file is _____.

6.10 The _____ command is used to keep the background jobs running even if we log out of the system.

6.11 The default nice value of a process is _____.

6.12 The command used to terminate a process is _____.

6.13 The _____ is an array of structures that contains an entry per process.

6.14 The term PCB stands for _____.

6.15 The _____represents the identifier of the parent process that created the process.

6.16 Program counter keeps the address of the _____ instruction to be executed by a process.

6.17 Files are internally represented by _____, which are maintained in the _____.

6.18 The _____ table keeps track of the files that are opened by the process.

6.19 When a process opens or creates a file, its _____ is returned by the kernel.

6.20 _____ state represents the state when the process is ready to run and is kept on secondary storage.

Multiple-choice Questions

6.1 The process in the Unix system that is created during bootstrapping is
(a) process 1   (c) process 0
(b) `init`   (d) `getty`

6.2 PID stands for
(a) process identification

(b) process is done
(c) parent input daemon
(d) performance is developing

6.3 A process includes three segments: text, data, and
(a) CPU   (c) scheduler
(b) queue   (d) stack

6.4 A process swapped to secondary storage and waiting for an event to occur is said to be
   (a) sleeping, swapped   (c) waiting
   (b) zombie   (d) secondary

6.5 When a higher priority process is to be executed, the current process is
   (a) terminated
   (b) swapped out
   (c) pre-empted
   (d) mailed to a colleague for processing

6.6 The smallest unit of processing is a
   (a) process   (c) bit
   (b) byte   (d) thread

6.7 A zombie process waits for its parent process to read its

   (a) PID
   (b) file descriptor table
   (c) exit status
   (d) U area file system

6.8 If a signal is delivered more than once, we say it is
   (a) queued   (c) flooded
   (b) not queued   (d) killed

6.9 The blocked signals of a process are represented by an array known as
   (a) blocked array   (c) signal mask
   (b) signal array   (d) masked array

6.10 The table that maps the virtual address to the physical address is known as
   (a) virtual table   (c) translation table
   (b) address table   (d) page map table

Programming Exercises

6.1 What are the following commands expected to do?
   (a) `$ ps -ef`
   (b) `$fg`
   (c) `$ bg %3`
   (d) `$ crontab -r`
   (e) `$ at -l`
   (f) `$ nice -n 10 sort mbacourse.txt`
   (g) `$ kill -9 10115`
   (h) Pressing Ctrl-c keys on the keyboard
   (i) Pressing Ctrl-z keys on the keyboard
   (j) Pressing Ctrl-\ keys on the keyboard

6.2 Write the commands for the following tasks:
   (a) To get the list of the processes of all users who are logged in to the system
   (b) To get complete information of the processes created by the user, charles
   (c) To get the list of system generated processes that are running at the current instant
   (d) To suspend a foreground job
   (e) To resume the suspended job
   (f) To stop a background job with job number 5

   (g) To terminate a background job with job number 5
   (h) To display all the jobs with their job numbers and current status
   (i) To schedule the job of sorting a file mbacourse.txt on the 5th day of every month at 10:30
   (j) To schedule the job of deleting all files with extension .bak on 1 January and 1 July every year
   (k) To see the list of commands supplied to the `crontab` file
   (l) To execute the shell file `message.sh` on 10 February at 4 p.m.
   (m) To execute the commands in the shell file, `message.sh`, in a batch
   (n) To sort the file, `mbacourse.txt`, in the background and ensure that the process is not terminated even if we log out of the system
   (o) Increase the priority of a command that sorts the file `mbacourse.txt`

Review Questions

6.1 Explain the following commands with examples:
   (a) `kill`   (d) `batch`
   (b) `crontab`   (e) `nohup`
   (c) `at`

6.2 Explain how the priority of a job can be changed.

6.3 Explain the difference between foreground and background jobs and how switching between them takes place.

6.4 What is a process and how can we know the status of a process running in a Unix system?

6.5 Explain the following terms related to a process:
(a) Process table   (c) Region table
(b) U area   (d) Zombie process

6.6 Explain the different states of a process.

6.7 Compare threads with processes.

6.8 What is the benefit of virtual memory and how is it implemented? Explain the role of page map table.

6.9 Explain the role of the following:
(a) Process control subsystem
(b) `cron` daemon in process scheduling

6.10 Explain the following:
(a) What are signals and their types?
(b) What are the two functions that are commonly used to send signals?

6.11 How does the `signal()` function perform signal handling? Explain with a running code.

Brain Teasers

6.1 If a new process is created and there is not enough primary memory, which state will it go into?

6.2 Assume that a process is asleep in the memory state waiting for an event to occur and that event happens. Which state will the process now switch to?

6.3 Why is communication and data sharing among threads faster than processes?

6.4 Correct the following command to view the list of processes of user, `chirag`:
`$ ps -f chirag`

6.5 Correct the error in the following statement: Virtual address comprises frame number and offset.

6.6 Correct the error in the following statement: In segmentation, the pages are of fixed size and are contiguous; hence, when a page expands, it results in overwriting of the content of the next page.

6.7 Correct the error in the following statement: When an application generates a virtual address that is not present in the physical memory, an exception is thrown, which is known as virtual fault.

■ ANSWERS TO OBJECTIVE-TYPE QUESTIONS ■

State True or False

6.1	True
6.2	True
6.3	False
6.4	False
6.5	False
6.6	True
6.7	True
6.8	False
6.9	True
6.10	True
6.11	True
6.12	False
6.13	False
6.14	True
6.15	True
6.16	False
6.17	True
6.18	False
6.19	True
6.20	True

Fill in the Blanks

6.1	scheduler
6.2	process identifier (PID)
6.3	ps
6.4	ps -e
6.5	Ctrl-z
6.6	fg
6.7	jobs
6.8	/usr/spool/
	cron/crontabs
6.9	crontab -r
6.10	nohup
6.11	20
6.12	kill
6.13	process table
6.14	process control block
6.15	parent process identifier (PPID)
6.16	next
6.17	inodes, inode table
6.18	user file descriptor
6.19	file descriptor
6.20	ready to run, swapped out

Multiple-choice Questions

6.1	(c)
6.2	(a)
6.3	(d)
6.4	(a)
6.5	(c)
6.6	(d)
6.7	(c)
6.8	(a)
6.9	(c)
6.10	(d)

System Calls

After studying this chapter, the reader will be conversant with the following:

- The role of system calls in performing different tasks
- Working of system calls related to file handling operations such as the system calls used in opening files, creating files, reading from files, writing to files, relocating file descriptors, closing files, linking to files, deleting files, changing file access permissions, accessing file information, and duplicating file descriptors
- System calls that perform tasks related to directory handling such as changing directory, opening directory, and reading directory
- System calls involved in process handling operations such as the `exec()` system call, the `fork` system call, and the `wait` system call
- Unix library functions and how they differ from system calls
- System calls that deal with memory management—allocating memory, freeing memory, and changing the size of allocated memory
- File locking and record locking, the implementation of read and write locks on the entire file and on small regions of the files, and how these locks compete with each other and might result in a deadlock
- Conditions that result in a deadlock situation and methods to solve the problem

7.1 INTRODUCTION

System calls are special functions that run in kernel mode and allow us to access kernel services. Hence, before we go deeper into understanding system calls, let us take a quick look at the user and kernel modes. You may recall that we have already discussed user and kernel modes in detail in Chapter 6.

7.1.1 Operation Modes

A process can operate in both user mode and kernel mode. While executing instructions, a process operates in the user mode. However, to access a file on the disk, memory, or some peripheral, system calls are used. Thus, to use a system call, the process switches to the kernel mode. Let us now discuss these modes and also understand the difference between them.

7.1.2 Kernel Mode

In kernel mode, the process has complete and unrestricted access to the underlying hardware. It can execute any CPU instruction and reference any memory address. Since the code executed in this mode can access the lowest level and security sensitive functions of the operating system, only trusted codes should be run in this mode, else, it may result in serious security vulnerabilities.

Note: Low-level functions are also known as system calls and are built into the operating system.

7.1.3 User Mode

In user mode, the process runs in restricted mode, that is, there are certain restrictions imposed on it. For example, in user mode, the process cannot access the memory locations used by the kernel, perform input/output (I/O) operations that may alter the global state of the system, or access kernel data structures. Being run in restricted mode (i.e., with limited permissions), the code run in user mode does not result in security vulnerabilities. This implies that it cannot access or overwrite system security related files.

The three common situations that occur when a process switches to the kernel mode from the user mode are as follows:

When an interrupt occurs In this situation, the status of the current running process is stored in the stack and the necessary code is run to serve the interrupt. This switching of modes happens in the kernel mode. After handling the interrupt, the process resumes execution from the place it was interrupted.

When process requires kernel services Kernel services are provided by switching to the kernel mode. If a user process needs to access a file from the disk, use a printer, or manage other peripherals, it needs to switch to the kernel mode. The kernel services are accessed by the respective system calls.

When an exception is raised Exceptions arise when some erroneous statement occurs in the program. The system switches to the kernel mode on the occurrence of an exception.

A system call is basically a request made by our program to the operating system to perform certain tasks such as managing the file system, controlling processes, and performing inter-process communication. The system calls execute the code in the kernel and thus the mode of a process is changed from the user to the kernel mode. The system calls are in the form of functions and are meant for performing all kinds of tasks such as managing files (creating, opening, closing, reading, writing, and deleting files), creating and ending processes, and allowing processes to communicate. There is a system call for each individual operation. In this chapter, we will discuss system calls belonging to the following three categories:

1. File-related system calls
2. Directory handling system calls
3. Process-related system calls

For performing file I/O or any I/O operations there are two completely different sets of functions:

High-level I/O functions High-level I/O functions, also known as standard I/O library functions, are the ones that call one or more low-level I/O functions to do their job because of the simple reason that high-level I/O are built on top of the low-level I/O functions. These functions are more portable and easier to operate when compared to low-level I/O functions. Example of high-level I/O functions include `fread()`, `fopen()`, `fwrite()`, and `fclose()`. These functions access the file through memory buffers, that is, the data is fetched from the file and is written into the file via buffers. The data to be written into the file is initially written into the memory buffer and when the buffer is full, the data is physically written into the disk.

Low-level I/O functions Low-level I/O functions, also known as system calls, are built into the operating system and are the functions on which the high-level functions are built. The low-level I/O functions are also referred to as unbuffered file I/O because the functions do not use any buffers and all the I/O operations are directly applied physically to the specified target (device). Example of low-level I/O functions include `read()`, `open()`, `write()`, and `close()`. The low-level I/O are part of the operating system and are executed in the system kernel. As a result, these functions have greater control over the system resources.

7.2 FILE-RELATED SYSTEM CALLS

As the name suggests, the system calls falling in this category help in performing file management tasks such as opening a file, reading file content, writing into the file, setting file pointer location, and duplicating file descriptors. Table 7.1 provides a list of all file-related system calls along with their functions. We will learn about each of these in detail in the following sections.

Table 7.1 File-related system calls

System call	Description
`open(filename, flags, mode)`	Opens a file with the specified flags and mode
`create(filename, mode)`	Creates a file with the specified mode
`read(fd, buf, n)`	Reads n bytes from an open file into the buffer `buf`
`write(fd, buf, n)`	Writes n bytes in the buffer `buf` to an open file
`lseek(fd, offset, location)`	Relocates the file descriptor `fd` at the specified offset from the given location
`close(fd)`	Closes an open file with file descriptor `fd`
`mknod(filename, mode, dev)`	Creates a regular file, special file, or directory with the given mode
`dup(fd)`	Makes a duplicate file descriptor `fd`
`dup2(fd1, fd2)`	Duplicates the file descriptor `fd1` with the name `fd2`
`link(f1, f2)`	Creates a link `f2` for the file `f1`
`symlink ()`	Makes a symbolic link to a file
`unlink(filename)`	Removes a link of the given filename
`stat(filename, buf)`	Returns status information of the given filename in the status buffer `buf`

(Contd)

Table 7.1 (*Contd*)

System call	Description
fstat(fd,buf)	Returns status information about the file with the file descriptor fd in the status buffer buf
lstat(symbolic_link,buf)	Returns status of the symbolic link in the buffer buf
access(filename, mode)	Checks for permissions in the given filename
chmod(filename, mode)	Changes the file/directory permissions
chown(filename, ownerID, groupdID)	Changes the owner and group of the given filename
umask(new mask)	Sets the file mode creation mask
ioctl(fd, command, arg)	Controls the functions of the specified devices

7.2.1 open(): Opening Files

The open() system call is used for opening an existing file as well as for creating a new file if it does not exist.

Syntax 1	int open(filename, flag);

Syntax 2	int open(filename, flag, mode);

Here, the first parameter, filename, corresponds to the filename to be opened or created. The second parameter, flag, defines how the file is going to be used. Some commonly used flag values are shown in Table 7.2.

The third parameter, mode, is used to specify the file access permissions for the new file. Commonly used modes are given in Table 7.3.

Table 7.2 Commonly used flag values

Flag	Description
O_RDONLY	Opens the file for reading only
O_WRONLY	Opens the file for writing only
O_RDWR	Opens the file for reading and writing
O_NONBLOCK	Non-blocking access
O_APPEND	Appends to the file
O_CREAT	Creates the file if it does not exist
O_TRUNC	Truncates the file size to 0 deleting older contents
O_EXCL	Opens files in exclusive mode; open() fails if the file already exists
O_SHLOCK	Obtains a shared lock
O_EXLOCK	Obtains an exclusive lock
O_DIRECT	Reduces the cache effects
O_FSYNC	For synchronous writing
O_NOFOLLOW	Does not follow symlink

Table 7.3 Commonly used mode values

Constant name	Description
S_IRWXU	Read, write, and execute permissions for the owner
S_IRUSR	Read permission for the owner
S_IWUSR	Write permission for the owner
S_IXUSR	Execute permission for the owner
S_IRWXG	Read, write, and execute permissions for the group
S_IRGRP	Read permission for the group
S_IWGRP	Write permission for the group
S_IXGRP	Execute permission for the group
S_IRWXO	Read, write, and execute permissions for others
S_IROTH	Read permission for others
S_IWOTH	Write permission for others
S_IXOTH	Execute permission for others

Here, RWX refers to read, write, and execute permissions, respectively.

The first syntax (Syntax1) is for opening an existing file and the second syntax (Syntax 2) is for creating a new file if it does not exist. Both formats return an integer called the *file descriptor*. The file descriptor is then used for reading from and writing into the file. If the file cannot be opened or created, the system call returns −1.

> **Note:** File descriptor—The kernel refers to any open file through a file descriptor. It is a non-negative integer that ranges from 0 through OPEN_MAX, the total number of files a process can open. OPEN_MAX is an operating system parameter with a default value of 4096. A file descriptor initially points to the beginning of the file and can be relocated in a file. The location of the file descriptor indicates the position in the file from where the next read or write operation may begin.

Examples

(a) `fp = open("xyz.txt", O_RDONLY);`

This command opens the file `xyz.txt` for a read only purpose. The file is opened and the file descriptor is assigned to `fp`.

(b) `fp = open("xyz.txt", O_CREAT|O_RDWR, S_IRWXU);`

This command creates the file `xyz.txt` for reading as well as writing purposes with read, write, and execute permissions only to the owner. The file descriptor of the created file is assigned to `fp`.

7.2.2 create(): Creating Files

The system call used for creating files is `create()`. It is not very popularly used as the files can be created through an `open()` system call too. The syntax for using this system call is as follows:

> Syntax   `int create(filename, mode)`

Here, `filename` is the name of the new file and `mode` defines the file's access permissions. `mode` refers to read, write, and execute permissions for the owner, group, and others, respectively. If the filename specified in the function does not exist, it is created with the specified mode. If the file already exists, its earlier contents will be deleted. The mode used in this system call is same as that discussed in Section 7.2.1.

> Example   `fp = create("xyz.txt", S_IRWXU);`

This command creates the file `xyz.txt` with read, write, and execute permissions for only the owner. The file descriptor of the newly created file is assigned to `fp`.

7.2.3 read(): Reading from Files

The system call for reading from a file is `read()`. The following is the syntax for using this system call:

> Syntax   `ssize_t read(int fd, void *buf, int size);`

Here, the first parameter, `fd`, is the file descriptor of the file that is returned from the `open()` or `create()` system calls. The second parameter `*buf` is a pointer pointing to the memory location where the data read from the file will be stored. The last parameter, `size`, specifies the number of bytes that we want to read from the file. The system call returns the number of bytes that are actually read from the file.

Example

The following segment of code reads up to 1024 bytes from the file, xyz.txt:

```
int n = 0;
int fp = open("xyz.txt", O_RDONLY);
void *buf = (char *) malloc(1024);
n = read(fp, buf, 1024);
```

In the aforementioned example, the file xyz.txt is opened in the read only mode and the file descriptor is assigned to a variable, fp. The file descriptor, fp, initially points to the beginning of the file. We set the size of the buffer buf (where data read from the file will be stored) to 1024 bytes. Finally, read() system call is invoked to read the said number of bytes from the file. The actual count of the number of bytes read from the file is assigned to the variable n.

Each file has a file descriptor that indicates the location in the file from where the next read or write operation will begin. The file descriptor automatically increments the number of bytes read from the file through the read() system call. In the aforementioned example, if the offset was zero before the read() call, and it actually reads 1024 bytes, then the offset will remain 1024 when the read() call returns.

7.2.4 write(): Writing to Files

The system call write() is used for writing the given content to a file. The syntax for using the system call is as follows:

Syntax   ssize_t write(int fd, void *buf, int size);

It writes the number of bytes, size, to the file pointed by file descriptor fd from the buffer pointed by *buf. The write operation starts at the location pointed to by the file descriptor fd. After the write operation, the file descriptor fd advances by the number of bytes that were successfully written. The function returns the actual number of bytes that are written into the file. If the system call fails, it returns a value −1.

Examples

(a)
```
int n = 0;
int fp = open("xyz.txt", O_CREAT|O_WRONLY|O_TRUNC, S_IRWXU);
n = write(fp, "Hello World!", 13);
```

In this example, the file xyz.txt is created in the write only mode; its earlier content, if any, is deleted and the owner of the file is given all the three—read, write, and execute—permissions for the newly created file. The file descriptor of the file is assigned to a variable, fp. The file descriptor fp initially points to the beginning of the file. Using the write() system call, we write the text Hello World! comprising 13 bytes (including the NULL character) into the file. If the write() call is successful, the count of the number of bytes written into the file is assigned to the variable n.

We have learnt about the read() and write() system calls. For understanding the practical implementation of these two system calls, let us write a program that involves the use of both these calls.

(b) The following program emulates the copy utility where two filenames are specified and the content from the first filename will be read and written into another filename.

```
copyemul.c
#include <sys/stat.h>
#include <fcntl.h>

main(int argc, char *argv[])
{
  int fd1, fd2;
  char buf[1024];
  long int n;

  if((fd1 = open(argv[1], O_RDONLY)) == -1)
  {
     perror("Source file does not exists ");
     exit(1);
  }
  if((fd2 = open(argv[2], O_CREAT|O_WRONLY|O_TRUNC, S_IRWXU)) == -1)
  {
     perror("Problem in creating the target file ");
     exit(1);
  }
  while((n=read(fd1, buf, 1024)) > 0)
  {
     if(write(fd2, buf, n) != n){
            perror("Error in writing into the target file");
            exit(2);
     }
  }
  close(fd1);
  close(fd2);
}
```

Output

```
$ gcc copyemul.c -o copyemul

$ cat xyz.txt
This is a test file

$ ./copyemul xyz.txt pqr.txt

$ cat pqr.txt
This is a test file
```

We can see in the aforementioned program that the first command line argument following the command script is considered the file from which we want to read the content. Hence, the file represented by the first command line argument is opened in the read only mode and its file descriptor is assigned to fd1. Similarly, the file represented by the following command line argument is considered to be the one into which we want to copy the content, hence it is opened in the write only mode. Its earlier content is truncated and read, write, and execute permissions for the owner are assigned to that file. The file descriptor of the second file is assigned to `fd2`. An error message will be displayed on the screen through the `perror()` function (described in Section 7.8.2) if an error occurs while opening either file. Once the two files are opened in the respective modes, through a `while` loop, a chunk of 1024 bytes is read from the first file, filled into the buffer `buf` and is written into the second file. The process continues until the first file is completed, thereby copying all the content of the first file into the second file. Again, an error message will be displayed if anything goes wrong in the reading or writing process. Finally, the two files are closed.

7.2.5 `lseek()`: Relocating File Descriptors

The file descriptor of the file initially points to the beginning of the file and indicates the location from where the next byte has to be read or written into the file. Through the `lseek()` call, we can relocate the file descriptor to any location in the file. It hence allows us to access a file randomly. In other words, a file descriptor is an integer value that represents the number of bytes from the beginning of the file and its value represents the location from where the next read or write operation can occur in the file. The syntax for using the `lseek()` system call is as follows:

Syntax   `long lseek(int fd, long offset, int location)`

A brief introduction of the arguments of this call is given in Table 7.4.

Table 7.4   Brief description of the arguments of `lseek()` call

Argument	Description
`fd`	This represents a file descriptor.
`Offset`	This represents the number of bytes that we want the file descriptor to move from the position represented by `location`.
`location`	This indicates whether the offset should be located relative to the beginning of the file (SEEK_SET or 0), from the current position of the file descriptor (SEEK_CUR or 1), or from the end of the file (SEEK_END or 2). The attributes, SEEK_SET, SEEK_CUR, and SEEK_END are represented by the constants 0, 1, and 2, respectively. The attribute SEEK_SET sets the file descriptor at the offset bytes *from* the beginning of the file; the value SEEK_CUR sets the file descriptor at its current location plus the *offset* bytes; and the value SEEK_END sets the file descriptor at the *offset* from the end of file.

If successful, `lseek()` returns a long integer that defines the location of the file descriptor measured in bytes from the beginning of the file. If unsuccessful, the position of the file descriptor does not change.

Examples

(a) The following example sets file descriptor `fd` at the 10th byte from the beginning of the file.
    `lseek(fd, 10, SEEK_SET);`
(b) The following example sets file descriptor `fd` at the last byte of the file.
    `lseek(fd, 0, SEEK_END);`
(c) The following example sets file descriptor `fd` at the 5th byte from the end of the file.
    `lseek(fd, -5, SEEK_END);`

7.2.6 `close()`: Closing Files

The `close()` system call is used for closing opened files.

Syntax `int close(int fd);`

To close a file, we pass its file descriptor to the `close()` system call. If successful, the call returns the value 0 and otherwise returns the value −1. On closing a file, the kernel releases all the resources used by it, provided no other file descriptor is still associated with it.

Example

The following example closes the file represented by the file pointer `fd`.

`close(fd);`

We will now write a program that makes use of all the system calls that we have seen till now.

The following program uses the system calls `open()`, `read()`, `lseek()`, `write()`, and `close()`. The program requires two filenames, which are passed as command line arguments, and the content of the first filename is read and written in reverse order into another file.

`openreadcall.c`

```c
#include <stdio.h>
#include <fcntl.h>
#include <sys/stat.h>

main(int argc, char *argv[])
{
    int fd1, fd2;
    char c;
    long int i=0, totalbytes=0;
    fd1=open(argv[1], O_RDONLY);
    fd2=open(argv[2], O_CREAT|O_WRONLY|O_TRUNC, S_IRWXU);
    while(read(fd1, &c, 1)>0)
        totalbytes++;
    while(++i <= totalbytes){
        lseek(fd1, -i, SEEK_END);
        read(fd1, &c, 1);
        write(fd2, &c, 1);
    }
    close(fd1);
    close(fd2);
}
```

Output

```
$ cat xyz.txt
This is a test file

$ ./openreadcall xyz.txt xyzreverse.txt
$ cat xyz.txt
This is a test file
```

```
$ cat xyzreverse.txt
elif tset a si sihT
```

We can see from the aforementioned program that the first command line argument following the command script that represents the file from which we want to read the content, is opened in the read only mode and its file descriptor is assigned to fd1. Similarly, the file represented by the following command line argument is considered to be the one into which we want to copy the content of the first file after reversing it. Hence it is opened in the write only mode; its earlier contents are truncated and the read, write, and execute permissions for the owner are assigned to that file. The file descriptor of the second file is assigned to fd2. Thereafter, we find the length or the total number of bytes in the first file by reading each of its characters and incrementing a counter, *totalbytes*, with every character that is read. Next, the file descriptor in the first file is positioned at the last character position through the lseek() system call and its last character is read and written into the second file. Again, the file descriptor is positioned at the second-last character position in the first file; this second-last character is read and written into the second file and the process continues until all the characters from the first file are written into the second file in reverse order. Finally, the two files are closed.

Table 7.5 Symbolic constants that represent different file types

Name	Description
S_IFIFO	FIFO-pipe
S_IFCHR	Character-oriented file
S_IFDIR	Directory
S_IFBLK	Block-oriented file
S_IFREG	Regular

Table 7.6 Symbolic constants representing the permissions for the new file

Name	Description
S_ISUID	Set user ID
S_ISGID	Set group ID
S_IRWXU	Read, write, and execute permissions for the owner
S_IRUSR	Read permission for the owner
S_IWUSR	Write permission for the owner
S_IXUSR	Execute permission for the owner
S_IRWXG	Read, write, and execute permissions for the group
S_IRGRP	Read permission for the group
S_IWGRP	Write permission for the group
S_IXGRP	Execute permission for the group
S_IRWXO	Read, write, and execute permissions for others
S_IROTH	Read permission for others
S_IWOTH	Write permission for others
S_IXOTH	Execute permission for others

7.2.7 mknod(): Creating Files

The system call, mknod(), is used to create a new regular, directory, or special file.

```
int mknod(const char *path, mode_t mode, dev_t dev);
```

Here, path represents the name of the file to be created; mode represents the file type of the newly created file; and dev represents the major and minor device numbers if the file to be created is a device file (character or block-oriented file).

The mode can be any of the following symbolic constants given in Table 7.5.

The mode parameter has the associated permissions that are OR'ed (connected with the OR operator, i.e., '|' operator) with the symbolic constants of the file types shown in Table 7.5. The permissions for the new file are represented by the symbolic constants shown in Table 7.6.

The dev parameter is ignored if the file type is not a character or block-oriented type. When successful, the method returns 0, otherwise it returns a value –1.

Example The following example creates a regular file, by the name stock.txt with read, write, and execute permissions to the *user* (owner) and only read permissions to the *group* and *other* users.

```
int   flag;
flag = mknod("stock.txt", S_IFREG | S_IRWXU| S_IRGRP | S_IROTH, 0);
```

In this example, the last parameter, dev, is ignored as it is a regular file and flag is assigned the returned status of the system call.

The following example creates a FIFO file with the name letter.txt that assigns read, write, and execute permissions to the user (owner), and read and execute permissions to the group and other users.

```
int   flag;
flag = mknod("letter.txt", S_FIFO | 0755, 0);
```

Again, the last parameter, dev, is ignored in the aforementioned statement as the file is a FIFO file.

7.2.8 dup() and dup2(): Duplicating File Descriptors

The dup system call is used for duplicating a file descriptor. You may recall that file descriptors are used for accessing files. Having more than one file descriptor for the same file necessitates a single file pointer to be shared by all file descriptors. It also means that an open file can be accessed or shared by several processes simultaneously. Hence, the dup system call duplicates the file descriptor fd returning a new descriptor. The dup2 system call copies one file descriptor to another specified file descriptor.

Syntax `int dup(int fd);`

Syntax `int dup2(int fd, int fd2);`

The dup system call returns the file descriptor that points to the same file as the fd descriptor. The dup2 system call makes the file descriptor fd2 point to the same file that the file descriptor fd is pointing at.

The system calls return or copy the file descriptor if successful and return a value of –1 otherwise.

Example

The following example demonstrates the use of dup() and dup2() system calls.

```
dupcall.c

#include <fcntl.h>

main()
{
    int fd1, fd2, fd3,fd4;
```

```
fd1 = open( "xyz.txt", O_RDWR | O_TRUNC );  /* file xyz.txt is opened and is
                                               represented by file descriptor fd1 */
fd2 = open( "pqr.txt", O_RDWR | O_TRUNC ); /* file pqr.txt is opened and is
                                              represented by file descriptor, fd2 */
write( fd1, "Hello", 6 );  /* The text, Hello is written in file xyz.txt */

write( fd2, "World", 6 );  /* The text, World is written in file pqr.txt */

fd3 = dup(fd1);  /* The file descriptor fd3 is set to point at the file where file
                    descriptor fd1 is pointing i.e. at file xyz.txt */

write( fd3, "Thanks", 7 );  /* The text, Thanks is written in the file xyz.txt */

fd4=dup(fd2);  /* The file descriptor fd4 is set to point at the file where file
                  descriptor fd2 is pointing i.e. at file pqr.txt */

dup2(fd1,fd2); /* The file descriptor leaves the file pqr.txt where it was earlier
                  pointing and is set to point at the file where file descriptor, fd1
                  is pointing i.e. at file xyz.txt */

close(fd1);  /* Close file with file descriptor fd1 */
close(fd4);  /* Close file with file descriptor fd4 */
}
```

Output

```
$ cat xyz.txt
This is a test file

$ cat pqr.txt
This is a test file

$ ./dupcall

$ cat xyz.txt
HelloThanks

$ cat pqr.txt
World
```

7.2.9 link() and symlink(): Linking to Files

To link to an existing file, the two system calls used are link() and symlink(). The difference between the two system calls is that while the link() system call creates a hard link, the symlink() system call creates a symbolic link. Table 7.7 shows the difference between a hard link and a symbolic link:

Table 7.7 Differences between hard links and symbolic links

Hard link	Symbolic link
In the case of a hard link, two filenames point to the same inode and the same set of data blocks. A hard link is a pointer to the file's inode.	A symbolic link has its own inode and hence consumes a small amount of disk space. A symbolic link is a file that contains the name of another file. It is like a pointer to the file's contents. Here, one file contains the actual data and the other file only contains the pointer to the first file's content.
A hard link cannot cross a file system, that is, both filenames must be in the same file system. It cannot be created to link a file from one file system to another file on another file system. Hard links only know information related to a particular system and hence cannot span file systems.	Symbolic links are more flexible than hard links. They can span file systems and even computer systems. A symbolic link can be created to link a file on one file system to a file on another file system.
A hard link to a directory cannot be created.	A symbolic link to a directory can be created.
In the case of a hard link, a file can be deleted without affecting the other. The system deletes the directory entry for one filename and leaves the data blocks untouched. The data blocks are only deleted when the link count goes to zero.	With a symbolic link, the two filenames are not the same. Deleting the link leaves the original file untouched but deleting or renaming the original file removes both the filename and the data. As a result, the link becomes useless.

The syntax for the `link()` system call that creates a hard link is as follows:

Syntax   `int link(const char *path1, const char *path2);`

Here, `path1` refers to the original filename and `path2` refers to the alias filename. The link count of the file referred to by `path1` will be incremented by 1.

The `link()` call creates a hard link to a file.

Example   `link("xyz.txt", "abc.txt");`

The file `xyz.txt` will have a hard link by the name `abc.txt`. The link `abc.txt` will be able to show the content of the file `xyz.txt`. If the original file `xyz.txt` is deleted, the link `abc.txt` can still be used to show the content of the file `xyz.txt`.

`link()` will fail and no link will be created if any of the following conditions occurs:

1. The file referenced by `path1` does not exist.
2. The file referenced by `path2` already exists or the directory referenced in `path2` does not have write permission.

The symbolic link is created by the `symlink()` system call. Table 7.7 shows how the symbolic link is different from the hard link that we learnt in Section 7.2.9.

Syntax   `int symlink(const char *path1, const char *path2);`

This syntax creates a symbolic link to the file referenced by `path1` in the name referenced by `path2`. The symbolic links to a file does not increment the file's link count.

We need to have write and execute permissions for the directory that contains the file for which these system calls are executed.

Example   `symlink("xyz.txt", "abc.txt");`

This example creates a symbolic link for the file xyz.txt with the name abc.txt. You may remember that xyz.txt is the file that contains the actual data and the filename abc.txt is just a pointer to the data blocks of xyz.txt. The file abc.txt will show the contents of the file xyz.txt. However, if the file xyz.txt is deleted, the symbolic link abc.txt will become useless, that is, it will lose its content too.

7.2.10 unlink(): Unlinking Files

The system call used for removing a link to a file is unlink():

Syntax   int unlink(const char *path);

The link specified through path is removed and the link count of the file referenced by the link is decremented by 1. When the link count of the file referenced by the link becomes 0 and is not accessed by any process, the file is removed, freeing up any space occupied by it. If the filename is the last link to a file that is still open by a process, the file will exist until the process closes the file. If the supplied path refers to a symbolic link, it is removed without affecting the file that is referenced by the symbolic link. The system call returns a value 0 if the unlinking was successful, and −1 on error.

Example   The following example decrements the link of file xyz.txt by 1. If the link count of the file has become 0, the file is deleted.

```
unlink("xyz.txt");
```

7.2.11 stat(), fstat(), and lstat(): Accessing File Status Information

The system calls that control the usage of files and also return their status information are stat, fstat, and lstat. Their syntax are as follows:

Syntax   int stat(const char *path, struct stat *buf);

Syntax   int fstat(int fd, struct stat *buf);

Syntax   int lstat(const char *path, struct stat *buf);

The meaning of the arguments used in all these three system calls is briefly explained in Table 7.8.

Table 7.8 Brief description of arguments used in stat(), fstat(), and lstat() system calls

Argument	Description
path	Represents the name and the relative or absolute path of the file
fd	Represents the file descriptor of the file
buf	Represents the pointer to the stat structure that contains the status information of the specified file

stat()   It fills the buffer buf with the status information of the specified file.

fstat()   It is same as the stat() system call. Instead of the filename, it accepts the file descriptor and fills the buffer buf with its status information.

lstat()   It returns information about a symbolic link rather than the file that it references. The difference between the stat()

Table 7.9 Brief description of the members of the stat structure

stat members	Description
st_mode	The file permissions and file-type information
st_ino	The inode number of the file
st_dev	The device on which the file resides
st_uid	The user ID of the file owner
st_gid	The group ID of the file owner
st_size	The file size
st_atime	The time the file was last accessed
st_ctime	The time the status of the file last changed permissions—owner, group, or content
st_mtime	The time the file was last modified
st_nlink	The count of the hard links to the file
st_blocks	The number of blocks of size 512 bytes that have been allocated

Table 7.10 Symbolic constants representing different file types

File-type flags	Description
S_IFBLK	Block special device
S_IFDIR	Directory
S_IFCHR	Character special device
S_IFIFO	FIFO—named pipe
S_IFREG	Regular file
S_IFLNK	Symbolic link

Table 7.11 Few of the masks used to test file permissions

Masks	Description
S_IRWXU	User's read/write/execute permissions
S_IRWXG	Group's read/write/execute permissions
S_IRWXO	Others' read/write/execute permissions

Table 7.12 Brief description of the macros used to determine file types

Macros	Description
S_ISBLK()	Test for block special file
S_ISCHR()	Test for character special file
S_ISDIR()	Test for directory
S_ISFIFO()	Test for pipe or FIFO
S_ISREG()	Test for regular file
S_ISLNK()	Test for symbolic link
S_ISSOCK()	Test for socket

and lstat() functions is that, if the specified filename refers to a link, the stat() function returns the information of the file referred by the link, whereas the lstat() function returns the information of the link itself.

The members of the structure, stat, are shown in Table 7.9.

The st_mode flags returned in the stat structure have a number of associated macros. These macros include *permissions* and *file-type* flags and some masks that can be used in testing for specific types and permissions (Table 7.10).

The masks to test file permissions are listed in Table 7.11.

Macros that can be used to determine file types are given in Table 7.12.

For example, to test whether the supplied name through command line arguments belongs to a regular file, directory, symbolic link, or something else, the code is as follows:

```
struct stat statusbuf;
mode_t modes;
stat(argv[1],&statusbuf);
modes = statusbuf.st_mode;
if (S_ISREG(modes)) printf("%s is a
regular file ", argv[1]);
else if (S_ISDIR(buf.st_mode))
printf("%s is a directory ", argv[1]);
...
...
...
```

Example The following example demonstrates the use of the fstat() system call and displays the inode number, size, and number of blocks associated with the file.

```
fstatcall.c
#include <fcntl.h>
#include <sys/stat.h>
```

```
main()
{
    struct stat statusbuf;
    int n, fp;
    fp = open("xyz.txt", O_WRONLY | O_CREAT, S_IREAD | S_IWRITE);
    if(fp == -1) /* Error in opening file */
        exit(-1);
    n = fstat(fp, &statusbuf);
    if(n == -1) /* The system call, fstat failed */
        exit(-1);
    printf("The inode number of the file is = %d\n", statusbuf.st_ino);
    printf("The size of the file is  = %d\n", statusbuf.st_size);
    printf("The number of blocks allocated to the file is = %d\n", statusbuf.st_
blocks);
}
```

Output

```
The inode number of the file is = 39816
The size of the file is  = 13
The number of blocks allocated to the file is = 2
```

Note: Whenever a system call or library function fails, it returns a value ▯1.

7.2.12 access(): Checking Permissions

The access() system call checks whether the user has the permissions to read, write, or perform other tasks on the specified file.

Syntax   `int access(const char *pathname, int mode);`

Here, pathname represents the file whose permissions have to be checked and mode represents the permissions that have to be checked for the file. The mode can be represented by the following symbolic constants:

1. F_OK: Checks whether the file exists
2. R_OK: Checks whether the file has read permission
3. W_OK: Checks whether the file has write permission
4. X_OK: Checks whether the file has execute permission

If we supply the symbolic link instead of filename in the access() system call, then the permissions of the file referred to by the symbolic link will be tested.

On success, that is, if all the requested permissions exist, the system call returns 0. If any requested permission is denied, the system call returns a value −1 and sets the external variable errno that describes the reason for error.

Example   The following program checks whether the file xyz.txt exists in the current directory. In addition, it checks if the user has read, write, or execute permissions for the file.

```
checkfile.c
#include <stdio.h>
#include <unistd.h>

main()
{
  char path[]="xyz.txt";

  if (access(path, F_OK) != 0)
    printf("The file, %s does not exist!\n", path);
  else
  {
    if (access(path, R_OK) == 0)
        printf("You have read access to the file, %s \n", path);
    if (access(path, W_OK) == 0)
        printf("You have write access to the file, %s \n", path);
    if (access(path, X_OK) == 0)
        printf("You have execute permission to the file, %s\n", path);
  }
}
```

Output

```
$ ls -al xyz.txt
-rwxr--r--   1 root   root   20 Feb 22 19:00 xyz.txt

$ ./checkfile
You have read access to the file, xyz.txt
You have write access to the file, xyz.txt
You have execute permission to the file, xyz.txt

$ chmod 544 xyz.txt

$ ls -al xyz.txt
-r-xr--r--   1 root root            20 Feb 22 19:00 xyz.txt

$ ./checkfile
You have read access to the file, xyz.txt
You have execute permission to the file, xyz.txt
```

7.2.13 chown(), lchown(), and fchown(): Changing Owner and Group of Files

To change the owner or group of the given files, the following system calls can be used:

Syntax   int cho wn(const char* filename, uid_t ownerID, gid_t groupID)

          int lchown(const char* filename, uid_t ownerID, gid_t groupID)
          int fchown(int fd, uid_t ownerID, gid_t groupID)

Table 7.13 Brief description of the arguments used in the `chown()`, `lchown()`, and `fchown()` system calls

Argument	Description
filename	Represents the name and relative or absolute path of the file
ownerID	Represents the ID of the owner, i.e., user ID
groupID	Represents the ID of the group
Fd	Represents the file descriptor of the file

The arguments used in the three system calls, `chown()`, `lchown()`, and `fchown()`, are briefly explained in Table 7.13.

The system call `chown()` changes the owner and group IDs of the specified filename to the supplied owner and group IDs, respectively. We substitute the value −1 in the system call for the owner ID or group ID that we want to keep unchanged.

System call `fchown()` is same as `chown()`, the only difference being that instead of the filename, it accepts the file descriptor of the file whose owner/group has to be changed.

The `lchown()` system call is used for changing the owner/group of a symbolic link.

Example   The following example changes the owner and group IDs of the file `xyz.txt` to 101 and 21 respectively. We assume that a user with ID 101 and a group with ID 21 already exist.

```
changeownergroup.c
main()
{
    int a,b,c;
    a = chown("xyz.txt",101, 21 );  /* Changes the owner and group to
                                        101 and 21 respectively */
    if ( a == -1 ) perror("Error in changing Owner ID and Group ID of
       the file xyz.txt");
    b = chown("xyz.txt",101, -1 );  /* Changes the owner of the file to
                                        5 keeping group ID unchanged */
    if ( b == -1 ) perror("Error in changing Owner ID of the file
       xyz.txt");
    c = chown("xyz.txt",-1, 21 );  /* Changes the group of the file to
                                       40 keeping owner ID unchanged */
    if ( c == -1 ) perror("Error in changing Group ID of the file
       xyz.txt");
}
```

Output

```
$ ls -al xyz.txt
-r-xr--r--  1 root  root        20 Feb 23 22:12 xyz.txt
$ ./changeownergroup
$ ls -al xyz.txt
-r-xr--r--  1 101   it          20 Feb 23 22:12 xyz.txt
```

In this example, we can see that the first `chown()` call demonstrates the changing owner as well as group IDs, whereas the second and third `chown()` calls change only the owner ID and group ID respectively. When unsuccessful, the system calls return a value −1, in which case, the error message is displayed via the `perror()` function.

7.2.14 chmod() and fchmod(): Changing Permissions of Files

To change the file/directory permissions for the three types of system users, user (owner), group, and other, the following system calls are used:

Syntax   `int chmod( const char* filename, int mode )`

`int fchmod( int fd, mode_t mode );`

A brief explanation of the arguments used in these system calls is given in Table 7.14.

Table 7.14   Brief description of the arguments used in the `chmod()` and `fchmod()` system calls

Argument	Description
filename	Represents the name of the file including its relative or absolute path
Mode	Represents the permissions that we wish to assign to the file/directory
fd	Represents the file descriptor of the file

Note: The mode parameter can have the values, that is, permissions specified in Table 7.3.

`chmod()` changes the mode (permissions) of the filename to the supplied mode, where the mode is specified as an octal number. Either the owner or super user can change the file's permissions. `fchmod()` works in the same manner as `chmod()` with the exception that it accepts the *file descriptor* of the file whose permissions we wish to change instead of the filename. Both methods return a value 0 when successful and a value −1 otherwise.

Example   The following example changes the permissions of the file `xyz.txt` to 744 (octal), which refers to read, write, and execute permissions for the user, and read permission for the group and other users.

```
changepermission.c
main()
{
  int a;
  a = chmod("xyz.txt", 0744);  /* Assigning r,w and x permissions to
                                  the User and only r permissions to the
                                  Group and Other for the file xyz.txt */
  if ( a==-1 ) perror("Error in changing permissions of the file
    xyz.txt");
}
```

Output
```
$ ls -al xyz.txt
-rw-r--r--   1 root          root          20 Feb 22 19:00 xyz.txt

$ ./changepermission

$ ls -al xyz.txt
-rwxr--r--   1 root          root          20 Feb 22 19:00 xyz.txt
```

7.2.15 umask(): Setting File Mode Creation Mask

The umask() system call sets the file mode creation mask. In simple language, it is a call that defines the default permissions for the files and directories when created. umask is basically used by the open() and mkdir() system calls to define the default permissions for the files and directories being created. The permissions can be specified either in the form of symbolic constants or in the form of a three-digit octal value.

Syntax   mod_t umask (mode_t new mask)

The system call returns the value of the previous mask.

Example   umask(S_IRGRP | S_IWGRP | S_IROTH | S_IWOTH);

          umask(0022);

The permission of the newly created file will be default file access mode -umask. Similarly, the permission of the newly created directory will be default directory access mode -umask.

   The default file access mode is 0666 and the default directory access mode is 0777.

   For example, if the value of umask is set to 0022 and a file is created without specifying the mode (it will have the default access mode, 0666):

```
flag = open("xyz.txt", O_WRONLY | O_TRUNC);
```

Then the newly created file, xyz.txt, will have the following access mode:

```
0666 - 0022 = 0644
```

The following command describes a case where the file is created with the mode 0544:

```
flag = open("xyz.txt", O_WRONLY | O_TRUNC, 0544);
```

The file xyz.txt will then have the following permissions:

```
0544 - 0022 =  0522
```

Similarly, if the value of umask is set to 0077, then the newly created directory will have the following access mode:

```
0777 - 0077 = 0700
```

7.2.16 utime(): Changing Access and Modification Times

The system call utime() is used to change the access and modification times of the specified filename.

Syntax   int utime(const char *filename, struct utimbuf *buf);

Here, filename represents the name of the file along with its relative or absolute path. The parameter buf represents the pointer to the utimbuf structure that contains the actime and modtime fields, which will be used to change the access and modification times of the file(s).

   The fields in the utimbuf structure are as follows:

```
struct utimbuf {
  time_t actime;  /* represents access time */
  time_t modtime; /* represents modification time */
};
```

If successful, the system call returns 0, else returns −1, and sets the errno variable describing the error.

Example The following example opens the file xyz.txt and changes its access and modification times to the system time at which the file was opened.

```
changetimes.c
#include <sys/stat.h>
#include <fcntl.h>
#include <utime.h>
main()
{
  int n, fp;
  struct stat statusbuf;
  struct utimbuf  timebuf;

  fp = open("xyz.txt", O_RDWR | O_TRUNC );
  if(fp == -1) /* Error in opening file */
    exit(-1);
  n = fstat(fp, &statusbuf);
  if(n == -1) /* The system call, fstat failed */
    exit(-1);
  close(fp);
  timebuf.actime  = statusbuf.st_atime;
  timebuf.modtime = statusbuf.st_mtime;
  if (utime("xyz.txt", &timebuf) < 0)      /* Error in changing access
                                              and modification times */
    exit(-1);
}
```

Output

```
$ ls -al xyz.txt
-r-xr--r--  1 101            it           20 Feb 23 22:12 xyz.txt
$ ./changetimes
$ ls -al xyz.txt
-r-xr--r--  1 101            it            0 Mar  1 16:19 xyz.txt
```

7.2.17 ioctl(): Controlling Devices

ioctl() is a system call that is used for controlling the functions of the specified devices.

Syntax int ioctl(int fd, int cmd, int arg)

The function represented by cmd is applied on the device whose file descriptor fd is provided. arg is optional and represents the arguments for the function cmd. The system calls return a value of −1 if unsuccessful.

Example The following example displays the screen height and width.

```
dispscreeninfo.c
#include <stdio.h>
#include <sys/ioctl.h>
#include <termios.h>

main(int argc, char **argv)
{
    struct winsize w;
    ioctl(0, TIOCSWINSZ, &w);
    printf("Screen width is %d and Screen height is %d\n", w.ws_col, w.ws_row);
}
```

Output

```
Screen width is 2053 and Screen height is 3018
```

The command TIOCSWINSZ that fills the information of the screen in the winsize structure sz, is executed. Using the ws_col and ws_row members of the winsize structure, the width and height of the screen are displayed.

The following are the members in the winsize structure.

```
struct winsize
{
unsigned short ws_row;       /* height of the screen i.e. number of rows */
unsigned short ws_col;       /* width of the screen i.e. number of columns */
unsigned short ws_xpixel;    /* width of the screen in terms of pixels */
unsigned short ws_ypixel;    /* height of the screen in pixels */
};
```

7.3 DIRECTORY HANDLING SYSTEM CALLS

The system calls in this category help us deal with the directory stream. We can create a new directory stream, change to any directory stream, read a stream, set our position in the directory stream, etc., via these system calls. The list of directory-related system calls are given in Table 7.15.

Table 7.15 List of directory handling system calls

System call	Description	System call	Description
mkdir(d)	Creates a new directory, d	telldir(d)	Returns the current position in the given directory stream
rmdir (d)	Removes directory d		
chdir(d)	Changes a directory to the specified directory, d	seekdir (d, loc)	Sets the directory entry pointer to the given location, loc, in the given directory stream
getcwd (buf, size)	Writes the name of the current working directory in the buffer of the given size	rewinddir(d)	Resets the position in the given directory stream to the beginning of the directory
opendir(d)	Opens the given directory stream	rename()	Changes the name or location of the file
readdir(d)	Reads the content of directory d	closedir(d)	Closes the given directory stream

7.3.1 `mkdir()` and `rmdir()`: Creating and Removing Directories

The system calls used for making and removing directories are `mkdir` and `rmdir` respectively. Let us first discuss the `mkdir()` system call.

Syntax   `int mkdir(const char *path, mode_t mode);`

This system call makes a new directory with `path` as its name. The permissions of the newly created directory are determined by the `mode` parameter. The permissions are the same as that of the `mode` parameter in the `open()` system call (refer to Table 7.3 for details).

If successful, the `mkdir()` system call returns 0; else it returns −1 if not successful.

Example

```
createdir.c
#include <sys/stat.h>
main()
{
  if (mkdir("/usr/experiments", S_IRWXU | S_IRGRP| S_IROTH) ==-1)
  {
    perror("Error in creating directory");
    exit(-1);
  }
  else
  printf("Directory successfully created");
}
```

Output

```
Directory successfully created
```

In the aforementioned example, the permissions of the newly created directory can also be specified in the octal format, as shown in the following example:

```
mkdir("/usr/experiments", 0744);
```

The system call for removing directories is `rmdir()`. Its syntax is as follows:

Syntax   `int rmdir(const char *path);`

Here, path represents the directory that we wish to remove. The directory will be removed provided it is empty. If successful, the `rmdir()` system call returns 0; if not successful, it returns −1.

Example

```
removedir.c
main()
{
  if (rmdir("/usr/projects") ==-1)
  {
    /* Error in removing projects directory */
    perror("Cannot remove the /usr/projects directory");
    exit(-1);
```

```
   }
   else
      printf("The /usr/projects directory successfully removed");
}
```

Output

```
$ ./removedir
Cannot remove the /usr/projects directory: File exists

$ ls /usr/projects
lockfile.txt pqr.txt xyz.txt

$ rm /usr/projects/*

$ ls /usr/projects

$ ./removedir
The /usr/projects directory successfully removed
```

This example tries to remove the `projects` directory that exists in the `usr` directory and displays an error if the directory could not be deleted.

7.3.2 `chdir()`: Changing Directories

The system call used to change the directory is `chdir()`. The `chdir()` system call changes our working directory to the specified one, that is, from the current working directory, our directory will change to the one whose path is specified. The syntax for using the `chdir()` system call is as follows:

Syntax   `int chdir(const char *path);`

Here, the `path` parameter represents the path of the directory.

Example   The following code changes the directory to the projects directory that exists in the `usr` directory and displays an error if unsuccessful.

```
changedir.c
main()
{
   if (chdir("/usr/projects") != 0)
   {
      perror("Cannot change to the projects directory");
      exit(1);
   }
   else
      printf("Changed to projects directory");
}
```

Output

```
Changed to projects directory
```

Note: For successful execution of the `chdir()` system call, the process must have execute permission for the directory.

Let us look at one more example that takes us to the desired directory by invoking the `chdir()` system call but this time, the call takes the name of the directory through command line arguments.

Example The following program emulates the `cd` command.

```
emulatecd.c
main(int argc,char **argv)
{
    if (argc < 2)
    {
        perror("Insufficient arguments ");
        exit(1);
    }
    if (chdir(argv[1]) != 0)
    {
        perror("Cannot change to the specified directory");
        exit(1);
    }
}
```

Output
```
$ ./emulatecd
Insufficient arguments : Error 0
$ ./emulatecd projects
Cannot change to the specified directory: No such file or directory
$ ./emulatecd accounts
$
```

In this program, we first check if the count of the command line argument is less than 2. If the directory name is not specified after the command line script, an error message, `Insufficient arguments`, is displayed through the `perror()` function and the program terminates setting its exit status as 1. If the command line argument is provided, then through the `chdir()` system call, the location of the current directory is changed to the specified directory. If an error occurs while changing directory, the following error message is displayed via the `perror()` function: `Cannot change to the specified directory`.

7.3.3 getcwd(): Determining Current Working Directory

We can know the current working directory by calling the `getcwd()` system call.

Syntax `char *getcwd(char *buf, size_t size);`

The `getcwd()` function writes the name of the current directory into the specified buffer, `buf`. The function returns `NULL` if the directory name exceeds the size of the buffer defined through the parameter, `size`. When successful, the function returns the buffer `buf` containing the name of the current directory.

Example The following example shows the path of the current working directory.

```
pathcurrentdir.c
#include <stdio.h>
main()
{
  char    buf[50];
  if (chdir("/usr/projects") != 0)
  {
    perror("Cannot change to the projects directory");
    exit(1);
  }
  if (getcwd(buf, 50) == NULL)
  {
    perror("The path of the working directory exceeds 50 characters");
    exit(1);
  }
  printf("Current working directory is %s\n", buf);
}
```

Output

```
Current working directory is /usr/projects
```

7.3.4 opendir( ): Opening Directories

The system call meant to open a directory is opendir(). The opendir() system call opens a directory stream represented by the specified directory name so that its contents can be read through the system call, readdir(). The system call will be able to open up to a total of {OPEN_MAX} files and directories. OPEN_MAX is an operating system parameter and its default value is 4096. On successful execution of opendir(), it returns a pointer to an object of type DIR; else, a NULL pointer is returned and errno is set to indicate the error. The type DIR represents a directory stream, which is an ordered sequence of all the directory entries in a particular directory. The syntax for using the opendir system call is as follows:

Syntax `DIR *opendir(const char *dirname);`

Here, dirname is a string that specifies the name of the directory to open. If the last component of dirname is a symbolic link, the function follows the symbolic link to open the directory referenced by it.

Example The following example opens the directory projects that exists in the usr directory and returns a pointer of type DIR and assigned to mydir.

```
DIR *mydir;
mydir=opendir ("/usr/projects");
```

7.3.5 readdir( ): Reading Directories

The system call used to read the content of a directory is readdir(). The syntax for using the system call is as follows:

Syntax   `struct dirent *readdir(DIR *dirp);`

The system call returns a pointer to a structure, `dirent`, which represents the directory entry at the current position in the directory stream specified through the argument `dirp`. You may recall that the directory stream `dirp` is the one we get on executing the `opendir()` system call. The structure `dirent` describes the directory entry that represents the file(s) in the specified directory stream.

The structure of `dirent` is as follows:

```
struct dirent
{
    long d_ino;
    off_t d_off;
    unsigned short d_reclen;
    char d_name [NAME_MAX+1];
}
```

The following points may be noted:

1. `d_ino` is an inode number.
2. `d_off` is the offset or distance from the start of the directory to this `dirent`.
3. `d_reclen` is the size of `d_name`, not counting the `NULL` terminator.
4. `d_name` is a `NULL`-terminated name of the file.

With every read operation, the system call buffers several directory entries. It also marks for update the `st_atime` field of the directory each time the directory is read. If successful, the system call returns a value 1; at the end of the directory, it returns a value 0; on error, it returns −1 and also sets the `errno` accordingly. The kind of errors that may occur are as follows:

1. EBADF: Occurs when the file descriptor `fd` is invalid.
2. EFAULT: Occurs when the argument points outside the calling process's address space.
3. EINVAL: Occurs when the result buffer is too small.
4. ENOENT: Occurs when the directory does not exist.
5. ENOTDIR: Occurs when the file descriptor does not refer to a directory.

Example   The following program shows filenames in the specified directory.

```
showfilenames.c
#include <dirent.h>
#include <errno.h>

main(int argc, char *argv[])
{
    DIR *mydir;
    struct dirent *files;

    if (argc == 2)
    {
```

```
        mydir = opendir(argv[1]);
        if (mydir)
        {
                while ((files = readdir(mydir)))
                        printf("%s\n", files->d_name);
        }
        else if (errno == ENOENT)
                perror("The specified directory does not exist.");
        else if (errno == ENOTDIR)
                perror("The specified file is not a directory.");
        else if (errno == EACCES)
                perror("You do not have the right to open this folder.");
        else
                perror("Error in finding file");
    }
  else
    perror("Insufficient number of arguments.");
}
```

Output

```
$ ./showfilenames
Insufficient number of arguments.: Error 0

$ ./showfilenames account
The specified directory does not exist.: No such file or directory

$ ./showfilenames xyz.txt
The specified file is not a directory.: Not a directory

$ ./showfilenames accounts
.
..
lockfile.txt
pqr.txt
xyz.txt
```

In the aforementioned program, we first check if the count of the command line argument
is 2, that is, if the name of the directory whose content we want to display is supplied after
the command line argument. In the case where the directory name is supplied through the
command line argument, the directory stream represented by the former is opened through
the opendir() system call. You may recall that the directory stream is an ordered sequence
of all the directory entries in a particular directory. Thereafter, through the readdir() system
call, each file entry in the specified directory is accessed from the directory stream and
assigned to the dirent structure. The dirent structure contains complete information of the
file entry accessed from the directory stream. Filenames are accessed and displayed through
the dirent structure.

7.3.6 `telldir()`, `seekdir()`, and `rewinddir()`: Knowing, Setting, and Resetting Position in Directory Streams

To determine the location to perform the next read/write operation in the directory stream, we first need to know our current position in the directory stream. Thereafter, we can set the position in the directory stream from where we need to perform some action.

Knowing our position in directory streams

The current position in a directory stream can be known through the system call `telldir()`.

Syntax   `long int telldir(DIR *dirp);`

The system call returns an integer value to indicate the current position in the directory stream specified through the parameter `dirp`. We get the pointer to the directory stream `dirp` on executing the `opendir()` system call.

Example   The following example shows the current position in the directory stream after one read in the specified directory.

```
DIR *mydir;
struct dirent *files;
mydir = opendir("/home/projects");
files = readdir(mydir);
printf("The current position in the directory stream is  %ld\n",
   telldir(mydir));
```

Setting position in directory streams

The system call used to set the directory entry pointer in the directory stream is `seekdir()`.

Syntax   `void seekdir(DIR *dirp, long int loc);`

Here, `dirp` represents the directory stream and the long integer parameter `loc` represents the location we wish to set the directory entry pointer in the directory stream. The next `readdir()` operation will begin from the `loc`. There is one restriction as far as `loc` is concerned. It must be the value that is returned from the earlier call to the `telldir()` function. If the value of `loc` is not obtained from the earlier call to the `telldir()` function, we might get unexpected results on subsequent call to the `readdir()` function.

Example   The following example shows the setting of the current position in the directory streams.

```
setposition.c
#include <dirent.h>
main()
{
   DIR *mydir;
   struct dirent *files;
```

```
    long int loc;
    mydir = opendir("/usr/projects");
    loc=telldir(mydir);
    printf("The current location in the directory stream is %ld\n", loc);
    seekdir(mydir,loc);   /* Current Position is set at 0th byte i.e. at the beginning
                          of the directory stream */
    files=readdir(mydir);
    printf("The first directory entry found in this directory is %s
    (current directory) \n", files->d_name);
    loc=telldir(mydir);
    seekdir(mydir,loc); /* Current Position is set at the location determined by
                        readdir() in the directory stream */
    printf("The current position in the directory stream is  %ld\n", loc);
}
```

Output

```
$ gcc setposition.c -o setposition
$ ./setposition
The current location in the directory stream is 0
The first directory entry found in this directory is . (current directory)
The current position in the directory stream is 12
```

Resetting position in directory streams

To reset our position in a directory stream, the rewinddir() system call is used.

Syntax   void rewinddir(DIR *dirp);

Our position in the given directory stream, dirp, will be reset to the beginning of the directory. The system call does not return any value.

Example   The following example shows how the current position in the directory stream is set to the beginning of the directory stream using the rewinddir() system call.

```
rewinddirectory.c
#include <dirent.h>

main()
{
    DIR *mydir;
    struct dirent *files;
    mydir = opendir("/usr/projects");
    files = readdir(mydir);
    printf("The current position in the directory stream is  %ld\n",
       telldir(mydir));
    rewinddir(mydir);  /* The current position is set to the beginning
       in the directory stream */
    printf("The current position in the directory stream is %ld\n", telldir(mydir));
```

```
}
```

Output

```
The current position in the directory stream is  12
The current position in the directory stream is 0
```

7.3.7 closedir(): Closing Directory Streams

The system call used to close the directory stream is closedir(). The system call closes the specified directory stream and frees the resources allocated to it. The call returns a value 0 on success and −1 otherwise.

Syntax   int closedir(DIR *dirp);

Examples

(a) The following example closes the directory stream.
```
DIR *mydir;
mydir = opendir("/home/projects");
closedir(mydir);
```

(b) The following program demonstrates the use of all the system calls related to directory streams: opendir(), readdir(), telldir(), seekdir(), rewinddir(), and closedir().
```
directorycalls.c
#include <dirent.h>
main(int argc, char *argv[])
{
    DIR *mydir;
    struct dirent *files;
    if (argc == 2)
    {
        mydir = opendir(argv[1]);
        if (mydir)
        {
            files = readdir(mydir);
            printf("The current position in the directory stream is %ld\n", telldir(mydir));
            seekdir(mydir,0);
            printf("The current position in the directory stream is %ld\n", telldir(mydir));
            files = readdir(mydir);
            printf("The current position in the directory stream is %ld\n", telldir(mydir));
            rewinddir(mydir);
            printf("The current position in the directory stream is %ld\n", telldir(mydir));
            closedir(mydir);
        }
        else
            perror("Error in opening directory");
    }
    else
```

```
            perror("Insufficient number of arguments.");
        }
```

Output

```
$ ./directorycalls
Insufficient number of arguments.: Error 0
$ ./directorycalls programs
Error in opening directory: No such file or directory
$ ./directorycalls accounts
The current position in the directory stream is 12
The current position in the directory stream is 0
The current position in the directory stream is 12
The current position in the directory stream is 0
```

7.4 PROCESS-RELATED SYSTEM CALLS

Unix provides several system calls that are used in process handling. These system calls perform several process-related tasks such as creating and ending a program, sending and receiving software interrupts, and allocating memory. Four system calls are provided for creating a process, waiting for a process to complete, and ending a process. These system calls are fork(), the exec() family, wait(), and exit(), described in Table 7.16.

Table 7.16 List of process-related system calls

System Call	Description
exec(filename, *argv)	Loads a file and executes it
fork()	Creates a new process
wait()	Waits for a child process
exit()	Terminates the current process

7.4.1 exec(): Replacing Executable Binaries with New Processes

The exec() system call replaces an executable binary file with a new process according to the specified arguments. There are several variants of the exec() system call; all of them perform the same task. They differ on the basis of the way the command line arguments are passed to it. Providing arguments in different data types to the exec() system call provides flexibility to the programmer. The prototypes for these calls are as follows:

```
int execl(const char *path, const char *arg0 [, arg1, ..., argn], NULL)
int execv(const char *path, char *const argv[]);
int execle(const char *path, const char* arg0 [, arg1, ..., argn], NULL, char *const envp[])
int execve(const char *path, char *const argv[], char *const envp[]);
int execlp(const char *path, const char *arg0 [, arg1, ..., argn], NULL)
int execvp(const char *path, char *const argv[])
```

Here, arg0, arg1, ... , argn represents the arguments to be passed to the new process—these arguments are pointers to NULL terminated strings. A NULL pointer terminates the argument list. path refers to the binary filename along with its path. argv is an array of character pointers that point to the arguments themselves. You may recall that arguments are character pointers to NULL-terminated strings. envp represents an array of character pointers to

NULL-terminated strings. These strings define the environment for the new process. The envp array is also terminated by a NULL pointer.

When the binary file is transformed to a process, that process replaces the process that executed the exec() system call (a new process is not created). The exec() system call returns −1 on failure.

Letters added to the end of exec indicate the type of arguments supplied to it. For example, l represents a list of arguments, v represents a vector—array of character pointers (argv), e represents environment variable list, and p indicates that the environment variable PATH be used while searching for the executable files.

Examples

(a) The following example executes the ls command, specifying the path name of the executable (/bin/ls) and using the argument, -l for the long format. The execl() call initiates the command or program in the same environment in which it is operating.
```
#include <unistd.h>
...
execl ("/bin/ls", "ls", "-l", (char *)0);
```

(b) The following command uses the execl() call. In this system call, we have to specify the environment for the command (ls) using the env argument.
```
#include <unistd.h>
char *env[] = { "USER=chirag", "PATH=/usr/bin", (char *) 0 };
...
execle ("/bin/ls", "ls", "-l", (char *)0, env);
```

(c) The following example uses the execlp() call. The call searches for the location of the ls command among the directories specified in the PATH environment variable.
```
#include <unistd.h>
...
execlp ("ls", "ls", "-l", (char *)0);
```

(d) The following example uses the execv() call. In this call, the arguments to the ls command are passed through the args array.
```
#include <unistd.h>
char *args[] = {"ls","-l", (char *) 0 };
...
execv ("/bin/ls", args);
```

(e) The following example uses the execve() call. In this call, the environment for the command through the env argument and the arguments to the command are passed through the args array.
```
#include <unistd.h>
char *args[] = {"ls","-l", (char *) 0 };
char *env[] = { "USER=chirag", "PATH=/usr/bin", (char *) 0 };
...
execve ("/bin/ls", args, env);
```

(f) The following example uses the execvp() call. The command searches for the location of the ls command among the directories specified by the PATH environment variable. In addition, the arguments to the command are passed through the args array.

```
#include <unistd.h>
char *args[] = {"ls","-l", (char *) 0 };
...
execvp ("ls", args);
```

7.4.2 fork(): Creating New Processes

The fork() system call creates a new process. The new process, also known as the child process, will have properties identical to its parent, but with a new process ID. The fork() system call does not take any argument and returns the process ID of the child process to the parent. It also returns a zero to the newly created child process.

Syntax   `#include <sys/types.h>`

`#include <unistd.h>`
`pid_t fork(void);`

The execution of the fork() system call results in the following conditions:

1. If successful, the fork() system call returns the process ID of the newly created child process to the parent and 0 to the newly created child process.
2. If unsuccessful, the fork() system call returns a negative value.

When a child process is created successfully, Unix makes an exact copy of the parent's address space and assigns it to the child. Therefore, the parent and child processes will have separate address spaces. Both processes start their execution right after the system call, fork(). Since both processes have identical but separate address spaces, those variables initialized before the fork() call have the same values in both address spaces.

Example   The following example executes the fork() system call and analyses its return value to know if the child process is created or the system call failed.

```
forkexample.c
#include <sys/types.h>

main()
{
    pid_t p;

    p  = fork();

    if (p == 0)
    {
        printf("This is a Child process\n");
    }
    else if(p > 0)
    {
        printf("This is a Parent process\n");
    }
    else if(p == -1)
```

```
        {
                printf("Fork was unsuccessful, process could not be created:\n");
        }
}
```

Output

```
This is a Child process
This is a Parent process
```

There is one more version of the fork() system call, the vfork() system call, which has been described next.

vfork(): Creating new processes suspending parent processes

In the case of the fork() system call, a copy of the address space of the parent process is created and assigned to the child process. On the other hand, in case of the vfork() system call the address space of the parent process is not copied. Instead, the parent process is suspended for a while and its address space is used by the child process. The parent process remains in a suspended state until either the child process exits or calls the exec() system call, in which case the parent's address space is released, allowing it to continue. While using the parent process's address space, there are many chances of the child process overwriting the data and stack of the former accidentally. The main benefit of the vfork() system call is that it is quite faster than the fork() system call as the memory is shared (between the parent and child process), which results in reducing the overheads of spawning a new process with a separate copy of the memory.

The vfork() system call helps in creating a new system context for an execve() operation that is used to execute a specified program. Using the fork() system call for this purpose is a time-consuming as well as a resource depleting operation for the simple reason that entire page table entries have to be copied from the parent to the child. This overhead is not required when creating a new system context for an execve() with the vfork() system call.

Syntax
```
#include <sys/types.h>

#include <unistd.h>
pid_t vfork(void);
```

Example   The following statement creates a child process and suspends the parent process if the vfork() call is successful.

```
pid_t p;
p = vfork( );
```

7.4.3 wait(): Waiting

If a process finishes its task and is killed, all of its child processes become orphans and are adopted by the init process. If the parent is a terminal control process, on completing its task it sends a hangup (SIGHUP) signal to all its children. To avoid such situations, we can suspend or make a parent process wait for some time until the child process finishes its task. To do so, the wait() system call is used. This implies that the wait() system call is used to block a parent process until one of its child processes either finishes its task or is suspended.

The wait() system call can thus be used to determine when a child process has completed its job. The call returns the PID of the completed child process along with its status. The status information allows the parent process to determine the exit status of the child process. The parent process resumes its execution when the wait() system call returns. If the calling process has no child process, the wait() system returns immediately with a value of −1.

Syntax   `#include <sys/types.h>`

`#include <sys/wait.h>`
`pid_t wait(int *status);`

Example   The following statement makes the parent process sleep until the child process finishes its job. The status of the child process, that is, how it is terminated, is returned through the status variable

`wait(&status);`

7.4.4 exit(): Terminating Processes

The exit() system call terminates the execution of a process and returns a value to its parent.

Syntax   `void exit(status)`

`int status;`

Here, status is an integer between 0 and 255 and is returned to the parent via wait() to represent an exit status of the process. The status value 0 indicates normal termination. When the exit() system call is called, all open file descriptors are closed and the child processes (of the process being terminated) will be known as orphans and will become the child process of the init process.

Examples

(a) The following statement demonstrates the normal termination of a process.
```
exit(0);
```
(b) The following program demonstrates the use of fork(), wait(), and exit() system calls

```
forkwaitexitcall.c
#include <sys/wait.h>
main()
{
    pid_t p;
    int status;

    p  = fork();

    if (p == 0)
    {
        printf("This is a Child process\n");
        exit(0);
```

```
            }
            else if(p > 0)
            {
                printf("This is a Parent process\n");
                wait(&status);  /* Makes the parent process to sleep until child
                                   process finishes its job. The status of the child
                                   process i.e. how it terminated is returned through
                                   status variable */
                printf("Parent is waiting for the child to finish");
                if (WIFEXITED(status))
                        printf("\nChild process terminated normally %d\n",
                            WEXITSTATUS(status)); /* WIFEXITED() is a macro that
                                    returns true if the process terminates normally */
            }
            else if(p == -1)
            {
            printf("Fork was unsuccessful, process could not be created:\n");
            }
        }
```

Output

```
This is a Child process
This is a Parent process
Parent is waiting for the child to finish
Child process terminated normally 0
```

7.5 INTERRUPTED SYSTEM CALL

While executing a system call, if an asynchronous signal (such as an interrupt or quit) occurs, the system call is said to be interrupted and returns an error condition. To understand the concept more clearly, we need to understand that system calls are divided into two categories:

1. Slow system calls
2. Rest of the system calls

Slow system calls represent those calls that wait for a condition to occur for an infinite time. This implies that these system calls can be blocked for ever. Some examples of such system calls include read(), write(), and pause().

The pause() system call, by default, puts the calling process into sleep until and unless a signal is caught by this process.

The read() system call can block the caller if the data does not appear at the desired source, which may be a pipe or a terminal device.

The write() system call can block the caller if the target is not ready to accept the incoming data.

When a system call is slow and a signal arrives while it is blocked or waiting, two consequences are possible. Either the operating system aborts the system call and sets errno to EINTR or it allows the system call to succeed with partial results. In any case, we have to test for the success of the system call and explicitly handle the returned error (if any). A solution to such a problem is to automatically restart the interrupted system calls from the beginning.

Example The following example demonstrates the interrupted system call. The user is prompted to enter some data through the read() system call. Now while the system call is being run, it is interrupted by invoking the SIGINT signal. When the read() system call is interrupted, the following message will be displayed: read: interrupted system call. Similarly, while the read() system call is being run, it is interrupted through another signal, SIGQUIT, which makes the system call read() restart, asking the user to re-enter the data.

interruptprog.c

```c
#include <stdio.h>
#include <errno.h>
#include <stdlib.h>
#include <unistd.h>
#include <signal.h>
void sig_handler (int signo)
{
    if (signo == SIGINT)
        printf("SIGINT has occurred\n");
    if (signo == SIGQUIT)
        printf("SIGQUIT has occurred. Restarting the read call\n");
}

int main() {
    struct sigaction sa;
    char buf;
    int n;

    sa.sa_handler = sig_handler;
    sigemptyset(&sa.sa_mask);
    sa.sa_flags = 0;
    if (sigaction(SIGINT, &sa, NULL)) exit(1);
    sa.sa_flags = SA_RESTART;
    if (sigaction(SIGQUIT, &sa, NULL))exit(1);
    n = read(0, &buf, 1);
    if(n < 0)
        if(errno == EINTR) perror("read");
    else
        printf("%c", buf);
    return 0;
}
```

Output

```
$ gcc interruptprog.c -o interruptprog

$ ./ interruptprog
hello^CSIGINT has occurred
read: Interrupted system call

$ ./interruptprog
thanks^\SIGQUIT has occured. Restarting the read call
grest^CSIGINT has occured
read: Interrupted system call
```

7.6 STANDARD C LIBRARY FUNCTIONS

We know that almost the whole of the Unix operating system is written in C. This fact enables us to readily use the standard C library functions while writing in C programs for the purpose of I/O operations and for making system calls. The library functions hence reduce much of our coding efforts. To use library functions in programs, all we need is to include its respective header file in the program. Some standard C library functions are given in Table 7.17.

Table 7.17 Brief description of library functions

Library function	Description
fopen()	Opens a stream
malloc()	Allocates memory
exit()	Terminates and exits from the program
getpid()	Gets the ID of the calling process
kill()	Kills a process
sleep()	Suspends the execution for an interval

7.6.1 Difference between System Calls and Library Functions

System calls and library functions have a common purpose of performing tasks that relieve us from critical programming. However, there are still some differences between the two. To make the difference between the system calls and library functions clear, their respective characteristics are listed as follows:

System calls

1. System calls are part of the operating system and are executed in the system kernel.
2. They are basically the entry points into the kernel. For requesting services from the kernel, our program needs to use system calls.
3. They execute in the kernel address space; hence, for running a system call, the program has to make a mode switch from the user mode to the kernel mode.
4. System calls usually cannot be replaced.
5. They are system dependent and hence not portable.
6. Being a part of the operating system, they can access any critical data (like the data related to system security) or hardware resource.

C Library functions

1. Library functions may invoke one or more system calls.
2. They are executed in the user address space.
3. They may be replaced, if desired.
4. There are no overheads in calling library functions.
5. They are not system dependent.
6. They provide comparatively more user interface and a richer set of features.
7. An appropriate header file has to be included for using library functions.

7.7 STREAMS AND FILE INPUT/OUTPUT LIBRARY FUNCTIONS

In Unix, everything is in the form of streams. This implies that all files are considered streams, data transferred between files is in the form of streams, data transferred from one command to another is in the form of streams, data transferred to any device including the printer is in the form of streams, etc. Streams, here, refer to a flow of bits.

Examples

(a) In the following example, a list of files and directories are transferred (in the form of a stream of bits) and saved into the file files.txt.

```
$ ls > files.txt
```

(b) Similarly, the following example sends file content to the printer in the form of a stream.

```
$ cat files.txt | lpr
```

There are three standard streams that are automatically opened when a program is started, namely stdin, stdout, and stderr. These are declared in stdio.h and represent the standard input, output, and error output respectively, which correspond to the low-level file descriptors 0, 1, and 2. Besides these three default file descriptors, there are others that are automatically assigned by the kernel when we open a file.

In this section, we will learn about the different library functions that help in performing different file I/O operations. These functions help in opening, closing, reading, and writing in the file stream. In addition, we can set the file pointer at the desired position in the file, flush the data in the buffer to the file, etc. The list of library functions for performing file I/O operations is given in Table 7.18.

Table 7.18 File I/O library functions

Function	Description
Fopen(filename, mode)	Opens a file stream in the given mode
Fread(ptr, size, n, stream)	Reads n number of items of a given size from the given file stream and stores it in the buffer pointed by ptr
Fwrite(ptr, size, n, stream)	Writes n number of items of a given size from the buffer pointed by ptr into the given file stream
Fclose(stream)	Closes the given file stream
Fflush(stream)	Flushes (writes) the buffered data into the file immediately

(Contd)

Table 7.18 *(Contd)*

Function	Description
Fseek(stream, offset, whence)	Sets the file pointer position at the given offset from the whence location in the file
fgetc(stream), getc(stream) and getchar()	Returns the next character from the given stream
fputc(c, stream), putc(c, stream), and putchar()	Writes a character to the given stream
Fgets(ptr, n, stream) and gets(ptr)	Reads text of n number of characters from the given stream and assigns it to the string pointed by pointer ptr

Note: The library functions in Table 7.18 such as fopen and fread are high level I/O functions and are implemented through low-level I/O functions such as open and read. We have discussed high-level and low-level I/O functions at the beginning of this chapter.

7.7.1 fopen(): Opening Files

The fopen library function is used for opening files.

Syntax   `FILE *fopen(const char *filename, const char *mode);`

It opens the file named by the filename parameter in the specified mode. The mode determines the purpose of opening the file, which is, whether it is supposed to be opened for reading, writing, updating, or appending. The mode can be any of the following (refer to Table 7.19).

Table 7.19 Brief description of the different modes in which a file can be opened

Mode	Description
"r" or "rb"	Opens the file for reading only
"w" or "wb"	Opens the file for writing and deletes its existing content, if any
"a" or "ab"	Opens the file for appending content—adding content to the end of file
"r+" or "rb+" or "r+b"	Opens the file for updating—reading and writing
"w+" or "wb+" or "w+b"	Opens the file for updating and deleting its existing content
"a+" or "ab+" or "a+b"	Opens the file for updating and appending content to the end of file

The character b in the aforementioned mode indicates that the file is a binary rather than a text file.

The mode parameter is a string and hence must be enclosed in double quotes. The function fopen(), if successful, returns a FILE * pointer pointing to the file, but a value NULL if it fails.

Example   The following example opens the binary file students.txt in write mode.

```
FILE *fp;
fp=fopen("students.txt","wb");
```

7.7.2 fwrite(): Writing into Files

The fwrite library accesses the data from the specified data buffer and writes them to the specified file. It returns the number of records successfully written into the file.

Syntax   `size_t fwrite (const void *ptr, size_t size, size_t nitems, FILE *stream);`

Here, `ptr` represents the pointer to the structure, an array, int, float, etc., containing the data to be written into the file. The file where we want to write the content is represented by the pointer `stream`. The argument `nitems` represents the number of records or structures to be written into the file and `size` represents the size of a single structure.

Example   The following example writes a student's record stored in the structure `stud` into the file `students.txt`.

```
writestudrecs.c
#include <stdio.h>
struct student
{
  int roll,marks;
  char name[20];
};
main()
{
  FILE *fp;
  struct student  stud;
  fp=fopen("students.txt","wb");
  stud.roll=101;
  strcpy(stud.name,"Chirag");
  stud.marks=95;
  fwrite(&stud,sizeof(struct student),1,fp);
}
```

Output

```
$ cat students.txt
cat: cannot open students.txt
$ ./writestudrecs
$ cat students.txt
e_Chiragtt?z??e??#
```

Note: Since the `students.txt` file is a binary file, we find some funny symbols in the file, which are machine-readable code.

7.7.3 fread(): Reading Data from Files

The `fread` library function is used to read data from the specified file.

Syntax   `size_t fread(void *ptr, size_t size, size_t nitems, FILE *stream);`

Data is read into the specified data buffer represented by the pointer `ptr` from the file represented by `stream`. The size of the *buffer* is specified as `size` and the number of items successfully read into the data buffer is represented by `nitems`.

Example The following example reads a student's record from the file students.txt and fills the information in the structure stud.

```
struct student
{
    int roll,marks;
    char name[20];
};
void main()
{
    FILE *fp;
    struct student  stud;
    fp=fopen("students.txt","rb");
    fread(&stud,sizeof(struct student),1,fp);
...
```

7.7.4 fclose(): Closing Files

The fclose library function closes the specified file. Any buffered data in the memory that is not yet flushed to the stream (file) is written into the stream before closing it. When a program ends, all the stream associated to files are automatically closed, that is, the fclose function is implicitly called when a program ends.

Syntax int fclose(FILE *stream);

Here, stream represents the pointer to the file stream that we wish to close.

Example The following example closes the file represented by the file pointer fp.

```
fclose(fp);
```

7.7.5 fflush(): Flushing out to Files

The fflush library function writes all buffered data in a stream to the associated file immediately. This library function is called to ensure that no important data is left in the buffer (which is volatile) and is successfully written into the file. The fclose function calls the fflush function implicitly so as to write the buffered content to the file before closing it.

Syntax int fflush(FILE *stream);

Here, stream refers to the stream that we wish to flush out.

Example The following example flushes the standard input device and writes the buffered content (if any) into the associated file.

```
fflush(stdin);
```

7.7.6 fseek(): Relocating File Pointers

The fseek function is equivalent to the lseek() system call and is used to set the position of the file pointer. The fseek function positions the file pointer in the stream for the next read or write operation.

Syntax   `int fseek(FILE *stream, long int offset, int whence);`

Here, `stream` represents the file and `offset` represents the number of bytes from `whence`. The argument `whence` refers to the location related to which the offset has to be set, that is, whether the offset has to be set from the *current*, *end*, or *beginning* of the file.

Example   The following sets the file pointer at the 0th byte, that is, at the beginning of the file.

`fseek(fp,0, SEEK_SET);`

7.7.7 `fgetc()`, `getc()`, and `getchar()`: Reading Characters

The `fgetc` function returns the next character from the specific stream, which may be a file or `stdin` (standard input). The function returns the EOF when either some error occurs or the end of file is reached.

Syntax   `int fgetc(FILE *stream);`

```
int getc(FILE *stream);
int getchar();
```

Here, `stream` represents the file from where we wish to read a character.

The `getc` function is equivalent to `fgetc`, except that it may be implemented as a macro.

The `getchar` function is equivalent to `getc(stdin)` and reads the next character from the standard input.

Note: The aforementioned functions return the character as `int`.

Example   The following example reads a character from the file pointed by file pointer `fp` and stores it in variable `c`.

`c = fgetc(fp);`

Writing characters

The `fputc` function writes a character to an output stream that may be a file or `stdout` (output stream). It returns either the value it has successfully written or the EOF on failure.

Syntax   `int fputc(int c, FILE *stream);`

```
int putc(int c, FILE *stream);
int putchar(int c);
```

Here, `c` represents the character that we wish to write into the file represented by `stream`.

The function `putc` is equivalent to `fputc`, the difference being it may be implemented as a macro. The `putchar` function is equivalent to `putc(c,stdout)` that writes a single character to the standard output.

Example   The following example writes the character in variable `c` into the file pointed by file pointer `fp`.

`fputc(c,fp);`

Example The following example demonstrates the use of `fgetc()` and `fputc()` functions. It makes a copy of the file `xyz.txt` with the name `pqr.txt` by reading each character sequentially from the file `xyz.txt` and writing into the file `pqr.txt`.

copyfile.c

```
#include <stdio.h>
main()
{
    int c;
    FILE *fp1, *fp2;
    fp1 = fopen("xyz.txt", "r");
    fp2 = fopen("pqr.txt", "w");
    while((c = fgetc(fp1)) != EOF)
        fputc(c,fp2);
    fclose(fp1);
    fclose(fp2);
}
```

Output

```
$ cat xyz.txt
This is a test file
$ cat pqr.txt
cat: cannot open pqr.txt
$ ./copyfile
$ cat pqr.txt
This is a test file
```

7.7.8 `fgets()` and `gets()`: Reading Strings

The `fgets` and `gets` functions are used for reading a string from specified streams. Their syntax is as follows:

Syntax `char *fgets(char *s, int n, FILE *stream);`

`char *gets(char *s);`

Here, `stream` represents the file stream from which the string has to be fetched or read. The string of size $n-1$ bytes will be read and assigned to the string represented by the pointer `s`.

The `fgets` function reads a string from the specified file. It reads the $n-1$ number of characters from the file represented by the stream and assigns it to the string pointed to by `s`. Either $n-1$ number of characters or characters up till the newline character (whichever appears first) are read into the string pointed by `s`. Why are $n-1$ number of characters read, and not n? This is because, a terminating NULL byte, `\0` is added to mark the end of the string pointed by `s`. When successful, the functions return a pointer to the string `s`. If the stream is at the end of a file, it sets the EOF indicator for the stream and returns a NULL pointer. In case of error, the function returns a NULL pointer and sets `errno` variable to indicate the type of error.

The gets function is similar to fgets, except that it reads from the standard input. All characters entered by the user except the newline character are read and assigned to the string pointed by s after appending a NULL byte, \0 to it.

Examples

(a) The following example reads 80 characters from the file pointed by the file pointer fp and stores it into the string k.

```
fgets(k,80,fp);
```

The following example reads the text from the keyboard and stores it into the string, k.

```
char k[60];
gets(k);
```

Since the size of variable k is 60, either the first 59 characters (one byte is left for the terminating NULL byte \0) or until the newline character (whichever appears earlier) is stored in the variable, k.

(b) The following program explains how to make use of fopen(), fread(), fwrite(), fseek(), and fclose() library functions to read and write a few records in the file randomly.

readwritestudrecs.c

```
/* Reading and writing students records  */
#include <stdio.h>

struct student
{
    int roll,marks;
    char name[20];
};

main()
{
    int i;
    FILE *fp;
    struct student stud;

  fp=fopen("students.txt","wb");
  printf("Enter roll, name and marks of three students\n");
  for (i=1;i<=3; i++)
  {
      scanf("%d %s %d", &stud.roll, stud.name, &stud.marks);
      fwrite(&stud,sizeof(struct student),1,fp);
  }
  fclose(fp);
  fp=fopen("students.txt","rb");
  printf("The records of the student in the file students.txt are as given
  below\n");
  for (i=1;i<=3; i++)
```

```
{
    fread(&stud,sizeof(struct student),1,fp);
    printf("%d %s %d\n", stud.roll, stud.name, stud.marks);
}
printf("Third student\'s record is \n");
fseek(fp,sizeof(struct student)*2, SEEK_SET);
fread(&stud,sizeof(struct student),1,fp);
printf("%d %s %d\n", stud.roll, stud.name, stud.marks);
printf("First student\'s record is \n");
fseek(fp,0, SEEK_SET);
fread(&stud,sizeof(struct student),1,fp);
printf("%d %s %d\n", stud.roll, stud.name, stud.marks);
fclose(fp);
}
```

Output

```
$ gcc readwritestudrecs.c -o readwritestudrecs
$ ./ readwritestudrecs
Enter roll, name and marks of the three students
101 chirag 85
102 john 75
103 naman 84

The records of the students in the file students.txt are as given below
101 chirag 85
102 john 75
103 naman 84

Third student's record is
103 naman 84

First student's record is
101 chirag 85
```

7.8 ERROR HANDLING

Errors often occur while creating or running applications. When an error occurs, the traditional approach that Unix prefers is assigning the error code to the special global variable, errno. The value in the errno variable is overwritten by the error code of the next error in the application. For a user-friendly and robust application, proper error handling must be implemented in an application.

By error handling, we mean that an error (if any), which occurs in the application, should not be displayed in critical error code (not understandable by a layman). It should instead be displayed in a user-friendly text message. In addition, on the occurrence of the error, the application should not crash in the middle of an operation and should instead exit gracefully after displaying the text error message and saving the data that was computed so far (if any).

To detect and handle errors, we will be using two functions, `perror()` and `strerror()`.

Note: The error codes are defined in the `errno.h` file.

7.8.1 Using strerror Function

The `strerror()` function displays an error message by accepting the error number argument, errno and returns a pointer to the corresponding message string.

Syntax `char *strerror(int errno);`

Here, errno contains the error code.

Example The following program demonstrates the `strerror()` function.

```
strerrorexample.c
#include <string.h>
#include <errno.h>

main ()
{
  FILE *fp;
  fp = fopen ("letter.txt","r");
  if (fp == NULL) printf ("Error in opening file: %s\n", strerror(errno));
}
```

Output

```
Error in opening file: No such file or directory
```

In this example, we try to open the file `letter.txt`. If, while opening the file, any error occurs, its description is displayed through the `strerror()` function.

`strerror_r()`is a function that is similar to the `strerror()` function. The difference between the two functions is that instead of returning a pointer to the corresponding error message, `strerror_r()` renders the message into an error buffer. In addition, the `strerror_f()` function is thread safe.

Syntax `int strerror_r(int errno, char *error_buf, size_t buffer_len);`

Here, `error_buf` is where the error message is rendered for a maximum of `buffer_len` characters.

7.8.2 perror(): Displaying Errors

The library function `perror` is used for displaying error messages. Whenever a system call or library function fails, it returns a value −1 and assigns a value to an external variable called errno. The value assigned to the errno variable is used by the `perror()` function to find the error message and write it to the standard error file descriptor.

Syntax `void perror(const char *s);`

Here, s represents the string that we wish to display along with the associated error message.

Example The following example demonstrates how the messages are displayed through the `perror()` library function.

```
demoperror.c
#include <stdio.h>
#include <errno.h>        //required when using perror() function

main (int argc, char *argv[])
{
    FILE *fp;
    fp = fopen(argv[1], "r");
    if(fp==NULL)
    {
        perror(argv[0]);  /* Displays demoperror.c: No such file or directory */
        perror(NULL);  /* Displays No such file or directory */
        perror("File could not be opened");  /* Displays File could not be opened: No
        such file or directory */
        printf("errno = %d\n", errno);  /* Displays errno=2 */
        exit(1);
    }
    printf("File exists and is opened for reading ");
    fclose(fp);
}
```

Output

```
$ ./demoperror
./demoperror: Bad address
Bad address
File could not be opened: Bad address
errno = 14

$ ./demoperror bank.lst
./demoperror: No such file or directory
No such file or directory
File could not be opened: No such file or directory
errno = 2

$ ./demoperror xyz.txt
File exists and is opened for reading
```

In the aforementioned example, the library function fopen() will return NULL value if it is unable to open the file whose name is supplied as command line argument. The returned NULL value will be assigned to the file pointer fp. The statement perror(argv[0]); prints the name of the program followed by a colon (:) and the associated error message No such file or directory. The statement perror(NULL); prints only the associated error message No such file or directory. The final statement, perror("File could not be opened"); prints the message File could not be opened followed by colon (:), which is followed by the associated error message, No such file or directory. The value assigned to the errno variable for this type of error is 2, which is also displayed at the end.

After understanding the two functions, `strerror()` and `perror()`, we will take a quick look at the difference between the two, as shown in Table 7.20.

Table 7.20 Difference between the `strerror` and `perror` functions

strerror()	perror()
It accepts an error number argument and returns a pointer to the corresponding message string.	It finds the error message corresponding to the `errno` variable and writes it to the standard error file descriptor.
The `strerror` function is declared in `string.h`.	The `perror` function is declared in `stdio.h`.

7.9 STREAM ERRORS

When an error occurs while executing a library function or system call, they return values such as −1, NULL, and EOF. Besides returning a value, they also assign a value to the `errno` variable to describe the error. The `errno` variable is an external variable.

```
extern int errno;
```

The value in `errno` variable can be used to diagnose the error. Its value must be checked immediately after the execution of the function or system call.

The standard `errno` values include the following:

1. E2BIG: The argument list passed to the function is too long.
2. EACCESS: Access denied! The user does not have permission to access a file, directory, etc.
3. EBADF: It refers to a bad file descriptor.
4. EBUSY: The requested resource is unavailable.
5. ECHILD: The `wait()` or `waitpid()` function tried to wait for a child process to exit, but all children have already exited.
6. EDEADLK: A resource deadlock would occur if the request continued.
7. EEXIST: The file or directory already exists.
8. EFAULT: One of the function arguments refers to an invalid address.
9. EINTR: The function was interrupted by a signal, which was caught by a signal handler in the program, and the signal handler returned normally.
10. EINVAL: It refers to an invalid argument passed to the function.
11. EIO: An I/O error occurred.
12. ENFILE: Too many files are already open in this process.
13. ENODEV: Device does not exist.
14. ENOENT: No file was found or the specified path name doesn't exist.
15. ENOEXEC: The file is not executable.
16. ENOLCK: No locks are available.
17. ENOMEM: The system is out of memory.
18. ENOSPC: No space is left on the device.
19. ENOTDIR: The specified path is not a directory.
20. ENOTEMPTY: The specified directory is not empty.
21. ENXIO: An I/O request is made to a special file for a device that does not exist.

22. EPERM: The operation is not permitted—no permission to access the specified resource.

23. EPIPE: The pipe to read from or write to does not exist.

We can also check the state of a file stream to determine whether an error has occurred or the end of file is reached. The syntax for checking the file streams is as follows:

Syntax
```
int ferror(FILE *stream);

int feof(FILE *stream);

void clearerr(FILE *stream);
```

Examples

(a) The ferror function tests the error indicator in the supplied stream and returns a nonzero value if it is set; otherwise, it returns zero.

```
if (ferror(stdin) != 0) fprintf(stderr,"Error in reading data");
```

(b) The feof function tests the end of file indicator within a stream and returns a nonzero value if it is set; otherwise it returns zero.

```
if (feof(stdin) != 0) fprintf(stderr,"File is over\n");
```

(c) The clearerr function clears the end of file and error indicators for the supplied stream. The function does not return any value.

```
clearerr(stdin);
```

7.10 FUNCTIONS FOR DYNAMIC MEMORY MANAGEMENT

Dynamic memory management means allocating the memory as and when required and releasing it when its purpose is complete. The released memory can then be reused by another process. The following are the functions used for managing memory:

malloc(size)   Allocated memory block of a given size

calloc(n, size)   Allocates n number of memory blocks of a given size and initializes the memory to zero

realloc(ptr, size)   Changes the size of the block of allocated memory, ptr, to the given size

free(ptr)   Releases the allocated memory block, ptr

7.10.1 malloc(): Allocating Memory Block

The malloc function allocates a memory block.

Syntax   `void* malloc(size_t size)`

Here, size determines the number of bytes of memory to allocate. If the allocation is successful, malloc returns a pointer to the memory. If memory allocation fails, it returns a NULL pointer. The allocated memory in this function is uninitialized, that is, it is raw memory.

Example   The following example allocates 10 bytes of memory to character type pointer k.

```
char *k,
k = (char *)malloc(10 * sizeof(char));
```

7.10.2 `calloc()`: Allocating Arrays of Memory Blocks

The `calloc()` function allocates an array of memory and initializes the entire memory to zero.

Syntax   `void* calloc(size_t nmemb, size_t size)`

Here, `nmemb` represents the number of elements in the array and the second argument is the `size` in bytes of each element. The function, if successful, returns a pointer to the allocated memory, and `NULL` otherwise.

Example   The following example allocates an array of memory to character type pointer k where the array consists of five elements and each element is assigned 10 bytes of memory.

```
char *k,
k = (char*) calloc (5, 10*sizeof(char));
```

7.10.3 `realloc()`: Resizing Allocated Memory

The `realloc()` function changes the size of the allocated memory. We can increase or decrease the size of the allocated memory through this function.

Syntax   `void* realloc (void *ptr, size_t size)`

Here, `ptr` represents the block of the memory whose *size* we wish to change. The new size is represented by the parameter, `size`. The function returns the pointer to the resized block of allocated memory. The newly allocated memory will be uninitialized. If the `ptr` argument is set to `NULL`, the function will be equivalent to the `malloc(size)` function. If the value of the `size` argument is set to zero, the function will be equivalent to `free(ptr)`.

Example   The following example reallocates 20 bytes of memory to character type pointer k.

```
char *k,
k = (char *)realloc(k, 20);
```

7.10.4 `free()`: Freeing Allocated Memory

The `free()` function deallocates or releases the block of allocated memory.

Syntax   `void free (void *ptr);`

Here, `ptr` refers to the block of memory pointed to by pointer `ptr` that we wish to release.

Examples

(a) The following example frees the memory assigned to character type pointer k.

```
free(k);
```

(b) The following program demonstrates the use of `malloc()`, `calloc()`, `realloc()`, and `free()` library functions.

```
memorymgmt.c
#include <malloc.h>

main()
{
    char *k, *t;  /* k and t are declared as character type pointers */
    int i;

    k = (char *)malloc(6 * sizeof(char));  /* Memory of 6 bytes is allocated to k  */
    strcpy(k, "Hello");              /* Text, Hello is stored in  k */
    printf("The string k contains the text: %s\n", k);
    /* The text, Hello in k is displayed on the screen */
    k = (char *)realloc(k, 13);    /* Reallocating the memory to k, incrementing the
allocated memory to 13 bytes */
    strcpy(k, "Hello World!");   /* Text, Hello World! is stored in k */
    printf("The string k now contains the text: %s\n", k);
    /* The text, Hello World! in k is displayed on the screen */
    free(k);                 /* freeing the memory allocated to k  */
    t = (char *) calloc (3, 20*sizeof(char)); /* Allocating 3 blocks of memory, each
                                       of 20 bytes to t */
    printf("Enter three names\n");
    for (i=0;i<=2;i++)
{
scanf("%s", t);
t+=20;
} /* Storing the names entered by user in t */
    printf("The three names entered are as follows \n");
t-=60;
    for (i=0;i<=2;i++)
{
printf("%s \n", t);
t+=20;
}
 /* Printing the names stored in t on the screen */
    free(t);  /* Freeing up memory allocated to t */
}
```

Output

```
$ gcc memorymgmt.c -o memorymgmt

$ ./memorymgmt
The string k contains the text: Hello
The string k now contains the text: Hello World!
```

```
Enter three names
Sanjay
Chirag
Naman

The three names entered are as follows
Sanjay
Chirag
Naman
```

7.11 FILE LOCKING

File locking is an essential task that is required in multi-user, multitasking operating systems to maintain file integrity. If a program is updating or writing into a file, it needs to be locked until the writing procedure is over so that another program that is supposed to read the file need not get obsolete content. The idea of file locking is to allow only one process at a time to update the content of a file, thereby avoiding any ambiguity and inconsistency. Only when the first process has completed its operations on the file, should the second process be allowed to manipulate the file, keeping the rest of the processes waiting. The file lock is created in an atomic way, that is, no other operation will take place while the file lock is being created. We can lock an entire file or some of its regions depending on our requirement.

7.11.1 Creating Lock Files

Lock files are created to limit access to the resources. The resources can be a file on the disk, memory, or other peripherals. To demonstrate exclusive access, that is, allowing only one process to access a file, we are going to see the creation of a lock file. The lock file is the one that is created and accessed by only one process at a time. Until the lock file (which was created by the earlier process) is deleted, no other process will be able to create another lock file.

Example   The following program shows the creation of an exclusive lock file.

```c
lockcreation.c
#include <fcntl.h>
#include <errno.h>

main()
{
   int fd;
   fd = open("lockfile.txt", O_RDWR | O_CREAT | O_EXCL, 0744);
   if (fd == -1) {
      printf("File could not be opened. Error number = %d\n", errno);
   }
   else {
      printf("File opened successfully");
   }
}
```

Output

```
$ ls lock*.txt
lock*.txt: No such file or directory
$ ./lockcreation
File opened successfully
$ ls lock*.txt
lockfile.txt
```

The program calls the open() system call to create a file, lockfile.txt, using the O_CREAT and O_EXCL flags. Mode 0744 indicates the permissions in octal form. The file will be created with read, write, and execute permissions assigned to the user (owner) and read permission to the group and other users. When this code is executed for the first time, it will create the file, lockfile.txt in exclusive mode but when the code is executed for the second time, the file will not be created because of the O_EXCL flag. The O_EXCL flag represents the exclusive flag and it opens the file only if it does not already exist.

Now, until and unless the file lockfile.txt is deleted manually, no other process can create the lock file and hence cannot access the file (or resource). To avoid the overhead of deleting lockfile.txt manually, we can modify this program in such a way that when the task of the process (that created the lock file) is complete, it deletes the file by itself, allowing another process to create the lock file. The code is modified to appear as follows.

```
lockcreation2.c
#include <fcntl.h>
#include <errno.h>

main()
{
   int fd;
   fd = open("lockfile.txt", O_RDWR | O_CREAT | O_EXCL, 0744);
   if (fd == -1) {
      printf("File is already locked\n");
   }
   else {
      printf("Process %d has created the lock file and is using it \n", getpid());
      /* Here the code that the process needs to execute exclusively  can be written */
      close(fd);
      unlink("lockfile.txt");
   }
}
```

Output

```
File is already locked
```

In the aforementioned code, the file is created in exclusive mode and while it is being used by the process, no other process will be able to create the lock file, lockfile.txt again. When the process (that created the lock file) is finished with its task, it closes the file and deletes it.

Deleting the file lockfile.txt indicates that the first process has completed its job (that it wished to run exclusively) and another process is welcome to create a lock file again.

7.11.2 Record Locking

Locking the entire file when a program is writing decreases the efficiency of the program. It is a better approach to lock only the region of the file that is being updated leaving the rest of the file to be accessed by other programs. Locking only a section or region of the file, allowing programs to access other parts of the file is called file region locking or simply, region locking. The system call used for locking regions of the file is the fcntl system call.

Syntax   `int fcntl(int fd, int command, struct flock *flock_structure);`

fcntl operates on open file descriptors and depending on the supplied command parameter, performs different tasks. The three command options for file locking are as follows:

1. F_GETLK
2. F_SETLK
3. F_SETLKW

The third parameter is a pointer to a struct flock that consists of the following members (refer to Table 7.21).

The l_type member indicates the type of lock. The following are the types of locks (refer to Table 7.22).

Table 7.21   Members of the flock structure

Value	Description
short l_type	It defines the type of desired lock. The available options are given here: F_RDLCK: Read only (shared) lock F_WRLCK: Write (exclusive) lock F_UNLCK: Unlocks the region
pid_t l_pid	It represents the process identifier requesting the lock.
short l_whence	It represents location in the file to define region. The available options are SEEK_SET, SEEK_CUR, and SEEK_END.
off_t l_start	It represents the start byte of the region of the file for which lock is requested.
off_t l_len	It represents the length of the region in bytes.

Table 7.22   Brief description of the types of locks

Value	Description
F_RDLCK	This value represents the read (shared) lock. The read lock is shareable among several processes. Since it does not change the content of the file, several processes can have a shared lock on the same regions of the file. If any process has a shared lock, then no process can get an exclusive lock on that region. The file must be opened and must have read or read/write access to get a read lock.
F_UNLCK	This indicates that the region is unlocked.
F_WRLCK	This value represents the exclusive (or 'write') lock. Only a single process can have an exclusive lock on any particular region of a file. Once a process has an exclusive lock, no other process will be able to get any other type of lock, neither read nor write lock on that region. The file must be opened and must have read/write access to get a write lock.

The l_whence, l_start, and l_len members define a region in a file to be locked. l_whence indicates the location in the file, that is, whether it is the beginning, current, or end of the file and is represented by the symbolic constants, SEEK_SET, SEEK_CUR, and SEEK_END. l_start represents the first byte related to the location specified in l_whence. The l_len parameter defines the number of bytes in the region. The l_pid parameter represents the process identifier holding a lock.

The three command options for file locking are as follows:

F_GETLK command

The F_GETLK command gets locking information of the file represented by the file descriptor fd. It is used for determining the current state of locks on a region of a file. The process requesting for a lock sets the values of the fields in the flock structure to indicate the type of the desired lock, region, etc. The fcntl call returns a value other than −1 if it is successful. If the file already has locks, the content in the flock structure is overwritten with the current status. If the fcntl call succeeds and the lock is granted, the content of fields in the flock structure remains unchanged.

F_SETLK command

The F_SETLK command attempts to lock or unlock the region of the file represented by the file descriptor fd. Again, the fields of the flock structure are set to define the region that we wish to lock, that is, the l_start, l_whence, and l_len fields are set to define the region. If the lock is successful, fcntl returns a value other than −1.

F_SETLKW command

The F_SETLKW command is same as the F_SETLK command with the difference that if it cannot obtain the lock, the call will wait until it gets the lock.

Note: When a file is closed, all the locks held on it are automatically cleared.

Types of locks

The various types of locks are as follows:

Read locks   The read (shareable) lock is acquired on a region (record) when a process wishes to only fetch content, but not update it. When a process locks a region through the read lock, other processes can also get read locked on the same region or a part of it, but no write lock can be acquired on that region. Being shareable in nature, several processes can get the read lock on the same region making it possible for all of them to read the content of the file simultaneously.

Write locks   The write (exclusive) lock is acquired by a process on a region when it wishes to update its content. To maintain file integrity and consistency, no other process can get the write lock or read lock on the same region (or part of it) that is already write locked by some other process. Until and unless the region is unlocked, no other process can lock the region through the read or write lock.

Examples   The following statements apply a read lock in the file lockfile.txt in the region that extends from the 5th byte to the 15th byte.

```
int fd, flag;
struct flock region;
fd = open("lockfile.txt", O_RDWR | O_CREAT, 0744);
region.l_type = F_RDLCK;
region.l_whence = SEEK_SET;
region.l_start = 5;
region.l_len = 10;
flag = fcntl(fd, F_SETLK, &region);
if (flag == -1) {
  printf("Region could not be locked\n");
} else {
  printf("Region successfully locked\n");
}
```

The following statements apply a write lock (exclusive lock) in the file lockfile.txt in the region that extends from the 20th byte to the 30th byte.

```
int fd, flag;
struct flock region;
fd = open("lockfile.txt", O_RDWR | O_CREAT, 0744);
region.l_type = F_WRLCK;
region.l_whence = SEEK_SET;
region.l_start = 20;
region.l_len = 10;
flag = fcntl(fd, F_SETLK, &region);
if (flag == -1) {
  printf("Region could not be locked\n");
} else {
  printf("Region successfully locked\n");
}
```

7.11.3 Competing Locks

When a region is locked with any lock, whether shareable or exclusive, there are quite a few chances that another process attempts to lock the same region—such a situation is one where different locks compete. When a region is locked by a read lock, which is shareable in nature, another process can lock the same region with a shareable lock but no exclusive lock. In case a region is locked by an exclusive lock, it cannot be locked by a lock of any type (neither read nor write) until and unless the region is unlocked.

Example   The following code demonstrates competing locks. We will see how certain regions are locked by shareable and exclusive locks.

```
competinglocks.c
#include <stdio.h>
#include <unistd.h>
#include <fcntl.h>
```

```
int main()
{
    int fd, flag;
    struct flock region;
    fd = open("lockfile.txt", O_RDWR | O_CREAT, 0744);
    if (!fd) {
        fprintf(stderr, "Unable to open lock file for read/write\n");
        exit(1);
    }
    region.l_type = F_RDLCK;
    region.l_whence = SEEK_SET;
    region.l_start = 5;
    region.l_len = 10;
    flag = fcntl(fd, F_SETLK, &region);
    if (flag == -1) {
        printf("Region could not be locked\n");
    } else {
        printf("Region successfully locked\n");
    }
    region.l_type = F_RDLCK;
    region.l_whence = SEEK_SET;
    region.l_start = 5;
    region.l_len = 5;
    flag = fcntl(fd, F_SETLK, &region);
    if (flag == -1) {
        printf("Region could not be locked\n");
    } else {
        printf("Region successfully locked\n");
    }
    region.l_type = F_WRLCK;
    region.l_whence = SEEK_SET;
    region.l_start = 20;
    region.l_len = 10;
    flag = fcntl(fd, F_SETLK, &region);
    if (flag == -1) {
        printf("Region could not be locked\n");
    } else {
        printf("Region successfully locked\n");
    }
    region.l_type = F_RDLCK;
    region.l_whence = SEEK_SET;
    region.l_start = 20;
    region.l_len = 5;
    flag = fcntl(fd, F_SETLK, &region);
```

```
      if (flag == -1) {
        printf("Region could not be locked\n");
      } else {
        printf("Region successfully locked\n");
      }
      region.l_type = F_UNLCK;
      region.l_whence = SEEK_SET;
      region.l_start = 20;
      region.l_len = 10;
      flag = fcntl(fd, F_SETLK, &region);
      if (flag == -1) {
        printf("Region could not be unlocked\n");
      } else {
        printf("Region successfully unlocked\n");
      }
      region.l_type = F_RDLCK;
      region.l_whence = SEEK_SET;
      region.l_start = 20;
      region.l_len = 5;
      flag = fcntl(fd, F_SETLK, &region);
      if (flag == -1) {
        printf("Region could not be locked\n");
      } else {
        printf("Region successfully locked\n");
      }
      close(fd);
}
```

Output

```
Region successfully locked
Region successfully locked
Region successfully locked
Region successfully locked
Region successfully unlocked
Region successfully locked
```

In the aforementioned code, we can see that a region from the 5th to the 15th byte is locked with a shareable (read) lock. Being under shareable lock, a region within the locked region from the 5th till the 10th byte is successfully re-locked in read lock mode. Thereafter, a region from the 20th till the 30th byte is locked with an exclusive (write) lock. An attempt to lock the same region (the 20th to the 30th byte) with read lock fails, as the write lock is an exclusive lock. The same region is then successfully unlocked. Once the exclusive lock is removed, the region from the 20th to the 30th byte is successfully locked with a read lock.

Note: When a region is locked with a shareable lock, another shareable lock can be created for the same region but not an exclusive lock. When a region is locked with an exclusive lock, no other lock can be created.

7.11.4 Deadlock

A deadlock is a situation in which the application hangs because two or more of its processes are unable to proceed as each is waiting for one of the others to release locks on certain regions. Let us assume that there are three running processes P1, P2, and P3, which have acquired write lock on regions R1, R2, and R3 respectively (refer to Fig. 7.1). In order to proceed, the process P1 wants the process P2 to release the write lock on region R2. Similarly, the process P2 is waiting for the process P3 to release the write lock on region R3. The process P3, on the other hand, is waiting for process P1 to release the lock on the region R1 to proceed further. Hence, there is a cycle of processes where each process is waiting for another to release the lock on a region to proceed. As a result, no process is able to finish its task and remains suspended for an infinite time. This situation where each process is stuck waiting for another process to release locks is known as deadlock.

The conditions that may result in a deadlock are as follows:

Mutual exclusion   Each region is locked by an exclusive lock (write lock). Shareable lock (read lock) on the required region does not exist, making it impossible for two or more processes to simultaneously access the same region.

Hold and wait   Processes are holding a lock on a region and waiting for locks on other region (without releasing existing locks).

No preemption   No process is ready to move back and release the region locked by it.

Circular wait   Each process is waiting to obtain a lock on the region that is already locked by another process.

The following are the ways to solve the deadlock problem:

Detection and recovery   If a deadlock occurs, take necessary action to resolve it. Action may include preempting a process and releasing the locks acquired by it. Deadlock can be detected by making a resource allocation/request graph and checking for cycles. Avoid making cycles by implementing the cycle detection algorithm.

Prevention   Prevent deadlocks by checking before assigning region locks. If granting of a lock on a region may result in a deadlock, it should not be granted.

Ignoring   In this approach, it is assumed that a deadlock will never occur. This approach is used when there is a large time gap between the occurrence of deadlocks. In addition, there is not much loss in efficiency or data during the deadlocks.

Avoidance   Deadlock can be avoided if the operating system knows in advance the requirement of resources by all the processes during their lifetime. The benefit of this information is that when a request for a resource

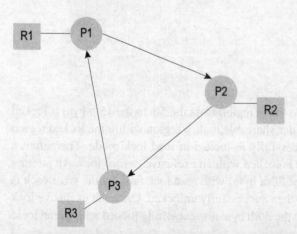

Fig. 7.1   Cycle appearing among three processes resulting in a deadlock

appears, the operating system will first check and ensure that the allocation of resources will not result in a deadlock. The operating system will therefore grant the resource only when it leads to a safe state. To determine whether the requested resource should be granted or not, the system must have the knowledge of resources currently available, the resources currently allocated to each process, and the future requests and releases of each process. One algorithm that is used for deadlock avoidance is the Banker's algorithm, which requires resource usage limit to be known in advance. Practically, it is not possible to know in advance what every process will request. This means that deadlock avoidance is often impossible.

In this chapter, we learnt about system calls of different categories including system calls that are dealt in file handling, directory handling, and process handling. We also saw different library functions. We discussed the library functions related to streams and the ones that are used in dynamic memory management. We also understood handling of stream errors. To maintain file integrity, we studied how a file and its regions are locked. Finally, we saw the conditions that may result in deadlock and how this problem can be solved.

■ SUMMARY ■

1. A system call is a request made to the operating system. It executes in the kernel address space.
2. Every open file is referred to using a file descriptor. The location of the file descriptor indicates the positions in the file from where the next read or write operation may begin.
3. The value of the file descriptor ranges from 0 through OPEN_MAX.
4. Besides the `create()` system call, a file can be created through the `open()` system call too.
5. The integer value represented by the file descriptor represents the distance, offset, or the number of bytes from the beginning of the file.
6. A file can be opened in several modes including read only, write only, reading and writing, append, and exclusive as desired.
7. File access permission for the new file can be defined in the `open()` system call. We can read the specified number of bytes from a given file through the `read()` system call.
8. The file descriptor automatically increments by the number of bytes read or within the file through the `read()` and `write()` system calls, respectively.
9. The location of the file descriptor in a file can be set through the `lseek()` system call.
10. We can have more than one name for a single file by linking to it via the `link()` system call.
11. The `unlink()` system call removes a given link to a file and also deletes the file if it is the last link.
12. To change the file access permission, the `chmod()` system call is used.
13. The system calls used to access status information of a file such as its inode number, protection mode, and time when it was last accessed or modified are `stat()`, `lstat()`, and `fstat()`.
14. The system call used for changing directory is `chdir()`. The system call used for opening a directory is `opendir()`. It returns a directory stream. The system call used for reading content of a directory is `readdir()`.
15. Each entry in a directory is read and stored into a `dirent` structure.
16. The `exec()` system call is used for transforming executable binary file into a process.
17. The `fork()` system call is used for creating a new process.
18. The system call `wait()` is used to make a process wait for some time to allow another process to finish.
19. The Unix library functions may invoke one or more system calls.
20. Unlike system calls, the library functions are executed in the user address space.
21. An appropriate header file has to be included in a program in order to use library functions.

22. The system calls are system dependent and hence not portable, whereas the library functions are not system dependent, and hence portable.

23. The library function `perror()` is used for displaying error messages.

24. Whenever a system call or library function fails, it returns a value −1 and assigns a value to an external variable called `errno`.

25. The system call `mknod()` is used to create a new regular, directory, or special file.

26. The `stat()` system call fills a buffer with status information of the specified filename.

27. When the link count of the file referenced by the link becomes 0 and is not accessed by any process, the file is removed freeing any space occupied by it.

28. The system call `chown()` changes the owner ID and group ID of the specified filename to the supplied ownerID and groupID, respectively.

29. `chmod()` changes the mode (permissions) of a filename to the supplied mode, where mode is specified as an octal number.

30. Only the owner or the super user can change a file's permissions.

31. `fchmod()` works in the same way as `chmod()` with the exception that it accepts the file descriptor of the file whose permissions we wish to change instead of the filename.

32. The `dup` system call is used for duplicating a file descriptor. It makes a duplicate of the supplied file descriptor and returns it.

33. The `dup2` system call copies one file descriptor to another specified file descriptor.

34. The symbolic link is created by the `symlink()` system call.

35. When the link count of the file referenced by the link becomes 0 and is not accessed by any process, the file is removed freeing up any space occupied by it.

36. The `access()` system call checks whether the user has the permissions to read, write, or perform other tasks on the specified file.

37. The `umask()` system call sets the file mode creation mask.

38. The three standard streams that are automatically opened when a program is started are `stdin`, `stdout`, and `stderr` having file descriptors 0, 1, and 2, respectively.

39. The `fopen` library function is used for opening files. The `fread` library function is used to read data from the specified file. The `fwrite` library function accesses data from the specified data buffer and writes them to the specified file. The `fclose` library function closes the specified file.

40. Any buffered data in the memory that is not yet flushed to the file stream is written into the stream before closing it.

41. The `fflush` library function converts all buffered data into a stream to be written immediately to the associated file.

42. The `getchar` function is equivalent to `getc(stdin)` and reads the next character from the standard input.

43. The `fputc` function writes a character to an output stream, which may be a file or `stdout` (output stream).

44. The `putchar` function is equivalent to `putc(c, stdout)` that writes a single character to the standard output.

45. The system calls used for making and removing directories are `mkdir` and `rmdir`, respectively.

46. We can know the current working directory by calling the `getcwd` system call.

47. The system call used to know our current position in a directory stream is `telldir()`. The system call used to set the directory entry pointer in the directory stream is `seekdir()`. The system call used to close the directory stream is `closedir()`.

48. The `malloc()` function allocates a memory block. The `calloc()` function allocates an array of memory and initializes all of the memory to zero. The `realloc()` function changes the size of the allocated memory.

49. If a program is updating or writing into a file, it needs to be locked until the writing procedure is over so that another program that is supposed to read the file does not get obsolete content.

50. When a region is locked with any lock, whether shareable or exclusive, there are chances that another process attempts to lock the same region; such a situation is one where different locks compete.

■ EXERCISES ■

Objective-type Questions

State True or False

7.1 The system calls execute in the user address space.

7.2 The Unix library functions may invoke one or more system calls.

7.3 The system calls are system dependent and hence are not portable.

7.4 System calls can perform all kinds of tasks except interprocess communication.

7.5 A file can be created through open() system call.

7.6 A file descriptor can be a negative integer.

7.7 A file descriptor points at the beginning of a file and its location cannot be changed.

7.8 On closing a file, all the resources allocated to it are freed.

7.9 By creating a link to a file, we basically create another filename for it.

7.10 The file descriptor cannot be duplicated.

7.11 The chmod() system call can change the links of the specified file.

7.12 Either the owner or the super user can change the file's permissions.

7.13 The fchmod() system call accepts the file descriptor of the file whose permissions we wish to change instead of the filename.

7.14 The ioctl system call is used for unlinking the specified file.

7.15 The dup system call is used for duplicating a file descriptor.

7.16 The default file descriptors for the three standard file streams, stdin, stdout, and stderr are 8, 9, and 10, respectively.

7.17 The symbolic link is created by the creat() system call.

7.18 The symbolic link to a file increments the file's link count by 2 instead of 1.

7.19 By unlink() system call, the link count of the file is decremented by one.

7.20 The umask() system call masks the files, that is, makes the file hidden for security reasons.

Fill in the Blanks

7.1 For executing system calls, the mode of a process is changed from _____ to _____.

7.2 The default value of operating system parameter OPEN_MAX is _____.

7.3 The O_TRUNC flag _____ older contents of the file.

7.4 The mode S_IRWXO when applied to a file will assign _____ permissions to _____.

7.5 The value SEEK_CUR in lseek() system call sets the file descriptor at its _____ plus the _____.

7.6 On failure, the system call close() returns a value _____.

7.7 For deleting files, the system call used is _____.

7.8 For successful execution of the chdir() system call, the process must have _____ permissions to the directory.

7.9 The structure _____ describes the directory entry that represent the files in the specified directory stream.

7.10 The ENOENT error occurs when _____ does not exists.

7.11 The exec() system call transforms an executable binary file into a _____.

7.12 The system call _____ can be used for knowing when a child process has completed its job.

7.13 The library function _____ is used for displaying error messages.

7.14 Whenever a system call or library function fails, it returns _____ value and assigns a value to an external variable called _____.

7.15 The system call _____ is used to create a new regular, directory, or special file.

7.16 The stat() system call is used for giving _____ of the specified filename.

7.17 The _____ system call returns information about a symbolic link itself rather than the file that it references.

7.18 The system call used for removing a link to a file is _____.

7.19 When the link count of the file referenced by the link becomes _____ and is not accessed by any process, the file is removed.

7.20 The system call chown() changes the _____ and _____ of the specified filename.

Multiple-choice Questions

7.1 The file's permissions can be changed either by the owner or the
    (a) group member   (c) super user
    (b) other user   (d) friend

7.2 The system call that copies one file descriptor to another specified file descriptor is
    (a) copy   (c) copy_fd
    (b) dup2   (d) make

7.3 The file descriptor assigned to the stderr stream is
    (a) 2   (b) 10   (c) 0   (d) 1

7.4 The system call by which a symbolic link is created is
    (a) symboliclink() (c) create()
    (b) slink()   (d) symlink()

7.5 The system call that checks whether the user has the permissions to read, write, or perform other tasks on the specified file is
    (a) check()   (c) permissions()
    (b) access()   (d) S_IRWXU

7.6 The standard stream for input is
    (a) keyboard   (c) standardin
    (b) instream   (d) stdin

7.7 The library function to read data from the specified file is
    (a) fread   (c) readfile
    (b) fetch   (d) readdata

7.8 The library function that is implicitly called when a program ends is
    (a) fclose   (c) terminate
    (b) bye   (d) fread

7.9 The library function used to set the position of the file pointer in the file is
    (a) fsetpos   (c) fflush
    (b) fclose   (d) fseek

7.10 The system call used to remove the empty directory is
    (a) deldir   (c) emptydir
    (b) remove   (d) rmdir

Programming Exercises

7.1 What are the following commands expected to do?
    (a) fp = open("xyz.txt", O_CREAT|O_WRONLY|O_TRUNC, S_IRWXU);
    (b) void *buf = (char *) malloc(512);
    (c) write(fd2, buf, n)
    (d) mknod("stock.txt", S_IFREG | S_IRWXU, dev);
    (e) fd2 = dup(fd1);
    (f) lseek(fd1, -10, SEEK_END);
    (g) stat("xyz.txt",&statusbuf);
    (h) chown("xyz.txt",2, 15)
    (i) chmod("xyz.txt", 0755);
    (j) c = fgetc(fp1);

7.2 Write down the commands for performing the following tasks:
    (a) To write a character in variable c in the file pointed by file pointer fp
    (b) To open the file xyz.txt in read mode
    (c) To read the content of the directory, projects.
    (d) To set the permission of the file xyz.txt to octal value 0765
    (e) To display an error message, "File does not exist"
    (f) To change the owner of the file xyz.txt to user with ID 25
    (g) To create a link of the file aa.txt with the name bb.txt
    (h) To write the text, "Good Morning" in the file xyz.txt pointed to by file pointer fp
    (i) To make a duplicate of the file descriptor fp with the name fq
    (j) To close the file pointed by the pointer, fp

Review Questions

7.1 Write short notes on the following system calls:
    (a) opendir()
    (b) lseek()
    (c) unlink()
    (d) wait()
    (e) write()

7.2 What are the system calls that are used for accessing file information? Explain these along with their syntax.

7.3 Which system call is used in opening a file? List all its flags and modes.

7.4 What are the differences between the following?

(a) `fork()` and `vfork()` system calls.

(b) System calls and library functions

7.5 Write a program that emulates the `cat` command, that is, displays the content of the specified file on the screen.

7.6 Explain the difference between the following:

(a) `calloc()` and `malloc()`

(b) read lock and `write` lock

(c) open and `fopen`

(d) `fgets` and `gets`

7.7 Explain the following:

(a) Deadlock

(b) File Locking

(c) `fflush`

7.8 How is a record or region locked in a file? Explain with a running code.

7.9 Explain the systems calls required in making, opening, reading, and closing a directory stream.

Brain Teasers

7.1 How will you set the file pointer in a file to read its last 5 bytes?

7.2 Can you emulate the `cat` command, that is, read the content of a file and display on the screen. How?

7.3 What flag will you use while opening a file so that its existing content is not deleted?

7.4 You are trying to create a link of the file `a.txt` with a name `b.txt` through the `link()` system call. However, the `link()` system call fails. What might be the reason?

7.5 `Unlink()` system call is removing the link of a file. In what situations does it delete a file?

7.6 I am trying to find the status information of a link through the `stat()` system call but am not able

to succeed. What is the mistake I am making?

7.7 Correct the mistake in the following statement for opening a file, `xyz.txt` in read only mode:
`open("xyz.txt", "r");`

7.8 Correct the mistake in the following statement for writing a text message `Hello` in the file referred to by the file descriptor to `fd`.
`fwrite( fd, "Hello", 6 );`

7.9 Correct the mistake in the following statement for setting the file pointer to the begining of the file:
`lseek(fd, 0, SEEK_END);`

7.10 Correct the mistake in the following statement for reading 1024 bytes from the file referred to by the file descriptor `fd` into the buffer `buf`:
`read(fd, 1024, buf);`

■ ANSWERS TO OBJECTIVE-TYPE QUESTIONS ■

State True or False

7.1	False
7.2	True
7.3	True
7.4	False
7.5	True
7.6	False
7.7	False
7.8	True
7.9	True
7.10	False
7.11	False
7.12	True
7.13	True
7.14	False
7.15	True
7.16	False
7.17	False
7.18	False
7.19	True
7.20	False

Fill in the Blanks

7.1 user mode, kernel mode

7.2 4096

7.3 deletes

7.4 (read, write, and execute), other

7.5 current location, offset

7.6 -1

7.7 unlink

7.8 read

7.9 dirent

7.10 directory

7.11 process

7.12 vfork

7.13 perror()

7.14 -1, errno

7.15 mknod()

7.16 status information

7.17 lstat()

7.18 unlink()

7.19 0

7.20 owner ID, group ID

Multiple-choice Questions

7.1 (c)
7.2 (b)
7.3 (a)
7.4 (d)
7.5 (b)
7.6 (d)
7.7 (a)
7.8 (a)
7.9 (d)
7.10 (d)

Editors in Unix

After studying this chapter, the reader will be conversant with the following:

- Stream editor (sed) used for filtering out the desired data from the specified file
- Sed commands for inserting lines, deleting lines, saving filtered content into another file, loading content of another file into the current file, and searching content that match specific patterns
- Visual editor, vi, for creating and editing files
- Different commands for searching through text, replacing text, saving content, navigating to different parts of the file, deleting text, copying and pasting text, among others
- Modeless editor, emacs, for creating and editing files
- Functioning of different emacs editor commands used in cursor movement, dealing with buffers, cutting and pasting content, and searching for and replacing content, among others.

8.1 INTRODUCTION

A text editor is a program that enables us to create and edit content in a computer file. It also provides several facilities. Some of these are listed here:

1. Search facility to quickly search for desired patterns
2. Navigation facility to navigate to a desired location in the file
3. Facility to copy and paste content
4. Facility to find and replace content

The following are the standard text editors available on most Unix systems:

ed   It is a line-oriented text editor for the Unix operating system that was originally written in PDP-11/20 assembler by Ken Thompson in 1971. It is an interactive program that is used to create, display, and modify text files. Editing in the ed editor is performed in two modes, the command mode and the input mode. When invoked, ed is initially in the command mode. In this mode, commands entered from the keyboard are executed to manipulate the contents of the editor buffer. The characters 'a' (append), 'i' (insert), or 'c' (change) when pressed, make the ed editor switch to the input mode. The input mode is particularly used to add text to a file.

ex   It is a line editor that is a more friendly version of ed, but is a bit more complicated to operate than the screen-based visual editor, vi. Initially, computers used printing terminals instead of CRTs and line numbers were used to identify regions of the file. To edit a region of the file, the programmer used to print a line via its line number on the printing terminal and give the editing command to correct or edit the line. The ex editor is still popular even though the vi editor is more comfortable to work with. The ex editor can be invoked from the vi editor and we can switch to the vi editor from the ex editor too.

vi   It is a visual editor that was originally written by Bill Joy in 1976. It is popularly used for creating and editing files. It is available on almost all Unix systems. It has no menus and for performing operations, a combination of keystrokes are used. Remembering commands might be a cumbersome task, but otherwise it is a fast and powerful editor. It operates in two modes: command mode and insert mode. To switch to the insert mode, the characters 'i' (input) or 'a' (append) are used. To switch to the command mode, the Esc key is pressed. Another editor that is distributed with most Unix systems and is an enhanced version of vi is the *vim* editor. It is a highly configurable text editor written by Bram Moolenaar. It provides both the command line as well as the graphical user interface. The enhanced features in vim that give it an edge over vi include multiple windows and buffers, multi-level undo, syntax highlighting, filename completion, and visual selection.

sed   It is a non-interactive stream editor that is popularly used for filtering out the desired data from the specified file. It reads input sequentially, applies the operations specified via the command line (or a sed script), and directs the processed data to the standard output. Many of the commands in sed are derived from the ed line editor.

emacs   It is a popular and powerful screen editor that is simpler to use when compared to the vi editor. It supports spell checking and enables us to edit and view multiple files simultaneously. Most emacs commands use either the Ctrl key or the Esc key.

pico   It stands for pine composer and is a file editor that was designed to be used with the pine mail system. It is a simple editor and is very easy to use. To create or edit a file using pico, execute the command in the following syntax:

```
pico filename
```

Here, filename is the file that we wish to create or edit through pico. On using this command, we get a screen to create or edit the file. The commands for editing in pico are invoked using the Ctrl key sequences. At the bottom of the screen, the status lines are displayed to indicate the commands that are currently active. To save the file and exit pico, the ^x command is used.

In this chapter, we will learn about the three editors: sed, vi, and emacs. We will now discuss each of these in detail.

8.2 STREAM EDITOR

The stream editor or sed is a tool that scans the specified file and filters out the desired data for us. The tool was designed by Lee McMohan and is derived from the *ed* line editor, the original editor of Unix. For filtering through sed, we have to supply a data stream (input data) and instructions that contain the criteria for filtering the desired data from the data stream. The instruction can be written either in the command line (if it is small) or separately in a script file.

The instruction is a combination of two components, an *address* and a *command*, where the address contains the filter condition that is applied on the data stream to extract the desired data. The command (containing action) is applied on the desired data for processing.

Syntax `sed options 'address action' file(s)`

The different options that are used with the sed editor are briefly described in Table 8.1.

Table 8.1 Brief description of options used with the sed editor

Cption	Description
-n	Suppresses duplicate line printing
-f	Reads instructions from a file
-e	Interprets the next string as an instruction or a set of instructions (for a single instruction, -e is optional)

The *address* in a syntax refers to the range of data of the *file(s)* on which we wish to apply the desired *action*.

The sed has two ways of addressing lines:

1. By line number
2. By specifying a pattern that occurs in a line

The address can be either a one line number to select a single line or a set of two to select a group of contiguous lines. In the absence of an *address*, sed acts on all lines of the specified file(s). The *action* results in the filtering of data and also performs insertion, deletion, or substitution of text.

8.2.1 Actions with Sed

The list of actions that can be performed using sed is shown in Table 8.2.

Examples

(a) To understand the working of sed, let us consider the file bank.lst with the following lines.

Table 8.2 List of actions performed while using sed

Command	Description
i\	Inserts text before the current line
a\	Appends text below the current line
c\	Changes text in the current line with the new text
d	Deletes line(s)
p	Prints line(s) on a standard output
q	Quits after reading up to the addressed line
=	Prints the line number addressed
s/s1/s2/	Substitutes string s1 with string s2
r filename	Places the contents of the file filename after line
w filename	Writes the addressed lines to the file, filename

```
101  Aditya    0      14/11/2012  current
102  Anil      10000  20/05/2011  saving
103  Naman     0      20/08/2009  current
104  Rama      10000  15/08/2010  saving
105  Jyotsna   5000   16/06/2012  saving
106  Mukesh    14000  20/12/2009  Current
107  Yashasvi  14500  30/11/2011  saving
108  Chirag    0      15/12/2012  current
109  Arya      16000  14/12/2010  Current
110  Puneet    130    16/11/2009  saving
```

We assume that the columns of the aforementioned bank.lst file represent the account number, customer's name, balance, date of opening of account, and type of account, respectively. We give the following command.

```
$ sed '3q' bank.lst
```

Output

```
101   Aditya   0       14/11/2012   current
102   Anil     10000   20/05/2011   saving
103   Naman    0       20/08/2009   current
```

We can see that q means quit. Hence, the aforementioned command quits after the third line and we get the first three lines as the output.

(b) `$ sed '1,2p' bank.lst`

This command prints the second line of the file twice.

```
101   Aditya     0       14/11/2012   current
101   Aditya     0       14/11/2012   current
102   Anil       10000   20/05/2011   saving
102   Anil       10000   20/05/2011   saving
103   Naman      0       20/08/2009   current
104   Rama       10000   15/08/2010   saving
105   Jyotsna    5000    16/06/2012   saving
106   Mukesh     14000   20/12/2009   Current
107   Yashasvi   14500   30/11/2011   saving
108   Chirag     0       15/12/2012   current
109   Arya       16000   14/12/2010   Current
110   Puneet     130     16/11/2009   saving
```

Note: By default, sed prints all lines on the standard output. Now, when we use the p command (which means print), the addressed lines will be printed twice.

-n option   It suppresses duplicate line printing.

Example   `$ sed -n '1,2p' bank.lst`

```
101   Aditya   0       14/11/2012   current
102   Anil     10000   20/05/2011   saving
```

This command prints only the first two lines of the file, `bank.lst`.

$ sign   This selects the last line of the file.

Example   `$ sed -n '$p' bank.lst`

```
110   Puneet   130   16/11/2009   saving
```

Negation operator (!)   The sed also has a negation operator (!), which can be used with any action. For instance, selecting the first two lines is the same as not selecting line 3 through the end.

Examples

(a) `$ sed -n '3,$!p' bnk.lst`

This command does not print from the third line till the end of the file, that is, it prints the first two lines.

```
        101     Aditya    0       14/11/2012    current
        102     Anil      10000   20/05/2011    saving
```

(b) `$ sed -n '3,$p' bank.lst`

This command prints from the third line till the end of the file.

```
        103     Naman     0       20/08/2009    current
        104     Rama      10000   15/08/2010    saving
        105     Jyotsna   5000    16/06/2012    saving
        106     Mukesh    14000   20/12/2009    Current
        107     Yashasvi  14500   30/11/2011    saving
        108     Chirag    0       15/12/2012    current
        109     Arya      16000   14/12/2010    Current
        110     Puneet    130     16/11/2009    saving
```

(c) `$ sed -n '$!p' bank.lst`

This command prints all the lines except the last line.

```
        101     Aditya    0       14/11/2012    current
        102     Anil      10000   20/05/2011    saving
        103     Naman     0       20/08/2009    current
        104     Rama      10000   15/08/2010    saving
        105     Jyotsna   5000    16/06/2012    saving
        106     Mukesh    14000   20/12/2009    Current
        107     Yashasvi  14500   30/11/2011    saving
        108     Chirag    0       15/12/2012    current
        109     Arya      16000   14/12/2010    Current
```

(d) `$ sed -n '5,7p' bank.lst`

This command prints from the fifth line to the seventh line.

```
        105     Jyotsna   5000    16/06/2012    saving
        106     Mukesh    14000   20/12/2009    Current
        107     Yashasvi  14500   30/11/2011    saving
```

(e) `$ sed -n '5,7!p' bank.lst`

This command prints all the lines except the fifth to seventh lines.

```
        101     Aditya    0       14/11/2012    current
        102     Anil      10000   20/05/2011    saving
        103     Naman     0       20/08/2009    current
        104     Rama      10000   15/08/2010    saving
        108     Chirag    0       15/12/2012    current
        109     Arya      16000   14/12/2010    Current
        110     Puneet    130     16/11/2009    saving
```

(f) `$ sed -n -e '1,2p' -e '7,9p' bank.lst`

This command prints from the first to second and the seventh to ninth lines.

```
        101     Aditya    0       14/11/2012    current
        102     Anil      10000   20/05/2011    saving
        107     Yashasvi  14500   30/11/2011    saving
        108     Chirag    0       15/12/2012    current
        109     Arya      16000   14/12/2010    Current
```

Adding text

The instruction $a is used for adding text to the existing file. Enter the instruction $a followed by a backslash (\) and press the Enter key. We can add as many lines as we want. Each line except the last will be terminated by the backslash (\). The backslash (\) is considered a line continuation character. On the other hand, sed identifies the line without the \ as the last line of input.

Syntax	`sed 'a\`
	`... /* lines to be appended */`
	`... /* lines to be appended */`
	`...`
	`'file`

Here, a\ represents the append command, which is then followed by the lines to be appended to the specified file.

Example	`$ sed 'a\`

```
117     vinay     4500      11/08/2011     current\
118     hitesh    3300      15/09/2012     saving
'bank.lst
```
Output
```
101     Aditya    0         14/11/2012     current
102     Anil      10000     20/05/2011     saving
103     Naman     0         20/08/2009     current
104     Rama      10000     15/08/2010     saving
105     Jyotsna   5000      16/06/2012     saving
106     Mukesh    14000     20/12/2009     Current
107     Yashasvi  14500     30/11/2011     saving
108     Chirag    0         15/12/2012     current
109     Arya      16000     14/12/2010     Current
110     Puneet    130       16/11/2009     saving
117     vinay     4500      11/08/2011     current
118     hitesh    3300      15/09/2012     saving
```

Similarly, i\ is used for inserting text before every line of the file.

Examples

(a) `$ sed 'i\`

    `this is bank file`

    `'bank.lst`

This command will print the text, `this is bank file`, before each line of the file.
```
this is bank file
101    Aditya   0        14/11/2012    current
this is bank file
102    Anil     10000    20/05/2011    saving
this is bank file
103    Naman    0        20/08/2009    current
```

```
            this is bank file
      104   Rama     10000   15/08/2010   saving
       :     :         :         :          :
       :     :         :         :          :
       :     :         :         :          :
```

(b) Similarly, the following command inserts a blank line before every line of the file.

```
      $ sed 'i\
      'bank.lst
      101   Aditya   0       14/11/2012   current

      102   Anil     10000   20/05/2011   saving

      103   Naman    0       20/08/2009   current

      104   Rama     10000   15/08/2010   saving
       :     :         :         :          :
       :     :         :         :          :
       :     :         :         :          :
```

(c) `$ sed -n '/current/p' bank.lst`

This command shows all the lines having the pattern current in it.

```
      101   Aditya   0       14/11/2012   current
      103   Naman    0       20/08/2009   current
      108   Chirag   0       15/12/2012   current
```

(d) `$ sed -n '/[Cc]urrent/p' bank.lst`

This command shows all the lines having the pattern current or Current in it.

```
      101   Aditya   0       14/11/2012   current
      103   Naman    0       20/08/2009   current
      106   Mukesh   14000   20/12/2009   Current
      108   Chirag   0       15/12/2012   current
      109   Arya     16000   14/12/2010   Current
```

w (write)   This command helps in writing the selected lines in a separate file.

Examples

(a) `$ sed -n '/current/w bkk.lst' bank.lst`

This command will write all records with pattern current into the file bkk.lst. Hence, bkk.lst will have the following data.

```
      $ cat bkk.lst
      101   Aditya   0       14/11/2012   current
      103   Naman    0       20/08/2009   current
      108   Chirag   0       15/12/2012   current
```

(b) `$ sed -n -e '/current/w bkk.lst' -e '/saving/w bkw.lst' bank.lst`

This command will write all the records with pattern current into the file bkk.lst and all the records having pattern saving into the file bkw.lst.

```
      $ cat bkw.lst
      102   Anil     10000   20/05/2011   saving
      104   Rama     10000   15/08/2010   saving
```

```
105    Jyotsna   5000    16/06/2012   saving
107    Yashasvi  14500   30/11/2011   saving
110    Puneet    130     16/11/2009   saving
```

Hence, bkk.1st will have all the records with pattern current and bkw.1st will have all the records with pattern saving as the output.

-f option When there are numerous editing instructions to be performed, it is better to use the -f option to accept an instruction from a file.

For example, the previous instructions could have been stored in a file, say, chirag.fil.

```
/current/w cfile
/saving/w sfile
```

sed is used with the -f filename option:

```
$ sed -n -f chirag.fil  bank.1st
```

The aforementioned statement reads the sed commands from the file, chirag.fil, and applies them to the file bank.1st.

Substitution

The strongest feature of sed is substitution. It allows us to replace a pattern in its input with some other pattern.

Syntax   sed [address]s/string1/string2/

Here, string1 will be replaced by string2 in all the lines specified by the address. If the address is not specified, the substitution will be performed for all the lines containing string1.

Examples

(a) `$ sed '1,5s/current/cur/' bank.1st`
   This command will replace the word current by cur in the first five lines of bank.1st.

```
101    Aditya    0       14/11/2012   cur
102    Anil      10000   20/05/2011   saving
103    Naman     0       20/08/2009   cur
104    Rama      10000   15/08/2010   saving
105    Jyotsna   5000    16/06/2012   saving
```

(b) `$ sed -n 's/current/fixed/p' bank.1st`
   It will display only the lines where the current pattern is replaced by the fixed pattern.

```
101    Aditya    0       14/11/2012   fixed
103    Naman     0       20/08/2009   fixed
108    Chirag    0       15/12/2012   fixed
```

(c) `$ sed 's/current/fixed/' bank.1st`
   This command will display all the lines of the file along with the lines where current is replaced by fixed.

```
101    Aditya    0       14/11/2012   fixed
102    Anil      10000   20/05/2011   saving
103    Naman     0       20/08/2009   fixed
104    Rama      10000   15/08/2010   saving
```

```
105    Jyotsna    5000     16/06/2012    saving
106    Mukesh     14000    20/12/2009    Current
107    Yashasvi   14500    30/11/2011    saving
108    Chirag     0        15/12/2012    fixed
109    Arya       16000    14/12/2010    Current
110    Puneet     130      16/11/2009    saving
```

(d) `$ sed 's/current/fixed/w bkk.1st' bank.1st`

This command displays all the lines but copies into `bkk.1st` only those lines of the current account replaced by fixed. The following output will be displayed on the screen.

```
101    Aditya     0        14/11/2012    fixed
102    Anil       10000    20/05/2011    saving
103    Naman      0        20/08/2009    fixed
104    Rama       10000    15/08/2010    saving
105    Jyotsna    5000     16/06/2012    saving
106    Mukesh     14000    20/12/2009    Current
107    Yashasvi   14500    30/11/2011    saving
108    Chirag     0        15/12/2012    fixed
109    Arya       16000    14/12/2010    Current
110    Puneet     130      16/11/2009    saving
```

The file `bkk.1st` will have the following records:

```
101    Aditya     0        14/11/2012    fixed
103    Naman      0        20/08/2009    fixed
108    Chirag     0        15/12/2012    fixed
```

(e) `$ sed = bank.1st`

This command prints line numbers as well as file contents on separate lines.

```
1
101    Aditya     0        14/11/2012    current
2
102    Anil       10000    20/05/2011    saving
3
103    Naman      0        20/08/2009    current
4
104    Rama       10000    15/08/2010    saving
:      :          :        :             :
:      :          :        :             :
:      :          :        :             :
```

(f) `$ sed -n 'p' bank.1st -r bkk.1st`

It prints the contents of the file `bkk.1st` after the contents of the file `bank.1st`.

```
101    Aditya     0        14/11/2012    current
102    Anil       10000    20/05/2011    saving
103    Naman      0        20/08/2009    current
104    Rama       10000    15/08/2010    saving
105    Jyotsna    5000     16/06/2012    saving
```

```
    106     Mukesh      14000     20/12/2009     Current
    107     Yashasvi    14500     30/11/2011     saving
    108     Chirag      0         15/12/2012     current
    109     Arya        16000     14/12/2010     Current
    110     Puneet      130       16/11/2009     saving
    101     Aditya      0         14/11/2012     fixed
    103     Naman       0         20/08/2009     fixed
    108     Chirag      0         15/12/2012     fixed
```

(g) $ sed '1,2 d' bank.lst

It will display all lines of the file except the first two.

```
    103     Naman       0         20/08/2009     current
    104     Rama        10000     15/08/2010     saving
    105     Jyotsna     5000      16/06/2012     saving
    106     Mukesh      14000     20/12/2009     Current
    107     Yashasvi    14500     30/11/2011     saving
    108     Chirag      0         15/12/2012     current
    109     Arya        16000     14/12/2010     Current
    110     Puneet      130       16/11/2009     saving
```

Notes:

1. To affect all lines, we may either use the global address `1,$`, or simply drop the address altogether. In the absence of an address, sed acts on all lines.

2. Remember that in the absence of the `-n` option and print (`p`) command, all lines will be displayed, irrespective of whether a substitution has been performed or not.

Context addressing

Context addressing is a mechanism in which we cannot directly address the lines on which we wish to apply the sed command. Instead, a regular expression is included, which is enclosed within slashes (/). The command mentioned in the sed will be applied only to the lines that match the supplied regular expression in the following syntax:

Syntax   sed "/regular_expression/command" filename

Here, the regular_expression is evaluated to find the address(s) of the filename onto which the command has to be applied.

Example   sed -n "/$1/p" 'bank.lst'

This script uses the shell parameter, $1 as a context address for searching through the file, bank.lst. The data supplied by the user is assigned to the shell parameter $1, which is then searched in the file bank.lst and displayed on the screen.

Regular expression

The regular expressions (also known as *regexp* in short) are used for pattern matching. It provides an efficient mechanism to search for the desired content in a given file. Regular expressions are built making use of certain special characters known as meta characters. A brief list of meta characters used in regular expressions is given in Table 8.3.

Table 8.3 Brief description of meta characters used in building regular expressions

Meta character	Description
[ ]	This matches anything inside the square brackets. For example, [ab] checks matches for a or b.
–	This is used to define a range. For example, [a-d] checks matches for the characters from a to d (inclusive).
^	The ^ (caret) within square brackets negates the expression. For example, [^a] matches anything except a. Similarly, [^ab] matches anything except a and b and [^a-d] matches everything except a to d.
?	This matches the preceding character 0 or 1 time. For example, an?d will check matches for ad and and.
*	This matches the preceding character 0 or more times. For example, an*d will check matches for ad, and, annd, among others.
+	This matches the previous character 1 or more time. For example, an+d will check matches for and and annd, among others.
{n}	This matches the preceding character(s) *n* number of times. For example,[0-9]{3} checks matches for any three-digit integer, such as 123 and 329.
{n,m}	This matches the preceding character at least *n* times but not more than *m* times. For example, [0-9] {3,5} will check matches for integers consisting of three to five digits, such as 123, 1234, and 29056, among others.
{n,}	This matches the preceding character *n* or more times. For example, [0-9]{3, } will check matches for integers consisting of three or more digits, such as 123, 1234, 12345, and 123456.
.(dot)	This matches any character. For example, a.b will match for a1b, abb, axb, and a b. Similarly, 1.2 will match for 112, 1 2, 1a2, 1x2, and so on. To find a floating value, we need to use the escape key, i.e., prefix dot (.) with a '\' backslash. For example, 1\.2 will match for 1.2.

The following points should be taken into account when using a regular expression:

1. A caret (^) at the beginning of a regular expression matches the null character at the beginning of a line.
2. A dollar sign ($) at the end of a regular expression matches the null character at the end of a line.
3. The characters (\n) match an embedded newline character.
4. A period (.) matches any character.
5. A regular expression followed by a star (*) matches any number of strings matching the regular expression.
6. A string of characters within square brackets ([ ]) matches any character in the string. If the first character of the string is a caret (^), the regular expression matches any character except the characters in the string.
7. To group regular expressions, they can be enclosed in sequences, '\(' and '\)'.

Examples

(a) $ sed -n '/th/' bank.lst
This matches the lines that contain the pattern 'th'.

(b) `/[Tt]he./`

This matches the lines that contain the pattern 'the' or 'The' followed by any character.

(c) `/./`

This matches all lines.

8.2.2 Remembered Patterns

Before discussing this topic, let us recall a few types of pattern matching in sed, as shown in the following examples.

Examples

(a) `$ sed -n '/[Cc]*/p' bank.lst`

This example matches the words beginning with character 'C' or 'c'.

(b) `$ sed -n '/[a-z]*/p' bank.lst`

This example matches all the words that begin with a lower-case character.

(c) `$ sed -n '/[a-z]/p' bank.lst`

This example matches a lower-case character.

Now, assume that we want to match *a repetitive pattern* or display duplicate words/characters. In such situations, we need a mechanism to name or number the pattern so that we can check if it is repeating. For naming or numbering a pattern, we need to enclose it within '\(' and '\)' as shown in the following syntax:

Syntax   `sed [options] \(remembered_pattern1\) [\(remembered_pattern2\)]… file_name`

Here, the options and actions are the same as those shown in Tables 8.1 and 8.2, respectively.

Each pattern enclosed within '\(' and '\)' is numbered from 1, as shown in Fig. 8.1.

We can see in the figure that the first pattern (`[Cc]`) that is enclosed in \(and \) is considered as pattern 1 and the second pattern (`[a-z]`) that is again enclosed within \(and \) is considered as pattern 2, and so on. In sed, the remembered patterns are represented by the sequence number preceded by a \ (backslash). This implies that remembered pattern 1 is represented by \1, remembered pattern 2 by \2, and so on. Note that we can have nine different remembered patterns. We can use these remembered patterns for matching repetitive patterns in sed.

Examples

(a) The following statement matches the duplicated characters.

`$ sed -n '/\([a-z]\)\1/p' bank.lst`

We can see that the pattern `\([a-z]\)` is considered remembered pattern 1 and represents a lower-case letter. The `\1` following the remembered pattern 1 represents the remembered pattern 1, that is, the patterns with repeated lower-case letters will be matched in the file, `bank.lst`.

`$ sed -n '/\ ([Cc]\) \ ([a-z]\) /p' bank.lst`

Remembered pattern 1   Remembered pattern 2

Fig. 8.1   Representation of the remembered patterns

(b) The following example matches the pattern that consists of three characters, where the first and third characters are exactly the same.

`$ sed -n '/\([a-z]\)\([a-z]\) \1/p' bank.lst`

By using these statements all the three characters in the file bank.1st are displayed in which the first and the third characters are the same (e.g., aba, bab, kmk).

(c) Similarly, the following example matches the pattern that consists of three characters and where the second and the third characters are exactly the same.

```
$ sed -n '/\([a-z]\)\([a-z]\) \2/p' bank.1st
```

By using these statements, all the three characters in the file bank.1st are displayed in which the second and the third characters are the same (e.g., abb, baa, kmm).

(d) The following example matches the duplicate words in the file bank.1st.

```
$ sed -n '/\([a-z][a-z]*\) \1/p' bank.1st
```

8.3 VISUAL EDITOR

Visual editor (vi editor), is a powerful and sophisticated tool for creating and editing files. The vi editor is basically a text editor that works on any type of terminal. It displays one full screen of text and allows us to enter text, edit text, search for desired content, navigate or scroll to any part of the text, and much more. The batch file named .exrc is executed from our home directory every time we load vi. The .exrc file can be used for customizing vi sessions.

The three common ways of starting a vi session are shown in Table 8.4.

Table 8.4   Brief description of the ways to start vi

Method	Description
vi filename	Opens the specified filename for editing
vi + n filename	Opens the filename at line *n* for editing
vi +/ pattern filename	Opens the filename where the specified pattern appears in the filename

Examples

(a) `$ vi a.txt`

This statement opens the file a.txt for editing. If a.txt is a new file, we get a blank screen where each blank line is marked by tilde characters (~).

(b) `$ vi +10 a.txt`

This statement opens the file a.txt at line 10 for editing.

(c) `$ vi +/saving a.txt`

This statement opens the file a.txt where the pattern, saving appears for the first time in the file.

Modes of operation

The vi editor has three modes of operation.

Command mode   Every key pressed in this mode is treated as a command.

Insert mode   Every key pressed in this mode will show up as text in the file.

Line editor mode   The line editor mode is also called the ex mode. It invokes the line editor ex and we can issue any ex command from within the vi editor.

When we invoke vi, we will be in the command mode. One can move into insert mode by pressing the a, I, A, or O keys and start inserting or appending text to the file. To get back to the command mode from insert mode, press the Esc key. To switch to line editor mode, type : (colon) from the command mode. The : (colon) will appear at the bottom of the screen and we can give any ex command. To exit from the line editor mode, we need to press either the Enter key or the Esc key.

We will now discuss the various categories of functions and commands under the vi editor.

8.3.1 Creating and Editing Files

To create a new file or edit an existing file, we use the following syntax:

Syntax   `$ vi {filename}`

Here, `filename` is the name by which we wish to open a file.

If the filename already exists, a copy of it is opened in a temporary buffer space. If the filename does not exist, a blank buffer is opened for it. We add content, edit it, and perform all the tasks on the content in the buffer. On giving the save command, this content is physically written onto the file on the disk.

Example   `$ vi a.txt`

By using this statement, the file `a.txt` will be created and we will get a blank screen (buffer) to create its content. A screen, shown in Fig. 8.2, will be displayed, where each blank line begins with a tilde. At the bottom of the screen, the name and status of the file is displayed.

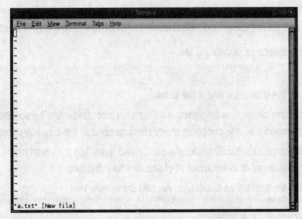

Fig. 8.2   Blank screen while creating a new file through vi

The vi editor always begins in the command mode. To switch to insert mode, we press the a, I, A, or O keys. To return to the command mode, we need to press the Esc key. To edit the content of the file, we need to be in the command mode only. There are a set of key combinations for editing content in a file: to insert text, delete text, search and replace text, navigate to a desired location in the file, etc. We just need to use the specified key combinations for applying the desired editing to the files. For each editing task, a set of key combinations are described in the tables that follow.

8.3.2 Inserting and Appending Text

As mentioned in Section 8.3, vi has two modes: the command mode and the insert mode. In the command mode, any key we press will be interpreted as commands. In the insert mode,

Table 8.5   List of commands to insert and append text

Command	Action
i	Inserts text to the left of the cursor
a	Appends text to the right of the cursor
I	Inserts text at the beginning of the line
A	Appends text to the end of the line

the keys pressed will form the content of the file. The keys used to insert or append text are shown in Table 8.5.

Example   Suppose the file a.txt in the vi editor appears as follows.

```
This is MCE Microchip Computer Education
Ajmer. We are working on vi editor.
```

```
It appears to be very interesting.
~
~
~
~
~
"a.txt" [New file]
```

Let us assume that the cursor is positioned at M (of MCE). On pressing i, the vi editor switches to the insert mode and any character we type will be inserted to the left of the cursor, that is, to the left of M. Similarly, on pressing a, the text typed will appear to the right of the cursor, that is, after M. On pressing I, the typed text will appear at the beginning of the line, that is, before the character T of This. On pressing A, the entered text will appear at the end of the line, that is, after the character n of Education.

8.3.3 Replacing Text

It is very common to commit mistakes while creating the content for a file. To correct these, the keys that we might require to replace and substitute content are shown in Table 8.6.

Table 8.6   List of commands to replace or substitute text

Command	Action
r	This replaces the character under the cursor.
R	This replaces the characters beginning with the character under the cursor until the Esc key is pressed, i.e., the overwrite mode remains on until the Esc key is pressed.
s	This substitutes one character under the cursor and goes into the insert mode. We can also specify the count of the number of characters to substitute.
S	This replaces the text with a blank line. We can insert new text.

Example   Consider the file a.txt (used in the example in Section 8.2.1) in the vi editor with the following initial content.

```
This is MCE Microchip Computer Education
Ajmer. We are working on vi editor.
It appears to be very interesting.
~
~
~
```

~

~

`"a.txt" [New file]`

Let us assume that the cursor is positioned at M (of MCE). On pressing r, whatever character we type will replace the character M. Similarly, on pressing R, the overwrite mode will become active and the text typed will replace the text beginning from character M of MCE until we press the Esc key. On pressing s, character M is replaced with the newly typed character and vi switches to the insert mode. On pressing S, a blank line is inserted at the position of character M so that we can type new text.

8.3.4 Inserting and Joining Lines

If we miss certain lines in the content and wish to insert lines below or above the current line or wish to join lines, we will require the keys shown in Table 8.7.

Table 8.7   List of commands to insert and join lines

Command	Action
o	It inserts a blank line below the current line.
O	It inserts a blank line above the current line.
J	It joins the current line with the line below. Position the cursor anywhere on the line to merge the lines, and press J to join the line below to the current line.

Example   Let us consider a.txt in the vi editor, which has the following content.

`This is MCE Microchip Computer Education`
`Ajmer. We are working on vi editor.`
`It appears to be very interesting.`
`~`
`~`
`~`
`~`
`~`
`~`
`"a.txt" [New file]`

Let us assume that the cursor is positioned at M (of MCE). On pressing o, a blank line will be inserted below the first line. On pressing O, a blank line will be inserted above the first line. On pressing J, the second line will be merged with the current first line.

8.3.5 Exiting and Writing to Files

The vi editor provides us with the facility to exit from it with or without saving the content. It also enables us to write to the file and continue entering or editing text.

In order to save the file, save and exit from the vi editor; to exit without saving or to perform similar kinds of operations, refer to the keys shown in Table 8.8.

Table 8.8 Commands to save the file and quit the vi editor

Command	Action
`:w`	Writes or saves the content to the file and continues editing, i.e., it does not quit vi
`:q`	Quits vi if the file is not modified
`:x`	Saves and quits file
`:wq`	Writes to the file and also quits vi
`ZZ`	Writes to the file and also quits vi
`:q!`	Quits vi without saving changes

Note: When we type the colon commands, the colon and the command appear in the lower left corner of our screen. On pressing the Enter key, the command is executed.

Example   Let us consider the file `a.txt` in the vi editor, which has the following content.

```
This is MCE Microchip Computer Education
Ajmer. We are working on vi editor.
It appears to be very interesting.
~
~
~
~
~

"a.txt" [New file]
```

On pressing Esc (if we are in the insert mode) followed by `:wq`, the content in the file will be saved and we can continue with our editing task. On pressing `:q`, we will exit from the vi editor if the file is the same as what was last saved and has not yet been modified. On pressing `:x`, `:wq`, or `ZZ`, the content in the file will be saved and we can quit from the vi editor. If we wish to exit from the vi editor without saving the content, we press `:q!`.

8.3.6 Navigating—Line Positioning and Cursor Positioning

For applying changes or adding content at the desired location in the file, we need to position the cursor at the desired location. The vi editor provides several commands to quickly navigate to the desired location in a line.

Though we can use arrow keys (in command mode) to navigate among the lines in a file, Table 8.9 shows the keys that we can use to quickly navigate to a desired location in the line.

Example   Assume that we are editing a file, `a.txt`, through the vi editor and has the following content.

Table 8.9 Brief description of line positioning and cursor commands

Command	Action
`h`	Moves the cursor one character to the left
`j`	Moves the cursor one line down
`k`	Moves the cursor one line up
`l`	Moves the cursor one character to the right
`Space bar`	Moves the cursor one character to the right
`Backspace`	Moves the cursor one character to the left
`$`	Moves the cursor to the last character of the line
`0 (zero)`	Moves the cursor to the first character of the line
`^`	Moves the cursor to the first non-blank character of the line

```
This is MCE Microchip Computer Education
Ajmer. We are working on vi editor.
It appears to be very interesting.
```

If the cursor is at the first character of the file, T, on pressing command j, we will be navigated to the next line, that is, to character A (of Ajmer). On pressing command k, we will be taken one line up, that is, to the character T (of This). On pressing command l or the space bar, we will be navigated one character to the right, that is, to character h (of This). On pressing command h or backspace, we will be navigated one character to the left, that is, to character T (of This). On pressing $, we will be navigated to the last character of the line, that is, to character n (of Education). On pressing 0, we will be navigated to the first character of the line, that is, to T (of This). If the cursor is at a blank space after This and we press ^, we will be navigated to the first non-blank character of the line, that is, to the character i of is.

8.3.7 Positioning Cursor on Words

Again, though we can use the arrow keys to navigate a file, Table 8.10 shows the keys that we can use to quickly position our cursor on the desired word in a file.

Table 8.10 Brief description of commands used for positioning the cursor on words

Command	Action
w	Moves the cursor to the first character of the next word
b	Moves the cursor to the first character of the previous word
e	Moves the cursor to the last character of the next word

Example Assume the cursor is at the first character in the file a.txt, whose initial content is as follows.

```
This is MCE Microchip Computer
Education
Ajmer. We are working on vi editor.
It appears to be very interesting.
```

On pressing command w, the cursor will move to the first character of the next word, that is, to character i (of is). On pressing command b, the cursor will move to the first character of the previous word, that is, to character T of This. On pressing command e, the cursor will be navigated to the last character of the next word, that is, to character s of is.

8.3.8 Positioning Cursor on Sentences

The vi editor provides commands to quickly locate the cursor on the desired sentence. A sentence is assumed to end with !, . (period), or ?. Table 8.11 shows the keys for positioning the cursor among sentences.

Table 8.11 Brief description of commands used for positioning the cursor on sentences

Command	Description
(	Moves the cursor to the beginning of the current sentence
)	Moves the cursor to the beginning of the next sentence

Example Assuming the cursor is at the first character in the file a.txt, that is, at character T of This, if we press the) command, it will be navigated to the beginning of the next sentence, that is, to character W of We. If the cursor is anywhere on the first sentence, say on character C of Computer, then on pressing the (command, it will be navigated to the beginning of the current sentence, that is, to character T of This.

8.3.9 Positioning Cursor on Paragraphs

Paragraphs are recognized by vi if they begin after a blank line. Make sure that each paragraph begins after a blank line. Table 8.12 shows the keys that we can use to navigate between paragraphs.

Table 8.12 Brief description of commands used for positioning the cursor on paragraphs

Command	Description
{	Moves the cursor to the beginning of the current paragraph
}	Moves the cursor to the beginning of the next paragraph

Example   Consider a file, a.txt which consists of the following two paragraphs.

```
This is MCE Microchip Computer Education
Ajmer. We are working on vi editor. It
appears to be very interesting.

Ajmer is a nice place to stay. FIRST it
is quite and calm. Secondly the distances
are small. Everything is in approach.
```

The first paragraph begins from the word This and ends with the word interesting. The second paragraph begins from the word Ajmer and ends at the word approach. If the cursor is at any word of the first paragraph say, character a of the word, are, then on pressing the } command, it will be navigated to the beginning of the next paragraph, that is, A of Ajmer. If the cursor is at any word of the first paragraph, say, at character w of working, then on pressing the { command, it will be navigated to the beginning of the current paragraph, that is, to character T of This.

8.3.10 Scrolling through Text

For faster navigation to the desired location in a file, we popularly use scrolling commands. Table 8.13 shows the keys that we can use to scroll to the next half screen, full screen, move to the previous half screen, full screen, and other similar operations.

8.3.11 Marking Text

If there are particular locations in a file that we wish to navigate frequently, vi enables us to mark those locations and we can directly navigate to those marked locations by using certain keys. Table 8.14 shows the commands we can use to mark locations and navigate to marked locations in a file.

Table 8.13 List of commands to scroll through a file

Command	Action
^u	Scrolls up half a page
^d	Scrolls down one full page
^b	Scrolls up one full page
^f	Scrolls down one full page
^e	Scrolls forward a line
^y	Scrolls backward a line

Table 8.14 List of commands for marking text

Command	Description
mk	Marks the current location as mark k
`k	Moves the cursor to the character marked by k
'k	Moves the cursor to the first character of the line marked k
``	Returns to the previous mark
"	Returns to the beginning of the line containing the previous mark

Example   Suppose a file, a.txt, consists of the following two paragraphs.

```
This is MCE Microchip Computer Education Ajmer. We are working on vi editor. It
appears to be very interesting.
Ajmer is a nice place to stay. FIRST it is quite and calm. Secondly the distances
are small. Everything is in approach.
```

Let us assume that we frequently need to visit the first and second paragraphs. For quicker navigation between paragraphs, we will mark the word MCE (any word) in the first paragraph and the word Ajmer in the second paragraph. We will position the cursor at character M of MCE and press mm to mark the location as m. Similarly, we will position the cursor to character A of Ajmer and press ma to mark the location as a. After marking the locations, we can navigate to the first paragraph at character M of MCE by pressing 'm. Similarly, we can move to the second paragraph to character A of Ajmer by pressing `a. On pressing 'm, the cursor will move to the first character of the line marked m, that is, to character T of This. If the cursor is at mark m, that is, at M of MCE, we can press `` to move to the previous mark, that is, to the mark a (to character A of Ajmer in the second paragraph). If the cursor is at mark a, that is, at character A of Ajmer, then on pressing ``, the cursor moves to the beginning of the line containing the previous mark, that is, to character T of This in the first paragraph.

8.3.12 Deleting and Undoing Text

When we commit mistakes while writing content in a file, we can correct them by deleting the undesired content. Table 8.15 shows the keys we can press to quickly delete content and also undo the changes, if required.

Table 8.15   Brief description of commands to delete and undo delete

Command	Action
x	Deletes the character at the cursor position
nx	Deletes n number of characters from the current cursor position
X	Deletes the character before the cursor position
dw	Deletes the current word
dd	Deletes the line where the cursor is
ndd	Deletes n number of lines
D or d$	Deletes a line from the cursor position till the end of the line
d^	Deletes a line from the cursor position to the beginning of the line
u	Undoes the last change and typing u again will redo the change
U	Undoes all changes to the current line

Example   Suppose a file, a.txt, consists of the following content.

```
This is MCE Microchip Computer Education Ajmer. We are working on vi editor. It
appears to be very interesting.
```

If the cursor is at character T of This, then the command x will delete character T of This. Pressing x thrice will delete three characters from the cursor position, that is, Thi of This will be deleted. If our cursor is at character h of This, then on pressing X, the character before the cursor position will be deleted, that is, character T will be deleted. On pressing dw the current word, This, will be deleted. On pressing dd, the current line, that is, the first line of the first paragraph will be deleted. On pressing 2dd, two lines, that is, the first two lines will be deleted. If the cursor is positioned at character C of Computer, then pressing D or d$ will delete the line from the cursor position till the end of the line, that is, the words Computer Education will be deleted. On pressing d^, the line from the cursor position till the beginning of the line is deleted, that is, This is MCE, will be deleted. On pressing u, the last delete command will be undone, that is, the words, This is MCE, will appear again. On pressing the U command again, the action will be redone, that is, the words This is MCE will be deleted again. On pressing the U command, the changes made in the current line will be undone.

8.3.13 Repeating Previous Commands

For repetitive editing, we might need to execute the same command several times. For such cases, the vi editor provides us a . (dot) command to repeat the last command. Similarly, if we have deleted a line by executing the dd command, we can delete another line by pressing. (dot). We can delete several lines by pressing .(dot) a few times.

Example   Assume that a file, a.txt, consists of the following content.

This is MCE Microchip Computer Education Ajmer. We are working on vi editor. It appears to be very interesting.

If the cursor is at the first line and we delete it using the dd command, then on pressing . (dot), the delete command will be repeated, that is, the second line will also be deleted. We can press . (dot) as many times as we want to delete more lines. Apart from delete, the . (dot) command can be used for repeating any previous command.

8.3.14 Going to Specified Lines

The vi editor provides us with the facility to directly go to any line of the file from our current location in the file. Table 8.16 shows the keys we can use to navigate to the required line of the file.

Assume that the file a.txt consists of the following content.

Table 8.16 Brief description of commands for navigating to a specified line

Command	Description
G	Goes to the last line of the file
nG	Goes to the nth line of the file

This is MCE Microchip Computer Education Ajmer. We are working on vi editor.
It appears to be very interesting.

If the cursor is at the first line and we press G, the cursor will be navigated to the last line of the file, that is, to the third line. On pressing 2G, the cursor will move to the second line of the file.

8.3.15 Searching for and Repeating Search Patterns

We can always search for the desired pattern in the given file. Not only can we search for a pattern, but also continue the search in either the forward or backward direction in the file. The continuation of the previous given search command in the forward or backward direction

Table 8.17 List of commands to search for and repeat desired patterns

Command	Description
/pattern	Searches for the specified pattern in the forward direction from the cursor position
?pattern	Searches for the specified pattern in the reverse direction from the cursor position
n	Repeats the last search command in the forward direction
N	Repeats the last search command in the opposite direction

is considered *repeating the search pattern*. Table 8.17 shows the keys for searching for a specified pattern in the file.

Example Assume that a file, a.txt, consists of the following content.

```
This is MCE Microchip Computer
Education
Ajmer. We are working on vi
editor. It is a fast editor.
It appears to be very interesting. Commands are hard to remember
```

The cursor is positioned at the first character of the file, that is, at T of This. To search for the word, are, we press the /are command. The cursor will be positioned at the first occurrence of the word, are, that is, on the second line. On pressing the n command, the search command will be repeated in the forward direction, moving the cursor to the next occurrence of the word are, that is, on the third line. On pressing character N, the search is repeated in the opposite direction, that is, towards the beginning of the file. The cursor will be positioned at the first occurrence of the word are, that is, on the second line. With the cursor on the second line, if we wish to search for the word is towards the beginning of the file from the current cursor position, press ?is. The cursor will be positioned at the word is that exists in the first line in the file.

8.3.16 Searching for Characters

Besides positioning the cursor at the desired word or pattern in the file, the vi editor also provides us with the facility to position the cursor at the desired character.

Table 8.18 lists the keys to search for a desired character in the file in the forward as well as in the backward direction.

Table 8.18 List of commands to search for a character

Command	Description
fx	Moves the cursor to the specified character, x, in the forward direction
Fx	Moves the cursor to the specified character, x, in the backward direction
tx	Moves the cursor just before the specified character, x, in the forward direction
Tx	Moves the cursor just after the specified character, x, in the backward direction
;	Continues the search specified in the command in the same direction and is used after the fx command
,	Continues the search specified in the command in the opposite direction and also works after the fx command

Assume that a file, a.txt, consists of the following content.

```
This is MCE Microchip Computer Education
Ajmer. We are working on vi editor. It is a fast editor.
```

```
It appears to be very interesting. Commands are hard to remember
```

If the cursor is positioned at the first character of the file, that is, at T of This and we wish the cursor to be positioned at character r (of Microchip), we press the fr command. On pressing tr, the cursor will be positioned just before character r, that is, under character c of Microchip. On pressing ; (semi colon), the search will continue in the forward direction and the cursor will move to the next character, r, that is, below character r of the word, Computer. If the cursor is positioned at the end of the first line and we press Fi, the cursor will search for character i in the reverse direction; hence, the cursor will be positioned to character i of the word Education. The command , (comma) continues the search in the opposite direction, that is, the cursor will be positioned below character 'i' of Microchip. The command Ti will continue the search in the reverse direction and positions the cursor after the character i, that is, under character c of Microchip.

8.3.17 Copying, Changing, Pasting, and Filtering Commands

While creating or editing content, we need to copy (or yank) and paste repetitive content. In addition, we need to cut and paste to move content from one location to another. The commands to copy the specified lines and paste them at the desired location are as follows (Table 8.19).

Table 8.19 Brief description of commands used to copy and paste lines

Command	Description
yy	Copies the current line
Nyy	Copies *n* number of lines
yw	Copies the current word
p	Pastes the copied text after the cursor
P	Pastes the copied text before the cursor
cc	Blanks out the entire line
C or c$	Overwrites the content from the place of the cursor until the Esc key is pressed
!	Executes commands external to vi for the purpose of filtering text
II	Edits the current paragraph
tr	Deletes or translate the filtered text

Example   Let us once again open the file, a.txt, which contains the following initial content.

```
This  is  MCE  Microchip  Computer
Education
Ajmer. We are working on vi editor.
It is a fast editor.
It appears to be very interesting.
Commands are hard to remember
```

Let us assume that the cursor is positioned at the first character of the file, that is, at T of This. The command yy will copy the entire first line into the memory. The command 3yy will copy all the three lines into the memory. The command yw will copy the word This into the memory. The command p will paste the copied content after the cursor, that is, after the character T of This command whereas the command P will paste the copied content before the cursor, that is, before character T of This. The command cc makes the entire line blank. The command C or c$ will switch the vi editor into the overwrite mode where any text typed will overwrite the existing content until the Esc key is pressed.

8.3.18 Set Commands

The escape colon commands enable us to set several configurations in the vi editor. Similarly, using these commands we can display line numbers, set the auto indent feature, display tabs and carriage returns, etc.

Table 8.20 Brief description of the commands to customize the vi session

Command	Action
:set nu	Numbers all the lines in the file, beginning from 1
:set nonu	Turns off line numbering
:set ai	Sets the auto indent feature
:set noai	Unsets the auto indent feature
:set ic	Ignores case when searching
:set ro	Changes the file type to read only
:set list	Displays the tabs and carriage returns
:set nolist	Turns off the list option
:set wrapmargin=n	Turns on word wrap n spaces from the right margin
:25	Moves to the 25th line of the file
:5,10d	Deletes lines starting from the 5th line to the 10th line

Table 8.20 shows the different commands that can be used to customize the vi editor.

On giving the :set nu command, all the lines in the file a.txt will be numbered. The first line is numbered 1, the second line is numbered 2, and so on, as shown in Fig. 8.3.

By default, the search operation in the vi editor is case sensitive. For example, if we give /Are command to search for the pattern 'are', the vi editor will respond displaying 'Pattern not found' on the screen, as shown in Fig. 8.4.

This is because the search is case sensitive; there are several 'are' but not a single pattern 'Are'. In order to compel the search command to ignore case, we give the command :set ic. With the :set ic command, the search command will perform case insensitive search. If we now search for pattern 'Are' by giving /Are command, the cursor will reach the first occurrence of the pattern, 'are' in the file, as shown in Fig. 8.5.

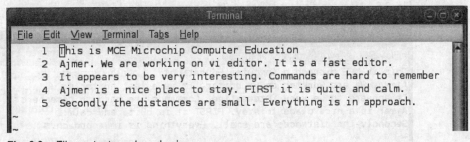

Fig. 8.3 File content numbered using: set nu

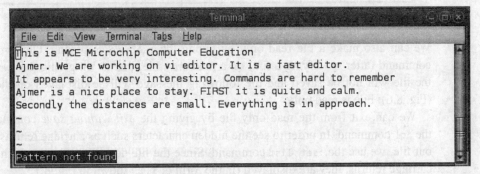

Fig. 8.4 'Pattern not found' displayed as search is case sensitive

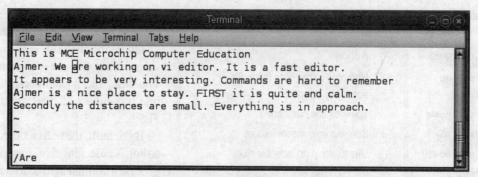

Fig. 8.5 Pattern found through case insensitive search

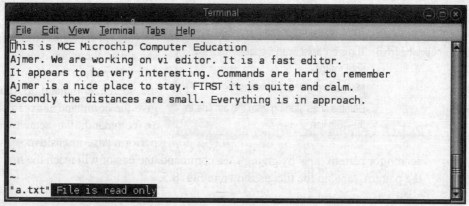

Fig. 8.6 Message displayed when we try to save a 'Read only' file

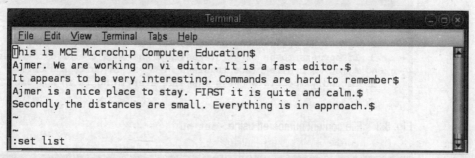

Fig. 8.7 Hidden characters displayed through `:set list` command

We can also make a file read only by giving the `:set ro` command. On giving the save command (after modifying a file) on a read only file, that is, on giving the `:wq` command, the file will not be saved and the following message will be displayed on the status bar (Fig. 8.6): File is read only.

We can exit from the read only file by giving the *exit without save* command, that is, the `:q!` command. In order to see the hidden characters such as carriage returns and tabs in our file, we use the `:set list` command. Since the file does not contain tab characters but carriage returns, they are displayed (in the form of $) as shown in Fig. 8.7.

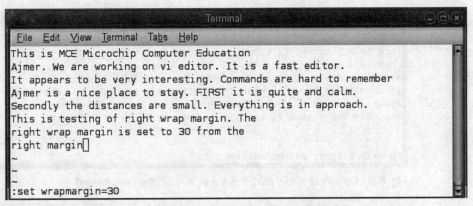

Fig. 8.8   Right margin set through the `:set wrapmargin` command

The right margin of the file can be set by the `:set wrapmargin` command. The content will wrap on to the next line when the cursor reaches the specified right margin. On setting the right margin to 30 spaces using `:set wrapmargin=30`, the cursor will wrap to the next line when the cursor reaches the right margin limit shown in Fig. 8.8.

8.3.19 Reading and Writing across Files

The vi editor provides us with the facility to share content among files, that is, we can paste content from other files into the current files and also write the selected content from the current file into a separate file. Apart from this, the output of an external command can also be pasted in the currently opened file. Table 8.21 briefly describes the commands to read and write content from the other file to the current file and vice versa.

Table 8.21   Brief description of the commands to read and write across files

Command	Description
`:r filename`	Places the text from the named file after the current line
`:nr filename`	Places the text after the line *n* from the file
`:r!command`	Places the output of the named command below the current line
`:n1, n2w newfile`	Writes lines starting from *n1* up to *n2* to the *newfile*

We already have a file, `a.txt`, with the aforementioned content. To see how the content can be shared between two files, we will create another file, `b.txt`, containing a single line of text:

```
This is a test file
```

Open the file, `a.txt` in the vi editor. Assuming the cursor is at the beginning of the file when we give the command `:r b.txt`, the content in the file, `b.txt` will be added in the current file below the current line. We can see that in Fig. 8.9, the text in the file `b.txt` is added to the file `a.txt` below the first line.

On giving the `:3r b.txt` command, the content of the file `b.txt` will be added after the third line in the current file `a.txt`, shown in Fig. 8.10.

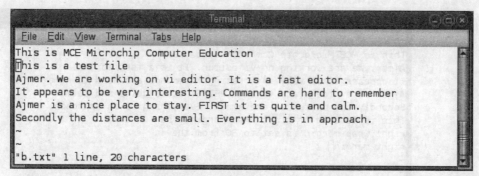

Fig. 8.9 Content of b.txt pasted in a.txt through the :r command

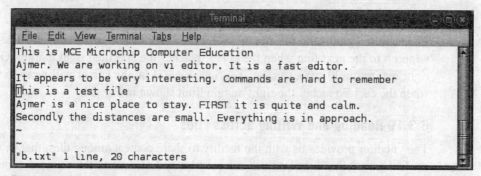

Fig. 8.10 Content of b.txt pasted into a.txt after the third line through the :3r command

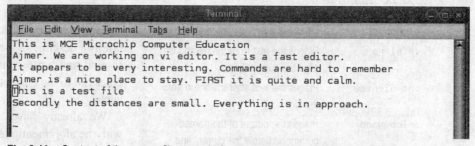

Fig. 8.11 Content of the b.txt file pasted after the current line, in the current file, a.txt, on executing the cat command

The vi editor provides us with the facility to run an external command within the vi editor and paste the output of that command below the current line in the opened file. Assuming that the cursor is on the fourth line in the file, a.txt, the command :r!cat b.txt pastes the content of the file b.txt below the fourth line in the current file a.txt, shown in Fig. 8.11.

We can also copy the desired content from the currently open file into a new file. We give the command :2,3w c.txt to copy the second and third line from the current file, a.txt. The status bar shows the message—c.txt' [New file] 2 lines—to indicate that a new file, c.txt, is created with the two lines from the current file shown in Fig. 8.12.

We can confirm if the new file, c.txt is created with the content from the a.txt file. Figure 8.13 shows the second and third lines copied into the file, c.txt.

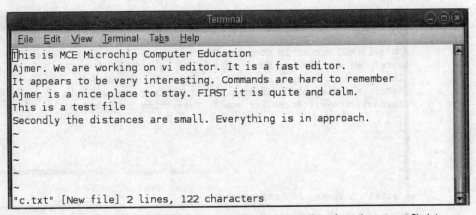

Fig. 8.12 Message displayed in the status bar on copying two lines from the current file into a new file, c.txt

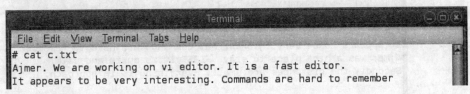

Fig. 8.13 Content copied into the file c.txt

8.3.20 Global Substitution—Find and Replace

We have seen the commands provided by the vi editor to search for different patterns in a file. In this section, we will see the manner in which the selected pattern can be replaced by the desired pattern. Table 8.22 shows a brief description of the commands to find and replace the desired patterns in a given file.

Table 8.22 Brief description of the commands to find and replace patterns

Command	Action
:s/pattern1/pattern2	Substitutes the first occurrence of pattern1 with pattern2 in the current line
:s/pattern1/pattern2/g	Substitutes all occurrences of pattern1 with pattern2 in the current line
:1,5s/pattern1/pattern2/g	Substitutes all occurrences of pattern1 from line 1 to line 5 with pattern2
:%s/pattern1/pattern2/g	Substitutes all occurrences of pattern1 with pattern2 in the file globally

We can now open the a.txt file in the vi editor to enter the commands for finding and replacing patterns in a file. The initial content in the file a.txt. is assumed to be as given in Fig. 8.14.

On navigating the cursor to the fourth line in the file we see that it contains two occurrences of the pattern 'is'. The command :s/is/was replaces the first occurrence of the pattern 'is' with the pattern 'was' shown in Fig. 8.15.

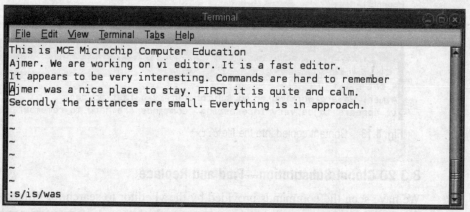

Fig. 8.14   Original content in the file `a.txt`

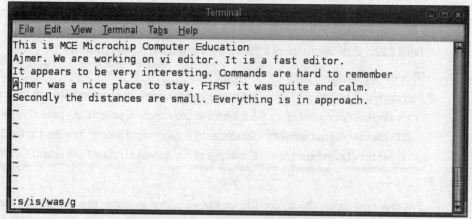

Fig. 8.15   First occurrence of the pattern 'is' replaced with 'was' in the current line

Fig. 8.16   All occurrence of the pattern 'is' replaced with the pattern 'was' in the current line

The command `:s/is/was/g` replaces all occurrence of the pattern 'is' in the current line with pattern 'was'. Both occurrences of the pattern 'is' in the fourth line will be converted to pattern 'was' as shown in Fig. 8.16.

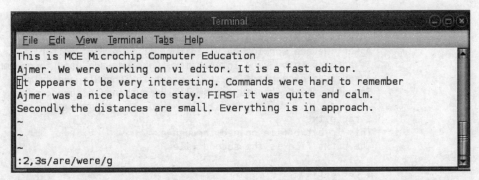

Fig. 8.17   All occurrence of the pattern 'are' replaced with the pattern 'were' in the second and third lines

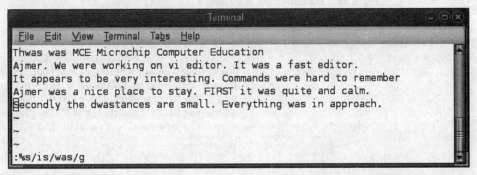

Fig. 8.18   All occurrence of the pattern 'is' replaced with the pattern 'was' in the entire file

The vi editor provides us with a facility to change patterns in specific lines only. The command :2,3s/are/were/g replaces the pattern 'are' with 'were' in the second and third line, as shown in Fig. 8.17.

The command %s/is/was/g replaces all the occurrence of the pattern 'is' with the pattern 'was' in the entire file even if it is a part of a word, as shown in Fig. 8.18.

8.3.21 Ex Mode—Line Editor Mode

Ex is a line editor that is commonly used for working with multiple files simultaneously. It helps in performing several operations including editing, copying, moving content from one file to another, switching from one file to another, and other similar actions.

This editor can be independently invoked from the command line as well as from the vi editor. To switch to ex (line editor) mode from within vi, type : (colon) from the command mode. The : (colon) will appear at the bottom of the screen and any ex command can be given. To exit from the ex mode, press either the Enter key or the Esc key. The following is the syntax to invoke the ex editor from the command line:

Syntax   ex file_name1 [file_name2] [file_name3]

In this section, we will assume that there exists three files, a.txt, b.txt, and c.txt, in our current directory with the content shown in Fig. 8.19.

```
$ cat a.txt
This is MCE Microchip Computer Education
Ajmer. We are working on vi editor. It is a fast editor.
It appears to be very interesting. Commands are hard to remember
Ajmer is a nice place to stay. First it is quite and calm.
Secondly the distances are small. Everything is in approach.

$ cat b.txt
This is b.txt file opened through ex
The b.txt file is the second file

$ cat c.txt
This is c.txt file opened through ex
The c.txt file is the third file
```

Fig. 8.19   Content of the three files, a.txt, b.txt, and c.txt

```
$ ex a.txt b.txt c.txt
3 files to edit
```

```
$ vi a.txt b.txt c.txt
This is MCE Microchip Computer Education
Ajmer. We are workig on vi editor. It is a fast
editor It appears to be very interesting. Commands
are hard to remember Ajmer is a nice place to
stay. First it is quite and calm. Secondly the
distances are small. Everything is in approach.
~
~
~
~
~
~
~
```

```
"a.txt" 5 lines, 283 characters
:
```

```
~
:▯
```

(a)   (b)

Fig. 8.20   Simultaneously opened files (a) ex line editor (b) vi editor

Example   `$ ex a.txt b.txt c.txt`

This command will simultaneously open the three files (a.txt, b.txt, and c.txt) in edit mode in the ex editor, as shown in Fig. 8.19.

We can open more than one file in the edit mode in the vi editor with the following syntax:

Syntax   `vi [filename1] [filename2][filename3]...`

Example   `vi a.txt b.txt c.txt`

This command (refer to Fig. 8.20a) will open all the three files (a.txt, b.txt, and c.txt) in command mode by default, with the first file, a.txt, as the current file. In order to switch to the ex-mode, we need to press colon (:), as shown in Fig. 8.20(b). The commands given in Table 8.23. are used while editing file(s) in the ex mode.

Table 8.23 Brief description of the commands used in ex mode

Command	Description
`:k1 [, k2][p]`	This displays line k1 of the current file on the screen. If k2 is also supplied, it displays lines in the range k1 to k2 on the screen. The default character, p, stands for printing on the screen. Writing 'p' alone will display the current line.
`:[+] [-] k`	+k will move k number of lines forward and display it. On the other hand, −k will move back k lines and display that.
`:s/pattern1/ pattern2/[g]`	This substitutes (replaces) the first pattern1 found in the current line with pattern2. For substituting all pattern1 with pattern2 globally in the current line, use the 'g' option.
`:r filename`	This reads the specified file and appends its content below the current line in the current file.
`:w filename`	This writes the edit buffer into the specified file, i.e., content of the currently open file will be written into the specified file.
`:n [!]`	This moves to the next file in the list and makes it the current file. The command is discarded if the current file is modified and not saved. The '!' command discards any changes made to the current file and moves on to the next file.
`: kn`	This advances k number of files in the list and makes it the current file
`:rew [!]`	This rewinds and opens the first file in the list. The command will be ignored and a warning message will be displayed if the current file is modified and is not yet saved. The '!' mark, when used, discards the changes made to the current file and moves on to the first file in the list.
`:ar`	This lists the currently open filenames.
`:e [!] [+n] filename`	This opens the specified file for editing. If the current buffer is modified and is not saved, a warning message will be displayed and the command is ignored. The '!' character will discard the changes made in the edit buffer and opens the specified file for editing. If +n is specified, the nth line is set as the current line.
`:r !commandname`	This runs the specified command and appends its output to the currently open file.
`:w`	This saves the currently open file.
`:q`	This quits editing.
`:q!`	This quits forcefully, discarding the changes

We assume that the three files, a.txt, b.txt, and c.txt, are simultaneously opened in the edit mode with the first file, a.txt as the current file. We know that a usual ex command consists of a line number followed by a command and ends with a carriage return.

Examples

(a) `: 1p`

This command will display the first line of the current file. The character p is the default, that is, the default action is printing the line. For example, the following command will display the 5th line of the current file.

`:5`

(b) To print more than one line, we can specify a range of line numbers separated by a comma. For example, the following command displays lines one to three.

```
:1,3
```

When we try to specify the line number beyond the length of the file, we get the following error message: `Not that many lines in buffer`.

(c) (i) A command without a line number is assumed to affect the current line. The following command will substitute the pattern 'is' with 'was' in the current line. The changed line will be reprinted.

```
:s/is/was/
```

(c) (ii) If the asked pattern is not found, the following message is displayed: `Substitute pattern match failed`. We can also specify the line where we need to apply substitution. For example, the following command substitutes the pattern 'is' with 'was' in the first line of the current file.

```
:1s/is/was/
```

(c) (iii) With the aforementioned command, only the first occurrence of the pattern 'is' in the first line will be replaced by 'was'. In order to replace all the 'is' patterns globally in the current line, we have to append 'g' to the command as follows.

```
:1s/is/was/g
```

(c) (iv) To substitute a pattern in a range of lines, we use the following command.

```
:1,5s/is/was/g
```

This command will replace all the patterns, 'is' found in lines one to five with the pattern, 'was'. If we do not use 'g', only the first occurrence of the pattern will be substituted. To apply substitution to the entire file, we use '$' that represents the last line in the edit buffer.

(c) (v) The following command substitutes the pattern, 'is' with 'was' in the entire file.

```
:1,$s/is/was/g
```

(d) The following command reads the specified file, `matter.txt`, and appends its contents after the current line.

```
:r matter.txt
```

(e) The following command writes the content in the edit buffer into the specified file `tmp.txt`.

```
:w tmp.txt
```

(f) We can also specify the range to write into the file. For example, the following command writes lines, from the first to the current one, of the edit buffer into the file `tmp2.txt`.

```
:1,.w tmp2.txt
```

In this command, . (dot) represents the current line.

(g) The following command moves forward four lines and displays it.

```
:+4
```

If there are not enough lines in the edit buffer, we get the following error message: Not
that many lines in buffer.

(h) The following command moves two lines backward and displays it.

    :-2

(i) We can move to the line containing the desired pattern. For example, the following
command moves to the line containing the pattern, editor.

    :/editor

(j) We can also mark any line with a specific term. The command used to mark any line is :k.
For example, the following command marks the current line as 'a'.

    :ka

(k) Now, we can refer to the current line as 'a'. To replace all the 'is' patterns by 'was'
patterns globally in the line, 'a', we will give the following command.

    :as/is/was/g

(l) The following command switches to the next file in the command line arguments list. The
command is discarded and a warning message is displayed if the current file is modified
and is not yet saved.

    :n

(m) To discard the changes made to the current file and move on to the next file in sequence,
use the ! mark after the n command as follows.

    :n!

(n) To rewind and open the first file in the arguments list, we use the :rew command.

    :rew

(o) This command will be ignored and a warning message will be displayed if the current
file is modified and is not yet saved. The following command discards the modifications
made to the current file and moves on to the first file in the arguments list.

    :rew!

(p) The following command opens the file matter.txt for editing.

    :e matter.txt

(q) If the current edit buffer is modified and not saved, a warning message will be displayed
and the following command will be ignored. The ! character will discard the changes
made in the edit buffer and open the specified file, matter.txt, for editing.

    :e! matter.txt

(r) The following command opens the file matter.txt and sets the third line as the current line.

    :e! +3 matter.txt

(s) To see the list of currently opened files, we use the following command.

    :ar

This command shows the list of filenames that are being edited. The current file will be enclosed in square brackets.

(t) The following command reads the specified file, `matter.txt`, and places it after the third line in the current file.

```
:3 r matter.txt
```

(u) The following command executes the specified command and the output of the command is appended to the current file.

```
:r !ls
```

This command will append the list of files and directory names to the current file.

(v) To save the current open file, we use the following command.

```
:w
```

This command saves the current file and a message is displayed indicating the same.

(w) The following command is used to quit the vi or ex editor.

```
:q
```

This command will be discarded if the edit buffer is modified and the content is not yet saved. When it succeeds, the command quits the current file and indicates the number of files that are still open in the edit buffer.

(x) The following command is used to force quit from the vi or ex editor without saving the content.

```
:q!
```

These examples are represented in Fig. 8.21.

```
: 1p
This is MCE Microchip Computer Education

:3p
It appears to be very interesting. Commands are hard to remember

:1,3
This is MCE Microchip Computer Education
Ajmer. We are working on vi editor. It is a fast editor
It appears to be very interesting. Commands are hard to remember

:6
Not that many lines in buffer

:5
Secondly the distances are small. Everything is in approach.

:s/is/was
Substitute pattern match failed
:Is is was
Thwas is MCE Microchip Computer Education
```

Fig. 8.21   Representation of the commands given in ex mode   *(Contd)*

```
:1,5s/is/was
Secondly the dwastances are small. Everything is in approach.

:1,$s/is/was
Secondly the dwastances are small. Everything is in approach.

:r matter.txt
"matter.txt" 3 lines, 132 characters

:w tmp.txt
"tmp.txt" [New file] 8 lines, 422 characters

:1,.w tmp2.txt
"tmp2.txt" [New file] 8 lines, 422 characters

:+4
Not that many lines in buffer

:p
It is going to rain today

:-2
Hello this is testing of interrupted system call command

:n
"b.txt" 2 lines, 73 characters

:1
This is b.txt file opened through ex

:n
"c.txt" 2 lines, 72 characters

:2
The c.txt file is the third file

:rew
3 files to edit
"a.txt" 5 lines, 283 characters

:1
This is MCE Microchip Computer Education

:e matter.txt
"matter.txt" 3 lines, 132 characters

:ar
[a.txt] b.txt c.txt

:r matter.txt
"matter.txt" 3 lines, 132 characters
```

Fig. 8.21 *(Contd)*

```
:r !ls
!
22 more lines in file after read
transact.txt

:r !cat matter.txt
!
It is going to rain today

:w
"a.txt" 33 lines, 777 characters

:q
2 more files to edit:q

$ cat rmp.txt
Thwas was MCE Microchip Computer Education
Ajmer. We are working on vi editor. It was a fast editor.
It appears to be very interesting. Commands are hard to remember
Ajmer was a nice place to stay. First it was quite and calm.
Secondly the dwastances are small. Everything was in approach.
Hello this is testing of interrupted system call command
I think it is working as per the expected result
It is going to rain today
```

Fig. 8.21   (Contd)

8.3.22 Abbreviating Text Input

For long text, we can define abbreviations that can be expanded to the text they represent. Abbreviations are like shortcuts for the frequently used long text and they help save typing time. To define an abbreviation, we use the following ex command.

Syntax   `:ab abbr text`

Here, abbr is a shortcut or an abbreviation for the specified text. In the insert mode, abbr (if it is a whole word and not a part of the word) will be expanded to the specified text.

Example   `:ab mce Microchip Computer Education`

This abbreviates the text Microchip Computer Education to the abbreviation mce. Now whenever we type mce in the insert mode, it will be expanded to the text, Microchip Computer Education. Expansion will occur when we press a non-alphanumeric character, a space, a carriage return, or the Esc key.

To disable an abbreviation, the command with the following syntax is used.

`:unab abbr`

Here, abbr represent the abbreviation that we wish to disable.

To display the list of defined abbreviations, the following command is used.

`:ab`

8.3.23 Mapping Keys of Keyboard

Mapping keys refer to the mechanism of mapping a complex command to a particular keystroke or sequence of keystrokes. Frequently used editing commands can be mapped to certain keys for convenience. Mapping can be done in modes such as the normal mode and insert mode. In normal mode, the following syntax is used for mapping:

Syntax `:map key_to_map command_to_execute`

In insert mode, the mapping is done with the `map!` command as follows:

Syntax `:map! key_to_map command_to_execute`

Example `:map <F2>Microchip Computer Education <CR>`

In this normal mode map command, the <F2> key is mapped to the text, `Microchip Computer Education`. On pressing the F2 key, the text `Microchip Computer Education` will be displayed along with a carriage return.

To view the list of defined maps, simply type `:map` or `:map!`, followed by the Enter key. All the defined maps will be displayed in the 'status bar.' To make maps permanent, add them to the `.vimrc` file.

Let us now understand how mapping is done in the insert mode.

Example `:map! m1Microchip Computer Education <CR>`

This command maps `m1` to the text, `Microchip Computer Education`, followed by carriage return `<CR>`. This map executes in the insert mode.

To unmap a mapped key, use the command with the following syntax.

Table 8.24 Brief description of the commands used in mapping in vi

Command	Description
`:map key` `command_sequence`	Defines the key as a sequence of editing commands
`:unmap key`	Disables the sequence of editing commands defined for a key
`:map`	Lists the keys that are currently mapped

Syntax `:unmap key`

Example `:unmap <F2>`

This statement unmaps the F2 key.

The list of commands used in mapping are given in Table 8.24.

8.3.24 Customizing vi Session

You may recall that the batch file named `.exrc` is executed every time vi is loaded. To customize the vi session, we open this file and write the desired statements in it.

For example, you can have the following features enabled in the file that you open or create through vi:

1. Lines are auto numbered
2. Auto indentation is enabled
3. Case is ignored while searching for content

For enabling these features in vi, we open the `.exrc` file in our home directory and write the following three lines and save it:

```
set nu
set ai
set ic
```

The next time we open or create any file, it will have the aforementioned three features enabled. We can write any number of set commands (refer to Section 8.3.18) in the .exrc file to suit our needs.

Advantages of vi

The following are the advantages of using the vi editor:

1. The vi editor is available on all Unix systems.
2. It is a bug-free editor.
3. Being a small program, it occupies less memory.
4. The vi editor is not column oriented, that is, we cannot modify the content of specific columns.
5. The vi editor can work with any kind of terminal.

The biggest disadvantage of the vi editor is that it uses many different commands, which are hard to remember.

After having learnt about the vi editor, let us take a look at another editor, that is, the emacs editor.

8.4 EMACS EDITOR

Emacs is one of the most popular screen editors in Unix. Again, like vi, emacs is also a text editor. Broadly, the following are the two differences between the vi and emacs editors:

1. Vi is a *modal* editor whereas emacs is a *modeless* editor. By modal editor we mean that the user has to switch between modes to enter/edit text and give commands. One mode is dedicated for adding or editing content in the editor and the other is for giving commands to the editor. Modeless editors, on the other hand, are those that when opened allow the user to enter text straight away by default. For giving editor commands in modeless editors, certain special keys such as Ctrl and Esc are designated. On pressing the special keys, the editor recognizes that the following text is not part of the content, but commands. Most of the editors today are of the modeless type.
2. The second difference between vi and emacs editors is size. The vi editor being small in size gets opened quickly, whereas it takes a comparatively longer time for the emacs editor to load.

The command to create a new file or edit an existing file through emacs has the following syntax:

Syntax   `emacs file_to_create/edit`

Emacs will run and open the specified file. When a file is loaded into emacs, it is initially loaded into a buffer. All the editing/insertions and changes are performed in the content that is in buffer. To update the actual file, the buffer must be saved.

We will now discuss the different commands used in emacs that include cursor movement, dealing with buffers, cutting and copying text, etc., in the subsequent sections. These commands are categorized on the basis of the tasks they perform.

The notation that is used while displaying the different commands is as follows:

1. C-x means to hold down the Ctrl key and press the x key.
2. Esc-x means to hold down the Esc key and press the x key.

8.4.1 Cursor Movements

While editing, we need to move the cursor to the desired location in the file. The syntax for this is as follows:

Syntax   C-x/Esc-x

Here, x is the character that designates the action to be taken.

The commands used in cursor movement are given in Table 8.25.

Table 8.25 Brief description of commands related to cursor movement

Commands	Description
C-p	Moves the cursor one line up
C-n	Moves the cursor one line down
C-f	Moves the cursor one character right
C-b	Moves the cursor one character back
C-a	Moves the cursor to the beginning of the line
C-e	Moves the cursor to the end of the line
C-v	Moves the cursor down a screen
Esc-v	Moves the cursor up a screen
Esc-<	Moves the cursor to the beginning of the buffer
Esc->	Moves the cursor to the end of the buffer
Esc-f	Moves the cursor one word forward
Esc-b	Moves the cursor one word backward
Esc-a	Moves the cursor back to the beginning of the sentence
Esc-e	Moves the cursor forward to the end of the sentence
Esc-]	Moves the cursor one paragraph forward
Esc-[	Moves the cursor one paragraph backward

8.4.2 Quitting Emacs

The command used to quit/terminate the emacs process is as follows:

Syntax   C-x C-c

The user will be asked to save any modified buffers. Emacs maintains a backup file when a file is saved. The name of the backup file is the original filename with a tilde (~) appended to the end.

8.4.3 Dealing with Buffers

Emacs supports multiple buffers. The user may load files into the buffers, switch between them, and copy text from one buffer to another.

The list of commands is given in Table 8.26.

Table 8.26   Brief description of commands dealing with buffer

Command	Description
C-x C-s	Saves the buffer into the file
C-x C-w	Writes the content of the buffer into a new filename and prompts the user for the new filename
C-x C-f	Reads a file into a buffer
C-x i	Inserts contents of a file into the current buffer
C-x b	Selects another buffer
C-x C-b	Lists all buffers that are currently active in emacs
C-x 2	Splits the screen to show two buffers
C-x 1	Goes back to one buffer on screen
C-x o	Switches the cursor to the other buffer

8.4.4 Cutting and Pasting

Before moving or copying text, it must be marked. The C-@ or C-Spacebar commands are used to mark the region for copying or moving. C-w cuts the region and Esc-w keys copy the region. Move the cursor to the position we want to move or copy the text and press C-y to paste the selected text.

The commands for deleting, cutting, and pasting the content are given in Table 8.27.

Table 8.27   Brief description of the commands for cutting and pasting

Command	Description
C-d	Deletes the character at the cursor
Esc-d	Deletes from the cursor till the end of the word
C-k	Erases till the end of the line
Esc-k	Erases till the end of the current sentence
C-@	Marks the beginning of the text to cut or copy
C-w	Cuts the text between the mark and current cursor position
Esc-w	Copies the text between the mark and current cursor position
C-y	Pastes the cut or copied content at the cursor position

8.4.5 Searching and Replacing

The emacs editor provides commands to search for the desired pattern in a file. We can not only search for the desired pattern but also replace it with the new pattern.

Table 8.28 Brief description of commands for searching and replacing text

Command	Description
C-s	Searches for the given string from the current cursor position in the forward direction in the buffer
C-r	Searches for the given string from the current cursor position in the backward direction
Esc-%	Prompts the user for the string to be replaced and the string to replace it with. Before replacing the string, the user will be asked for confirmation and the user can select any of the following keys in response to confirmation: 1. Space bar: Replaces the string and moves on to the next match 2. Delete key: Skips without replacing and moves on to the next match 3. !: Replaces all the remaining matches 4. Esc key: Stops replacing

For searching and replacing the content in a file, we use the commands given in Table 8.28.

While using the commands for searching and replacing, a prompt will appear at the bottom where the user can type in the text to search or replace. Searching begins immediately as the user types the characters. As the characters are typed emacs begins its search procedure. Similarly, to search for the word *an*, on typing character, *a*, emacs will move to the first occurrence of the character *a*. On typing the next character, *n*, the emacs will move to the first occurrence of the word *an,* and so on. To stop a search, press the Esc key.

8.4.6 Miscellaneous Commands

Some miscellaneous commands in emacs are listed in Table 8.29.

Table 8.29 Brief description of the miscellaneous commands in emacs

Command	Description
C-g	Aborts a partially typed command
C-x u	Undoes the last change to the buffer
C-l	Redraws the screen
C-h	Starts the emacs online help
Esc-$	Checks the spelling of the word at that point

Thus, we have discussed the three important editors in Unix— sed, vi, and emacs—in this chapter. We have seen the commands required in writing, deleting, and modifying content, as well as navigating to the desired content, searching and replacing content, cutting, copying, and pasting content, and so on.

■ SUMMARY ■

1. Ed is a line-oriented text editor for the Unix operating system written by Ken Thompson in 1971. Editing in the ed editor is done through the command and input modes.

2. Ex is a line editor that is a friendlier version of ed but is a bit more complex to operate when compared to the screen-based visual editor, vi. The ex editor can be invoked from the vi editor and can be switched to the vi editor from the ex editor too.

3. Vi is a visual editor that was originally written by Bill Joy in 1976. It operates in the command and insert modes. To switch to the insert mode from the command mode in the vi editor, characters 'i' (input) or 'a' (append) are pressed. To switch to the command mode from the insert mode in the vi editor, press the Esc key.

4. Letters typed in the command mode in vi are treated as commands.

5. Another editor that is distributed with most Unix systems and is an enhanced version of vi is the vim editor. The vim editor is a highly configurable text editor written by Bram Moolenaar.

6. The stream editor :sed is popularly used for filtering out the desired data from the specified file. The stream editor, sed was designed by Lee McMohan and is derived from the ed line editor.

7. For filtering through sed, we have to supply a data stream (input data) and instructions that contain criteria for filtering the desired data from the data stream.

8. Emacs is a popular and powerful screen editor that is simpler to use than the vi editor. Most of the emacs commands use either the Ctrl key or the Esc key.

9. Pico stands for pine composer and is a file editor that was designed to be used with the pine mail system. The commands for editing in pico are invoked by Ctrl key sequences. To save a file and exit pico, the ^x command is used.

10. The -n option in sed suppresses duplicate line printing.

11. In sed, the -f option is used to accept instructions from a file. The file should have a .fil extension.

12. The instruction $a in sed is used for adding text to the existing file.

13. The backslash (\) in sed is considered a line continuation character.

14. The instruction i\ in sed is used for inserting text before every line of the file.

15. The w (write) command helps in writing the selected lines in a separate file.

16. The $ sign in sed represents the last line of the file.

17. The negation operator (!) can be in sed's action.

18. The p command in sed is for printing the result of the filtering of data. It is the default action.

19. The s command in sed is for substituting a string by another string in a file.

20. The vi editor can be customized with the help of the .exrc file, which is executed every time vi is loaded.

21. When a file is loaded into emacs, it is initially loaded into a buffer. All the editing/insertions and changes are performed in the content that is in the buffer.

22. Context addressing is a mechanism where we cannot directly address the lines on which we wish to apply the sed command. Instead, a regular expression is included, enclosed within slashes (/).

23. The regular expressions, also known as regexp in short, is used for pattern matching.

24. Regular expressions are built making use of certain special characters known as meta characters.

25. A caret (^) at the beginning of a regular expression matches the null character at the beginning of a line.

26. A string of characters in square brackets ([ ]) in a regular expression matches any character in the string.

27. In remembered patterns, we use a mechanism to name or number the pattern so that it can be checked for repetition.

28. For naming or numbering a pattern, we need to enclose it within '\(' and '\)'.

29. In the vi editor, the x command deletes the character at the cursor position.

30. In the vi editor, the dd command deletes the line where the cursor is.

31. In the vi editor, the yy command copies the current line.

32. In the vi editor, the p command pastes the copied text after the cursor.

33. In the vi editor, the :r filename command places the text from the named file after the current line.

34. The :ab command is used for defining abbreviations.

35. The :unab command is used to disable abbreviations.

36. Mapping keys refer to a mechanism of mapping a complex command to a particular keystroke or sequence of keystrokes.
37. The `:map` command is used for mapping keys.
38. The `:unmap` command is used for unmapping keys.
39. While vi is a modal editor, emacs is a modeless editor.
40. The vi editor is smaller in size than the emacs editor.
41. The `C-x C-c` command is used to quit/terminate the emacs process.
42. The ex is a line editor that is commonly used for working with multiple files simultaneously.
43. The ex editor can be independently invoked from the command line as well as from the vi editor.
44. To switch to the ex (line editor) mode from within vi, type : (colon) from the command mode.

■ EXERCISES ■

Objective-type Questions

State True or False

8.1 The print option is always on by default with sed.
8.2 To select the last line of the file, we use the ^ option.
8.3 The option q with sed is for quitting after displaying the addressed line.
8.4 The w command is used for writing the selected lines in a separate file.
8.5 We cannot print the contents of a file followed by the contents of another file in sed.
8.6 The l option is for printing line numbers along with the file contents.
8.7 The vi editor has two modes of operation.
8.8 We can switch to the insert mode from the command mode in the vi editor by pressing character e or E.
8.9 The :w command is for writing into the file and continuing editing.
8.10 The $ command in vi is for moving the cursor to the last character of the line.

8.11 The Fx command in vi moves the cursor to the specified character, x, in the forward direction.
8.12 The { command in vi moves the cursor to the beginning of the current sentence.
8.13 To delete a line in vi, the dd command is used.
8.14 The :set nu command is for removing line numbering while displaying the file contents.
8.15 When a file is loaded into emacs, it is initially loaded into a buffer.
8.16 Emacs supports multiple buffers but the user cannot switch between them.
8.17 In emacs, a string can be searched for in the forward as well as in the backward direction.
8.18 Emacs supports spell checking too.
8.19 The command to quit from emacs is C-x C-c.
8.20 Emacs is a graphic editor like vi.

Fill in the Blanks

8.1 The _____ option is used for suppressing duplicate line printing in sed.
8.2 The command to print the first line of the file, bank.1st is _____.
8.3 The _____ option is used in sed to accept instructions from a file.
8.4 In sed, for adding text to the existing file _____ is used.
8.5 In sed, for inserting text before every line of the file, the _____ option is used.
8.6 The command _____ is used in vi to delete a line from the cursor position to the beginning of the line.
8.7 To go back to the command mode from the insert mode in the vi editor, we press _____.
8.8 The _____ command in vi moves the cursor to the first character of the previous word.
8.9 To scroll down one full page, the _____ command is used in vi.
8.10 To go to the *n*th line of a file, the _____ command is used in vi.
8.11 To repeat the last search command in the opposite direction, _____ is used in vi.
8.12 The _____ command in emacs displays online help.
8.13 In emacs, the _____ command is used for pasting content at the position of the cursor.

8.14 To see the list of all currently active buffers in emacs, the _____ command is used.

8.15 The command Esc-] in emacs is used for moving the cursor _____ one paragraph.

Multiple-choice Questions

8.1 sed stands for
(a) solid editor   (c) stream editor
(b) searching editor   (d) sleeping editor

8.2 Editing in ed editor is done in
(a) two modes   (c) a single mode
(b) three modes   (d) four modes

8.3 The option used with the sed editor to read instructions from a file is
(a) -file   (b) -o   (c) -1   (d) -f

8.4 The sed editor is derived from
(a) vi editor   (c) vim editor
(b) ed editor   (d) emacs editor

8.5 The pattern is enclosed in '\(' and '\)' to match for
(a) deleted pattern   (c) filtered pattern
(b) printed pattern   (d) repetitive pattern

8.6 The .exrc file is executed every time the
(a) line is appended to sed
(b) vi editor is loaded
(c) pico editor is loaded
(d) sed editor is loaded

8.7 In the vi editor, when : (colon) is pressed in the command mode, it switches to
(a) ex mode   (c) nothing will happen
(b) insert mode   (d) print mode

8.8 The command used to number all the lines in the vi editor is
(a) :set list   (c) :set ro
(b) :set ai   (d) :set nu

8.9 The command C-a in the emacs editor will
(a) move the cursor down one screen
(b) move the cursor to the beginning of a line
(c) move the cursor one paragraph forward
(d) move the cursor one line up

8.10 The command to delete the character at the cursor in the emacs editor is
(a) C-d   (b) C-k   (c) C-w   (d) C-y

Programming Exercises

8.1 Write the commands for performing the following tasks in sed:
(a) To print all the lines of the file bank.lst except lines three to six
(b) To display the first four lines and the eighth line to the eleventh line of the file bank.lst
(c) To display all the lines from the file letter.txt where the word Charles has occurred
(d) To replace the word Charles by Peters in the file letter.txt
(e) To replace the word Charles by Peters in the file letter.txt and copy the lines where replacement occurs into the file latest.txt
(f) To display the last line of the file letter.txt

8.2 Write the commands for performing the following tasks in the vi editor:
(a) To write to the file and quit the vi editor
(b) To move the cursor to the first character of the line
(c) To move the cursor to the beginning of the current paragraph
(d) To search for the word Charles in the forward direction from the cursor position
(e) To move to the tenth line of the file

(f) To copy n number of lines

8.3 Write the commands for performing the following tasks in the emacs editor:
(a) To check the spelling of the word at a particular point
(b) To search for the given string in the backward direction from the current cursor position.
(c) To mark the beginning of the text to cut or copy
(d) To split the screen to show two buffers
(e) To move the cursor to the beginning of the line
(f) To undo the last change made to the buffer

8.4 Consider a file, school.txt, with the following content:

```
A101    John      XI    80
A102    Caroline  XI    75
A103    Susan     XI    92
A104    David     XII   82
A105    Kelly     XII   84
A106    Candace   XII   90
```

(a) What will the output of the following commands be?
(i) $ sed -n '2,$!p' school.txt

(ii) `$ sed -n '1,3p' school.txt`

(iii) `$ sed -n '3,6p' school.txt`

(iv) `$ sed -n -e '1,2p'  -e  '4,6p'`
   `school.txt`

(v) `$ sed -n '/[Xx]I/p' school.txt`

(vi) `$ sed '3,5 d' school.txt`

(b) What tasks will the following commands perform in the vi editor?

(i) `Tx`

(ii) `j`

(iii) `d$`

(iv) `:set noai`

(v) `: s/Charles/Peters/g`

(vi) `:5,10 w a.txt`

(c) What tasks will the following commands perform in the emacs editor?

(i) `Esc-k`

(ii) `C-x C-f`

(iii) `Esc->`

(iv) `Esc-w`

(v) `C-k`

(vi) `Esc-e`

Review Questions

8.1 (a) Explain any two options that are used while using the sed editor.

(b) Explain the following commands of sed with examples:

(i) To substitute string s1 with s2

(ii) Write an address line to another file

(iii) Change text in the current line with new text

8.2 Write short notes on the following:

(a) Context addressing

(b) Remembered pattern

8.3 (a) Explain any two common ways of starting a vi session.

(b) What are the two modes of operation in the vi editor and what are the keys pressed to switch between the two modes?

(c) Write down the commands for the following in the vi editor:

(i) Cut and copy text

(ii) Delete and undo delete operation

(iii) Search for a desired pattern in the file

(iv) Substitute a pattern with another pattern globally

8.4 Can we deal with multiple files in vi? If yes, write the commands for the same.

8.5 (a) Explain what you mean by mapping keys.

(b) Explain how abbreviations are created in vi.

8.6 (a) Explain two differences between the vi and emacs editors.

(b) Does emacs supports multiple buffers? If yes, write the commands that deal with buffers.

8.7 What is a regular expression? Explain the concept including a few meta characters used in creating a regular expression.

8.8 Explain the commands that are used in the vi editor for copying content from the current file to a new file and for pasting content from another file.

8.9 Explain the set commands that can be used for configuring the vi session.

Brain Teasers

8.1 What is the error in the following command to print the last line of the file, `school.txt`?
`$ sed -n '^p' school.txt`

8.2 Correct the mistake in the following command to print only the first three lines of the file, `school.txt`.
`$ sed '1,3p' school.txt`

8.3 Correct the mistake in the following command to write all records with pattern `XI` from the file `school.txt` into the file `eleventh.lst`.
`$ sed -n '/XI/p eleventh.lst' school.txt`

8.4 Remove the mistake from the following command to substitute the pattern 'XI' in the file

`school.txt` with the pattern 'Class XI'.
`$ sed 'd/XI/Class XI/' school.txt`

8.5 I am trying to read the content of the file `accounts.txt` and place it after the current line in vi through the following command:
`:r! accounts.txt`
However, the command is not working. Identify and correct the mistake.

8.6 The following command for ignoring case while searching is not working in vi. Find the error.
`:set ignorecase`

8.7 Correct the error in the following command to move the cursor to character 'z' in the forward direction in vi.

`Fz`

8.8 What is the mistake in unmapping a key, F3 in vi?

`:umap <F3>`

8.9 Correct the error in the following command to

move the cursor down one screen in the emacs editor:

`Esc-v`

8.10 Correct the mistake in the following command to list all the currently active buffers in emacs.

`C-x b`

■ ANSWERS TO OBJECTIVE-TYPE QUESTIONS ■

State True or False

8.1	True
8.2	False
8.3	True
8.4	True
8.5	False
8.6	False
8.7	True
8.8	False
8.9	True
8.10	True
8.11	False
8.12	False
8.13	True
8.14	False
8.15	True
8.16	False
8.17	True
8.18	True
8.19	True
8.20	False

Fill in the Blanks

8.1	`-n`
8.2	`$ sed -n '1p' bank.lst`
8.3	`-f`
8.4	`$a\`
8.5	`i\`
8.6	`d^`
8.7	the Esc key
8.8	`b`
8.9	`^f`
8.10	`nG`
8.11	`N`
8.12	`C-h`
8.13	`C-y`
8.14	`C-x C-b`
8.15	forward

Multiple-choice Questions

8.1	stream editor
8.2	two modes
8.3	`-f`
8.4	ed editor
8.5	repetitive pattern
8.6	vi editor is loaded
8.7	ex mode
8.8	`:set nu`
8.9	Moves cursor to beginning of the line
8.10	`C-d`

AWK Script

After studying this chapter, the reader will be conversant with the following:

- Role of the AWK command in filtering and processing content
- Different functions used in AWK for printing results, formatting output, and searching for desired patterns
- Different operators that include comparison operators, logical operators, arithmetic operators, string functions, arithmetic functions, and search and substitute functions
- Built-in variables to perform desired operations quickly and with the least effort
- Different loops to perform repetitive tasks, taking input from the user to perform operation on the desired content

9.1 AWK COMMAND

The AWK command is a programming language that is executed by the AWK interpreter. It is a commonly used text processing tool and a powerful text filtering tool designed for processing structured data records. It divides the input into different records on the basis of the record separator encountered. By default, the record separator is a newline character. The individual records are then divided into fields on the basis of the field separators. Based on the patterns specified, AWK applies the desired modifications to the records and displays the report if desired. AWK is found on all Unix systems and is very fast, easy to learn, and extremely flexible. The name AWK comes from the last names of its creators Alfred Aho, Peter Weinberger, and Brian Kernighan.

9.1.1 Versions

There are, in all, three versions of AWK, the original AWK, NAWK, and GAWK. The following is a brief description of the three versions:

AWK It is a powerful language to manipulate and process text files. It is also very helpful in filtering out desired information from a file in record format. Besides filtering, even computation can be applied to the filtered out records. AWK is the original version that was written by Alfred Aho, Peter Weinberger, and Brian Kernighan in 1977.

NAWK The original AWK was enhanced by its original authors to create its enhanced version known as NAWK, 'new awk'.

GAWK It is an AWK version that was released by the free software foundation under the GNU. All Linux distributions come with GAWK. It is fully compatible with AWK and NAWK.

Note: All the features and functions are not available in the original AWK. They are available in NAWK and/or GAWK. For example, the most popular functions, such as `gsub()`, `getline`, and `system()`, are supported in NAWK but not in AWK.

9.1.2 Advantages and Disadvantages of Using AWK Filters

The following are the advantages of using an AWK filter:

1. It uses very simple patterns and actions that are easy to learn.
2. It is quite small in size.
3. It is an interpreted language, hence it consumes fewer resources.
4. It accomplishes complex filtering tasks with minimum instructions.
5. It considers text files as records and fields.
6. It applies the desired filtering and processing operations on the fields and generates formatted reports.

The following are the disadvantages of using AWK filters:

1. It processes the file sequentially, hence consumes much time in filtering.
2. It is not suitable for filtering large volume of data.

To summarize, AWK has features for filtering, text processing, and writing reports. It operates at the field level and can easily access, transform, and format individual fields in a record.

The syntax for using the AWK command is as follows:

Syntax   `awk '/pattern/ {action}' file(s)`

Here, `pattern` is a regular expression that defines the address on which action has to be applied, and `action` is one or more commands that we want to apply on the matching patterns. If `pattern` is omitted, AWK performs the specified actions for each input line of the file(s).

Note: If the address is missing, the action applies to all lines of the file. If the action is missing, the entire line will be printed. Either the address or the action is necessary but both must be enclosed within a pair of single quotes.

Example   Consider a file `bank.1st`, with the following content.

```
101    Aditya     0       14/11/2012    current
102    Anil       10000   20/05/2011    saving
103    Naman      0       20/08/2009    current
104    Rama       10000   15/08/2010    saving
105    Jyotsna    5000    16/06/2012    saving
```

106	Mukesh	14000	20/12/2009	current
107	Yashasvi	14500	30/11/2011	saving
108	Chirag	0	15/12/2012	current
109	Arya	16000	14/12/2010	current
110	Puneet	130	16/11/2009	saving

```
$ awk '{ print }' bank.lst
```

This command will print *all the records* of the file bank.lst. It is because we have not specified any criteria or filter condition. The print command in AWK displays the filtered records. We will now learn more about this command.

9.2 print: PRINTING RESULTS

The print command is used for displaying messages, fields, variables, etc. AWK automatically divides input lines into fields on the basis of the field separators. A field is a set of characters that are separated by one or more field separators. The default field separators are tab and space. On reading a line, its parsed fields are assigned individual numbers to access them. This implies that the first field is accessed as $1, the second field as $2, and so on. In the aforementioned file bank.lst, the first column, that is, account numbers, is represented by $1, customer names by $2, balance by $3, and so on. $1, $2, etc., are also known as special variables. One of the special variables, $0, represents the whole line.

> Syntax   `print [special variables]`

Here, special variables represent the comma separated special variables, $1, $2, etc.

If print statement is used without any special variable, it prints the entire line.

> Example   The following example displays selected fields of the input file.

```
$ awk '{ print $1,$2,$3 }' bank.lst
```

This command will print only the first three fields of each record of the file bank.lst. The fields are delimited by either space or tab. The parameters $1, $2, $3, etc., represent the fields separated by spaces or tabs. A contiguous sequence of spaces or tabs can be considered a delimiter.

101	Aditya	0
102	Anil	10000
103	Naman	0
104	Rama	10000
105	Jyotsna	5000
106	Mukesh	14000
107	Yashasvi	14500
108	Chirag	0
109	Arya	16000
110	Puneet	130

Note: AWK uses the special variable $0 to indicate the entire line.

9.3 `printf`: FORMATTING OUTPUT

We can format the output of the AWK command using the `printf` command instead of the print command. `printf` is a statement used for displaying formatted data (similar to the `printf` statement of the C language).

Syntax `printf "format string", special_variable1, special_variable2, ...`

Here, the format string consists of format specifiers that define the format in which we wish to display the special variables. The format specifiers are specified for each special variable being displayed and usually specify the data type and width or space assigned to each.

The list of format specifiers that are most commonly used in the `printf` statement is as follows:

Format specifier	What is displayed
%d	Integers
%f	Float
%s	Strings
%c	Character
%e	Number in scientific (exponential) notation

Note: The `printf` statement does not automatically append a newline to its output. It only displays the content specified in the format string. To append a new line, we need to add a newline character '\n' at the end in the format string.

Example The following example displays the `bank.lst` file in a formatted pattern.

```
$ awk '{ printf "%6d %-20s %7d \n",$1,$2,$3 }' bank.lst
```

This command will print the first field in the field width of six digits (if the field has only a few digits, it is padded with white spaces), the second field is displayed in the field width of 20 characters. The − (minus) sign in %−20s is for left alignment. The last field is displayed in the field width of seven digits. The output of the aforementioned command is as follows:

```
101    Aditya       0
102    Anil         10000
103    Naman        0
104    Rama         10000
105    Jyotsna      5000
106    Mukesh       14000
107    Yashasvi     14500
108    Chirag       0
109    Arya         16000
110    Puneet       130
```

9.4 DISPLAYING CONTENT OF SPECIFIED PATTERNS

Instead of displaying all lines, we can also display only those lines from the input file that have the given specific pattern. For doing this, we will follow the given syntax:

Syntax awk '/pattern/ {action}' file(s)

Example The following example displays only the lines that have the given pattern.

$ awk '/current/ { print }' bank.lst

This command selects all customers having current account in bank.lst, that is, all lines/records having the pattern current are displayed.

```
101     Aditya      0       14/11/2012      current
103     Naman       0       20/08/2009      current
108     Chirag      0       15/12/2012      current
```

Printing is the default action of AWK. We can omit it as given here:

$ awk '/current/' bank.lst

It gives the same output as the aforementioned command.

The single quotes around the pattern are optional. We can also omit it as shown in the following syntax:

$ awk /current/ bank.lst

Again, it gives the same output as the aforementioned command, that is, all the lines with the pattern current are displayed. We can omit the single quotes; however, it is good practice to place the pattern and action within the quotes.

You may recall that a single complete line of the input file is represented by $0. Let us apply it to the file, bank.lst:

$ awk '/current/' { print $0 }' bank.lst

$0 refers to the complete record. Hence, this command will print all the lines/records from the bank.lst file that have the pattern current in it.

The following example displays specific fields of the file that match the given pattern.

$ awk '/saving/ { print $2,$3,$4 }' bank.lst

Only the second, third, and fourth fields of the file bank.lst that have the pattern saving are displayed. The , (comma) is used to delimit the field specifications. This ensures that each field is separated from the other by a space. If we do not place a comma, the fields will be displayed without any space in between.

Output

```
Anil        10000       20/05/2011
Rama        10000       15/08/2010
Jyotsna     5000        16/06/2012
Yashasvi    14500       30/11/2011
Puneet      130         16/11/2009
```

9.5 COMPARISON OPERATORS

For comparing values in the fields, we require comparison operators. The fields combine with comparison operators to make expressions. Only the fields that match the given expressions are displayed. The operators used for comparison are shown in Table 9.1.

Table 9.1 Brief description of the expressions made by comparison operators

Operator	Description
x < y	Returns true if x is less than y
x <= y	Returns true if x is less than or equal to y
x == y	Returns true if x is equal to y
x > y	Returns true if x is greater than y
x >= y	Returns true if x is greater than or equal to y
x != y	Returns true if x is not equal to y
x ~ y	Returns true if string x matches the regular expression represented by y
x !~ y	Returns true if string x does not match the regular expression represented by y

Note: While comparing operands with comparison operators, if both the operands are numeric, a numeric comparison is made, otherwise the operands are compared as strings.

Examples

(a) `$2 <= 500`

It returns true if the value of the second field is less than or equal to 500.

`$1 ~ /saving/`

It returns true if the value of the first field matches the pattern saving.

`$1 !~ /saving/`

It returns true if the value of the first field does not match the pattern saving.

(b) The following example has become more precise with the application of comparison operators. Instead of searching for the pattern current anywhere in the input line, the following example checks for the existence of the pattern current in the fifth field.

```
$ awk '$5 == "current" ' bank.lst
```

Only the records/lines having the pattern current in the fifth field will be displayed. Here, == is the 'equal to' operator.

(c) The following example gives the inverse output of the preceding example.

```
$ awk '$5 != "current" ' bank.lst
```

The records/lines *not having* (!= stands for not equal to) the pattern current in the fifth field will be displayed as follows:

```
102     Anil      10000     20/05/2011     saving
104     Rama      10000     15/08/2010     saving
105     Jyotsna   5000      16/06/2012     saving
107     Yashasvi  14500     30/11/2011     saving
110     Puneet    130       16/11/2009     saving
```

(d) `$ awk '$3 > 10000' bank.lst`

The records having the balance >10000 will be displayed as follows:

```
106     Mukesh    14000     20/12/2009     current
107     Yashasvi  14500     30/11/2011     saving
109     Arya      16000     14/12/2010     current
```

9.5.1 ~ and !~: Matching Regular Expressions

A regular expression is a way of expressing strings or patterns that we are searching for. A regular expression is formed by writing a pattern along with a couple of operators enclosed by slashes (/). The ~ and !~ are the two operators that are used while comparing regular expressions. The meaning of ~ is that it matches and that of !~ is that it does not match.

Examples

(a) The following example shows all the records from the file bank.1st that have the pattern current in the fifth field.

```
$ awk '$5 ~/current/' bank.1st
```

(b) The following example shows all the records from the file bank.1st that do not have the pattern current in the fifth field.

```
$ awk '$5 !~ /current/' bank.1st
```

While matching the expressions, the two meta characters that are frequently used are ^ (which means matches at the beginning) and $ (which means matches at the end).

Examples

(a) The following example shows all the records from the file bank.1st in which the fifth field ends with the character t.

```
$ awk '$5 ~/t$/' bank.1st
```

(b) The following example shows all the records from the file bank.1st in which the fifth field begins with character t.

```
$ awk '$5 ~/^t/' bank.1st
```

(c) `$ awk '/[Cc]urrent/' bank.1st`

It displays all the lines having the pattern current or Current in them.

101	Aditya	0	14/11/2012	current
103	Naman	0	20/08/2009	current
106	Mukesh	14000	20/12/2009	current
108	Chirag	0	15/12/2012	current
109	Arya	16000	14/12/2010	current

For matching an expression given anywhere in a field, AWK offers the ~ and !~ operators to match and not match, respectively. The expression must be enclosed in // (slashes).

Examples

(a) `$ awk '$5 ~/saving/' bank.1st`

It prints all the records having the pattern saving in the fifth field in the file bank.1st.

102	Anil	10000	20/05/2011	saving
104	Rama	10000	15/08/2010	saving
105	Jyotsna	5000	16/06/2012	saving
107	Yashasvi	14500	30/11/2011	saving
110	Puneet	130	16/11/2009	saving

(b) `$ awk '$5 ~/[cC]urrent/' bank.1st`

It prints all the records having the pattern current or Current in the fifth field in the file bank.1st.

101	Aditya	0	14/11/2012	current
103	Naman	0	20/08/2009	current
106	Mukesh	14000	20/12/2009	current

```
          108     Chirag     0        15/12/2012     current
          109     Arya       16000    14/12/2010     current
```

(c) `$ awk '$5 ~ "current" ' bank.lst`

It prints all the records having the `current` pattern in their fifth field.

```
          101     Aditya     0        14/11/2012     current
          103     Naman      0        20/08/2009     current
          106     Mukesh     14000    20/12/2009     current
          108     Chirag     0        15/12/2012     current
          109     Arya       16000    14/12/2010     current
```

(d) `$ awk '$5 ~/t$/' bank.lst`

It displays all the records having t as the last character in the fifth field. The `$` symbol represents the end of the field.

```
          101     Aditya     0        14/11/2012     current
          103     Naman      0        20/08/2009     current
          106     Mukesh     14000    20/12/2009     current
          108     Chirag     0        15/12/2012     current
          109     Arya       16000    14/12/2010     current
```

While pattern matching, we can also replace slashes (`//`) with double quotes as follows:

`$ awk '$5 ~ "t$" ' bank.lst`

It gives the same result as the aforementioned command.

(e) `$ awk '$5 !~ "t$" ' bank.lst`

It displays all the records not having t as the ending character in the fifth field in the file bank.lst.

```
          102     Anil       10000    20/05/2011     saving
          104     Rama       10000    15/08/2010     saving
          105     Jyotsna    5000     16/06/2012     saving
          107     Yashasvi   14500    30/11/2011     saving
          110     Puneet     130      16/11/2009     saving
```

(f) `$ nawk '$2 ~  "^A" ' bank.lst`

It displays all the records that start with the character A in the second field. `^` stands for the beginning of the field.

```
          101     Aditya     0        14/11/2012     current
          102     Anil       10000    20/05/2011     saving
          109     Arya       16000    14/12/2010     current
```

Note: To match a string at the beginning of the field, precede the search pattern by `^`. Similarly, use `$` for matching a pattern at the end of a field.

9.6 COMPOUND EXPRESSIONS

When two or more expressions are combined to check for a particular condition, they are termed compound expressions. Compound expressions are constructed using the compound operators (also known as logical operators) shown in Table 9.2.

Table 9.2 Brief description of logical operators

Symbol	Operator	Description
&&	And	Results true when all the expressions are true
||	Or	Results true when any of the expressions is true
!	Not	Reverses (negates) the logical expression

Examples

(a) $ awk 'NR >= 3 && NR <= 7 { print NR,$0 }' bank.lst

It prints all the records/lines from record number 3 to record number 7, along with their record number.

```
3   103   Naman      0       20/08/2009   current
4   104   Rama       10000   15/08/2010   saving
5   105   Jyotsna    5000    16/06/2012   saving
6   106   Mukesh     14000   20/12/2009   current
7   107   Yashasvi   14500   30/11/2011   saving
```

(b) $ awk 'NR == 3, NR == 5 { print NR,$0 }' bank.lst

It prints records from the third till the fifth, with their record number. The , (comma) specifies the range of records.

Output

```
3   103   Naman      0       20/08/2009   current
4   104   Rama       10000   15/08/2010   saving
5   105   Jyotsna    5000    16/06/2012   saving
```

(c) $ awk 'NR == 3 || NR ==5 { print NR,$0 }' bank.lst

It prints the records/lines having record number 3 or record number 5, along with their record number.

Output

```
3   103   Naman      0       20/08/2009   current
5   105   Jyotsna    5000    16/06/2012   saving
```

(d) $ awk 'NR<2 || NR>4 { print NR,$0 }' bank.lst

It prints all the records /lines having a record number less than 2 or greater than 4, along with their record number.

Output

```
1    101   Aditya     0       14/11/2012   current
5    105   Jyotsna    5000    16/06/2012   saving
6    106   Mukesh     14000   20/12/2009   current
7    107   Yashasvi   14500   30/11/2011   saving
8    108   Chirag     0       15/12/2012   current
9    109   Arya       16000   14/12/2010   current
10   110   Puneet     130     16/11/2009   saving
```

(e) $ awk '! NR >= 3 { print NR,$0 }' bank.lst

It prints all the records/lines whose record number is less than 3, along with their record number.

```
101   Aditya   0       14/11/2012   current
102   Anil     10000   20/05/2011   saving
```

(f) Consider a file `text.1st`, having the following content.
```
This is Solaris Unix Operating System
Ajmer. We are working on awk scripts
It appears to be very interesting
$ awk '{ print NF }' text.1st
```
It counts the number of fields in each line/record of the file `text.1st` and displays them. NF refers to the number of fields.

Output

```
6
7
6
```

(g) `$ awk '{ print $NF }' text.1st`
It prints the last field (word) of each record/line of the file `text.1st`. `$NF` refers to the last field.
```
System
scripts
interesting
```

(h) `$ awk '$2 ~ "^A" && $5 ~ "t$" ' bank.1st`
It displays all records having A as the starting character in the second field, as well as t as the ending character in the fifth field. Only records that satisfy both the conditions are displayed because of the *and* operator (`&&`).

```
101    Aditya     0         14/11/2012    current
109    Arya       16000     14/12/2010    Current
```

(h) (i) `$ awk '$2 ~ "^A" || $5 ~ "t$" ' bank.1st`
It displays all the records having A as the starting character in the second field or t as the ending character in the fifth field. The records satisfying either of the conditions are displayed.

```
101    Aditya     0         14/11/2012    current
102    Anil       10000     20/05/2011    saving
103    Naman      0         20/08/2009    current
106    Mukesh     14000     20/12/2009    current
108    Chirag     0         15/12/2012    current
109    Arya       16000     14/12/2010    current
```

(j) `$ awk '$5 ~/saving/ || $5 ~/current/' bank.1st`
It displays all the records having the pattern saving or current in the fifth field.

```
101    Aditya     0         14/11/2012    current
102    Anil       10000     20/05/2011    saving
103    Naman      0         20/08/2009    current
104    Rama       10000     15/08/2010    saving
105    Jyotsna    5000      16/06/2012    saving
107    Yashasvi   14500     30/11/2011    saving
108    Chirag     0         15/12/2012    current
110    Puneet     130       16/11/2009    saving
```

(k) `$ awk '$4 ~ /^20.*09$/' bank.lst`

It displays all the records having 20 as the starting digit and 09 as the ending digit in the fourth field of the file `bank.lst`.

```
103    Naman    0        20/08/2009    current
106    Mukesh   14000    20/12/2009    current
```

(l) `$ awk '$4 ~/^20.*09$/ && $2 ~/^N/' bank.lst`

It displays all the records having 20 as the starting digit and 09 as the ending digit in the fourth field of the file `bank.lst` and N as the starting character in the second field of the same file.

```
103    Naman    0        20/08/2009    current
```

9.7 ARITHMETIC OPERATORS

Arithmetic operators are used to perform arithmetic operations. The list of arithmetic operators that can be used in AWK is shown in Table 9.3.

Table 9.3 Brief description of arithmetic operators used in AWK

Operator	Description
*	Multiply
/	Divide
%	Mod (returns remainder)
+	Add
–	Subtract
++	Increments value by 1
––	Decrements value by 1
+=	Adds the value

AWK can perform computation on numbers using the arithmetic operators +, –, *, /, and % (modules).

Example `$ awk '$3 == "saving" {> printf "%20 s %d %20s %f\n", $2,$3,$4,$3*0.05}' bank.lst`

This command will print the customer name, balance, date, and interest (5% of balance) as follows:

```
Anil      10000    20/05/2011    500.00
Rama      10000    15/08/2010    500.00
Jyotsna   5000     16/06/2012    250.00
Yashasvi  14500    30/11/2011    725.00
Puneet    130      16/11/2009    65.00
```

You will find more examples of arithmetic operators in the following sections.

9.8 BEGIN AND END SECTIONS

When we have to print something before processing the first line, we use the Begin section. Similarly, the End section is useful in printing the total values after the processing is finished. The middle portion will be applied to all the lines/records of the file. In other words, the Begin and End sections are executed only once but the middle portion is executed for every line/record.

The syntax of the AWK command for using Begin and End sections is as follows:

```
awk '
BEGIN { actions }
/pattern/ { actions }
/pattern/ { actions }
END { actions }
' files
```

Note: The Begin and End sections are optional.

Example

```
$ awk BEGIN{
        printf "Records in the bank.lst file are :\n"
}
{ print $1, $2, $3 }' bank.lst
```

This example prints the first, second, and third fields of the file bank.lst. At the top, the following header will be displayed along with the line feed: Records in the bank.lst file are.

9.9 USER-DEFINED VARIABLES

The user-defined variables in AWK are similar to the variables that we use in a traditional programming language. They are meant for holding intermediate as well as final results of computation in the script.

Syntax   variable_name=value

Here, variable_name is the name of the variable and value is the value assigned to it. A variable_name can consist of only letters, numbers, and underscores and cannot begin with a number.

Example

```
total=0
account="saving"
```

These examples create the two variables total and account, respectively. The total variable is initialized to value 0 and the account variable is initialized to saving.

Note: No type declaration is required for defining variables in AWK. By default, variables are initialized to zero or a null string.

Example   The following is the file bank.lst, which we created in Section 9.1.

```
101    Aditya      0       14/11/2012    current
102    Anil        10000   20/05/2011    saving
103    Naman       0       20/08/2009    current
104    Rama        10000   15/08/2010    saving
105    Jyotsna     5000    16/06/2012    saving
106    Mukesh      14000   20/12/2009    current
107    Yashasvi    14500   30/11/2011    saving
108    Chirag      0       15/12/2012    current
109    Arya        16000   14/12/2010    current
110    Puneet      130     16/11/2009    saving
```

The following script adds the contents of the third field of the file bank.lst into the variable total. At the end, the total is displayed.

```
totalbal.awk
{total+=$3}
END{print "Total Amount In Bank Is " ,total}
$ awk -f totalbal.awk bank.lst
```

Output

```
Total Amount In Bank Is 69630
```

The following script displays all the records of the file bank.lst, counts the number of records, and also prints the average balance.

```
countrecs.awk
BEGIN{
    printf "Records are :\n\n"
}
{
  printf"%5d %-20s %d %15s %10s\n",$1,$2,$3,$4,$5
  c++;
  tot+=$3
}
END{
  printf"\n\t The Number Of Records Are %d\n",c
  printf"\n\t The Average Balance Is %.2f\n",tot/c
}
$ awk -f countrecs.awk bank.lst
```

Output

```
Records are :
101    Aditya      0        14/11/2012    current
102    Anil        10000    20/05/2011    saving
103    Naman       0        20/08/2009    current
104    Rama        10000    15/08/2010    saving
105    Jyotsna     5000     16/06/2012    saving
106    Mukesh      14000    20/12/2009    current
107    Yashasvi    14500    30/11/2011    saving
108    Chirag      0        15/12/2012    current
109    Arya        16000    14/12/2010    current
110    Puneet      130      16/11/2009    saving
The Number Of Records Are 10
The Average Balance Is 6963.00
```

The following script adds the third field of the file bank.lst and if the third field is 0, skips to the next record. In other words, only the contents of the third field that are non-zero are added into the total variable. Besides this, counting is also done for the number of customers with non-zero balance and the average balance is computed.

```
addnonzero.awk
$3==0{next}
```

```
{
  total +=$3
  count++
}
END {avrg = total/count
  printf "Total Amount     :%d\n",total
  printf "Number Of Customer :%d\n ",count
  printf "Average Amount In Bank  :%9.2f\n",avrg
}
```

$ awk -f addnonzero.awk bank.lst

Output

```
Total Amount       :69630
Number Of Customer :7
Average Amount In Bank: 9947.14
```

9.10 if else STATEMENT

During programming we may come across a situation where we wish to apply conditional branching, that is, we wish to apply specific processing on columns that satisfy given criteria. The if else statement is used to implement such criteria.

An if else statement is a conditional statement that is used for choosing one set of statements out of the two depending on the validity of the logical expression included.

```
if (logical expression)
{
  ...
  ...
}
else
{
  ...
  ...
}
```

If the logical expression is true, then the statement in if block will execute, otherwise the statements of else block will be executed.

Examples

(a) $ awk '{ if($3 > 10000) print "interest =" $3*.05; else print "interest=" $3*.06 }' bank.lst
It prints the interest as 5% of the balance if the balance is more than 10,000, otherwise it prints the interest as 6% of the balance, from the file bank.lst.
```
interest=0
interest=600
```

```
interest=0
interest=600
interest=300
interest=700
interest=725
interest=0
interest=800
interest=7.8
```

The script calculates the average balance in the `saving` account of the file `bank.1st`. This is to say that the total balance of all the customers with `saving` account is computed and the total is divided by the number of customers with `saving` account. If the average balance is more than 100,000, the following message is displayed: `Quite Good`. Otherwise the following message is displayed: `below Average`.

avgbalance.awk

```
{
  if ($5 == "saving")
  {
          bal +=$3
          c++
  }
}
END{
          avg=bal/c
          if(avg > 100000)
          print "Average balance in saving accounts is Quite Good",avg
          else
          print "Average balance in saving account is below Average",avg
}
$ awk -f avgbalance.awk bank.1st
```

Output

```
Average balance in saving account is below Average 7926
```

The script displays the records of the file `bank.1st` having a balance >= 15,000 and also having the pattern `current` in the fifth field.

currentbal.awk

```
{
  if($3 >= 15000 && $5=="current")
          print $0
}
$ awk -f currentbal.awk bank.1st
```

Output

```
109      Arya      16000    14/12/2010        current
```

(b) This script finds the maximum and minimum balance in the bank.1st file.

```
maxminbal.awk
{
  if (NR==1)
  {
          min=$3
  }
  if (max < $3)
  {
          max=$3
  }
  if (min > $3)
  {
          min=$3
  }
}
END{
  print "Maximum balance is ", max
  print "Minimum balance is ", min
}
$ awk -f maxminbal.awk bank.1st
```

Output

```
Maximum balance is  16000
Minimum balance is  0
```

(c) The following script removes the first four lines from the file bank.1st and stores the rest of the lines in the file passed as the command line argument. If we enter the same file name as source file # in the command line argument, it will remove the first four lines from the file source file.

```
removefour.awk
awk 'NR >4{
  print $0 > "'$1'"
}' bank.1st
$./removefour.awk bkk.1st
```

All the lines from the file bank.1st will be copied into the file bkk.1st except the first four lines. When we see the contents of the file bkk.1st, its contents will be as given here:

Output

```
$ cat bkk.1st
105   Jyotsna    5000    16/06/2012   saving
106   Mukesh     14000   20/12/2009   current
107   Yashasvi   14500   30/11/2011   saving
108   Chirag     0       15/12/2012   current
```

```
109   Arya      16000   14/12/2010   current
110   Puneet    130     16/11/2009   saving
```

9.11 BUILT-IN VARIABLES

In addition to the variables that we can define, AWK provides several built-in variables that are predefined and ready-to-use. The complete list of these variables is given in Table 9.4.

Table 9.4   Built-in variables in AWK

Variable	Description	Variable	Description
FS	Input field separator	FILENAME	Name of the current file
RS	Input record separator	ARGC	Number of command-line arguments
OFS	Output field separator	ARGV	Command-line argument array
ORS	Output record separator	RLENGTH	Length of string matched by a built-in string function
NF	Number of non-empty fields in current record		
NR	Number of records read from all files	RSTART	Start of string matched by a built-in string function

Examples

(a) $ awk 'NR >0' bank.lst

This statement prints all the records of the file having record number >0. Since the record number begins from 1, all the records of the file bank.lst are displayed.

```
101   Aditya    0       14/11/2012   current
102   Anil      10000   20/05/2011   saving
103   Naman     0       20/08/2009   current
104   Rama      10000   15/08/2010   saving
105   Jyotsna   5000    16/06/2012   saving
106   Mukesh    14000   20/12/2009   current
107   Yashasvi  14500   30/11/2011   saving
108   Chirag    0       15/12/2012   current
109   Arya      16000   14/12/2010   current
110   Puneet    130     16/11/2009   saving
```

(b) $ awk 'NR >0 { print NR,$0 }' bank.lst

This statement prints all the records of the file bank.lst along with their record number (line number). The built-in variable, NR, represents the row or record number and $0 represents the complete input line.

Output

```
1   101   Aditya    0       14/11/2012   current
2   102   Anil      10000   20/05/2011   saving
3   103   Naman     0       20/08/2009   current
```

4	104	Rama	10000	15/08/2010	saving
5	105	Jyotsna	5000	16/06/2012	saving
6	106	Mukesh	14000	20/12/2009	current
7	107	Yashasvi	14500	30/11/2011	saving
8	108	Chirag	0	15/12/2012	current
9	109	Arya	16000	14/12/2010	current
10	110	Puneet	130	16/11/2009	saving

(c) $ awk 'NR ==3 { print NR,$0 }' bank.lst

It prints only the third record, that is, record number 3 will be displayed.

Output

```
3 103 Naman 0 20/08/2009 current
```

It is now time to understand field separators.

A record in AWK is split into fields on the basis of the field separator. By default, the field separator is a blank space or a tab space. In order to specify our own field separator, the two built-in variables that are popularly used are FS and OFS.

9.11.1 fs: Field Separator

It represents the input field separator, that is, it splits an input record into fields on the basis of this separator. The FS may be in the form of a single character or a regular expression. The default value of the field separator is a single space.

Examples

(a) FS = ","

This example describes input field separator as , (comma), which means that each occurrence of a , in the input record separates two fields.

(b) FS = "\t"

This example describes the input field separator as a tab space, which means that the input record is separated into fields on each occurrence of a tab character.

9.11.2 OFS: Output Field Separator

It represents the output field separator, that is, it is an output equivalent of the AWK FS variable. It determines the field separator used while displaying fields via the print statement. By default, AWK OFS is a single space. We set the OFS character to a comma (,) as follows:

```
OFS=","
```

Then the following print statement displays the fields of the file bank.lst separated by a , (comma):

```
print $1, $2, $3 } bank.lst
```

Similarly, the following value of the OFS will separate the fields by a tab space when printed:

```
OFS="\t"
```

Example $ awk 'BEGIN { OFS = "\t" } { print $1, $2, $3 }' bank.lst

It prints the first, second, and third fields of the file `bank.1st`. The fields will be separated by a tab space. `OFS` stands for output field separator. In the absence of the `OFS`, the default output field separator is a white space.

9.12 CHANGING INPUT FIELD SEPARATOR

The input field separator, `FS`, helps in specifying how and where an input line be split into fields. The default value for `FS` is space and tab. We can manually set `FS` to any other character depending on our requirement. To change `FS`, we either specify it through the `-F` option or in a `BEGIN` pattern.

Note: We can even store AWK commands in files and then use it at run time. The extension of the file is `.awk`.

Examples

(a) Let us store the following commands in the file `dispjustify.awk`.

```
BEGIN{FS="|"}{
        printf"%20s %d %-20s\n",$1,$2,$3
        # by %20s the string will be right justified and by %-20s, the string will
be left justified
}
```

Note: No quotes are used to enclose the AWK program.

(b) Consider the file `bnk.1st`.

```
Aditya|5000|current|14/11/2012
Anil|13000|current|15/12/1987
Naman|15000|saving|16/10/1982
Rama|10000|saving|19/09/1982
Jyotsna|15000|current|20/10/1956
Mukesh|14000|saving|21/05/1985
Yashasvi|14500|current|21/11/1982
Chirag|12500|saving|12/11/1984
Arya|16000|current|16/01/1973
Puneet|13000|saving|20/02/1970
```

The AWK commands that are stored in a file can be accessed with the `-f` filename option.

```
$ awk  -f dispjustify.awk  bnk.1st
```

Where `-f` is the option in AWK that is used to execute the AWK script stored in the file. In this script, we have set `FS`, that is, input field separator to '|'. This means the file on which this script will be applied must have fields separated by a '|'.

The following will be the output.

```
Aditya    5000    current
Anil      13000   current
Naman     15000   saving
Rama      10000   saving
```

```
Jyotsna      15000    current
Mukesh       14000    saving
Yashasvi     14500    current
Chirag       12500    saving
Arya         16000    current
Puneet       13000    saving
```

(c) Consider a file `comp.1st`.

```
PC XT        1986     100      150000
PC AT        1990     200      125000
PC P1        1995     125      100000
PC PII       1996     100      80000
PC PIII      1999     150      70000
PC PIII      2000     25       60000
```

The following script prints the total number of computers, as well as the total number of computers, made after 1998.

```
totalcomp.awk
BEGIN{
  FS="\t"
}
{
  print $0
  totno +=$3
  if ($2 >1998)
    tot +=$3
}
END{
    print "Total number of computers ", totno
    print "Total number of computers made after 1998 are ", tot
}
$ awk -f totalcomp.awk comp.lst
```

Output

```
PC XT        1986     100      150000
PC AT        1990     200      125000
PC P1        1995     125      100000
PC PII       1996     100      80000
PC PIII      1999     150      70000
PC PIII      2000     25       60000
Total number of computers  700
Total number of computers made after 1998 are 175
```

9.13 FUNCTIONS

Functions are small modules/subroutines, which, once written, can be called as many times as we want, hence avoiding repetition of statements. Functions also make a program clear and systematic.

Example   Consider a file `data.1st`.

```
45        91
kamal     sunil
82        15
31        44
manish    anil
Rama      ravi
```

The following script prints the larger value first followed by the smaller value out of the two values (of each line/record) in the given file (using functions).

`largersmaller.awk`

```
{
    printf "%15s %15s \n", larger($1,$2), smaller($1,$2)
}
function larger(m,n)
{
    return m > n ? m:n
}
function smaller(m,n)
{
    return m < n ? m : n
}
```

Output

```
$ cat data.1st
45        91
kamal     sunil
82        15
31        44
manish    anil
Rama      ravi
$ nawk -f largersmaller.awk data.1st
            91        45
         sunil     kamal
            82        15
            44        31
        manish      anil
          ravi      Rama
```

AWK also has several built-in functions, performing both arithmetic and string operations.

9.13.1 String Functions

AWK includes numerous string functions that can be used to determine the length of a string, extract a part of a string, split a string into an array, and much more. A few of the built-in string functions are listed in Table 9.5.

Table 9.5 Built-in string functions in AWK

Function	Description
length(x)	It returns the length of the argument x. If the argument is not supplied, it finds out the length of the entire line.
substr(s1,s2,s3)	It returns a portion of the string of length s3, starting from position s2 in the string s1.
Index(s1,s2)	It returns the position of the string s2 in the string s1. It returns 0 if t is not present.
Split(s,a)	It splits the string s into an array a and optionally returns the number of fields. The field separator is specified by FS.
system("cmd")	It runs the Unix command, cmd, and returns its exit status.

The string functions will now be discussed in detail.

length() The length() function determines the length of its arguments, and if no arguments are present, Table 9.5 it assumes the entire line as its argument.

Syntax   length [(argument)]

Here, argument, if supplied, makes the length function return its length.

Examples

(a) Consider the file text.1st.

```
This is Solaris Unix Operating System
Ajmer. We are working on awk scripts
It appears to be very interesting
```

(a) (i) $ awk '{ print length }' text.1st
It displays the length (the number of characters) of each line/record of the file text.1st.

Output

```
37
36
33
```

(a) (ii) $ awk 'length ($2) >4' bank.1st
It displays all the records where the second field is more than four characters long.

Output

```
101    Aditya     0        14/11/2012    current
103    Naman      0        20/08/2009    current
105    Jyotsna    5000     16/06/2012    saving
106    Mukesh     14000    20/12/2009    current
107    Yashasvi   14500    30/11/2011    saving
108    Chirag     0        15/12/2012    current
110    Puneet     130      16/11/2009    saving
```

(b) Consider a file text.lst.

```
This is Solaris Unix Operating System
Ajmer. We are working on awk scripts
It appears to be very interesting
```

(b) (i) The following script prints the complete line, as well as the number of characters in each line of the file text.lst.

linechars.awk

```
{
  print $0, "\t", n=length($0)
  c +=n
}
END {print "Total characters in ",FILENAME, "are", c}
# FILENAME is the reserved word which designates the script file name
$ awk -f  linechars.awk text.lst
```

Output

```
This is Solaris Unix Operating System    37
Ajmer. We are working on awk scripts     36
It appears to be very interesting        33
Total characters in  text.lst  are       106
```

(b) (ii) The following script counts the number of lines and the words in each line and at the end prints the total number of lines and words in the file.

counttotlw.awk

```
BEGIN{print "Line No\t Words \t Line"}
{
  print NR,"\t",NF,"\t" $0
  w+=NF
}
END{
  print "\nTotals:"
  print "Words: \t" w
  print "Lines:\t" NR
}
```

In this script, NF, that is, the number of fields (number of words) are added to the variable, w (for every line).

```
$ awk -f counttotlw.awk text.lst
```

Output

```
Line No  Words  Line
1        6      This is Solaris Unix Operating System
2        7      Ajmer. We are working on awk scripts
3        6      It appears to be very interesting
```

```
Total:
Words:     19
Lines:     3
```

(b) (iii) The following script prints the average number of words per line. First, it computes the total number of lines and the total number of words in the file and then prints the average.

avgwords.awk

```
{
  totw +=NF
  l++
  print $0
}
END{
  print "Total number of words in ",FILENAME, "are", totw
  print "Total number of lines are ",l
  printf "Average number of words per line is %d\n", totw/l
}
$ awk -f avgwords.awk text.lst
```

Output

```
This is Solaris Unix Operating System
Ajmer. We are working on awk scripts
It appears to be very interesting
Total number of words in  text.lst  are  19
Total number of lines are  3
Average number of words per line is 6
```

index()   The index() function determines the position of a string within a larger string.

Syntax   index(main_string, string_to_search)

Here, main_string is the string in which string_to_search has to be searched for. If the string_to_search is found in the main_string, its index location will be returned, otherwise 0 will be returned.

(a) x = index("abcde", "b")

This returns the value 2.

(b) The following script counts the number of customers with current account.

countcurrent.awk

```
# Counting the number of customers with current account
{
  n=index($0, "current")
  if (n>0)
  {
    c++
  }
}
END{
```

```
    print "The number of customers with current account is ", c
}
$ awk -f countcurrent.awk bank.lst
```

Output

The number of customers with current account is five.

The script checks if the desired pattern exists in the string fed by the user.

checkpattern.awk

```
BEGIN{print "Enter a string followed by Enter key. To quit, press ^d"}
{
  n=index($0,"M")
  print "'M' is found at location ",n," in word ",$0
  n=index($0,"ic")
  print "'ic' is found at location ",n," in word ",$0
  n=index($0,"chip")
  print "'chip' is found at location ",n," in word ",$0
}
```

Output

```
$ awk -f checkpattern.awk
Enter a string followed by Enter key. To quit, press ^d
Microchip
'M' is found at location 1 in word Microchip
'ic' is found at location 2 in word Microchip
'chip' is found at location 6 in word Microchip

Silicon chips
'M' is found at location 0 in word Silicon chips
'ic' is found at location 4 in word Silicon chips
'chip' is found at location 9 in word Silicon chips
```

(c) Consider a file matter.1st.

```
We are trying an awk script
Ajmer is a nice place to stay
FIRST it is quiet and calm
Secondly the distances are small
Everything is in approach
Many visiting places END
Even Mayo college is in Ajmer
Always work hard
Who knows when the talent is required
India is supposed to be super power
Indians are very hard working
WASHINGTON D C is in America
New Delhi is in India
Sydney is in Australia
```

(c) (i) The script prints all the lines from the given file, from the line starting with the word FIRST, till the line that ends with the word, END.

beginfirst.awk

```
{
  if($1=="FIRST")
    start=NR
  if ($NF=="END")
  {
    print $0
    exit
  }
  if (NR >= start  && start != 0)
    print $0
}
```

In this script, the line where the first word is 'FIRST' is found, and the variable start is set equal to that line number. Then, until and unless the line where the last word is 'END' occurs, all the lines in between are printed. However, if the line where the first word is 'FIRST' does not exist, the value of the variable start is set to 0 and nothing will be displayed.

```
$ awk -f beginfirst.awk matter.lst
```

Output

```
FIRST it is quiet and calm
Secondly the distances are small
Everything is in approach
Many visiting places END
```

(c) (ii) The following script prints all the lines from the given file, starting from line number 7 till the line that starts with the word WASHINGTON DC.

fromline7.awk

```
{
  start=7
  n=index($0,"WASHINGTON DC")
  if (n>0)
  {
        print $0
        exit
  }
  if (NR >= start)
        print $0
}
```

```
$ awk -f fromline7.awk matter.lst
```

Output

```
Even Mayo college is in Ajmer
Always work hard
Who knows when the talent is required
```

```
India is supposed to be super power
Indians are very hard working
WASHINGTON D C is in America
```

substr() The substr() function is used for extracting a part of a string. It takes three arguments as follows:

Syntax   substr(stg,s,n)

The first argument, stg, represents the string to be used for extraction, s represents the starting point of extraction, and n indicates the number of characters to be extracted.

Examples

(a) substr($1,3,1)
It extracts the third character of the first field.

(b) substr($1,1,4)
It extracts the first four characters of the first field

(c) substr($1,2,3)
It extracts three characters from the second position of the first field

(d) $ awk 'substr($2,1,1) == "A" && substr($5,1,3) == "cur" ' bank.lst
It displays all the records having A as the first character in the second field and cur as the first three characters in the fifth field of the file bank.lst.

```
101    Aditya    0        14/11/2012   current
109    Arya      16000    14/12/2010   current
```

(e) $ awk 'substr($4,9,2) == "09" ' bank.lst
It displays all the records having 82 as the last two digits in the fourth field of the file bank.lst.

```
103    Naman     0        20/08/2009   current
106    Mukesh    14000    20/12/2009   current
110    Puneet    130      16/11/2009   saving
```

(e) (i) The following script prints records having the pattern Saving or saving in it.

```
dispsaving.awk
BEGIN{OFS="\t"}
{
n=substr($5,1,1)
if(n=="S" || n=="s")
{
        print $0
}
}
$ awk -f dispsaving.awk  bank.lst
```

Output

```
102    Anil      10000    20/05/2011   saving
104    Rama      10000    15/08/2010   saving
105    Jyotsna   5000     16/06/2012   saving
```

```
107    Yashasvi  14500    30/11/2011    saving
110    Puneet    130      16/11/2009    saving
```

(e) (ii) The following script takes the first name and surname as input and prints them after interchanging the two names.

```
interchange.awk
BEGIN{print "Enter first name and sur name. To quit press  ^d"}
{
  n=index($0," ")
  s=substr($0,n)
  f=substr($0,1,n-1)
  print "Name after interchanging first and sur name is ",s,f
}
```

Output

```
$ awk -f interchange.awk
Enter first name and sur name. To quit press ^d
Anil Sharma
Name after interchainging first and sur name is Sharma Anil
Sunil Arora
Name after interchainging first and sur name is Arora Sunil
```

split() The split() function splits a string on the basis of a given delimiter and stores the split elements in an array. It takes three arguments, a string to be split (first argument), an array (second argument), and the delimiter, which is used as the third argument.

Syntax   split(stg,array_name,"pattern")

Here, stg represents the string that we wish to split, where the given pattern (*delimiter*) occurs in the string. The split string is stored in the given array_name.

Examples

(a) split ($1,k, " ")
    It will split field1 into different components wherever space occurs. The components are then stored in the array k. This implies that if the $1 field has Manoj Kumar Sharma, then Manoj will be stored in k[1], Kumar will be stored in k[2], and Sharma will be stored in k[3].

(b) Consider the file salary.1st.

```
Anil,Sharma      5000
Sunil,Arora      4500
Charles,Peters   5300
$ nawk 'split($1, p, ",") { print p[2] " " p[1] }' salary.1st
```
    It will split the first field ($1) into parts wherever the delimiter comma (,) appears and stores those parts in the array p (p[1] containing the first part, p[2] containing the second part, and so on). After splitting, the array p[2], containing the surname is displayed, followed by a blank space, which is then followed by the array p[1]. The

names are displayed from the file `salary.lst` after interchanging the first name and the surname.

Output

```
Sharma Anil
Arora Sunil
Peters Charles
```

(c) Consider a file `salary.lst`.

```
Anil,Sharma      5000
Sunil,Arora      4500
Charles,Peters   5300
```

(c) (i) The script prints the salary and then the name of the person, interchanging the first name and surname after removing the , (comma) from the name.

```
salintchange.awk
BEGIN{FS="\t"}
{
  split($0,n)
  split(n[1],lnm,",")
  print n[2],lnm[2],lnm[1]
}
$ awk -f salintchange.awk salary.lst
```

Output

```
5000    Sharma Anil
4500    Arora Sunil
5300    Peters Charles
```

Note: The `split()` function is supported by NAWK but not AWK.

system() The `system()` function accepts any Unix command within double quotes as an argument, and executes the command. System commands or utilities are used in the AWK script using a pipe. This implies that the system command is written as a string within double quotes and the result of the system command is piped into the script through pipe line (|). The piped result is read into the script with a `getline` command.

Examples

(a) `system("tput clear")`
`system("date")`
The command returns 0 (success) or 1 (failure), which can then be used in the script.

(b) The following script demonstrates execution of the date system command and displays the first and fourth fields of the command output.

```
demogetline.awk
BEGIN{
  "date" | getline
  print($1,$4)
}
```

Output

```
$ date
Tuesday 6 March 2012 10:47:10 PM IST
$ nawk -f demogetline.awk
Tuesday 2012
```

(c) When there are multiple lines of output from the system command, they must be read with a loop, as shown in the following script.

```
demogetline2.awk
BEGIN{
  "date" | getline
  print($1,$4)
  while("who" | getline)
    print($1,$2)
}
```

Output

```
$ date
Tuesday 6 March 2012 11:03:58 PM IST
$ who
root    console   Mar 6 22:33   (:0)
root    pts/3     Mar 6 22:34   (:0.0)
$ nawk -f demogetline2.awk
Tuesday 2012
root console
root pts/3
```

9.13.2 Arithmetic Functions

Commonly used arithmetic operations such as computing square root, sine, and cosine can be easily performed in AWK as it provides the respective arithmetic functions for the same. The list of arithmetic functions is given in Table 9.6.

Table 9.6 Brief description of commonly used arithmetic functions in AWK

Function	Description
Int	It truncates floating-point value to integer.
rand()	It returns a random number between 0 and 1.
Srand(x)	It sets the seed or starting point for random numbers to be generated. If called without an argument, it uses the time of the day to generate the seed. If we do not provide or set a seed, the rand() function will return the same values every time it is run.
cos(x)	It returns the cosine of x.
exp(x)	It returns the exponent.
log(x)	It returns the natural logarithm (base e) of x.
sin(x)	It returns the sine of x.
sqrt(x)	It returns the square root of x.

Examples

(a)
```
BEGIN {
print sin(90*p/180)
}
```
This example will print the output 1 as sin(p/2) is 1.

(b)
```
BEGIN {
print exp(1)
}
```
This example will return an exponent of 1 (e^1), that is, 2.71828.

(c)
```
BEGIN {
print 10/3
}
```
This example will print the result 3.333.

(d)
```
BEGIN {
print int(10/3)
}
```
This example will print the result 3 as `int()` truncates the decimals from the result.

(e)
```
BEGIN {
print rand()
}
```
As mentioned in Table 9.6, the `rand()` function generates a random floating-point number between 0 and 1. Hence, this example might display the output as 0.231072.

(f)
```
BEGIN {
print rand()
srand()
print rand()
}
```
This example might display the following output.
```
0.231072.
0.639201
```
We get a result that is the same as the one obtained in Example (e) because when the `rand()` function is called without calling the `srand()` function, AWK acts as if the `srand()` is called with a constant argument causing the `rand()` function to begin from the same starting point every time the program is run. On calling the `srand()` function, it generates a seed on the basis of the time of the day making the `rand()` function generate a new value.

(g) `$ awk '{ print sqrt($3) }' bank.lst`
It prints the square root of the balance of the file `bank.lst`.

(h) `$ awk '{ print sin(3.1414/2) }' bank.lst`
It prints 1 (because sin $\pi/2$ =1) 10 times because there are 10 records/lines in the file `bank.lst`.

(i) `$ awk '{ if($3 <10000) print }' bank.lst`
It prints only the records with a balance (third field) less than 10,000 in the file `bank.lst`.

```
101     Aditya      0       14/11/2012      current
103     Naman       0       20/08/2009      current
105     Jyotsna     5000    16/06/2012      saving
108     Chirag      0       15/12/2012      current
110     Puneet      130     16/11/2009      saving
```

(j) `$ awk '{ if ($3 > 10000) print "good"; else print "bad" }' bank.lst`

It prints a message, good, if the balance is greater than 10,000 and otherwise prints bad (only the message, good or bad, will be displayed with no records).

```
bad
bad
bad
bad
bad
good
good
bad
good
bad
```

(k) Consider a file, bnk.lst, in which the delimiter used between fields is | instead of spaces or tabs.

```
Aditya|5000|current|14/11/2012
Anil|13000|current|15/12/1987
Naman|15000|saving|16/10/1982
Rama|10000|saving|19/09/1982
Jyotsna|15000|current|20/10/1956
Mukesh|14000|saving|21/05/1985
Yashasvi|14500|current|21/11/1982
Chirag|12500|saving|12/11/1984
Arya|16000|current|16/01/1973
Puneet|13000|saving|20/02/1970
```

(k) (i) `$ awk '$0 ~/^A.*7$/' bnk.lst`

This displays all the records having A as the starting character and 7 as the ending character in the file bnk.lst.

Output

```
Anil|13000|current|15/12/1987
```

(k) (ii) `$ awk '$0 ~/^[A-W]/' bnk.lst`

It displays all the records starting from any character in the range A to W in the file bnk.lst.

Output

```
Aditya|5000|current|14/11/2012
Anil|13000|current|15/12/1987
Naman|15000|saving|16/10/1982
```

```
Rama|10000|saving|19/09/1982
Jyotsna|15000|current|20/10/1956
Mukesh|14000|saving|21/05/1985
Chirag|12500|saving|12/11/1984
Arya|16000|current|16/01/1973
Puneet|13000|saving|20/02/1970
```

(k) (iii) `$ awk '$0 !~/^[A-W]/' bnk.lst`

It displays all the records not starting from any character in the range A to W in the file bnk.lst.

Output

```
Yashasvi|14500|current|21/11/1982
```

9.14 LOOPS

Loops are used for executing a set of commands on the given input a specified number of times or until the specified logical expression is true. We are going to study three loops.

9.14.1 for Loop

The for loop is used for repeating a set of statements.

Syntax `for(variable=initial value; final condition; increment/decrement)`

```
{
...
...
...
}
```

A variable will be assigned an initial value. Until the variable reaches the final condition, the body of the loop is executed, and the value of the variable increases/decreases with every execution.

Examples

(a) `$ awk '{ for (k=1;k<=2;k++) printf "%s\n", $0 }' bank.lst`

It displays each record of the file bank.lst two times.

101	Aditya	0	14/11/2012	current
101	Aditya	0	14/11/2012	current
102	Anil	10000	20/05/2011	saving
102	Anil	10000	20/05/2011	saving
103	Naman	0	20/08/2009	current
103	Naman	0	20/08/2009	current
104	Rama	10000	15/08/2010	saving
104	Rama	10000	15/08/2010	saving
105	Jyotsna	5000	16/06/2012	saving
105	Jyotsna	5000	16/06/2012	saving
106	Mukesh	14000	20/12/2009	current

```
106     Mukesh      14000     20/12/2009    current
107     Yashasvi    14500     30/11/2011    saving
107     Yashasvi    14500     30/11/2011    saving
108     Chirag      0         15/12/2012    current
108     Chirag      0         15/12/2012    current
109     Arya        16000     14/12/2010    current
109     Arya        16000     14/12/2010    current
110     Puneet      130       16/11/2009    saving
110     Puneet      130       16/11/2009    saving
```

This command can also be written in two or more lines as shown.

```
$ awk '{
    for (k=1;k<=2;k++)
        printf "%s\n", $0
    }' bank.lst
```

(b) The following script prints the total of all the columns of each record.

```
totalcols.awk
BEGIN{
    FS="\t"
    OFS="\t"
}
{
    tot=0
    for (i=1;i<=NF;i++)
        tot+=$i
    print $0,tot
}
```

```
$ awk -f totalcols.awk data.dat
```

The contents of the file data.dat are as follows.

```
10      20      30      40
11      21      31      41
12      22      32      42
```

The output will be as follows.

```
10      20      30      40      100
11      21      31      41      104
12      22      32      42      108
```

(c) Consider a file school.1st.

```
101     anil    45      66      78
102     kamal   79      43      76
103     ajay    87      41      65
```

(c) (i) The following script prints the record of each school student and also prints the total marks.

```
totalmarks.awk
BEGIN{print "Print Total"}
```

```
{total=$3+$4+$5}
{print $1,$2,$3"+"$4"+"$5"="total}
$ awk -f totalmarks.awk school.lst
```

Output
```
Print Total
101 anil 45+66+78=189
102 kamal 79+43+76=198
103 ajay 87+41+65=193
```

(c) (ii) The following script prints the roll number, name, and the average marks acquired by each student.

avgmarks.awk
```
{
   total=0
   count=0
   for (i=3;i<=NF;i++)
   {
       total +=$i
       count++
   }
   if (count > 0){
      avrg=total/count
      print ($1,$2,avrg)
   }
}
$ awk -f avgmarks.awk school.lst
```

Output
```
101 anil 63
102 kamal 66
103 ajay 64.3333
```

(d) Consider a file txt.lst.
```
This is Solaris Unix Operating System
Ajmer. We are working on awk scripts
It appears to be very interesting
```

Note: There are two blank lines in this file.

(d) (i) The following script prints all the lines after the blank line.

followblank.awk
```
n == 1 {print $0;n = 0}
$0 ~/^$/ {n=1}
# If the line is blank (i.e. start and end  ^- start, $-end are same), above
line will set the value # of n=1. So, this script prints all the lines following
the blank line
$ awk -f followblank.awk txt.lst
```

Output

```
Ajmer. We are working on awk scripts
It appears to be very interesting
```

(d) (ii) The following script prints the lines before the blank line.

```
beforeblank.awk
$0 ~/^$/ && NR !=1 {print k}
{k=$0}
# This script prints the lines before the blank line. The line is first saved in
the variable k
$ awk -f beforeblank.awk txt.lst
```

Output

```
This is Solaris Unix Operating System
Ajmer. We are working on awk scripts
```

(d) (iii) The following script counts the number of blank lines in a file.

```
countblank.awk
# Counting the number of blank lines
$0 ~/^$/ {n=n+1}
END{
    print "The number of blank lines are ",n
}

$ awk -f countblank.awk txt.lst
```

Output

```
The number of blank lines is 2.
```

(d) (iv) The following script inserts the two lines in between the file.

```
inserttwo.awk
# It inserts two lines :
# Hello World !
# Thank you
# after second line in the given file
NR !=3 {print $0}
NR == 3{print "Hello World!"; print "Thank you" ;print $0}
$ awk -f inserttwo.awk text.lst
```

Output

```
This is Solaris Unix Operating System
Ajmer. We are working on awk scripts
Hello World!
Thank you
It appears to be very interesting
```

(d) (v) The following script prints the matter from the file 10 characters at a time.

tenchar.awk

```
# This script prints the matter from the file 10 characters at a time.
{
    n=length($0)
    if (n<=10)
        print $0
    else
    {
        for (i=1;n>10;i+=10)
        {
            print substr($0,i,10)
            n-=10
        }
        print substr($0,i)
    }
}
$ awk -f tenchar.awk text.lst
```

Output

```
This is Solaris Unix Operating System Ajmer. We are working on awk scripts It
appears to be very interesting
```

9.14.2 do while Loop

It is the loop used for repeating a set of statements.

Syntax   do

```
        {
            ...
            ...
            ...
            ...
        }while(logical expression)
```

As we can see from the syntax in the 'do while' loop, the logical expression is checked at the end of the loop, so the loop will execute at least once, even if the logical expression is false.

Example   The following script prints the roll number, name, and average marks acquired by each student (IInd method).

avgmarks2.awk

```
{
    FS="\t"
    OFS="\t"
    total =0
```

```
        count =0
        i = 3
}
NF > 1{
    do
    {
        total +=$i
        count++
        i++
    }while(i <=NF)
    avrg=total/count
    print($1,$2,avrg)
}
```

Output

```
$ nawk -f avgmarks2.awk school.lst
101  anil    63
102  kamal   66
103  ajay    64.3333
```

9.14.3 while Loop

In the while loop, the logical expression is validated only in the beginning, so the loop will not execute at all if the logical expression is false.

Syntax
```
while (logical expression)
        {
            ...
            ...
            ...
            ...
        }
```

Example   The following script prints the roll number, name, and average marks acquired by each student (IIIrd method).

avgmarks3.awk
```
{
    tot = 0
    c = 0
    i = 3
    while(i <= NF)
    {
        tot +=$i
        c++
        i++
```

```
    }
    if(c > 0)
    {
       avg = tot/c
       print ($1,$2,avg)
    }
}
$ awk -f avgmarks3.awk school.lst
```

Output

```
101 anil 63
102 kamal 66
103 ajay 64.3333
```

9.15 GETTING INPUT FROM USER

In order to enhance user interaction, we require the user to input a value (or values) in the script. The command used for doing so is `getline`.

9.15.1 `getline` Command: Reading Input

The `getline` command is used for reading a line (record). Data can be fed using the keyboard or from the file.

Syntax   `getline variable < file`

If we write `/dev/tty` instead of `file`, then the data will be read from the terminal (keyboard).

Examples

(a) The following script displays the records of the customers having an account number greater than the value entered by the user.

```
desiredact.awk
BEGIN{
  printf "Enter the a/c no: "
  getline act < "/dev/tty"
  printf "Records of customers are:\n\n"
}
$1 > act {printf "%-20s %.2f %20s %20s\n",$2,$3,$4,$5}
```

If the value of `$1` (account no.) is greater than the value entered by the user in the variable act, then the record is displayed. By %-20s, the string is left aligned and by %20s, the string is right aligned

Output

```
$ nawk -f desiredact.awk bank.lst
Enter the a/c no: 105
```

```
Records of customers are:
Mukesh      14000.00    20/12/2009    current
Yashasvi    14500.00    30/11/2011    saving
Chirag      0.00        15/12/2012    current
Arya        16000.00    14/12/2010    current
Puneet      130.00      16/11/2009    saving
```

Note: You may recall that some functions such as getline, gsub(), and system() are supported in NAWK but not AWK.

(b) The following script displays the records of the customers having an account number and balance greater than the values entered by the user.

```
actbal.awk
BEGIN{
printf "Enter account number: "
  getline acc <"/dev/tty"
  printf "Enter balance: "
  getline bal <"/dev/tty"
  print "Records are: " }
$1 > acc && $3 > bal{printf "%5d %-20s %d\n",$1,$2,$3}
```

Output

```
$ nawk -f actbal.awk bank.lst
Enter account number: 105
Enter balance: 10000
Records are:
106         Mukesh        14000
107         Yashasvi      14500
109         Arya          16000
```

(c) Consider the file address.lst.

```
Anil Sharma
22/1 Sri Nagar Road
Ajmer

Sunil Arora
43/19 Vaishali Nagar
Jaipur

Chirag Harwani
15, Chirag Enclave
New Delhi
```

The following script prints the first and last fields of the record of the file address.lst.

```
lastfield.awk
BEGIN{FS="\n"; RS=""}
{
```

```
    print($1,"\t", $NF)
}
#$NF prints the last field contents
$ awk -f lastfield.awk address.lst
```

Output

```
Anil Sharma       Ajmer
Sunil Arora       Jaipur
Chirag Harwani    New Delhi
```

9.16 SEARCH AND SUBSTITUTE FUNCTIONS

Searching for a pattern is the most preferred operation with AWK scripts. In addition, we come across situations where we wish to search for a pattern and substitute it with some other pattern. By substitute, we mean replacing a regular expression found in a string with another string. The substitution can be done for the first occurrence or for the global occurrence of the regular expression. The list of commonly used search and substitute functions is as given in Table 9.7.

Table 9.7 Brief description of commonly used search and substitute functions in AWK

Function	Description
Delete array [element]	This deletes the specified element of the array.
Sub(r, s [,t])	This substitutes the first occurrence of the regular expression r by s in the string t. If the string t is not supplied, $0 (entire line/record) is considered. The function returns 1 if successful and 0 otherwise.
Gsub(r,s)	This substitutes s in place of r globally in $0 (entire line/record) and returns the number of substitution made.
Gsub(r,s,t)	This substitutes s in place of r globally in the string t and returns the number of substitutions made.
match(s,r)	This searches the string s for a substring r. The index of r is returned or zero is returned.
Toupper(str)	This converts the given string into upper case.
Tolower(str)	This converts the given string into lower case.

Through the AWK script we can replace a pattern or content in a given file with the desired content. We will use two functions, sub() and gsub(), for substituting file content. Let us see how.

9.16.1 sub()

Substitution function replaces a pattern with another pattern in a given string.

Syntax sub (pattern to be replaced, new pattern, string in which pattern is to be replaced)

The function replaces the pattern to be replaced with the new pattern in the string, String in which pattern is to be replaced. If the string in which pattern is to be replaced is not supplied, $0, that is, the entire line is considered.

This function returns 1 (true) if the substitution is successful and 0 (false) if the target string could not be found and the substitution could not be made.

Example   Consider the file shp.lst.

```
101    Tea       50
102    Coffee    32
103    Sugar     55
102    Coffee    65
101    Tea       69
101    Tea       35
102    Coffee    69
103    Sugar     97
103    Sugar     36
102    Coffee    35
```

(a) The following script replaces the word Tea with the word Brooke Bond in a given file and displays those lines where the replacement is performed.

replacewrd.awk

```
{
  t = sub(/Tea/,"Brooke Bond",$0)
}
{
  if(t > 0)
    print NR,$0
}
```

Output

```
$ nawk -f replacewrd.awk shp.lst
1  101   Brooke Bond   50
5  101   Brooke Bond   69
6  101   Brooke Bond   35
```

(b) The following script replaces a string with another string of a particular record/line only.

replacestr.awk

```
{
  if(NR == 5)
    sub (/Tea/,"Brooke Bond")
  print $0
}
```

Output

```
$ cat shp.lst
101    Tea         50
102    Coffee      32
103    Sugar       55
102    Coffee      65
101    Tea         69
101    Tea         35
102    Coffee      69
103    Sugar       97
103    Sugar       36
102    Coffee      35
$ nawk -f replacestr.awk shp.lst
101    Tea         50
102    Coffee      32
103    Sugar       55
102    Coffee      65
101    Brooke Bond 69
101    Tea         35
102    Coffee      69
103    Sugar       97
103    Sugar       36
102    Coffee      35
```

9.16.2 gsub()

The global substitution function changes all occurrences of a value by another value. The format for the global substitution function is identical to sub. The only difference is that it replaces all occurrences of the matching text.

Syntax   There are two syntaxes for using the gsub() command.

`gsub(r,s)`

Here, r is the expression or pattern that is substituted by s globally in $0 (entire line/record). The function returns the number of substitutions made.

`gsub(r,s,t)`

Here, r is the expression or pattern that is substituted by s globally in the string t. The function returns the number of substitutions made.

Example   The following script replaces the string Tea with Brooke Bond in the whole file.

repstrglob.awk

```
{
   gsub (/Tea/,"Brooke Bond",$0)
}
```

```
{
  if(index($0,"Brooke Bond"))
    print NR,$0
}
```

Output

```
$ cat shp.lst
101   Tea      50
102   Coffee   32
103   Sugar    55
102   Coffee   65
101   Tea      69
101   Tea      35
102   Coffee   69
103   Sugar    97
103   Sugar    36
102   Coffee   35
$ nawk -f repstrglob.awk shp.lst
1   101   Brooke Bond   50
5   101   Brooke Bond   69
6   101   Brooke Bond   35
```

9.16.3 match()

The match string function returns the starting position of the matching expression in the line. If there is no matching string, it returns 0. In addition, it sets two system variables—RSTART to the starting position and RLENGTH to the length of the matching text string.

Syntax   position = match (string in which to search, pattern to search)

Examples

(a) {if (match($0, /^.*,/) > 0)
    print NR, substr ($0 , RSTART, RLENGTH)
    }

This example prints lines that start with any character but end with a , (comma).

The following is a detailed example that demonstrates the use of the match() function.

(b) Consider a file bank1.lst, with the content as provided.

```
101   Aditya     0       14/11/2012   current
102   Anil       10000   20/05/2011   saving
103   Naman      0       20/08/2009   Current
104   Rama       10000   15/08/2010   saving
105   Jyotsna    5000    16/06/2012   saving
106   Mukesh     14000   20/12/2009   current
107   Yashasvi   14500   30/11/2011   saving
108   Chirag     0       15/12/2012   Current
```

```
109    Arya       16000   14/12/2010   Current
110    Puneet     130     16/11/2009   saving
```

The following script counts the number of customers with current or Current accounts.

```
countcurrent2.awk
# Counting the number of customers with current or Current account
{
  match($0, /[Cc]urrent/)
  if (RSTART>0)
  {
          c++
  }
}
END{
  print "The number of customers with current account is ", c
}
```

Output

```
$ cat bank1.lst
101    Aditya     0       14/11/2012   current
102    Anil       10000   20/05/2011   saving
103    Naman      0       20/08/2009   Current
104    Rama       10000   15/08/2010   saving
105    Jyotsna    5000    16/06/2012   saving
106    Mukesh     14000   20/12/2009   current
107    Yashasvi   14500   30/11/2011   saving
108    Chirag     0       15/12/2012   Current
109    Arya       16000   14/12/2010   Current
110    Puneet     130     16/11/2009   saving
$ nawk -f councurrent2.awk bank1.lst
The number of customers with current account is 5
```

9.16.4 toupper()

The toupper() function converts lower-case characters in a string into upper case. Characters that are not in lower case are left unchanged.

Syntax   toupper(str)

Here, str represents the string that will be converted into upper case.

9.16.5 tolower()

The tolower() function converts upper-case characters into lower case without disturbing characters that are not in upper case.

Syntax   tolower(str)

Here, str represents the string that will be converted into lower case.

Examples

(a) The following script replaces all the occurrences of the pattern tea or Tea with its upper case format, that is, TEA, in the given file.

```
repupper.awk
{
  match($0,/[Tt]ea/)
  t=toupper(substr($0,RSTART,RLENGTH))
  gsub(/[Tt]ea/,t)
  print $0
}
```

Output

```
$ cat shp.lst
101    Tea       50
102    Coffee    32
103    Sugar     55
102    Coffee    65
101    Tea       69
101    Tea       35
102    Coffee    69
103    Sugar     97
103    Sugar     36
102    Coffee    35

$ nawk -f repupper.awk shp.lst
101    Tea       50
102    Coffee    32
103    Sugar     55
102    Coffee    65
101    Tea       69
101    Tea       35
102    Coffee    69
103    Sugar     97
103    Sugar     36
102    Coffee    35
```

(b) Consider a file, letter.1st, with the following content.

```
tea
coffee
tea
sugar
coffee
coffee
sugar
tea
```

The following script displays all the lines from the given file starting with the specified character.

```
linesfromchar.awk
BEGIN{
   print "Enter a character: "
   getline c <"/dev/tty"
}
{
   n=substr($0,1,1)
   n=toupper(n)
   c=toupper(c)
   if (n==c)
   {
       print $0
   }
}
```

Output

```
$ cat letter.lst
tea
coffee
tea
sugar
coffee
coffee
sugar
tea
$ nawk -f linesfromchar.awk letter.lst
Enter a character: t
tea
tea
tea
```

(c) Consider a file, matter.1st, with the following content.

```
We are trying an awk script
Ajmer is a nice place to stay
FIRST it is quiet and calm
Secondly the distances are small
Everything is in approach
Many visiting places END
Even Mayo college is in Ajmer
Always work hard
Who knows when the talent is required
India is supposed to be super power
Indians are very hard working
```

```
WASHINGTON DC is in America
New Delhi is in India
Sydney is in Australia
```

The following script searches for a word in any case (lower case or upper case) in the file and displays the matching lines.

```
searchword.awk
BEGIN{
  print "Enter the word"
  getline c <"/dev/tty"
  }
{
  n=toupper($0)
  c=toupper(c)
  k=index(n,c)
  if (k>0)
  {
      print $0
  }
}
$ nawk -f searchword.awk matter.lst
```

Output

```
Enter the word
india
India is supposed to be super power
Indians are very hard working
New Delhi is in India
```

(d) Consider a file, text.1st, with the following content.

```
This is Solaris Unix Operating System
Ajmer. We are working on awk scripts
It appears to be very interesting
```

(d) (i) The following script changes the case of the words in the file. The words starting with lower case are converted to upper case and the words starting with upper case characters are converted to lower case.

```
changecase.awk
{
    for(i=1;i<=NF;i++)
    {
        h=substr($i,1,1)
        if( h>="a" && h<="z")
                printf "%s", toupper($i)
        else
                if (h>="A" && h<="Z")
```

```
                        printf "%s", tolower($i)
            else
                        printf "%s", $i
    }
    printf "\n"
}
```

Output

```
$ cat text.lst
This is Solaris Unix Operating System
Ajmer. We are working on awk scripts
It appears to be very interesting

$ nawk -f changecase.awk text.lst
this IS solaris unix operating system
ajmer. we ARE WORKING ON AWK SCRIPTS
it APPEARS TO BE VERY INTERESTING
```

(d) (ii) The following script changes the case of the words in the file into lower case.

```
intolower.awk
{
    print tolower($0)
}
```

Output

```
$ cat text.lst
This is Solaris Unix Operating System
Ajmer. We are working on awk scripts
It appears to be very interesting

$ nawk -f intolower.awk text.lst
this is solaris unix operating system
ajmer. we are working on awk scripts
it appears to be very interesting
```

(d) (iii) The following script changes the case of the words in the file into upper case.

```
convupper.awk
{
print toupper($0)
}
```

Output

```
$ cat text.lst
This is Solaris Unix Operating System
Ajmer. We are working on awk scripts
It appears to be very interesting
```

```
$ nawk -f convupper.awk text.lst
THIS IS SOLARIS UNIX OPERATING SYSTEM
AJMER. WE ARE WORKING ON AWK SCRIPTS
IT APPEARS TO BE VERY INTERESTING
```

(d) (iv) The following script toggles the case of each character in the file, that is, the characters in lower case are converted into upper case and characters in upper case are converted into lower case.

togglecase.awk

```
{
    for(i=1;i<=NF;i++)
    {
        n=length($i)
        for(j=1;j<=n;j++)
        {
            h=substr($i,j,1)
            if( h>="a" && h<="z")
                printf "%c",toupper(h)
            else
                if (h>="A" && h<="Z")
                    printf "%c",tolower(h)
                else
                    printf "%c",h
        }
        printf " "
    }
    printf "\n"
}
```

Output

```
$ cat text.lst
This is Solaris Unix Operating System
Ajmer. We are working on awk scripts
It appears to be very interesting

$ nawk -f convupper.awk text.lst
tHIS IS sOLARIS uNIX oPERATING sYSTEM
aJMER. wE ARE WORKING ON AWK SCRIPTS
iT APPEARS TO BE VERY INTERESTING
```

(e) This example shows how to access each word of the file followed by extracting each character of the word and converting its case as desired. In the following example, we will extend the same concept, but this time, we will learn to access the desired number of columns and use them in computation.

Consider a file, `data.dat`, with the initial content as follows.

```
10      20          30      40
11      21          31      41
12      22          32      42
```

(e) (i) The following script adds the given number of columns from the given file. The number of columns to be added is passed as a command line argument.

```
addcols.awk
awk 'BEGIN{
  OFS="\t"
  print "Total of",'$1', "columns"
}
{
  tot=0;
  for(i=1;i<='$1';i++)
    tot +=$i
  gtot=gtot+tot
  print $0,tot
}
END{
  print "Grand Total",gtot
}' data.dat
$./addcols.awk 2
```

Note: This AWK script is executed the way a shell script is executed, that is, `./` followed by the script name, which is then followed by the command line arguments.

Output

```
Total of        2       columns
10      20          30      40          30
11      21          31      41          32
12      22          32      42          34
Grand Total     96
$./addcols.awk 3
```

Output

```
Total of        3       columns
10      20          30      40          60
11      21          31      41          63
12      22          32      42          66
Grand Total     189
```

Examples   (a) The following example focuses on the input and output field separators, displaying content of columns that satisfy given criteria, displaying desired rows of the file, performing computation on the specified column content, and applying string functions on specific columns of the file.

Consider a file `cont.1st`.

```
CIS          8650     262     Asia
Canada       3852     24      North America
China        3692     866     Asia
USA          3615     219     North America
Brazil       3286     116     South America
Australia    2968     14      Australia
India        1269     637     Asia
Argentina    1072     26      South America
Sudan        968      19      Africa
Algeria      920      8       Africa
```

In this file, the columns specify the country, its area, population (in millions), and the continent to which it belongs.

(a) (i) The following script displays the countries of the Asian continent that have a population of more than 500 million.

```
popasia.awk
BEGIN{
  IFS="\t"
  OFS="\t"
  print "Country\tArea\tPOP\tContinents"
}
{
  if($4 == "Asia" && $3 >= 500)
    print $1,$2,$3,$4
}
$ awk -f popasia.awk cont.1st
```

Output

```
Country    Area     POP     Continents
China      3692     866     Asia
India      1269     637     Asia
```

(a) (ii) The following script prints the first five records of the file `cont.1st`.

```
firstfive.awk

BEGIN{
  FS="\t"
  OFS="\t"
  print "Country\tArea\tPOP\tContinents"
}
{
  if(NR <=5)
```

```
    print $1,$2,$3,$4
}
$ awk -f firstfive.awk cont.lst
```

Output

```
Country  Area   POP    Continents
CIS      8650   262    Asia
Canada   3852   24     North America
China    3692   866    Asia
USA      3615   219    North America
Brazil   3286   116    South America
```

(a) (iii) The following script prints each record preceded by its record number and a colon, with no extra blanks from the file cont.1st.

```
recnumcolon.awk
BEGIN{
    FS="\t"
    print "Country Area POP Continents"
}
{
    print NR,":",$1,$2,$3,$4
}
$ awk -f recnumcolon.awk cont.lst
```

Output

```
Country Area POP Continents
1 : CIS 8650 262 Asia
2 : Canada 3852 24 North America
3 : China 3692 866 Asia
4 : USA 3615 219 North America
5 : Brazil 3286 116 South America
6 : Australia 2968 14 Australia
7 : India 1269 637 Asia
8 : Argentina 1072 26 South America
9 : Sudan 968 19 Africa
10 : Algeria 920 18 Africa
```

(a) (iv) The following script prints those records whose country name begins with the letters S through Z from the file cont.1st.

```
countrysz.awk
BEGIN{
    FS="\t"
    OFS="\t"
    print "Country\tArea\tPOP\tContinents"
}
```

```
{
    h=substr ($1,1,1)
    if ((h>="S" && h<="Z") || (h>="s" && h<="z"))
        print $1,$2,$3,$4
}
$ awk -f countrysz.awk cont.lst
```

Output

Country	Area	POP	Continents
USA	3615	219	North America
Sudan	968	19	Africa

(a) (v) The following script is used to display all the records of the file cont.lst and at the end print the total area and total population.

```
totareapop.awk
BEGIN{
    FS="\t"
    print"COUNTRY""\t\t""AREA""\t""POP""\t""CONTINENT"}
{
    printf "%-15s %d\t%d\t%-20s\n", $1,$2,$3,$4
    tot +=$2
    total +=$3
}
END{
    print "============================================="
    print "Total" "\t\t" tot "\t" total
    print "============================================="
}
$ awk -f totareapop.awk cont.lst
```

Output

COUNTRY	AREA	POP	CONTINENT
CIS	8650	262	Asia
Canada	3852	24	North America
China	3692	866	Asia
USA	3615	219	North America
Brazil	3286	116	South America
Australia	2968	14	Australia
India	1269	637	Asia
Argentina	1072	26	South America
Sudan	968	19	Africa
Algeria	920	18	Africa

```
=============================================
Total          30292   2201
=============================================
```

(a) (vi) The following script prints the contents of the file countries abbreviating the country names to their first three characters from the file cont.1st.

```
abbrthree.awk
BEGIN{
    FS="\t"
    OFS="\t"
    print "Country\tArea\tPOP\tContinents"
}
{
    h=substr($1,1,3)
    print h,$2,$3,$4
}
$ awk -f abbrthree.awk cont.1st
```

Output

Country	Area	POP	Continents
CIS	8650	262	Asia
Can	3852	24	North America
Chi	3692	866	Asia
USA	3615	219	North America
Bra	3286	116	South America
Aus	2968	14	Australia
Ind	1269	637	Asia
Arg	1072	26	South America
Sud	968	19	Africa
Alg	920	18	Africa

(a) (vii) The following script displays the total area and population in each of the continents from the file cont.1st. Continent name is the first column, total population is the second column, and the total area is the third column.

```
popareacont.awk
BEGIN{
    FS="\t"
    print "Continent\tTotal Pop\tTotal Area"
}
{
    totp[$4]+=$3
    tota[$4]+=$2
}
END{
    for(i in totp)
    {
```

```
                    printf "%-15s %d\t\t%d\n",i,totp[i],tota[i]
        }
}
$ awk -f popareacont.awk cont.lst
```

Output

```
Continent          Total Pop    Total Area
South America          142         4358
Africa                  37         1888
Asia                  1765        13611
Australia               14         2968
North America          243         7467
```

(b) The following example demonstrates the usage of field separators (FS and OFS) and number of fields (NF).

Consider a file, text.1st, having the following content.

```
This is Solaris Unix Operating System
Ajmer. We are working on awk scripts
It appears to be very interesting
```

The following script prints each line of the file in reverse order. Reverse, here, does not mean upside down; instead, it means that the first word of the line is printed last, the second word is printed second last, and so on.

```
reversefile.awk
BEGIN{
    FS=" "
    OFS=" "
}
{
    for(i=NF;i>=1;i--)
    {
          printf "%s ",$i
    }
    printf"\n"
}
$ awk -f reversefile.awk text.1st
```

Output

```
System Operating Unix Solaris is This
scripts awk on working are We Ajmer.
interesting very be to appears It
```

9.17 COPYING RESULTS INTO ANOTHER FILE

Till now, we have used AWK scripts for displaying filtered content, applying desired processing on the filtered content, and displaying the results in the form of a report on the screen. We will now learn how to store the filtered and processed report in another file through a few examples.

Examples

Consider the file bank.lst, which we have been using. The following are its contents for reference.

```
101    Aditya      0        14/11/2012    current
102    Anil        10000    20/05/2011    saving
103    Naman       0        20/08/2009    current
104    Rama        10000    15/08/2010    saving
105    Jyotsna     5000     16/06/2012    saving
106    Mukesh      14000    20/12/2009    current
107    Yashasvi    14500    30/11/2011    saving
108    Chirag      0        15/12/2012    current
109    Arya        16000    14/12/2010    current
110    Puneet      130      16/11/2009    saving
```

(a) The following script will copy all the lines (records) of the file bank.lst and store them in another file bkw.lst.

```
copylines.awk
BEGIN{
  while (( getline f < "bank.lst")>0)
  {
        print f > "bkw.lst"
  }
}
```

Output

```
S cat bkw.lst
cat: cannot open bkw,lst
$ nawk -f copylines.awk

$ cat bkw1.lst
101        Aditya        0        14/11/2012    current
102        Anil          10000    20/05/2011    saving
103        Naman         0        20/08/2009    current
104        Rama          10000    15/08/2010    saving
105        Jyotsna       5000     16/06/2012    saving
106        Mukesh        14000    20/12/2009    current
107        Yashasvi      14500    30/11/2011    saving
108        Chirag        0        15/12/2012    current
```

109	Arya	16000	14/12/2010	current
110	Puneet	130	16/11/2009	saving

(b) The following script will copy all the lines (records) of one file and store them in another file. The filenames will be passed as command line arguments.

```
copylines2.awk
nawk 'BEGIN{
  while (( getline f < "'$1'")>0)
  {
      print f > "'$2'"
  }
}'
```

Output

```
S cat bb.lst
cat: cannot open bb,lst
$ ./copylines2.awk bank.lst bb.lst
$ cat bb.lst
    101     Aditya      0       14/11/2012      current
    102     Anil        10000   20/05/2011      saving
    103     Naman       0       20/08/2009      current
    104     Rama        10000   15/08/2010      saving
    105     Jyotsna     5000    16/06/2012      saving
    106     Mukesh      14000   20/12/2009      current
    107     Yashasvi    14500   30/11/2011      saving
    108     Chirag      0       15/12/2012      current
    109     Arya        16000   14/12/2010      current
    110     Puneet      130     16/11/2009      saving
```

The contents of the file bank.lst are copied into another file bb.lst.

(c) The following script will copy all the records having the specified pattern from a given file into another file. The filename is passed as a command line argument.

```
copypattern.awk
awk '/current/{
print $0 > "'$1'"
}' bank.lst
$./copypattern.awk bnkcur.lst
```

All records from bank.lst with pattern 'current' are copied into the file bnkcur.lst. The following content in the file bnkcur.lst confirms this.

```
cat bnkcur.lst
    101     Aditya      0       14/11/2012      current
    103     Naman       0       20/08/2009      current
    106     Mukesh      14000   20/12/2009      current
    108     Chirag      0       15/12/2012      current
    109     Arya        16000   14/12/2010      current
```

9.18 DELETING CONTENT FROM FILES

Not only can we filter the desired content from a file but also delete it if desired. We will now see the procedure for deleting content from a file that satisfies a given criteria.

Examples

(a) The following script deletes the lines from a given file that does not have the specified pattern.

```
delnotpattern.awk
nawk 'BEGIN{
  printf "Enter a word: "
  getline w < "/dev/tty"
  while (( getline k < "'$1'")>0)
  {
      n=index (k, w)
      if (n >0)
              print k > "'$1'"
  }
}'
```

Output

```
$ cat bank.lst
101     Aditya    0         14/11/2012    current
102     Anil      10000     20/05/2011    saving
103     Naman     0         20/08/2009    current
104     Rama      10000     15/08/2010    saving
105     Jyotsna   5000      16/06/2012    saving
106     Mukesh    14000     20/12/2009    current
107     Yashasvi  14500     30/11/2011    saving
108     Chirag    0         15/12/2012    current
109     Arya      16000     14/12/2010    current
110     Puneet    130       16/11/2009    saving
$ ./delnotpattern.awk bank.lst
Enter a word: current
$ cat bank.lst
101     Aditya    0         14/11/2012    current
103     Naman     0         20/08/2009    current
106     Mukesh    14000     20/12/2009    current
108     Chirag    0         15/12/2012    current
109     Arya      16000     14/12/2010    current
```

We can see that all the lines in the file bank.lst are erased except the lines/records having the pattern current in it.

(b) The following script removes lines with the specified pattern in the file.

```
removepattern.awk
# This script removes the lines with the specified pattern in file
```

```
nawk 'BEGIN{
  printf "Enter a word: "
  getline w < "/dev/tty"
  while (( getline k < "'$1'")>0)
  {
          n=index (k, w)
          if (n ==0)
                  print k > "'$1'"
  }
}'
```

Output

```
$ cat bank.lst
101    Aditya     0       14/11/2012    current
102    Anil       10000   20/05/2011    saving
103    Naman      0       20/08/2009    current
104    Rama       10000   15/08/2010    saving
105    Jyotsna    5000    16/06/2012    saving
106    Mukesh     14000   20/12/2009    current
107    Yashasvi   14500   30/11/2011    saving
108    Chirag     0       15/12/2012    current
109    Arya       16000   14/12/2010    current
110    Puneet     130     16/11/2009    saving
$ ./removepattern.awk bank.lst
Enter a word: current
$ cat bank.lst
102    Anil       10000   20/05/2011    saving
104    Rama       10000   15/08/2010    saving
105    Jyotsna    5000    16/06/2012    saving
107    Yashasvi   14500   30/11/2011    saving
110    Puneet     130     16/11/2009    saving
```

We can see in the output that all the lines in the file bank.lst with the pattern current are erased.

9.19 ARRAYS

As the name suggests, the term array refers to a sequential set of allocated memory. In other words, when a set of sequential memory is assigned to a variable, it is commonly known as array. The content to the allocated memory is assigned as well as referenced via indices. The index value begins from 1 (instead of 0 as in traditional programming languages).

Examples

(a) The following example assigns the value 10 to the index 4 of the array p:

```
p[4]=10
```

(b) The following examples access the value stored in the index 4 of the array p:

```
print p[4]
p[4]=[4]-2
```

(c) Consider the file bank.1st that we have been using. The following is its content for reference.

101	Aditya	0	14/11/2012	current
102	Anil	10000	20/05/2011	saving
103	Naman	0	20/08/2009	current
104	Rama	10000	15/08/2010	saving
105	Jyotsna	5000	16/06/2012	saving
106	Mukesh	14000	20/12/2009	current
107	Yashasvi	14500	30/11/2011	saving
108	Chirag	0	15/12/2012	current
109	Arya	16000	14/12/2010	current
110	Puneet	130	16/11/2009	saving

The following script prints all the records of the file bank.1st in reverse order.

```
reverserec.awk
{lines [NR] = $0}
END{
    for(i=NR;i>0;i-)
        print lines[i]

}
```

All the lines will be stored in array lines using the lines[NR]=$0 command, that is, the first line of the file will be stored in lines[1], the second line in lines[2], and so on. NR is set to the total number of records. The for loop is executed in reverse order to print the file in reverse.

```
$ awk -f reverserec.awk bank.1st
```

Output

110	Puneet	130	16/11/2009	saving
109	Arya	16000	14/12/2010	current
108	Chirag	0	15/12/2012	current
107	Yashasvi	14500	30/11/2011	saving
106	Mukesh	14000	20/12/2009	current
105	Jyotsna	5000	16/06/2012	saving
104	Rama	10000	15/08/2010	saving
103	Naman	0	20/08/2009	current
102	Anil	10000	20/05/2011	saving
101	Aditya	0	14/11/2012	current

(d) Consider a file shop.1st.

101	sales	Sugar	50	16
102	sales	Tea	55	10

103	purchase	Coffee	60	15
101	sales	Sugar	65	52
102	purchase	Tea	04	50
103	purchase	Coffee	15	40
103	sales	Coffee	40	10
102	purchase	Tea	18	52
101	sales	Sugar	56	58
103	sales	Coffee	98	90

The following script prints the average quantity and average sales price, that is, the quantities and prices of sold items are added and then divided by the number of records added.

avgqtysp.awk

```
BEGIN{
   FS="\t"
   printf "Code      A/c     Name   Qty    Sp\n"
}
/sales/
{
   c=c+1;
   tot[1]+=$4;
   tot[2]+=$5;
}
END{
   printf "Average Quantity is %.3f And Average Selling Price is %.3f \n",tot[1]/
c,tot[2]/c
}
$ awk -f avgqtysp.awk shop.lst
```

Output

```
Code  A/c    Name    Qty  Sp
101   sales  Sugar   50   16
102   sales  Tea     55   10
101   sales  Sugar   65   52
103   sales  Coffee  40   10
101   sales  Sugar   56   58
103   sales  Coffee  98   90
Average Quantity is 46.100 And Average Selling Price is 39.300
```

We can see that in this AWK script, the contents of the fourth field and the fifth field of the file shop.1st are added to the tot[1] and tot[2] array, respectively.

9.20 ASSOCIATIVE ARRAYS

Associative arrays are those arrays in which we can use any string as an index of the array instead of using the traditional indices, 1, 2,..., etc. Besides strings, we can use any expression at the place of the index in an associative array.

Examples

(a) `k[tea]=50;`

`p[anil]=10;`

The strings `tea` and `anil` are the indices or keys of the associative arrays `k` and `p` respectively. The numbers 50 and 10 are the values of the respective keys of the associative arrays.

(b) Consider a file `letter.1st`.

```
tea
coffee
tea
sugar
coffee
coffee
sugar
tea
```

The following script counts the frequency of every word in the file `letter.1st`.

`countfreq.awk`

```
{k[$0]++}
END{
    for(i in k)
            print(i,"\t", k[i])
}
$ awk -f countfreq.awk letter.1st
```

Output

```
tea      3
coffee   3
sugar    2
```

In this script, using `k[$0]++`, the array with subscripts tea, coffee, or sugar will be made, (i.e., `k[tea]`, `k[coffee]`, `k[sugar]` will be made and its value will be set equal to the number of times that item has occurred). This implies that the value of `k[tea]` will be 3 (because the item tea has occurred three times). Similarly, the value of `k[coffee]` will be 3 and `k[sugar]` will be 2.

(c) Consider the file `shp.1st`.

101	Tea	50
102	Coffee	32
103	Sugar	55
102	Coffee	65
101	Tea	69
101	Tea	35
102	Coffee	69
103	Sugar	97
103	Sugar	36
102	Coffee	35

The following script displays the total quantity of each item sold and in the end it also displays the grand total.

```
soldqty.awk
{sumqty [$2]+=$3}
END{
        for(i in sumqty)
        {
            print i,":",sumqty[i]
            gqty += sumqty[i]
        }
print "Grand Total Of Quantity ",":",gqty
}
$ awk -f soldqty.awk shp.lst
```

Output

```
Sugar : 188
Tea : 154
Coffee : 201
Grand Total Of Quantity  : 543
```

In this script, by using the `sumqty[$2]` command, an array with subscript having the names of the 2nd field (`$2`), that is, `Tea`, `Coffee`, `Sugar` will be made, that is, `sumqty[Tea]`, `sumqty[Coffee]`, `sumqty[Sugar]` will be made and in this array, the total of the 3rd field (`$3`), that is, quantity will be stored.

(d) Consider a file `sales.1st`.

```
Anil      4
Sunil     3
Kamal     8
Anil      2
Sunil     9
Kamal     1
Anil      5
Sunil     4
Kamal     7
```

(d) (i) The following script displays the total quantity of items sold by each salesman and, in the end, displays the grand total of sold quantities.

```
soldsales.awk
BEGIN{
    print "Sales man Name\t Sales made"
}
{sales[$1]+=$2}
END{
    for(i in sales)
    {
        print i,"\t\t",sales[i]
                gtot += sales[i]
```

```
        }
        print "Grand Total Of Sales ",gtot
        }
$ awk -f soldsales.awk sales.lst
```

Output

```
Sales man Name          Sales made
Sunil 16
Anil   11
Kamal  16
Grand Total Of Sales        43
```

(d) (ii) The following script demonstrates how an item can be deleted from an array. First the total quantity of each item is computed and stored in an array, and then an element is deleted from an array.

```
delarray.awk
BEGIN{OFS = "\t"}
{sumqty[$2]+=$3}
END{
  print "Deleting sugar index entry"
  delete sumqty["Sugar"]
    for(i in sumqty)
    {
        print i,":",sumqty[i]
        gqty +=sumqty[i]
    }
  print "Grand total of quantity",":",gqty
}
```

Output

```
$ cat shp.lst
101     Tea       50
102     Coffee    32
103     Sugar     55
102     Coffee    65
101     Tea       69
101     Tea       35
102     Coffee    69
103     Sugar     97
103     Sugar     36
102     Coffee    35
$ nawk -f delarray.awk shp.lst
Deleting sugar idex entry
Tea: 154
Coffee:  201
Crand total of quantity:     355
```

(e) The following script prints all the words that are four characters long and which have occurred five or more times.

Consider a file mat.lst.

```
must have are is and were have and is must
must is and were have must
were must and is were is and were must
wordsoccur.awk
BEGIN{
  FS=" "
}
{
  split($0,k)
  # all the words are stored in the array k
  for(i in k)
       j[k[i]]++
  # Counting the frequency of each word and storing in the array j
}
END{
  for(i in j)
  {
          if (length(i) ==4 && j[i] >=5)
             print(i, "\t", j[i])
  }
}
$ awk -f wordsoccur.awk mat.lst
```

Output

```
must       6
were       5
```

(f) The script merges the two files, bank.lst and shp.lst, horizontally, that is, the lines of bank.lst and shp.lst will be displayed adjacent to each other. Once one file is completed, the second file is displayed at the bottom.

The content of the two files, bank.lst and shp.lst, which will be merged is as follows.

bank.lst

```
101    Aditya     0        14/11/2012    current
102    Anil       10000    20/05/2011    saving
103    Naman      0        20/08/2009    current
104    Rama       10000    15/08/2010    saving
105    Jyotsna    5000     16/06/2012    saving
106    Mukesh     14000    20/12/2009    current
107    Yashasvi   14500    30/11/2011    saving
108    Chirag     0        15/12/2012    current
109    Arya       16000    14/12/2010    current
110    Puneet     130      16/11/2009    saving
```

shp.lst

101	Tea	50
102	Coffee	32
103	Sugar	55
102	Coffee	65
101	Tea	69
101	Tea	35
102	Coffee	69
103	Sugar	97
103	Sugar	36
102	Coffee	35

The AWK script that merges the content of two files, bank.1st and shp.1st, horizontally is as follows.

mergefiles.awk

```
BEGIN{
while ((getline f < "bank.1st")>0\
  && (getline s < "shp.1st")>0)
{
  print f,s
}
while ((getline f < "bank.1st")>0)
  {print f}
while ((getline first < "shp.1st")>0)
  {print s}
}
# Above script will merge the two files horizontally
```

Output

```
$ cat bank1.1st
101   Aditya     0       14/11/2012   current
102   Anil       10000   20/05/2011   saving
103   Naman      0       20/08/2009   current
104   Rama       10000   15/08/2010   saving
105   Jyotsna    5000    16/06/2012   saving
106   Mukesh     14000   20/12/2009   current
107   Yashasvi   14500   30/11/2011   saving
108   Chirag     0       15/12/2012   current
109   Arya       16000   14/12/2010   current
110   Puneet     130     16/11/2009   saving
$ cat shp.1st
101   Tea        50
102   Coffee     32
103   Sugar      55
102   Coffee     65
```

```
101     Tea        69
101     Tea        35
102     Coffee     69
103     Sugar      97
103     Sugar      36
102     Coffee     35
$ nawk -f mergefiles.awk
101     Aditya     0       14/11/2012   current 101   Tea      50
102     Anil       10000   20/05/2011   saving  102   Coffee   32
103     Naman      0       20/08/2009   current 103   Sugar    55
104     Rama       10000   15/08/2010   saving  102   Coffee   65
105     Jyotsna    5000    16/06/2012   saving  101   Tea      69
106     Mukesh     14000   20/12/2009   current 101   Tea      35
107     Yashasvi   14500   30/11/2011   saving  102   Coffee   69
108     Chirag     0       15/12/2012   current 103   Sugar    97
109     Arya       16000   14/12/2010   current 103   Sugar    36
110     Puneet     130     16/11/2009   saving  102   Coffee   35
```

In this chapter, we learnt the different patterns and actions that are used in AWK filters to search for desired content from a file and display results in the form of a report. We discussed how to display formatted output, use different operators, built-in variables, and the functions to perform desired processing on the filtered records. We also explained how to copy content from one file that matches the given pattern, into another file. We also understood how to make use of conditional statements and loops for performing repetitive tasks. Finally, we talked about geting input from the user and using arrays in AWK scripts.

■ SUMMARY ■

1. The AWK command is a programming language that is executed by the AWK interpreter.
2. AWK is a commonly used text processing tool and a powerful text filtering tool designed for processing structured data records.
3. AWK operates at the field level and can easily access, transform, and format individual fields in a record.
4. The print command in AWK is used for displaying messages, fields, variables, etc. If field specifiers are not specified, it prints the entire line.
5. AWK automatically divides input lines into fields on the basis of the field separators. Each field is assigned an individual number to access them. For instance, the first field is accessed as $1, second field as $2, and so on.
6. When two or more expressions are combined to

check for a particular condition, they are termed as a compound expression.
7. Compound expressions are constructed using compound operators, also known as logical operators (&& (AND), || (OR), and ! (NOT) operator).
8. For matching anywhere in a field, AWK offers the ~ and !~ operators to match and not match, respectively. The ^ symbol represents the beginning of the field. The $ symbol represents the end of the field.
9. The length() function determines the length of its arguments, and if no arguments are present, it assumes the entire line as its argument.
10. The index() function determines the position of a string within a larger string.
11. This substr() function is used for extracting a part of a string.

12. The `system()` function accepts any Unix command within double quotes as an argument, and executes the command.

13. The `split()` function splits a string on the basis of a given delimiter and stores the split elements in an array.

14. An 'if else' statement is a conditional statement that is used for choosing one set of statements out of two depending on the validity of the logical expression included.

15. To print something before processing the first line in the output, the Begin section is used in AWK.

16. The End section in AWK is used for printing ending remarks, totals, summaries, etc., after the processing is over.

17. OFS stands for output field separator. The default output field separator is a white space.

18. The input field separator, FS, helps in specifying how and where to split an input line into fields.

19. AWK commands can be stored in files and can be used at run time. The extension of the file is `.awk`.

20. This –f option is used in AWK to execute the AWK script stored in the file.

21. The user-defined variables in AWK are similar to the variables used in traditional programming languages and are used for holding intermediate as well as final results of computation in the script.

22. No type declaration is required for defining variables in AWK. By default, variables are initialized to zero or a null string.

23. The `getline` command is used for reading a line (record). Data can be fed in using the keyboard or from the file.

24. For reading input from the terminal (keyboard), `/dev/tty` is used with the `getline` command.

25. The `$NF` variable represents the last field of the line/record.

26. The value of the NR variable is automatically set to the total number of records.

27. In the 'do while' loop, the logical expression is validated at the end of the loop, hence the loop will execute at least once, even if the logical expression is false.

28. In the while loop, the logical expression is validated only in the beginning, hence the loop will not execute at all if the logical expression is false.

29. Substitution function `sub()` replaces a pattern with another pattern in a given string.

30. Global substitution function `gsub()` replaces all occurrences of a value with another value.

31. The match string function returns the starting position of the matching expression in the line. If there is no matching string, it returns 0.

32. The match string function sets two system variables: `RSTART` to the starting position and `RLENGTH` to the length of the matching text string.

33. The `toupper()` function converts lower-case characters in a string to their upper-case values. Any characters that are not lower case are left unchanged.

34. The `tolower()` function converts upper-case characters to their corresponding lower-case values without disturbing characters that are not upper case.

35. Functions are small modules/subroutines, which, once written, can be called as many times as we want, hence avoiding repetition of statements. Functions make a program clear and systematic.

■ EXERCISES ■

Objective-type Questions

State True or False

9.1 The AWK command is a programming language that is executed by the AWK interpreter.

9.2 AWK is a commonly used stream editor

9.3 AWK divides the input into different records on

the basis of the record separator encountered.

9.4 The default field separators are newline character and . (period).

9.5 Each field in AWK is assigned an individual number to access them. For instance, the first field is accessed as $1 and second field as $2.

9.6 The special variable, $10, represents the entire line.

9.7 Compound expressions are not possible while working with AWK.

9.8 The ~ operator in AWK is used for matching patterns anywhere in the field.

9.9 The !~ symbol represents the end of the field.

9.10 The length() function, if no arguments are specified, assumes the entire line as its argument.

9.11 This substr() function is used for substituting a given string with another string.

9.12 The system() function is used for checking the computer system for any virus.

9.13 To print something before processing the first line in output, the Begin section is used in AWK.

9.14 The End section in AWK is used for printing ending remarks, totals, summaries, etc., after the processing is completed.

9.15 The Begin and End sections are executed for every line/record but the code between the Begin and End section is executed only once.

Fill in the Blanks

9.1 In AWK, the record separator by default is a _____.

9.2 The records in AWK are divided into _____ on the basis of the _____.

9.3 The name AWK comes from the last names of its creators _____, _____, and _____.

9.4 The _____ statement is used for displaying data in the formatted way.

9.5 The built-in variable _____ represents the row or record number.

9.6 When two or more expressions are combined to check for a particular condition, they are termed _____.

9.7 The _____ symbol represents the beginning of the field in AWK.

9.8 The _____ function determines the position of a string within a larger string.

9.9 The _____ function splits a string on the basis of a given delimiter and stores the split elements in an array.

9.10 OFS stands for _____.

9.11 The _____ option is used in AWK to execute the awk script stored in the file.

9.12 The _____ command is used for reading input from the keyboard or from the file.

9.13 The _____ function replaces a pattern with another pattern in a given string.

9.14 The _____ function returns the starting position of the matching expression in the line.

9.15 The _____ function converts lower-case characters in a string to their upper-case values.

Multiple-choice Questions

9.1 To represent the entire line, the special variable used is
(a) $0   (c) $10
(b) $1   (d) $v

9.2 The $NF variable represents the
(a) first field   (c) last field
(b) second field   (d) second last field

9.3 AWK commands can be stored in a file with the extension
(a) .a   (c) .k
(b) .awk   (d) .aw

9.4 The /dev/tty is used with the getline command to
(a) get device information
(b) read device configuration from disk
(c) display terminal information
(d) read input from the keyboard

9.5 If the match string function finds no matching string, it returns
(a) −1   (c) infinite
(b) 0   (d) 1

9.6 The %f in printf is used for displaying
(a) float value   (c) filename
(b) string   (d) integer value

9.7 The built-in variable that represents the name of the current file is
(a) FILE
(b) CURRENT
(c) NAME
(d) FILENAME

9.8 To negate or reverse the logical expression, the operator used is
   (a) %   (c) !
   (b) /   (d) ||
9.9 The built-in variable for the output record separator is
   (a) ORS
   (b) ORSP
   (c) OFS
   (d) RS
9.10 The arithmetic function used to find the square root of a value is
   (a) root()
   (b) sroot()
   (c) sqroot()
   (d) sqrt()

Programming Exercises

9.1 Consider a file, stock.lst, which contains the product code, product name, price, quantity, and category of product as follows.

```
101   Jeans      1000   10   garments
102   Camera     5000   3    electronics
103   Trousers   1200   5    garments
104   Laptop     40000  15   electronics
105   CellPhone  8000   8    electronics
```

With respect to this file, stock.lst, what will the output of the following commands be?
   (a) $ awk '/garment/' stock.lst
   (b) $ awk '/electronics/ { print $2,$4 }' stock.lst
   (c) $ awk '$4 < 10' stock.lst
   (d) $ awk 'NR >0 { print NR,$0 }' stock.lst
   (e) $ awk 'NR == 2, NR == 4 { print NR,$0 }' stock.lst
   (f) $ awk '{ print NF }' stock.lst
   (g) $ awk '{ print $NF }' stock.lst
   (h) $ awk '$5 ~/s$/' stock.lst
   (i) $ awk '$2 ~ "^C" ' stock.lst
   (j) $ awk '$2 ~ "^C" && $4 < 5 ' stock.lst

9.2 Considering the file stock.list as the input file, write the commands for performing the following tasks.
   (a) To print only the code of the electronics products
   (b) To print the information of the products whose price is in the range 5000–10,000
   (c) To print all the products except jeans
   (d) To print the third record in the file
   (e) To print the product whose code is 102
   (f) To print the products whose product names begin from any character between a to d
   (g) To print all the products whose product name is more than six characters long.
   (h) To print all the products whose quantity is less than 10
   (i) To print all the products whose product name is laptop
   (j) To print the product name and price of all the garment product whose code is less than 103 and whose price is more than 800
   (k) To print only the product names of the products whose quantity is between 10 and 15.
   (l) To print all the products whose product name begins with the character 'C'

9.3 Consider a file, school.lst, with the following content.

```
101   Anil     science    45   60   105
102   Rama     commerce   55   30   85
103   Sunil    science    35   20   55
104   Peter    commerce   75   70   145
105   Sanjay   science    95   80   175
```

Write the AWK scripts to do the following:
   (a) Count the number of students with roll >= 105
   (b) Count the number of commerce students
   (c) Count the number of science students whose roll <= 103
   (d) Count the number of students having total >= 100

9.4 Consider a file, data.lst, with the following content.

```
AnilSharma     VaishaliNagar   science    45   67
ManojGupta     SriNagarRoad    commerce   66   89
KamalSharma    ShastriNagar    commerce   81   32
RamaSharma     VaishaliNagar   commerce   45   91
ChiragHarwani  VaishaliNagar   science    34   63
```

Write the AWK script for the following:
   (a) Show all the lines/records between the specified range, to be entered by the user
   (b) Show all the records having the pattern Vaishali Nagar in it
   (c) Replace the pattern science with commerce
   (d) Print all the contents of this file along with the total of two subjects of each student
   (e) Show all the records with surname 'Sharma'

Review Questions

9.1 Explain the meaning of the following statements with examples:
   (a) `printf`   (b) `gsub`   (c) `getline`
9.2 Explain how arrays and associative arrays are used in AWK.
9.3 Considering the aforementioned file, `stock.lst`, write the complete AWK scripts for the following:
   (a) Print the first, second, and fifth fields of the file `stock.lst` separated by a tab space
   (b) Print all the rows of the products with the total quantity, that is, the fourth column at the end
   (c) Print all the rows of the products along with the count of the products whose quantity is less than 10, and the total of the prices of all products
   (d) Print all the rows of the products along with the count of the products that belong to the electronics category, and whose quantity is less than 10
   (e) Print all the rows of the products having code

equal to the value entered by the user.
9.4 Explain the purpose of the following:
   (a) Begin and End sections   (c) For loop
   (b) If else statement   (d) Match
9.5 Explain the purpose of the following string functions with examples:
   (a) `index()`   (b) `substr()`   (c) `split(0`
9.6 Does AWK support arithmetic functions? If yes, then write the commands for the following tasks:
   (a) Print the sine of 180°
   (b) Print three random numbers
   (c) Print the square root of the number entered by the user
9.7 Explain with examples the use of the following built-in variables:
   (a) NF
   (b) OFS
   (c) NR
   (d) RSTART
   (e) FILENAME

Brain Teasers

9.1 The following code for displaying the first four columns of the file `bank.lst` is not working correctly. Correct the code

```
$ awk '{ printf $1,$2,$3 }' bank.lst
```

9.2 What is wrong in the following code for displaying the first five rows of the file `bank.lst`?

```
$ awk '$NR <=5 { print $0 }' bank.lst
```

9.3 Find out the error in the following code to show the records where the second column begins with 'A' and ends with 'Z'.

```
$ awk '$2 ~ "^A" || $2 == "$Z" ' bank.lst
```

9.4 What is wrong in the following code for adding the content of the third column of the given file and printing the total at the end?

```
BEGIN{
tot=0
   tot+=$3
}
END{
   printf "\The total sum is %d\n", tot
}
```

9.5 The following code is for replacing the text sun

with moon in a text file and displaying the lines where substitution occurs. Find out why the code is not working.

```
{
t = sub(/sun/,"moon",$1)
}
{
   if(t ==0)
       print $0
}
```

9.6 Correct the error in the following code that asks the user to enter a string and displays that entire line in lower case, where the string is found.

```
BEGIN{
   print "Enter the word "
   getline c >"/dev/tty"
}
{
   n=toupper($0)
   c=tolower(c)
   k=index(n,c)
   if (k<0)
   {
```

```
    print tolower($0)
    }
}
```

9.7 Find out the error in the following code for displaying the total number of words and lines in a file

```
    {
    w+=$NF
}
END{
    print "Words: " w
    print "Lines:" NF
}
```

9.8 Correct the error in the following code that displays a file in reverse order.

```
{ lines [NF] = $1 }
END{
    for(i=NR;i>=0;i--)
```

```
    print lines[0]
}
```

9.9 Correct the following code that searches for the line that begins with the word Sun and displays all the lines of the file from that line onwards till the end of the file.

```
{
    if($1=="Sun")
            start=$NF
    if (NR >= start )
            print $1
}
```

9.10 Correct the following program that displays the current month and year

```
BEGIN{
"date" | getty
print($1,$4)
}
```

■ ANSWERS TO OBJECTIVE-TYPE QUESTIONS ■

State True or False

9.1 True
9.2 False
9.3 True
9.4 False
9.5 True
9.6 False
9.7 False
9.8 True
9.9 False
9.10 True
9.11 False

9.12 False
9.13 True
9.14 True
9.15 False

Fill in the Blanks

9.1 newline character
9.2 fields, field separators
9.3 Alfred Aho, Peter Weinberger, and Brian Kernighan
9.4 printf

9.5 NR
9.6 compound expression
9.7 ^
9.8 index()
9.9 split()
9.10 output field separator
9.11 -f
9.12 getline
9.13 sub()
9.14 match
9.15 toupper()

Multiple-choice Questions

9.1 (a)
9.2 (c)
9.3 (b)
9.4 (d)
9.5 (b)
9.6 (a)
9.7 (d)
9.8 (c)
9.9 (a)
9.10 (d)

Bourne Shell Programming

After studying this chapter, the reader will be conversant with the following:

- Creating and running simple Bourne shell scripts
- Using command line parameters in the shell scripts
- Using conditional statements and loops to make the desired commands execute a specified number of times
- Reading input, displaying output, testing data, translating content, and searching for patterns in files using different commands
- Displaying the exit status of the commands, applying command substitution, and sending and receiving messages with other users
- Creating and using functions, setting and displaying terminal configurations, managing positional parameters, and using fetch options in the command line

10.1 INTRODUCTION

Bourne shell was one of the major shells used in the early versions of the Unix operating system. It was written by Stephen Bourne at Bell Labs. Often known as the command interpreter, the Bourne shell provides a user interface to the rich set of Unix utilities. It reads the commands from the terminal or file and executes them. It is represented by the dollar '$' command line prompt.

The Bourne shell provides variables, flow control constructs, and functions to write user-friendly and interactive shell scripts. Apart from this, it provides interactive features that include job control, command line editing, history, and aliases. In addition, it supports 'quoting' to remove the special meaning of certain meta characters.

Note: Bourne again shell (Bash) is similar to the Bourne shell; however it has additional features like command line editing.

Features of Bourne shell

As discussed, the Bourne shell is the original Unix shell that was developed at Bell Labs by Stephen Bourne. Being a shell, it provides user interface, interprets commands, and provides an environment to work on the Unix system. Bourne shell provides several features. A few of them are listed here:

1. Allows execution of commands and scripts
2. Provides a set of built-in commands and utilities
3. Enables execution of commands in the background
4. Provides input/output redirection, pipes, and filters
5. Enables command substitution by using back quotes
6. Provides commands for loops and conditional branching
7. Supports pattern matching operators (?, *)

We can make the Bourne shell execute desired tasks through scripting. We will now learn the procedure of writing and executing shell scripts.

10.2 BEGINNING BOURNE SHELL SCRIPTING

A shell program (also known as a shell script) is a collection of a series of commands for a Unix shell, such as the Bourne shell, Korn shell, and C shell. No separate compiler is required to execute these shell scripts as the shell itself interprets and executes them. The shell scripts include both Unix commands as well as built-in functions in the shell. Each shell has a different mechanism for executing the commands in the shell script and hence the shell script of one shell may not execute on another shell. Most shell scripts are written for the Bourne shell, as this is the most commonly used shell.

This chapter focuses on understanding how to write scripts for the Bourne shell and its enhanced version, Bourne again shell. Before beginning with shell scripting, we will discuss some of the frequently used commands in shell scripts. These commands here are explained with respect to the Bourne shell. The relevant useful commands are repeated in Chapters 11 and 12 with respect to Korn and C shells, respectively.

10.2.1 echo: Displaying Messages and Values

You may recall we have already discussed this command in Chapter 3. The echo command is used for displaying messages or values of the variables/expression.

Syntax	`echo "Messages/$Variables"`

Notes:
1. Quotation marks are optional in the echo command. If quotations are not used in the echo command, extra white spaces are automatically removed on the display.
2. All variables in the echo command have to be preceded by a $ sign.

Example	`echo "Welcome to MCE"`

Output

```
Welcome to MCE
```

Example   n=15

```
          echo "The value of n is $n"
```

Output

```
The value of n is 15
```

The character n used in the output is a variable. Variables are explained in detail in the following section.

10.2.2 Variables

We can use variables in our shell scripts, and assign values to them using the following syntax:

Syntax   `Variable = value`

To retrieve the value of a variable, place a dollar sign ($) in front of the variable name.

Note: Do not introduce any spaces on either side of the equal to sign (=). Variable names must begin with a letter or an underscore character (_). We can also use letters, underscores, or numbers for naming variables.

10.2.3 expr: Evaluating Expressions

The expr command is used to evaluate a specified expression.

Syntax   `expr arg1 operator arg2 ...`

Here, arg1, arg2, ... represent the arguments that combine with operators to form the expression to be evaluated.

Examples

(a) `$ x=3`
(b) `$ y=5`

Output

```
expr  $x + $y
8
```

The aforementioned example adds the values of variables x and y. Similarly, the following example displays the value of the addition of the values of variables x and y assigned to variable z.

```
z=`expr $x+ $y`
$ echo $z
8
```

The following example adds constants 3 and 5.

```
$ expr 3 + 5
8
```

The following example multiplies values 3 and 2.

```
$ expr 3 \* 2
6
```

The * (asterisk) is escaped by a \ (backslash) to be treated as the multiplication symbol, hence multiplying 3 by 2.

Note: Asterisk (*) refers to all files in the current directory. Hence \ (backslash) is used to escape it, that is, * is treated as the multiplication symbol.

10.2.4 let: Assigning and Evaluating Expressions

The let command is used for assigning values to the variables as well as for evaluating the expression. It is the same as the expr command but it does not require the $ (dollar sign) with the variables.

Syntax `let variable1=value/expression [variable2=value/expression]...`

Examples

(a) `$ let x=15+10`
    `$ echo $x`
    `25`

(b) `$((15*10))`
    `25`

Note: A set of double parentheses, '((' and '))' may be used instead of the let command.

(c) `$ x=22 y=28 z=5`
    `$((z=x+y+z))`
    `$ echo $z`
    `55`

10.2.5 bc: Base Conversion

The bc command has already been discussed in Chapter 2. The calculator (or base conversion) mode is invoked by typing the bc command at the shell prompt and thereafter the $ prompt disappears. The input to the calculator is taken line by line. We need to first enter an expression, after which the Unix command produces the result.

Examples

(a) `$ bc`
    `10/2*2`
    `10`
    `2.5*2.5+2`
    `8.25`
    `quit`
    On typing quit, the bc command ends.

Note: In order to get precise answers while working with a floating point number, we set the variable *scale* to a value equal to the number of digits after the decimal point.

(b) `$ bc`
    `scale=1`
    `25/2`
    `12.50`

After setting the scale variable, if the answer of an expression is more than the value of the scale set, then the scale value is ignored and the correct answer is displayed.

Another useful feature of bc is *base conversion*.

(c)
```
$ bc
ibase = 2
obase = 16
1010
A
quit
```

By setting the variables, ibase to 2 and obase to 16, all the input values are taken as binary numbers while all the output values are displayed in hexadecimal format.

bc also supports functions such as sqrt, cosine, sine, and tangent. sqrt() is an in-built function whereas s() and c(), which stand for sine and cosine respectively, would work only when bc is invoked with the –1 option.

(d)
```
$ bc
sqrt(49)
7
```

(e)
```
$ bc -1
scale =2
s(3.14)
0
```

bc also allows setting up of variables. These variables can be used in programs.

(f)
```
$ bc
for (i=1; i<=5; i=i+1) i
1
2
3
4
5
quit
```

> **Note:** expr is capable of carrying out only integer arithmetic. To carry out arithmetic on real numbers the bc command is used.

(g)
```
a=81.3
b=15.7
c=`echo $a + $b | bc`
d=`echo $a \* $b | bc`
echo $c $d
```

Output

```
97.0 1276.41
```

10.2.6 factor: Factorizing Numbers

The factor command is used to factorize the given number and print its prime factors. When factor is invoked without an argument, it waits for a number to be typed and prints the factors of the number entered. It then waits for another number and exits if it encounters a zero or any non-numerical character.

Syntax `factor [number]`

Example
```
$ factor
15
    3
    5
28
    2
    2
    7
q
$
```

10.2.7 units: Scale Conversion

The `units` command converts quantities expressed in various standard scales to their equivalents in other scales.

```
$ units
you have : inch
you want : cm
*2.540000e+00
/3.937008e-01
```

This output means that to convert inches into centimeters, we need to multiply the inches with 2.54 or divide inches by 0.3937008.

The `units` command understands distance through units such as cms, metres, kms, inches, feet, miles, nautical miles, and yards and the quantity of liquids in litres, quarts, and gallons.

10.3 WRITING SHELL SCRIPTS

The following points should be taken into account while writing a shell script:

1. Comments should be preceded with a #. A comment split over multiple lines must have a # at the beginning of each line.
2. More than one assignment can be done in a single statement.
3. Multiplication symbol * must always be preceded by a \, otherwise the shell will treat it as a wild-card character. The wild character (*) usually represents any number of characters or numbers. You may recall that `ls *` displays all filenames in the current directory comprising any number of characters or numerals.

To type a script, we open the vi editor with the following command:

```
$ vi dispmessage
```

In the file dispmessage, enter the following text:

```
#!/bin/bash
echo -n "Hello! "
echo "You are Welcome"
echo "We are working in directory `pwd`"
echo "Todays date is `date`"
```

Save the file by pressing Esc:wq, that is, first press the Esc key and then press :wq where w is for saving the file and q is for quitting from the vi editor. To execute the aforementioned shell program, we type the following:

```
$ ./dispmessage
```

Output

```
Hello! You are Welcome
We are working in directory /Unixcode
Todays date is Saturday 3 March 2012 09:54:44 PM IST
```

The # symbol, as mentioned, is for writing comments.

echo prints all messages on the screen. We can write messages in double quotes.

If we pass the -n command line parameter to echo, then it would not end its output with a *newline*.

Hence, the following echo command output will also appear on the same line. Therefore, the following two lines will give the output on the same line:

```
echo -n "Hello! "
echo "You are Welcome"
```

Output

```
Hello! You are Welcome
echo "We are working in directory  `pwd`  "
```

The accent marks (back quotes) surrounding the pwd command imply that the shell should execute the command between the accent marks and then substitute the output of the command in the string passed to the echo command.

We can print the date and time with the date command:

```
$ date
Saturday 3 March 2012 09:54:44 PM IST
```

Before executing a shell script, it must be made executable by the chmod command as shown:

```
$ chmod 700 dispmessage
```

Here, 7 is for owner and is assigned read (4), write (2), and execute (1) permissions. Group and others are assigned 0 permissions, that is, others and group members would not be able to read, write, or execute the file.

Predefined variable Predefined variables can be divided into two categories—shell variables and environment variables. Shell variables are used to customize the shell itself. Environmental variables control the user environment and can be exported to subshells.

10.4 COMMAND LINE PARAMETERS

Shell scripts can read up to *nine command line parameters* or arguments into special variables. These command line parameters appear as specially named shell script variables. The command line parameters are named $1, $2, $3, up to $9.

The name of the executable script is stored in $0.

The first argument is read by the shell into the parameter $1, the second argument into $2, and so on.

$# is the count of the number of arguments and $* represents all command line arguments.

Example   Consider the following example that demonstrates the usage of command line parameters in a shell script.

```
$ vi commandparam
#!/bin/bash
echo "The number of parameters are $#"
echo  "The parameters are $*"
echo "The parameters are $1 $2 $3"
echo  "The shell script command is $0"
```

If we execute the aforementioned shell script in the following way,

```
$ ./commandparam a.txt 10 b.txt 25
```

./commandparam will be stored in $0.

a.txt will be assigned to $1.

10 will be assigned to $2.

b.txt will be assigned to $3.

25 will be assigned to $4.

a.txt 10 b.txt 25 will be collectively stored in $*.

$# will be assigned the counting of arguments, that is, 4

Output

```
$ ./commandparam a.txt 10 b.txt 25
The number of parameters are 4
The parameters are a.txt 10 b.txt 25
The parameters are a.txt 10 b.txt
The shell script command is ./commandparam
```

Note: If we pass less than nine command line parameters, the extra variables have a *null value*.

10.5 read: READING INPUT FROM USERS

The read command is used to read the input typed by the user into shell variables.

Syntax   `read variable_name`

Examples

(a) The following script prompts the user to enter his/her first and last names. It then displays the name as well as that particular day's date and time on the screen.

```
demoread
#!/bin/bash
echo -n "Enter your first name "
read f
echo -n "Enter your last name "
read l
echo "Your name is $f $l"
$. /demoread
```

Output

```
Enter your first name arun
Enter your last name sharma
Your name is arun sharma
```

(b) The following script prints that particular day's date only.

```
printdate
#!/bin/bash
m=`date +%d/%m/%Y`
echo "Current system date is $m"
```

Output

```
Current system date is 26/02/2012
```

Note: To execute any Unix command from a shell script, it has to be enclosed in back quotes. It is for this reason that the date command is enclosed in back quotes.

(c) The following script only prints the system time.

```
printtime
#!/bin/bash
echo "The system time is `date +%H:%M:%S`"
```

Output

```
The system time is 10:14:59
```

10.6 for LOOP

Loops are used for executing a command or a set of commands for each value of the given set.

Syntax   for variable

```
        in list_of_values
    do
        command 1
        command 1
        ...
        ...
    done
```

The variable in this syntax will be assigned one of the values from the *list_of_values* and the commands between *do* and *done* will be executed on that variable. This is repeated till all the commands between *do* and *done* are executed for each value assigned to the variables.

Examples

(a) The following script prints the sequence of numbers from 1 to 5.

```
dispsequence
#!/bin/bash
for x in 1 2 3 4 5
do
  echo "The value of x is $x"
done
```

Output

```
The value of x is 1
The value of x is 2
The value of x is 3
The value of x is 4
The value of x is 5
```

As we can see in this output, the variable x will first be assigned a value 1, following which the body of the loop is executed, that is, the echo command is executed. Thereafter, the variable, x, will get another value, 2, and the body is executed. This is repeated till the loop is executed for each value assigned to the variables.

(b) The following script prints all the filenames in the current directory that begin with the character b.

```
filescurdirectory
#!/bin/bash
for k in b*
do
  echo "File name is $k"
done
$./filescurdirectory
```

Note: The * is considered a wild-card character that represents any number of alphanumerals.

In the aforementioned script, variable *k* will be assigned a file (if it exists) from the hard disk having the first character as b, followed by any number of characters or numerals. The filenames will be assigned to variable *k* one by one.

Output

```
File name is b.1st
File name is bank.1st
```

(c) The following script shows the contents of all the files in the current directory starting with the character b.

```
filesbeginb
#!/bin/bash
```

```
for f in b*
do
  cat $f
done
```

Output

```
This is a test file
1001    Charles    15000    saving
1002    Kiran      10000    current
1003    Anushka    12000    current
1004    John       8000     saving
1005    Enna       11000    current
```

Assuming that there are two files, b.1st and bank.1st, which begin with the character b in the current directory, the aforementioned output shows the content of the two files.

Note: ? is a wild-card character that represents a single alphanumeral (character, numeral, or symbol). The * is a wild-card character and represents any number of alphanumerals.

(d) The following script prints the command line arguments sent while executing the script.

```
dispcommandargs
#!/bin/bash
for arg
in $*
do
  echo $arg
done
```

Note: $* will be assigned all the parameters sent from the command line. The variable *arg* will be assigned one parameter at a time and then displayed.

Output

```
$ ./dispcommandargs xyz.txt bank.1st school.xt
xyz.txt
bank.1st
school.txt
```

(e) The following script copies the contents of all the files starting with character b and which have the extension .1st in the specified directory, specified by the user, into the file mce.dat.

```
copyfilescontent
#!/bin/bash
echo -n "Enter name of directory: "
read a
for filename
in b*.1st
do
```

```
    cat $filename >> $a/merge.dat
done
```

Output

```
$ ls b*.lst
b.lst    bank.lst
$ cat b.lst
This is a test file
$ cat bank.lst
1001    Charles    15000    saving
1002    Kiran      10000    current
1003    Anushka    12000    current
1004    John       8000     saving
1005    Enna       11000    current
$ ./copyfilescontent
Enter name of directory: accounts
$ cd accounts
$ cat merge.dat
This is a test file
1001    Charles    15000    saving
1002    Kiran      10000    current
1003    Anushka    12000    current
1004    John       8000     saving
1005    Enna       11000    current
```

(f) The following script does not display anything on the screen though the filenames beginning with character b and with extension .1st, and their file contents will be stored in the file hh.bat.

```
copyfilescontent2
#!/bin/bash
for f in b*.lst
do
  echo $f
  cat $f
done > hh.bat
```

Output

```
$ ls b*.lst
b.lst    bank.lst
$ cat b.lst
This is a test file
$ cat bank.lst
1001    Charles    15000    saving
1002    Kiran      10000    current
1003    Anushka    12000    current
```

```
1004    John     8000     saving
1005    Enna     11000    current
$ ./copyfilescontent2
$ cat hh.bat
b.lst
This is a test file
bank.lst
1001    Charles  15000    saving
1002    Kiran    10000    current
1003    Anushka  12000    current
1004    John     8000     saving
1005    Enna     11000    current
```

(g) The following script prints the contents of the file with one word on each line. The filename will be passed as a command line argument.

fileoneword

```
#!/bin/bash
for k
in  `cat $1`
dos
  echo $k
done
```

Output

```
$ cat xyz.txt
Ths is a test file
$ ./fileoneword xyz.txt
Ths is a test file
```

10.7 while LOOP

The while loop is used for repeating a set of statements for the time the specified logical expression is true.

Syntax   while [logical expression]

```
        do
          ...
          ...
          ...
        done
```

Examples

(a) The following script displays the sequence of numbers from 1 to 10.

```
#!/bin/bash
n=1
```

```
while [ $n -le 10 ]
do
  echo $n
  (( n++ ))
done
```

Removing extra spaces

Extra spaces can easily be removed using the echo command. If the echo's argument is quoted, it prints its argument as such, that is, with tabs or multiple spaces in between. However, if the argument is used without quotes in the echo command, then the extra spaces are automatically removed from the arguments.

(b) The following script removes the extra spaces in the lines of the file and displays them on the screen. The filename is passed as a command line argument.

removeextra
```
#!/bin/bash
cat $1 | while read k
do
  echo $k
done
```

Output
```
$ cat school.txt
101    Anil    75
102    Chirag  82
103    Kanika  70
104    Naman   88
105    Suman   68
106    John    83
$ ./removeextra school.txt
101 Anil 75
102 Chirag 82
103 Kanika 70
104 Naman 88
105 Suman 68
106 John 83
```

The lines of the file school.tst will be assigned to the variable *k* through the while loop one by one, and then echoed on the screen.

(c) The following script displays the contents of the file phone.1st on the screen after removing extra blank spaces.

removeextra2
```
#!/bin/bash
while read k
do
  echo $k
```

```
done < school.txt
$./removeextra2
```

Output

```
101    Anil     75
102    Chirag   82
103    kanika   70
104    Naman    88
105    Suman    68
106    John     83
```

(d) The following script will read line by line from one file and store it in another file after removing the extra spaces. The filenames are passed as command line arguments.

```
removeextrastore
#!/bin/bash
cat $1 | while read k
do
  echo $k
done > $2
```

Output

```
$ ./removeextrastore school.txt sch.txt
$ cat school.txt
101    Anil     75
102    Chirag   82
103    kanika   70
104    Naman    88
105    Suman    68
106    John     83
$ cat sch.txt
101    Anil     75
102    Chirag   82
103    Kanika   70
104    Naman    88
105    Suman    68
106    John     83
```

It can be observed that in the output, each line of the file school.txt will be assigned to the variable *k* through the while loop and its contents will be directed to the file sch.txt.

10.8 until LOOP

The until loop is used for repeating a set of statements for the time the specified logical expression is false. The moment the logical expression becomes true, the control will come out of the loop.

Syntax   until logical expression

       do

         ...

         ...

         ...

       done

Example   The following script stores the sequence of numbers from 1 to 100 in the file d.bat.

```
storeseqinfile
#!/bin/bash
n=1
until test $n -gt 10
do
   echo $n >> d.bat
   ((n=n+1))
done
```

Output

```
$ ./storeseqinfile
$ cat d.bat
1
2
3
4
5
6
7
8
9
10
```

Note: The redirection symbol >> is used for appending the contents in the file (without affecting the earlier data). The redirection symbol > creates the new file (the previous data, if any, will be erased).

10.9 if STATEMENT

The if statement is used for selecting a set of statements out of the two sets depending on the validity of the logical expression included.

Syntax   if (logical expression) then

        command1

        command2

        ...

       else

        command1

```
        command2
        ...
    fi
```

The if statement ends with the fi command. The shell executes the code of the then statement if the logical expression is true, otherwise the code of the else statement is executed.

Note: The else part of the statement is optional.

Examples

(a) The following script compares the value in a variable, *n*, and prints the message accordingly.

```
#!/bin/bash
n=10
if [ $n -eq 10 ]
then
    echo "The number is equal to 10"
else
    echo "The number is not equal to 10"
fi
```

Output

```
The number is equal to 10
```

(b) The following script compares marks and prints First Division if the marks are >=60, and otherwise prints Second Division.

```
#!/bin/bash
m=60
if [ $m -ge 60 ]
then
    echo "First Division"
else
    echo "Second Division"
fi
```

Output

```
First Division
```

10.10 BOURNE SHELL COMMANDS

Bourne shell commands are built-in compiled and executable programs or scripts located in their respective directories on the Unix system. Shell, as we know, is a command interpreter and when we type a command, the command interpreter searches for it in the local directory as well as in the directories listed in the PATH variable. If the command is found, it is executed and its output is displayed on the screen. In case the command is not found, the following error message is displayed: command not found.

Flow control is an essential requirement in scripting. Testing of expressions and their output plays a major role in the flow control of a script. We will now learn how testing of expressions is performed.

10.10.1 `test`: Testing Expressions for Validity

To gain more flexibility with if statements, we use the Bourne shell's `test` command. The `test` command returns true if the expression included is valid and otherwise returns false.

Table 10.1 Brief description of the options used with the `test` command

Option	Description
`-a file`	Returns true if the file has at least one character
`-e file`	Returns true if the file exists
`-f file`	Returns true if the file exists and is a regular file
`-r file`	Returns true if the file exists and is readable
`-w file`	Returns true if the file exists and is writeable
`-x file`	Returns true if the file exists and is executable
`-d file`	Returns true if the file exists and is a directory
`-s file`	Returns true if the file exists and has a size greater than zero

Table 10.2 Brief description of the operators used for numeric comparison in the `test` command

Operator	Description
`-eq`	Equal to
`-ne`	Not equal to
`-gt`	Greater than
`-ge`	Greater than or equal to
`-lt`	Less than
`-le`	Less than or equal to

Table 10.3 Brief description of the operators used for string comparison in the `test` command

Operator	Description
`-n str`	Returns true if the string str is not a null string
`-z str`	Returns true if the string str is a null string
`s1=s2`	Returns true if the string s1 is equal to s2
`s1!=s2`	Returns true if the string s1 is not equal to s2

The `test` command can be used to test various file attributes, that is, we can test if a file has the necessary read, write, or executable permissions. The options that are used with the `test` command are briefly explained in Table 10.1.

All the aforementioned options for test return false if the named file does not exist. While working with numerals, we need certain operators for numeric comparison. Table 10.2 shows the list of operators that can be used for comparing numerals in the `test` command.

Besides numbers, we might also need to compare strings. The list of operators used for string comparison with the `test` command is shown in Table 10.3.

Examples

(a) The following shell script checks whether the two strings sent as command line arguments are the same.

comparestrings

```
#!/bin/bash
if test $1 = $2
then
    echo "Both strings are same"
else
    echo "Strings are not same"
fi
```

Output

```
$ ./comparestrings hello hi
Strings are not same
$ ./comparestrings hello Hello
Strings are not same
$ ./comparestrings hello hello
Both strings are same
```

(b) In the following shell script, we enter a name and check whether it is a file, directory, or something else.

```
checktype
#!/bin/bash
echo -n "Enter the name: "
read f
if test -f $f
then
    echo "$f is a file"
    else
            if test -d $f
            then
            echo "$f is a directory"
            else
            echo "$f is something else"
            fi
    fi
```

Output

```
$ ./checktype
Enter the name: xyz.txt
xyz.txt is a file
$ ./checktype
Enter the name: accounts
accounts is a directory
$ ./checktype
Enter the name: projects.lst
projects.lst is something else
```

(c) The following script will copy the file (sent as a command line argument) into the home directory of the user (provided the argument sent is a file and the user has read permission for it).

```
copyintohome
#!/bin/bash
k=`whoami`
if test $# -lt 1 -o $# -gt 1
then
  echo "The number of arguments are not correct"
  exit
fi
if test ! -f $1
then
  echo "The argument sent is not a file"
exit
fi
```

```
if test ! -r $1
then
  echo "You don't have the permission to copy the file"
  exit
fi
cp $1 /usr/$k
```

Output

```
$ ./copyintohome
The number of arguments are not correct
$ ./copyintohome accounts
The argument sent is not a file
$ ./copyintohome xyz.txt
$ ls /usr/root
xyz.txt
```

Note: -o is the logical *or operator* used to connect two or more expressions/statements. Or operator returns true if either of the statements is true.

10.10.2 [ ]: Test Command

Since test is a frequently used command, there exists a shorthand method of writing it. A pair of rectangular brackets enclosing the expression can replace the test command, that is, test $x -eq $y can be written as [$x -eq $y].

Examples

(a) The following script displays the sequence of numbers from 1 to 10.
```
demowhile
#!/bin/bash
i=1
while [ $i -le 10 ]
do
  echo $i
  ((i = i+1))
done
```

Output

```
1
2
3
4
5
6
7
8
9
10
```

The counter is set to 1 and the while loop is executed for the time the counter is 1e (less than or equal to) 10

(b) The following script is used to enter a few numbers and print their sum.

```
printsum
#!/bin/bash
echo "Enter few numbers and press ^d to see the total"
s=0
while read k; do
  let s=s+k
done
echo "Sum is $s"
```

Output

```
Enter few numbers and press ^d to see the total
5
8
2
^d
Sum is 15
```

In the aforementioned script the while read k statement makes an infinite loop that continuously prompts for the values of variable *k*. The contents of this variable will then be added to the variable *s*. The control releases from the infinite loop when the user presses Ctrl-d and the sum stored in the variable *s* will be displayed on the screen.

(c) The following script prints the sum of a few numbers entered by the user. In order to quit, we can enter −1.

```
sumoffewnum
#!/bin/bash
# The script computes the sum of few entered numbers
echo "Enter the numbers to be added, enter -1 to quit"
s=0
read h
while test $h != -1
do
  s=`expr $s + $h`
  read h
done
echo "The sum is $s"
```

Output

```
Enter the numbers to be added, enter -1 to quit
9
2
6
```

```
0
4
-1
The sum is 21
```

(d) The following script computes the sum of *n* numbers entered by the user.

```
sumofn
#!/bin/bash
echo -n "How many numbers are there? "
read n
s=0
x=1
while test $x -le $n
do
  echo -n "Enter a  number: "
  read h
  s=`expr $s + $h`
  ((x=x+1))
done
echo "The sum is $s"
```

Output

```
$ ./sumofn
How many numbers are there? 4
Enter a number: 8
Enter a number: 0
Enter a number: 4
Enter a number: 1
The sum is 13
```

(e) The following script checks if the given filename has come into existence. The script will keep checking after every minute if the filename that is passed through the command line argument exists or not. The loop continues to execute until the file comes into existence.

```
checkfileexist
#!/bin/bash
while test ! -s $1
do
    sleep 60
    done
echo "$1 exists now"
```

Output

```
$./checkfileexist bank.lst
bank.lst exists now
```

10.10.3 tr: Applying Translation

The tr command is used for translating a set of strings with another, that is, we specify two sets of strings and each character in the first set of characters is replaced with a corresponding character in the second specified set. The first character in the first set is replaced by the first character in the second set; the second character in the first set is replaced by the second character in the second set, and so on. The strings are specified using quotes.

Syntax   tr [options] [set1 [set2]]

The characters specified in set1 are mapped to the corresponding characters in set2.

The various options used in the tr command are described in Table 10.4.

Table 10.4   Brief description of the options used in the tr command

Option	Description
-d	Deletes specified characters in set1 from the input supplied
-s	Squeezes repeated characters specified in set1 into a single character
-c	Applies translation on the complement of the characters mentioned in set1, that is, on the characters that are not specified in set1

Examples

(a) $ tr "aeiou" "AEIOU"

After giving this command, all the vowels in the sentences we type will be converted into upper case as shown:

```
it is very easy to use
It Is vEry EAsy tO UsE
```

We can type as many lines as we wish. After completing the entry of data, we must key an end of file (Ctrl-d, also designated as ^d). Unix translates one line at a time, changing the specified characters until it finds the end of the file.

When the translated strings are of different lengths, the result depends on which string is shorter. If string 2 is shorter, the unmatched characters will all be changed to the last character in string 2. On the other hand, if string 1 is shorter, the extra characters in string 2 are ignored.

```
$ tr "aeiou" "AE?"
It is very easy to use
It ?s vEry EAsy t?  ?sE
$ tr "aei" "AEIOU"
It is very easy to  use
It is vEry EAsy to usE
```

Deleting matching characters

To delete matching characters in the translation, we use the delete option (-d).

(b) $ tr -d "aeiouAEIOU"

```
It is very easy to use
t s vry sy t s
```

This command will remove the upper as well as the lower-case vowels.

(c) tr -d "a-z"

```
HALLOW hallow
```

```
HALLOW
```

This command removes lower-case letters.

We can also specify the range of characters to translate.

(d) To change all the lower-case characters to upper case, the following command is used.

```
$ tr '[a-z]' '[A-Z]' < school
```

–s option   This substitutes all the specified characters with another specified character and displays the results.

(e) The following example substitutes all A's with character B in the file school.txt.

```
$ tr –s AB < school.txt
```

Note: Substitution is a default option.

–d option   This deletes specified characters from the given input and displays the result.

(f) The following example deletes all occurrences of the character B from the file school. txt and displays the result.

```
$ tr –d B < school.txt
```

–c option   This tells tr not to match the specified characters.

(g) The following example deletes all characters except character B from the file school.txt and displays the result.

```
$ tr –cd B < school.txt
```

Squeeze option   This deletes consecutive occurrences of the same character in the output.

For example, if after the translation of the letter 'i' to the letter 's', the output contains a string of consecutive occurrences of 's', then only one character 's' is displayed and the remaining occurrences of 's' are deleted.

(h) `$ tr –s "i" "s"`

It will replace all i's by s and consecutive occurrences of s will be replaced by a single s.

```
this is my stick
ths s my stsck
```

(i) The following script accepts the word 'oak' as an answer, regardless of whether upper-case or lower-case letters are used anywhere in the word, to the question asked, 'What kind of tree bears acorns?'

```
acceptans
echo "What kind of tree bears acorns?"
read ans
ans=`echo $ans | tr a-z A-Z`
if [ $ans == "OAK" ]
then
 echo "Correct Answer"
else
echo "Sorry the answer is wrong"
fi
```

Output
```
$./acceptans
What kind of tree bears acorns?
banana
Sorry the answer is wrong
$./acceptans
What kind of tree bears acorns?
Oak
Correct Answer
```

We first ask the user to enter the answer, which is then stored in the variable *ans*. The answer is then translated into upper case by the tr command and then compared with the actual answer (which is already in upper case).

(j) The following script changes the case of the string entered through the keyboard (upper case is converted to lower case and vice versa). To exit from the script, press Ctrl-d.

changecase
```
#!/bin/bash
echo "Enter a string"
read k
echo $k | tr '[a-z][A-Z]' '[A-Z][a-z]'
```

Output
```
Enter a string
Hello
hELLO
```

(k) The following script changes the case of the file and stores it in another file. The file names are sent as command line arguments.

changecaseinfile
```
#!/bin/bash
cat $1 | tr '[a-z][A-Z]' '[A-Z][a-z]' > $2
```

Output
```
$ cat xyz.txt
This is a test file
$ cat pqr.txt
cat: cannot open pqr.txt
$ ./changecaseinfile xyz.txt pqr.txt
$ cat xyz.txt
This is a test file
$ cat pqr.txt
tHIS IS A TEST FILE
```

(l) The following script will copy the contents of the file a.bat and b.bat, one after the other, into the file c.bat. The filenames are sent through command line arguments.

```
copyfilecontent3
#!/bin/bash
if test $# -ne 3
then
  echo The number of arguments passed are less than 3
  exit
else
  cat $2 > $1
  cat $3 >> $1
  echo The file after merging the two files $2 and $3 are
  cat $1
fi
```

Output

```
$ cat a.txt
Today is Sunday. It may rain.
I am tired.
$ cat b.txt
This is a test file
$ ./copyfilecontent3 merge.txt a.txt b.txt
The file after merging the two files a.txt and b.txt are
Today is Sunday. It may rain.
I am tired.
This is a test file
```

10.10.4 wc: Counting Lines, Words, and Characters

The wc command is used to find the number of source code lines in any application program developed in the Unix environment. By default, it gives all the three counts—characters, words, and lines—of any given file.

Syntax   wc [options] filename

The options and arguments used in the wc command are briefly explained in Table 10.5.

Table 10.5 Brief description of the options used in the wc command

Option	Description
-l	It returns the total number of lines in a file.
-w	It returns the total number of words in a file.
-c	It returns the total number of characters in a file.
filename	It is the name of the file whose number of characters, words, or lines we wish to know.

Examples

(a) $ wc phone.lst

It will display the number of lines, words, and characters in this file. We can use the -l, -w, and -c option along with the wc command if we wish to view only the number of lines, words, or characters in the file respectively.

$ wc -l phone.lst

It will give the number of lines in the file. Similarly, the -w option will give the total number of words in a file and the -c option will give the total number of characters in a file.

(b) The following script merges the three files, chapter 1, chapter 2, and chapter 3, into the file book and counts the number of lines in it.

```
mergefiles
#!/bin/bash
cat school.txt > book
cat course.txt >> book
cat xyz.txt >> book
n=`cat book | wc -l`
echo "There are $n number of lines in the file book"
$./mergefiles
```

Output

```
There are 13 number of lines in the file book
```

> **Note:** wc -l counts the number of lines in the output of the cat book command (contents of book file). The output is then stored in the variable *n*.

(c) The following script counts the number of persons logged in.

```
countlogged
#!/bin/bash
n=`who | wc -l`
echo "There are $n users logged onto the system"
```

Output

```
There are 3 users logged onto the system
```

10.10.5 grep: Searching Patterns

grep is a utility program that searches the file(s) for lines with a matching pattern. Lines that match the pattern are printed on the standard output.

To find all the lines containing the string mce in the file a.bat, we use the following command:

```
$ grep mce a.bat
```

The aforementioned command will search all the lines in the file a.bat containing the string mce and display all those lines on standard output along with the line number where the pattern was located. If a pattern containing more than a single word is searched for, it can be enclosed in quotes.

Syntax   grep option pattern filenames

The options used with the grep command are briefly explained in Table 10.6.

Table 10.6 Brief description of the options used in the grep command

Option	Description
-c	Displays the count of the number of occurrences
-l	Displays the list of filenames only
-n	Displays line numbers along with lines
-v	Displays all the lines except those matching the expression
-I	Ignores case for matching
-h	Omits filenames when handling multiple files

The pattern refers to the *regular expression,* that is, the character(s) or string we wish to search for in the specified file(s). If the pattern consists of characters, then the expressions that can be formed using characters are shown in Table 10.7.

Table 10.7   Brief description of the expressions that can be formed using characters

Expression	Description
*	Matches zero or more occurrences of previous characters
[pqr]	Matches a single character, p, q, or r
[c1 - c2]	Matches the range between c1 and c2
[^pqr]	Matches a single character which may be p, q, or r at the beginning of the line

While writing patterns consisting of strings, different expressions can be formed. The expressions that can be formed using strings are shown in Table 10.8.

Table 10.8   Brief description of the expressions that can be formed using strings

Pattern	Description
Pat	Matches the given pattern
?	Matches zero or one single character
*	Repeats the pattern zero or more times
^pat	Matches the pattern pat at the beginning of the line
pat$	Matches the pattern pat at the end of the line
? (pat1|pat2|...)	Matches zero or one of any of the patterns
@(pat1|pat2|...)	Matches exactly one of the patterns
*(pat1|pat2|...)	Matches zero or more of the patterns
+(pat1|pat2|...)	Matches one or more of the patterns
!(pat1|pat2|...)	Matches anything except any of the patterns

Consider the file `bank.lst` with the following content.

```
101    Aditya     0       14/11/2012   current
102    Anil       10000   20/05/2011   saving
103    Naman      0       20/08/2009   Current
104    Rama       10000   15/08/2010   saving
105    Jyotsna    5000    16/06/2012   saving
106    Mukesh     14000   20/12/2009   current
107    Yashasvi   14500   30/11/2011   saving
108    Chirag     0       15/12/2012   Current
109    Arya       16000   14/12/2010   Current
110    Puneet     130     16/11/2009   saving
```

Examples

(a) $ grep "[mM]ic*[rR]ochip bank.lst

This example searches a line having the pattern mic/Mic with any number of occurrences of the character c, then r/R, and then chip in the file bank.1st. Since the file bank.1st shown in the command does not have the pattern Microchip, nothing will appear in the output.

While writing patterns, different characters or string expressions can be made. Table 10.9 shows the examples of the patterns that can be built using different character and string expressions.

Table 10.9 Different examples of the expressions that can be formed using characters and strings

Pattern	Matches
?(Mce)	'Mce' or nothing
?(Mce|MCE)	'Mce', 'MCE', or nothing
@(Mce|MCE)	'Mce' or 'MCE'
Mce	Matches only Mce and nothing else
[Hh]*	Matches any word beginning with upper- or lower-case H
[Hh]?	Matches any two characters beginning with upper- or lower-case H
[Hh]	Matches any word containing an upper- or lower-case H
H|h	Matches only one character, upper- or lower-case H
[aeiouAEIOU]	Matches only one character and it must be a vowel (a, e, i, o, or u)
[0-9]	Matches one digit in the range 0–9
[a-z A-Z]	Matches an alphabetic character

(b) $ grep current bank.1st

Output

```
101    Aditya  0       14/11/2012   current
106    Mukesh  14000   20/12/2009   current
```

Note: Quotation is not desired here because it is required only when the search string consists of more than one word.

(c) $ grep current bank.1st bnk.1st

The string current is searched in both the files, bank.1st and bnk.1st, and the filenames are also displayed on the left side of the result.

(d) $ grep 'Chirag' bank.1st

It will search for the name Chirag in the file bank.1st.

Output

```
108    Chirag  0       15/12/2012      Current
```

(e) $ grep -c current bank.1st

-c counts the number of times the pattern current has occurred in the file bank.1st.

(f) $ grep -n current bank.1st

-n is used to display the line number containing the pattern along with the line.

(g) `$ grep -v current bank.lst`

-v is inverse, that is, it selects all the lines not containing the pattern current.

Output

```
102    Anil       10000    20/05/2011    saving
103    Naman      0        20/08/2009    Current
104    Rama       10000    15/08/2010    saving
105    Jyotsna    5000     16/06/2012    saving
107    Yashasvi   14500    30/11/2011    saving
108    Chirag     0        15/12/2012    Current
109    Arya       16000    14/12/2010    Current
110    Puneet     130      16/11/2009    saving
```

(h) `$ grep -l current *.lst`

-l lists only the filenames containing the pattern.

(i) `$ grep -i current bank.lst`

-i ignores case while searching for the pattern, that is, it shows records having current or Current, that is, current in any case (lower case/upper case).

Output

```
101    Aditya     0        14/11/2012    current
103    Naman      0        20/08/2009    Current
106    Mukesh     14000    20/12/2009    current
108    Chirag     0        15/12/2012    Current
109    Arya       16000    14/12/2010    Current
```

(j) `$ grep -e current -e Current bank.lst`

This shows records having the pattern current or Current. -e stands for the or operator. The output will be the same as in the aforementioned example.

(k) `$ grep -2 -i Jyotsna bank.lst`

This shows two lines above and below the line containing the pattern Jyotsna.

(l) `$ grep "r" bank.lst`

This shows all records having the character r in them anywhere.

Output

```
101    Aditya     0        14/11/2012    current
103    Naman      0        20/08/2009    Current
106    Mukesh     14000    20/12/2009    current
108    Chirag     0        15/12/2012    Current
109    Arya       16000    14/12/2010    Current
```

(m) `$ grep "r*" bank.lst`

It means that r can appear any number of times including zero. It displays all the records that have or do not have this character.

(n) `$ grep "^1" bank.lst`

All lines starting with 1 are shown.

Output

```
101    Aditya    0       14/11/2012    current
102    Anil      10000   20/05/2011    saving
103    Naman     0       20/08/2009    Current
104    Rama      10000   15/08/2010    saving
105    Jyotsna   5000    16/06/2012    saving
106    Mukesh    14000   20/12/2009    current
107    Yashasvi  14500   30/11/2011    saving
108    Chirag    0       15/12/2012    Current
109    Arya      16000   14/12/2010    Current
110    Puneet    130     16/11/2009    saving
```

Note: ^ means the pattern is matched at the beginning of the line. $ signifies that the pattern is at the end of the line.

(o) `$ grep "^11" bank.lst`

It will print all the lines starting with 11.

Output

```
110    Puneet    130     16/11/2009    saving
```

(p) `$ grep [Cc]urrent bank.lst`

It displays records having the pattern current or Current.

Output

```
101    Aditya    0       14/11/2012    current
103    Naman     0       20/08/2009    Current
106    Mukesh    14000   20/12/2009    current
108    Chirag    0       15/12/2012    Current
109    Arya      16000   14/12/2010    Current
```

(q) `grep -h "current" *.lst`

It displays all the lines having the pattern current without the filenames on its left.

(r) `grep ".....nt" bank.lst`

It displays all records having the pattern current or Current. Five dots (.....) implies that any five characters having nt at the end are displayed.

Output

```
101    Aditya    0       14/11/2012    current
103    Naman     0       20/08/2009    Current
106    Mukesh    14000   20/12/2009    current
108    Chirag    0       15/12/2012    Current
109    Arya      16000   14/12/2010    Current
```

(s) `grep "cu...nt" bank.lst`

It displays all records having the pattern current in the file bank.lst.

Output

```
101    Aditya    0        14/11/2012    current
106    Mukesh    14000    20/12/2009    current
```

(t) `grep "t$" bank.lst`

It displays all records having character t at the end, that is, all records having the pattern current or Current at the end of the line are displayed.

Output

```
101    Aditya    0        14/11/2012    current
103    Naman     0        20/08/2009    Current
106    Mukesh    14000    20/12/2009    current
108    Chirag    0        15/12/2012    Current
109    Arya      16000    14/12/2010    Current
```

10.10.6 egrep: Searching Extended Regular Expressions

Extending grep (egrep) extends the pattern matching capabilities of grep. By pattern matching, we mean searching extended regular expressions. It offers all the options of grep but its most useful feature is the facility to specify more than one pattern for search.

Syntax   `egrep [options] [regular_expression] [files]`

The options of egrep are the same as that of grep. regular_expression refers to the pattern that we wish to search for in the given files.

More than one pattern (separated by pipelines) can be searched for. The expressions used by egrep are shown in Table 10.10.

Table 10.10   Brief description of the expressions used by the egrep command

Expression	Description
ch+	Matches one or more occurrences of the character ch
ch?	Matches zero or one occurrence of the character ch
exp1 | exp2	Matches the expressions exp1 or exp2
(x1 | x2) x3	Matches the expressions x1x3 or x2x3

Notes:
1. + matches one or more instances of the previous character.
2. ? matches zero or one occurrence of the previous character.

Examples

(a) `$ egrep "r" bank.lst`

(b) `$ egrep "r+" bank.lst`

It matches one or more occurrences of character r.

(c) `$ egrep "r?" bank.lst`

It matches zero or one occurrence of character r, that is, it shows all records.

(d) `$ egrep '^[A-D].*f$' bank.lst`

It displays all records beginning with any character from A to D and ending with character g.

Note: The pattern can also be saved in a file.

Consider the file chirag.lst with the following syntax.

`current|saving`

(e) `$ egrep -f chirag.lst bank.lst`

It displays all the records having the pattern `current` or `saving` in it.

(f) The following script lists all the ordinary files with names starting with a vowel.

filesbeginvowel

```bash
#!/bin/bash
for f in *
do
  if test -f $f
  then
    echo $f >> tmp.lst
  fi
done
grep "^[aeiou]" tmp.lst
$./filesbeginvowel
```

Output

```
acceptans
accountslist
accountswithr
usrnme
```

(g) The following script counts the number of blank lines in the file named `c.txt`.

countblank

```bash
#!/bin/bash
n=`grep ^$ c.txt | wc -l`
echo There are $n lines blank in the file, c.txt
```

Output

```
$ cat c.txt
Today is Sunday. It may rain.
I am tired.
This is a test file
$ ./countblank
There are 3 lines blank in the file, c.txt
```

Note: ^ is used for start (beginning) and $ is for end. When ^$ are the same, that is, if the beginning and end of the line are the same, it means the line is blank

(h) The following script counts the number of links in the file. The filename is sent as a command line argument.

countlinks

```bash
#!/bin/bash
n=`ls -i $1`
# Storing the inode number of the file sent as command line argument in the
variable n
ls -ilR > tmp.lst
```

```
k=`grep $n tmp.lst | wc -l`
echo "There are $k links of $1 file"
```

Output

```
$ ./countlinks xyz.txt
There are          1 links of xyz.txt file
$ ln xyz.txt x.txt
$./countlinks xyz.txt
There are          2 links of xyz.txt file
```

> **Note:** In the aforementioned script, `ls -ilR` command options perform the following functions:
> `i` is to display the inode number
> `l` is to display the long listing
> `R` is for recursive display, that is, subdirectories are also included

10.10.7 Command Substitution

We can execute a command by enclosing it within two grave accent marks, also called backquotes (`` ` ``). The shell replaces the command and the grave marks with the output from the command.

Examples

(a) `workingdir='pwd'`
  `echo 'The present working directory is $workingdir'`
  In this example, the `pwd` command is executed and its output is then assigned to the variable `workingdir`.
  We can also write this example as follows:
  `echo 'The present working directory is' `` `pwd` ``
  The normal output obtained by executing the `date` command is as follows:
  ```
  $date
  Thu Dec 10 13:10:05 MDT 2012
  ```

(b) The following script demonstrates the use of the `set` command. It displays the current weekday, month, day, time, and year.
  ```
  demoset
  #!/bin/bash
  set `date`
  echo $*
  echo
  echo 'Week day:' $1
  echo 'Month:' $3
  echo 'Day:' $2
  echo 'Time:' $5 $6
  echo 'Year:' $4
  ```

Output

```
Saturday 25 February 2012 02:45:40 PM IST
Week day: Saturday
Month: February
Day: 25
Time: 02:45:40 PM
Year:  2012
```

The first command of the aforementioned script uses the grave accent marks to set the command line argument variables to the output of the date command. Remember, the entire string between grave accents (`...`) is taken as the command to be executed and is replaced with the output from the command.

(c) The following script demonstrates the execution of the commands through the grave accent marks. The system date and current working directory path are displayed through the script.

```
demograve
#!/bin/bash
directory='pwd'
todaydate='date'
echo "Present working directory is $directory"
echo "Today date is $todaydate"
```

Output

```
Present working directory is /UnixCode
Today date is Saturday 25 February 2012 02:16:54 PM IST
```

10.10.8 cut: Slicing Input

The cut command is used for slicing (cutting) a file vertically. It identifies both the fields and the columns.

Syntax   cut [options] filename

The options that can be used with the cut command are shown in Table 10.11.

Table 10.11   Brief description of the options used in the cut command

Option	Description
-c	This is used for cutting columns.
-f	This is used for cutting fields. The fields are assumed to be separated by tab space.
filename	This represents the file from which we wish to cut the desired columns or fields.

Example

(a) $ cut -c 6-22,30-35 bnk.lst
This retrieves characters 6–22 and 30–35 columns (characters) from the file bnk.lst.

(b) $ cut -f2 bank.lst
We get field number 2 of the file bank. 1st provided the fields are separated by tab space.

Files usually do not contain fixed length records and the fields may be delimited by some other character other than tab such as ',' and '|'. Hence, we use -d (delimiter) to specify the field delimiter.

(c) `$ cut -f2,3 -d "," txt.lst`

It will show the second and third fields of the file `txt.lst`. Each word of the file `txt.lst` is delimited by a , (comma).

Text files can be handled as textual databases by Unix with each word in the file being taken as a field. To understand cutting and pasting better, let us create two files with the following names—`Names` and `Telephone`.

The `Names` file may have the following contents.

```
101     Anil
102     Ravi
103     Sunil
104     Chirag
105     Raju
```

The `Telephone` file may have the following content.

```
101     2429193
102     2627312
103     2456789
104     2646189
105     2547856
```

Note: Here each word is separated by a 'tab' character.

(d) Now if we wish to cut out only the second word (field) from the file `Names`, we give the following command.

`$ cut -f2     Names`

We get the following output on the screen.

```
Anil
Ravi
Sunil
Chirag
Raju
```

(e) `$ cut -f2     Telephone`

```
2429193
2627312
2456789
2646189
2547856
```

We can save the output by redirecting standard output to a file.

(f) `$ cut -f2 Name > nn`

(g) `$ cut -f2 Telephone > tt`

The names and telephone numbers will be saved in two files, `nn` and `tt` respectively.

10.10.9 paste: Pasting Content

The `paste` command is used to join textual data together. It is very useful to put together textual information located in various files.

Syntax   `paste [-d delimiter] [files]`

Here, `delimiter` specifies the character(s) to be used while pasting or joining content.

Examples

(a) `$ paste nn tt`

The output will be as follows.

```
Anil      2429193
Ravi      2627312
Sunil     2456789
Chirag    2646189
Raju      2547856
```

Note: By default, paste uses the tab character for pasting files but we can specify a delimiter of our choice with the -d option.

(b) `$ paste -d"|" school.lst merit.lst`

It will join the two files with the help of the | delimiter and not *tab*.

`$ cut -d"|" -f1,4- p.lst | paste -d"|" - q.lst`

It will cut the first, fourth, and all fields after the fourth field from `p.lst` and paste them before all the fields of `q.lst` (– sign is used before `q.lst`). If – (hyphen) is used after `q.lst`, it would have pasted the fields after fields of `q.lst`.

(c) The following script prints any one of these messages.
Good Morning if the time is between 00:00 to 11:59.
Good Evening if the time is between 12:00 to 17:59 (between 12 to 5:59 p.m.).
Good Night at all other times.

```
wishme
#!/bin/bash
h=`date +"%T" | cut -c1-2`
if test $h -lt 12
then
    echo "Good Morning"
else
    if test $h -lt 18
    then
        echo "Good Evening"
    else
        echo "Good Night"
    fi
fi
```

Output

Good Morning

10.10.10 sort: Sorting Input

The sort command is used for sorting and merging files. We can sort even on the fields of a file where fields can be separated by a white space, tab, or special symbol.

Syntax   `sort filename`

All lines in the filename are ordered by treating the entire line as the key field.

`sort +p1 - p2 filename`

This limits the sort to a key field beginning with p1 and ending with field p2, where p1 and p2 are field numbers. If p2 is omitted, the key field extends from p1 to the end of the line.

We can sort the numerals as well as text in upper and lower case. In addition, we can eliminate duplicate lines while sorting. Table 10.12 shows the options applicable to the sort command.

Table 10.12   Brief description of the options used in the sort command

Option	Description
-n	Sorts numerical values instead of ASCII, ignoring blanks and tabs
-r	Sorts in reverse order
-f	Sorts upper and lower case together, that is, ignores differences in case.
-u	Displays unique lines, that is, eliminates duplicate lines in the output
-b	Ignores leading spaces while sorting
filename	Represents the file to be sorted

Examples

(a) `sort +2 -4 bnk.lst`

It skips the first two fields and uses the third and fourth fields for sorting the file bnk.lst.

(b) `sort +3 -4 bnk.lst`

It skips the first three fields and uses the fourth field for sorting the file bnk.lst.

(c) `sort +2 bnk.lst`

It skips the first two fields and uses the third field and rest of the fields up till the end of the line for sorting the file bnk.lst.

(d) `sort bnk.lst -o bank.lst`

It sorts bnk.lst and stores the result in bank.lst.

(e) `sort +0-1 bnk.lst`

It sorts the first field.

(f) `sort +1 -4 bnk.lst`

It sorts fields from the second to the fourth.

(g) `sort +2b bnk.lst`

It sorts the third field, ignoring leading blank spaces.

(h) `sort +2bf bnk.lst`

f is used to ignore the upper and lower case distinction.

It sorts the third field, ignoring leading blank spaces and sorts upper and lower case data together.

(i) `sort -n +2 -3 a.bat`

The -n option is used for sorting the file on numerical values rather than ASCII values. It sorts the file a.bat on the third field, considering it to be a numerical field.

(j) `sort -r link.lst`

It sorts in reverse order.

(k) `sort -nu +2 -3 a.bat`

-u eliminates duplicate lines in the sorted output.

It sorts the file a.bat on the third field after eliminating duplicate lines.

(l) Suppose file1 contains records having the roll number, name, and marks of the students and file2 contains records with the roll number and two subject names chosen by the student. To create a file, file3 from file1 and file2 with records of the roll number, name, and two subjects of the student, the file must be sorted on roll number.

file1

```
101    Anil     75
102    Chirag   82
103    kanika   70
104    Naman    88
105    Suman    68
106    John     83
```

file2

```
101    Science  Maths
102    Arts     English
103    Science  Computer
104    Arts     Sanskrit
105    Arts     Politics
106    Science  Biology
```

The following script demonstrates the usage of sort, cut, and paste commands.

```
cutpastesort
#!/bin/bash
sort file1 -o file1
sort file2 -o file2
cut -f1 file1 > rollnum
cut -f2 file1 > name
cut -f2 file2 > sub1
cut -f3 file2 > sub2
paste rollnum name sub1 sub2 > file3
sort file3 -o file3
```

Output

```
$ cat file1
101    Anil     75
102    Chirag   82
```

```
103    kanika    70
104    Naman     88
105    Suman     68
106    John      83
$ cat file2
101    Science   Maths
102    Arts      English
103    Science   Computer
104    Arts      Sanskrit
105    Arts      Politics
106    Science   Biology
$ ./cutpastesort
$ cat file3
101    Anil      Science    Maths
102    Chirag    Arts       English
103    Kanika    Science    Computer
104    Naman     Arts       Sanskrit
105    Suman     Arts       Politics
106    John      Science    Biology
```

Two files, file1 and file2, are sorted first. Thereafter, field 1, that is, roll numbers from file1 are extracted and stored in the file rollnum. Field 2, that is, name from file1 is extracted and stored in the file name. Field 2, that is, subject 1 from file2 is extracted and stored in file sub1. Field 3, that is, subject 2 from file2 is extracted and stored in file sub2. At the end, the contents from the files, rollnum, name, sub1, and sub2 are pasted onto the file file3. Finally, file3 is sorted.

(m) The following script sorts a file on a given field and stores the sorted content in another file. The file school.txt is sorted on the basis of its third field, marks, and the sorted rows are stored in the file skk.txt.

sortandstore
```
#!/bin/bash
sort -n +2 -3 school.txt > skk.txt
```

Output

```
$ cat school.txt
101    Anil      75
102    Chirag    82
103    Kanika    70
104    Naman     88
105    Suman     68
106    John      83
$ ./sortandstore
$ cat skk.txt
```

```
105    Suman    68
103    kanika   70
101    Anil     75
102    Chirag   82
106    John     83
104    Naman    88
```

We can see that `skk.txt` contains the rows sorted on the marks field. In the aforementioned script, options used in the `sort` command are described as follows:

-n   is used for numerical comparison.

+2   skips two fields to reach the beginning of the sort field.

-3   means that we have to include everything up till the third field for sorting (−4 implies that we have to consider the third as well as the fourth fields for sorting).

(n) The following script will print the names of all the files in the given directory having the specified heading (the first line) in them. The directory name and the heading, that is, the text is passed as a command line argument.

```
fileswithhead
#!/bin/bash
cd $1
for f in *
do
    k=`head -1 $f`
    if $k == $2
    then
        echo $f
    fi
done
$./fileswithhead accounts Employees Report
```

First, we go into the directory, *accounts*, using the `cd` command. Then, we search each file in that directory. Extract the first line of every file using the head command, and match that first line extracted with the pattern (employees report) that we are looking for. The names of the files having the same first line as that of the pattern are then displayed.

Output

```
Report.txt
emp.txt
```

(o) The following script extracts the specified range of lines from a given file and stores them in another file.

```
copyrangeinfile
#!/bin/bash
# extracts $2-$3 lines from $1 and place then in $4
head -$3 $1 | tail +$2 > $4
```

Output

```
$ ./copyrangeinfile school.txt 2 4 range.txt
$ cat school.txt
101    Anil     75
102    Chirag   82
103    Kanika   70
104    Naman    88
105    Suman    68
106    John     83
$ cat range.txt
102    Chirag   82
103    Kanika   70
104    Naman    88
```

The aforementioned script extracts lines, from the second till the fourth, from the file, school.txt and stores them in the file range.txt.

Initially, the first four lines are extracted from the file school.txt. From these first four lines, the first two are skipped and lines from the third till the end, that is, the fourth line will be stored in the file range.txt.

Note: Tail +*n* skips *n*-1 lines and extracts from the *n*th line till the end of the file.

(p) The following script displays the last 10 files present in the current directory.

```
lastten
#!/bin/bash
ls > tmp
tail -10 tmp
```

Output

```
bank.lst
school.txt
temp.lst
tmp.lst
usrnme
wishme
wishme2
x.txt
xyz.txt
yy.txt
```

(q) The following script looks for the filenames in the given directory having the specified heading (the first line) in them. Then, the number of lines in the files is counted and a message is displayed on the following basis.

The file is *small-sized* if the number of lines in the file is less than 50.

The file is *medium-sized* if the number of lines in the file is less than 100.

The file is *large-sized* otherwise.

```
filesheadingsize
#!/bin/bash
cd $1
for f in *
do
  k=`head -1 $f'
  if test $k -eq $2
  then
    n=`cat $f | wc -l`
    if test $n -lt 50
    then
      echo "The file $f is small sized"
    else
      if test $n -lt 100
      then
        echo "The file $f is medium sized"
      else
        echo "The file $f is large sized"
      fi
    fi
  fi
fi
done
```

Output

```
$./filesheadingsize accounts "Employees Report"
The file a.txt is small sized
The file k.txt is small sized
The file d.txt is large sized
The file b.txt is medium sized
```

This output confirms that the first line in the files a.txt, k.txt, d.txt, and b.txt is Employees Report. The output also gives information about their sizes.

(r) The script reverses the given file, that is, the last line is printed first, followed by the second last line, and so on. The first line will be printed at the bottom.

```
reversefile
#!/bin/bash
# reversing the file
n=`cat $1 | wc -l'
x=1
while test $n -gt 0
do
  tail -$x $1 > k
  h=`head -1 k`
  echo "$h"
  ((n=n-1))
```

```
    ((x=x+1))
```

```
$ cat school.txt
101    Anil     75
102    Chirag   82
103    kanika   70
104    Naman    88
105    Suman    68
106    John     83
$ ./reversefile school.txt
106    John     83
105    Suman    68
104    Naman    88
103    Kanika   70
102    Chirag   82
101    Anil     75
```

First, we count the number of lines in the file. Then the last line of the file is extracted and stored in a temporary file *k*. After that, the first line of file *k* is displayed (i.e., the last line is displayed). Thereafter, the last two lines of the file are extracted and stored in the file *k* and again the first line of this file, that is, the second last line will be displayed, and so on.

10.10.11 uniq: Eliminating and Displaying Duplicate Lines

The uniq command deletes duplicate lines (only one line is kept and the rest are deleted) in the output. Only adjacent duplicate lines are deleted. To delete non-adjacent lines, the file must be sorted.

Syntax   uniq [options] filename

The options shown in this syntax are briefly described in Table 10.13.

Table 10.13   Brief description of the options used with the uniq command

Option	Description
-u	Displays only unique lines
-d	Displays only duplicate lines
-c	Displays all lines with duplicate count
-f	Skips leading fields before checking for duplicate text
-s	Skips leading characters before checking for duplicate text

Note: Until and unless the –f option is used, the whole line is used for comparison.

Examples

(a) $ uniq mce.txt

It prints all the non-duplicated lines of the file mce.txt. Only one line of the duplicated lines is displayed.

(b) $ uniq -u mce.txt

It suppresses the output of the duplicated lines and lists only the unique lines in the file mce.txt (the duplicated lines are not displayed even once).

(c) $ uniq -d mce.txt

It displays the duplicated lines only once.

(d) $ uniq -c mce.txt

All lines are preceded by a number showing the number of times the line has occurred in the file.

(e) While the default compares the whole line to determine if two lines are duplicate, we can also specify where the comparison is to begin. The skip duplicate fields option (-f) *skips the number of fields* specified starting at the beginning of the line.

$ uniq -d -f 2 mce.txt

It will skip the first two fields and start comparing from the third field onwards till the end of the line and displays that line once, if found similar.

(f) We can also specify the number of characters that are to be skipped before starting the comparison using the -s option.

$ uniq -d -s 5 mce.txt

10.10.12 /dev/null: Suppressing Echo

The /dev/null is used when we do not want to echo the output of any command on the screen. In order to suppress the output of certain commands, we divert the standard output (STDOUT) to the /dev/null directory instead of the screen. The three streams that we come across while scripting are as follows:

STDIN—Standard input stream It is used for entering data. Its file descriptor is 0.

STDOUT—Standard output stream It is used for displaying output on the screen. Its file descriptor is 1.

STDERR—Standard error stream It deals with errors. Its file descriptor is 2.

Syntax   command > /dev/null [2>&1]

In the aforementioned syntax, we can see that the output of the command, which was supposed to be sent to the standard output (STDOUT), is suppressed by sending it to the /dev/null directory. The 2>&1, if used, redirects the standard error stream, 2 (STDERR) to the same place where 1 that is, STDOUT is being sent, /dev/null. Hence, the errors will also not appear on the screen.

To understand the concept more clearly, observe the following situations:

command > file   The stdout is redirected to the file, overwriting it if the file exists.

command > /dev/null   The stdout is redirected to /dev/null, suppressing the output on the screen.

command < file   The command takes input from the file instead of the standard input device.

2 > file   The stderr is redirected to the file, overwriting it if file exists

2>&1   The stderr is redirected to the same location where stdout is being redirected.

Examples

(a) The following shell script is used to find whether the given file exists in the current directory or not.

```
checkincurdir
#!/bin/bash
echo -n "Enter the file name to search: "
read f
ls -R > tmp.lst
if grep $f tmp.lst >/dev/null
then
  echo "$f exists in the current directory"
else
  echo "$f does not exist in the current directory"
fi
```

Output

```
$ ./checkincurdir
Enter the file name to search: xyz.txt
xyz.txt exists in the current directory
$ ./checkincurdir
Enter the file name to search: letter.txt
letter.txt does not exist in the current directory
```

Usually, the output of grep is displayed on the screen, that is, the lines having the file name (stored in variable $f) in tmp.lst file are displayed on the screen. However, since we do not want to see those lines on the screen but just want to know if the statement results in true or not, we suppress the output by redirecting it to the /dev/null directory.

(b) The following script searches for a pattern in the files of the current directory and prints the line containing the pattern as well as the names of the files containing the pattern.

```
searchpatinfiles
#!/bin/bash
echo -n "Enter the pattern to search: "
read k
for f in *
do
  if grep $k $f
  then
    echo The file, $f contains the pattern, $k
  fi
done
```

Output

```
Enter the pattern to search: Chirag
Chirag|11, Amrapali Circle Jaipur
```

```
The file, address.lst contains the pattern, Chirag
102   Chirag   82
The file, bank.txt contains the pattern, Chirag
```

(c) The following script searches for the pattern in the files of the current directory and prints only the names of the files containing the pattern.

```
searchpatinfiles2
#!/bin/bash
echo -n "Enter the pattern to search: "
read k
for f in *
do
if grep $k $f >/dev/null
then
  echo The file, $f contains the pattern, $k
fi
done
```

Output

```
Enter the pattern to search: Chirag
The file, address.lst contains the pattern, Chirag
The file, bank.txt contains the pattern, Chirag
```

(d) The following script prompts for the username and indicates (via a display) if the user has a login account in the system or not (i.e., the username is searched for in the file named passwd (in the etc directory). The user has the login account on the system only if the passwd file contains the username.

```
checkiflogged
#!/bin/bash
echo -n "Enter the user name to search: "
read n
if grep "$n" /etc/passwd > /dev/null
then
  echo "User exists"
else
  echo "Sorry! User does not exist"
fi
```

Output

```
$ ./checkiflogged
Enter the user name to search: chirag
User exists
$ ./checkiflogged
Enter the user name to search: john
Sorry! User does not exist
```

(e) The following shell script is used to read a name and indicate (via a display if that person is authorized to use the system or not). If the person is authorized, it displays whether that person is currently logged in or not.

```
checkauthoriz
#!/bin/bash
echo -n "Enter the name of the person: "
read u
cut -f1,5 -d":" /etc/passwd > tmp
if grep $u tmp > /dev/null
then
  if who |grep $u > /dev/null
  then
      echo "$u is the authorized person and is currently logged in"
  else
      echo "$u is the authorized person but is not logged in"
  fi
else
  echo "$u is not the authorized person to use this system"
fi
```

Output

```
$ ./checkauthoriz
Enter the name of the person: john
john is not the authorized person to use this system

$ ./checkauthoriz
Enter the name of the person: chirag
chirag is the authorized person but is not logged in

$ ./checkauthoriz
Enter the name of the person: root
root is the authorized person and is currently logged in
```

The person who has a login account (i.e. his/her name is in the /etc/passwd file) is the authorized person to use the system. Hence, we first check whether the login name exists in the passwd file and after that we check whether the user is currently logged in or not, through the who command.

(f) The following script displays the usernames having a login account in the machine.

```
accountslist
cut -f1,5 -d: /etc/passwd
$./accountlist
```

The following are the contents of the passwd file.

```
root:x:0:0:root:/root:/bin/bash
bin:x:1:1:bin:/bin:/sbin/nologin
daemon:x:2:2:daemon:/sbin:/sbin/nologin
```

```
adm:x:3:4:adm:/var/adm:/sbin/nologin
kanika:x:500:500:kanika:/home/kanika:/bin/bash
vikash:x:501:501:vikash:/home/vikash:/bin/bash
jyotika:x:502:512:jyotika:/home/jyotika:/bin/bash
neeraj:x:503:503:neeraj:/home/neeraj:/bin/bash
archana:x:504:504:archana:/home/archana:/bin/bash
geeta:x:505:505:geeta:/home/geeta:/bin/bash
fateh:x:506:506:fateh singh:/home/fateh:/bin/bash
anil:x:507:507::/home/anil:/bin/bash
```

We need to display the field numbers 1 and 5 to display the existing login names in the passwd file. Since the fields are delimited by : (colon), we use the -d option with the cut command.

The following is the output of the aforementioned script.

```
root:root
bin:bin
daemon:daemon
adm:adm
kanika:kanika
vikash:vikash
jyotika:jyotika
neeraj:neeraj
archana:archana
geeta:geeta
fateh:fateh singh
anil:
```

(g) This script prints the names of the users beginning with character r and having a login account (whether logged in or not).

```
accountswithr
cut -f1 -d":" /etc/passwd > usrnme
grep "^r" usrnme
$./accountswithr
```

All the usernames in the /etc/passwd file are first stored in the file usrnme. From that file, the names (lines) beginning with character r are displayed.

Output

```
ravi
rahul
root
```

10.10.13 Logical Operators

The following are the three logical operators:

1. && (And operator)
2. || (Or operator)
3. ! (Not operator)

&&—And operator

When we use && to connect two statements, the second statement is executed only when the first succeeds.

Examples

```
$ grep "mce" a.lst  && echo "record exists"
```

Now, the message record exists will appear only when the string mce is found in the file a.lst.

||—Or operator

It is used to execute the command following it only when the previous command fails.

Examples

(a) `$ grep 'mce' a.lst || echo "record  not found"`

It will display the message record not found only when the word mce is not found.

(b) The following script checks if a pattern occurs in the specified file or not. The pattern and the files are sent as command line arguments.

```
checkpattern
#!/bin/bash
grep $1 $2 || exit
echo "Record is found"
```

Output

```
$ ./checkpattern test xyz.txt
This is a test file
Record is found
$ ./checkpattern hello xyz.txt
$
```

If the grep command succeeds (i.e., the pattern is found) then the next half (after the || operator), that is, the exit command, will not execute and the message Record is found will be displayed on the screen. On the other hand, if the grep command does not succeed, that is, the test string is not found in the file names.lst, then the command exit will be executed, which takes the control to the shell prompt. In that case, the message Record is found is not displayed on the screen.

The aforementioned script can also be written as follows:

```
checkpattern2
#!/bin/bash
if grep $1 $2 > /dev/null
then echo "$1 is found in file $2"
else echo "$1 is not found in file $2"
fi
```

!—Not operator

The not operator performs negation, that is, it reverses the meaning of the logical expression. The following examples use the not operator to search for files and eliminates directories from the search.

Examples

(a) The following script displays the first five executable files of the given directory. The directory name will be specified through the command line argument.

```
fiveexec
#!/bin/bash
cd $1
x=1
for filename
in *
do
    if test ! -d $filename -a -x $filename -a $x -le 5
    then
        echo $filename
        ((x=x+1))
    fi
done
```

Output

```
$ ./fiveexec accounts
bank.lst
bk.lst
pqr.txt
range.txt
ravi.txt
text.lst
```

Note: -a is the logical and operator that is used to connect two or more commands/expressions. This operator returns true if all the expressions connected with this operator are true.

Using the `cd` command, we first go into the specified directory. Then, through the `test` command, we check each file of the specified directory and test the following conditions:

1. It should not be a directory
2. It should be executable
3. The counter (x) should be less than five.

If all the conditions are true, the filename is displayed and the counter (x) is incremented by one.

(b) The following script displays all the filenames in the current directory having the first character as an alphabet from a to b and the second character as a numeral.

```
findfileab
#!/bin/bash
ls * >tmp.lst
grep "^[a-b][0-9]" tmp.lst
```

Output

```
a1.lst
b7.txt
```

Note: The symbol ^ means beginning with.

All the filenames are first stored in the temporary file `tmp.1st`. Thereafter, all the lines in the file `tmp.1st` are searched and the lines beginning with a or b followed by any numeral from 0 to 9 are displayed on the screen.

(c) The following script prints the names of the users who are currently logged in and whose names begin with character r.

```
loggednames
#!/bin/bash
who | cut -f1 -d":" > usrnme
grep "^r" usrnme
```

Output

```
root    console  Feb 26 07
root    pts/3    Feb 26 07
ravi    pts/4    Feb 26 07
rahul   pts/5    Feb 26 07
```

(d) The following script counts the number of directories in the current directory.

```
countdir
#!/bin/bash
n=0
for f in *
do
  if test -d $f
  then
      ((n++))
  fi
done
echo "The number of directories are $n"
```

Output

```
The number of directories are 1
```

10.10.14 exec: Execute Command

The exec command is used to open and close files in the script. There are several options to open a file. Table 10.14 gives a brief description of the options available to open a file with the exec command.

Table 10.14 Brief description of the options used to open a file with the exec command

Option	Description
exec 0< filename	File is opened for input
exec 1> filename	File is opened for output
exec 2> filename	File is opened for writing errors

1. A file stream descriptor is created to represent each file. For standard files, the file descriptors are 0 (standard input), 1 (standard output), and 2 (standard error).

2. To designate that a file is for input, we use an input redirection token (<).

3. To designate that a file is for output or for error, we use an output redirection token (>).

When we open a file as input, we redirect it to standard input (0). Once opened, we can use the read command in a loop to read the specified file one line at a time. Similarly, when we open a file as output, we can redirect the standard output to it.

Closing files

The end of the script automatically closes all open files but we can also close them explicitly.

The following is the command to close an input file:

```
exec  0<&-
```

The following is the command to close an output file:

```
exec 1>&-
```

To close an output file and then open it as input, we use the redirection substitution operators to first close the output (4>&-) and then open it as input (4<&). The number indicates which stream descriptor is being closed.

Examples

(a) The following script reverses the sentences of the file sent as an argument.

```
sentreversfile
#!/bin/bash
exec 0< $1
while read k
do
    n=${#k}
    while (( $n >0))
do
    h=$(expr "$k" : ".*\(.\)")
    echo -n "$h"
    k=$(expr "$k" : '\(.*\).')
    ((n=n-1))
done
    echo
done
exec 0<&-
```

Output

```
$ cat a.txt
Today is Sunday. It may rain.
I am tired.
$ ./sentreversfile a.txt
```

```
.niar ya tI .yadnuS si yadoT
.derit ma I
```

The file a.txt is opened for input. Thereafter, by using the while loop, each line of the file is assigned to the variable *k* one by one. The length of each line is calculated and the last character of that line is displayed. This last character is then removed from that line and again the last character of the modified line is displayed. This process is repeated for the whole line and for all the lines of the file. In the end, the respective file is closed.

(b) The following script reverses the sentences of the file and stores it in another file sent as a command line argument.

```
sentreverstore
#!/bin/bash
exec 0< $1
exec 1> $2
while read k
do
  n=${#k}
  while (( $n >0))
  do
    h=$(expr "$k" : '.*\(.\)')
    echo -n "$h"
    k=$(expr "$k" : '\(.*\).')
    ((n=n-1))
  done
  echo
done
```

Output

```
$ cat a.txt
Today is Sunday. It may rain.
I am tired.
$ ./sentreverstore a.txt b.txt
$ cat b.txt
.niar yam tI .yadnuS si yadoT
.derit ma I
```

(c) The following script is used for copying alternate lines from one file into another file and the filenames are sent as command line arguments.

```
copyalternate
#!/bin/bash
exec 0< $1
exec 3> $2
x=1
while read k
do
```

```
(( m = x % 2 ))
  if [ $m != 0 ]
  then
         echo $k 1>&3
  fi
  ((x=x+1))
done
exec 0<&-
exec 3>&-
```

Output

```
$ cat school.txt
101    Anil    75
102    Chirag  82
103    kanika  70
104    Naman   88
105    Suman   68
106    John    83
$ ./copyalternate school.txt sch.txt
$ cat sch.txt
101    Anil    75
103    kanika  70
105    Suman   68
```

The file school.txt is opened in the input mode (its file descriptor is set to 0) and the file sch.txt is opened in the output mode (its file descriptor is set to 3). A variable *x* is used and its initial value is set to 1. The value of the variable *x* is incremented by 1 after every line is read. Using the while loop, each line of the file is assigned to the variable *k* one by one. If the value of the variable *x* is odd, only those lines are written into the file sch.txt (the % operator returns the remainder—the lines that have 0 as the remainder are even lines and the lines that have a remainder that is non-zero are odd lines). At the end, the respective files are closed.

(d) The following script demonstrates the exec command. Three file names will be supplied to this script, bnk.1st, current.1st, and saving.1st. The file bnk.1st will be split into two files, current.1st and saving.1st, where the current.1st file will store the lines having the pattern 'current' whereas saving.1st will have the pattern 'saving'.

```
splitfile
#!/bin/bash
# Splitting the bank file into two files : one having the pattern current account
and other
# having the pattern saving account. The file names are sent as command line
arguments
exec 0<$1
exec 3>$2
```

```
exec 4>$3
while read k
do
  echo "$k" | egrep 'current' 1>&3
  echo "$k" | egrep 'saving' 1>&4
done
exec 0<&-
exec 3>&-
exec 4>&-
```

Output

```
$ cat bnk.lst
1001    Charles    15000    saving
1002    Kiran      10000    current
1003    Anushka    12000    current
1004    John       8000     saving
1005    Enna       11000    current
$ ./splitfile bnk.lst current.lst saving.lst
$ cat current.lst
1002    Kiran      10000    current
1003    Anushka    12000    current
1005    Enna       11000    current
$ cat saving.lst
1001    Charles    15000    saving
1004    John       8000     saving
```

The file bnk.lst is opened in the input mode (its file descriptor is set to 0), the file current.lst is opened in the output mode (its file descriptor is set to 3), and the file saving.lst is opened in the output mode (its file descriptor is set to 4). Using the while loop, each line of the file is assigned to the variable *k* one by one. If variable *k* has the pattern current, then it is stored in the file current.lst (file descriptor 3) and if the line has the pattern saving, it is stored in the file saving.lst (file descriptor 4). In the end, the respective files are closed.

(e) The following shell script displays the file type, number of links, the permissions, the owner name, and the group name of the specified file.

```
fileinfo
#!/bin/bash
ls -l >tmp
echo -n "Enter the file name whose details are required: "
read k
exec 0< tmp
while read f
do
  if echo "$f" | egrep $k >/dev/null
```

```
        then
          flt=`echo "$f" | cut -c1`
          perm=`echo "$f" | cut -c2-10`
          lnk=`echo "$f" | cut -c14`
          own=`echo "$f" | cut -c16-23`
          grp=`echo "$f" | cut -c25-32`
          echo "The file type is $flt"
          echo "The permissions of file are $perm"
          echo "The number of links are $lnk"
          echo "The owner of the file is $own"
          echo "The group is $grp"
        fi
     done
```

Output

```
$ ls -al bank.lst
-rw-r--r--      2 root  it     124 Feb 26 12:54 bank.lst
$ ./fileinfo
Enter the file name whose details are required: bank.lst
The file type is -
The permissions of file are rw-r--r--
The number of links are 2
The owner of the file is root
The group is it
```

The long listing of the current directory is first stored in a temporary file `tmp`. After storing the long listing in the `tmp` file, through the while loop, each line of the file is assigned to variable *f* one by one. Then, through the `cut` command we extract the desired parameters, permissions, links, etc., of the line having the specified filename.

10.10.15 `sleep`: Suspending Execution

The `sleep` command is used for inserting some delay, that is, to temporarily suspend the execution of a program for some seconds.

Syntax   `sleep t`

Here, `t` is the time in seconds.

Examples

(a) `$ sleep 100`

This statement waits for 100 seconds.

The `sleep` command requires one argument, the number of seconds to pause (sleep). The shell suspends script execution for the specified duration when the `sleep` command is executed. It is often executed in a background script.

(b) The following script waits in an infinite loop until the file `bk.lst` is made executable. In other words, the script will check whether the file `bk.lst` has the execute permission or not.

If it has, the script exits onto the prompt. However, if the file bk.1st does not have execute permission, the script waits for a minute and rechecks for execute permission. In this way, the script checks whether the file bk.1st has execute permission after every minute.

```
checkexec
#!/bin/bash
while [ ! -x bank.1st]
do
    sleep 60
done
```

In the aforementioned script, the while loop will execute when the bank.1st file is not made an executable file. There will be no output or message displayed on the screen.

10.10.16 exit: Terminating Programs

The exit command prematurely terminates a program. When the exit statement is encountered in a script, execution is halted and control is returned to the calling program.

Syntax exit

% operator It returns the remainder. The following are examples:

Examples

(a) 14 % 2 will return 0

(b) 13 % 2 will return 1

(c) The following script is used to enter a number and print if it is a prime number or not.

```
findprime
#!/bin/bash
echo -n "Enter a number: "
read n
i=2
while [[ i -lt n ]]
do
    ((m = n % i))
    if test $m -eq 0
    then
            echo "The number, $n is not prime number"
            exit
    fi
    ((i=i+1))
done
echo "The number, $n is a prime number"
```

Output

```
Enter a number: 9
The number, 9 is not prime number
```

```
Enter a number: 17
The number, 17 is a prime number
```

A number *n* is a prime number if it is not divisible by any number between 2 and *n*−1. In this shell script, we start dividing the variable *n* by number 2 and above. If the number is divided by any number between 2 and *n*−1 (the remainder returned is 0), we exit from the loop, and indicate that the number is not prime.

10.10.17 $?: Observing Exit Status

The $? symbol stores the exit status of the last command. It has a value 0 if the command succeeds and a non-zero value if the command fails. To find out if a command executes successfully or not, simply echo $? after the command is used. Table 10.15 shows the possible values of the exit status.

Table 10.15 Brief description of a few of the exit statuses

Exit value	Exit status
0	Success
Non Zero	Failure
2	Incorrect usage
126	Not executable
127	Command not found

Examples

(a) If the command executes successfully, the exit status is 0, as shown in the following example.
```
$ grep Chirag bank.lst
108 Chirag 0 15/12/2012 Current
$ echo $?
0
```

(b) If the command is not successful, a non-zero value is returned, as shown in the following example.
```
$ grep Bintu bank.lst
$ echo $?
1
```

(c) If the command being run does not exist, the exit status returned is 127, as shown here.
```
$ greep Chirag bank.lst
-bash: greep: command not found
$ echo $?
127
```

(d) The following script copies all the lines from one file having the specified pattern into another file. The filenames will be passed as command line arguments.
```
copypattern
#!/bin/bash
if test $# -ne 3
then
    echo "You have not entered 3 arguments"
exit 3
else
    if grep $1 $2 > $3
```

```
    then
        echo "$1 pattern found in file, $2. File by name $3 is created containing
        the pattern"
    else
        echo "$1 pattern not found in file, $2"
    fi
    fi
```

Output

```
$./copypattern saving bank.lst
You have not entered 3 arguments
$ echo $?
3
```

The aforementioned value, 3, has come from the exit argument.

```
$./copypattern saving bank.lst savingrec.out
$ cat savingrec.out
102     Anil      10000    20/05/2011      saving
104     Rama      10000    15/08/2010      saving
105     Jyoti     5000     16/06/2012      saving
107     Yashasvi  14500    30/11/2011      saving
110     Puneet    130      16/11/2009      saving
```

We can see that the file savingrec.out will have all the lines with the pattern saving in it.

(e) The following script emails the user when he/she logs in, indicating by how many minutes he/she is late.

```
mailtologged
#!/bin/bash
m=0
while true
do
  who | grep $1 > /dev/null
  if test $? -eq 0
  then
    echo "You have logged $m minutes late | mail $1"
    break
  else
    sleep 60
    ((m=m+1))
  fi
done
```

Output

```
$./mailtologged ravi
```

This script will go into an infinite loop waiting for the user, ravi, to log in. When ravi logs in, a mail will be sent to him indicating how many minutes late he is.

(f) (i) The following script searches for a given string in the specified file.

```
searchstrinfile
#!/bin/bash
echo -n "Enter the string to search: "
read s
if [ -z $s ]
then
  echo "You have not entered the string"
  exit 1
else
  echo -n "Enter the file to be used: "
  read f
  if [ -z $f ]
  then
    echo "You have not entered the file name"
    exit 2
  else
    grep $s $f || echo "Pattern not found"
  fi
fi
```

Output

```
$ ./searchstrinfile
Enter the string to search:
You have not entered the string
$ ./searchstrinfile
Enter the string to search: Vinay
Enter the file to be used:
You have not entered the file name
$ ./searchstrinfile
Enter the string to search: Vinay
Enter the file to be used: bank.1st
Pattern not found
$ ./searchstrinfile
Enter the string to search: John
Enter the file to be used: bank.1st
1004    John    8000    saving
```

-n returns true if string is not a null string.

-z returns true if string is a null string.

Note: -z is same as !-n.

The command after the || operator will be executed if the command before the || operator, that is, the grep command does not succeed (i.e., it returns false).

Note: Test also permits the checking of more than one conditions in the same line using -a (and) and -o (or) operators.

(f) (ii) The following script searches for a given string in the specified file (second method).

```
searchstrinfile2
#!/bin/bash
echo -n "Enter the string to search and the filename: "
read s f
if [ -n "$s" -a -n "$f" ]
then
  grep "$s" $f || echo "Pattern not found"
else
  echo "At least one input is a null string"
  exit 1
fi
```

Output

```
$ ./searchstrinfile2
Enter the string to search and the filename: vinay
At least one input is a null string
$ ./searchstrinfile2
Enter the string to search and the filename: bank.lst
At least one input is a null string
$ ./searchstrinfile2
Enter the string to search and the filename: vinay bank.lst
Pattern not found
$ ./searchsrinfile2
Enter the string to search and the filename: John bank.lst
1004    John      8000      saving
```

(g) The script continuously checks whether the user root (any user) is logged in to the machine or not after every minute. The script goes into an infinite loop and exits only when the user root logs in to the machine.

```
checkiflogged2
#!/bin/bash
until who | grep root
do
  sleep 60
done
```

Output

```
root    console   Mar    2 16:40  (:0)
```

(h) The script displays the contents of the specified file and if the file is not available, it waits for the file to be available and checks if the file is available or not (i.e., created or copied) after every five seconds. The moment the file is available, its contents are displayed on the screen.

```
checkifavail
#!/bin/bash
if [ -r $1 ]
then
  cat $1
else
  until [ -r $1 ]
  do
    echo "File, $1 is not available .. waiting"
    sleep 5
  done
  echo "File, $1 is available, its content is as given below:"
  cat $1
fi
```

Output

```
$ ./checkifavail xyz.txt
File, xyz.txt is not available .. waiting
File, xyz.txt is not available .. waiting
File, xyz.txt is not available .. waiting
File, xyz.txt is available, its content is as given below:
This is a test file
```

The shell script waits in an infinite loop until the file xyz.1st does not become available. The script first checks whether the file exists or not. If it exists, its contents will be displayed on the screen, otherwise the control remains in an infinite loop and checks every five seconds to see if the file has come into existence or not.

(i) The following shell script waits in an infinite loop as long as the file bank.1st is made readable. If the file is created and is readable, the loop is terminated and the shell script change case is executed.

```
checkifreadable
#!/bin/bash
while [ ! -r bank.1st ]
do
  sleep 60
done
./changecase
```

Output

```
$ ./checkifreadable
Enter a string
hello
HELLO
```

The aforementioned script waits in an infinite loop until the file bank.1st is made readable. On making the file, bank.1st, readable, the loop breaks and the script, changecase will be executed. The message `Enter a string` in the output appears from the execution of the `changecase` script.

(j) The following script waits for the specified user to log in. If the user is not currently logged in, it checks after every minute to find out if the user is logged in or not.

```
checkiflogged3
#!/bin/bash
echo -n "Enter the name of the person: "
read n
until who | grep $n
do
echo "Waiting for $n to log in"
sleep 60
done
echo "$n is logged in"
$./checkiflogged3
```

Output

```
Enter the name of the person: root
root        console     Mar  2 16:40    (:0)
root        pts/3       Mar  2 17:41    (:0.0)
root is logged in
```

(k) The following script waits for the specified user to log in. If the user is not currently logged in, it checks after every minute to ascertain if the user is logged in or not and also prints the time at which the user logged in.

```
loggedintime
#!/bin/bash
until who | grep $1
do
  echo "waiting for $1 to log in"
  sleep 60
done
echo "$1 is logged in at `date +%H:%M:%S` time"
$ ./loggedintime root
```

Output

```
waiting for root to log in
waiting for root to log in
root        console     Feb 26 07:41    (:0)
root is logged in at 07:41:00 time
```

10.10.18 tty: Terminal Command

The tty utility is used to show the name of the terminal we are using. Unix treats each terminal as a file, which means that the name of our terminal is actually the name of a file.

`tty [-s]`

Here, `-s` means silent mode. It will not print anything on the screen and returns only the exit status.

Example `$ tty`
`        /dev/tty2`

The output shows that the name of the terminal is `/dev/tty2` or, more simply, `tty2`. In Unix, the name of a terminal usually has the prefix `tty`.

10.10.19 write: Sending and Receiving Messages

With the `write` command, messages are sent one line at a time, that is, the text is collected until we press Enter. We can type as many lines as we need to complete our message; we terminate the message with either an end of file (Ctrl-d) or a `cancel` command (Ctrl-c). When we terminate the message, the recipient receives the last line and the end of transmission (<EOT>) to indicate that the transmission is complete.

Syntax `write    options    user_id    terminal`

Example The following command sends a message to ravi on `/dev/tty3`.

```
$ write ravi tty3
Happy Diwali
Coming home today ?
```

When we are done typing, enter Ctrl-d (it is the ASCII character of EOF (end of file). If we want to get the attention of the person at the other end, we can type Ctrl-g, which is the ASCII character, BEL (bell).

On the receiver's terminal, complete information is displayed, such as the name of sender, the system the message is coming from, the sender's terminal ID, and the date and time when the message was sent.

The following message will appear on Ravi's terminal.

```
Message from chirag on tty2 [Sun Nov 16 21:21:25]
Happy Diwali
Coming home today ?
Eof
```

The receiver can turn our message off by typing the `mesg n` command. If we send a message to the user who has turned off the messages, we get the following error.

```
Can no longer write to /dev/tty3
```

On sending a message to a user who is not logged on, we get the following error message.
```
Ravi is not logged on.
```

Notes:

1. To allow write messages, use the `mesg y` command.

2. To prevent write messages, use the `mesg n` command.

10.10.20 `mesg`: Controlling Delivery of Messages

It is in our control to allow or disallow user(s) from sending messages to our terminal. To determine whether incoming messages are allowed on our terminal or not, use the `tty` command:

```
$ tty
/dev/tty04
```

We have to then use the `ls -l` command to see the permissions:

```
$ ls -l /dev/tty04
crw--w----1 chirag     tty        136,    1 dec 4  13:47 /dev/tty04
```

The permission flags on this terminal show that the person is logged in and has read and write permissions and the group member has write permission. If the group has write permission, the terminal can receive messages from other users, we can use the `mesg` command to change the permissions setting that controls the receipts of messages. We can turn messaging off our terminal by giving the following command:

```
$ mesg n
$ ls -l /dev/tty04
cr---w----1 chirag     tty        136,    1 dec 4  13:47 /dev/tty04
```

The *n* option turns off the device node's permission bit that allows other users to write to our terminal. To turn on messaging, enter the following command:

```
$ mesg y
```

Instead of using `ls` to look at how the access bits are set, we can run `mesg` without an argument to determine whether the setting is *y* or *n*.

```
$ mesg
```

If we get the output, *y*, it means the `mesg` is set to *y* and otherwise it is set to *n*.

Example   The script waits for the user to log in. If the user is not logged in, it checks every minute to ascertain if the user is logged in or not. The moment he logs in, a message is sent to him.

```
msgtologged
#!/bin/bash
until who | grep $1 >/dev/null
do
    sleep 60
```

```
done
write $1 << MSG
Hello how are you
late today?
MSG
```

Output

```
$ ./msgtologged root
root is logged on more than one place.
You are connected to "console".
Other locations are:
pts/3
Hello how are you
late today?
```

10.10.21 wall: Broadcasting Message

Similar to the write command, the wall utility is also used for sending messages. There are two differences between the wall and write commands. Firstly, we can type as many lines of text as we want (by pressing Ctrl-d after the lines). Secondly, instead of sending the message to a person specified on the command line, *wall sends the message to everybody who is logged in.* The wall is an abbreviation of *write to all.*

Syntax wall [message]

Example The following example broadcasts a message to all the currently logged in users, directing them to shutdown their machines.

```
$ wall
Please shut down your machines
Going for lunch
Ctrl d
```

Output

```
Broadcast message from root (pts/1) (Wed Nov 15 20:30:05 2012): Please shut down
your machines
Going for lunch
```

10.10.22 stty: Setting and Configuring Terminals

The stty command is used to set and display the configuration of a terminal. We can configure terminal parameters, such as turning on or off screen echo and setting the erase characters. The stty command is commonly used for setting different functions to the appropriate key on our terminal. The different functions that can be assigned to the respective control characters are listed in Table 10.16.

Table 10.16 Brief description of the functions and control characters that stty can change

Function	Description	Control characters
eof	End of file character—Exits from a program	^d (Ctrl-d)
erase	Erases the previous character	^\? (DELETE)
kill	Erases the entire line	^u (Ctrl-u)
werase	Erases the previous word	^w (Ctrl-w)
intr	Interrupts the current job	^c (Ctrl-c)
quit	Terminates the current job, creates a core file	^\\ (Ctrl-\)
susp	Pauses the current job and puts it in the background	^z (Ctrl-z)
rprnt	Redisplays the current line	^r (Ctr-r)

We can use the stty command to change control characters. The syntax for changing control characters is as follows.

Syntax `stty function control_character`

Here, function is one of the functions—erase, kill, or terminate—that we want to reassign to the given control_character. The control characters are represented through a two-character combination; the first is a caret (^) that represents the Ctrl key and a character. We may need to assign a \ before the character to prevent the shell from interpreting it as a wild card and a \ before the ^ to prevent some Bourne shells from interpreting it as a pipe. Otherwise, we may also include the quotes around the control characters to avoid incorrect interpretation.

Note: No two tasks can be assigned the same control character.

Examples

(a) stty erase \^z.
Ctrl-z keys will be treated as delete.
(b) stty kill '^y'
The entire line will now be deleted using the Ctrl-y keys.
(c) stty eof \^e
The eof, which was Ctrl-d, is changed to Ctrl-e.
(d) stty erase ^h
For erasing characters, we use the Ctrl-h keys instead of the delete key.

As mentioned in this section, the stty command can also be used for setting terminal configuration. The most common options used with the stty command for the configuration of terminal settings is as follows:

Syntax `stty [-a][-g] [echo][sane][olcuc][iuclc][icanon][isig]`

The options and arguments shown in the aforementioned syntax are briefly described in Table 10.17.

Table 10.17 Brief description of the options used with the `stty` command

Option	Description
-a	Displays all the settings for the terminal
-g	Displays the current settings in the stty-readable form—the format that can be used as an argument to another stty command
stty echo	Restores screen echo
stty sane	Sets the terminal configuration to a setting that can be used with a majority of the terminals, that is, default setting
stty olcuc	Maps lower case to upper case on output
stty iuclc	Maps upper case to lower case on input
stty icanon	Turns on the canonical mode and requires Enter key to read
stty isig	Enables interrupt, quit, and suspend special characters (INTR, QUIT, SWTCH, and SUSP).

If any of the options listed is prefixed by a - (hyphen) their action will be reversed.

If we use the `stty` command without any options or arguments, it shows the current common setting of our terminal such as baud rate and delete key settings.

Examples

(a) The following script is used for reading the password.

```
readingpass
#!/bin/bash
printf "Enter password: "
stty -echo
read password
stty echo
printf "The    password    entered    is
$password\n"
```

Output

```
Enter password:
The password entered is gold
```

Note: The password that we type does not appear on the screen.

(b) The following script is used for reading one character at a time without pressing the Enter key. The shell exits on pressing #.

```
readchars
#!/bin/bash
old_tty_settings=$(stty -g)    # Saving old settings
stty -icanon min 0 time 0
# min n - indicates the number of characters accepted
# time t - indicates the time allowed between each character
key=""
while [ "$key" != "#" ]
do
    printf "Type a key: "
    key=""
    while [ "$key" = "" ]
    do
        read key
    done
    printf "\nThe key typed is $key\n"
done
stty icanon
stty "$old_tty_settings"        # Restoring old settings.
```

Output

```
$ ./readchars
Type a key: t
The key typed is t
Type a key: 2
The key typed is 2
Type a key: @
The key typed is @
Type a key: #
The key typed is #
```

(c) The following shell script is used to implement terminal locking. The shell script locks the terminal until the correct password ('hello') is entered. The user cannot terminate the script using Ctrl-c, Ctrl-\, Ctrl-z, or Ctrl-d.

```
lockterminal
#!/bin/bash
echo "Enter password"
stty -echo
read pswd
stty echo
if [ $pswd = "mce" ];then
echo "You are Welcome"
exit
else
echo "The terminal is locked"
stty -echo
stty -isig
while [ "$pswd" != "mce" ]
do
  echo "Enter the password again"
  read pswd
done
stty isig
stty echo
echo "The terminal is unlocked"
fi
```

Output

```
$ ./lockterminal
Enter password
The terminal is locked
Enter the password again
Enter the password again
The terminal is unlocked
```

(d) The following script keeps asking for the password till the user enters the correct password mce. In addition, while typing the password, it will not echo on the screen.

```
checkpasswd
#!/bin/bash
while true
do
  echo  "Enter password"
  stty -echo
  read h
  stty sane
  if [ $h = "mce" ]
  then
          echo "Welcome"
          break
  else
          echo "Wrong password try again"
  fi
done
```

Output

```
Enter password
Wrong password try again
Enter password
Wrong password try again
Enter password
Welcome
```

We will keep getting the message Wrong password try again until we enter the correct password mce.

Note: The password we type will not echo on the screen.

(e) The following shell scripts prompt the user to enter the login name. If the name is not in the LOGFILE, it displays Sorry! You cannot work, otherwise it asks for the password. The password file is not echoed. It checks the password with file PASSWORD and if it does not match, displays ACCESS DENIED. The LOGFILE and PASSWORD are not actual system files but user generated files.

```
logincheck
#!/bin/bash
echo -n "Enter login name: "
read n
if grep $n LOGFILE >/dev/null
then
  echo -n "Enter password: "
  stty -echo
  read p
```

```
            stty sane
            if grep $p PASSWORD >/dev/null
            then
                    echo "Welcome"
                else
                    echo "Access Denied"
                fi
        else
        echo ."Sorry! You cannot work"
        fi
```

Output

```
$./logincheck
Enter login name: naman
Sorry! You cannot work
$./logincheck
Enter login name: chirag
Enter password:
Access Denied
$./logincheck
Enter login name: chirag
Enter password:
Welcome
```

10.10.23 w;who: Activities of Logged in User

The w;who command is used to obtain information related to the activities of users who are logged in users. These include the users' logging time and terminals on which they are logged.

Syntax   w;who

Output

USER	TTY	FROM	LOGIN@	IDLE
root	pts/0	-	Feb 19 11:06	(:0)
ravi	pts/1	-	Feb 17 11:23	2days
ajay	pts/2	-	Feb 19 12:10	(0.15s)

10.10.24 last: Listing Last Logged

The last command indicates all those who have logged in and out, when, from where, and also the time during which they have been connected.

Syntax   last

Output

root	pts/3	:0.0	Sat Mar 3 23:45	still logged in
root	console	:0	Sat Mar 3 23:44	still logged in
ravi	pts/3	:0.0	Sat Mar 3 23:14 - 23:32 (00:17)

chirag	pts/4	:0.0	Sat Mar	3 23:01 - 23:14	(00:13)
rahul	pts/5	:0.0	Sat Mar	3 21:51 - 22:19	(00:28)
root	console	:0	Sat Mar	3 21:50 - down	(01:08)
reboot	system boot		Sat Mar	3 21:49	
reboot	system down		Sat Mar	3 21:48	

wtmp begins Mon Feb 20 23:30

Example   The following script displays the login names of all users who have logged off in the last 10 minutes.

```
loggedofflast
#!/bin/bash
dd=`date +%d`
hh=`date +%H`
mm=`date +%M`
last >tmp
num=`cat tmp | wc -l`
((num=num-1))
head -$num tmp > ttmp
exec 0< ttmp
while read f
do
    n=`echo "$f" | cut -c1-9`
    d=`echo "$f" | cut -c49-50`
    h=`echo "$f" | cut -c52-53`
    m=`echo "$f" | cut -c55-56`
    ((difm = mm - m))
    ((difh = hh-h))
    ((mint = difm + difh * 60))
echo $difm
echo $difh
echo $mint
    if test $d -eq $dd
    then
        if test $mint -le 10
        then
            echo $n
        fi
    fi
done
```

Output

```
./loggedofflast
chirag
ravi
```

First, we extract the current day, hour, and minute from the date command and store them in the variables *dd*, *hh*, and *mm* respectively. Then, the output of the last command is stored in a temporary file tmp. The last command contains all the details of the users, their terminals, the time spent by them, whether they are currently working or logged out, etc. Using the while loop, each line of the tmp file is assigned to variable *f* one by one. From the variable, *f*, we cut the username, the day, hour, and minute the user logged in and store them in the variables *n*, *d*, *h*, and *m* respectively. Thereafter, we find the difference in the minutes and hours, that is, the hour the user logged in is subtracted from the current hour and the minute the user logged in is subtracted from the current minute. The difference of time is computed in minutes (hour difference is multiplied by 60). Then, if the current day and the login day of the user is the same and the difference between the minutes is <=10, then the username is displayed.

10.10.25 case Statement

The case statement helps in choosing one out of several sets of statements depending on the value of the specified expression. At instances where several 'if else' statements are desired, it is better to use the case statement.

Syntax
```
case  variable in

    value1)
        command1
        command2
        ...
        ...;;
    value2)
        command1
        command2
        ...
        ...;;
        command1
        command2
        ...
        ...;;
    esac
```

Examples

(a) In the following script, when we enter any number between 0 and 9, it is displayed in words.
```
numinwords
#!/bin/bash
echo -n "Enter a digit between 0 to 9: "
read n
echo -n "You have entered $n. In words, it is "
case $n in
  0) echo "zero";;
```

```
      1) echo "one";;
      2) echo "two";;
      3) echo "three";;
      4) echo "four";;
      5) echo "five";;
      6) echo "six";;
      7) echo "seven";;
      8) echo "eight";;
      9) echo "nine";;
      *) echo "not displayed as the number is out of range"
    esac
```

Output

```
$ ./numinwords
Enter a digit between 0 to 9: 3
You have entered 3. In words, it is three
$ ./numinwords
Enter a digit between 0 to 9: 9
You have entered 9. In words, it is nine
$ ./numinwords
Enter a digit between 0 to 9: 12
You have entered 12. In words, it is not displayed as the number is out of range
```

(b) The following script demonstrates the creation of a menu using the case statement.

```
demomenu
#!/bin/bash
echo "MENU"
echo "1: List of files"
echo "2: Processes of user"
echo "3: Today's date"
echo "4: Users of system"
echo "5: Exit to prompt"
echo "Enter your choice"
read choice
case $choice in
  1)ls -l;;
  2)ps -f;;
  3)date;;
  4)who;;
  5)exit
esac
```

Output

```
$./demomenu
MENU
```

```
1: List of files
2: Processes of user
3: Today's date
4: Users of system
5: Exit to prompt
Enter your choice
1
total 8
-rw-r--r--    1 root    root    20 Feb 10  2006 b.lst
-rwxr-xr-x    1 root    root    124 Feb 10  2006 bank.lst
-rw-r--r--    1 root    root    20 Feb 25 18:07 c.txt
-rw-r--r--    1 root    root    112 Feb 25 18:07 course.txt
-rw-r--r--    1 root    root    20 Feb 25 18:07 xyz.txt
./demomenu
MENU
1: List of files
2: Processes of user
3: Today's date
4: Users of system
5: Exit to prompt
Enter your choice
2
  UID    PID    PPID    C    STIME TTY        TIME CMD
  root   1347   1346    0    10:28:18 syscon    0:00 ps -f
  root   1346   1321    0    10:28:17 syscon    0:00 /bin/bash ./demomenu
  root   1321   1318    0    10:23:00 syscon    0:00 sh
./demomenu
MENU
1: List of files
2: Processes of user
3: Today's date
4: Users of system
5: Exit to prompt
Enter your choice
3
Saturday 3 March 2012 10:29:08 AM IST
./demomenu
MENU
1: List of files
2: Processes of user
3: Today's date
4: Users of system
5: Exit to prompt
```

```
Enter your choice
4
root   console   Mar 3 10:18   (:0)
root   pts/3     Mar 3 10:22   (:0.0)
./demomenu
MENU
1: List of files
2: Processes of user
3: Today's date
4: Users of system
5: Exit to prompt
Enter your choice
5
#
```

(c) The following script will prompt the user to enter a few pairs of names and addresses and store them in the file address.1st.

```
nameaddstore
#!/bin/bash
k=y
while [ "$k" = "y" ]
do
  echo -n "Enter the name and the address: "
  read n a
  echo "$n|$a" >> address.1st
  echo -n "Want to enter more(y/n)? "
  read h
  case $h in
          y*|Y*) k=y;;
          n*|N*) k=n;;
          *) k=y;;
  esac
done
```

Output

```
$ ./nameaddstore
Enter the name and the address: John 20, Hill View Street Ajmer
Want to enter more(y/n)? y
Enter the name and the address: Chirag 11, Amrapali Circle Jaipur
Want to enter more(y/n)? n
$ cat address.1st
John|20, Hill View Street Ajmer
Chirag|11, Amrapali Circle Jaipur
```

(d) The following script will print any one of these messages.

Good Morning if the time is between 00:00 to 09:59 or 10:00 to 11:59.

Good Afternoon if the time is between 12:00 to 17:59.

Good Evening if the time is between 18:00 to 19:59.

Good Night at all other times

```
wishme2
#/bin/bash
h=`date +"%T" | cut -c1-2`
case $h in
  0?:?? | 1[01]:??) echo "Good Morning";;
  1[2-7]:??) echo "Good Afternoon";;
  1[89]:??) echo "Good Evening";;
  *) echo "Good Night"
esac
```

Output

```
Good Night
```

The aforementioned script will extract the first and second characters, that is, hour along with minutes from the *date +'%T'* output and store it in the variable, *h*. Then, if the value in variable *h* is between 00:00 to 11:59, the message Good Morning is displayed. If the value in variable *h* is between 12:00 to 17:59, the message Good Afternoon is displayed. If the value in variable *h* is between 18:00 to 19:59, the message Good Evening is displayed. In all other cases, the message Good Night is displayed.

10.10.26 Functions

Functions are small modules, which, once written, can be called as many times as desired, hence avoiding repetition of statements.

```
function_name ()

{
    statement
    statement
    .
    .statement
    return value
}
```

Examples

(a) The following script prints the sum of sequence numbers. The limit is entered through the command line arguments (using functions).

```
demofunc
#!/bin/bash
sum()
{
    s=0
    x=1
```

```
        while test $x -le $1
        do
                ((s=s+x))
                ((x=x+1))
        done
        return $s
}
sum $1
echo "The sum of $1 sequence number is $?"
```

Output

```
$ ./demofunc 5
The sum of 5 sequence number is 15
$ ./demofunc 10
The sum of 10 sequence number is 55
```

Note: The output, that is, the value returned by the function is displayed with the help of $?.

(b) The following script checks whether the command line argument sent is a numeral or non-numeral (using functions).

```
checkargtype
#!/bin/bash
check()
{
  ((x=$1+1)) > /dev/null 2>&1
  if [ $? != 0 ]
  then
        echo "The number is not numeric"
  else
        echo "The number is numeric"
  fi
}
check $1
```

Output

```
$ ./checkargtype 5
The number is numeric
$ ./checkargtype xyz.txt
The number is not numeric
```

Note: We can redirect output to /dev/null for suppressing echo on the screen. To redirect the output of a standard error (with file descriptor 2) to /dev/null, we use the following syntax:
`command >/dev/null 2>&1.`

(c) The following script compares the two strings passed as command line arguments and indicates if the first string is smaller or larger than the other string.

```
strcmpfunc
#!/bin/bash
strcmp()
{
 if [ $1 = $2 ]
 then
        echo "$1 is same as $2"
 else
        echo $1 > tmp.lst
        echo $2 >> tmp.lst
        sm=`sort tmp.lst | head -1`
        if [ $sm = $1 ]
        then
             echo "$1 is smaller then $2"
        else
             echo "$1 is larger then $2"
        fi
 fi
}
strcmp $1 $2
```

Output

```
$ ./strcmpfunc sanjay sandeep
sanjay is larger then sandeep
$ ./strcmpfunc kelly sandra
Kelly is smaller then sandra
```

10.10.27 select: Creating Menus

The select loop is a special loop designed to create menus. A menu is a list of options displayed on the monitor.

Syntax   select variable in menu_opt1 menu_opt2...menu_optn

```
        do
           case $variable in
                menu_opt1)  command1;;
                menu_opt2)  command2;;
                menu_optn)  commandn;;
           esac
        done
```

Here, menu_opt1, menu_opt2, ..., menu_optn represents menu options, and command1, command2, ..., commandn represents the commands we wish to execute when the corresponding menu option is selected.

(a) demomenu2

```
#!/bin/bash
select k in month year quit
do
  case $k in
        month)cal;;
        year) yr=`date +%Y`
              cal $yr;;
        quit) echo Bye Bye
              exit;;
        *)echo Please try again
  esac
done
```

Output

```
$./demomenu2
1) month
2) year
3) quit
#? 1

   March 2012
 S  M Tu  W Th  F  S
             1  2  3
 4  5  6  7  8  9 10
11 12 13 14 15 16 17
18 19 20 21 22 23 24
25 26 27 28 29 30 31
#? 2

                    2012
   Jan               Feb               Mar
 S  M Tu  W Th  F  S    S  M Tu  W Th  F  S    S  M Tu  W Th  F  S
 1  2  3  4  5  6  7          1  2  3  4                   1  2  3
 8  9 10 11 12 13 14    5  6  7  8  9 10 11    4  5  6  7  8  9 10
15 16 17 18 19 20 21   12 13 14 15 16 17 18   11 12 13 14 15 16 17
22 23 24 25 26 27 28   19 20 21 22 23 24 25   18 19 20 21 22 23 24
29 30 31               26 27 28 29            25 26 27 28 29 30 31

   Apr               May               Jun
 S  M Tu  W Th  F  S    S  M Tu  W Th  F  S    S  M Tu  W Th  F  S
 1  2  3  4  5  6  7       1  2  3  4  5                      1  2
 8  9 10 11 12 13 14    6  7  8  9 10 11 12    3  4  5  6  7  8  9
15 16 17 18 19 20 21   13 14 15 16 17 18 19   10 11 12 13 14 15 16
22 23 24 25 26 27 28   20 21 22 23 24 25 26   17 18 19 20 21 22 23
29 30                  27 28 29 30 31         24 25 26 27 28 29 30
```

```
    Jul                     Aug                     Sep
 S  M Tu  W Th  F  S      S  M Tu  W Th  F  S      S  M Tu  W Th  F  S
 1  2  3  4  5  6  7                  1  2  3  4                     1
 8  9 10 11 12 13 14      5  6  7  8  9 10 11      2  3  4  5  6  7  8
15 16 17 18 19 20 21     12 13 14 15 16 17 18      9 10 11 12 13 14 15
22 23 24 25 26 27 28     19 20 21 22 23 24 25     16 17 18 19 20 21 22
29 30 31                 26 27 28 29 30 31        23 24 25 26 27 28 29
                                                  30

    Oct                     Nov                     Dec
 S  M Tu  W Th  F  S      S  M Tu  W Th  F  S      S  M Tu  W Th  F  S
    1  2  3  4  5  6                  1  2  3                        1
 7  8  9 10 11 12 13      4  5  6  7  8  9 10      2  3  4  5  6  7  8
14 15 16 17 18 19 20     11 12 13 14 15 16 17      9 10 11 12 13 14 15
21 22 23 24 25 26 27     18 19 20 21 22 23 24     16 17 18 19 20 21 22
28 29 30 31              25 26 27 28 29 30        23 24 25 26 27 28 29
                                                  30 31

#? 3
Bye Bye
```

(b) The following script converts the contents of a given file in the current directory into upper case.

```
filetoupper
#!/bin/bash
ls > tmp.lst
echo -n "Enter the file name: "
read f
if grep $f tmp.lst >> /dev/null
then
  cat $f | tr '[a-z]' '[A-Z]' > $f
  echo "The file is converted to upper case"
else
  echo "Sorry! The file does not exist"
fi
```

All the filenames are first stored in a temporary file, `tmp.lst`. Then the filename entered by the user is searched in the file `tmp.lst` and if present, the contents of that file are translated by the `tr` command and again stored in the same file. If the filename is not present in the file `tmp.lst` then the following message is displayed: `Sorry the file is not present`.

Output

```
$ cat xyz.txt
This is a test file
$ ./filetoupper
Enter the file name: xyz.txt
```

```
The file is converted to upper case
$ cat xyz.txt
THIS IS A TEST FILE
```

(c) The following script prompts the user to enter the distance between two cities in kilo-metres and converts it into metres and centimetres.

```
kmintomtr
#!/bin/bash
echo -n "Enter the distance between two cities in km: "
read k
m=`expr $k \* 1000`
cm=`expr $m \* 100`
echo "Distance in meters is $m"
echo "The distance in centimeters is $cm"
```

Output

```
$./kmintomtr
Enter the distance between two cities in km: 15
Distance in meters is 15000
The distance in centimeters is 1500000
```

10.10.28 basename: Extracting Base Filename

The basename command extracts the base filename from an absolute path name.

Syntax   basename string [extension]

Here, string refers to the filename along with its path. If extension is not provided, only the filename (after stripping the path) is returned. If extension is supplied, the filename is returned after deleting its extension (and path).

Examples

(a) The following syntax displays a.txt on the screen.
```
$ basename /mce/project/a.txt
```
When basename is used with the second argument, it strips off the string from the first argument as shown:
```
$ basename ajmer.txt txt
```
ajmer is returned.

(b) The following script renames the files with a secondary name .doc to one having a .bat extension.

```
renameext
#!/bin/bash
for k in *.dat
do
  p=`basename $k dat`
  mv $k ${p}bat
done
```

Output

```
$ ls *.dat
b.dat     tmp.dat
$ ./renameext
$ ls *.dat
*.dat: No such file or directory
$ ls *.bat
b.bat     tmp.bat
```

(c) The following script copies the lines from one file into another after replacing a given pattern by another pattern.

```
copyafterreplace
# Replacing a pattern in one file and copying into another file
#!/bin/bash
sed s/were/are/g $1 > $2
$ cat temp.lst
We were tired
It was raining
We were hungry
$ ./copyafterreplace temp.lst tt.lst
$ cat tt.lst
We are tired
It was raining
We are hungry
```

We can see that all the words 'were' from the file temp.lst are replaced by 'are' and written into the file tt.lst.

(d) The following script demonstrates the procedure for replacing a pattern from a file and copying it into another file.

```
copyafterreplace2
#!/bin/bash
# Replacing a pattern in one file and copying into another file (II nd method)
echo Enter the pattern to replace
read k
echo Enter the new pattern
read h
sed s/$k/$h/g $1 > $2
```

Output

```
$ ./copyafterreplace2 temp.lst tmp.lst
Enter the pattern to replace
were
Enter the new pattern
are
$ cat temp.lst
```

```
We were tired
It was raining
We were hungry
$ cat tmp.lst
We are tired
It was raining
We are hungry
```

(e) The following script prompts for a string and prints its length (counts the number of characters in it).

```
stringlength
#!/bin/bash
echo -n "Enter a string: "
read k
n=${#k}
echo "The length of the string, $k is $n"
```

Note: `${#stg}` calculates the length of the string `stg`.

Output

```
$./stringlength
Enter a string: chirag
The length of the string, chirag is 6
```

10.10.29 expr—Advanced Features

The `expr` command is also used for extracting a part of a string. The different expressions that can be formed with the `expr` command are shown in Table 10.18.

Table 10.18 Brief description of the expressions formed with the `expr` command

Expression	Description
Expr "stg" : '\(.\)'	Extracts the first character from the string stg
expr "stg" : '\(..\)'	Extracts the first two characters from the string stg
expr "stg" : '\(...\)'	Extracts the first three characters from the string stg
expr "stg" : '.*\(.\)'	Extracts the last character from the string stg
expr "stg" : '.*\(..\)'	Extracts the last two characters from the string stg
expr "stg" : '.*\(....\)'	Extracts the last four characters from the string stg
expr "stg" : '\(.*\).'	Extracts all the characters except the last character from the string stg
expr "stg" : '\(.*\)...'	Extracts all the characters from the string stg leaving the last three characters
expr "stg" : '...\(..\)'	Extracts the fourth and fifth characters from the string stg
expr "stg" : '..\(....\)'	Extracts characters from the third to the sixth, from the string stg

Examples

(a) The following script reverses a string entered by the keyboard. Blank spaces between the words, if any, are removed.

```
stringreverse
#!/bin/bash
echo -n "Enter a string: "
read k
n=${#k}
while (( $n >0))
do
  h=$(expr "$k" : '.*\(.\)')
  echo -n $h
  k=$(expr "$k" : '\(.*\).')
  ((n=n-1))
done
echo
```

Output

```
$ ./stringreverse
Enter a string: education
noitacude
$ ./stringreverse
Enter a string: Hello World!
!dlroWolleH
```

It extracts the last character from the string, *k*, and stores it in the variable, *h*. The contents of the variable *h* are displayed on the screen. Thereafter, the last character is removed from the string, *k*, and the process is repeated.

(b) The following script reverses a sentence entered by the keyboard. The extra blank spaces between the words are kept as such.

```
sentencereverse
#!/bin/bash
echo -n "Enter a sentence: "
read k
n=${#k}
while (( $n >0))
do
  h=$(expr "$k" : '.*\(.\)')
  echo -n "$h"
  k=$(expr "$k" : '\(.*\).')
  ((n=n-1))
done
echo
```

Output

```
Enter a sentence: It may rain
niar yam tI
```

> **Note:** When a variable in the echo command is enclosed in double quotes, the extra blank spaces in the contents of that variable are retained, otherwise they are removed.

10.10.30 getopts: Handling Options in Command Line

The getopts command reads the command line and if there are options, takes each option one by one, validates it, and then handles it.

Options with no values

The simplest case is when we allow only options without any value.

Examples

(a) ls -l

Options with no values are defined by a minus sign and a letter. The option can be separated or combined with each other.

Syntax   getopts   xyz   variable

The user can use -x, -y, -z, -xy, -xz, or -xyz options. Whenever an option is used, it will be assigned to the specified variable.

Each use of the getopts command gets the next option from the command line and stores the option (without the minus sign) in its variable. If we want to get all the options, we need to use a loop.

> **Notes:**
> 1. The getopts *exit status* is true when there are more options; it is false when all options have been processed.
>
> 2. The getopts command stores a question mark (?) in its variable if the *option is not in the list of valid options*. We can use this value to detect invalid options and exit if the user enters a wrong option.

(b) The following script demonstrates handling of options in a command line. It checks if the option passed in the command line is an a or c and displays a message accordingly.

```
demoopt
#!/bin/bash
while getopts ac variable
#above command means, a and c are the allowed options
do
case $variable in
  a) echo "a option will be processed";;
  c) echo "c option will be processed";;
esac
done
```

The option (beginning with a hyphen, -) we enter will be assigned to a variable and the case statement will execute accordingly.

Output

```
$./demoopt  -a
a option will be processed
$./demoopt  -c
c option will be processed
$./demoopt  -ac
a option will be processed
c option will be processed
$./demoopt  -a -c
a option will be processed
c option will be processed
```

Options with values

In the getopts command, there is a pre-defined variable called OPTARG, which holds the value for the option.

Syntax   `getopts x:y: variable # x, y are the allowed options with values`

Note: If an option needs a value, it must be followed by a colon (:).

(c) The following script converts the distance entered in kilometres into metres, decimetres, and centimetres depending on the option passed to the script.

```
demoopt2
#!/bin/bash
getopts d:c: op
case $op
  in
        d) k=$OPTARG
           ans=`expr $k \* 10000`
                echo "The $k km is converted to $ans decimetre";;
        c) k=$OPTARG
           ans=`expr $k \* 100000`
                echo "The $k km is converted to $ans centimetre";;
        \?)k=$1;
           ans=`expr $k \* 1000`
                echo "The $1 km is converted to $ans metre";;
esac
```

Output

```
$ ./demoopt2 10
The 10 km is converted to 10000 metre
$ ./demoopt2 -d 10
The 10 km is converted to 100000 decimetre
$ ./demoopt2 -c 10
The 10 km is converted to 1000000 centimetre
```

There is another built-in variable, OPTIND, which provides the number of arguments after the options in the command line. It can be used to shift the options out of the positional parameters so that the first parameter ($1) holds the first actual argument.

(d) The following script demonstrates the use of the shift command. It displays the option used while running the script and displays the command line parameter after shifting it once.

demoopt3

```
#!/bin/bash
#demonstrating getopts command
while getopts a:b: k
do
  case $k in
        a) echo You have entered a option ;;
        b) echo You have entered b option ;;
  esac
done
shift `expr $OPTIND - 1`
echo The command line argument sent is $1
```

Output

```
$ ./demoopt3 -a 10 20
You have entered a option
The command line argument sent is 20
$ ./demoopt3 -b 10 20 30
You have entered b option
The command line argument sent is 20
$ ./demoopt3 -a 10 -b 20 30
You have entered a option
You have entered b option
The command line argument sent is 30
```

In the first execution of the script, the value of the OPTIND variable will be set to 2. Then, using the shift command, 20 will be stored in $1.

In the second execution of the aforementioned script, the value of the OPTIND variable will be set to 3. Then, with the shift command, 20 will be stored in $1 and 30 will be stored in $2.

In the third execution of the script, there are two options, a and b. The value of the OPTIND variable will be set to 2. After this, using the shift command, 30 will be stored in $1, which is then displayed.

(e) The following script displays the options sent to the script and the arguments sent with each option.

demoopt4

```
#!/bin/bash
#demonstrating getopts command
```

```
while getopts a:b: k
do
  case $k in
          a) echo You have entered a option, the argument with a is $OPTARG  ;;
          b) echo You have entered b option, the argument with b is $OPTARG  ;;
  esac
done
shift `expr $OPTIND - 1`
echo The command line argument sent is $1
```

Output

```
$ ./demoopt4 -a 10 20
You have entered a option, the argument with a is 10
The command line argument sent is 20
$ ./demoopt4 -b 10 20 30
You have entered b option, the argument with b is 10
The command line argument sent is 20
$ ./demoopt4 -a 10 -b 20 30
You have entered a option, the argument with a is 10
You have entered b option, the argument with b is 20
The command line argument sent is 30
```

In the first example, the value of the OPTIND variable will be set to 2. Then, using the shift command, 20 will be stored in $1. In the second example, the value of the OPTIND variable will be set to 3. And then, using the shift command, 20 will be stored in $1 and 30 will be stored in $2.

10.10.31 set: Setting Positional Parameters

The set command parses an input string and places each separate part of the string into a different positional parameter. We can set the IFS to any desired token and use set to parse the data accordingly.

Syntax   `set input_data/command`

Examples

(a) The following script demonstrates the usage of the set command to assign values to the positional parameters.

```
demoset2
#!/bin/bash
set $(date)
echo Date is $*
k="$2 $3 $4"
echo Today is $k
```

Output

```
Date is Saturday 3 March 2012 11:27:03 AM IST
Today is 3 March 2012
```

As we can see in the output, the date command is split and assigned to parameters $1, $2, $3, and so on by the set command and we display the desired parameter.

(b) The following script demonstrates the setting values of the positional parameters through the set command.

```
demoset3
#!/bin/bash
echo The first parameter is $1
echo The second parameter is $2
set hello
echo After set operation, there are $# parameters
echo The first parameter is $1
echo The second parameter is $2
set 1 2
echo After set operation, there are $# parameters
echo The first parameter is $1
echo The second parameter is $2
```

Output

```
$ ./demoset3 xyz.txt pqr.txt
The first parameter is xyz.txt
The second parameter is pqr.txt
After set operation,there are 1 parameters
The first parameter is hello
The seond parameter is
After set operation, there are 2 parameters
The first parameter is 1
The second parameter is 2
```

We can see in the aforementioned output that by using the set command, we can change the values of the command line arguments while executing the script.

10.10.32 shift: Shifting Command Line Arguments

The shift command moves the values in the parameters towards the beginning of the parameter list.

Syntax   shift [n]

Here, n is an integer that determines the number of command line arguments to be shifted to the left. If n is not used, then with every shift command execution, the command line arguments are shifted to the left, that is, $2 shifts to $1, $3 shifts to $2, and so on. If the integer n specified is 2, then the command line arguments will shift two places to the left, that is, $3 will shift into $1, and $4 will shift into $2, and so on.

Example   The following script demonstrates the parameter passing to the script.

```
demoshift
#/bin/bash
echo There are $# parameters
while [ $# -gt 0 ]
do
   echo $1
shift
done
```

Output

```
$ ./demoshift xyz.txt 15 bank.lst 9 school.txt
There are 5 parameters
xyz.txt
15
bank.lst
9
school.txt
```

10.10.33 at: Scheduling Execution

By using the at command, we can schedule the execution of command(s) or program at some particular time.

Syntax   at time [date]

Examples

(a) The following example schedules to list the content of the working directory. It changes the current directory to ajmer and lists its contents at 1:20 p.m.

```
$ at 1320
ls
cd ajmer
ls
Ctrl-d
$
```

(b) The following example schedules to execute the script chirag.sh at 2 p.m.

```
$ at 14
chirag
```

(c) The following example schedules to execute the commands written in file.sh at 3 a.m.

```
$ at 3am <file
$
```

Time can be expressed in the 24-hour system (e.g., 2130) or in the 12-hour system (e.g., 9:30 p.m.).

(d) The following script demonstrates the list of users logged in between 10:00 a.m. and 10:59 a.m.

```
listlogged
#!/bin/bash
who -u | cut -c1-9,30-34 > tmp.lst
cat tmp.lst | while read f
do
    set $f
    echo $2 > tmp2.lst
    hr='cat tmp2.lst | cut -f1 -d":"'
    mn='cat tmp2.lst | cut -f2 -d":"'
    if test  $hr -ge 10 -a $mn -ge 00 -a $hr -le 10 -a $hr -le 59
    then
            echo $f
    fi
done
```

10.11 TRAPPING SIGNALS

In the following shell scripts, we will learn to perform certain actions in response to a signal. We will create a function and through the `trap` command, we will bind the function to the signal so that on the occurrence of the signal, the function is executed.

Examples

(a) The following shell script executes a function on the occurrence of the `hangup` signal.

```
demotrap
#!/bin/bash
hangupfunc()
{
    echo "Received Hangup (SIGHUP) signal"
}
trap hangupfunc SIGHUP
while true ; do
    sleep 1
done
exit 0
```

While executing the aforementioned shell script, we send the *HUP* signal to the process ID to see if the associated function, `hangupfunc`, executes.

(b) In the following shell script, a specific function is executed on exit of the script.

```
demotrap2
#!/bin/bash
function exitfunc()
{
    echo " Received EXIT signal"
```

```
}
trap exitfunc EXIT
while true ; do
    sleep 1
done
exit 0
```

Output

```
^C Received EXIT signal
```

While executing the aforementioned shell script, we break the script to see if the associated function, exitfunc, executes.

trap command

The trap command is used to execute a command when a signal is received by our script.

Syntax   `trap cmd signals`

Here, signals is a list of signals to interrupt and cmd is a command to execute when one of the signals is received. If cmd is missing then nothing will happen on receiving the signal.

Note: Two signals SIGKILL and SIGSTOP cannot be trapped.

Examples

(a) `trap "ls" 1 2 3 15`
(b) `trap "ls" SIGHUP SIGINT SIGQUIT SIGTERM`

These examples will display the listing of the directory on the occurrence of the given signals. We can also use signal names in place of signal numbers.

In this chapter, we learnt how to create and execute Bourne shell scripts. We also learnt to pass command line parameters in the shell scripts, use conditional statements and loops to execute the desired commands a specified number of times. We learnt to read user input, test different conditions, search patterns, translate content, and observe the exit status of the commands. We learnt to apply command substitution, send and receive messages to other users, create and use functions, set and display terminal configurations, and manage positional parameters.

■ SUMMARY ■

1. Shell program (also known as shell scripts) is a collection of a series of commands for a Unix shell, such as the Bourne shell, sh, or C shell csh.
2. Shell scripts include both Unix commands as well as built-in functions in the shell.
3. The echo command is used for displaying messages or values of the variables/expression.
4. All variables in the echo command have to be preceded by a $ sign.
5. Quotation marks are optional in the echo command. If quotations are not used in the echo command, then extra white spaces are automatically removed on display.
6. The expr command is used to perform arithmetical

operations on integers.

7. For multiplication, the asterisk (*) is escaped by \ (backslash), that is, * is treated as a multiplication symbol.

8. The let statement is used for assigning the values to variables as well as for evaluating the expression.

9. The `let` command is the same as the `expr` command but it does not requires the $ (dollar sign) with the variables.

10. A set of double parentheses, '((' and '))' may be used to represent the `let` command.

11. The calculator called bc (base conversion) is invoked by typing bc at the shell prompt. Typing quit ends the bc command.

12. The `expr` command is capable of carrying out only integer arithmetic. To carry out arithmetical operations on real numbers, the bc command is used.

13. The `factor` command factorizes the number and prints its prime factors.

14. The `units` command converts quantities expressed in various standard scales to their equivalents in other scales.

15. Comments should be preceded with a #.

16. If we pass the −n command line parameter to echo, then it will not end its output with a newline.

17. Shell scripts can read up to nine command line parameters. The first argument is read by the shell into the parameter $1, the second argument into $2, and so on.

18. $# stores the count of the number of command line arguments.

19. All command line arguments passed are stored in $*.

20. Variable names must begin with a letter or an underscore character (_).

21. To retrieve the value of a variable, place a dollar sign ($) in front of the variable name.

22. The `read` command is used to read the input typed by the user into shell variables.

23. Loops are used for executing a command or a set of commands for each value of the given set.

24. Asterisk (*) is a wild-card character and it refers to any number of characters.

25. The ? is considered a wild-card character that represents a single alphanumeral.

26. The `if` command is used for selecting a set of statements out of two sets depending on the validity of the logical expression included.

27. The `test` command returns true if the expression included is valid and false otherwise.

28. The `tr` command is used for translating a set of strings with the other.

29. The `wc` command is used to find the counts of characters, words, and lines in a given file.

30. grep is a utility program that searches file(s) for lines that contain a matching pattern.

31. egrep extends the pattern matching capabilities of grep.

32. The cut command is used for slicing (cutting) a file vertically. It identifies both the fields and columns.

33. The `paste` command is used to join textual data together.

34. A pair of rectangular brackets enclosing the expression can be used for the `test` command.

35. The `exit` command prematurely terminates a program.

36. The `until` loop is used for repeating a set of statements for the time the specified logical expression is false.

37. If echo's argument is used without quotes, the extra spaces are automatically removed from the arguments.

38. The `sleep` command is used for inserting some delay, that is, to temporarily suspend the execution of a program for some seconds.

39. The $? symbol stores the exit status of the `last` command.

40. The $? symbol gets the value 0 if the command succeeds and a non-zero value if the command fails.

41. /dev/null is used to suppress the output of certain commands and not display them on the screen.

42. We can execute a command by enclosing it within two grave accent marks also called backquotes (`).

43. The `tty` utility is used to show the name of the terminal we are using.

44. We can send messages to other users sitting on other terminals and can receive messages through the `write` command.

45. We can turn off messaging at our terminal using the `mesg n` command.

46. With the `write` command, messages are sent one line at a time, that is, the text is collected until we press Enter.

47. The `wall` command sends the message to all those who are logged in.

48. The `useradd` command is used to add new users to the system.

49. The `usermod` command is used for modifying some of the parameters of the newly added user.

50. The `userdel` command is used to remove users.

51. The `sort` command is used for sorting and merging files.

52. The `case` statement helps in choosing one set of statements out of several set of statements depending on the value of the specified expression.

53. The `select` loop is a special loop designed to create menus.

54. The `basename` command extracts the base filename from an absolute path name.

55. The `exec` command is used to open and close files in the script.

56. To close an input file, the `exec 0<&-` command is used.

57. To close an output file, the `exec 1>&-` command is used.

58. The `w;who` command is used to get information related to the activities of the users who are logged in, such as their logging time and terminals on which they are logged.

59. The `last` command tells us who have logged in and out, when, from where and also the time they have been connected.

60. The `getopts` command reads the command line and if there are options, takes each option one by one, validates it, and then handles it.

61. The `OPTIND` is a built-in variable that provides the number of arguments after the options in the command line.

62. The `set` command parses an input string and places each separate part of the string into a different positional parameter.

63. The `shift` command moves the values in the parameters towards the beginning of the parameter list.

64. Functions are small modules, which, once written can be called as many times as desired, hence avoiding repetition of statements.

65. The `stty` command is used to set and display a terminal's configuration.

66. The `uniq` command deletes duplicate lines (only one line is kept and the rest are deleted) in the output.

67. With the `at` command, we can schedule the execution of command(s) or programs at some particular time.

68. The `trap` command is used to execute a command when a signal is received by our script.

■ EXERCISES ■

Objective-type Questions

State True or False

10.1 The shell script is a collection of Unix commands and certain built-in functions.

10.2 The `expr` command can perform arithmetical operations on integers.

10.3 Using the `bc` command, we enter the calculator mode.

10.4 The `units` command is used for converting values in one standard scale to another scale.

10.5 We cannot perform more than one assignment in a single statement.

10.6 `$*` represents the count of the number of command line arguments.

10.7 With the `tr` command, we can not only translate characters but also delete matching characters.

10.8 We can specify more than one pattern for searching with the `egrep` utility.

10.9 We cannot use logical operators in shell scripts.

10.10 When pattern matching, '`^`' designates the beginning and '`$`' designates the ending.

10.11 `-a` is the logical OR operator used to connect two or more commands/expressions.

10.12 The `cut` command is used for slicing (cutting) a file vertically.

10.13 The `-f` option in the `cut` command is used for cutting files.

10.14 By default, the `paste` command uses the tab character for pasting files.

10.15 The `test` command can be represented by a pair of rectangular brackets.

10.16 The until loop is used for repeating a set of statements for the time the logical expression included is true.

10.17 $? gains a non zero value if the command succeeds and a 0 value if the command fails.

10.18 The /dev/null is used when we do not want to echo the output of any command on the screen.

10.19 If two commands are connected through the logical OR operator (||), the command on the right of the || operator will be executed only if the command on the left of the || operator does not succeed.

10.20 The –n option in the test command returns true for a null string.

10.21 We can execute a command by enclosing it within two grave accent marks also called back quotes (`).

10.22 Unix treats each terminal as a hardware peripheral.

10.23 We can send and receive messages with the users sitting on other terminals through the echo command.

10.24 With the write command, messages are written onto the printer.

10.25 The wall command is used for sending a message to all those who are logged in.

10.26 The userdel command is used to remove users.

10.27 The tail+n command skips *n*–1 lines and extracts from the *n*th line up till the end of the file.

10.28 For sorting numerical values, the -*n* option is used with the sort command.

10.29 The case statement helps in changing the case of the letters, that is, to convert lower-case letters to upper case and vice versa.

10.30 The select loop is a special loop designed to create menus.

10.31 In the exec command, to designate that a file is for input, we use an input redirection token(<).

10.32 The w;who command is used to get the information related to the activities of the deleted users.

10.33 The last command tells us who have logged in and out, when, and from where they have logged in.

10.34 The exit status of getopts returns false when all options are processed.

10.35 Functions are small modules, which, once written can be called as many times as desired, hence avoiding repetition of statements.

10.36 The stty sane command displays all the settings of the terminal.

10.37 The shift command moves the values in the parameters towards the end of the parameter list.

10.38 The trap command is used to trap a set of commands in a loop from where they cannot come out.

10.39 The command duplicate –c is used to count the duplicate lines in a file.

10.40 The two signals SIGKILL and SIGSTOP cannot be trapped.

Fill in the Blanks

10.1 The variables in shell script have to be preceded by _____.

10.2 The comments in shell script are preceded by the _____ symbol.

10.3 The let command can be replaced by _____.

10.4 To come out of calculator mode, we use the _____ command.

10.5 The command used to factorize a number is _____.

10.6 The multiplication sign in shell script must be preceded by a _____ otherwise it will be treated as a wild-card character.

10.7 The option used with the echo command to avoid outputting a new line character is _____.

10.8 Predefined variables are of two categories: _____ and _____.

10.9 The command used to count the number of lines, word, and characters in a file is _____.

10.10 The utility program used to search for the string with the specified pattern in a file(s) is _____.

10.11 The and operator evaluates to _____ if any of the expressions connected with this operator is false.

10.12 The option _____ in the cut command is used for cutting columns.

10.13 The _____ option is used to specify our own delimiter in the paste command.

10.14 The _____ command is used for temporarily suspending the execution of a program for some seconds.

10.15 The _____ symbol stores the exit status of the `last` command.

10.16 The `-z` option when used with the `test` command returns _____ if string is a null string.

10.17 The names of the users who have a login account is present in the _____ file.

10.18 The redirection symbol, _____, when diverting output to a file, overwrites its existing content if any.

10.19 To exit from an infinite loop, _____ can be pressed.

10.20 In a test statement, the and operator is represented by _____.

10.21 The _____ utility is used to show the name of the terminal we are using.

10.22 The _____ command can be used to change the permissions setting that controls the receipt of messages.

10.23 The _____ command is used for sending and receiving messages.

10.24 The _____ keys can be used to cancel the `write` command.

10.25 The _____ command is used to add new users to the system.

10.26 The _____ option in the `sort` command is used to remove duplicate lines.

10.27 The _____ option in the case statement represents the default condition.

10.28 To extract the base filename from an absolute path name, the _____ command is used.

10.29 To modify the parameters of an existing user, the _____ command is used.

10.30 To sort a file in the reverse order, the _____ option is used with the `sort` command.

10.31 Using the `exec 0< filename` command, the file is opened for _____.

10.32 To close an input file, the command used in exec is _____.

10.33 The _____ command is used for reading the command line and validating the options in it.

10.34 In the `getopts` command, the predefined variable that holds the values for the options is _____.

10.35 The built-in variable _____ provides the number of arguments after the options in the command line.

10.36 The _____ command is used to set and display a terminal's configuration.

10.37 The _____ command parses an input string and places each separate part of the string into a different positional parameter.

10.38 The _____ command deletes duplicate lines in the output.

10.39 The value returned by a function is displayed with the help of _____.

10.40 The option of the `stty` command that is used to map lower case to upper case in the output is _____.

Programming Exercises

10.1 What will the following commands do?

(a) `expr 10 \* 3`

(b)
```
$ bc
scale=2
17/3
```

(c)
```
for x in 2 4 9 12
do
echo "$x"
done
```

(d)
```
for filename in $*
do
    cat $filename
done
```

(e) `for f in a*`

```
do
    cat $f >> allfiles.txt
done
```

(f)
```
ls * >tmp.lst
grep "^[aeiou]" tmp.lst
```

(g)
```
x=1
for k in *
do
    if test  -d $k -a $x -le 3
    then
        echo $k
        ((x=x+1))
    fi
done
```

(h) `$ cut -f1,4 school.txt`

(i) `$ paste -d"," a.txt b.txt`

(j)
```
i=5
while [ $i -ge 1 ]
do
      echo $i
      ((i--))
done
```

(k)
```
if [ -r a.txt ]
then
      cat a.txt
fi
```

(l) `echo "'date +%H:%M:%S' time"`

(m)
```
set 'date'
echo $1, $6
```

(n)
```
$ write bintu tty5
Merry Christmas!!
```

(o) `# useradd -u 105 -g accounts -c "Bintu"`

(p) `sort +1 -3 school.txt`

10.2 Write a shell script to add four numerals sent through a command line argument.

10.3 Write a shell script to enter the name and three subject marks of a student and calculate the total and percentage (considering MM marks = 100) and print

(a) `First division` if percentage >= 60

(b) `Second division` if percentage >= 45 and < 60

(c) `Third division` in other cases

10.4 Write a shell script to read the lines from one file and store them into another file after converting all the vowels from the first file into upper case. The filenames will be sent as command line arguments.

10.5 Write a shell script to show all the files in the current directory whose name begins and ends with a vowel.

10.6 Write a shell script to count the number of non blank lines in a file.

10.7 Write a shell script to print the average of n

numerals.

10.8 Write a shell script to print the specified range of lines from a given file.

10.9 Write a shell script to count the number of files in the current directory having the specified pattern.

10.10 Write a shell script that takes the first 10 lines from one file and the last 10 lines from the second file and stores them in a third file. The filenames will be sent as command line arguments.

10.11 Write a shell script to count the number of files in the current directory beginning with the specified character.

10.12 Consider a file `school.dat` with the following fields: Roll, Name, and Marks. Write a shell script to sort the file in descending order of marks.

10.13 Show the names of the last five subdirectories in the current directory.

10.14 Show the names of all the files having less than five lines in them.

10.15 Write a shell script to count the number of persons currently logged in to the system. The script should stay in an infinite loop and keep counting the logged in users after every one minute. The script should terminate when the number of persons logged in is more than five.

10.16 Write a shell script that accepts the name of a user, and prints the entered name in reverse and also prints the length of the entered name.

10.17 Consider a file, `school.txt`, containing records of the eleventh and twelfth grade students. The eleventh grade and twelfth grade is represented as XI and XII respectively. Write a shell script to copy the records of the eleventh grade students into the file `eleventh.txt`.

10.18 Write a shell script that displays the login names of all users who have logged off in the last one hour.

10.19 Write a shell script that prints the sum of n even numbers. The limit is entered through the command line arguments (using functions).

Review Questions

10.1 Explain the following commands with syntax and examples:

(a) `echo`   (b) `wall`

(c) `set`   (d) `let`

(e) `paste`

10.2 Explain the concept of command line parameters with a running script.

10.3 Explain the different loops that can be used in Bourne shell scripts with examples.

10.4 Explain the use of the `tr` command in translating

the contents of a file.

10.5 Explain in detail the use of the grep command. How does it differ from the egrep command?

10.6 Explain what the `shift` command does to the positional parameters with a running script.

10.7 Explain how positional parameters are set with the `set` command.

10.8 Explain how the options and command line arguments that are passed to a script with a running script, can be read.

10.9 What is the role of the `expr` command with relation to strings?

Brain Teasers

10.1 The following code is not displaying today's date. Correct the code.

```
echo "Today's date is date "
```

10.2 The following code is not displaying the count of the number of command line arguments passed. Correct the code.

```
echo -n "The number of parameters are $*"
```

10.3 The following code for displaying words of the file a.txt one below the other is not working. Find the error in the code.

```
for k in cat a.txt
do
    echo $k
done
```

10.4 Find out the error in the following code for displaying the names of all the files that begin with the character a and for which we have read permission.

```
for f in a*
do
    if test -d $f -a test ! -r $f
    then
        echo $f
    fi
done
```

10.5 The following code for deleting all the upper-case letters in the input is not working. Find out the error.

```
$ tr -s "A-Z"
```

10.6 Correct the error in the following code for converting a string entered in the variable *t* into upper case.

```
echo "Enter a string"
read $t
t=`echo $t | tr A-Za-z`
```

10.7 Find out the error in the following code for finding out the total number of upper-case characters in the files a.txt and b.txt:

```
cat a.txt | tr -s "a-z" > kk
cat b.txt | tr -s "a-z" > kk
n='cat kk | wc -c'
echo "The total number of characters
that are in upper case in files a.txt and
b.txt are $n"
```

10.8 The following code for displaying the count of the lines ending with character *t* in the file a.txt is not working. Find out the error.

```
n='grep ^t a.txt | wc -l'
echo "There are $n lines that end with
character t in the file a.txt"
```

10.9 Find out the error in the following code for printing the count of the number of sub directories in the current directory.

```
for k in a*
do
    if test -r $k
    then
        echo $k >aa
    fi
done
n='cat aa | wc -c'
echo  "There  are  $n  number  of
subdirectories in the current directory
that begins with character a "
```

10.10 Correct the following program that prompts the user to enter two names and indicates if the two names entered are the same or not.

```
echo "Enter first name "
read $a
echo "Enter second name "
read $b
if grep $a = $b
then
    echo "Both names are same"
```

```
else
    echo "The two names are different"
done
```

10.11 The following code is not extracting 'hour' from the date correctly. Correct the code.

```
h=`date | cut -c10-11`
echo $h
```

10.12 The following code is not displaying the sum of the first five sequence numbers correctly. Find the error.

```
s=0
k=1
while [$k -ge 5]
do
    ((s=s+k))
    [k=k+1]
endwhile
echo "Sum of first five sequence numbers
is $s"
```

10.13 Find out the error in the following code that runs infinitely asking the user to enter a filename. The code will keep asking for the filename until a valid filename is entered.

```
echo -n "Enter a file name"
read t
while test  -f $f
do
    echo "$f is not a file. Try again"
    wait 60
done
```

10.14 What is wrong in the following code for displaying all the filenames that end with a numerical digit?

```
ls * >tmp.lst
grep "^[0-9]" tmp.lst
```

10.15 The following code for finding whether the entered number is even or odd is not working. Find the errors.

```
echo "Enter a number"
read n
((m = n / 2))
if test m -eq 0
then
    echo "The number is an even number"
else
    echo "The number is an odd number"
```

```
fi
```

10.16 Correct the error in the following code for counting the number of files and directories in the current directory.

```
x=0
y=0
for k in *
do
    if test -f $z
    then
        ((x=x+1))
    fi
    if test -d $z
    then
        [[y=y+1]]
    fi
done
echo "The number of files are $x and
directories are $y"
```

10.17 Find out the error in the following code for reading the content of one file and storing it in another file after converting into upper case. The two filenames are passed as command line arguments.

```
if test $# -ne 4
then
    echo "You have not entered 2 arguments"
    exit
else
    cat $1 | tr A-Za-z  > $2
fi
```

10.18 Correct the error in the following code that prompts the user for a filename and indicates if the file exists in the current directory or not.

```
echo "Enter the file name to search"
read n
ls * >tmp.lst
if grep "n" tmp.lst > /device/null
then
    echo "Sorry, the file does not exists
"
else
    echo "The file exists in the current
directory"
fi
```

10.19 Find out the error in the following code for

finding specified pattern in the files that begins with a vowel.

```
echo "Enter the pattern to search"
read k
ls * >tmp.lst
grep "^[aeiou]" tmp.lst> files.lst
```

```
grep "k" files.txt
```

10.20 Correct the following program that displays the list of users who are logged in and whose names begin with characters a to d.

```
who > usrnme
tr "$[a-d]" usrnme
```

■ ANSWERS TO OBJECTIVE-TYPE QUESTIONS ■

State True or False

10.1 True	10.22 False	10.2 #	10.22 mesg
10.2 True	10.23 False	10.3 (())	10.23 write
10.3 True	10.24 False	10.4 quit	10.24 Ctrl-c
10.4 True	10.25 True	10.5 factor	10.25 useradd
10.5 False	10.26 True	10.6 \	10.26 -u
10.6 False	10.27 True	10.7 -n	10.27 *)
10.7 True	10.28 True	10.8 shell variables,	10.28 basename
10.8 True	10.29 False	environment	10.29 usermod
10.9 False	10.30 True	variables	10.30 -r
10.10 True	10.31 True	10.9 wc	10.31 input
10.11 False	10.32 False	10.10 grep	10.32 exec 0<&-
10.12 True	10.33 True	10.11 false	10.33 getopts
10.13 False	10.34 True	10.12 -c	10.34 OPTARG
10.14 True	10.35 True	10.13 -d	10.35 OPTIND
10.15 True	10.36 False	10.14 sleep	10.36 stty
10.16 False	10.37 False	10.15 $?	10.37 set
10.17 False	10.38 False	10.16 true	10.38 uniq
10.18 True	10.39 False	10.17 /etc/passwd	10.39 $?
10.19 True	10.40 True	10.18 >	10.40 olcuc
10.20 False		10.19 Ctrl-d	
10.21 True	**Fill in the Blanks**	10.20 -a	
	10.1 $	10.21 tty	

Korn Shell Programming

After studying this chapter, the reader will be conversant with the following:

- Introduction to and features of Korn shell
- Command line editing, filename completion, command name aliasing, command history substitution, Korn shell meta characters
- Operators—arithmetic, logical, and relational operators
- Creating shell variables and setting shell prompts
- Defining variables, environment variables, and DISPLAY environment variable
- Basic input/output (I/O) commands
- Command line arguments
- If else and case statements
- Testing strings and files
- Loops—while, until, and for
- Arrays—indexed and associative arrays
- Functions, passing arguments to functions, returning values, local and global variables, recursion
- I/O redirection

11.1 INTRODUCTION

The Korn shell or ksh is a command and scripting language created by David Korn of Bell Labs. The first version of ksh was released in 1983. Its next version came out in 1988, which was adopted by system V Release 4 Unix. The latest version, the 1993 version, is a major rewrite of the 1988 version. The Korn shell is almost entirely backward compatible with the Bourne shell, which means that Bourne shell users can use it right away.

11.2 FEATURES

In addition to its Bourne shell compatibility, the Korn shell includes the best features of C shell, besides having several advantages of its own. The important features of Korn shell include the following:

Command-line editing   This allows using vi or emacs style editing commands on the command lines.

Control structures   This supports popular control structures such as loops, conditional statements, and select statements.

Filename completion   This supports the filename feature, that is, on entering a few beginning characters of a file, its complete name and possible suggestions are displayed automatically.

Command history   This supports command history that helps in recalling and reusing previously given commands.

Command aliases   This supports a command aliases feature, which helps in assigning smaller names to long and frequently used commands.

Debugging   This supports a debugging feature that helps in debugging shell codes.

Regular expressions   This supports applications of regular expressions that are popularly used in utilities such as grep and egrep for enhanced searching.

Monitoring jobs   This provides the facility to monitor background and foreground jobs.

We will now discuss some of the features of the Korn shell in detail.

11.2.1 Command Line Editing

The Korn shell has editing modes that allow us to edit command lines with editing commands similar to those of the two most popular Unix editors, vi and emacs. There are two ways of entering the editing mode. First, we can set our editing mode by using the environment variable *VISUAL*. The Korn shell checks to see if this variable defines either vi or emacs. We can also set VISUAL by putting the following line in our .profile or environment file:

```
VISUAL=$(whence emacs)
or
VISUAL=$(whence vi)
```

Using the command whence, the complete path name of the specified editor is searched and stored in the environment variable VISUAL.

The second way of selecting an editing mode is to set the option explicitly with the set -o command:

```
$ set -o emacs
or
$ set -o vi
```

These two commands help in setting a default editing mode similar to emacs and vi editors, respectively.

Though we have studied vi and emacs editors in detail in Chapter 8, let us take a small recap here.

Using vi

There are several vi commands for moving around the command lines and editing them. We know that the vi editor operates in two main modes, the command and insert modes. In the

Table 11.1 Keys for cursor movement in command mode in vi

Key	Description
l	Moves the cursor one character forward
h	Moves the cursor one character back
w	Moves the cursor one word forward
b	Moves the cursor one word back
fx	Finds the character x in the line
0	Moves the cursor to the start of the line
$	Moves the cursor to the end of the line

Table 11.2 Keys for performing editing tasks in the command mode in vi

Key	Description
x	It deletes the character at the position of the cursor. It can be preceded by a number.
X	It deletes the character behind the cursor. It can be preceded by a number.
~	It changes the case of the character at the position of the cursor. It can be preceded by a number.
u	It undoes the last change made to the line.
U	It undoes all changes made to the line.

command mode, single keys move the cursor, delete characters, and perform other actions. In the insert mode, single keys are typed into the command line. The list of keys used in cursor movement is shown in Table 11.1.

The keys, l, h, w, f, and b, can be preceded by a number. For instance, 5l moves the cursor forward by five characters. Similarly, 2w will move the cursor forward by two words; 2fa finds the second occurrence of character *a* in the line. The list of keys used in performing editing tasks is shown in Table 11.2.

To enter the insert mode, press a, A, i, or I. To exit to the command mode, press the Esc key.

On pressing the Enter key, the command that appears on the command line will be executed. After having learnt about the editing mode in vi, let us take a look at the keys required for editing in emacs mode.

Note: Students are advised to refer to Chapter 8 for an explanation on the vi editor.

Using emacs

The keys for cursor movement in the emacs editor are different from that used in the vi mode. The list of keys used in cursor movement in the emacs mode is shown in Table 11.3. To edit commands, the key pairs shown in Table 11.4 are used.

Do remember that command line editing applies to the current command being typed or retrieved from history.

Note: Students are advised to refer to Chapter 8 for an explanation on the emacs editor.

Table 11.3 Key pairs for cursor movement in emacs

Key pair	Description
Ctrl-f	Moves the cursor one character forward
Ctrl-b	Moves the cursor one character back
Esc-f	Moves the cursor one word forward
Esc-b	Moves the cursor one word back
Ctrl-a	Moves the cursor to the beginning of the line
Ctrl-e	Moves the cursor to the end of the line

Table 11.4 Key pairs for editing in emacs

Key pair	Description
Ctrl-d	Deletes the character at the cursor
Esc-d	Deletes the current word
Ctrl-c~	Capitalizes the current character
Esc-l	Converts the current character to lower case

11.2.2 Filename Completion

By filename completion, we mean that when we type in a partial name of a file, and press certain specific keys, the shell will automatically complete the name of the file for us. We will now discuss filename completion in the vi as well as the emacs modes.

In the vi mode, backslash (\) is the command that tells the Korn shell to perform filename completion.

If we type in a word, press the Esc key to enter the *control mode*, and then press the \ (back slash) key, the complete filename matching the typed word will appear. If no filename matches the typed characters, we get a beep sound, and no filename will appear.

If more than one file begins with the characters typed, the shell will complete the name up to the point where the names differ. To be more specific, we need to type more characters and reuse the Esc key if desired. If there is exactly one file that begins with the characters typed and that is a regular file, the shell will type the rest of the filename. If there is no file but a directory that begins with the characters typed, the shell will complete the filename, followed by a slash.

After the Esc key, we can either press = to get the numbered list of matching filenames to select the filename that we desire, or press * to expand the filename and replace it with the list of matching filenames.

In the emacs mode, we need to press the Esc key twice to complete the filename. For instance, in the vi mode, we can press the = key after the Esc key to expand the filename and display the numbered list of matching filenames to select from. In addition, we can press * after the Esc key to expand the filename and replace it with the list of matching filenames.

Let us now discuss the ways by which the Korn shell relieves us from typing lengthy commands.

11.2.3 Command Name Aliasing

Both ksh and csh provide command name aliasing that not only allows us to rename commands but also saves a lot of keystrokes while typing frequently used lengthy commands.

Syntax	`alias alias_name=command`

Here, `alias_name` is the alias that we want to use for the specified command.

Examples

(a) To alias the `cat inventory.txt` command to `ci`, use the following command in the Korn shell.

```
alias ci='cat inventory.txt'
```

On creating the alias, `ci`, whenever we type the command `ci`, the shell will substitute it with the string `cat inventory.txt` before executing it.

(b) `alias changedir= 'set dirname=projects; cd $dirname; unset dirname'`

This command creates an alias by the name `changedir` that sets the value of the shell variable `dirname` to the directory, `projects`, changes the directory to `projects`, and removes the shell variable `dirname` from the environment by unsetting it.

Note: Enclosing the alias string within single quotes (') will prevent the shell from interpreting special characters.

(c) To remove an alias, the `unalias` command is used. The following command will remove the `changedir` alias that we just created.

```
unalias changedir
```

The alias `changedir` will be removed.

11.2.4 Command History Substitution

The Korn shell keeps an ordered list of the commands that we give in the command line, allowing us to retrieve them when desired. We can reuse all or part of the previously entered commands depending on our requirement. Each command in the list is given a command number depending on the sequence it was issued. To view the command history list, we type the following:

```
history
```

Retrieving commands from command history in Korn shell

When using the Korn shell, the number of commands stored by the shell is controlled by the `HISTSIZE` environment variable.

Syntax   `HISTSIZE=number_of_lines_to_store_in_command_history`

Example   To set the length of the history list to 80 lines, use the following command.

```
HISTSIZE=80;export HISTSIZE
```

By default, the history size is set to 128 lines.

In the emacs editing mode, the key pairs, Ctrl-p and Ctrl-n, are used to display earlier commands and forward command in the command history respectively. After editing the command line, if desired, press the return key to issue the command to the shell.

In the vi editor, we use _ (underscore) in the *control mode* to get the last argument of the previous command, or *n_* to get the *n*th argument of the previous command. In case of the emacs editor, we can use Esc_ for the same purpose.

Whether it is searching for text in a file or searching a file or directory, or representing some unknown text, we need to make use of meta characters. This is discussed in the following section.

11.3 KORN SHELL META CHARACTERS

Meta characters are characters that render a special meaning to the shell. The list of Korn shell meta characters is given in Table 11.5.

Table 11.5   List of Korn shell meta characters

Character	Meaning
\	This is the escape character. It disables the special meaning of the character that it precedes.
*	This is the wild card match for zero or more characters.
?	This is the wild card match for one character.

(Contd)

Table 11.5 (*Contd*)

Character	Meaning
[abc]	This matches one character specified within the brackets, a, b, or c.
[!abc]	This matches one character not specified within the brackets, a, b, or c.
[a-z]	This matches one character in the range between a and z.
<	This redirects the standard input. The input comes from the specified file instead of the terminal.
>	This redirects the standard output. The output is sent to the specified file instead of the terminal.
>>	This appends the standard output to the end of a specified file.
|	The pipe character connects the standard output of one command to the standard input of another command.
&	When appended to a command, it makes the process run in the background.
~	It represents the path of a user's home directory.
.	It represents the current directory.
..	It represents the parent to the current directory.
/	It represents the root directory.
'	It represents a string with variable substitution.
"	It represents a string with variable substitution. It also preserves the embedded spaces and new lines if any.
`	Back quotes around a command string tell the shell to run the command and use the output in place of the string.
( )	It groups commands together for execution.
;	It separates commands on a command line.

We have been using these meta characters in different commands such as in ls, grep, and expressions. We will further be using them in the Korn shell scripts in this chapter.

11.4 OPERATORS

Korn shell supports several operators such as arithmetic and logical, relational, string, and file test operators. We will learn about these operators as we proceed further in this chapter.

11.4.1 Arithmetic and Logical Operators

Arithmetical operators are used for different computing tasks while logical help in creating logical conditions or expressions used in conditional statements and loops.

The list of arithmetic and logic operators is as shown in Table 11.6.

Table 11.6 Arithmetic and logical operators

Operator	Description	Operator	Description	Operator	Description	Operator	Description
+	Unary plus	+	Add	!=	Comparison for non-equality	&&	Logical 'AND'
-	Unary minus	-	Subtract	=~	Pattern matching	||	Logical 'OR'

(*Contd*)

Table 11.6 (*Contd*)

Operator	Description	Operator	Description	Operator	Description	Operator	Description
!~	Binary inversion (one's complement)	<<	Left shift	&	Bitwise 'and'	++	Increment
*	Multiply	>>	Right shift	^	Bitwise 'exclusive or'	--	Decrement
/	Divide	==	Comparison for equality	|	Bitwise 'inclusive or'	=	Assignment
%	Modulo						

We can see that these operators include arithmetic operators such as +, -, and * for writing arithmetical expressions, bitwise operators (<<, >>, &) to operate on bits of the specified integers, and logical operators (AND, OR) to combine logical expressions.

Table 11.7 Relational operators

Operator	Description
-eq	equal to
-ne	not equal to
-lt	less than
-gt	greater than
-le	less than or equal to
-ge	greater than or equal to

11.4.2 Relational Operators

The relational operators are mainly used for comparing objects. If two numerals are being compared, the operators listed in Table 11.7 can be used.

We will learn about other operators as we proceed in this chapter. After understanding operators, we need to understand the types of variables as they play a major role in shell scripts.

11.5 VARIABLES

Variables, as we know, are used for holding and passing information. Variables in Unix are of two categories, shell variables and environment variables.

11.5.1 Shell Variables

As the name suggests, shell variables belong to the shell and contain values that are visible and applicable only to the current instance of the shell. We can set values for the shell variables, print them, and use them in expressions but their scope is limited to the current instance of the shell. It is for this reason that shell variables are also termed as *local variables*. By convention, shell variables are written in lower case.

Creating shell variables

Variable names can be a single character, a collection of characters, or digits. They can also include underscores but cannot begin with a digit.

The following are examples of a few valid variable names:

```
a
radius
```

```
volume2
area_rectangle
```

These are a few valid variable names. We cannot begin a variable name with a digit. For instance, 2volume is an invalid variable name.

Assigning values to shell variables

To assign a value to a variable, we use the following format:

```
variable=value
```

An equal to sign is used between the variable and the value without any space—neither before nor after the equal sign. If a space has to be used in the value, the value must be placed within quotes.

Example
```
message="Are you sure?"
radius=5
```

Exporting variables

The shell variables discussed here are only available to the current shell. As previously mentioned, these are local variables and the child processes of the current shell will not be able to access them. Hence, in order to pass the shell variables to a subshell, we need to export them using the export command. Variables that are exported are referred to as environment variables.

An environment variable is a shell variable that is exported or published to the environment so that it is accessible to the child processes of the current shell too. To set the values of the environment variables, we use either of the following formats:

```
$ VARNAME=new value
$ export VARNAME
```
or
```
$ export VARNAME=new value
```

The second format assigns as well as exports the variable.

Example
```
PS1=':${PWD#HOME/}:!$'
PATH="$PATH:/usr/John/bin"
export PS1 PATH
```

The export command makes the value of the variable available to other processes too. Usually when we declare, initialize, read, and modify variables, they are local to that process. When a process forks a child process, the parent process does not automatically pass the value of the variable to the child process. To pass the value of the variable to the child process, we use the export command. It is a one-way transition; we can export variables from the parent to the child process but vice versa is not possible.

11.5.2 Environment Variables

Environment variables, also known as global variables, are available to all the shells. Whenever a new shell is created, it inherits all of its parent's environment variables but it does not inherit any shell variable. This implies that the environment variables are accessible to any child process of the current shell and hence have a great impact on the working of the new shell too, but the same is not true for local variables. By convention, environment variables have upper case names. Some of the important environment variables are listed in Table 11.8.

Table 11.8 List of environment variables

Environment variable	Description
EDITOR	It is used to decide the editor the user wishes to use.
	Examples:
	EDITOR=vi
	EDITOR=emacs
VISUAL	It is used to specify a default visual editor, overriding the EDITOR variable.
	Example: VISUAL=vi
	The Korn shell first checks the value of the VISUAL environment variable. If it is defined, it uses the specified command line editor. If the VISUAL environment variable is undefined, the Korn Shell checks the value of the EDITOR environment variable and uses the editor specified in it, if defined.
HOME	It is the home directory of the user. We can set this variable to override the setting in /etc/passwd that represents the home directory. The tilde symbol ~ refers to the home directory.
	Example: HOME=/home/john
ENV	Besides the .profile file (if it exists), the Korn shell uses the start-up file specified by this variable.
	Example: ENV=$HOME/.kshrc
	Basically the start-up file can be any filename with any extension, not necessarily, .kshrc. The .profile file is read once on logging in, whereas the file specified through the ENV environment variable is read every time the Korn shell is invoked.
LOGNAME	It specifies the name of the user.
	Example: LOGNAME=john
HOSTNAME	This variable is used by several commands to identify the current host. Hence, the name of the current system is assigned to this variable.
	Example: HOSTNAME=$(uname -n)
	Here, the variable uname is meant for displaying the system's configuration information. The option -n is used for displaying the name of the machine.
PWD	It contains the absolute path name of the current working directory. Its value is automatically set by the cd command.
MAIL	This indicates the location of the incoming local e-mail. The mail reader uses this variable to find the mailbox. If not set, the default location where mails are dropped is /var/mail/username.
MAILCHECK	The MAILCHECK variable specifies the time interval in which the shell will check for new mail. If not set or set to zero, new mail is checked before each new prompt is displayed. The default value of this environment variable is 600 seconds, that is, 10 minutes.

(Contd)

Table 11.8 (Contd)

Environment variable	Description
MAILPATH	This environment variable is used when we have multiple mailboxes. It contains a colon-separated list of mailbox files to check for the new mails. If set, the environment variable overrides the MAIL variable.
	If MAILPATH is not set, there is no default.
	Example: `MAILPATH=/home/john/mbox:/news/mbox`.
	On getting a new mail, the Korn shell displays this message on our terminal just before the prompt:
	`you have mail in the mailbox file.`
	To modify the mail notification message, append a ? to the path specified in the MAILPATH environment variable followed by the custom message that we wish to display on getting a new mail:
	`MAILPATH=/home/john/mbox? ' New mail has arrived. Please check $_'`
	Here, _ (underscore) is substituted for the name of the mailbox file.
PAGER	This message indicates if there is more information to be viewed. It is used by programs created for viewing a file.
	Examples:
	`PAGER=less`
	`PAGER=more`
CDPATH	It defines a list of colon-separated directories that the shell checks when a full path name is not given to the `cd` command. It makes the directory navigation easier as each directory in CDPATH is searched from left to right for a directory that matches the `cd` argument. Let us assume that our CDPATH is set as follows:
	`CDPATH=:/home/john:/etc:/var`
	The CDPATH environment variable indicates the shell to check the current directory first, `/home/john`: `/etc`, and then `/var` when the `cd` command is issued without a full path name.
	Note: The colon (:) alone in CDPATH stands for the current directory.
	Assume that we give the following `cd` command:
	`cd progs`
	The shell will search for the progs directory in the current directory followed by the `/home/john` directory and then the `/etc` and `/var` directories. Assuming the progs directory exists in the `/home/john` directory, our directory will change to the `/home/john/progs` directory.
	There is no default value for the CDPATH environment variable and hence this feature is disabled if the environment variable is not set.
PATH	It contains a list of colon separated directories to search for the file of the issued command. Each directory in PATH is searched from left to right. The command is executed only if the file is found, otherwise an error message is displayed.
	Example: `PATH=:/bin:/usr/bin`
	Here, : (colon) alone represents the current directory.

(Contd)

Table 11.8 (*Contd*)

Environment variable	Description
	The value in the PATH environment variable asks the shell to check the current directory, the /bin directory, then /usr/bin for the issued command.
	If not set, the default value for PATH is /bin:/usr/bin.
PS1	It controls the appearance of the primary prompt. It uses several escape characters to display the desired information in the prompt.
PS2	It is the secondary prompt and is usually displayed when we break a long Unix command on multiple lines by pressing the Enter key, mid-command. The PS2 prompt by default appears as >, which means that Unix is waiting for the rest of the command. By setting the PS2 environment variable, we can modify the default PS2 prompt > to display the desired information.
PS3	It defines the prompt for selecting an option in an interactive menu created through the select command. Default prompt is #?.
PS4	It defines the *execution trace* prompt that precedes each line of an execution trace. The default *execution trace prompt* is + (plus).
HISTFILE	It is used to specify the path name of the file where the list of commands, that is, command history is saved. By default, the history file for bash is .bash_history and that for the Korn shell is .sh_history. We need to delete the commands from the history file each time we log in or else the number of commands stored in it becomes quite large. We can also issue a command in the .profile file to delete the history file: rm .sh_history By implementing this command, the earlier commands will be deleted each time we log in to the computer.
HISTSIZE	The value specified through this environment variable decides the number of commands that are kept in the history file. You may recall that the history file makes the previously entered commands accessible by the shell. By default, 512 commands are stored for the root user and 128 commands for other users.
USER	The username is stored here.

The values of most of the aforementioned environment variables automatically change on the basis of user actions. For example, the environment variable, PWD, stands for present working directory and its value is the directory where the user is currently working. If the user changes the directory, then the new directory where the user has moved to is assigned to the PWD variable.

A sample start-up file, .profile, containing different shell and environment variables may appear as follows:

```
.profile file
set -o allexport
TERM=vt102
LOGNAME=john
HOSTNAME=$(uname -n)
```

```
HISTSIZE=50
EDITOR=vi
MAIL=/usr/spool/mail/$LOGNAME
HOME=/home/john
SHELL=/bin/ksh
ENV=$HOME/doit.kshrc
PWD=$(pwd)
PATH=$HOME/bin:/usr/bin:/usr/local:/etc:/bin:/home/john/bin:/usr/local/bin:.
PS1="$HOSTNAME ! $"
PS2="Continue....>"
stty erase \^H intr \^C susp \^Z quit \^\\
set +o allexport
```

The set -o allexport statement in the aforementioned sample start-up file sets the allexport option, hence all variables defined in the script will automatically be exported making it available to subshells. The last statement of the start-up file set +o allexport switches off the allexport statement and stops the export of variables.

Besides the .profile file, the Korn shell uses the start-up file specified by the ENV variable. In the sample .profile file, the ENV variable refers to the start-up file doit.kshrc.

A sample .kshrc file may appear as follows:

```
doit.kshrc
if [ -z "$VISUAL" -a -z "$EDITOR" ]; then
    set -o vi
fi
set -o ignoreeof
set -o noclobber
```

This start-up file shows that if the VISUAL and the EDITOR variables are not set, then vi is set as the default editor while editing a command line. It also disables ^D from logging out. Thus, the exit command can only be used to exit the shell. In addition, it will not allow a user to overwrite a file with the same filename.

To display all environment variables and their values, we can use any of the following commands:

```
$ set or
$ printenv or
$ env
```

Let us understand the role of environment variables in controlling the appearance of our shell prompt.

11.6 SETTING SHELL PROMPTS

A default shell prompt displays the host name and current working directory. We can customize our prompt to display desired information. The appearance of shell prompt is controlled through the special shell variables PS1, PS2, PS3, and PS4.

11.6.1 PS1 Variable

Out of these special shell variables, the one that controls the appearance of the primary prompt is PS1. To display the current prompt setting, we can echo the PS1 variable:

```
$ echo $PS1
```

Let us learn more about the procedure of changing the appearance of the primary prompt. To modify the prompt, we can assign the backslash escaped special characters to PS1 as shown in Table 11.9. After assigning the escape characters to the PS1 variable, press the Enter key.

Table 11.9   Escape characters to be used with the PS1 variable

Escape character	Displays
\d	Date in *Weekday Month Date* format (Example, "Fri Dec 15")
\H	Host name
\n	Newline
\r	Carriage return
\s	Name of the shell
\t	Current time in 24-hour HH:MM:SS format
\T	Current time in 12-hour HH:MM:SS format
\@	Current time in 12-hour a.m./p.m. format
\A	Current time in 24-hour HH:MM format
\u	Username of the current user
\v	Version of bash
\w	Current working directory
\nnn	Character corresponding to the octal number nnn
\\	Backslash
\[	Begins a sequence of non-printing characters
\]	Ends a sequence of non-printing characters

Examples

(a) Let us try to set the prompt so that it can display today's date.

```
$PS1="\d $"
```

The prompt will change in this way.

```
Fri Dec 15 $
```

(b) Now we will set the prompt to display time, username, and current directory.

```
Fri Dec 15 $ PS1="[\t\u\w] $"
```

The prompt will change in this way.

```
[18:30:15 John~] $
```

11.6.2 PS2 **Variable**

The PS2 variable defines the secondary prompt that is displayed when a Unix script extends to multiple lines. The default PS2 prompt appears as >.

Example
```
echo "Number of argument
> are $#"
```
We can see that the prompt '>' appears when the echo command is extended to the next line asking for the rest of the statement. The '>' prompt is the default output of the PS2 variable. Let us modify it in this way.

```
PS2="Continue….>"
```

Now, the shell will prompt for the rest of the statement through the following prompt.

```
echo "Number of argument
Continue….> are $#"
```

11.6.3 PS3 **Variable**

The PS3 variable defines the select prompt, which is used in selecting an option from an interactive menu. The default prompt is #?. Before we understand more about the PS3 prompt, let us learn about the select command.

select **command**

The select command is used for creating an interactive menu. The syntax for using the select command is as follows:

Syntax
```
select variable in option1 option2...optionN
        do
            case $variable in
                option1)   command1;;
                option2)   command2;;
                optionN)   commandN;;
            esac
        done
```
Here, option1, option2, ..., optionN represents valid menu options, and command1, command2, ..., commandN represents the commands that will be executed when the corresponding menu option is selected by the user.

Example   The following shell script demonstrates how an interactive menu is created using the select command and its default prompt.

```
interactmenu.ksh
#!/bin/ksh
select i in Date Listing Users Exit
do
    case $i in
        Date)  date;;
```

```
            Listing) ls;;
            Users) who;;
            Exit) exit;;
      esac
done
```

We can see that four menu options are provided through the `select` command. The respective actions to be taken on the selection of any command are shown via case statements. On execution of the aforementioned shell script, we will have the following output.

```
$ ./interactmentu.ksh
1) Data
2) Listing
3) Users
4) Exit
#? 1
Monday 27 February 2012 10:32:50 AM IST
#? 2
checkargs.ksh      checkextexec.ksh    dispfiletypeoutput      project
checkexec.ksh      dispfiletype.ksh    interactmenu.ksh
#? 3
root            console         Feb 27 09:09          (:0)
root            pts/3           Feb 27 09:09          (:0.0)
root            pts/4           Feb 27 09:10          (:0.0)
#? 4
$
```

We can see that the default prompt displayed for the `select` command prompt is '#?', which is not very user-friendly. Let us now change the default prompt using the following PS3 command.

```
PS3="Select an option(1-4): "
```

Next, we will modify the select prompt by applying the aforementioned PS3 prompt in the shell script.

```
modiprompt.ksh

#!/bin/ksh
PS3="Select an option(1-4): "
select i in Date Listing Users Exit
do
   case $i in
      Date) date;;
      Listing) ls;;
      Users) who;;
      Exit) exit;;
   esac
```

done

The output will now display the following modified PS3 prompt.

```
$ ./modiprompt.ksh
1) Data
2) Listing
3) Users
4) Exit
Select an option(1-4): 1
Monday 27 February 2012 10:59:56 AM IST
Select an option(1-4): 2
checkargs.ksh        interactmenu.ksh        listfilesdiroutput
checkexec.ksh        interactmenuoutput.png  modiprompt.ksh
checkextexec.ksh     listfilesdir.ksh        project
dispfiletype.ksh     listfilesdir2.ksh
dispfiletypeoutput   listfilesdir2output

Select an option(1-4): 3
root    console   Feb 27 09:09   ( :0)
root    pts/3     Feb 27 09:09   ( :0.0)
root    pts/4     Feb 27 09:10   ( :0.0)

Select an option(1-4): 4
$
```

In this output, we can see that the prompt for the select command is changed to Select an option (1-4): through the PS3 prompt.

11.6.4 PS4 Variable

The PS4 variable is used for changing the execution trace prompt. The default execution trace prompt is + (the plus sign). The execution trace is a great tool for debugging shell scripts. It lists each command before the shell runs it. To enable the execution trace for a shell script, we need to add the set -x statement at the beginning.

Example The following script demonstrates how to enable execution trace prompt.

```
demoset.ksh
#!/bin/ksh
set -x
for i in 1 2 3
do
  echo $i
done
exit
```

Output

```
+ echo 1
```

```
1
+ echo 2
2
+ echo 3
3
+ exit
```

We can see that the trace lines displaying the output of the script appear in the default prompt, along with a + (plus) sign.

To display the shell script name along with the line numbers of the commands in the script, we make use of the LINENO variable to set the PS4 prompt in the following way.

```
PS4='$0.$LINENO+ '
```

To display the line numbers only in square brackets along with the trace line, enclose the LINENO variable in square brackets in the PS4 prompt in the following way.

```
PS4='[${LINENO}]+'
```

On executing the set PS4 variable, the output of this script displays the line numbers along with the trace line.

Output
```
[5]+echo 1
1
[5]+echo 2
2
[5]+echo 3
3
[7]+exit
```

The numbers in the square brackets are the line numbers in the scripts that display the output.

We will now see how the environment variables control the display and terminal.

11.7 SETTING DISPLAY ENVIRONMENT VARIABLE

For running certain applications, the DISPLAY environment variable must be set correctly as it plays a major role in the X Window System. X Windows is a client/server model, where the communication is performed using the X protocol. In this model, the output of the program that is run on a remote Unix system can be seen on our local display. This implies that the program and the user interface can be on different machines. The client's machine is known as the workstation or the X terminal.

11.7.1 Terminal

A terminal might be a text-based teletype terminal (tty) or a graphics-based terminal. Before being used, a terminal needs to be configured and for that we need to define the environment variable, TERM, with an appropriate value that best describes the terminal. The most common values assigned to the TERM environment variables for configuring the terminals are *vt100* and *xterm* and they work for almost all types of terminals.

Note: The terminal can always be configured manually using the stty command.

To display some content on the client's screen, the client asks a server on the specified host to draw windows for it.

11.7.2 Display

A display is a virtual screen that is created by the X server on a particular host. When an X client program wants to open a window, it looks in the Unix environment variable DISPLAY for the IP address of a host, which has an X server it can contact. Each display on a machine is assigned a display number (beginning at 0) when the X server for that display is started. Each display has a set of windows where each screen is assigned a screen number (beginning at 0). If the screen number is not given, screen 0 will be used.

Every X server has a display name in the following format:

```
hostname:displaynumber.screennumber
```

Here, hostname specifies the name of the machine to which the display is physically connected. The displaynumber refers to the display or monitor number and screennumber refers to the screen or window on a monitor. The following is an example:

```
DISPLAY="hostname:0"
export DISPLAY
```

The client will try to contact the X server on 'host name' and ask for a window on display number zero.

11.8 STEPS TO CREATE AND RUN KORN SHELL SCRIPTS

The following are the steps for creating and running a Korn shell script:

1. Create a script with extension .ksh using any editor. For instance, to create a script by the name kornsh1.ksh through the vi editor, open the vi editor as follows:

   ```
   vi kornsh1.ksh
   ```

2. Type the script content, save it, and exit from the editor.
3. Before executing a shell script, it must be assigned execute permissions. To assign these permissions, run the following command:

   ```
   chmod +x kornsh1.ksh
   ```

4. To run the Korn shell script, give the following command:

   ```
   $./kornsh1.ksh
   ```

   Here, . (dot) represents the current directory.
   In order to execute scripts by typing its name alone, the current directory containing the shell script must be defined in the PATH variable. On specifying the current directory in the PATH variable, we can run scripts without using . (dot) in the command as follows:

   ```
   $ kornsh1.ksh
   ```

We will first create the code for the Korn shell script using the aforementioned steps through the following example.

Example The following script demonstrates how computation is performed and the result is displayed in a Korn script.

arearect.ksh

```
#!/bin/ksh
l=5
b=6
((a=l*b))
echo "Area of rectangle is $a"
```

Output
```
Area of rectangle is 30
```

Let us understand the usage of the first line of the script that begins with the following statement.

```
#!/bin/ksh
```

On executing a shell script, the commands are passed to an interpreter for processing and running it. Since many shells exist, we need to inform the current running shell program that the script being executed is a Korn Shell script, and hence has to be interpreted by the ksh interpreter and not by csh, sh, bash, tcsh, or any other interpreter. The first line of the script does the job of indicating which interpreter has to be used for executing the shell. The line contains special characters beginning with '#!'.

Normally a hash sign (#) represents a comment line; hence, a line beginning with # is not interpreted by the shell. In the case where the hash sign is immediately followed by an exclamation mark (!), and is in the first line of the script, the characters after the exclamation mark are considered as the program name to be used for running and interpreting the rest of the script. Hence, the first line of the script, `#!/bin/ksh`, invokes the Korn shell interpreter to execute the script.

While assigning a value to a shell variable, we do not need to use a dollar sign. While accessing the value of the variable, it needs to be prefixed by the $ sign. If the variable name is immediately followed by some other content, then for readability and clear separation, it must be enclosed in curly braces ({ }).

Since we will require variables in shell scripts for storing data and results, let us recall the syntax for creating shell variables.

Syntax `variable=value`

It is to be remembered that no spaces are allowed around the = (equal to) sign. The value can be numerical, a string, or an expression and can be enclosed in double or single quotes if desired.

Examples
```
p="Hello World!"
q=10
r=
```

These examples assign the string Hello World! to the variable p, value 10 is assigned to the variable q, whereas the variable r is not set. You may recall that if a shell variable is not set, then the null string is substituted for it, which means that nothing will appear on the screen when printed.

> **Note:** The value of a variable is accessed by preceding its name with a dollar sign ($).

11.9 BASIC INPUT/OUTPUT COMMANDS

In this section, we are going to learn about the basic input/output (I/O) commands that are required in almost all shell scripts. The basic commands include the commands to accept input from the user and to display messages and results.

11.9.1 echo

The echo statement displays messages, arguments, variables, etc., terminated by a newline, to the screen. In order to keep the extra white spaces within the data being displayed, it needs to be enclosed in quotes. Escape characters that can be used in the echo command are given in Table 11.10.

Table 11.10   List of escape characters to be used with echo and printf commands

Escape character	Usage	Escape character	Usage
\b	Backspace	\t	Tab
\c	Print line without newline (works in some versions)	\v	Vertical tab
		\\	Single backslash
\f	Form-feed	\0n	ASCII character with octal (base-8) value n, where n is 1 to 3 digits
\n	Newline		
\r	Carriage return		

A common option used with the echo command is -n, which suppresses the newline making the cursor remain on the same line after displaying the output so that the successive read or write begins from there.

Examples

(a) This example displays the text message "The files in the directory are".

```
echo "The files in the directory are"
```

(b) This example displays the value in the variable x.

```
echo $x
```

(c) This example displays the message Thanks and Bye on two separate lines.

```
echo "Thanks\nBye"
```

After displaying the text, Thanks, the newline character, \n makes the cursor move on to the next line.

Note: We need to use a double backslash while using escape sequences if the string that contains them is not enclosed in quotes.

11.9.2 print

It is the most popularly used command in Korn shell for displaying messages and results on the screen. The output displayed via the print statement is terminated by a newline. It uses the same escape conventions that we discussed in the echo command. The two common options used with the print command are -n and -r:

1. -n suppress newline.
2. -r raw mode ignores the escape sequences.

Examples

(a) The following example prints the text Hello World! on the screen.

```
print  "Hello World! "
```

(b) This example prints the values in the variables x and y.

```
print  $x $y
```

(c) This example prints the text messages Thanks and Bye on the same line.

```
print  -n "Thanks"
print "Bye"
```

Though Thanks and Bye are printed through two different print statements, the option -n used with the first print statement suppresses the newline character after printing the text Thanks and hence prints the text Bye also on the same line.

11.9.3 read

The read command is used for reading values from the keyboard into the shell variables.

Syntax   read var1 var2 ...

This statement takes a line from the standard input and breaks it into words on the basis of the delimiter specified in the variable IFS. The default delimiters are space, TAB, and newline. The words are then assigned to the variables var1, var2, etc.

Example   The following script prompts the user to enter a name and print its name back along with a hello message.

readinput.ksh

```
#!/bin/ksh
print -n "Enter your Name: "
read name
print Hello $name
```

Output

```
Enter your Name: John
Hello John
```

11.9.4 printf

The printf command is used for displaying formatted output. It does not include a newline character in its output and hence the escape sequence \n is explicitly used for getting a newline in the printf statement.

Syntax `printf "Message format specifiers" argument list`

Here, Message is the text content that we want to display and format specifiers are for formatting the arguments supplied in the argument list to display the output in the desired format. The list of format specifiers used in the printf command is given in Table 11.11.

Table 11.11 List of format specifiers to be used in the printf command

Format specifier	Description
%c	Prints a character
%d	Prints a decimal integer
%i	Prints a decimal integer
%o	Displays unsigned octal number
%s	Displays a string
%u	Displays unsigned decimal value
%x	Displays unsigned hexadecimal number and a to f in lower case for numbers 10 to 15
%X	Displays unsigned hexadecimal number and a to f in upper case for numbers 10 to 15
%f	Displays floating-point number

Table 11.12 List of flags to be used in the printf command

Flags	Description
-	Left justifies the formatted value within the field
space	Prefixes positive values with a space and negative values with a minus sign
+	Prefixes every numeric value with a sign, plus sign for positive and minus sign for negative values
0	Pads the output with zeros and not spaces, applies only to numeric formats

Along with the format specifiers, we can use certain flags too in the printf statement that helps in aligning, padding, or prefixing the content. The syntax for using the flags is as follows:

Syntax `%flags width format-specifier`

Here, the width is a numeric value to specify the width assigned to an argument. The list of flags is given in Table 11.12.

Note: If printf cannot perform a format conversion, it returns a non-zero exit status.

By default, the contents are right justified. By using flags, we can change the justification.

Examples

(a) `printf "%20s \n" Hello`

The string, Hello, will be displayed right justified in the allowable width of 20 characters.

(b) `printf "%-20s \n" Hello`

The string, Hello, will be displayed left justified in the allowable width of 20 characters.

(c) `printf "%+d %+d" 10 -20`

The numerals will be displayed along with the sign prefix. The output will be +10 -20.

(d) `printf "%08d " 10`

The numeral 10 will be displayed in the allowable width of eight digits padded with 0s on the left side.

11.9.5 typeset

The `typeset` command is used to define variables. The following is the syntax for using the `typeset` command:

Syntax `typeset [+-attributes] [name[=value]]`

The list of attributes used in this command is shown in Table 11.13.

Table 11.13 List of attributes used in the `typeset` command

Attribute	Meaning
-	Used to set attributes after setting values
+	Used to unset attributes after setting values
-A arr	Defines the associative array arr
-E n	Defines the exponential number n that specifies the significant digits
-F n	Defines floating-point number n that specifies the number of decimal places
-I n	Defines the integer of base n
-l	Converts upper-case characters to lower case
-r	Marks the variable as read-only
-u	Converts lower-case characters to upper case

Examples

(a) `$typeset -i x=500`

This command will define the variable x as an integer and assign the value 500 to it.

(b) `$typeset -i8 y=15`

This command will define the variable y as an octal integer and assign the value 15 to it. A valid base is between base 2 and base 36.

(c) If we want the variable to always contain a hexadecimal number, then the following command is used.

`typeset -i16 hexvalue`

After the hexvalue variable is typeset to base 16, any value assigned to it will be automatically converted to hexadecimal. We can also typeset a variable after a number is assigned to it.

(d) In order to quickly convert any base number (base 2 through base 36) to base 10, the following syntax is used:

`echo $((base#number))`

(e) The following command converts the base-16 number, ae09f, to its base-10 equivalent.

```
$ echo $((16#ae09f))
16652452
```

Using both these techniques, we can convert bases of any number.

(f) The following command converts base 10 to base 16.

```
$ typeset -i16 hexvalue
$ hexvalue=2091
$ echo $hexvalue
16#3487
```

(g) The following command converts base 8, octal, to base 16, hexadecimal.

```
$ typeset -i16 hexvalue
$ hexvalue=8#2075
$ echo $hexvalue
16#3487
```

In the aforementioned example, we assigned the octal number, 2075, to the hexvalue variable by specifying the number base followed by the base-8 number, `hexvalue=8#2075`. When this base-8 number is assigned to the hexvalue variable, it is automatically converted to base 16.

We can also use the `printf` command to convert number bases. The `printf` command accepts base-10 integer values and converts the number to the specified number base. The following options are available:

1. o: It accepts a base-10 integer and prints the number in octal.
2. x: It accepts a base-10 integer and prints the number in hexadecimal

11.9.6 Converting Base 10 to Octal

```
$ printf %o 6541
$ printf %x 6541
```

The added percent sign (%) before the `printf` command option tells the `printf` command that the following lower-case letter specifies the base conversion. If the following letter is o, it means the number needs to be converted to octal and the letter x indicates that the number needs to be converted into hexa.

To get a list of exported objects available to the current environment, the following commands may be used:

```
$ typeset -x              # list of exported variables
$ typeset -fx             # list of exported functions
$ typeset -r radius=10    # defines a read only variable
$ typeset -i2 x           # deciares x as binary integer
$ typeset -i8 y           # declares y as octal integer
```

Examples

(a) The following example takes an input value of base 10 and coverts it into base 16, 8, and 2 respectively.

```
convbase.ksh

#!/bin/ksh
print -n "Enter a value "
read n
integer -i10 value=$n
print "Original value is $value"
typeset -i16 value
print "Value in hexa form is $value"
typeset -i8 value
```

```
print "Value in octal form is $value"
typeset -i2 value
print "Value in binary form is $value"
```

Output

```
$ ./convbase.ksh
Enter a value 32
Original value is 32
Value in hexa form is 16#20
Value in octal form is 8#40
Value in binary form is 2#100000

$ ./convbase.ksh
Enter a value 100
Original value is 100
Value in hexa form is 16#64
Value in octal form is 8#144
Value in binary form is 2#1100100
```

(b) The following shell script takes a string from the user and prints it along with its upper-case and lower-case versions.

changecase.ksh

```
#!/bin/ksh
print -n  "Enter a string: "
read str
print "The original string is $str"
typeset -u  str
print "The string in upper case is $str"
typeset -l str
print "The string in lower case is $str"
```

Output

```
Enter a string: Hello
The original string is Hello
The string in upper case is HELLO
The string in lower case is hello
```

11.9.7 unset

For removing a variable or function from our shell environment, the unset command is used.

Syntax   unset [-fv] name(s)

Here, the option -f removes the definition of the given function name. -v removes the attribute and the value of the given variable name(s). This option is default.

Note: The variables that are set for read only cannot be removed.

Examples

(a) `$ unset x`

(b) `$ unset factorial`

(c) The following script demonstrates the setting and unsetting of variables.

```
export radius=10
echo $radius
unset $radius
echo $radius
```

The aforementioned script will first display 10 as the value of the variable radius. Next it will display nothing, that is, a null character, because the variable radius is unset. The unset variable does not display anything.

11.10 VARIABLE SUBSTITUTION

After a value is assigned to a variable, it needs to be substituted by its value in a script. A variable name can be substituted by its respective value. Table 11.14 lists the formats in which the variables in the script will be substituted by their respective value.

If a shell variable is not set then the null string is substituted for it. For example, if the variable *d* is not set then the following statements will not echo anything:

```
echo $d or echo ${d}
```

Note: The colon (:) shown in the aforementioned format is optional. If it is included, the var must be set and not be null.

Table 11.14 List of formats of variable substitution

Format	Description
${ var }	Uses the value of var
${ var1 :- var2 }	Uses var1 if set, otherwise uses var2
${ var1 := var2 }	Uses var1 if set otherwise uses var2 and assigns its value to var1
${ var1 :? var2 }	Uses var1 if set, otherwise prints var2 and exits, and if var2 is not supplied, it prints the message 'parameter null or not set'
${ var1 :+ var2 }	Uses var2 if var1 is set, otherwise uses no variable

The following examples demonstrate variable substitution:

```
p=Hello
q=World
r=
```

Assuming that the value for the variable r is not set and the values of the variables p and q are Hello and World respectively, the following are the examples and their output on variable substitution:

```
$ echo ${p}World!
```

We can see that braces are needed for separation. The aforementioned example displays HelloWorld!.

```
$ echo ${p-$q}
```

This will display the value of p or q; since p is set, the following message will be displayed:

```
Hello
$ echo ${r-`date`}
```

If r is not set, the date command is executed. We get the following output:

```
Sat Mar 15 18:13:25 EST 2012
$ echo ${r="Great"}
```

The variable r will be assigned the string Great, which is also displayed on the screen.

```
$ echo ${r:="Work"}
```

Since r is already set, it will print its value as follows:

```
Great
$ echo ${r?Work}
```

It will display the string already assigned to r:

```
Great
```

11.11 COMMAND LINE ARGUMENTS

While executing a script, we can pass the data to it for processing in the form of command line arguments. The data typed beyond the script name is treated as command line arguments. These command line arguments can be accessed in the shell script through *positional parameters* that are represented in the $n format. For instance, the positional parameter $0 represents the command line script, $1 represents the first argument, and $2 represents the second argument. The list of positional parameters is given in Table 11.15.

Table 11.15   List of positional parameters

Variable	Description
$0	It represents the name of the command or script being executed.
$n	It represents the positional parameter passed to the script, where *n* is a number between 1 and 9 indicating the position of the argument from the script. For instance, $1 represents the first argument that follows the command script and $2 represents the second argument from the command script. The arguments exceeding the 9th position need to be enclosed in curly braces. For example, the 10th argument has to be used as ${10}.
$#	It represents the count of the number of positional parameters passed to the script.
$*	It represents a list of all command line arguments.
$@	It represents an individually double-quoted list of all command line arguments.
$!	It represents the PID (process ID) number of the last background command.
$$	It represents the PID (process ID) number of the current process.
$?	It represents a numerical value indicating the exit status of the last executed command.

The # variable is used for ascertaining the length or count of the positional parameters. If followed by a variable or expression, it determines the length or count of the given variable or expression also. The following three formats explain the same:

${# var}   This displays the length of var.

${#*}   This displays the number of positional parameters.

${#@}   Like ${#*}, this also displays the number of positional parameters.

Examples

(a) The following shell script demonstrates how command line arguments are displayed using different positional parameters. The script prints the command line arguments, their count, command script, etc.

```
positionparm.ksh
```

```
#!/bin/ksh
print "Number of argument are $#"
print "The command line arguments passed are $*"
print "Number of argument are ${#*}"
print "Number of argument are ${#@}"
print "The shell script name is $0"
print "The first argument is $1"
print "The second argument is $2"
print "The above print command returned $?"
```

Assume we execute this shell script by passing the following command line arguments.

```
$ ./positionparm.ksh xyz.txt 10 4 bank.lst
Number of argument are 4
The command line arguments passed are xyz.txt 10 4 bank.lst
Number of argument are 4
Number of argument are 4
The shell script name is ./positionparm.ksh
The first argument is xyz.txt
The second argument is 10
The above print command returned 0
```

The command line arguments can be accessed using $1, $2, till $9. We cannot use the same notation for command line arguments greater than nine. We need to use curly braces for arguments ${10}, ${11}, and so on. Let us look at the following two examples.

```
echo "The 10th argument is : $10"
```

It will print the content of $1 followed by 0.

```
echo "The 10th argument is : ${10}"
```

It will print the content of the tenth argument $10.

(b) The following script concatenates two strings. Besides demonstrating string concatenation, the script displays the length of the individual strings along with the concatenated string using the ${# var } format.

strconcat.ksh

```
#!/bin/ksh
print -n "Enter two strings: "
read str1
read str2
print "The two strings entered are $str1 and $str2"
print "The length of the first string is ${#str1} and of second string is ${#str2}"
str3="$str1$str2"
print "The concatenated string is $str3"
print "The length of the concatenated string is ${#str3}"
```

Output

```
Enter two strings: birds
fly
The two strings entered are birds and fly
The length of the first string is 5 and of second string is 3
The concatenated string is birdsfly
The length of the concatenated string is 8
```

11.11.1 shift: Shifting Positional Parameters

The shift command shifts or renames the positional parameters, $1, $2, etc., which was discussed in Chapter 10.

Syntax   shift [n]

On giving the command shift n, the (n+1)th positional parameter becomes the positional parameter $1; the (n+2)th positional parameter becomes the positional parameter $2, and so on. The value of n supplied must be between zero and the count of positional parameters. The command fails to supply a negative value or value greater than the count of positional parameters. The default value for the shift command is 1. The value of $# that represents the count of the positional parameters will be automatically updated on the execution of the shift command. The command returns 0 on successful execution and 1 on failure.

Example   The following script demonstrates the impact of the shift command.

demoshift.ksh

```
#!/bin/ksh
print "Number of argument are $#"
print "The command line arguments passed are $*"
print "The first argument is $1"
print "The second argument is $2"
shift 2
print "Number of argument are $#"
```

```
print "The command line arguments passed are $*"
print "The first argument is $1"
print "The second argument is $2"
```

Assume we execute this shell script by passing the following command line arguments.

```
$ ./demoshift.ksh xyz.txt 10 4 bank.lst
Number of argument are 4
The command line arguments passed are xyz.txt 10 4 bank.lst
The first argument is xyz.txt
The second argument is 10
Number of argument are 2
The command line arguments passed are 4 bank.lst
The first argument is 4
The second argument is bank.lst
```

Through the output, we realize that the shift 2 command shifts the positional parameter $3 to $1 and parameter $4 to $2, and also updates the value of the parameter $# to 2.

11.11.2 set: Handling Positional Parameters

The set command is used for changing the positional parameters. The positional parameters cannot be set through the assignment statement and we have already seen how to set them through command line arguments. We can set or change them via the set command. The command replaces the values of the positional parameters with the new values if they are already set. The positional parameter $# will be automatically updated to display the count of the currently set positional parameters.

Syntax   set [data list][`executable command`]

Here, data list can be any text or numerical content delimited by a space. The first word will be assigned to the positional parameter $1, the second word to positional parameter $2, and so on. Similarly, if the output of the executable command has more than one item, which can be a word, character, or number, they will be assigned to the corresponding positional parameters, that is, the first item will be assigned to positional parameter $1, second item to positional parameter $2, and so on.

Example   The following script demonstrates how the positional parameters are set and changed via the set command.

setposparm.ksh

```
#!/bin/ksh
set a b c
print "Number of argument are $#"
print "The command line arguments passed are $*"
print "The first argument is $1"
print "The second argument is $2"
```

```
set one two
print "Number of argument are $#"
print "The command line arguments passed are $*"
print "The first argument is $1"
print "The second argument is $2"
set `date`
print "Number of argument are $#"
print "The command line arguments passed are $*"
print "The first argument is $1"
print "The second argument is $2"
```

We will get the following output.

```
./setposparm.ksh
Number of argument are 3
The command line arguments passed are a b c
The first argument is a
The second argument is b
Number of argument are 2
The command line arguments passed are one two
The first argument is one
The second argument is two
Number of argument are 7
The command line arguments passed are Monday 27 February 2012 02:59:50 PM IST
The first argument is Monday
The second argument is 27
```

We can see that the command set a b c assigns a, b, and c to the positional parameters $1, $2, and $3 respectively. Similarly, the command set one two will assign the words one and two to the positional parameters $1 and $2 respectively. The final command set `date` substitutes the output of the date command, hence assigning the output Monday 27 February 2012 02:59:50 PM IST to the positional parameters $1, $2, $3, $4, $5, $6, and $7, respectively.

11.11.3 test Command

We have learnt about the test command in detail in Chapter 10. We may recall that the test command is used for checking or comparing expressions where the expression is a boolean expression resulting in *true* or *false* values. The test command includes several operators that help in checking properties of files, strings, and integers. The test command can also be represented by a square bracket. The expression within the bracket can have leading and trailing blanks for separation.

Syntax   `[[ boolean expression ]]`

Examples

(a) The following example tests whether the number of command line arguments is 0.
   `[[ $# -eq 0 ]]`

(b) The following example tests whether the length of the string name is zero.

```
[[ -z $name ]]
```

(c) The following example tests whether the filename specified through variable $file is a file.

```
[[ -f $file ]]
```

In a Korn shell, apart from single brackets, we can also use double brackets. There is no difference between the two, as both represent the test command. We will learn about different test operators as we proceed in the chapter.

11.12 PATTERN-MATCHING OPERATORS

The Korn shell provides several pattern-matching operators, as given in Table 11.16, which we can use to strip off or remove the desired pattern from the given variable or string.

Table 11.16   List of pattern matching operators

Operator	Description
${ var # pattern }	Displays the value of var after removing the shortest matching pattern from the left
${ var ## pattern }	Same as the pattern #, but removes the longest matching pattern from the left
${ var % pattern }	Displays the value of var after removing the pattern from the right
${ var %% pattern }	Same as the pattern %, but removes the longest matching pattern

Example   The following shell script deletes characters from the beginning as well as from the end of a given string using pattern matching operators.

delchars.ksh

```
#!/bin/ksh
print -n  "Enter a string: "
read str
print "The original string is $str"
print "The string after deleting first 2 characters is ${str#??}"
print "The string after deleting the last 2 characters is ${str%??}"
```

Output

```
Enter a string: education
The original string is education
The string after deleting first 2 characters is ucation
The string after deleting the last 2 characters is educati
```

11.12.1 If Else Statement

The if else statement is a flow control construct that result in conditional jumping. Through this statement, we can make the shell script branch to the desired block of statement(s) depending on the basis of the logical expression included. The logical expression can be built with the help of the `test` command combined with different operators. The if else statement has the following syntax:

Syntax
```
if condition
then
     block of statements
[elif condition
then
     block of statements ...]
[else
     block of statements ]
fi
```

Here, `condition` refers to the logical expression that is built either using relational operators or the `test` command with its different operators. The simplest form of the if statement consists of only the if clause and its statements execute only when the logical expression is true. If the else clause is included, its statements will execute if the logical expression is false. We can also use the *elif* clause, which is the combination of 'else if' clauses in case we have more conditions to check.

Examples

(a) The following shell script uses the `test` command to check if the command line arguments are passed to the script or not.

checkargs.ksh
```
#!/bin/ksh
if [[ $# -eq 0 ]]
then
        print "No command line arguments are passed"
fi
```

Output
```
$ ./checkargs.ksh
No command line arguments are passed
$ ./checkargs.ksh a.txt
$
```

The parameter `$#` is compared with the relation operator `-eq` to see if any command line argument is passed to the script. If none of the command line arguments are passed to the shell script, its value will be 0, hence displaying the message, `No command line arguments are passed`.

(b) The following script checks if the two words exist in the given file where the words and the file will be supplied as command line arguments.

checkwords.ksh
```
#!/bin/ksh
if grep $2 $1 || grep $3 $1
```

```
then
        print "The words $2 or $3 exists in the file $1"
fi
```

Output

```
$ cat school.txt
101 Anil     75
102 Chirag   82
103 Kanika   70
104 Naman    88
105 Suman    68
106 John     83
$ ./checkwords.ksh school.txt chirag Naman
102 Chirag   82
The words Chirag or Naman exists in the file school.txt
```

While using the logical expressions consisting of commands connected with the logical AND operator (&&) or the logical OR operator (||), we need to remember the following two points:

1. If the two commands are connected through the logical AND operator, the shell executes the second command only if the first command results in a true value.
2. If the two commands are connected through the logical OR operator, the shell executes the second command only if the first command results in a false value.

The conditional statement, if else, which we have discussed here, is combined with certain testing operators to implement string and file-related conditions. Let us see how.

11.13 TESTING STRINGS

Korn shell provides several test operators that we can use for manipulating strings. We can use these test operators for performing several tasks including comparing and handling strings. For instance, we can test whether the given string is empty, the given file contains the specified characters, two strings are equal, and a string is alphabetically smaller than the other string. The list of string operators used in testing strings is shown in Table 11.17.

Table 11.17   List of Korn shell string operators

Operator	True if
-n string	The string is of non zero length
-z string	The string is of zero length
string1=string2	The two strings are equal
string1!=string2	The two strings are not equal
string=pattern	The pattern matches the string
string!=pattern	The pattern does not match the string
string1<string2	string1 is less than string2 alphabetically
string1>string2	string1 is greater than string2 alphabetically

Examples

(a) The following shell script asks for the username. If a username is entered, a welcome message is displayed and if an empty string is entered, the following message is displayed: You have entered a zero length string. The test operator, -z, is used to check whether a zero length string is entered.

```
welcomemsg.ksh
#!/bin/ksh
print -n "Enter your Name: "
read name
if [[ -z $name ]];then
    print "You have entered a zero length string "
else
    print "Welcome! $name"
fi
```

Output

```
$ ./welcomemsg.ksh
Enter your Name:
You have entered a zero length string
$ ./welcomemsg.ksh
Enter your Name: John
Welcome! John
```

We can also use the -n test operator for the aforementioned shell script as shown in the following code.

```
welcomemsg2.ksh
#!/bin/ksh
print -n "Enter your Name "
read name
if [[ -n $name ]];then
    print "Welcome! $name"
else
    print "You have entered a zero length string "
fi
```

Output

```
$ ./welcomemsg2.ksh
Enter your Name:
You have entered a zero length string
$ ./welcomemsg2.ksh
Enter your Name: John
Welcome! John
```

The aforementioned shell script checks if the string of non-zero length is entered and displays either a welcome message or the following message: You have entered a zero length string.

(b) The following shell script checks if the user has entered an authorized username or not.

```
authorize.ksh
#!/bin/ksh
print -n "Enter your Name "
```

```
read name
if [[ $name = "John" ]];then
        print "Welcome, ${name}!"
else
        print "Sorry! You are not authorized"
fi
```

Output

```
$ ./authorize.ksh
Enter your Name Chirag
Sorry! You are not authorized
$ ./authorize.ksh
Enter your Name John
Welcome, John!
```

(c) The following shell script concatenates the two strings.

strconcat2.ksh

```
#!/bin/ksh
print -n "Enter two strings: "
read str1 str2
str="$str1$str2"
print "The two strings are $str1 and $str2 and their concatenation is $str"
```

Output

```
Enter two strings: birds fly
The two strings are birds and fly and their concatenation is birdsfly
```

This shell script asks the user to enter two strings. The two strings entered are assigned to the variables str1 and str2 respectively. The two strings are concatenated and assigned to string str. The individual strings are displayed along with the concatenated string.

(d) The following script prompts the user to enter marks. If the marks entered are greater than or equal to 60, the following message is displayed: First Division. Otherwise the message Second Division will be displayed.

demoifelse.ksh

```
#!/bin/ksh
print -n "Enter marks: "
read m
if ((m >= 60 ))
then
        print "First Division"
else
        print "Second Division"
fi
```

Output

```
$ ./demoifelse.ksh
Enter marks: 80
First Division
```

```
$ ./demoifelse.ksh
Enter marks: 50
Second Division
```

In this shell script, we can see that (( )) are used along with the relational operator >= to check if the marks entered by the user in the variable *m* is greater than or equal to 60. If the marks in the variable *m* are greater than or equal to 60, a message, First Division, is displayed or else, the message Second Division is displayed. We can replace the (( )) with double square brackets as follows:

demoifelse2.ksh

```
#!/bin/ksh
print -n "Enter marks: "
read m
if [[ $m -ge 60 ]]
then
    print "First Division"
else
    print "Second Division"
fi
```

Output

The output of this script will be the same as that of the demoifelse.ksh script

```
$ ./demoifelse2.ksh
Enter marks: 70
First Division
```

```
$ ./demoifelse2.ksh
Enter marks: 50
Second Division
```

(e) The following script prompts the user to enter marks. If the marks entered are greater than or equal to 60, the following message is displayed: First Division. If the marks are greater than or equal to 45 but less than 60, the following message is displayed: Second Division. In other cases, the following message will be displayed: Third Division.

In this script, we will use the *nested if else* statements. Nested if else statement means using another if else statement within the if or else block of the existing if else statement. In the following script, within the *else* block of the *if else* statement, we will make use of another *if else* statement.

nestedif.ksh

```
#!/bin/ksh
print -n "Enter marks: "
```

```
read m
if [[ $m -ge 60 ]]
then
    print "First Division"
else
    if [[ $m -ge 45 ]]
    then
            print "Second Division"
    else
            print "Third Division"
    fi
fi
```

Output

```
$ ./nestedif.ksh
Enter marks: 70
First Division

$ ./nestedif.ksh
Enter marks: 50
Second Division

$ ./nestedif.ksh
Enter marks: 40
Third Division
```

We can see that if the marks entered in the variable m are greater than 60, then the message First Division will be displayed. If the marks entered are less than 60, the *else* block will be executed. Within the else block, the logical expression of the nested *if else* statement is evaluated. If the marks in the variable *m* are greater than or equal to 45, the *if* block will be executed, displaying the message Second Division on the screen. If the marks in variable *m* are less than 45, then the *else* block will be executed, displaying the message Third Division on the screen.

We can also make use of the *elif* block in the *if else* statement instead of a nested *if else* statement. The aforementioned shell script is rewritten using the *elif* block of the *if else* statement for checking the following condition: If marks are greater than or equal to 45 but less than 60.

The shell script has the following code.

```
demoelif.ksh
#!/bin/ksh
print -n "Enter marks: "
read m
if [[ $m -ge 60 ]]
then
    print "First Division"
elif [[ $m -ge 45 ]]
```

```
then
    print "Second Division"
else
    print "Third Division"
fi
```

Output

```
$ ./demoelif.ksh
Enter marks: 70
First Division

$ ./demoelif.ksh
Enter marks: 50
Second Division

$ ./demoelif.ksh
Enter marks: 40
Third Division
```

Basically, the *else* and *if* blocks are merged in the *elif* block. The *elif* block is preferred over a nested if else statement as it is more readable and requires only a single fi statement to close the if else statement. This relieves the programmer from keeping a record of the number of if statements and ending each of them through their corresponding fi statements.

(f) The following script asks the user to enter marks and displays the messages on the following basis.

1. Displays the message First Division if the marks entered are >= 60
2. Displays the message Second Division if the marks entered are >= 45 and < 60
3. Displays the message Third Division if the marks entered are >=36 and <45
4. Displays the message Fail for other conditions

Let us rewrite the aforementioned shell script, nestedif.ksh, using the logical and operator. The code of the shell script connecting conditions through the and operator is as follows:

demoand.ksh

```
#!/bin/ksh
print -n "Enter marks: "
read m
if [[ $m -ge 60 ]]
then
    print "First Division"
fi
if [[ $m -ge 45 && $m -lt 60 ]]
then
    print "Second Division"
fi
if [[ $m -ge 36 && $m -lt 45 ]]
then
    print "Third Division"
```

```
fi
if [[ $m -lt 36 ]]
then
    print "Fail"
fi
```

Output

```
$ ./demoand.ksh
Enter marks: 80
First Division

$ ./demoand.ksh
Enter marks: 50
Second Division

$ ./demoand.ksh
Enter marks: 40
Third Division

$ ./demoand.ksh
Enter marks: 30
Fail
```

Testing files

Korn shell provides several test operators to test various properties associated with a Unix file. The test operators for testing file properties are listed in Table 11.18.

Table 11.18   List of file testing operators

Operator	True if
-d filename	Filename exists and is a directory
-e filename	Filename exists
-f filename	Filename is a text file
-r filename	Filename is readable
-w filename	Filename is writable
-x filename	Filename is executable
-s filename	Filename is not empty
-l filename	Filename exists and is a symbolic link
-o filename	User is the owner of the filename
-g filename	Group ID of the user is the same as that of the filename

Examples

(a) The following shell script checks if the filename supplied through the command line argument is a regular file or not. If it is a regular file, then the script checks whether the file is executable or not.

```
checkexec.ksh
#!/bin/ksh
if [[ -f $1 ]]
then
  if [[ -x $1 ]]
  then
    print "$1 is an  executable file"
else
    print "$1 is a non executable
file"
fi
else
print "$1 is not a regular file"
fi
```

Output

```
$ ls -al xyz.txt
-rw-r--r--  1 root  root  20 Feb 26 15:48 xyz.txt
$ ./checkexec.ksh xyz.txt
xyz.txt is a non executable file
$ chmod 755 xyz.txt
$ ls -al xyz.txt
-rwxr-xr-x        1 root  root              20 Feb 26 15:48 xyz.txt
$ ./checkexec.ksh xyz.txt
xyz.txt is an executable file
$ ./checkexec.ksh accounts
accounts is not a regular file
```

In the aforementioned script, we see that the –f test operator checks if the filename passed through the command line argument is a regular file or not. If it is not a regular file, the else statement will be executed displaying the message the file is not a regular file. If the filename is a regular file, the –x *test* operator is used to check if it is executable or not and hence the messages are displayed accordingly.

(b) The following shell script checks several things, including whether any file exists by the name supplied as the command line argument and whether the filename supplied is a directory, a regular file, or a special file.

findfiletype.ksh

```
#!/bin/ksh
if [[ ! -e $1 ]]; then
    print "file $1 does not exist."
elif [[ -d $1 ]]; then
    print "$1 is a directory "
elif [[ -f $1 ]]; then
    print "$1 is a regular file."
else
    print "$1 is a special type of file."
fi
```

Output

```
$ ./findfiletype.ksh school.txt
school.txt is a regular file.

$ ./findfiletype.ksh accounts
accounts is a directory

$ ./findfiletype.ksh course.lst
file course.lst does not exist.
```

We can see that this script uses the -e test operator to check whether the filename supplied as command line argument exists or not. Through the test operators -d and –f, the script checks if the filename is a directory or a regular file. If the file is none of these, it is declared as a special type of file.

(c) The following shell script asks the user to enter a value between 1 and 4 and prints it in the text form. This implies that if the user enters 1, the script will display it in text, that is, *One*. If the user enters a value 2, it will be displayed as *Two*, and so on.

```
numintoword.ksh
#!/bin/ksh
print -n "Enter a value between 1 and 4: "
read n
if [[ $n -eq 1 ]]
then
    print One
elif [[ $n -eq 2 ]]
then
    print Two
elif [[ $n -eq 3 ]]
then
    print Three
else
    print Four
fi
```

Output

```
$ ./numintoword.ksh
Enter a value between 1 and 4: 1
One

$ ./numintoword.ksh
Enter a value between 1 and 4: 2
Two

$ ./numintoword.ksh
Enter a value between 1 and 4: 3
Three

$ ./numintoword.ksh
Enter a value between 1 and 4: 4
Four
```

We can see in this script that the -eq relation operator is used to check if the value entered is 1, 2, 3, or 4 and it is accordingly displayed in the text form.

When there are many conditions to check for, then instead of using the if else statement combined with many elif statements, it is always more advisable to use the case...esac statement, which is discussed in the following section.

11.14 case...esac STATEMENT

The case statement is a multi-conditional statement that helps in selecting and executing a desired block of statements out of several blocks depending on the included condition. The case statement begins with the word case and ends with the reverse, esac.

In addition to characters and integers, we can also test strings using the case statement. The string pattern may contain wild-card characters.

Syntax
```
case expression in

    pattern1 ) statements
    ;;
    pattern2 ) statements
    ;;
    * ) statements
esac
```

The expression in case statement is matched with the patterns included. The patterns can include wild cards and several patterns can be combined by using pipe characters (|). The pipe character when used for combining patterns, acts as the logical OR operator. If the expression matches any one of the patterns, its corresponding statements are executed. When several patterns are combined through pipe characters, if the expression matches any of the combined patterns, the statements following the pattern are executed. Each set of statements is terminated by double semicolons to represent the end of the block of statements. If no matching pattern is found, the statement following the * pattern that represents the default condition is executed until the double semicolons or esac is reached.

Examples

(a) The following script demonstrates the use of the case…esac statement. It prints the number entered (between 1 and 4) in words.

```
numintoword2.ksh
#!/bin/ksh
print -n "Enter a value between 1 and 4: "
read n
case $n in
  1) print "One"
  ;;
  2) print "Two"
  ;;
  3) print "Three"
  ;;
  4) print "Four"
  ;;
  *) print "The number is out of range"
  ;;
esac
```

The output of this script is the same as that of numintoword.ksh as given here.

```
$ ./numintoword2.ksh
Enter a valur between 1 and 4: 1
One
```

```
$ ./numintoword2.ksh
Enter a value between 1 and 4: 2
Two

$ ./numintoword2.ksh
Enter a value between 1 and 4: 3
Three

$ ./numintoword2.ksh
Enter a value between 1 and 4: 4
Four
$ ./numintoword2.ksh
Enter a value between 1 and 4: 5
The number is out of range
```

(b) The following shell script requests the user for the filename to delete. The provided name
is checked to see if it is a file and is then deleted after confirmation from the user.

delfile.ksh

```
#!/bin/ksh
print -n "Enter file name to delete: "
read filename
if [[ -f $filename ]]
then
    print -n "Sure want to delete this file yes/no? "
    read ans
    case $ans in
          y*) rm ${filename}
                    print "The file is deleted"
                    ;;
          n*) print "The file is not deleted"
                    ;;
          *) print "Please enter either yes or no"
    esac
else
    print "$filename is not a file"
fi
```

Output

```
$ ./delfile.ksh
Enter file name to delete: accounts
accounts is not a file

$ ./delfile.ksh
Enter file name to delete: abc.txt
Sure want to delete this file yes/no? no
The file is not deleted
```

```
$ ls abc.txt
abc.txt
$ ./delfile.ksh
Enter file name to delete: abc.txt
Sure want to delete this file yes/no? yes
The file is deleted
$ ls abc.txt
abc.txt: No such file or directory
```

The filename entered by the user is assigned to the variable *filename*. Through the -f test operator, it is checked to see whether the supplied filename is a file. When it is confirmed that the supplied name is of a file, the user is asked for confirmation to delete the file. The response from the user is assigned to the variable *ans*. The *case* statement checks the user's response. If the user has entered yes, the file is deleted and a confirmation message is displayed. If the user has entered no, the file is not deleted and the user is informed about the same. If anything else besides yes or no is entered, the following message is displayed: Please enter either yes or no.

Sometimes, we need to repeat or execute a set of statements several times. For such kinds of repetitive tasks, we make use of loops. The Korn shell provides three looping constructs, while, until, and for. Let us start with the first looping construct, the while loop.

11.15 while LOOP

The while loop is used for executing a block of statements until the included logical expression holds true.

Syntax   while [[logical expression]] ; do

statements
        done

The logical expression is evaluated and only when it returns a boolean value, true, are the statements within the while loop executed. The statements of the while loop are enclosed between the keywords, do and done.

Examples

(a) The following shell script displays all the command line arguments passed to the script.

```
demowhile.ksh
#!/bin/ksh
while [[ $# -ne 0 ]]; do
   print $1
   shift
done
```

Assume we execute the aforementioned shell script by passing the following command line arguments.

```
$ ./demowhile.ksh xyz.txt 10 4 bank.lst
xyz.txt
10
4
bank.lst
```

We can see that with every `shift` command, the positional parameter `$2` will become `$1`, `$3` will become `$2` and so on, hence printing the next successive positional parameter via the `$1` parameter.

(b) The following shell script displays the sequence of numbers from 1 to 10.

```
dispsequence.ksh
#!/bin/ksh
x=1
y=10
while [ $x -le $y ]; do
    echo $x
    ((x=x+1))
done
```

Output

```
1
2
3
4
5
6
7
8
9
10
```

The two variables x and y are initialized to values 1 and 10 respectively. A test condition is applied in the while loop to execute the loop for the time the value of variable x is less than or equal to the value of the variable y. In the while loop, the value of variable x is displayed, that is, 1. After that, the value of the variable x is incremented by 1 making it 2. Again the while loop will execute as value of variable x, that is, 2 is still less than the value of variable y, that is, 10. Thus, value 2 will be displayed on the screen following which the value of the variable x will be incremented and so on.

(c) The following shell script displays the sequence of numbers from 10 to 1.

```
seqreverse.ksh
#!/bin/ksh
n=10
while [[ $n -gt 0 ]]; do
    print "$n"
```

```
        let n=n-1
done
```

Output
```
10
9
8
7
6
5
4
3
2
1
```

The value of the variable *n* is initialized to 10. The logical expression in the while loop will make it execute while the value of the variable *n* is greater than 0. In the while loop, the value of the variable *n* is displayed, that is, 10, following which its value is decremented by 1, making it 9. Since the logical expression in the while loop is still true, the while loop will execute displaying the value of the variable *n*, 9, followed by another decrementation of its value by 1. The while loop will execute until the value of the variable *n* reduces to 0.

11.16 break: BREAKING OUT OF LOOPS

The break statement terminates a loop and exits from it.

Syntax   Break

Example   The following shell script displays numerical values from 1 to 10 using the infinite while loop. The script uses break statement to exit from the loop.

demobreak.ksh

```
#!/bin/ksh
n=1
while :
do
    print "$n"
    let n=n+1
    if [[ n -gt 10 ]]
    then
        break
    fi
done
```

Output
```
1
2
```

```
3
4
5
6
7
8
9
10
```

In this script, we can see that the variable *n* is initialized to value 1. Since there is no logical expression in the while loop, it will never terminate and is hence considered an infinite loop. In the while loop, the value of the variable *n* is displayed, that is, value 1 will appear on the screen. Thereafter, the value of the variable *n* is incremented by 1 making its value 2. In the while loop, through the if statement, the value of the variable *n* is checked to see if it is greater than 10. If the value of variable *n* is greater than 10, the break statement will terminate the while loop. If the value of the variable *n* is less than or equal to 10, the while loop will execute and display its value and then increment it by 1. The process continues until the while loop terminates through the break statement when value of the variable *n* exceeds value 10.

11.17 continue: SKIPPING STATEMENTS IN LOOPS

The continue statement skips or bypasses the body of the loop and executes the loop with the next iteration.

Syntax   continue

Examples

(a) The following shell script displays the sequence of numbers from 1 to 10 except value 7.

democontinue.ksh

```
#!/bin/ksh
n=0
while [[ $n -le 10 ]]; do
    let n=n+1
    if [[ n -eq 7 ]]
    then
            continue
    fi
    print "$n"
done
```

Output

```
1
2
3
4
5
```

```
6
8
9
10
11
```

The variable *n* is initialized to value 0. The while loop is set to execute if the value of variable *n* is less than or equal to 10. In the while loop, the value of the variable *n* is incremented by 1. In addition, the value of variable *n* is checked to determine whether it is equal to 7. When the value of the variable *n* is equal to 7, through the `continue` statement, the body of the while loop is skipped bypassing the `print` statement to execute the loop with the next iteration. Following the if statement is the print statement to display the value of the variable *n*. All the sequence numbers will be displayed from 1 to 10 except the value 7 for the simple reason that through the *continue* statement, the print statement is bypassed and the value of the variable *n* is incremented to move ahead with the next successive value.

(b) The following shell script keeps asking for a numerical value until `no` is entered. The script displays the square of the numerical value entered.

squrenum.ksh

```
#!/bin/ksh
wantmore="yes"
while [[ $wantmore == "yes" ]];  do
    print -n "Enter a value: "
    read m
    let n=m*m
    print "Entered value is $m and its square is $n"
    print -n "Want to try more yes/no: "
    read wantmore
done
```

Output

```
$ ./squarenum.ksh
Enter a value: 4
Entered value is 4 and its square is 16
Want to try more yes/no: yes
Enter a value: 9
Entered value is 9 and its square is 81
Want to try more yes/no: no
```

A string yes is assigned to a variable, `wantmore`. The while loop is set to execute if the value of the variable wantmore is yes. In the while loop the user is asked to enter a value that is assigned to the variable *m*. The entered value and its square are then displayed. The user is asked if there are more numerical values whose squares are required. If user enters yes, that will be assigned to the variable wantmore and hence result in the execution of the while loop. The user can exit from the loop by entering `no` when prompted.

11.18 until LOOP

Unlike the while loop where the block of statements execute as long as the boolean expression evaluates to true, the until loop executes as long as the logical expression evaluates to false.

Syntax   until [[logical expression]] ; do

        statements

   done

If the logical expression results in a boolean value false, the statements in the until loop that are enclosed within the do and done keywords are executed.

Examples

(a) The following shell script will display the sequence of numbers from 1 to 5.

dispsequence2.ksh

```
#!/bin/ksh
i=1
until ((i>5)); do
  print "$i"
  let i=i+1
done
```

Output

```
1
2
3
4
5
```

The value of the variable *i* is set to 1. The until loop executes as long as the included logical expression evaluates to false. The logical expression in the until loop will return true only when the value of the variable *i* becomes greater than five and hence, will only display the first five sequence of numbers on the screen.

(b) The following shell scripts keeps checking for the given user to log in to the system every 60 seconds. The script terminates only when the specified user logs in. The name of the user will be passed as a command line argument.

checklogin.ksh

```
#!/bin/ksh
until who | egrep $1; do
  sleep 60
done
```

Output

```
$ ./checklogin.ksh root
root       console       Feb 26 15:27       (:0)
root       pts/3         Feb 26 15:28       (:0.0)
```

In this example, the who command displays the list of users that are currently logged in. Until the name of the user supplied through the command line argument appears in the users list produced by the who command, the script will first wait for 60 seconds. The until loop is executed again to check if the username appears in the who command.

(c) The following script displays the square of the number entered by the user. The script keeps asking for the number and hence displays its square value until the user wishes to exit. We have already created the script using the while loop. Let us rewrite it through the until loop.

```ksh
squarenum2.ksh
#!/bin/ksh
until [[ $wantmore = "no" ]]; do
    print -n "Enter a value: "
    read m
    let n=m*m
    print "Entered value is $m and its square is $n"
    print -n "Want to try more, yes/no: "
    read wantmore
done
```

Output
```
$ ./squarenum2.ksh
Enter a value: 4
Entered value is 4 and its square is 16
Want to try more, yes/no: yes
Enter a value: 9
Entered value is 9 and its square is 81
Want to try more, yes/no: no
```

The until loop keeps executing until the value of the variable wantmore is set to *no*. The script prompts the user to enter a number and then displays it along with its square value. Thereafter, the user is prompted if he wishes to input more numerals. The choice entered by the user is assigned to the variable wantmore. The until loop will execute for any text assigned to the variable wantmore except the text 'no', which results in the termination of the until loop.

11.19 for LOOP

The for loop is used for applying a set of statements on all the elements of a given set of values. There are two formats of using the for loop. The first format is as follows:

Syntax   for variable in set_of_values

```
    do
        statements
    done
```

The variable is assigned a value from the set_of_values and the body of the loop is executed, that is, the statements enclosed within the *do* and *done* keywords are executed.

After an iteration, the second value from the set_of_values is assigned to the variable and again the statements in the body of the for loop are executed. The procedure continues until all the values in the set_of_values are assigned to the variable.

The following is the second format of using the for loop:

```
for (( [expr1]; [expr2]; [expr3] ))
do
    statements
done
```

The arithmetic expression expr1 is evaluated first. Usually it consists of initialization of a variable. The expression expr2 is always evaluated before executing the body of the loop. The expression expr2 must return a non-zero or true value for executing the statements enclosed within the do and done keywords. The arithmetic expression expr3 is evaluated after the execution of the for loop and usually results in incrementing or decrementing the variable used in the expression expr1.

Examples

(a) The following shell script displays the list of files and directories in the current directory.

listfilesdir.ksh

```
#!/bin/ksh
for i in *
do
    print $i
done
```

Output

```
bank
checkargs.ksh
checkexec.ksh
dispfiletype.ksh
interactmenu.ksh
listfilesdir.ksh
prod
```

Asterisk is a wild card that matches for zero or more of any character in a filename. Hence, all the filenames in the current directory are assigned to the variable *i* one by one. The body of the for loop will execute with every filename assignment. Using the for loop, each filename is displayed on the screen. The aforementioned shell script can also be rewritten in the following way.

listfilesdir2.ksh
```
#!/bin/ksh
for i in $(ls)
do
    print $i
done
```

Output

```
bank
checkargs.ksh
checkexec.ksh
dispfiletype.ksh
interactmenu.ksh
listfilesdir.ksh
prod
```

The ls command is executed and its output, that is, the list of files and directories will be assigned to the variable *i*. The variable *i* will be assigned the names of files and directories one by one and they will be displayed on the screen through the for loop.

(b) The following shell script prints filenames that consists of four characters.

```
filesfourchar.ksh
#!/bin/ksh
for i in ????
do
    print $1
done
```

Output

```
bank
prod
```

'?' is a wild card that matches exactly one character in a filename. Hence, all the filenames in the current directory that consist of exactly four characters are assigned to variable *i* one by one. On using the for loop, each filename assigned to variable *i* is displayed on the screen.

(c) The following script displays the words in the file letter.txt one by one.

```
dispwords.ksh
#!/bin/ksh
for k in $(cat  xyz.txt)
do
    print "$k"
done
```

Output

```
This
is
a
test
file
```

Through the cat command, the complete content of the file letter.txt will be assigned to the variable *k*, one word at a time. Each of the words assigned to the variable *k* is then displayed on the screen.

(d) The following shell script checks all the users provided in the variable userslist to see if any of them is logged in.

checklogin2.ksh

```
#!/bin/ksh
userslist="chirag root john"
for person in $userslist
do
    finger $person
    print
done
```

Output

```
Login name: chirag
Directory: /home/chirag  Shell: /bin/sh
Last login Sat Feb 25 12:47 on pts4
No unread mail
No Plan.

Login name: root          In real life: Super-User
Directory: /              Shell: /sbin/sh
On since Feb 26 15:27:53 on console from :0
Mail last read Sun Feb 26 08:17:49 2012
No Plan.

Login name: john
Directory: /home/john     Shell: /bin/sh
On since Feb 26 15:28:52 on pts/3 from :0.0
29 seconds Idle Time
```

The names of the users whose login status we need to know are stored in the variable userslist. Using the for loop, each name is fetched one at a time through the finger command, and tested to see whether the user is logged in.

(e) The following shell script displays the names of the users from the password file.

disppasswd.ksh

```
#!/bin/ksh
for username in $(cat /etc/passwd | cut -f1 -d":")
do
print $username
done
```

Output

```
root
daemon
bin
sys
```

```
adm
lp
uucp
nuucp
smmsp
listen
gdm
webservd
postgres
ravi
rahul
chirag
```

This shell script retrieves the names of the users from the passwd file by using the cut command. The passwd file is assumed to be located in the etc folder and the first field in it delimited by : (colon) consists of the usernames. These usernames are assigned to the variable *username* one by one and are then displayed on the screen.

(f) The following shell script displays the sequence of numbers from 1 to 10.

```
dispsequence3.ksh

#!/bin/ksh
for i in 1 2 3 4 5
do
    print "$i"
done
```

Output
```
1
2
3
4
5
```

We can see in the aforementioned script that a set is defined as comprising values 1, 2, 3, 4, and 5. The variable *i* will be assigned one value from the set with every iteration that also gets displayed on the screen.

(g) The following script displays the text message Hello World! five times.

```
disphello5.ksh

#!/bin/ksh
for i in {1..5}
do
    echo "Hello World"
done
```

Output
```
Hello World
Hello World
Hello World
Hello World
Hello World
```

The variable *i* in the for loop is assigned a range of sequence numbers from 1 to 5 one by one. With every new value assigned, the for loop is executed to print the text Hello World!

(h) The following script prints the sequence of numbers from 1 to 10.

dispsequence4.ksh

```
#!/bin/ksh
for i in 1 2 3 4 5
do
    print $i
done
```

Output
```
1
2
3
4
5
```

In the for loop, the variable *i* is initialized to value 1, its increment step is set to plus 1 and the logical expression is set to execute the loop as long as the value of the variable *i* is less than or equal to 10. Therefore, the for loop is set to execute 10 times by assigning values from 1 to 10 to variable *i*. In the for loop, the value of the variable *i* is displayed.

(i) The following script displays the names of the files and directories in the current directory and also indicates if it is a file or a directory.

```
dispfiletype.ksh
#!/bin/ksh
for file in $(ls);do
   if [[ -d $file ]];then
        print "$file is a directory"
   else
        print "$file is not a directory"
   fi
done
```

Output
```
checkargs.ksh is not a directory
checkexec.ksh is not a directory
```

```
checkextexec.ksh is not a directory
dispfiletype.ksh is not a directory
project is a directory
```

The ls command is executed retrieving the names of files and directories in the current directory. The retrieved list of files and directories is assigned to the variable file one by one. The filename assigned to the variable file is tested through the –d *operator* to know if it is a directory or not and a message is accordingly displayed on the screen.

(j) The following script searches for the files with extension .sh in the current directory and checks if it is executable or not. The executable shell scripts are executed one by one.

checkextexec.ksh

```
#!/bin/ksh
for i in *.ksh
do
    if [ -x $i ]; then
        ./$i
    fi
done
unset i
```

Output

The output of this script comprises the output of the execution of all the executable shell scripts in the current directory as follows.

```
$ ./checkextexec.ksh
The array elements are
15
9
12
2
6
The sum is 15
Area of rectangle is 30
Enter your Name Chirag
Sorry! You are not authorized
Hello World!
Hello World!
Hello World!
The value of x in function is 10
The value returned by the function is 15
Enter a string: education
The original string is education
The string in upper case is EDUCATION
The string in lower case is education
```

Note: The execution of this shell script will stop if any of the executed shell script contains an error.

The aforementioned code sets up a variable *i* containing the names of all the files in the current directory whose filenames ends in `.sh`. It then checks each of the files to see if it is executable. The executable file is then run in the context of the current shell using the dot command (`. $i`). After all the files in the current directory are checked, the variable *i* is unset, that is, removed from memory.

(k) The following script moves the files with extension `.1st` and `.txt` to user's *data* directory and the files with extension `.c` and `.o` to the *programs* directory. The filenames will be passed as command line arguments.

```
movefiles.ksh

#!/bin/ksh
for file in $*; do
    case $file in
            *.1st|*.txt) mv $file ${HOME}/data ;;
            *.[co]) mv $file ${HOME}/programs;;
            *) print $file not moved ;;
    esac
done
```

Output
```
$ ls /data
$ ls /programs

$ ./movefiles.ksh pqr.1st xyz.txt a.dat arearect.c
a.dat not moved
$ ls /data
pqr.1st xyz.txt
$ ls /programs
arearect.c
```

The files `pqr.1st` and `xyz.txt` will be moved to the *data* directory present in the user's home directory and the file `arearect.c` will be moved to the *programs* directory in the user's home directory. The file `a.dat` will not be moved as it does not match any of the specified patterns.

11.20 ARRAYS

An array is a variable that can store one or more values. In general, there are two kinds of arrays, one-dimensional and two-dimensional where one dimensional array consists of either rows or columns, whereas two dimensional arrays consist of both rows as well as columns. Korn shell supports one-dimensional array. The Korn shell has two types of arrays: indexed and associative.

11.20.1 Indexed Array

In an indexed array, each element of the array is indexed by a value. The lowest value of an index is 0 and the upper range is at least 4,095. It is through the help of an index that the elements in an array can be accessed randomly. To specify the maximum size of an indexed array, use the following format:

Syntax   `typeset -u variable[n] command`

Here, n is the upper bound of the array and `variable` is the name of the array.

Examples

(a) `typeset -u p[10]`

This example declares an indexed array p that can contain a maximum of 10 values.
To assign values to the array, we make use of their indexes:

```
p[0]=15
p[1]=9
p[2]=12
```

In the aforementioned examples, the values 0, 1, and 2 in square brackets are known as indexes. Indexes begin with 0 value, that is, the first value of an array is located at index 0, the second value is located at index 1, and so on. Hence, the values 15, 9, and 12 will be assigned to array p at index locations 0, 1, and 2 respectively. If we do not specify an index location while using an array, the default index location 0 is considered. Consider the following example:

```
p=25
```

This example will assign value 25 to the array at index location 0.
To assign multiple values to an array, we use the following syntax:

```
set -A array_name value1 value2 ... valuen
```

(b) `$ set -A p 15 9 12`
    `$ set -A names Ajay Manish Bharat Gunjan Omy`

The first example creates an indexed array consisting of three elements 15, 9, and 12 assigned to the index locations 0, 1, and 2 respectively. Similarly, the second example will create an indexed array consisting of five elements, Ajay, Manish, Bharat, Gunjan, and Omy, assigned to index locations 0, 1, 2, 3, and 4.

Note: We can also use an arithmetic expression for the index. The only point to remember is that it must be a positive integer, that is, it cannot be negative, nor can it have a decimal point.

Indexes are very helpful in accessing an array element randomly. To access an array element, we use the following syntax:

```
${array_name[index]}
```

The following example accesses the second value, that is, the element at index location 1 in array p.

```
$ echo ${p[1]}
```

The output will be 9.

We can also access more than one value at a time from an array, as shown in the following examples:

```
$ echo ${p[*]}
$ echo ${p[@]}
```

Both these examples will display all the elements of the array p.

Sometimes, we need to display indexes instead of elements at particular index locations. To display index locations, we use the following syntax:

Syntax   `${!array_name[index]}`

Examples

(a) `$echo ${!p[2]}`

It will display the index value 2 instead of 12, which is the value stored at index location 2 in the array p.

(b) `$echo ${!p[*]}`

(c) `$echo {!p[@]}`

These two examples will list all indexes in the array p.

Let us now take a look at the second type of arrays, associative array.

11.20.2 Associative Array

In an associative array, the index can be an arbitrary string. The indexes are usually considered keys and the array elements are considered values; hence, associative arrays are commonly termed *key/value* pairs. The *value* of any key from an associate array can be accessed by referring to it as the index in the array.

Associative arrays must be declared with typeset -A:

```
$ typeset –Ai names
```

The array *names* is declared as an associative array that can store integer values. The subscript of the associative array can be strings. We can define the following three elements for the associative array names:

```
$ names["ajay"]=10
$ names["manish"]=15
$ names["bharat"]=7
```

We can see that the first element has a key, *ajay* and its value is 10. Similarly, the second and third elements consist of keys, *manish* and *bharat* and values 15 and 7, respectively.

To assign multiple values to an associative array, we can write as follows:

```
$ names=([ajay]=10 [manish]=15 [bharat]=7)
```

The procedure for accessing elements from an associative array is the same as in an indexed array, that is, via referring to their index.

```
print "Marks of ajay is ${names[ajay])"
```

Marks of ajay is 10

The following is the command to print the entire array.

```
print ${names[@]}
10 15 7
```

Example   The following script creates an indexed array p of five elements and displays its elements through the while loop.

```
indexedarr.ksh
#! /bin/ksh
set -A p 15 9 12 2 6
echo "The array elements are "
x=0
while [ $x -lt ${#p[@]} ]; do
    echo "${p[$x]}"
    let x=x+1
done
```

Output

```
The array elements are
15
9
12
2
6
```

An indexed array p is initialized with values 15, 9, 12, 2, and 6 respectively. A variable *x* is initialized to value 0. A while loop is executed till the length of the array. In the while loop, after displaying an array element of the index location designated by variable *x*, the value of variable *x* is incremented by 1 to access the next array element in sequence.

11.21 FUNCTIONS

Functions are small modules or subprograms that are created to perform some task. A function once created can be called several times, hence helping in avoiding repetition of statements. Functions help in dividing a large shell script into small manageable chunks. Functions also increase readability of shell scripts. Similar to built-in commands, a function can be simply called by entering its name. A function must be defined before it is called, hence a function needs to be defined at the beginning of the script.

Defining functions

Functions are defined with the keyword function followed by the function name. The function name is followed by curly braces, which in turn is followed by the body of the function.

Syntax   `function function_name {`
                      `statements`
                `}`

The statements within the curly braces form the body of the function.

Examples

(a) The following script demonstrates creating and calling a function. It displays the message
`Hello World!`

`demofunc.ksh`

```
#!/bin/ksh
function disp  {
  echo "Hello World!"
}
disp
```

Output

`Hello World!`

(b) Once a function is created, it can be called several times, as shown in the following shell
    script. This script demonstrates calling a function several times in a loop. It displays the
    message `Hello World!` thrice.

`callfunc.ksh`

```
#!/bin/ksh
function disp {
  echo "Hello World!"
}
i=1
while ((i<=3))
do
  disp
  let i=i+1
done
```

Output

```
Hello World!
Hello World!
Hello World!
```

The arguments passed to a function are accessible via the standard positional parameter
mechanism.

11.21.1 return Command

The `return` command returns the flow of control from the function back to the caller. It might
also carry the value to be returned to the caller. The following is the syntax for using the
return statement:

Syntax   `return [value]`

The value returned by the return statement is assigned to the exit code, that is, the exit status is set equal to the value returned by the function. The exit code or status is then accessed from the caller via the $? variable. When return is used without an argument, the function call returns with the exit code of the last command in the function.

11.21.2 Passing Arguments to Functions

Arguments can be passed to a function while calling it. While calling a function, the function name can be followed by the argument that we want to pass to it. The arguments passed to the function are accessible inside the function through positional parameters.

Syntax   `function_name arg1 arg2...`

The arguments arg1, arg2, etc., can be accessed inside the function through positional parameters. For instance, arg1 can be accessed through positional parameter $1 and arg2 can be accessed through positional parameter $2.

Examples

(a) The following script adds two numbers by passing them as arguments to a function.
addnumfunc.ksh

```
#!/bin/ksh
function sum {
  ((sum=$1+$2))
  return $sum
}
sum 10 5
print The sum is $?
```

Output

```
The sum is 15
```

By default, the variables used in a function are global in nature, that is, any changes made to the variables inside the function will also be visible outside the function.

(b) The following script demonstrates global variables.
demoglobal.ksh

```
#!/bin/ksh
dispval() {
  print "The value of x in function is $x"
  ((x=x+5))
  return $x
}
x=2
dispval
print "The value of x outside the function is $x"
```

Output

```
The value of x in function is 2
The value of x outside the function is 7
```

The variable x in the aforementioned script is acting as a global variable. It is initialized to value 2. The value of variable x is accessed, used in the function, and displayed on the screen. The shell script displays its value as follows:

```
The value of x in function is 2
```

After displaying the value of variable x, its value is incremented by five in the function, making its value 7. On returning to the main body from the function, when we display the value of x, it prints the modified value of x:

```
The value of x outside the function is 7
```

This confirms that the value of variable x is not local to the function but is acting as a global variable.

11.21.3 Creating Local Variables

The typeset command helps in creation of local variables, that is, variables created using the typeset command is limited to the scope of the function in which it is created. The variable will not be visible outside the body of the function and will appear undefined. The variable's scope is limited to the function in which it is defined and in all the functions that are called by it.

If a variable of the same name already exists, it will resume its original value when the function returns.

Example   The following script demonstrates a local variable.

```
demolocal.ksh
#!/bin/ksh
x=2
dispval() {
  typeset x
  x=$1
  print "The value of x in function is $x"
  x=x+5
  return $x
}
dispval 10
print "The value of x outside the function is $x"
```

Output

```
The value of x in function is 10
The value of x outside the function is 2
```

The shell script defines variable x in the main body of the shell script and initializes it to value 2. The variable x in the function *dispval* is different from the variable in the main body and is a local variable to the function, that is, its scope is limited within the body of the function. The argument 10 passed to it will be assigned to the variable x in the function. On printing the value of variable x, the shell script displays its value as follows:

```
The value of x in function is 10
```

After displaying the value of variable *x*, its value is incremented by 5 in the function, making its value 15. On returning to the main body from the function, the variable *x* of the function is lost and that of the main body becomes active. On displaying the value of *x* in the main body, it prints its original value:

```
The value of x outside the function is 2
```

This confirms that the variable *x* defined in the function is local to the function and it loses its definition when it exits from the function.

11.21.4 Recursion

Recursion is a procedure when a function calls itself. In recursive functions, since a function call statement appears inside the body of the function, we need to take special care in defining the *exit* condition from the function, else the function will keep calling itself infinitely.

Examples

(a) The following shell script displays the text Hello World! three times using recursion.

```
recursion.ksh

#!/bin/ksh
function disp {
    if (($1<=0))
    then
            return
    else
            typeset x
echo "Hello World!"
            ((x=$1-1))
            disp $x
    fi
}
disp 3
```

Output
```
Hello World!
Hello World!
Hello World!
```

The function disp is called with argument 3. Argument 3 is accessed in the disp function through the positional parameter $1. The exit condition is checked to see if the value of the positional parameter is less than or equal to 0. The function is supposed to exit when the value of the positional parameter becomes 0. The text Hello World! is displayed and after every display, the value of the positional parameter $1 is decremented by 1 and assigned to the local variable *x*. Thereafter, recursive call to the *disp* function is made with the decremented value of *x* and the procedure is repeated until the value of the positional parameter reaches value 0 and the function exits.

(b) The following shell script calculates and displays the factorial of a number entered through recursive function call.

factorial.ksh

```
#!/bin/ksh
function factorial {
    if (( $1 <= 1 ))
    then
            return 1
    else
            typeset x
            typeset result
            (( x = $1 - 1 ))
            factorial $x
            (( result = $? * $1))
            return $result
    fi
}
print -n "Enter a value: "
read m
factorial $m
echo The factorial of $m is $?
```

Output

```
Enter a value: 5
The factorial of 5 is 120
```

The user is asked to enter a value whose factorial is desired and is assigned to variable *m*. The value in variable *m* is passed to the *factorial* function. In the function, two local variables, *x* and *result* are used, where the variable *x* is meant to control the execution of the function and the variable *result* is meant to store the factorial of the number. The value passed to the function is decremented by 1 and a recursive call to the *factorial* function is made with the decremented value and the procedure is repeated until the value of the positional parameter reaches 1 and the function exits by returning value 1. The factorial of the number in variable *result* is returned and displayed. We can have a list of currently available functions using the following command.

$ typeset -f

By default, a function is not available to subshells. To make it available to subshells, we need to export it using the following command.

typeset –fx function-name

To list the exported functions, we need to use the following command.

typeset -fx

We can remove function definitions by using the unset -f command.

```
$ unset -f function_name
```

We can supply multiple function names to the unset -f command.

After understanding creation and execution of functions recursively, we will now see how a script can be terminated abruptly if desired and how its return status can be observed.

11.22 exit()

The exit() function terminates a script and returns the status to the parent process. The returned status can be used in analysing the execution of a script. Basically, successful execution of a script returns a value 0, whereas an unsuccessful one returns a non-zero value, which can then be used to analyse where the error occurred. The exit function may return a value in the 0–255 range.

Example exit 0

This sets the return status of the shell to 0. This return status can be used to determine the status of an executed shell script.

Note: When a script ends with an exit that has no parameter, the exit status of the script will be set to the exit status of the last command executed in the script.

11.23 $?

It reads the exit status of the last command executed. We can also use it after a function call to ascertain the status of the execution of the function.

Example The following script compares two files and if no differences are found, removes the second file.

```
comparefiles.ksh
#!/bin/ksh
if [[ $# -ne 2 ]]; then
    print "Insufficient number of command line arguments"
    exit 1
fi
diff $1 $2 > /dev/null
if [[ $? -eq 0 ]]; then
    rm $2
    print "Both files are exactly same, hence $2 removed"
else
    print "The two files, $1 and $2 differ"
fi
```

Output

```
$ cat xyz.txt
This is a test file

$ cat abc.txt
This is a test file
```

```
$ cat pqr.txt
Hello! how are you doing?
$ ./comparefiles.ksh xyz.txt abc.txt
Both files are exactly same, hence abc.txt removed
$ cat abc.txt
cat: cannot open abc.txt
$ ./comparefiles.ksh xyz.txt pqr.txt
The two files, xyz.txt and pqr.txt differ
```

The script terminates and exits in the middle setting the exit status as 1 if the user does not provides two filenames to compare via command line arguments. If two command line arguments are supplied, through the `diff` command, it is checked to see if there is any difference between the two. The value of `$?` is checked to ascertain if the `diff` command is successful. Recall `$?` represents the exit status of the last command. If the two files are found to be exactly the same, that is, if the `diff` command is successful, its exit status will be 0. The script, on finding the value of `$?` equal to 0, will remove the second file and display a message confirming the same. If the two files differ, the exit status will not be zero and hence no file will be deleted.

11.24 INPUT/OUTPUT REDIRECTION

A program usually needs some input to perform some processing and displays some output in response. It might also display errors, if any. In other words, a program deals with three streams, standard input, standard output, and standard error:

Standard input   The default input is taken from the standard input device, that is, keyboard It is also known as stdin.

Standard output   The default output goes to the user terminal. It is also known as stdout.

Standard error   The default output goes to the user terminal. It is also known as stderr.

A file stream descriptor is assigned to each of the aforementioned standard streams. Standard input has a file descriptor of 0, standard output uses 1, and the number 2 is used by standard error. File descriptors, as we know, are the numbers that are associated with a file and help in identifying the file.

Usually, stdin gets its input from the standard input device and both stdout and stderr direct output to the terminal by default. Unix, through I/O redirection, provides us with a capability to change the location from where standard input comes or where output goes. This is to say that we can modify the default and set the input to come from a file and the output to be directed to some other file or be passed as input to another command. The I/O redirection is accomplished using redirection operators. There are two types of redirection operators:

Output redirection operator   The output redirection operator is represented by the `>` (greater than) symbol.

Syntax   `command > output_file`

It directs the output of the command to the output_file.

Input redirection operator The input redirection operator is represented by the < (less than) symbol.

Syntax `command < input_file`

It provides the input to the command from the input_file.

To designate that a file is for input, we use an input redirection operator (<). To designate that a file is for output or error, we use an output redirection operator (>). Knowing the file descriptor numbers of the standard streams and input and output redirection operators, we can represent the standard input redirection operator as 0<, the standard output redirection operator as 1>, and the standard error redirection operator as 2>.

Examples

(a) `exec 0< tmp`

Instead of from the standard input device, the input will be taken from the file `tmp`.

(b) `exec 1 > temp`

Instead of the terminal, the standard output will be sent to the file `temp`.

(c) `exec 2> tmpdata`

Instead of the terminal, the error stream will be sent to the file `tmpdata`.

(d) `$ ls > tmp`

The list of files and directories will be sent to the file `tmp`, overwriting its earlier contents.

(e) `ls > /dev/null`

The list of files and directories will not appear on the standard output and will be sent to the special file `/dev/null` also referred to as the 'bit bucket'. The `/dev/null` file discards all data written to it. It is usually used to suppress the output on the screen.

(f) `1>&3 -`

It informs the shell to redirect the output of the standard output stdout to the same place where output of the file descriptor 3 is sent.

(g) `2>&1`

It informs the shell to redirect the output of standard error 2 to the same place where output of the standard output stdout is sent.

(h) `ls > /dev/null 2>&1`

The list of files and directories is sent to the special file `/dev/null` and the 2>&1 indicates that the output of error channel 2 will also be redirected to the standard output stdout, thus no output will be sent to the terminal but instead sent to the `/dev/null` file.

(i) `ls > tmp 2>&1`

The list of files and directories is sent to the file `tmp` overwriting its earlier content and the 2>&1 indicates that the output of error channel 2 will also be redirected to the same place where standard output *stdout* is sent, that is, to the file `tmp`.

(j) To close an input file, the following command is used.

```
exec 0<&-
```

(k) To close an output file, the following command is used.

```
exec 1>&-
```

(l) To close an output file with file descriptor 3, the following command is used.

```
exec 3>&-
```

(m) To close an input file with file descriptor 3, the following command is used.

```
exec 3<&-
```

(n) The following shell script checks if the filename passed as a command line argument exists or not.

```
checkfileexist.ksh
#!/bin/ksh
ls -l $1 > /dev/null 2>&1
if [[ $? != 0 ]]; then
    print "The file, $1 does not exists"
    exit
else
    print "The file, $1 exists"
fi
```

Output

```
$ ./checkfileexist.ksh xyz.txt
The file, xyz.txt exists
$ ./checkfileexist.ksh bank.lst
The file, bank.lst does not exists
```

We can see that the ls command with its long list option (-l) is executed with the filename passed as a command line argument. The list of files and directories matching the command line argument is sent to the special file /dev/null and 2>&1, that is, output of error channel. Hence, no output will appear on the screen but will be sent to the /dev/null file. The status of $? is checked to ascertain the exit status of the last executed command. Students may recall that successful execution of a command or script returns an exit status 0, whereas an unsuccessful one returns a non-zero value. If the value of $? is 0, it means the execution of the ls command was successful and hence the filename passed as a command line argument exists in the current directory. A non-zero value in $? means the ls command was not successful and the given file does not exist.

(o) The following script demonstrates redirecting of the standard output and standard error.

```
redirect.ksh
#!/bin/ksh
ls  > tmpfile 2>&1
```

```
    if [[ $? = 0 ]]; then
        print "The list of files and directories is saved in tmpfile"
    else
        print "The redirection failed and list of files and directories is not saved
    in the tmpfile"
    fi
```

Output

```
$ ./redirect.ksh
The list of files and directories is saved in tmpfile
$ cat tmpfile
arearect.c
checkargs.ksh
checkexec.ksh
checkextexec.ksh
dispfiletype.ksh
```

The list of files and directories is sent to the file `tmpfile` overwriting its earlier content. In addition, the output of error channel 2 will also be redirected to the same place where standard output `stdout` is sent, that is, to the file `tmpfile`. By observing the status of `$?`, the script indicates whether the redirection of the list of files and directories was successful or not. It may be recalled at this point that if the last command is successful, the status of the `exit` command is 0.

(p) The following script demonstrates redirection by concatenating the content of the two files into a third file. The filenames will be passed as command line arguments.

```
concatfiles.ksh
#!/bin/ksh
if [[ (-f $1) && (-f $2) && (-r $1) && (-r $2) ]]
then
    exec 3< $1
    exec 4< $2
    exec 5> $3
else
    print "Sorry, files are not readable regular files"
    exit 2
fi
while read -u3 line; do
    print -u5 "$line"
done
while read -u4 line; do
    print -u5 "$line"
done
exec 3<&-
exec 4<&-
exec 5>&-
```

Output

```
$ cat pqr.txt
Hello! how are you doing?

$ cat xyz.txt
This is a test file

$ ./concatfiles.ksh
Sorry, files are not readable regular files

$ ./concatfiles.ksh accounts
Sorry, files are not readable regular files

$ ./concatfiles.ksh pqr.txt xyz.txt aaa.txt
$ cat aaa.txt

Hello! how are you doing?
This is a test file
```

The filenames passed as the first and second command line arguments are opened for input and the filename passed as the third command line argument is opened for output. The script first checks if the first two filenames passed as command line arguments are regular files and we have the read permission to access their content. If either of the files is not a regular file or we do not have the read permission for the same, an error message is displayed and we exit from the application setting the exit status to value 2. If the files are readable regular files, every line of the first file is read and written into the third file. After copying all the content from the first file, all the lines from the second file are read and written into the third file. Finally, the three files are closed.

This chapter focuses on understanding the Korn Shell scripting stepwise. We have seen different features of the Korn Shell programming including command line editing, file name completion, command name aliasing, and command history substitution. We got an overview of Korn shell meta characters, arithmetic operators, logical operators, and relational operators. In addition, we have seen the usage of shell variables and environment variables. We will learn to use command line arguments, if else statements, case statements, loops, and arrays. Finally, we also touched upon using functions, passing arguments to a function, returning values, local and global variables, recursion, and applying I/O redirection.

■ SUMMARY ■

1. The Korn shell or ksh is a command and scripting language created by David Korn of Bell Labs. It supports several features such as command-line editing, filename completion, command history, command aliases, and monitoring background and foreground jobs.

2. Korn shell allows us to edit command lines with editing commands similar to the two Unix editors vi and emacs.

3. In filename completion, we type some initial characters of the file and the rest of the filename is completed by the shell.

4. Command name aliasing helps rename commands and also saves a lot of keystrokes for frequently used lengthy commands.

5. Command history helps in finding out the commands we issued earlier.

6. The number of commands stored by the shell is controlled by the HISTSIZE environment variable.

7. Broadly, there are two types of variables, shell variables and environment variables. Shell variables are local variables and are visible and applicable only to the current instance of the shell, whereas environment variables are global variables and are available to all the shells.

8. The VISUAL and EDITOR variables are used to specify a default visual editor.

9. The symbol ~ (tilde) represents the user's home directory.

10. The ENV variable specifies the start-up file besides the `.profile` file.

11. The LOGNAME and USER variables represent the user's name.

12. The HOSTNAME variable is used to identify the current host.

13. The MAIL variable specifies the location of the incoming local e-mail.

14. The MAILCHECK variable specifies the time interval in which the shell will check for new mail.

15. The MAILPATH variable is used to specify the colon separated list of mailboxes.

16. The PAGER variable is used to represent the text that appears when the entire output of a command cannot be displayed on the current screen and the shell needs to indicate that there is more information to be viewed.

17. The CDPATH variable defines a list of colon-separated directories that the shell checks when a full path name is not provided in the `cd` command.

18. The PATH variable contains a list of colon separated directories to search for a file for the issued command.

19. The variable PS1 controls the appearance of the primary prompt.

20. The variable PS2 controls the appearance of the secondary prompt that is displayed when a long Unix command is split on multiple lines by pressing the Enter key in the middle of the command. The default prompt is >.

21. The PS3 prompt controls the appearance of the prompt used for selecting an option in an interactive menu created through the `select` command. The default prompt is #?.

22. The PS4 prompt defines the prompt that precedes each line of an execution trace. The default execution trace prompt is + (plus).

23. The HISTFILE variable is used to specify the path name of the file where the list of previous commands, that is, command history, is saved. By default, the history file for the Korn shell is *.sh_history*.

24. The HISTSIZE variable decides the number of commands that are kept in the history file.

25. The TERM environment variable is used for configuring the terminals.

26. A display is a virtual screen that is created by the X server on a particular host.

27. The `unset` command is used to remove a variable or function from the shell environment.

28. The first line in the Korn shell script, #!/bin/ksh, informs the shell that the script is a Korn shell script and hence has to be interpreted by the ksh interpreter.

29. A line beginning with # is treated as a comment line and hence not interpreted by the shell.

30. If the variable name is followed immediately by some other content, then for readability and clear separation, it must be enclosed in curly braces ({ }).

31. The echo statement displays messages, arguments, variables etc., terminated by a newline, to the screen. To suppress newline in the `echo` command, it must be used with -n option.

32. The `print` command is the most popularly used command in Korn shell for displaying messages and results on the screen. The output displayed via the print statement is terminated by a newline.

33. The `read` command is used for reading values from the keyboard into the shell variables.

34. The `printf` command is used for displaying formatted output. It uses format specifiers for formatting the content being displayed in the desired format.

35. The `typeset` command is used to define variables.

36. The format specifier %o and %x used in the `printf` command converts the given numbers to octal and hexa respectively.

37. The parameter $# represents the count of the number of positional parameters passed to the script; $* represents a list of all command line arguments; and $? represents the exit status of the last executed command.

38. The `shift` command shifts or renames the positional parameters $1, $2, etc.

39. The `test` command is used for checking or comparing expressions resulting in true or false values. It

includes several operators for checking properties of files, strings, and integers.

40. The `test` command can also be represented by a square bracket.

41. While using the if else statement, we can also use the *elif* clause, which is a combination of 'else if' clauses when we have more conditions to check.

42. If two commands are connected through the logical AND operator, the shell executes the second command only if the first command results in a true value. If two commands are connected through the logical OR operator, the shell executes the second command only if the first command results in a false value.

43. The `exit()` function terminates a script and returns the status to the parent process. The exit status of a successfully executed command or script is 0 and a non-zero value refers to an unsuccessful execution. The exit function may return a value in the 0–255 range.

44. Pattern-matching operators can be used to strip off or remove the desired pattern from the given variable or string.

45. String test operators can be used for comparing strings, knowing if a string is empty, of non-zero length, or contains desired characters.

46. File test operators are used for testing various attributes of a file such as whether it is a file or directory, whether it exists or not, and whether it is readable, executable, or writable.

47. The while loop is for executing a set of statements as long as the included logical expression is true.

48. The until loop executes as long as the included logical expression evaluates to false.

49. The for loop is used for applying a set of statements on all the elements of a given set of values.

50. An array is a variable that can store one or more values. Arrays are of two types, indexed and associative.

51. In an indexed array, each element of the array is indexed by a value. The lowest value of an index is 0 and the upper value is at least 4095.

52. An associative array consists of key/value pairs.

53. Functions are the small modules or subprograms that are created to perform some task.

54. The `return` command returns the flow of control from the function back to the caller.

55. While calling a function, the function name can be followed by the argument to be passed to it.

56. The arguments passed to a function are accessed through the positional parameters.

57. The `typeset` command helps in the creation of local variables of a function.

58. The value returned by the return statement is accessed through the exit status, that is, through the `$?` variable.

59. Recursion is a procedure wherein a function calls itself.

60. To make the functions available to subshells, export them using the following command:

    `typeset -fx function-name`

61. A program deals with three streams, standard input, standard output, and standard error.

62. The file descriptor for standard input is 0, standard output is 1, and that of standard error is 2.

63. To suppress the output from getting displayed on the screen, it is directed to the special file `/dev/null` also referred to as the 'bit bucket'.

■ EXERCISES ■

Objective-type Questions

State True or False

11.1 The Korn shell was developed by David Korn.

11.2 The Korn shell is not compatible with the Bourne shell.

11.3 The Korn shell does not support the feature to monitor background and foreground jobs.

11.4 Command name aliasing helps in renaming commands and saves keystrokes for lengthy commands.

11.5 The meta character ~ represents the user's current directory.

11.6 The scope of the shell variables is limited to the current instance of the shell.

11.7 A shell variable name can begin with a digit.

11.8 The environment variable PS2 controls the appearance of the prompt that appears when a long command is split by pressing the Enter key in the middle.

11.9 The ENV variable defines the path of the

.profile file.

11.10 In emacs editing mode, the key pair Ctrl-p is used to display previous commands in the command history.

11.11 The . (dot) in the command line represents the current directory.

11.12 To avoid default newline in the echo command, it is used with the -n option.

11.13 The printf command is not terminated by newline by default.

11.14 The flag - (hyphen) in the printf command right justifies the content being displayed.

11.15 We cannot declare an octal integer with the typeset command.

11.16 The positional parameter $1 represents the shell script to which the command line arguments are passed.

11.17 The ${# var } format represents the length of the variable.

11.18 The shift command, besides renaming the positional parameters, also changes the value of the $# parameter.

11.19 The values of positional parameters can be changed only using the command line arguments.

11.20 If the two commands are connected through the logical AND operator, the shell executes the second command only if the first command

results in a false value.

11.21 The exit function may return a value in the 0–255 range.

11.22 The test operator –z is used to check whether a zero length string is entered.

11.23 We cannot use wild-card characters in the pattern of case statements.

11.24 The while loop executes as long as the included logical expression evaluates to true.

11.25 The break statement terminates the application.

11.26 The continue statement skips the body of the loop and begins with the next iteration.

11.27 Similar to the while loop, the until loop also executes as long as the included logical expression evaluates to true.

11.28 The for loop is used for applying a set of statements on all the elements of a given set of values.

11.29 In an indexed array, the lowest index value is 1.

11.30 An index in an associative array can be a string.

11.31 Functions help in dividing a large application into small modules, hence making it manageable.

11.32 The arguments passed to a function are accessed through positional parameters.

11.33 A function cannot return a value.

11.34 The typeset command can be used to define read only variables.

11.35 A function can make a recursive call to itself.

Fill in the Blanks

11.1 The Korn shell was developed at _____.

11.2 The feature that helps in recalling and reusing previously given commands is known as _____.

11.3 Korn shell allow us to edit command lines with editing commands similar to the Unix editors, _____ and _____.

11.4 The vi editor operates in two main modes, _____ and _____.

11.5 The _____ variable is used to set the history size.

11.6 The shell variables are also known as _____.

11.7 To make the shell variables accessible to subshells, we need to _____ them.

11.8 The two environment variables used for defining the default editor are _____ and _____.

11.9 The _____ environment variable defines

a list of directories that the shell checks when the full path name is not given in the cd command.

11.10 The PS4 variable is for changing the _____ prompt.

11.11 The first line of the Korn shell script must be _____ to inform the shell that the script needs to be interpreted by the ksh interpreter.

11.12 The data that is passed to the shell script while executing it through command line is known as _____.

11.13 The exit status of the last executed command or script is represented by _____.

11.14 To check if the file is readable, the _____ option is used with the test command.

11.15 A script that is successfully executed, returns a value _____, and _____ value in case of any failure.

11.16 The _____ clause indicates the end of an

if else statement.

11.17 If in a script, branching is required, then instead of using several if else statements, it is better to use the _____ command.

11.18 A block of statements in a case statement is terminated by _____.

11.19 The default pattern in a case statement is represented by _____.

11.20 The file test operator to know if the file is an executable file is _____.

11.21 The statement _____ is used to terminate and exit from a loop.

11.22 The _____ loop is commonly used for applying a set of statements on all elements of a given set of values.

11.23 Arrays are of two types: _____ and _____.

11.24 Associative arrays are declared by the _____ command.

11.25 _____ statement is used to return from the function back to the caller.

11.26 The value returned from a function is accessed through _____.

11.27 A program deals with three streams, _____, _____, and _____.

11.28 The file descriptor for standard input is _____, standard output is _____, and standard error is _____.

Programming Exercises

11.1 Write the commands to do the following:
   (a) Convert a number of base 10 to a number of base 8
   (b) Convert a string to lower case
   (c) Print all the command line arguments passed to the shell script
   (d) Set the length of the history list to 50 lines
   (e) Check if the string str is of non-zero length
   (f) Check if the file by name filename exists or not

11.2 What will the following commands do?
   (a) `$ set -o emacs`
   (b) `printf "%-20s \n" str`

   (c) `$ typeset -i8 value`
   (d) `typeset -l str`
   (e) `print "${#str}"`

11.3 Write the commands to do the following:
   (a) Create an indexed array of five elements
   (b) Display all the elements in the array p
   (c) Send the list of files and directories to a special file /dev/null
   (d) Redirect the output of standard error 2 to the same place where output of the standard output stdout is sent
   (e) Close an output file

Review Questions

11.1 Write short notes on the following:
   (a) Command name aliasing
   (b) DISPLAY environment variable
   (c) MAILPATH variable
   (d) Meta characters
   (e) Command line editing

11.2 Explain the filename completion feature in detail.

11.3 How can the PS3 variable be used to change the prompt of an interactive menu? Explain with an example.

11.4 What are shell variables? How are they set and unset? Is there any way to make them global? If yes, how?

11.5 Explain the following commands with syntax and examples:
   (a) typeset
   (b) if else

   (c) case
   (d) printf
   (e) exit

11.6 Write Korn shell scripts for the following:
   (a) Ask the user to enter his/her name, address, and e-mail address and display the entered information
   (b) Concatenate two strings and convert it into upper case
   (c) Print the average of three numerical values passed as command line arguments
   (d) Enter a string and a pattern and display the string after removing the given pattern from it
   (e) Display the names of all the executable files in the current directory
   (f) Ask the user to enter two numerical values and print their addition, subtraction, multi-

plication, and division depending on the users' choice. The user may enter character a, s, m, or d to indicate whether he/she wishes to view addition, subtraction, multiplication, or division. Use the case statement for this script.

11.7 Explain variable substitution in detail.

11.8 How is data passed to a shell script using command line arguments?

11.9 What is the impact of `shift` and `set` commands on the positional parameters? Explain.

11.10 Explain different string and file test operators with examples.

11.11 Explain the following with syntax and examples:
(a) while   (c) for   (e) exit
(b) until   (d) indexed array

11.12 Write Korn shell scripts for the following:
(a) Print the table of 9 up till 90
(b) Print the sequence of numbers between the two entered values
(c) Print the average of the values: 18, 2, 91, 25, and 10
(d) Print the names of all readable files in the current directory
(e) Print the sum of three values passed to a function named addo

11.13 Explain recursion in detail with an example.

11.14 What is I/O redirection? Explain.

11.15 How is an associate array different from an indexed array?

11.16 How are arguments passed to a function and how is a value returned by it?

Brain Teasers

11.1 The following code is not displaying the value of the tenth command line argument. Correct the code.
```
echo "The 10th argument is : $10"
```

11.2 The following code is not deleting the first two characters of the supplied string. Find the error.
```
print "${str%??}"
```

11.3 The following code for displaying the supplied command line arguments is not working. Correct the code.
```
#!/bin/ksh
while [[ $@ -ne 0 ]]; do
print $1
shift -1
done
```

11.4 Find the error in the following code for ascertaining if the supplied argument is a readable directory.
```
#!/bin/ksh
if [[ -e $1 ]]
then
    if [[ -g $1 ]]
    then
        print "$1 is a readable directory"
    fi
fi
```

11.5 Correct the following code for printing the sequence of numbers from 1 to 10.
```
#!/bin/ksh
```

```
i=1
until ((i<=10)); do
    print "i"
    (( i=i+1))
done
```

11.6 Correct the error in the following code for counting the number of files and directories in the current directory.
```
#!/bin/ksh
n=0
for i in cat ls
do
    [[n=n+1]]
done
print $n
```

11.7 Find the error in the following code for displaying the elements of an array in reverse order.
```
#! /bin/ksh
set -A p 10 3 8 1 5
echo "The array elements in reverse order are "
let x=${p[@]} -1
while [ $x -ge 0 ]; do
    echo "{p[x]}"
    let x=x-1
done
```

11.8 The following code for displaying the text Hello World thrice does not work. Find the error.
```
#!/bin/ksh
```

```
for i in [1..3]
do
    print "Hello World"
did
```

11.9 I wish to send a list of files and directories to a file `tmp.lst` and also to the output of the standard error channel. Find the error in the following code for doing so.

```
ls > tmp.lst 3>&2
```

11.10 Correct the following program that computes multiplication of two values through a function.

```
#!/bin/ksh
function mult {
    ((x=$1*$2))
    return x
}
multiply 2 6
print The multiplication is $*
```

■ **ANSWERS TO OBJECTIVE-TYPE QUESTIONS** ■

State True or False

11.1	True
11.2	False
11.3	False
11.4	True
11.5	False
11.6	True
11.7	False
11.8	True
11.9	False
11.10	True
11.11	True
11.12	True
11.13	True
11.14	False
11.15	False
11.16	False
11.17	True
11.18	True
11.19	False
11.20	False
11.21	True
11.22	True
11.23	False
11.24	True
11.25	False
11.26	True
11.27	False
11.28	True
11.29	False
11.30	True
11.31	True
11.32	True
11.33	False
11.34	True
11.35	True

Fill in the Blanks

11.1	Bell Labs
11.2	Command history
11.3	vi, emacs
11.4	command mode, insert mode
11.5	HISTSIZE
11.6	local variables
11.7	export
11.8	EDITOR, VISUAL
11.9	CDPATH
11.10	execution trace
11.11	#!/bin/ksh
11.12	command line arguments
11.13	$?
11.14	-r
11.15	0, non-zero
11.16	fi
11.17	case
11.18	;;
11.19	*)
11.20	-x
11.21	break
11.22	for
11.23	Indexed array, Associative Array
11.24	typeset -A
11.25	return
11.26	$?
11.27	standard input, standard output, and standard error
11.28	0, 1, 2

C Shell
Programming

After studying this chapter, the reader will be conversant with the following:

- C shell and its different features
- Using command history to retrieve commands from the history file
- Command substitution and filename substitution (globbing)
- Filename completion and aliases
- Job control, running jobs in background, and suspending, resuming, and killing jobs
- Environment variables, shell variables, and built-in shell variables
- Customizing the shell
- Using C shell operators
- Understanding, creating, and running simple C shell scripts
- Different flow control statements in C shell scripts
- Loops, arrays, and display errors

12.1 C SHELL

The C shell is a shell developed by Bill Joy at the University of California at Berkeley. Bill Joy is also the author of the vi text editor. It uses C programming language as a syntax model and has powerful interactive features.

12.1.1 Features

The most important features of the C shell include the commands, constructs, and arrays, which are syntactically similar to C language. You may recall that the Unix system is written in C language, so the C shell's first objective was to provide a C-like platform to the users. The following are the other major features provided by the C shell:

Command history   Allows the user to recall and reuse previously given commands.

Command substitution   Substitutes the output of the command at the place of command.

Filename substitution—Globbing Searches and replaces the pattern consisting of wild-card characters with the file(s) matching the given pattern.

Filename completion Displays and suggests the complete name(s) of the files on the basis of the initial characters typed by us.

Aliases Helps in assigning shortcuts to long and frequently used commands, renaming commands, and assigning user defined names for a sequence of commands.

Job control Helps in monitoring background and foreground jobs.

We will discuss the aforementioned features in detail in the subsequent sections.

12.1.2 Command History

In the command history feature, the list of commands implemented in the C shell is saved for future use. The commands can be retrieved from the history either fully or partially. By retrieving commands from the history, we can recall the commands we had given earlier and also reuse them without typing them again.

Syntax `history [ -r ] [-h]`

The `-r` option is used to print history lines in reverse order, from the most recent to the oldest.

The `-h` option prints history lines without line numbers.

To display all the lines that are stored in the history, simply use the history command without any option:

`%history`

We will get a list of commands in the history list preceded by a line number.

The number of lines stored in the history list is determined by the amount of memory available to the shell. We can also specify the number of lines that we want stored in the history of the start-up file `.cshrc` (which will be discussed in Section 12.2.1). The following command is an example:

`set history=80`

This command will enable the C shell to store 80 commands.

Retrieving commands from history

In order to retrieve commands from the history list, the exclamation point (!) character, also known as the 'bang operator', is used. We can be more specific in retrieving the desired previous command by giving the line numbers or text patterns with the bang character.

Note: The exclamation point will be treated as the bang operator, that is, the history-substitution character even if it is quoted. We must precede it with \ (backslash) to remove its special meaning.

The bang operator can be used in two formats, `!!` and `!number`. The `!!` symbol is replaced with the previous command line. The `!n` symbol is replaced with the command in the history list represented by the line number `n`. The different formats for referring to command history are given in Table 12.1.

Table 12.1 List of formats used to refer to previous commands in the command history

Format	Replaced with
!!	The last command in the history
!n	The command represented by the specified line number n in the command history.
!-n	The command with the line number n from the most recent command
!string	The last command that begins with `string`
!?string?	The last command that contains `string` anywhere in the command line

Examples

(a) !!

This retrieves the last command.

(b) !8

This retrieves command number 8 from the history list.

(c) !-4

This retrieves the fourth most recent command.

(d) !cd

This retrieves the last command that begins with the letters `cd`.

A colon (:) is used to create a new command from the previous command. Each argument in the command is referenced through its position. The command name itself is numbered zero. The list of expressions used in selecting arguments from the command history is given in Table 12.2.

Table 12.2 List of argument selectors from the command history

Expression	Specification
0	First word of the command, that is, the command name
n	The nth argument of the command, 0 refers to the command name and its arguments are numbered from 1
^	First argument of the command
$	Last argument of the command
%	Argument matching the specified string
m-n	Substitutes arguments from m through n of the history line
m-	Argument from the mth location till the second last argument
-n	The first argument of the history line through to the nth argument, it is the same as 0-n
M*	Arguments beginning with the mth word through to the last argument of the line, it is the same as m-$
*	All arguments of the command line

Examples

(a) !:3

This recalls the third argument from the last command.

(b) `!:*`

This recalls all the arguments from the last command.

(c) `md !10:2`

This performs an `md` on the second argument from the command number 10.

(d) `md !10:$`

This performs an `md` on the last item from the command number 10.

(e) `!cd:^`

This retrieves the first argument of the last command that started with `cd`.

(f) `!cd:1`

This is same as the preceding example. It retrieves the first argument of the last command that started with `cd`.

(g) `!cd:$`

This retrieves the last argument of the last command that started with `cd`.

(h) `!$`

This retrieves the last argument of the last command.

12.1.3 Command Substitution

Command substitution implies that the output of the command is substituted in the place of the command. To be substituted, the command has to be enclosed in ` ` `. The output from such a command is split into separate words at the occurrence of blanks, tabs, and newlines. The output then replaces the command.

Example   `d=`date``

The variable `d` is assigned the output of the `date` command. The `date` command, as we know, displays the current system date as follows:

`Sat and the year is 2011`

Wherever the variable `d` is used in the script, it will be replaced with the system date as shown here.

12.1.4 Filename Substitution—Globbing

As the name suggests, filename substitution refers to the process of finding the file(s) beginning with the characters typed by us. The characters typed by the user will be replaced by the file name matching the typed characters. The procedure of filename substitution is also known as *globbing*. For filename substitution, the characters or the words that we type must contain any of the following characters: *, ?, [, {, -, or ~. The word carrying any of the said characters will then be used for retrieving an alphabetically sorted list of filenames that match its characters.

We will now discuss the role of characters *, ?, -, or ~ in finding a given file.

1. The character * matches any string of characters, including the null string.
2. The character ? matches any single character.
3. A pair of characters separated by a hyphen (-) matches any character between the two (inclusive).

4. The character ~ at the beginning of a filename refers to home directories. The user's home directory is substituted in the place of ~.

> **Note:** The character ~ will only be replaced by the home directory of the user if it appears at the beginning of the word and is followed by a character or /; it will otherwise be treated as a simple symbol.

Examples

(a) `ls a{b,c,d}e`

This statement will show the filenames that consist of three characters and which begin and end with characters a and e respectively (e.g., abe ace ade).

(b) `ls *.txt`

This statement will show the list of filenames that have the extension .tx.

(c) `ls [abc]*`

This statement will show the list of filenames that begin with a, b, or c.

(d) `ls [a-d]*`

This statement will show the list of filenames that begin with any character from a to d.

(e) `ls a???.txt`

This statement will show the list of filenames that consist of four characters and which begin with character a and have the extension .txt.

(f) `cd ~john`

This statement will change the directory to the home directory of the user, john, that is, to /usr/john directory.

(g) `ls ~john/progs/{try1,try2 try3}.c`

This statement will display the files /usr/john/progs/try1.c, /usr/john/progs/try2.c, and /usr/john/try3.c.

To turn off the filename substitution feature, set the noglob variable through the following command.

`set noglob`

12.1.5 Filename Completion

As the name suggests, filename completion means that the shell will guide the user by displaying or completing the filename on the basis of the initial characters typed. It can also suggest expected filenames by searching the directory that matches the initial characters typed by the user.

To turn on filename completion, we need to set the C shell variable, filec, through the following command:

`set filec`

We have to add this command in the C shell start-up file .cshrc.

To complete a file or directory name, we only need to type few of its starting characters and press the Esc key. On pressing the Esc key, the shell completes the filename if it is uniquely identified or stops with a beep sound after typing a few characters, asking the user to type a few more characters to distinguish the file. In this case, we need to type a few more characters and press the Esc key again to initiate file completion.

In order to list all the possible filenames or directories on the basis of the typed characters, press Ctrl-d. The directories will appear with the trailing / character.

Examples

Let us assume that our current directory contains the following files and directories.

```
project.txt progs/ program1.c programs2.c
```

Observe the following file completion commands:

(a) `%ls prEsc`

This command will display `pro` and then the terminal will beep as there are multiple matches beginning with the word `pro`.

(b) `%ls projEsc`

It will uniquely identify and display the filename `project.txt`.

(c) `ls prog^D`

It will display the files and directories that begin with the word `prog`.

(d) `progs/ program1.c programs2.c`

For making the task of typing long commands easier, the C shell supports the concept of aliases, which is discussed in the next section.

12.1.6 Aliases

Aliases can be used to rename the existing commands, create a short cut for longer commands and define new commands that may be a combination of a sequence of commands. The syntax for creating an alias is as follows:

Syntax   `alias name text`

The name will become the alias of the command(s) represented by `text`. Now, whenever we use this `name`, the C shell will replace it with the sequence of commands specified in the `text`.

Examples

(a) `alias pri printenv`

In this example, `pri` will act as an alias of the `printenv` command. Now if we type `pri` on the command line, it will be replaced by the `printenv` command before executing.

(b) `alias h history -r`

This statement will declare letter `h` as an alias of the `history -r` command. Hence, `h` will be replaced by the `history -r` command before being executed.

(c) To view all current aliases, just write alias on the command line without any argument:

`alias`

(d) To remove a previously defined alias, specify its name in the `unalias` command:

`unalias alias_name`

C shell also supports the feature of job control. For example, we can suspend and resume jobs, switch background jobs to foreground and vice versa, and kill jobs. We will now learn about this feature in detail.

12.1.7 Job Control

The C shell supports a job control feature that allows us to do the following tasks:

1. Run processes in the background
2. Bring background jobs to the foreground when required
3. Suspend current jobs
4. Resume suspended jobs
5. Kill jobs

A process can be set to execute in the background by following its command with an ampersand (&) symbol.

Syntax   `command&`

Therefore, any command can be set to run in the background by suffixing an ampersand (&) symbol to the command.

On executing a job in the background, its information appears on the screen, which may be as follows:

```
$ lp a.txt&
[3] 20971
```

This statement indicates that the `print` command is placed in the background, and its job ID is 3 and process ID is 20971. To bring a job to the foreground, the `fg` command is used. Similarly, in order to bring the aforementioned background job with ID 3 to the foreground, we use the following command:

```
fg 3
```

> **Note:** The jobs that do not require terminal input and have no time constraints can be run in the background.

We can also suspend or stop a running job by pressing ^z, which sends a *STOP* signal to the current job. The suspended jobs do not execute but they consume system memory. The suspended job can be put in the background with the `bg` command or can be resumed in the foreground with the `fg` command. To get the list of jobs, we give the command `jobs` without any argument, as follows:

```
jobs -l
```

This command displays the list of jobs along with their IDs. We can use the job IDs to control specific jobs. For referring to a job, the `%` character is used. The following examples will make things more clear.

Examples

(a) `%1`

This brings the job with ID 1 to the foreground.

(b) `%1 &`

This takes the job with ID 1 to the background.

(c) `%+` or `%%`

This refers to the current job.

(d) %-

This refers to the previous job.

Syntax   To terminate a job, we can use the Ctrl-c interrupt or the `kill` command with the following syntax:

```
kill job_id
```

Example   The following statement is an example.

```
kill 3
```

This will terminate the job with ID 3.

The `kill` command can also be used to suspend a background job with the following syntax:

Syntax   `kill - STOP job_id`

The following statement is an example:

Example   `kill -STOP 3`

This will suspend the background job with ID 3.

The summary of all the aforementioned commands used in controlling jobs is given in Table 12.3.

Table 12.3   Summary of commands used to control jobs

Command	Function
`bg [job_id]`	Executes a job with a given ID in the background (default is current job)
`fg [job_id]`	Executes a job of the given ID in the foreground
`kill [signal] [job_id]`	Terminates a process or sends a signal where the signal usually used is the STOP signal
`jobs [-l]`	Lists the foreground and background jobs with their process IDs
`Ctrl-c`	Terminates the foreground job
`Ctrl-z`	Suspends the foreground job

After looking at the features of the C shell, we will discuss the different start-up files that the C shell uses when invoked.

12.2 START-UP FILES

When we log in to a Unix system, if we get the per cent sign (%) as the command line prompt, then our logon shell is the C shell. If we do not get the % sign prompt, it implies that our logon shell is either the Bourne shell or Korn shell. We can interactively invoke the C shell from the command line by using the following command:

```
$ csh
%
```

The C shell executes three files, .cshrc, .login, and .logout, which are located in the user's home directory and indicated by the HOME environment variable. These files can be used for customizing the C shell environment. Let us learn about the files in detail.

12.2.1 .cshrc File

The .cshrc file is executed every time one of the following occurs:

1. The C shell is invoked
2. We log in to the system
3. A C shell script is executed
4. A new process is forked

It is executed before the .login file and contains instructions to define or customize the C shell environment. We can use this file to set variables and parameters that are local to a shell. The instructions that are commonly stored in this file include directory paths, shell variables, and aliases.

The following is a sample .cshrc file:

```
#!/bin/csh
# Sample .cshrc file
set history=50
set savehist=50
set ignoreeof noclobber
if ($?prompt) then
   set prompt=$user ">"
endif
alias h history
alias lo logout
```

The .cshrc file declares to store or remember 50 lines of history, that is, previous commands and also declares to save 50 commands in a login session. Besides this, it will prevent the user from logging out of the shell on pressing Ctrl-d by accident. The file also defines the primary shell prompt as well as h and lo as alias (shortcuts) for the commands history and logout respectively.

12.2.2 .login File

The .login file is executed when we log in to the system. The .login file is read only once when we log in and hence contains the commands that we want to execute only once, that is, at the beginning of each session. The file usually contains instructions to set up terminal settings and environment variables.

The following is a sample .login file:

```
#!/bin/csh
# Sample .login file
stty erase ^H intr ^C susp ^Z quit ^\\
echo "You are Welcome"
```

This .login file displays a welcome message to the user. Besides this, the file also configures the terminal through the stty command. The stty command assigns some functions to certain keys pairs as follows:

1. Ctrl-h key pairs will be used to delete or erase the previous character.
2. Ctrl-c key pairs will be used to interrupt the current job.
3. Ctrl-z key pairs will be used to suspend or pause the current job.
4. Ctrl-\ key pairs will used to terminate the current job.

12.2.3 .logout File

The .logout file contains commands that are run when the user logs out of the system. Usually, it contains the commands that we wish to execute before the user exits.

Example   The following sample .logout file indicates that the user has logged out of the system and displays the current system date.

```
#!/bin/csh
echo -n "Logged out of the system "
date
```

In the preceding start-up files, we observed that different variables are defined and set in order to configure or customize the shell. Let us learn about these variables in detail.

12.3 VARIABLES

Variables are used for holding and passing information. In this section, we will discuss the several types of variables such as environment variables, shell variables, and built-in shell variables that play a major role in configuring a shell and have a great impact on its working. Let us begin with environment variables.

12.3.1 Environment Variables

Environment variables are variables that are defined in our start-up files to inform the shell about our environment. Whenever we start a new shell, these variables are passed to the invoked shell. In addition, these variables are passed to all processes that are run from the current shell and hence these variables are also known as *global variables*. The environment variables have a great impact on the working of a shell. For example, an environment variable, PATH, specifies the list of directories where the shell can find the executable programs. Now, when the user types a command, the shell searches through the directories listed in the PATH environment variable for the executable program that matches the command typed by the user. The command will not execute if the shell is unable to find the executable program of the command in the directories listed in the PATH environment variable. The environment variables usually appear in upper case. Some of the most commonly used environment variables are shown in Table 12.4.

Table 12.4 List of a few environment variables

Environment variable	Description
PATH	This is a list of directories in which the shell searches for commands and programs. If a program is in a directory that is not in the path, the shell will not be able to find it.
EDITOR	This variable is used to decide the editor the user wishes to use.
SHELL	This variable displays the name of the shell.
HOME	This variable points to the user's home directory.
TERM	This variable informs us of the type of the user's terminal. The C shell uses the terminal definitions given in the termcap file. Typical terminal types are vt100 or xterm.
TERMCAP	This variable specifies the file containing terminal definitions.
DISPLAY	This environment variable is set while using an X device and is used to keep track of the display the graphics should be created on.
PRINTER	This variable defines the name of the default printer.

To change or assign a value to an environment variable, we use the following syntax:

Syntax `setenv environment_variable value`

Example `setenv TERM vt100`

Note: The setenv command does not use the = operator.

The changes will remain in effect until we log out or invoke a new shell. To change an environment variable permanently, we need to define it in the file .cshrc. The changes will come into effect the next time we log in or invoke an instance of the shell. To make the changes come into effect immediately, we give the following command:

`source .cshrc`

To append a value at the end of an environment variable, we use the following syntax:

Syntax `setenv VARIABLE ${VARIABLE}:value_to_append`

This will append the value, value_to_append, to the end of the current value of the variable.
  To remove an environment variable, we use the unsetenv command.

Examples

(a) To remove the environment variable, TERM, we can use the following command.

```
% unsetenv TERM
```

(b) To display the list of all currently set environment variables, the printenv command is used.

```
% printenv
HOME=/home/john
```

```
SHELL=/bin/csh
PATH=(/home/john/bin /bin /usr/bin /usr/local/bin)
USER=john
TERM=vt100
EDITOR=emacs
```

This list of currently set environment variables gives information about the home directory, shell, path directories, username, terminal, and default editor of the user.

12.3.2 Shell Variables

Unlike environment variables, shell variables are local variables as they contain values that are visible and applicable only to the current instance of the shell. In other words, the scope of shell variables is limited to the current instance of the shell. The C shell automatically sets values to a few shell variables such as argv, cwd, home, path, prompt, shell, status, term, and user. The shell variables usually appear in lower case. The list of pre-defined shell variables is given in Table 12.5.

Table 12.5   List of predefined shell variables

Predefined variable	Description
argv	The list of arguments passed to the current command is assigned to it.
cwd	It contains the full path name of the current directory.
home	It is the home directory of the user, initialized from the HOME environment variable.
path	It is the list of directories that the shell is supposed to search in, for the commands to execute. It is initialized from the PATH environment variable.
prompt	It is a string that represents the shell prompt for an interactive input. The default prompt for the C shell is %.
shell	The path name of the shell program currently in use is assigned to it. The default path name for the C shell is /bin/csh.
status	The exit status of the last command is assigned to this variable. Usually, successful commands return value 0, and failure or unsuccessful commands return a value of 1.
term	The name of the terminal type is assigned to it. It gets a value from the TERM environment variable. The default value is /etc/ttytype.
user	The login name of the user is assigned to it. It gets a value from the USER environment variable

Note: When a C shell is started, it will set the value of shell variables (home, path, term, and user) same as the environment variables (HOME, PATH, TERM, and USER).

12.3.3 Built-in Shell Variables

Besides the aforementioned predefined shell variables, there are several built-in shell variables that have special functions. The list of the built-in shell variables that have special meanings is shown in Table 12.6.

Table 12.6 List of built-in shell variables

Variables	Description
autologout	Contains the number of minutes the shell can be idle before it automatically logs out
Cdpath	Specifies a list of directories to be searched by the chdir or cd command to find subdirectories
Echo	When set, causes each command and its arguments to echo before it is executed
history	Sets the number of lines of history (previous commands) to be remembered
histchars	Changes the history substitution characters, '!' and '^'
ignoreeof	Prevents logging out of the shell with Ctrl-d
mail	Specifies the files where the shell checks for mail
noglob	Avoids filename expansion
notify	When set, the shell sends asynchronous notification of changes in the job status
noclobber	Prevents overwriting of files when using redirection
savehist	Defines the number of history commands to save from one login session to the next
time	If set, displays the statistical lines showing the resources used by the command that takes more than the specified CPU time in execution
verbose	Causes the words of each command to display after history substitution

A list of the current shell variables using the set command is as follows:

```
% set
```

We may get the following output.

```
argv()
ignoreof
history 40
home /home/john
path (/home/john/bin /bin /usr/bin /usr/local/bin)
noclobber
shell /bin/csh
```

This list of shell variables, besides displaying the information of home, path, and shell of the user, also informs that the command line argument's array is currently empty, accidental logging out of the shell by pressing Ctrl-d is not allowed, 40 lines will be stored in the history to remember, and the existing files will not be overwritten while using redirection.

To assign value to a shell variable, the set command is used.

Syntax	set shell_variable=value

Example	set history=50

This example will set the history to store 50 lines.

12.3.4 Unsetting Variable

To delete or unset a shell variable, we use the unset command.

Syntax   % unset variable_name

The unset command completely removes the variable from memory. The command to remove the shell variable, history, which we just created, is as follows:

% unset history

We will now see the practical aspects of the variables that we discussed here. Let us use some of these variables to customize the shell as per our requirement.

12.4 CUSTOMIZING SHELLS

In Section 12.3, we learnt about the different types of variables and their usages. Now we will learn about the various roles (e.g., how they can be used in changing the appearance of a primary prompt, changing the special characters used in retrieving previous commands from history, and defining the location of mailbox files) played by the three variables, that is, prompt, histchars, and mail variables, in the working of a shell.

12.4.1 Setting Primary Prompt

We can set the appearance of the primary prompt using the set command. We can make the user's name, time, current working directory, history number, etc., appear in the primary prompt. The list of different symbols that we can use to customize the primary prompt is shown in Table 12.7.

Table 12.7   List of symbols used in customizing primary prompt

Symbol	Displays
$cwd	Current working directory
$cwd:t	Current working directory with the user's home directory represented by '~'
'uname -n'	Full host name
`hostname -s`	Host name up to the first '.'
%B or %b	Start/Stop boldfacing mode
%U or %u	Start/Stop underline mode
`whoami`	Username
%h	Current history number
%t	Time of day in the 12-hour system, hh:mm a.m./p.m.
%T	Time of day in the 24-hour system, hh:mm
%p	Time of day in the 12-hour system with seconds hh:mm:ss a.m./p.m.
%P	Time of day in the 24-hour system with seconds hh:mm:ss
%D	The day in two digits, 'dd' format
%w	The month in three character format, 'Jan'
%W	The month in two digits, 'nn' format
%y	The year in two digits, 'yy' format
%Y	The year in four digits, 'yyyy' format
%d	The weekday in three characters, 'Mon' format

We can use these symbols to get the desired information to appear in the primary prompt. Let us look at the following examples.

Examples

(a) `set prompt="${cwd} >"`

It sets the prompt to the current working directory.

`/usr/john>`

(b) `set prompt = $user " > "`

It sets the prompt to the user's name.

`john>`

(c) `set prompt = "\! $user > "`

It sets the prompt to the number of the current history event followed by the user's name and > character.

`209john>`

12.4.2 Changing History Characters

We have already discussed in Section 12.1.2 that while retrieving previously issued commands from the command history, special characters, such as ! (exclamation point) and ^ (caret), are commonly used. By using the `histchars` variable, we can replace or change these two special history characters, ! and ^ with any characters of our choice that do not have special meaning or the ones that are not frequently used. The syntax for replacing the two characters is as follows:

Syntax   `set histchars="char1char2"`

Here, `char1` replaces the ! character and `char2` replaces the ^ character.

Example   `% set histchars='@#'`

Using this statement, the history characters are changed. This implies that while accessing the `history` command, in the place of ! and ^, we will now use @ and # respectively. It also means that instead of using the `!!` command that was earlier used for accessing the last command from the history, we need to now use the `@@` command. Similarly, instead of using the command `!:^`, which was earlier used to retrieve the first argument of the last command, we now need to use the `@:#` command.

12.4.3 Setting `mail` Variable

The `mail` variable is used to inform the shell about the file to check for incoming mail.

Syntax   `set mail = (time_interval file_to_check)`

This syntax will make the shell check `file_to_check` periodically for mails in the specified `time_interval`. If `time_interval` is not specified, a default of five minutes is considered.

Examples

(a) In the following file, we set the `mail` variable.

```
set mail=(/usr/spool/mail/john)
```

By assigning this file to the `mail` variable, we are asking the shell to check this file after five minutes to see if any mail has arrived there. The shell will notify us in case any new mail arrives in the file. We can also change the time interval for checking the mail from five minutes to any desired time. The following example does the same.

(b) `set mail=(60 /usr/spool/mail/john)`

This statement asks the shell to check the mailbox of the user, `john`, every 60 seconds. It is to be remembered that if the first word of the value of the `mail` variable is a numeric, it specifies a time interval in seconds for the shell. If we specify multiple mail files, the shell displays the message along with the name of the file where the mail has arrived.

Sending mail

Let us quickly take a look at the command that is used to send mail. To send mail to a user, we use the `mail` program. The following is the syntax for sending mail:

```
mail username_to_receive_mail
message...
message...
EOT
```

Example   `mail john`

```
This is a test for checking if the mail
program is working
EOT
```

The first line, `mail john` will execute the mail program that is used to send messages. Here, `john` is the argument that indicates the name of the user to whom the mail is to be sent. Thereafter, we can type the message or text that we want to send to the user, `john`. We end the message with ^D, which sends an end of file marker to the mail program. On receiving the ^D command, the mail program echoes the characters EOT and transmits our message to the specified user.

Before we begin with the creation of C shell scripts, it is essential to have basic knowledge of C shell operators. Hence, let us take a quick look at the different C shell operators.

12.5 C SHELL OPERATORS

Almost all basic expressions in a shell script require the usage of arithmetical operators. The arithmetical operators include not only the basic addition, subtraction, multiplication, and division operators but much more. A list of different arithmetical operators is shown in Table 12.8.

Table 12.8 List of arithmetical operators

Operator	Description	Operator	Description
( )	Grouping and changing precedence	-	Subtract
		<<	Left shift
~	Complement of 1	>>	Right shift
*	Multiply	&	Bitwise 'AND'
/	Divide	^	Bitwise 'exclusive OR'
%	Modulo	|	Bitwise 'inclusive OR'
+	Add		

Examples

The following examples will help in understanding the purpose of these operators better.

(a) `@c=$a+$b`

This adds the values of variables a and b and assigns the addition to variable c.

(b) `@d=($a+$b) * $c`

This adds the values of variables a and b and the total is multiplied with the value of variable c and finally the result is stored in variable d. It is because of the parentheses that addition operator is performed before multiplication.

(c) `@c=$a % 5`

This applies the modulo operator to the value of variable a. Modulo operation here divides the value of variable a by five and the remainder will be stored in variable c.

(d) `@d=$a<<1`

This left shifts the value in variable a by 1 bit. Every left shift operation multiplies the value by two and a right shift divides the value by 2. Hence, the value in variable a is multiplied by two and the result is assigned to variable d.

(e) `@e=$a&$b`

The bitwise AND operation is applied on the bits of values of variables a and b and the result is stored in variable e. While using bitwise operators, the operation is applied on the bit structure of the number. In a bitwise AND operation, the resulting bit is 1, only when both the bits being compared are 1.

(f) `@f=$a^$b`

The bitwise exclusive OR operation is applied on the values of variables a and b and the result is assigned to variable f. In a bitwise OR (exclusive) operation, the resulting bit is set to 1 only when either of the bits being compared is 1. This implies that it will result in 0 if both the compared bits are 1.

(g) `@g=$a|$b`

The bitwise inclusive OR operation is applied to the values of variables a and b, and the result is assigned to variable g. In a bitwise OR (inclusive) operation, the resulting bit is set to 1 when either or both the bits being compared are 1.

After arithmetical operators, let us take a look at the assignment operators. The assignment operators include the operators that perform certain operations on the data before being assigned to the specific variable. Table 12.9 provides a list of assignment operators.

Table 12.9 List of assignment operators

Operator	Description
++	Increments
--	Decrements
=	Assigns
*=	Multiplies the left side value by the right side value and updates the left side
/=	Divides the left side value by the right side value and updates the left side
+=	Adds the left side value to the right side value and updates the left side
-=	Subtracts the left side value from the right side value and updates the left side

Table 12.10 List of comparison operators

Operator	Meaning
==	Equal to
!=	Not equal
>	Greater than
<	Less than
>=	Greater or equal to
<=	Less than or equal to
!	Logical NOT
&&	Logical AND
||	Logical OR

The following examples will make the concept of these assignment operators more clear.

(a) @a++

The value in variable a will be incremented by 1.

(b) @b=$a

The value in variable a will be assigned to variable b.

(c) @c+=$a

The values in variables c and a will be added and the sum will be stored in variable c.

(d) @c/=$a

The value in variable c will be divided by the value in variable a and the result will be stored in variable c.

Whether it is a logical expression in a loop or a criterion in a branching statement, conditional operators are used in almost all logical expressions. Table 12.10 shows the list of comparison operators.

Examples

The following examples will help us understand the purpose of the preceding operators in a better way.

(a) ($a==5)

This returns true if the value in variable a is equal to 5

(b) ($a !=5)

This returns true if the value in variable a is not equal to 5

(c) ($a <=10)

This returns true if the value in variable a is less than or equal to 10

(d) (!$a==5)

The result of the logical expression is reversed. This implies that if the value in variable a is equal to 5, then the resulting Boolean value that is *true* will be reversed to *false* and vice versa.

(e) ($a > 2 && $b < 1)

Since the two logical expressions are connected through the logical AND operator, the combination evaluates to true only when both the individual logical expressions are *true*, that is, when variable a is greater than 2 and variable b is less than 1.

Now, we will discuss how to create and execute some C shell scripts.

12.6 WRITING AND EXECUTING FIRST C SHELL SCRIPT

We can use any editor to write a C shell script. We will now create a file by the name removearg.csh and type the following content in it:

```
removearg.csh
#!/bin/csh
rm $argv[1]
```

The first line, `#!/bin/csh`, specifies that the shell to be executed is the C shell, csh. The second line removes the file whose name is passed through the command line argument. Assume that the aforementioned shell script is executed as follows:

```
% removearg.csh inventory.txt
```

The script will delete the filename assigned to the `$argv[1]` array. The script name removearg. csh will be assigned to `$argv[0]` and the filename inventory.txt will be assigned to the `$argv[1]` array. The file inventory.txt is hence deleted.

We can execute C shell scripts using the source command. This command makes the C shell read commands from a file.

| Syntax | `source scriptname` |

When debugging C shell scripts, it is best to use the csh command.

| Syntax | `csh -x scriptname` |

The `-x` option sets the echo variable so that commands are echoed to standard error.

In the aforementioned shell script, we have used command line arguments. The command line arguments and related variables are treated as special shell variables. Table 12.11 shows the list of special shell variables.

Table 12.11 List of special shell variables

Variable	Meaning
${0}	The name of the script being run
$?variable_name	Returns true if the variable name is defined and otherwise returns false
$n	The value of the nth positional parameter passed to the script
$argv[n]	The value of the nth argument passed to the script
$#argv	The number of arguments passed to the script
$argv[*]	All the arguments supplied to the script
$argv[x-y]	The arguments from x to y passed to the script, that is, the arguments in the argv array between index locations, x and y are returned
$$	Process identification number of the current process

Let us understand these special shell variables through a running example.

Example   Let us create another shell script by the name `commandargs.csh` and write the following code to demonstrate how command line arguments are passed and accessed in a C shell script.

commandargs.csh

```
#! /bin/csh
echo "The script name is: ${0}"
echo "Number of arguments are: $#argv"
echo "First argument is $argv[1] and second argument is $argv[2]"
echo "All of the arguments are: $argv[*]"
echo "Second and third arguments are: $argv [2-3]"
echo "All arguments except the first are: $argv[2-$#argv]"
```

Let us pass the following command line arguments to the preceding shell while executing it.

```
$ ./commandargs.csh xyz.txt 10 4 bank.lst
The script name is: ./commandargs.csh
Numberv of arguments are: 4
First argument is xyz.txt and second argument is 10
All of the argument are: xyz.txt 10 4 bank. lst
Second and third arguments are: 10 4
All arguments except the first are: 10 4 bank.Lst
```

The command line arguments `xyz.txt`, `10`, `4`, and `bank.lst` will be assigned to the command line argument array, `argv`, and will be stored at index locations `argv[1]`, `argv[2]`, `argv[3]`, and `argv[4]` respectively.

We can see that the predefined shell variable, `argv`, plays a major role in passing data to the shell script. The C shell borrowed the concept of using the `argv` array from the C programming language. The name of the shell script is assigned to the element `argv[0]`. The element `$argv[1]` is equivalent to `$1`, that is, the first positional parameter that is assigned the value of the command line argument that follows immediately after the name of the shell script. The second and the following command line arguments are assigned to the elements `argv[2]`, `argv[3]`, etc. The first *echo* statement in the aforementioned script displays the script name `commandargs.csh`. The second *echo* statement displays the count or the number of command line arguments passed to the script. Since four command line arguments are passed to the script, the echo statement displays value 4. The third echo statement displays the values in the elements `argv[1]` and `argv[2]` of the command line arguments array, hence `xyz.txt` and `10` are displayed. The fourth echo statement displays all the command line arguments passed to the script. The fifth echo statement displays the second and third command line arguments and the last echo statement displays all the command line arguments except the first command line argument.

We observed in the preceding two scripts that only one command is written in a single line. However, we can also write more than one command in a single line as discussed in the following section.

Writing multiple commands on lines Usually, the shell assumes a single command on a line considering the first word in the line to be the command name and the following words as arguments to that command. To write multiple commands on a single line, we use a semicolon (;) at the end of the command. On finding a semicolon (;), the shell interprets the word following it as a new command, with the rest of the words as arguments to the new command.

For example, the following command line is basically three commands in one line:

```
@x=10; echo "Hello World!"; set name="Ajay"
```

What happens if we come across a command that is too long to fit in a single line? In such a case, we split the command as discussed in the following section.

Splitting commands in more than one line The shell usually assumes the end of command on finding a newline character. In order to continue a long command onto the new line, we need to escape the newline character. On ending a line with a backslash (\), the newline character is escaped and the shell does not interpret it as the end of the command.

Besides using command line arguments, data can also be passed to the shell script by interactively asking the user for the same.

For creating interactive shell scripts, we need to add the statement that enables users to enter data so that the shell scripts take action on the basis of the entered data. Hence, the next thing is to understand how to read data from the user.

12.6.1 Reading Data

For reading data from the keyboard and assigning it to a variable(s), we initialize it to hold the special parameter $<. The parameter $< prompts the user to enter some data. The entered data is then assigned to the desired variable.

Syntax   `set variable_name = $<`

The data typed by the user up till the Enter key is assigned to `variable_name`.

Examples

(a) `set filename = $<`

Using this statement, everything typed by the user will be assigned to the variable `filename` till the Enter key is pressed. In other words, $< substitutes a line from the standard input device—the keyboard.

(b) The following shell script asks the user to enter a filename. The entered filename is then displayed.

```
readinput.csh
#!/bin/csh
echo -n "Enter a file name: "
set filename = $<
echo The file name entered is $filename
```

Output

```
Enter a file name: xyz.txt
The file name entered is xyz.txt
```

The option -n that is used with the echo command suppresses the newline character so that the next output or input occurs on the line of the output of the previous echo command.

The aforementioned shell script asks the user to enter a filename that is assigned to the variable filename, which is then displayed on the screen. A shell variable used in a command is prefixed with a dollar sign ($). $ tells the command interpreter that the user wants the variable's value and not its name. We can also use curly braces ${filename} if the variable is immediately followed by some text. The curly braces help in separating variable from the attached text, if any.

filename used in the aforementioned shell script is a user defined shell variable. We will now learn more about user defined shell variables.

12.6.2 User-defined Shell Variables

We have discussed predefined shell and built-in shell variables that play a major role in the working of a shell. Now we will discuss the variables used to hold data and results in shell scripts. These variables are called user defined variables.

The commands for defining and removing shell variables is the same for all types—the set command is used to define variables and the unset command to delete variables. To define a new variable or modify the value of an existing variable, we use the following syntax:

Syntax   `set variable_name=value`

Here, variable_name is the name of the variable that can be up to 20 letters or digits long and can include underscores but not begin with a number. value is the data that we want to assign to the variable.

Example   `set str="Hello World!"`

Using this statement, a string variable, str, is initialized to the string Hello World!
To initialize integer variables, we use the following syntax:

Syntax   `@ variable=value`

Example   `@1=10`

Note: There must be a space between the @ command and the variable name. We can see that for integers, the declaration begins with the @ character instead of set.

To assign a null value to a variable, don't assign any value to it.

`set area`

This example will assign a null value to the variable area.

To assign a list of values to the variable, enclose them in parentheses.

`set variable_name=(value1 value2 value3)`

Example   `set studentnames = (Ajay Omy Manish Bharat)`

This example will assign the strings Ajay, Omy, Manish, and Bharat to the variable studentnames. Now, studentnames is not a simple variable but an array. To assign value to the nth word in the variable, we use the index to specify the location as shown in the following syntax:

Syntax   `set variable_name[n]=value`

Example   To assign a string, Gunjan, to the second index location in the array studentnames, the following command is used.

`set studentnames[2]="Gunjan"`

The set command issued without arguments will display all the shell variables.

To prepend a value to an existing shell variable, we use the following syntax:

Syntax   `set name=prepend_value${name}`

Example   `set new_list=Sanjay${studentnames}`

This example will prepend the string, Sanjay, to the existing strings in the studentnames array and assign them to the array new_list.

A similar syntax can be used to append a value to an existing shell variable.

Syntax   `set name=${name}append_value`

Example   `set new_list=${studentnames}Puneet`

This example will append the string, Puneet, to the existing strings in the studentnames array and assign them to the array new_list.

To find the length of a variable, that is, to find the number of characters in a string or the numbers of words or numerals in an array, the following syntax is used:

Syntax   `$#variable_name`

This syntax will return zero if the variable is assigned a null value and an error if the variable is not set.

Examples

(a) `str="Hello"`
    `echo $#str`
    This example will display the length of the string, str, that is, it will display value 5:
(b) `echo $#studentnames`
    This example displays the count of the elements in the array, studentnames.
(c) The following shell script demonstrates the assignment of strings and numerical to different variables.
    `demovariables.csh`

    ```
    #!/bin/csh
    set firstfile=xyz.txt
    set secondfile=uvw.txt
    ```

```
cp $firstfile $secondfile
@ length = 8
@ breadth = 5
@ area =  $length * $breadth
echo Area of rectangle is $area
unset $area
```

Output
```
Area of rectangle is 40
```

The two filenames, xyz.txt and uvw.txt, are assigned to the two variables, firstfile and secondfile, respectively and a copy of the file xyz.txt is made in the name uvw.txt. Similarly, numerical values, 8 and 5, are assigned to the two variables, length and breadth respectively and their values are multiplied and stored in the area variable, which is then displayed. Finally, the variable area is removed from memory through the unset command.

(d) The following shell demonstrates how to perform floating point operations in C shell.

floatoperat.csh

```
#!/bin/csh
set a = 1234.56
set b = 99.99
set c = `echo $a + $b | bc`
set d = `echo $a \* $b | bc`
echo Sum of floating point numbers is $c
echo Multiplication of floating point numbers is $d
```

Output
```
Sum of floating point numbers is 1334.55
Multiplication of floating point numbers is 123443.65
```

C shell cannot do floating point arithmetic; hence the bc calculator program is used in the shell script to perform floating point arithmetic. We can see that two floating point values are assigned to the two variables, a and b, respectively. The two values are added and multiplied using the bc calculator, assigned to the two variables c and d respectively, and hence displayed.

The C shell does not provide a way to read multiple values in a single command.

(e) The following shell script allows the user to enter two values simultaneously. The two values are then separated through the cut command.

readmultiple.csh
```
#!/bin/csh
printf "Enter two values "
set numbers = "$<"
@ a = `echo "$numbers" | cut -f1 -d " "`
@ b = `echo "$numbers" | cut -f2 -d " "`
@ sum = $a + $b
echo The two numbers are $a and $b and their sum is $sum
```

Output

```
Enter two values 10 20
The two numbers are 10 and 20 and their sum is 30
```

The two values entered by the user are assigned to the variable numbers. Assume that the user entered two values, 10 20, which will be assigned to this variable. On the basis of the space delimiter, the two values are cut or separated and assigned to the variables, a and b, respectively. The two values and their sum are then displayed.

Usually, the script executes statements in sequence, but sometimes we need to control this sequence of flow on the basis of certain conditions. We will now learn about the different flow control statements used in shell scripting.

12.7 FLOW CONTROLLING STATEMENTS

The C shell supports changing the flow of the script conditionally, that is, on the basis of certain conditions, the script can be set to execute a desired set of statements. The if-then-else statement is one of the commands that is popularly used in directing the flow of the script.

12.7.1 if-then-else Statements

The if-then-else statement is used in conditional branching, that is, we can make it execute a set of statements out of two depending on the validity of the logical expression included. The syntax for using the if-then-else statement is as follows:

```
if (logical expression) then
    statements
[else if (logical expression) then
    statements ]
[else
    statements]
endif
```

The logical expression in parentheses is evaluated, returning a Boolean value, true (1) or false (1). The statements in the *if* block will be executed when the logical expression evaluates to true, otherwise the statements in the optional *else* block will be executed. An if-else statement is terminated by the endif keyword.

While dealing with files, we need to know their attributes, such as whether it is a file or directory, if it exists or not, and whether it has desired permissions. To know file attributes, file testing operators are used. Let us understand how they are used.

File testing operators

C shell provides several test operators to know the status of a file. The complete list of file testing operators used to test the different attributes of the files is shown in Table 12.12.

Table 12.12 List of file testing operators

Operator	Returns true if
-d	File is a directory
-e	File exists
-f	File is a plain file
-o	User owns file
-r	User has read permission
-w	User has write permission
-x	User has execute permission
-z	File has a length of zero

Examples

(a) The following script checks if the filename supplied as a command line argument exists or not. If the file exists, it is deleted.

```
checkexist.csh
#!/bin/csh
if ( -e $argv[1] ) then
rm $1
endif
```

Output
```
$ ls -l xyz.txt
-rw-r--r--   1 root  root    20 Mar 10 22:33 xyz.txt
```

```
$ ./checkexist.csh
Subscript out of range
$ ./checkexist.csh xyz.txt

$ ls -l xyz.txt
xyz.txt: No such file or directory
```

-e is one of the file operators that checks if the file exists. If the file exists, it is deleted using the rm command.

(b) The following shell script deletes the two files whose names are supplied as command line arguments.

```
delfiles.csh
#!/bin/csh
if ( -e $argv[1] && -e $argv[2]) then
    rm $argv[1]  $argv[2]
endif
```

Output
```
$ ls x*.txt
x.txt    xyz.txt
$ ./delfiles.csh
Subscript out of range
$ ./delfiles.csh abc.txt
Subscript out of range
$ ./delfiles.csh x.txt abc.txt

$ ls x*.txt
x.txt    xyz.txt
$ ./delfiles.csh x. txt xyz.txt

$ ls x*.txt
x*.txt: No such file or directory
```

Through the -e file operators, it is checked if both the files exist. They are deleted only if both the files exist. Assume that the two filenames that are supplied through command line arguments to the shell script are x.txt and xyz.txt. Now, only if both the files, x.txt and xyz.txt, exist, will the two files be deleted, otherwise nothing will happen.

The only limitation that we might observe in the aforementioned shell script is that if either file exists, nothing will happen and the script simply terminates without any message to the user. What if we want the user to be informed that no action has taken place as neither of the files exist? Let us modify the script to inform the user.

delfiles2.csh

```
#!/bin/csh
if ( -e $argv[1] && -e $argv[2]) then
    rm $argv[1]  $argv[2]
    echo "Both files, argv[1] and argv[2] are deleted"
else
    echo "Either of the file does not exists, no file will be deleted
endif
```

Output

```
$ ls x*.txt
x.txt xyz.txt

$ ./delfiles2.csh
Subscript out of range

$ ./delfiles2.csh x.txt abc.txt
Either of the file does not exists, no file will be deleted

$ ls x*.txt
x.txt xyz.txt

$ ./delfiles2.csh x.txt xyz.txt
Both files, x.txt and xyz.txt are deleted

$ ls x*.txt
x*.txt: No such file or directory
```

In the aforementioned shell script, if both the filenames passed through command line arguments exist, then the if block of the if else statement will be executed deleting both the files. If either of the files does not exist, the else block of the if else statement does not delete any file and simply displays the message Either of the files does not exist, no file will be deleted.

After executing a command, it is quite natural that we become curious to know whether it was successfully executed or not. To know the status of the last command or script we make use of the $? variable. Let us learn more about this.

$? Variable

It reads the exit status of the last command executed. We can also use it after a function call to know the status of the execution of the function. It returns 0 if the last command or script was successfully executed and otherwise returns a non-zero value.

Examples

(a) The following shell script checks if the given text exists in the given file. Both the text and filename will be supplied through command line arguments.

checkpattern.csh

```csh
#!/bin/csh
if ( { grep $argv[1]  $argv[2] } ) then
    echo The text, $argv[1] found in the file, $argv[2]
else
    echo The text, $argv[1] not found in the file, $argv[2]
endif
```

Output

```
$ cat school.txt
101     Anil       75
102     Chirag     82
103     Kanika     70
104     Naman      88
105     Suman      68
106     John       83

$ ./checkpattern.csh Chirag school.txt
102     Chirag     82
The text, Chirag found in the file, school.txt

$ ./checkpattern.csh Sanjay school.txt
The text, Sanjay not found in the file, school.txt
```

In the output, we first check if the word Chirag exists in the file school.txt. The script uses the grep command to find out if the text Chirag appears in the file school.txt. After the grep command, its exit status, that is, $? is tested. You may recall that if the last command is successful, its exit status, that is, $? is 0, otherwise it is non-zero. Through the if else statement, the exit status is checked and if it is 0 implying that the text, Chirag, is found in the given file school.txt, a message informing the same is displayed. If the exit status is non-zero, it implies that the text, Chirag does not exist in the school.txt file and hence a message informing the same is displayed.

(b) In the following script, we implement a validity check to see if the user has supplied the command line arguments or not.

checkargs.csh

```csh
#!/bin/csh
if ( $#argv == 0 ) then
    echo No file name passed as command line argument
else  if ( -e $argv[1] && -e $argv[2]) then
    rm $argv[1]  $argv[2]
endif
```

Output

```
$ ls *.txt
pqr.txt xyz.txt
$ ./checkargs.csh
No file name passed as command line argument
Subscript out of range
$ ./checkargs.csh xyz.txt pqr.txt
$ ls *.txt
*.txt: No such file or directory
```

$#argv counts the number of command line arguments passed to the shell script and its value is 0 if no command line argument is passed to the shell script. The shell script checks if the value of $#argv parameter is equal to 0 in which case, a message, No file name passed as command line argument, is displayed on the screen. The script checks if both the files exist through the -e operators. Only if both the files exist are the two files deleted.

(c) The following scripts take action on the basis of the number of command line arguments passed to the shell script. If two or more command line arguments are passed, the second command line argument will be displayed. If one command line argument is passed, it is displayed and if no command line argument is passed, a message, No command line argument supplied, is displayed.

dispargs.csh

```
#!/bin/csh
if ( $#argv >= 2 ) then
    echo $argv[2]
else if ( $#argv == 1 ) then
    echo $argv[1]
else
    echo No command line argument supplied
endif
```

Output

```
$ ./dispargs.csh
No command line argument supplied
$ ./dispargs.csh school.txt
school.txt
$ ./dispargs.csh school.txt 10
10
$ ./dispargs.csh school.txt 10 bank.lst
10
```

(d) The following script makes a copy of a file. Both the source and target filenames will be provided as command line arguments to the shell script. Before applying the copy command, cp, the shell script performs some validations.

```
copyfile.csh
#!/bin/csh
if ( ! -e $argv[1] ) then
    echo The source file, $1 file does not exists
else
    if ( -e $argv[2] ) then
        echo A file by name $2 already exists
    else
        cp $argv[1]  $argv[2]
    endif
endif
```

Output

```
$ ./copyfile.csh
Subscript out of range
$ ./copyfile.csh abc.txt
The source file, abc.txt file does not exists
$ ./copyfile.csh xyz.txt pqr.txt
A file by name pqr.txt already exists
$ ./copyfile.csh xyz.txt uvw.txt
$ cat xyz.txt
This is a test file
$ cat uvw.txt
This is a test file
```

The aforementioned shell script first checks if the source file whose copy is to be made exists or not. If not, an error message source file does not exist is displayed. Thereafter the shell script checks whether the target file, that is, the file to be created through the copy command, exists. If a file already exists in the target filename, again an error message is displayed stating the file already exists by this name. In the case where the two errors do not occur, a copy of the source file is made in the target filename.

(e) The following shell script demonstrates string comparison. The user is asked to enter either yes or no. On entering yes, the list of files and directories is displayed.

```
stringcompare.csh
#!/bin/csh
echo -n "Want to see list of files and directories yes/no? "
set ans = $<
if ($ans == "yes") then
    ls
endif
```

Output

```
$ ./stringcompare.csh
Want to see list of files and directories yes/no? no
```

```
$ ./stringcompare.csh
Want to see list of files and directories yes/no? yes
addext.csh              checkexistoutput.png    delfiledir.csh
addextoutput.png        convlower.csh.          delfilediroutput.png
BANK.TXT                convloweroutput.png     fileslower.csh
```

(f) The aforementioned shell script will display the list of files and directories when the user enters yes but will not display anything if the user enters the string no. Let us modify the script to inform the user that he has responded by entering no.

```
stringcompare2.csh
#!/bin/csh
echo -n "Want to see list of files and directories yes/no? "
set ans = $<
if ($ans == "yes") then
  ls
else
  echo "You have entered No"
endif
```

Output

```
$ ./stringcompare2.csh
Want to see list of files and directories yes/no? no
You have entered No
$ ./stringcompare2.csh
Want to see list of files and directories yes/no? yes
addext.csh              checkexistoutput.png    delfiledir.csh
addextoutput.png        convlower.csh.          delfilediroutput.png
BANK.TXT                convloweroutput.png     fileslower.csh
```

(g) The only limitation that we can see in the preceding script is that even when the user enters something other than yes or no, the output of the script will be You have entered No. The preceding script can be made more precise as given here.

```
stringcompare3.csh
#!/bin/csh
echo -n "Want to see list of files and directories yes/no? "
set ans = $<
if ($ans == "yes") then
  ls
else if ($ans == "no") then
  echo "You have entered No"
  else
    echo "You have entered something other than yes or no"
endif
```

Output

```
$ ./stringcompare3.csh
Want to see list of files and directories yes/no? no
You have entered No

$ ./stringcompare3.csh
Want to see list of files and directories yes/no? y
You have entered something other than yes or no

$ ./stringcompare3.csh
Want to see list of files and directories yes/no? yes
addext.csh              checkexistoutput.png    delfiledir.csh
addextoutput.png        convlower.csh.          delfstrediroutput.png
BANK.TXT                convloweroutput.png     fileslower.csh
```

We can see that the response entered by the user is assigned to variable ans. If the variable, ans, is assigned *yes*, then the ls command is executed to display the names of files and directories in the current directory. If the variable, ans, is not assigned the text, *yes*, then the *else if* statement checks if it is assigned *no*. If the ans variable contains *no*, then the message You have entered no is displayed. In case the ans variable is assigned neither *yes* nor *no*, a message, You have entered something other than yes or no is displayed.

(h) The following shell script moves the filename entered by the user to a directory named projects. The directory projects does not exist and is created by the shell script.

movefiles.csh

```
#!/bin/csh
echo -n "Enter a file name "
set filename = $<
if (-e $filename) then
    if (! -d ~/projects) then
        mkdir ~/projects
    endif
    mv $filename ~/projects
else
    echo The file $filename does not exist
    exit
endif
```

Output

```
$ ls xyz.txt
xyz.txt
$ ls /projects
/projects: No such file or directory

$ ./movefiles.csh
Enter a file name bank.lst
The file bank.lst does not exist
```

```
$ ./movefiles.csh
Enter a file name xyz.txt
$ ls xyz.txt
xyz.txt: No such file or directory
$ ls /projects
xyz.txt
```

The filename entered by the user is assigned to filename. Through the -e operator, a test is carried out to check if a file in that name exists. If no file exists by that name, an error message stating filename does not exist is displayed. Once it is confirmed that a file exists in the given filename, the shell scripts test if the projects directory exists or not. If the projects directory does not exist, it is created and finally the file is moved into that directory.

(i) The following shell script demonstrates the use of the *if else* statements in performing several types of conditional branching. The script asks the user to enter a student name and displays its marks. For instance, if the name entered is *ajay*, its assumed marks is displayed. Similarly, the marks of other studentnames are also displayed.

demoifelse.csh

```
#!/bin/csh
echo -n "Enter a name: "
set name = $<
if ( $name == "ajay" ) then
    echo Marks of $name is 50
else if ( $name == "manish" ) then
    echo Marks of $name is 70
else if ( $name == "omy" ) then
    echo Marks of $name is 80
else
    echo Marks of $name is 85
endif
```

Output

```
$ ./demoifelse.csh
Enter a name: ajay
Marks of ajay is 50
$ ./demoifelse.csh
Enter a name: manish
Marks of manish is 70
$ ./demoifelse.csh
Enter a name: omy
Marks of omy is 80
$ ./demoifelse.csh
Enter a name: bharat
Marks of bharat is 85
```

The script asks the user to enter the name of the student, which is assigned to the variable, `name`. Thereafter string comparison is done to see if the entered name is `ajay`, `manish`, `omy`, or something else and the corresponding marks of the name is displayed.

Can we jump to any desired statement in a shell script? Yes, C shell supports branching to any statement using the `goto` statement.

12.7.2 Branching with goto

In general, commands in a shell script are executed one after another in succession. Using the `goto` command, we can change the flow of the program in a desired manner.

Syntax   `goto label`

The shell will search for the statement that begins with the specified label followed by a colon (:). On finding the given label, the execution resumes with the statement following the label. If the given label is not found, then an error message is displayed followed by the termination of the script.

Examples

(a) The following shell script displays the sequence of numbers from 1 to 10.

dispsequence.csh

```
#!/bin/csh
@ count = 1
dispvalue:
echo $count
@ count++
if ($count <=10) goto dispvalue
```

Output

```
1
2
3
4
5
6
7
8
9
10
```

A variable, `count`, is initialized to value 1. The value of this variable is displayed, printing 1 on the screen. The value of the `count` variable is then incremented by 1 followed by comparing it with the final value 10. If the value of the `count` variable is less than 10, a branch or jump will take place at the top in the script where the label `dispvalue` occurs, hence displaying the incremented value of the variable. This is followed by another increment of the value of the variable. In other words, the script will keep branching or jumping to the top statement in the script, repeatedly executing the statements in between until the value of this variable exceeds the value 10.

(b) The following shell script asks the user to enter a number and prints the message indicating whether the entered number is *even* or *odd*. The script will continue to execute a desired number of times.

evenodd.csh

```
#!/bin/csh
morevalue:
echo -n "Enter a number: "
set n = $<
if ($n % 2 == 0) then
    echo "The number is even"
else
    echo "The number is odd"
endif
echo -n "More numerical yes/no? "
set ans = $<
if ($ans == "yes") goto morevalue
```

Output

```
$ ./evenodd.csh
Enter a number: 20
The number is even
More numerical yes/no? yes
Enter a number: 5
The number is odd
More numerical yes/no? yes
Enter a number: 10
The number is even
More numerical yes/no? no
```

The user is prompted to enter a value, which is assigned to the variable n. The mod operator is applied to the value in this variable and the resulting remainder is tested. The modulo 2 operation results in 0 for even values and 1 for odd values. Hence, an appropriate message indicating whether the entered number is even or odd is displayed, depending on the result of the *mod* operation. The user is then asked if there are more numerals to be tested. If the user enters *yes*, the script will branch or jump to the top where the label, *morevalue* occurs, hence repeating the procedure of asking another numerical value and testing it for even or odd. The script continues to execute until the user enters *no*.

(c) The following shell script asks the user to enter a number between 1 and 4 and prints it in words. The user is asked to re-enter a value if a value outside the range is entered.

numinwords.csh
#!/bin/csh

```
entervalue:
echo -n "Enter a number between 1 and 4: "
set numb = $<
if ($numb == 1) then
    echo "One"
else if ($numb == 2) then
    echo "Two"
else if ($numb == 3) then
    echo "Three"
else if ($numb == 4) then
    echo "Four"
else
    echo "Invalid value. Please try again"
    goto entervalue
endif
```

Output

```
$ ./numinwords.csh
Enter a number between 1 and 4: 2
Two

$ ./numinwords.csh
Enter a number between 1 and 4: 4
Four
$ ./numinwords.csh
Enter a number between 1 and 4: 9
Invalid value. Please try again
Enter a number between 1 and 4: 5
Invalid value. Please try again
Enter a number between 1 and 4: 1
One
```

The value entered by the user is assigned to the variable numb. Through the series of checks via the if else statement, the value in this variable is tested and accordingly its value in text form is displayed. If the value in the variable does not fall within the range 1–4, the script will branch or jump to the top of the label, entervalue, asking the user to re-enter a value within the range 1–4. The script will keep jumping to the top and asking the user for a new value until a value within the range is entered.

The exit status of the script or the last command is heavily used for determining whether their execution was a success or a failure. Let us learn more about the exit command.

12.7.3 exit Command

The exit command terminates a script and returns the status to the parent process. The returned status can be used in analysing the execution of a script. Successful execution of a script returns a value 0, whereas an unsuccessful one returns a non-zero value. This can then be used to analyse and debug the script. The exit command may return a value in the 0–255 range.

Syntax   `exit [n]`

Here, n is the exit status returned to the parent process.

Examples

(a) `exit 0`

The aforementioned command sets the return status of the shell to 0. This return status can be used to determine the status of an executed shell script.

Note: When a script ends with an exit that has no parameter, the exit status of the script will be set to the exit status of the last command executed in the script.

(b) The following script asks the user to enter a number and checks if the entered number is even or odd and hence sets the exit status accordingly.

evenodd2.csh

```
#!/bin/csh
echo -n "Enter a number: "
set n = $<
if ( $n % 2 == 0) then
   exit 1
else
   exit 2
endif
```

Output

```
$ ./evenodd2.csh
Enter a number: 10
$ echo $?
1
$ ./evenodd2.csh
Enter a number: 7
$ echo $?
2
```

In this example, if the value entered by the user is an even value, the execution of the *mod* operator on it will result in the value 0 and hence will set the return status of the script to 1. Similarly, if the value entered by the user is an odd value, the return status of the script will be set to 2.

After execution of the script, we can echo $? to ascertain the exit status of the script. On the basis of the output displayed by $? we can know the location where the script terminated. Not only can we use $? to know the exit points of the script, but also to debug it. In addition, we can put the aforementioned code in a function, and in the statement following the function call, we can use $? to ascertain the return status of the function and accordingly take further action.

Sometimes, we come across a situation where we have to check several conditions and hence, we have to use a bunch of if else statements. Instead, we can also substitute the if else statements with the switch statement (discussed in detail in the following section), which is easier to use and more readable.

12.7.4 `switch`, `case`, `breaksw`, and `endsw` Statements

The switch statement is a substitute for several if else statements. This implies that when we need several branchings to occur in a shell script, the switch statement is preferred as it is more readable when compared to a cluster of if else statements. In the switch statement, an expression is supplied to be evaluated followed by a series of *case* statements. Each *case* statement carries a pattern followed by statement(s). If the pattern associated with the *case* statement matches with the expression of the `switch` statement, the statements of that case will be executed. The block of statements of each *case* statement is terminated by the `breaksw` keyword. The `breaksw` statement is used to exit from the `switch` statement. In case the expression of the `switch` statement doesn't match any value of the *case* statement, the statements associated with the *default* statement will be executed. The switch statement ends with the `endsw` keyword.

Syntax
```
switch (expression)

         case pattern1:
                statements
                breaksw
         case pattern2:
                statements
                breaksw
             : : :
             : : :
         default:
                statements
                breaksw
      endsw
```

Examples

(a) The following shell script prompts the user to enter the filename to delete. The entered filename is deleted after confirmation.

delfile.csh

```
#!/bin/csh
echo -n "Enter file name to delete: "
set filename = $<
echo -n "Sure, want to delete this file yes/no? "
set reply=$<
switch ($reply)
   case [Yy]*:
        rm $filename
```

```
            echo "File $filename is deleted"
            breaksw
        default:
            echo "File not deleted"
            breaksw
    endsw
```

Output

```
$ ls -l sch.txt
-rw-r--r--         1 root  root    6 Mar 10 23:17 sch.txt
$ ./delfile.csh
Enter file name to delete: sch.txt
Sure, want to delete this file yes/no? no
File not deleted

$ ls -l sch.txt
-rw-r--r--         1 root  root    6 Mar 10 23:17 sch.txt
$ ./delfile.csh
Enter file name to delete: sch.txt
Sure, want to delete this file yes/no? yes
File sch.txt is deleted

$ ls -l sch.txt
sch.txt: No such file or directory
```

The entered filename is assigned to the variable `filename`. The user is then asked for confirmation before deleting the file. If the user enters Yes or yes, the file is deleted. The pattern [Yy]* finds a match for any word that begins with the letter y, be it in upper or lower case. If the user enters something else, the file is not deleted and a message informing the same is displayed.

(b) The following shell script checks the command line argument passed to it and accordingly displays a message.

```
checkargs2.csh
#!/bin/csh
switch ($1)
    case ajay:
        echo "The argument passed is ajay"
        breaksw
    case  a?:
        echo "The argument passed is two letter word beginning with
            letter a"
        breaksw
    case a*:
        echo "The argument passed is a word beginning with letter a "
        breaksw
```

```
    default:
        echo "The argument passed is something else"
        breaksw
endsw
```

Output

```
$ ./checkargs2.csh ajay
The argument passed is ajay
$ ./checkargs2.csh an
The argument passed is two letter word beginning with letter a
$ ./cneckargs2.csh ability
The argument passed is a word beginning with letter a
$ ./checkargs2.csh chirag
The argument passed is something else
```

In the aforementioned script, the student name passed as a command line argument is checked through the switch command for the following things:
1. If it is the word, ajay
2. If it is the word consisting of two characters beginning with character a
3. If it is a word of any number of characters or digits beginning with character a
4. If it is some other text

An appropriate message is displayed depending on the command line argument passed to the script.

(c) The following script asks the user to enter a student name. If the student name entered is ajay, manish, or omy, then their respective assumed marks 50, 70, and 80 are displayed. If a student name other than these three is entered, a default mark of 85 is displayed and the exit status is set to 1 before exiting the script.

demoswitch.csh

```
#!/bin/csh
echo -n "Please enter a name: "
set name = $<
switch ( $name )
    case [Aa]jay:
        echo Marks of $name is 50
        breaksw
    case [Mm]anish:
        echo Marks of $name is 70
        breaksw
    case [Oo]my:
        echo Marks of $name is 80
        breaksw
    default:
        echo Marks of $name is 85
    exit 1
endsw
```

Output

```
$ ./demoswitch.csh
Please enter a name: ajay
Marks of ajay is 50

$ ./demoswitch.csh
Please enter a name: Manish
Marks of Manish is 70

$ ./demoswitch.csh
Please enter a name: omy
Marks of omy is 80

$ ./demoswitch.csh
Please enter a name: bharat
Marks of bharat is 85
```

(d) The following script asks the user to enter a filename to delete. If the entered name is not of a file, the script ends by displaying a message stating that the entered name is not a file. If the entered name is of a file, the user is asked for confirmation to delete the file. The response entered by the user is assigned to the variable *ans*. If the user responds by entering yes, the file is deleted. If the user types no, the file is not deleted. A message, Please enter either yes or no, is displayed if the user types a text other than yes or no.

delfile2.csh

```
#!/bin/csh
echo -n "Enter file name to delete: "
set filename = $<
if (-f $filename) then
    echo -n "Sure want to delete this file yes/no: "
    set ans = $<
    switch ($ans)
        case [yY][eE][sS]:
            rm ${filename}
            echo "The file is deleted"
            breaksw
        case [nN][oO]:
            echo "The file is not deleted"
            breaksw
        default:
            echo "Please enter either yes or no"
            breaksw
    endsw
else
    echo "$filename is not a file"
endif
```

Output

```
$ ./delfile2.csh
```

```
Enter file name to delete: accounts
accounts is not a file
$ ./delfile2.csh
Enter file name to delete: xyz.txt
Sure want to delete this file yes/no: n
Please enter either yes or no
$ ./delfile2.csh
Enter file name to delete: xyz.txt
Sure want to delete this file yes/no: y
Please enter either yes or no
$ ./delfile2.csh
Enter file name to delete: xyz.txt
Sure want to delete this file yes/no: no
The file is not deleted
$ ./delfile2.csh
Enter file name to delete: xyz.txt
Sure want to delete this file yes/no: yes
The file is deleted
$ ls xyz.txt
xyz.txt: No such file or directory
```

Sometimes we need to execute a few statements several times. We can do so with the help of loops. Let us begin with the study of loops.

12.8 LOOPS

As the name suggests, loops refer to an enclosed set of statements tied with a logical expression. The loop will execute as long as the logical expression is true, that is, all the enclosed statements will keep executing until the knot of the loop opens. The knot of the loop opens when the included logical expression evaluates to false. Let us begin by learning about the while loop.

12.8.1 while end Loop

A loop, as we know, is used for repeating a set of statements a specified number of times. The while loop allows us to execute a set of statements as long as the specified logical expression is true.

Syntax   `while (logical expression)`

        `statements`
    `end`

If the logical expression evaluates to the Boolean value, true, the statements in the body of the while loop are executed. After an iteration, on reaching the *end* statement of the while loop, again the logical expression is evaluated. If the logical expression again evaluates to *true*, the body of the while loop is executed, otherwise the loop exits and the execution of the shell script continues from the statement following the *end* statement. The statements in the body of the while loop will keep executing as long as the logical expression evaluates to *true*.

Example   The following script displays the sequence of numbers from 1 to 10.

dispseq.csh

```
#!/bin/csh
@count = 1
while ($count <= 10)
   echo $count
   set count = `expr $count +1`
end
```

Output

```
1
2
3
4
5
6
7
8
9
10
```

The variable count is initialized to value 1. In the while loop, the value of this variable is displayed, following which its value is incremented by 1. The loop will execute until the value of the count variable becomes more than 10. In the preceding script we observe that the value of the count variable is incremented via the expr command.

Let us modify the script to increment the value of the count variable through the increment operator ++.

dispseq2.csh

```
@ count = 1
@ limit=10
while ( $count <= $limit )
   echo $count
   @ count++
end
```

Output

```
1
2
3
4
5
```

6

7

8

9

10

The variables count and limit are set to values 1 and 10 respectively. The while loop is set to execute as long as the value of the count variable is less than the limit variable. In the while loop, the value of this variable is displayed following which its value is incremented by one.

Examples

(a) The following script displays the sequence of numbers from 10 to 1.

```
seqreverse.csh
#!/bin/csh
@ n = 10
while ($n)
    echo $n
    @ n--
end
```

Output

10

9

8

7

6

5

4

3

2

1

The variable n is set to value 10. The while loop will execute until its logical expression evaluates to false. Any value other than 0 is considered true and the value 0 is considered false. It means that the while loop will execute until the value of this variable becomes 0. In the while loop, the value of the variable is displayed following which its value is decremented by one. Hence, the loop will display values from 10 to 1.

(b) The following shell script displays the multiplication table of 5 from 5 till 50, that is, the output will be 5, 10, 15, ..., 50.

```
table5.csh
#!/bin/csh
@count = 1
while ($count <= 10)
    set $num=`expr $count \* 5`
    echo $num
    set count = `expr $count +1`
end
```

Output
```
5
10
15
20
25
30
35
40
45
50
```

We can see that a variable, count, is initialized to value 1. A while loop is made to execute until the value of the count variable becomes greater than 10. The value of this variable is multiplied by five to print the table.

(c) The following script displays the message Hello World! five times.

```
disphello.csh
#!/bin/csh
@ n = 1
while ($n <=5)
    echo Hello World
    @ n++
end
```

Output

```
Hello World
Hello World
Hello World
Hello World
Hello World
```

We can see that n is initialized to value 1 and the while loop is set to execute five times, that is, until the value of n exceeds 5. In the while loop, the message Hello World is displayed and the value of variable n is incremented by 1. This implies that the while loop will execute five times, displaying the message, Hello World, in each iteration.

12.8.2 repeat Command

The repeat command is used for repeatedly executing a command a specified number of times.

Syntax   repeat count command

Here, count is an integer value representing the times of repetition. A zero value for count suppresses the execution of the command.

Examples

(a) repeat 5 echo Hello World
This statement displays the text Hello World five times.

(b) `repeat 5 echo Hello World! >xyz.txt`

Five lines of the text `Hello World!` will be written in the file `xyz.txt`.

(c) The following script displays all the command line arguments that are passed to the shell script.

`dispallargs.csh`

```
#!/bin/csh
while ($#argv != 0 )
    echo $argv[1]
    shift
end
```

Output

```
$ ./dispallargs.csh school.txt 10 4 bank.lst
school.txt
10
4
bank.lst
```

You may recall that the `shift` command shifts or renames the elements in the command line arguments array `$argv[1]`, `$argv[2]`, etc. On giving the command without the parameters, the default value 1 is considered and hence the element in `$argv[2]` is assigned to the `$argv[1]` element, the value of `$argv[3]` element is assigned to the `$argv[2]` element, and so on. In addition, the value of `$#argv` that represents the count of the command line arguments is also automatically reduced by one on execution of the `shift` command.

In the aforementioned script the command line arguments `school.txt`, `10`, `4`, and `bank.lst` will be assigned to the positional parameters `$argv[1]`, `$argv[2]`, `$argv[3]`, and `$argv[4]` respectively. On displaying the value `argv[1]`, the value in this positional parameter, `school.txt`, is displayed. In the while loop, on executing the `shift` command, the positional parameter, `$argv[2]`, is renamed `$argv[1]`, `$argv[3]` is renamed `$argv[2]`, `$argv[4]` is renamed `$argv[3]`, and `$#argv` is decremented to 3. Again, the while loop executes, displaying the value in the positional parameter, `$argv[1]`, which was earlier `$argv[2]` (`10`). The loop continues until the count of the argument `$#argv` becomes 0. The count of the command line arguments, `$#argv`, becomes 0 when all the arguments are shifted or renamed.

(d) The following shell script checks the status of all the command line arguments. If the command line arguments include the name of any file, then the count of the number of lines in it is displayed. For other command line arguments, the message, `The file is not a regular file`, is displayed.

`countlines.csh`

```
while ($#argv)
    if (-f $argv[1])
        wc -l $argv[1]
    else
        echo "$argv[1] is not a regular file"
```

```
        endif
        shift
```

```
$ ./countlines.csh school.txt xyz.txt merge.txt
    6 school.txt
    1 xyz.txt
    2 merge.txt
```

The next loop that we are going to discuss is the one that is commonly used to apply a set of statements or a desired processing on a set of values. The name of the loop is foreach end loop. We will now learn more about it.

12.8.3 foreach end Loop

The foreach loop is used for iterating through the values provided in the given list.

Syntax
```
foreach var (list)
        statements;
    end
```

The variable var will be assigned the values given in the list one by one. The list may contain strings, numerals, and even wild-card expressions. The statements between foreach and end keywords are executed once for each item in the list. This implies that var is assigned the first value from the list and the body of the loop is executed. Then, the second value from the list is assigned to the variable, var, and again the loop is executed. The procedure is repeated for all the values in the list. The current value from the set can be accessed with the variable $var.

Example   The following shell script displays the sequence of numbers from 1 to 10.

dispsequence2.csh

```
#!/bin/csh
foreach i ( 1 2 3 4 5 6 7 8 9 10 )
        echo $i
end
```

Output

```
1
2
3
4
5
6
7
8
9
10
```

The variable, i, is assigned a value from the set and the loop is executed. After an iteration, the next value in the set is picked up, assigned to this variable, and the loop is executed again.

The procedure continues and all the values in the set are assigned to the variable i. The next statement will help us in skipping the body of a loop.

continue statement

The continue command takes no arguments and is used to skip the following statements in the loop and re-invoke the loop with the next iteration. This implies that the execution resumes from the first statement in the loop with the next iterative value after skipping the statements following the continue command.

Example The following shell script displays all the even values between 1 and 10.

dispeven.csh

```
#!/bin/csh
foreach i ( 1 2 3 4 5 6 7 8 9 10 )
   if ( $i % 2 == 1 ) then
      continue
   endif
   echo $i
end
```

Output

```
2
4
6
8
10
```

The variable i is assigned a value from the set of given values, one by one. The *mod* operator is applied to each value assigned to this variable. If the result of the mod operator is 1, meaning the value in the variable, i is odd, as a consequence, the continue statement is executed resulting in the skipping of the body of the foreach loop. Not only is the body of the foreach loop skipped but the next value in the set is picked up by this variable. If the result of the mod operator is 0, meaning the value in the variable i is even, its value is displayed on the screen.

In case we want to break and exit from the loop, we generally use the break statement, which is discussed in the subsequent section.

break statement

The break command terminates the current loop and exits from it. The command can be used with both the loops, foreach and while. The script resumes execution from the statement following the end statement of the loop.

Note: In case of nested loops, the break statement terminates the current loop and not the outer loop.

Examples

(a) The shell script displays the first 10 numbers in sequence.

```
dispsequence3.csh
#!/bin/csh
```

```
foreach i ( 1 2 3 4 5 6 7 8 9 10 11 12)
    if ( $i == 11 ) then
        break
    endif
    echo $i
end
```

Output

```
1
2
3
4
5
6
7
8
9
10
```

The variable i will be assigned the values specified in the given set one by one. For every value assigned to the variable, the body of the foreach loop is executed printing the value in the variable i. In this loop, a check is made to see if the value of the variable is equal to 11 in which case the loop is terminated. The script displays all the values specified in the set until it comes across the value 11.

(b) The following shell script adds a few numerical values specified in the set.

dispvalset.csh addfewset.csh

```
#!/bin/csh
@ s=0
foreach i ( 5 8 6 9 2 )
    @ s +=$i
end
echo "The sum of values is $s"
```

Output

```
The sum of values is 30
```

Variable i is assigned the values given in the set one by one. With every value assigned to the variable, the body of the foreach loop is executed where the value in variable i is added to variable s. When all the values in the set are processed, their addition stored in variable s is displayed.

(c) The following shell script displays values in a given set one by one.

dispvalset.csh

```
#!/bin/csh
echo The names of students are
foreach studentnames(ajay manish omy bharat gunjan)
    echo $studentnames
end
```

Output

```
The names of students are
ajay
manish
omy
bharat
gunjan
```

The variable studentnames is assigned values from the given set one by one. With every value assigned to this variable, the body of the foreach loop is executed to display the value assigned to it. Firstly, the studentnames variable will be assigned the text, ajay, and the loop is executed. In the foreach loop, the value assigned to the studentnames variable, that is, ajay, is displayed. After the first iteration, the next value in the set, manish, will be assigned to the studentnames variable, and again the loop is executed to display the text manish assigned to it. The loop continues to execute until all the text in the set are displayed via the studentnames variable.

(d) The following shell script displays all the names of the files and directories in the current directory after converting them to lower case.

fileslower.csh

```
#!/bin/csh
foreach file (`ls`)
    echo $file | tr '[A-Z]' '[a-z]'
end
```

Output

```
$ ls
BANK.TXT    fileslower.csh    school.txt    xyz.txt
$ ./fileslower.csh
bank.txt
fileslower.csh
school.txt
xyz.txt
```

The ls command is executed and the resulting names of all the files and directories in the current directory are assigned to the variable file one by one. Through the foreach loop, each name assigned to the file variable is displayed on the screen after translating the upper-case characters in the filename, if any, to lower case. Hence, all the names of the files and directories are displayed in lower-case letters.

(e) The following shell script displays all the names of the files and directories in the current directory that have the extension .png.

disppng.csh

```
#!/bin/csh
foreach i ( *.png )
    echo ${i}
end
```

Output

```
addextoutput.png
checkargs2output.png
checkargsoutput.png
countlinesoutput.png
delfile2output.png
delfiledtroutput.png
dispargsoutput.png
dispexistoutput.png
```

The names of the files and directories in the current directory that have the extension .png are assigned to variable i one by one. Through the foreach loop, all the names assigned to the variable are displayed on the screen.

(f) The following shell script accesses every command line argument passed to it. If the command line argument includes the name of an existing file, its name is displayed.

dispexist.csh

```
#!/bin/csh
foreach file ($argv[*])
    if (-e $file) then
        echo $file
    endif
end
```

Output

```
$ ./dispexist.csh school.txt abc.txt bank.lst xyz.txt
school.txt
xyz.txt
```

The $argv[*] parameter represents the list of command line arguments passed to the script. Through the foreach loop, each command line argument is accessed from the $argv[*] parameter and assigned to the variable file. The file test operator -e checks if any file exists in the current directory by the name assigned to the file variable. If the name in the file variable matches with an existing file, that filename is displayed.

(g) The following shell script displays the names of all the directories in the current directory.

alldirs.csh

```
#!/bin/csh
foreach file ( `ls` )
    if ( ! -f $file ) then
        echo $file
    endif
end
```

Output

```
$ ./alldirs
accounts
```

The ls command is executed and the resulting names of all the files and directories in the current directory are assigned to variable file one by one. Through the foreach loop, each name assigned to file is tested through the file test operator, -f, to know if it belongs to a file. If the name in variable file is not of a file (i.e., it represents a directory), the name is displayed. The procedure is repeated for all the directory names in the current directory.

(h) The following shell script adds an extension .new to all the names of the files that are in upper case in the current directory.

addext.csh

```
#!/bin/csh
foreach i ([A-Z]*)
    mv $i $i.new
end
```

Output

```
$ ls B*.*
BANK.TXT
$ ls S*.*
School.1st School.txt
$ ./addext.csh
$ ls B*.*
BANK.TXT.new
$ ls S*.*
School.1st.new School.txt.new
```

All the names of the files and directories beginning with upper-case letters in the current directory are assigned to variable i one by one. Through the foreach loop, each filename in the variable is moved or renamed by adding an extension .new to it. For instance, if the filename is BANK.TXT, it will be renamed BANK.TXT.new.

(i) The following shell script makes copies of all the files in the current directory having the extension .txt with the extension .dat.

copydiffext.csh

```
#!/bin/csh
foreach file (*.txt)
    set newfile = `basename $file .txt`
    cp $file $newfile.dat
end
```

Output

```
$ ls *.txt
bank.txt school.txt
$ ls *.dat
*.dat: No such file or directory
$ ./copydiffext.csh
$ ls *.txt
bank.txt school.txt
$ ls *.dat
bank.dat school.dat
```

All the names of files with the extension .txt in the current directory are assigned to variable file one by one. The *basename*, that is, primary name of the file is extracted from the filename after removing its extension, .txt, and assigned to the variable newfile. Thereafter, a copy of the file is made by adding the extension .dat to the extracted primary name.

(j) The following shell script converts all the files and directory names in the current directory to lower case.

```
convlower.csh
#!/bin/csh
foreach file (`ls`)
    set newfile = `echo $file | tr '[A-Z]' '[a-z]'`
    if ($newfile == $file) then
        continue
    endif
    mv $file $newfile
end
```

Output
```
$ ls B*.*
BANK.TXT
$ ls S*.*
School.1st School.txt
$ ./convlower.csh
$ ls B*.*
B*.*: No such file or directory
$ ls b*.*
bank.txt
$ ls S*.*
S*.*: No Such file or directory
$ ls s*.*
school.1st     stringcompare2output.png.new
school.txt     stringcompare3.csh.new
```

The ls command is executed to assign all the names of files and directories in the current directory to the file variable one by one. Through the foreach loop, every name assigned to variable file is translated to lower-case letters and assigned to variable newfile. A check is made to ascertain if the file or directory name is already in lower case. If this is the case, no action is taken and the next file in the sequence is picked up. If the file or directory name is not in lower case, it is renamed in its lower-case form that is stored in the variable newfile.

(k) The following shell script checks each of the command line arguments passed to the script and informs which of them are options and which are filenames.

```
checkargs3.csh
#!/bin/csh
foreach arg ($argv)
```

```
        if ( $arg =~ -* ) then
            echo $arg Argument is an option
        else
            echo $arg Argument is a filename
        endif
    end
```

Output

```
$ ./checkargs3.csh -a
-a Argument is an option
$ ./checkargs3.csh xyz.txt
xyz.txt Argument is a filename
```

As we know, all the command line arguments passed to the shell script are assigned to the array $argv. Using the foreach loop, each command line argument in the $argv array is picked and assigned to variable arg one by one. The argument assigned to the arg variable is checked to see if it begins with a - (hyphen). If the arg variable begins with a hyphen, it means it is an option, otherwise it is a filename and a message is displayed on the screen accordingly.

(l) The following shell script retrieves the names of files and directories in the current directory and assigns each name to variable file. Each name assigned to this variable is checked to ascertain if it is a file or directory and accordingly a message is displayed asking if the given file or directory has to be deleted. If the user enters *yes*, the specified file or directory is deleted.

delfiledir.csh

```
#! /bin/csh
foreach file (`ls`)
    if ( -f $file ) then
        echo -n "Delete the file ${file} (y/n)?"
    else
        echo -n "Delete this directory ${file} (y/n)? "
    endif
    set ans = $<
    switch ($ans)
        case n:
            breaksw
        case y:
            rm -r $file
            breaksw
    endsw
end
```

Output

```
$ ./delfiledir.csh
Delete the file a.dat (y/n)?y
Delete the file a.txt (y/n)?n
```

```
Delete the file bank.dat (y/n)?y
Delete the file bank.txt (y/n)?n
Delete the file checkexist.csh (y/n)?n
Delete the file convlower.csh (y/n)?n
Delete this directory projects (y/n)? y
```

The ls command is executed and all the names of the files and directories are assigned to variable file one by one. Each name assigned to this variable is tested using the -f operator to find out if it is a file or directory. If the name assigned to the file variable is of a file, the message, Delete the file file_name (y/n)? is displayed, otherwise, a message, Delete this directory directory_name (y/n)? is displayed. The response typed by the user is assigned to the variable, ans. If the user types the character n, indicating that no file or directory be deleted, the script exits from the switch statement without doing anything to the said file or directory. If the user types character y, confirming the said file or directory be deleted, then through rm -r, the said file or directory is recursively deleted. The procedure is repeated for every file or directory assigned to the file variable. We will now learn how to deal with a collection of values through arrays.

12.9 ARRAYS

Arrays are a set of consecutive memory locations where each memory location stores an item. Each item in an array is accessed through subscripts beginning from 1. An array is created by enclosing some data in parentheses.

Syntax   `array_name(data1 data2 data3...)`

The data within the parentheses is separated by a space. The data can be enclosed in single quotes, back quotes, or double quotes as desired.

Examples

(a) `set countries=(U.S.A U.K. India Australia)`
This example creates an array, countries, consisting of four elements, U.S.A, U.K., India, and Australia. These array elements can be accessed using the subscripts 1, 2, 3, and 4. Observe the following examples:
(i) `echo countries[2]`
This displays the second array element U.K.
(ii) `echo countries[4]`
This displays the fourth array element Australia.
(iii) `echo countries[2-3]`
This displays the second and third array elements U.K. and India.
(iv) `echo countries[3-]`
This displays elements from the third array till the end, that is, India Australia.
(v) `echo $#countries`
This displays the length of the array countries.
(vi) `set places=($countries)`
This creates an array places and assigns all the array elements of countries to it.

(vii) `set countries=($countries Japan)`

This adds an element `Japan` to the end of an existing array.

(viii) `set countries=(China $countries)`

This adds an element `China` to the beginning of an existing array.

(ix) `set countries=()`

This makes the `countries` array empty.

(x) `unset countries`

This removes the definition of the array `countries`.

(b) The following shell script demonstrates how an array is defined and how its elements are accessed.

`demoarray.csh`

```
#! /bin/csh
set studentnames = (ajay manish omy bharat gunjan)
echo "The list of student names is $studentnames "
echo "The list of student names is shown below:"
foreach name($studentnames)
    echo "$name"
end
```

Output

```
The list of student names is ajay manish omy bharat gunjan
The list of student names is shown below:
ajay
manish
omy
bharat
gunjan
```

An array, `studentnames`, is defined consisting of five elements, `ajay`, `manish`, `omy`, `bharat`, and `gunjan`. The first echo statement displays the complete array with all its elements in a row. Thereafter, using `foreach`, all the array elements of the `studentnames` array are accessed and assigned to variable `name` one by one and displayed on the screen.

(c) The following shell script displays the length of an array and accesses its element using the subscripts.

`arrayaccess.csh`

```
#!/bin/csh
set studentnames = (ajay manish omy bharat gunjan)
echo Number of student names are $#studentnames
echo The first name  is $studentnames[1]
echo The second name is $studentnames[2]
echo The last name is $studentnames[$#studentnames]
```

Output

```
Number of student names are 5
The first name is ajay
```

```
The second name is manish
The last name is gunjan
```

The first echo statement displays the length of studentnames. Knowing that the first array element is found at subscript 1, the next two echo statements will print the first and second elements of the name array respectively. Since $#studentnames returns the length of the array, that is, 5, the third echo statement will display the array element at subscript location 5, that is, the last element of the array.

(d) The following shell script displays all the elements of the studentnames array.

```
disparray.csh
#!/bin/csh
set studentnames = (Ajay Bharat Omy Manish Gunjan)
@ i = 1
while( $i <= $#studentnames )
    echo "$studentnames[$i]"
    @ i++
end
```

Output

```
Ajay
Bharat
Omy
Manish
Gunjan
```

In order to access array elements using the subscript, variable i is initialized to value 1, as an array begins from the subscript location 1. A while loop is executed up till the length of the array accessing each array element using variable i as its subscript. After displaying each array element, the value of i is incremented by 1 to access the next element. The loop executes until the value of the variable exceeds the length of the array.

(e) The following shell script displays all the elements of the studentnames array using the shift command.

```
disparray2.csh
#!/bin/csh
set studentnames = (ajay manish omy bharat gunjan)
while ( $#studentnames > 0 )
    echo "$studentnames[1]"
    shift studentnames
end
```

Output

```
ajay
manish
omy
bharat
gunjan
```

A while loop is executed as long as the length of the studentnames array is greater than or equal to 1. Within the loop, the first array element is displayed. After displaying the first element, the array is shifted. The shift command shifts the second array element to the first subscript location, third array element to the second subscript location, and so on, hence reducing the size of the array by one. In other words, the value of the studentnames[2] element will be assigned to studentnames[1], studentnames[3] element will be assigned to studentnames[2], and so on. After every shift command, the loop executes to display the studentnames[1] element, which is nothing but the next element in sequence. This implies that the shift command is executed in a loop to left shift the array elements to the location, studentnames[1], one by one. The procedure is repeated until the array size reduces to 0.

Note: The shift command when used with an array not only reduces the size of the array by 1 but also shifts the array elements towards the first subscript location.

(f) The following shell script determines if the student name passed as the command line argument to the shell script exists in the given array or not.

searcharray.csh

```
#!/bin/csh
set studentnames = (ajay bharat manish gunjan omy)
while ($argv[1] != $studentnames[1])
    shift studentnames
    if ($#studentnames == 0) then
        echo "$argv[1] is not present in the list of student names"
        exit 1
    endif
end
echo "$argv[1] is present in the list of student names"
```

Output

```
$ ./searcharray.csh
Subscript out of range
$ ./searcharray.csh ajay
ajay is present in the list of student names
$ ./searcharray.csh omy
omy is present in the list of student names
$ ./searcharray.csh sanjay
sanjay is not present in the list of student names
```

The studentnames array is made up of five elements, ajay, bharat, manish, gunjan, and omy. A while loop is used to check if the student name sent as a command line argument matches with the first array element, name[1]. If they match, then a message is displayed indicating that the supplied student name is present in the list of student names. If they do not match, the studentnames array is shifted through the shift command. You may recall that the shift command left shifts the array element, that is, the studentnames[2] element will shift to the `studentnames[1]` location, `studentnames[3]` will shift to the `studentnames[2]` location, and so on reducing the size of the array by 1. This loop is used again to check if the student name sent through the command line argument matches with the array element `studentnames[1]`. The `studentnames[1]` element is basically the second array element shifted to the `studentnames[1]` location. The while loop continues to execute till either the array size is reduced to zero or a match is found. If the array size reduces to 0, a message is displayed informing us that the supplied student name is not present in the list of student names, and the script is terminated setting the exit status to value 1.

(g) The following shell script creates an array from the `date` command and displays the desired information from it.

```
arrfromdate.csh
#!/bin/csh
echo Date is `date`
set today=`date`
echo Today is $today[1] and the year is $today[4]
```

Output

```
Date is Monday 27 February 2012 03:45:06 PM IST
Today is Monday and the year is 2012
```

The first `echo` command displays the system date. The system date is then assigned to the variable `today`. This variable will then act as an array consisting of six elements. The first and sixth elements of the array that represent the week, day, and year are displayed.

C shell also supports associative arrays. Associative arrays take subscripts, like ordinary arrays do, but here the subscripts are arbitrary strings (or keys) associated with the value stored in the element of the array. We need to use `typeset -A` to create an associative array.

Syntax   `typeset –A assoc_array_name`

Here, `assoc_array_name` represents the associative array.

Example   `typeset -A capitals`
          `capitals=(India Delhi Australia  Sydney  UK London )`

The two preceding statements define an associative array by the name `capitals` consisting of three countries and their respective capitals. The countries `India`, `Australia`, and `UK` are the keys of the associative array and the capitals of these countries, `Delhi`, `Sydney`, and `London`, are the values of the respective keys.

The following example prints the value of the key `Australia` from the associative array, `capitals`.

```
print ${capitals['Australia']}
```

While writing scripts it is quite natural to come across certain errors. Let us see how errors that might occur in a script are displayed.

12.10 DISPLAYING ERRORS

When we expect some error to occur in a procedure or script, we pass it to the perror() function. If an error occurs in the procedure or script that is passed to the perror() function, the error message is sent to the standard error file descriptor stderr and also the value of the global variable errno is set. We can also display the description of the error by passing the errno variable to the strerror() function. To display all the error messages that are defined in a global error list array sys_errlist[], we can make use of a for loop to display its array elements from 0 to one less than sys_nerr, where sys_nerr is the number of error messages defined in the sys_errlist array. The list of terms that we use to display errors is given in Table 12.13.

Table 12.13 List of terms used to display errors

Term	Description
sys_nerr	It represents the number of error messages defined in sys_errlist.
sys_errlist[]	It is the global error list used to access and display error messages. The respective error messages are retrieved using errno as index in the sys_errlist.
strerror() function	It returns a string that describes the error of the code passed to it in the argument, errnum, as follows: `char *strerror(int errnum);`
strerror_r() function	It is similar to strerror() and returns the string that describes the error of the error code passed to it in the argument errnum. However, the string is returned in the supplied buffer buf of length n. The function returns 0 on success and -1 on failure as follows: `int strerror_r(int errnum, char *buf, size_t n);`
perror() function	It displays the error message corresponding to the current value of the global variable errno and writes it, followed by a newline, to the standard error file descriptor stderr. In other words, this function converts the error code into human readable form. The variable errno is set when errors occur during a call to a system or library function. The name of the program where error may occur or the file on which system calls are applied is passed to the perror() function as an argument. `public static void perror(String s)` Here, s is the program or filename.
	Note: When a system call fails, it usually returns -1 and sets the variable errno to a value describing the error.

Example The following shell script uses the strerror() function to print all the error messages.

```
printerrors.c
# include <stdio.h>
```

```
int main () {
    int i;
    extern    int sys_nerr
    printf ("Total number of errors are: %d\n", sys_nerr);
    for (i =0; i < sys_nerr; i++)
        printf ("%d: %s\n", i, strerror (i) );
    exit (0);
}
```

Assume there are certain errors in the system and their details are available in the array sys_errlist. The length of the sys_errlist array, that is, the number of errors, is accessed through the sys_nerr integer. With the help of a for loop, the error codes are passed to the strerror() function and the text messages describing the errors returned by it are displayed.

onintr command

The onintr command is used to specify the action to be taken when the shell receives a signal. The command can be used in the command line as well as in the shell script. When used within a shell script, the command causes most signals to terminate the shell script. When used in the command line, the command resets earlier signal handling applied by the earlier onintr commands and restores the normal default signal actions for all the signals. Not only can the onintr command be used to specify the action to initiate on the occurrence of a signal but also be used to disable and ignore all signals.

Syntax   onintr label

Here, label is the statement that the script will jump to on the occurrence of a signal. This implies that when the user presses the interrupt key, often configured to be Ctrl-c, the script will jump to the statement label to do the desired task.

Note: We can use the stty -a command to display all the settings for the terminal.

Example   The following shell script will ask the user to enter a number and will indicate if the entered number is even or odd. The script will keep executing in an infinite loop until the user interrupts the script by pressing the Ctrl-c command.

evenodd3.csh

```
#!/bin/csh
onintr close
while (1)
    echo -n "Enter a number: "
    set n = $<
    if ($n % 2 == 0) then
        echo The number, $n is even
    else
        echo The number, $n is odd
    endif
end
```

```
close:
echo Script ends
```

Output

```
$ ./evenodd3.csh
Enter a number: 20
The number, 20 is even
Enter a number: 7
The number, 7 is odd
Enter a number: 4
The number, 4 is even
Enter a number: ^C
Script ends
```

On occurrence of the interrupt, the script will jump to the label, close, which exits from the infinite while loop and hence terminates the script. Until the interrupt key is pressed, the user is asked for a number and the script will display whether the entered number is even or odd.

In this chapter, we learnt about C shell and its different features. We saw how to use command history to retrieve commands from the history file, apply command substitution, filename substitution, filename completion, and aliases to rename existing commands. We also discussed how to control jobs, run them in the background, and suspend, resume, and kill them. We then dealt with the purpose of environment variables, shell variables, and built-in shell variables. We discussed the use of C shell operators, creation and running of simple C shell scripts, use of different flow controlling statements, loops, arrays, and display of errors.

■ SUMMARY ■

1. The C shell was developed by Bill Joy at the University of California at Berkeley.
2. The C shell has a syntax similar to the C programming language.
3. C shell supports features such as command history, command substitution, filename substitution, filename completion, aliases, and job control.
4. The history command without any options displays all the lines that are stored in the history.
5. The !! symbol is replaced with the previous command line; the !n symbol is replaced with the command in the history list represented by the line number n.
6. The filename substitution also known as globbing uses the characters typed by us to find the file(s) beginning with those characters and replaces the characters typed by us.
7. While using filename substitution, the character ~ (tilde), if it appears at the beginning of the word and is followed by a character or /, will be replaced by the home directory of the user.
8. Filename completion makes the shell display or complete the filename on the basis of the initial characters typed by the user.
9. Aliases can be used for renaming existing commands, creating shorthand for longer commands, and to define new commands that may be a combination of a sequence of commands.
10. The unalias command is used to remove a previously defined alias.
11. A process can be set to execute in the background by following its command with an ampersand (&) symbol.
12. To bring a job to the foreground, the fg command is used.
13. The command jobs -l displays the list of jobs along with their IDs.
14. Ctrl-z can be used to suspend or stop a running job.
15. The C shell, when invoked, executes three files located in the user's home directory: .cshrc, .login,

and .logout.

16. The .login file is read only once when we log in and hence contains the commands that we want to execute only once, that is, at the beginning of each session.

17. The .cshrc file usually contains instructions that include directory paths, shell variables, and aliases and the .login file contains set-up terminal settings and environment variables.

18. The .logout file contains commands that are run when the user logs out of the system.

19. The environment variables are also known as global variables as these variables are passed to the newly started shell. In addition, these variables are passed to all processes run from the current shell. Usually, these variables are written in upper case.

20. The setenv command is used to change or assign a value to an environment variable.

21. The unsetenv command is used to remove an environment variable.

22. The printenv command is used to display the list of all currently set environment variables.

23. Shell variables are local variables as they belong to a shell and contain values that are visible and applicable only to the current instance of the shell.

24. The set command is used to assign a value to a shell variable.

25. To delete or remove a shell variable, the unset command is used.

26. By setting the prompt variable, we can control the appearance of the primary prompt.

27. By setting the histchars variable, we can change the special history characters, ! (exclamation point) and ^ (caret).

28. By setting the mail variable, we can specify the file that the shell needs to check for mail. In addition, we can specify the interval in which the shell should check for incoming mail. The default time interval in which the shell looks for the mail is five minutes.

29. The command line arguments passed to a script are stored in the argv[] array.

30. $#argv refers to the number of arguments passed to the script.

31. To write multiple commands on a single line, we need to separate them with semicolon (;).

32. In order to continue a long command onto a new line, end the line with a backslash (\).

33. For reading data from the keyboard into a variable, we initialize it to hold the special parameter $<. The $<

substitutes a line from the standard input device—the keyboard.

34. The @ symbol is used instead of set command to initialize integer variables.

35. To assign a list of values to the variable, enclose them in parentheses.

36. To find the length of a variable, prefix the variable by $#. This implies that $#variable_name finds out the length of variable_name.

37. The C shell cannot do floating point arithmetic; hence the bc calculator program is used in the shell script to perform floating point arithmetic.

38. The if-then-else statement is used in conditional branching, that is, it usually contains two sets of statements and a logical expression. If the logical expression is true, the set of statements associated with 'if' is executed, otherwise the set of statements associated with 'else' is executed.

39. There are several file testing operators that are used in testing different attributes of the files.

40. The $? parameter indicates the exit status of the last command executed.

41. The exit status of the last command is 0 if it is successfully executed, otherwise it returns a non -zero value.

42. Through the goto command, we can change the flow of the program in a desired manner.

43. The exit command terminates a script and returns the status to the parent process.

44. The repeat command is used for repeatedly executing a command a specified number of times.

45. The goto command jumps to the statement in the script that is prefixed by a given label. The label must be followed by a colon (:).

46. The exit command terminates a script and returns the status to the parent process.

47. The switch statement is a substitute to several if else statements.

48. The while loop executes a set of statements as long as the specified logical expression is true.

49. The repeat command is used for repeatedly executing a command a specified number of times.

50. The foreach loop is used for iterating through the values provided in the given list.

51. The continue command skips the following statements in the loop and re-invokes the loop with the next iteration.

52. The break command terminates the current loop and exits from it.

53. An array is a set of consecutive memory locations where each memory location stores an item. Each item in an array is accessed through the subscript, where subscripts begin from one.

54. An array is created by enclosing data in parentheses.

55. Procedures are small modules that are created to perform some specific task or processing.

56. A procedure is defined by the proc statement. In addition, a procedure may or may not include a return statement. The procedure body ends with the end statement.

57. The unproc statement is used to discard procedures.

58. By default, the variables used in a procedure are global in nature.

■ EXERCISES ■

Objective-type Questions

State True or False

12.1 The exclamation point (!) character also known as bang operator is used to retrieve commands from the history list.

12.2 While accessing arguments of the earlier commands, the $ and ^ symbols represent the first and last arguments respectively.

12.3 The Boolean value false is also numerically represented as 0.

12.4 The exit status of the last command or script is automatically set to a non-zero value if it is successfully executed.

12.5 When the count in the repeat command is 0, the repeat command will not execute at all.

12.6 The shift command when used with an array does not reduce the size of the array.

12.7 The break command terminates the current loop and exits from it.

12.8 The foreach loop is used for iterating through the values provided in the given list.

12.9 Procedures are small modules that are created to do a specific task or processing.

12.10 For reading data from the keyboard and assigning to a variable (pr variables), we initialize it to hold the special parameter $<.

12.11 The continue command can only be used in loops.

12.12 We can write multiple commands on a single line if they are separated by a semicolon (;).

12.13 By setting the mail variable, we can set the time interval for the shell to check for incoming mail.

12.14 The unalias command can be used to remove previously defined aliases.

12.15 On pressing ^Z, the background job will switch to the foreground.

Fill in the Blanks

12.1 When invoked, the C shell executes three files in the user's home directory, _____, _____, and _____.

12.2 The _____ is used to access arguments of the earlier commands.

12.3 In filename substitution, the _____ is replaced by the home directory of the user.

12.4 To turn on filename completion, we need to set the _____ variable.

12.5 By following a command with an _____, the process will execute in the background.

12.6 While using the filename completion feature, press _____ to list all the possible filenames or directories on the basis of the typed characters.

12.7 The _____ command displays the list of jobs along with their IDs.

12.8 The file test operator, _____, is used for testing the read permission of the file.

12.9 To know the exit status of the last executed command, _____ is used.

12.10 On using the goto statement, the shell searches for the given label that is followed by a _____.

12.11 The sys_nerr represents the number of errors messages defined in _____.

12.12 To continue a long command onto the new line, we need to end the line with _____.

12.13 Through the histchars variable, we can change

the history substitution characters _____ and _____.

12.14 To terminate a job, we use the _____

command.

12.15 The subscript in an array begins with the value, _____.

Programming Exercises

12.1 What will these commands do?
  (a) `set history=80`
  (b) `!-4`
  (c) `!$`
  (d) `jobs -l`
  (e) `alias h history`

12.2 Write the commands with examples for doing the following tasks.
  (a) Display the username and current working directory in primary prompt
  (b) Retrieve the last command that begins with gr
  (c) Show the list of files and directories that consists of four characters, and begins with characters from a to d and ends with any numeral
  (d) Create an alias by the name fi for finger command

  (e) Exit from the script with status 4

12.3 Write shell scripts for the following:
  (a) Display all the names of files that carry the text `hello`
  (b) Move all the files in the current directory to the directory that is supplied through the command line argument
  (c) Check the size of the filenames passed through command line arguments to the script and print their names with the prefix `small file` and `large file` depending on whether their size is less than or greater than 100 KB.
  (d) Display the elements of an array in reverse order
  (e) Ask the user to enter a single key and display whether the entered key is a numeral, character, or something else

Review Questions

12.1 Write short notes on the following:
  (a) Filename substitution
  (b) Filename completion
  (c) Aliases
  (d) Command history
  (e) Repeat command

12.2 Explain the three start-up files `.cshrc`, `.login`, and `.logout` along with their sample content.

12.3 Explain how the `strerror()` function is used to display error messages.

12.4 How are arrays created and used in C shell

scripts? Explain with a running script.

12.5 Explains the different loops used in C shell scripts.

12.6 What is the role of break and continue commands in loops? Explain with running examples.

12.7 How can `$?` be used to read the `exit` status? Explain with a running script.

12.8 How are history characters changed? Explain.

12.9 Explain a few shell variables.

12.10 What is the role of environment variables?

Brain Teasers

12.1 What is wrong in the following code to set the Ctrl-h key pair to erase the previous character and the Ctrl-c key pair to interrupt the current job?

```
stty erase  intr ^C ^H
```

12.2 Correct the following code for displaying all arguments except the first.

```
echo "All arguments except the first
are: $argc[2-${0}]"
```

12.3 Correct the following code to multiply two values.

```
#!/bin/csh
@ x = 8
@ y = 5
m =  x* y
echo Multiplication is m
```

12.4 Find the error in the following code.

```
#!/bin/csh
```

```
echo -n "Enter either y or n "
set x = $>
if ( x = "y" ) then
    echo You have entered yes
else
    echo You have entered no
endif
```

12.5 Correct the following code to print 'Hello' three times.

```
#!/bin/csh
@ x = 1
dispmsg:
echo "Hello"
x++
if (x <=3) goto dispmsg
```

12.6 Correct the error in the following code asking the user to enter *y* or *n* and displaying what option has been entered.

```
#!/bin/csh
echo -n "Please either y or n "
x = $<
switch ( x )
    case [yY]:
        echo You have entered Yes
        breaksw
    case [nN]:
        echo You have entered No
        breaksw
    defaulter:
        echo Please enter either y or n
endsw
```

12.7 Find the error in the following while loop to print the multiplication table of 9 till 90.

```
#!/bin/csh
@x = 9
while (x <= 90)
    echo $x
    x = expr $x +9
end
```

12.8 The following code for displaying all the command line arguments is not working. Correct the error.

```
#!/bin/csh
while ($#argv != 0 )
    echo $argv[0]
    argv++
end
```

12.9 Correct the following code for displaying the first five numbers in a sequence.

```
#!/bin/csh
foreach i ( 1 2 3 4 5  )
    if ( $i == 1 ) then
        continue
    else
        break
    endif
    echo $i
end
```

12.10 What is wrong in the following code for displaying the elements of a set? Correct the code.

```
#!/bin/csh
echo The names of students are
while  student(john,  manisha,  chirag,
suman, naman)
    echo student
end
```

Different Tools and Debuggers

After studying this chapter, the reader will be conversant with the following:

- Language development tools, Yacc, Lex, and M4
- Text-formatting tools, troff and nroff
- Preprocessors for nroff and troff—tbl, eqn, and pic
- Debugger tools, dbx, adb, and sdb
- Strip—discarding symbols from object files
- Version control systems

13.1 LANGUAGE DEVELOPMENT TOOLS—YACC, LEX, AND M4

In this section, we are going to learn about the tools that analyse text in the given file(s). After having observed and matched them with the laid standards, such tools produce an output, which can be used in further language development of the file(s). The language development tools that we are going to learn are as follows:

Yacc This compiler reads the grammar specifications and accordingly generates parsing tables and driver routines.

Lex It searches for the required regular expressions in a file, takes appropriate actions against them, and produces programs that are used in a simple lexical analysis of the text.

M4 It is a macro processor that reads the given m4 template as well as expands and processes macros in the input file to produce an output.

13.1.1 Yet Another Compiler–Compiler

Yet another compiler–compiler (yacc) is a compiler that reads the grammar specifications in the specified file and generates parsing tables and driver routines to the file y.tab.c.

Syntax   yacc [-b file_prefix] [-d] [-l] [-v] [-Q [y | n]] [-p sym_prefix] file

A brief description of the options used in the yacc command is given in Table 13.1.

Table 13.1 Brief description of options used in the `yacc` command

Option	Description
`-b file_prefix`	It uses the given `file_prefix` as the prefix for all output files. By default, the prefix for all output files is y. By using this parameter, the code file, `y.tab.c`, the header file, `y.tab.h`, and the description file, `y.output`, will be changed to `file_prefix.tab.c`, `file_prefix.tab.h`, and `file_prefix.output`, respectively.
`-d`	It generates the file `y.tab.h` with the `#define` statements that associate the `yacc`'s token codes with the user-declared token names.
`-l`	The code produced in `y.tab.c` will not contain any `#line` directives. The `#line` directives help the C compiler in relating errors in the generated code with the original code. Hence, the `-l` option is used when debugging is complete.
`-v`	It generates the file `y.output`, which contains a description of the parsing tables and other diagnosed information.
`-Q [y|n]`	`-Qy` writes the version information about `yacc` in `y.tab.c`. The `-Qn` option (default) writes no version information.
`-p sym_prefix`	It changes the prefix prepended to `yacc`-generated symbols to the string represented by `sym_prefix`. The default prefix is the string yy.
`File`	It represents the filename with the complete path for which parsing tables and driver routines should be created.

13.1.2 Lexical Analyser

Lexical analyser (lex) takes an input stream and generates programs that can be used in a simple lexical analysis of the text. The input file contains regular expressions and the actions that are to be executed when expressions are found in the input stream. For example, the following command produces the C source by the name `lex.yy.c` for the lexical analyser:

```
lex a.l
```

Syntax   `lex [-n] [-t] [-v] file`

A brief description of the options used in the `lex` command is given in Table 13.2.

Table 13.2 Brief description of options used in the `lex` command

Option	Description
`-t`	It sends the lex's output to the standard output rather than to the file `lex.yy.c`.
`-v`	It prints a one-line summary of the statistics of the generated analyser.
`-n`	It suppresses the summary of the statistics written with the `-v` option (default).
`file`	It represents the input filename.

The generated C source can be compiled as shown here:

```
% cc lex.yy.c -ll
```

This command executes the associated C action for each identified regular expression.

The following lex program converts upper case to lower case, removes blanks at the end of lines, and replaces multiple blanks with single blanks:

```
%%
[A-Z] putchar(yytext[0]+'a'-'A');
```

```
[ ]+$
[ ]+ putchar(' ');
```

Example   Assume the C program is as follows.

```
{
        int a=10;
        printf("%d\n",a);
}
```

The lexical analyser will break the input stream into a series of tokens as described here.

```
{
int
a
=
10
;
printf
(
"%d\n"
,
a
)
;
}
```

13.1.3 m4

m4 is a Unix macro processor. It considers an m4 template as input and after having expanded and processed the macros, it produces output on the standard output. Macros can be either built-in or user defined, and can take any number of arguments. The m4 has built-in functions that are used for including files, running commands, managing text, performing computation, and so on.

Syntax   `m4 [-e] [-s] [ -Dname [=val]] [-U name] [filename]`

A brief description of the options used in the m4 command is given in Table 13.3.

Note: m4 cannot include more than nine nested files.

Table 13.3   Brief description of options used in the m4 command

Option	Description
-e	It operates interactively. Interrupts are ignored and the output is unbuffered.
-D name[=val]	It defines the given names to the specified val. If the val is not specified, the names are defined to NULL.
-U name	It undefines, i.e., deletes the defined names.
-s	It enables line sync output for the C preprocessor.
Filename	It represents the text file that is to be processed. If no filename is given, the standard input is read.

Creating macros

Macros can be created with the following syntax:

```
name(arg1,arg2, ..., argn)
```

The opening parenthesis, '(', should immediately follow the name of the macro. If this is not the case, then it is considered a macro call. A macro name can consist of alphanumeric characters as well as underscores beginning with a character.

The m4 comes with an initial set of built-in macros. In order to create new macros, the define() macro is used. The following statement shows how a macro is created:

```
define(USA, United States of America)
```

In the aforementioned define() macro described, we find two parameters, USA and the United States of America. In the input, wherever the term USA appears, it will be expanded as United States of America. There should not be any white space between the macro name and the opening parenthesis. Any white space before the parameters is ignored. By default, the newline character is also echoed in the output. To suppress this newline character, we use the 'delete to newline' (dnl) macro shown here:

```
define(USA, United States of America)dnl
```

This macro will replace the term USA in the input stream with United States of America without the following newline character. There should not be any space between the end of the macro and the dnl.

Assume the following input is provided to m4:

```
define(USA, United States of America)
I live in USA
'USA' stands for USA
```

It will then give the following output:

```
I live in United States of America
'USA' stands for United States of America
```

When a string is quoted, it is not expanded.

In order to give definitions on the command line, the -D option is used in the following example:

```
m4 -D USA="United States of America"  a.m4
```

The hash character (#) is used for comments; the comments are echoed to the output.

Quoted strings are also used in defining macros.

```
define(USA, 'United States of America')
```

While expanding the macros, the quotes will be stripped off. The quoted strings can also include newline characters:

```
define(USA, 'United States
of
America')
```

Assume the following input is provided to m4:

```
I live in USA
```

The term USA will then be expanded as follows:

```
I live in United States
```

```
of
America
```

13.2 TEXT-FORMATTING TOOLS

In this section, we are going to learn about the different text-formatting tools that format a given document and, hence, its appearance. The tools enable the formatted document to appear similar to a typeset document, manual pages, etc. The two most popular tools that we are going to discuss here are as follows:

troff   It formats the given document such that it appears similar to a typeset document.

nroff   It produces output for terminal windows, line printers, and typewriter-like devices.

13.2.1 troff

troff (pronounced 'tee-roff') is a text-formatting tool that formats the document such that it appears similar to a typeset document.

> **Syntax**   troff [-a] [-F directory_name] [-i] [-T name] filename

A brief description of the options used in the troff command is given in Table 13.4.

The most common formatting commands that are used with the troff command are provided in Table 13.5.

The default vertical spacing is dependent on the text processor. In nroff, the default vertical spacing is 1/6" and for troff, it is 12 points.

Table 13.4   Brief description of options used in the troff command

Option	Description
-a	It generates an ASCII version of the formatted output.
-F directory_name	It searches the given directory, directory_name for font width, or terminal tables. If the directory_name is not specified, the system default directory is used.
-i	It reads the standard input after all the specified input files are read.
-T name	It prepares the output for the specified device instead of the default PostScript printer.
filename	It represents the file that is to be processed.

Table 13.5   Brief description of formatting commands used with troff command

Formatting command	Description
.fi	This fills the text with input (default setting).
.nf	This does not fill the text. The right margin appears ragged.
.br	This breaks the filling and starts a new block of text. The same action can be done by starting a line of text with a space.
.ad	This controls adjustment. Valid arguments are as follows:
	1: Adjusts only the left margin
	r: Adjusts only the right margin
	c: Centres each line
	b or n: Adjusts both margins
.ce n:	Centres the next *n* lines without filling the text

Table 13.6 Brief description of units used in space measurement in the `troff` command

Option	Description
I	inch
c	centimetre
p	pica
m	em
n	en
p	point
u	unit
v	vertical space

```
troff filename | hplj
```

The units used for `troff` space measurement are provided in Table 13.6.

| Example | `$ troff a.txt` |

This statement runs `troff` on the file a.txt.

The output produced by `troff` is device independent and requires to be post-processed before it can be accepted by most printers. The syntax for post-processing the input file is as follows:

| Syntax | `troff filename | postprocessor` |

| Example | To post-process the `troff` output for the hp laser jet printer, the subsequent statement is used.

In order to use `troff`, we need to specify the command that indicates how we want to format the text. The command is usually placed on a new line beginning with a period. For example, the following command changes the point size of the text on the subsequent lines to 20 points.

```
.ps 20
Hello
```

The text `Hello` will appear in 20-point size.

Note: One point is 1/72 inch.

If the specified point size is not of the legal size, it is rounded up to the next valid value, with a maximum of 36. If no point size is specified, the previous size is considered. The default point size is 10.

The backslash character (\) is used for applying `troff` commands and for inserting special characters in the text. For example, the following statement will make the text appear in 20-point size:

```
\s20Hello
```

This statement will make the text `Hello` appear in 20-point size.

The set point size is considered in the following command. For example, the following text will make the text `World` appear in 25-point size and the text `Bye` to appear in 15-point size:

```
\s+5World\s-5Bye
```

We can see that the point size is specified in terms of the previously set point size.

Note: The `\s0` command will consider the previous point size value.

13.2.2 nroff

`nroff` (or new roff) is a text-formatting tool that produces output for terminal windows, line printers, and typewriter-like devices. It is mostly used to format manual pages or help files.

Syntax   `nroff [-o pages] [-h] [-i] [-T name] [filename]`

A brief description of the options used in the `nroff` command is given in Table 13.7.

Table 13.7   Brief description of options used in the `nroff` command

Option	Description
-o pages	It displays only the specified pages. The page numbers can be comma separated and a hyphen can be used to represent a range of pages.
-h	It uses TAB characters for horizontal spacing.
-i	It reads the standard input after the input files are read.
-T name	It prepares output for a device of the specified name. Valid options are as follows: ascii, ascii8, latin1, utf8, nippon, and cp1047
filename	It represents the document that needs to be formatted for display. If no filename argument is present, nroff reads from the standard input.

Example   `nroff a.txt`

This statement formats the file `a.txt`.

An `nroff` command is written just above the line of the text to which we wish to apply it. The command begins with a period, followed by two letters that represent the command, which is again optionally followed by a number that represents the number of spaces, lines, or tabs.

Example   `.in 5`

This statement indents the following text by five spaces.

13.3 PREPROCESSORS FOR nroff AND troff

In this section, we are going to discuss the preprocessor tools that format tables, mathematical equations, pictures, etc., into commands that are understandable by the text-formatting tools `troff` and `nroff`. The preprocessors that we are going to discuss are as follows:

tbl   It formats tables into commands and escape sequences that `nroff`/`troff` can understand.

eqn   It typesets mathematical equations and compiles descriptions of equations embedded within `troff` input files into commands that are understandable by `troff`.

pic   It is a graphics language preprocessor that compiles pictures embedded within `troff` input files into commands that are understandable by `troff`.

Each of these preprocessors translates codes into `nroff`/`troff` requests.

13.3.1 tbl

`tbl` is a preprocessor that formats tables for `nroff`/`troff`. It compiles descriptions of tables embedded within `troff` input files into commands and escape sequences that `nroff`/`troff` can understand.

Syntax	`tbl [options] [filename]`

Here, `filename` represents the input file that is to be processed. If instead of an input file we want to read from the standard input device, a hyphen (-) is substituted for the filename.

Example	`$ tbl file`

As evident from this statement, the commands between each `.TS`/`.TE` macro pair (in the file) are converted into a printable table. The remaining commands are passed through, unchanged.

An input file may exhibit coding in the following format.

```
.TS H
options;
format1
format2.
Column Titles
.TH
Item1  Item2  Item3
Item1  Item2  Item3 ...
.TE
```

We can see that a table definition begins with a `.TS` macro (or a `.TS H` macro if the table is long enough to cross a page boundary) followed by options and one or more format lines. The column titles are represented by the `.TH` macro. The data in the table columns are separated by a tab or the designated tab symbol. The table definition ends with a `.TE` macro. The meaning of the most commonly used `tbl` macros is briefly described in Table 13.8.

Table 13.8 Brief description of macros used in the `tbl` command

Macro	Description
`.TS`	It starts a table.
`.TE`	It ends a table.
`.TS H`	It is used when the table extends to more than one page.
`.TH`	It is used after column titles to separate them from other data.

Options used with `tbl`

Options help in controlling the appearance of the entire table. They are either comma-separated or separated by spaces, and the line ends with a semicolon. Table 13.9 displays the commonly used options for defining table(s).

Table 13.9 Brief description of options used in the `tbl` command

Option	Description
`center`	It centres the table. By default, the table is left justified.
`expand`	It expands the table to full page width.
`box`	It encloses the table in a box.
`double box`	It encloses the table in a double box.
`allbox`	It encloses each item of the table in a box.
`tab(x)`	It separates the items in the input data by the specified character 'x' instead of a tab.
`linesize(n)`	It sets the lines to *n* point size.

Formats used with `tbl`

The formats help in laying out the individual columns and rows of the table. Each line contains a key letter for each column of the table. The column entries should be separated by spaces, and the format section should end with a period. Each line of the format corresponds to one line of the table. The key letters used in the line are given in Table 13.10.

Table 13.10 Brief description of the key letters used in laying columns and rows in the `tbl` command

Keys	Description
c,C	It centres data within the column.
r,R	It right justifies data within the column.
l,L	It left justifies data within the column.
n,N	It aligns numerical data in the column, i.e., hundredth value will appear below the hundred's place, tenth value will appear below the ten's place, unit value will appear below the ones's place, and so on.
s,S	It horizontally spans the previous column data into the current column.
a,A	It aligns text data in the column.
^	It vertically spans data from the previous row into the current row.
_,-	It replaces the current data with a horizontal line.
=	It replaces the current data with a double horizontal line.
|	It displays a vertical bar. It can be used to display a line at the edge of the table.
||	It displays a double vertical bar. It can be used to display a double line at the edge of the table.

The key letters that are used to lay columns and rows in the `tbl` command are followed by key specifiers. The list of key specifiers is given in Table 13.11.

Table 13.11 Brief description of the key specifiers used after key letters while laying columns and rows in the `tbl` command

Key specifiers	Description
b	It makes the data bold.
i	It makes the data italic.
fx	It applies the font x.
p n	It changes the point size to *n* units.
v n	It sets the vertical line spacing to *n* points.
t	It begins or pushes the vertically spanned data to the top row of range.
e	It ensures that all columns are of equal width.
w(n)	It sets a minimum column width to *n* size, where *n* can be in any of the `troff` units. If no unit is given, en units are used.
n	It sets the amount of separation (in ens) between columns. The default separation is 3 en.

While writing the code for the `tbl` file, we should consider the following points:

1. Long commands can be continued onto the next line by placing backlash (\) as the last character on the line.

2. If a line consists of '_' or '=', a single or double horizontal line will be drawn across the full width of the table.

3. If the data consists of only '\$_' or '\$=', a single or double horizontal line will be drawn across the full width of the column.

4. If the data consists of only '_' or '\=', a single or double line will be drawn equal to the field width.

5. A data item consisting of only '\Rx' fills the column width by repeating the character 'x'.

6. A long block of text can be treated as a single table entry if it begins with 'tab T {'and ends with 'T} tab'.

13.3.2 eqn

eqn is a preprocessor that is used for typesetting mathematical equations for troff. It compiles descriptions of equations embedded within troff input files into commands that are understandable by troff. Thereafter, the output of eqn is processed with troff.

Syntax	eqn [-d xy] [-s n] [-p n] [-m n] [filename]

A brief description of the options used in the eqn command is given in Table 13.12.

Table 13.12   Brief description of options used in the eqn command

Option	Description
-d xy	It uses x and y as delimiters for the left and right end, respectively, of the input line.
-p n	It reduces the size of superscripts and subscripts by *n* points. The default reduction in size is of 3 points. The subscripts and superscripts are 70% of the size of the surrounding text.
-s n	It reduces the point size by *n* points.
-m n	It sets the minimum point size to *n*. The eqn will not reduce the size of subscripts or superscripts to a size smaller than *n*.
filename	It represents the troff input file. If the filename is not provided or a hyphen (-) is used instead of the filename, the data will be read from the standard input.

Several macros are used in eqn. The macros refer to very small functions. They carry the keywords to write the desired mathematics. A macro may contain parameters in the form of $n, where n is between 1 and 9. The parameter(s) are replaced by the respective arguments that are passed while calling the macro. A macro is called by specifying its name (by which it is defined through the define command) followed by a left parenthesis, which, in turn, is followed by the arguments that we wish to pass to the macro. The arguments are separated by a comma (,). The argument list is followed by a right parenthesis.

The following macros are used in eqn:

.EQ   It starts typesetting mathematics.

.EN   It ends typesetting mathematics.

Besides macros, eqn also uses fonts. The eqn uses at least two fonts to set an equation, an italic font for letters and a roman font for other components of the equation. The italic keyword uses the current italic font, whereas the roman keyword uses the current roman font.

Keywords recognized by eqn

The following keywords, given in Table 13.13, are used in eqn.

Table 13.13 Brief description of the keywords used in the eqn command

Keyword	Description
back n	It moves backward horizontally by *n* units, where *n* is 1/100th of an em.
bold	It applies bold style.
ccol	It centre aligns a column of a matrix.
cpile	It makes a centrally aligned pile.
define	It creates a macro or a short name for a frequently used long text.
delim xy	It defines the characters to mark the left and right ends of an eqn equation. The delimiters can be turned off through delim off statement.
down n	It moves down *n* units, where *n* is 1/100th of an em.
fat	It widens the current font.
font x	It switches to the specified font.
from	It represents the lower limit in summations, integrals, etc.
fwd n	It moves forward horizontally by *n* units, where *n* is 1/100th of an em.
gfont x	It sets the specified global font for all equations.
gsize n	It sets the specified global size for all equations.
italic	It changes style to italic.
lcol	It left justifies a column of a matrix.
left	It creates big brackets, big braces, big bars, etc.
lineup	It lines up marks in equations on different lines.
lpile	It left justifies the elements of a pile.
mark	It remembers the horizontal position in an equation. It is used with lineup.
matrix	It creates a matrix.
over	It makes a fraction.
pile	It makes a vertical pile with elements centred above each other.
rcol	It right justifies a column of a matrix.
right	It creates big brackets, big braces, big bars, etc. It should have a matching left.
roman	It sets the following constant in roman.
rpile	It right justifies the elements of a pile.
size n	It changes the size of the font to *n* units.
sqrt	It takes the square root of the following equation.

(Contd)

Table 13.13 (*Contd*)

Keyword	Description
sub	It starts a subscript.
sup	It starts a superscript.
tdefine	It makes a definition for the eqn.
to	It represents the upper limit that is used in summations, integrals, etc.
up n	It moves up *n* units, where *n* represents 1/100th of an em.
~	It inserts an extra space into the output.
^	It inserts a space that is equal to one half of the size of the space applied by ~.
{ }	It is used to combine elements into a unit.

13.3.3 pic

pic compiles pictures embedded within troff input files into commands to make them understandable by these text-formatting tools.

> Syntax   pic [options] [filename]

Here, filename represents the input file that will be processed to produce a desired picture. If the filename is not provided or a hyphen (-) is supplied for the filename, the data will be read from the standard input.

pic macros

Each picture starts with a line beginning with the .PS macro and ends with a line beginning with the .PE macro. The .PS and .PE macros, respectively, are used to turn the preprocessor on and off. Table 13.14 describes the macros used in pic.

Table 13.14 Brief description of the macros used in the pic command

Macro	Description
.PS [height [width]]	It begins the pic description. The height and width are optional parameters that specify the desired height and width of the picture.
.PS < filename	Commands will be read from the specified filename and will be placed in the current statement.
.PE	It ends the pic description.

We can also define a scale for a pic description. By default, the scale is 1 to 1, that is, 1 unit is equal to 1" (by default). We use the following statement to declare a different scale:

scale = n

This statement declares that 1 unit is equal to one- nth of an inch.

For drawing basic objects, such as boxes, circles, ellipses, lines, arrows, arcs, spline curves, and text, via pic, there are appropriate commands for each. The command may be followed by the respective options that are explained in Table 13.15.

Table 13.15 Brief description of the commands used in the `pic` command

Command	Description
`arc [clk] [options] ["text"]`	It draws an arc that is 1/4th of a circle. By default, a counter-clockwise arc is drawn. The clk option is used for drawing a clockwise arc.
`arrow [options] ["text"]`	It draws an arrow.
`box [options] ["text"]`	It draws a box.
`circle [options] ["text"]`	It draws a circle.
`ellipse [options] ["text"]`	It draws an ellipse.
`line [options] ["text"]`	It draws a line.
`move [options] ["text"]`	It moves the position in the drawing.
`spline [options] ["text"]`	It draws a line with a slope.
`"text"`	It displays text centred at the current point.

Options

The commands for drawing objects such as arcs, arrows, boxes, etc., can use the options listed in Table 13.16.

Table 13.16 Brief description of the options used in the commands of `pic` command

Option	Description
`right [n]`	It moves towards the right by n units.
`left [n]`	It moves towards the left by n units.
`up [n]`	It moves upwards by n units.
`down [n]`	It moves downwards by n units. To move diagonally, two directions are used.
`rad n`	It creates the primitive (circle, arc, ellipse, etc.) of radius n units.
`diam n`	It creates the primitive (circle, arc, ellipse, etc.) of diameter n units.
`ht n`	It creates the primitive of height n units.
`wid n`	It creates the primitive of width n units. For an arrow, height and width represent the arrowhead size.
`same`	It creates the primitive using the same dimensions used in the recent matching primitive.
`at point`	It centres the primitive at the specified point.
`from point1 to point2`	It draws the primitive from `point1` to `point2`.
`->`	It directs the arrowhead forward.
`<-`	It directs the arrowhead backward.
`<->`	It directs the arrowhead in both directions.
`chop n m`	It chops off n units from the beginning and m units from the end of the primitive. Only one argument is used to chop equal units from both ends.
`dotted`	It draws the primitive using dotted lines.

(Contd)

Table 13.16 (*Contd*)

Option	Description
dashed	It draws the primitive using dashed lines.
invis	It draws the primitive using invisible lines. The default is a solid line.
then	It continues the given primitive in a new direction. It is used only with lines, splines, moves, and arrows.
Text	It displays the text. The text should be enclosed within quotes. By default, the text is always displayed at the centre within the object. The following options can be used to align the text:
	Ljust It left justifies the text. The text appears vertically centered.
	Rjust It right justifies the text. The text appears vertically centered.
	Above It displays the text above the centre of the object.
	Below It displays the text below the cenre of the object.

By default, each object begins at the point where the last object left off. If a sequence of commands is provided enclosed in curly braces ({ }), then pic returns to the position before the first brace.

Note: The points may be expressed as either absolute cartesian coordinates or in relation to the existing objects.

The objects can be referred to by their position shown in the following examples:

2nd circle: It refers to the second circle.

1st box: It refers to the first box.

3rd line: It refers to the third line.

last ellipse: It refers to the last ellipse.

The objects drawn can also be given unique names by declaring their names in initial caps as shown in the following example:

```
Circle1: circle rad 2 right from last arc.ne
```

This statement defines a circle by name Circle1 that is of radius 2 units and is drawn on the right of the last arc in its north-east direction. Valid corners of the object can be specified by any of the following constants shown in Table 13.17.

Table 13.17 Brief description of the corners of the objects created in the pic command

Corner	Represents	Corner	Represents
n	North	se	South-east
s	South	sw	South-west
e	East	t	Top (same as n)
w	West	b	Bottom (same as s)
ne	North-east	r	Right (same as e)
nw	North-west	l	Left (same as w)

Table 13.18 Brief description of the attributes of the objects created in the `pic` command

Attribute	Description
.x	It refers to the x-coordinate of the object.
.y	It refers to the y-coordinate of the object.
.ht	It refers to the height of the object.
.wid	It refers to the width of the object.
.rad	It refers to the radius of the object.

The objects' physical attributes are referred to in Table 13.18.

The following sections discuss loops, conditional statements, and other commands frequently used in `pic`.

13.3.4 Commands Used in `pic`

To compile pictures, we need to understand the different types of commands. Examples include the loops to repeat a set of statements, conditional statements to choose a set of statements out of two, reading content from specific files, and resetting variables. Let us start with loops.

Loops: Repeating sets of commands

The for loop is used for repeating a set of commands a specified number of times.

Syntax `for variable = expr1 to expr2 [by [*]expr3]`

```
do
{
body
}
```

The `variable` is initialized to `expr1`, and the loop will continue to execute until the value of the `variable` becomes more than `expr2`. After each execution of the loop, the value in `variable` is incremented by `expr3`. If `by` is not used, the default value by which `variable` is incremented is 1. If `expr3` is prefixed by *, the value of `expr3` is not added to the variable but is multiplied.

Conditional statement

The `if` statement is used for conditional branching, that is, depending on the value of the logical expression, one set of statements out of the two is chosen to be executed.

Syntax `if expr then`

```
        statement(s)
else
        statement(s)
```

Depending on the value of the logical expression, `expr`, either the `if` or `else` statement(s) will be executed.

Including contents from specified files

We can include content or code from another file at the current point in the file.

Syntax `copy "filename"`

This syntax will include the code or content of the entire filename at the current point in the file. The following syntax is used for including only the desired content from another file:

Syntax `copy ["filename"] thru`

```
{
    body
} [until "exit_cond"]
```

Or

`copy ["filename"] thru macro [until "exit_cond"]`

These syntaxes execute the body of the loop once for every line of the filename. If the filename is not given, lines are taken from the current input to the .PE macro. If an until clause is specified, lines will be read until the line with the first word exit_cond appears.

Example

```
.PS
copy thru % circle at ($1,$2) % until "END"
1 2
3 4
5 6
END
box
.PE
```

This is equivalent to the following.

```
.PS
circle at (1,2)
circle at (3,4)
circle at (5,6)
box
.PE
```

Resetting variables

The reset command is used to reset or re-initialize the given set of variables to their default values.

Syntax `reset variable1, variable2, ...`

This syntax resets pre-defined variables, variable1, variable2, ..., etc., to their default values. If no arguments are given, all pre-defined variables will be reset to their default values.

13.4 DEBUGGER TOOLS

When a program crashes, displays errors, or does not give the expected results, we say that it carries a bug. The process of removing the error and making the program yield the expected results is known as *debugging*. The traditional way of debugging is to display the intermediate results so as to isolate the bug statement or module. The echo command is inserted at several places in these program to display these intermediate results.

A debugger is a software that makes the job of debugging a program easier for us. It runs the program in the debugging mode instead of in the normal mode and does the following tasks:

1. It enables us to suspend execution of the program at desired places.
2. It executes various commands in the suspended mode in order to know the state of the intermediate results.
3. It displays the values of the variables as the program progresses.
4. It resumes execution of the program.

13.4.1 dbx

dbx is an interactive, command-line debugging tool. It can be used to ascertain the location of the bug in our program, the flow of execution, memory consumption by different parts of the program, etc.

Table 13.19 Brief description of the options used in the dbx command

Option	Description
-c cmd	It runs dbx command after initialization.
- pid	It debugs a currently running program by specifying its process ID.
-r	It executes the specified object_file and waits for the user's response from the keyboard.
-s file	It reads initialization commands from the start-up file dbxinit.

Syntax dbx [options] [object_file [core_file]]

A brief description of the options used in the dbx command is given in Table 13.19.

Examples

(a) $ dbx a.out core

This statement debugs the object file a.out and the core file. We can identify the location of error in our program or the reason for not getting the correct results along with the memory status by examining the core file.

(b) $ dbx - 1201

This statement debugs the running program whose process identifier (PID) is 1201.

In order to debug a program, first compile it with the -g flag and then invoke the debugger with the following syntax:

dbx object_filename

At the dbx prompt, execute the run command:

dbx> run

In order to pass arguments or redirect the input or output of our program, we use the following syntax:

dbx> run [arguments][>output_file][<input_file]

Here, output_file and input_file are meant for providing desired redirections to the dbx tool.

Setting breakpoints

Breakpoints are locations in the program at which we wish to suspend program execution. When the program is suspended at a breakpoint, we can examine the state of the program and the values of variables to see whether the program is running as expected up till the breakpoint. Several types of breakpoints can be set. The simplest type of breakpoint is a stop breakpoint. We can set this in a function or in any statement.

Example   `dbx> stop in calculate`

This statement places a breakpoint in the function `calculate`.

```
dbx> stop at "area.c":10
```

This statement places a breakpoint at line 10 in the source file `area.c`.

In order to continue execution of the program after it has stopped at a breakpoint, the `cont` command is used. In order to get a list of all current breakpoints, the `status` command is used. The `step` and `next` commands are used to step through the program one statement at a time. Both commands execute one statement of a program and then stop. In case of functions, the `step` command steps into the function, whereas the `next` command steps over the function. Another command, `step up`, continues execution until the current function returns control to the caller function.

Viewing call stacks

The call stack represents all the currently active functions. In a stack structure, the functions and their arguments are kept in the order in which they were called. A stack trace helps in knowing when a function was called and when it returned. In order to display a stack trace, the `where` command is used.

To see the intermediate results, we usually display the values of the variables or expressions at a breakpoint using the `print` command:

```
dbx> stop at "area.c":10
dbx> run
dbx> where
[1] printf(0x10938, 0x20a84, 0x0, 0x0, 0x0, 0x0), at 0xef763418
=>[2] printf(msg = 0x20a84 "welcome\n"), line 6 in "area.c"
[3] main(argc = 1, argv = 0xefffe93c), line 10 in "area.c"
dbx> print a
```

These statements place a breakpoint at line 10 in the source file `area.c`. The source file is run until the breakpoint, the stack trace is displayed at the breakpoint, and the value of the variable, *a*, is displayed at the breakpoint.

13.4.2 adb

`adb` is a general-purpose debugger. It enables us to view the core files resulting from aborted programs and to display output at the given addresses in order to isolate the statements resulting in an error. `adb` is invoked through the following syntax:

```
adb object_file corefile
```

Here, `object_file` is an executable Unix file, and `corefile` is a core image file.

Example   `$ adb a.out core`

A hyphen (-) is used to ignore a filename. The following statement is used to specify only the core image file.

`$ adb - core`

We can examine locations in both the files:

?: It is used to examine the contents of the `object_file`.

/: It is used to examine the `corefile`.

Syntax   `address [?][/] format`

adb maintains a current address called dot. Different formats are used to specify the type of data that we wish to display. The characters that represent the format of display are given in Table 13.20.

Table 13.20   Brief description of the characters representing the display format in the adb command

Character	Description
b	It represents a byte.
c	It represents a character.
o	It represents an octal.
d	It represents a decimal.
f	It represents a floating point.
i	It represents an instruction.
s	It represents a null-terminated character string.
a	It represents the value of a dot.
u	It represents an unsigned integer.
n	It represents a newline.
r	It represents a blank space.

Examples

(a) `0193?i`

It sets a dot (current address) to octal 193 and prints the instruction at that address.

(b) `.,5/b`

It prints five bytes starting at the dot.

(c) `.,2/d`

It prints two decimal numbers starting at the dot.

When used with the ? or / requests, the current address can be advanced further by typing a newline, and it can be decremented by typing ˆ.

13.4.3 sdb

The symbolic debugger (sdb) is used for examining core images of programs and for finding and removing bugs from them. When debugging a core image, sdb indicates the line(s) that are responsible for the error in the program, and enables us to access all the variables symbolically and check their status to isolate what went wrong.

Table 13.21   Brief description of the options used in the sdb command

Options	Description
-e	It ignores symbolic data.
-w	It makes the specified object_file and core_file writable.
-W	It suppresses warning messages for older files.

Syntax   `sdb [ options ] [ object_file [ core_file [ dir ]]]`

In order to ignore the core image file, a hyphen (-) is substituted at its place. A brief description of the options used in the sdb command is given in Table 13.21 and the commands that are available for sdb are given in Table 13.22.

Table 13.22   Brief description of the commands used in the `sdb` command

Command	Description
`t`	It displays the stack trace of the suspended program.
`T`	It displays the top line of the stack trace.
`variable/`	It displays the value of the specified variable.
`address/` and `address:?`	It displays content beginning at the specified address.
`line?`	It displays machine instruction corresponding to the given line.
`variable=`	It displays the address of the specified variable.
`variable!value`	It assigns value to the specified variable.
`x`	It displays the machine registers and the machine instructions.
`X`	It displays the current machine instruction.
`e filename`	It changes the current source file to the specified filename.
`/regular expression//` and `?regular expression??`	It searches for instances of the specified regular expression in source files.
`p`	It displays the current line.
`z`	It displays 10 lines starting at the current line. It also advances the current line by 10.
`w`	It displays 10 lines around the current line.
`number`	It sets the current line to the specified line number.
`count+`	It advances the current line by the specified count. It also displays the new current line.
`count-`	It takes the current line back by the specified count. It also displays the new current line.
`r arguments`	It runs the program with the given arguments.
`R`	It runs the program with no arguments.
`c`	It continues the execution of a stopped program.
`C`	It continues the execution of a stopped program and passes the signal to the program that stopped the program.
`line g`	It resumes execution of the stopped program at the specified line.
`s`	It runs the program for a single statement.
`S`	It runs the program for a single statement but does not stop within the called functions.
`i`	It runs the program for one machine instruction and ignores the signal that stopped the program.
`I`	It runs the program for one machine instruction and passes the signal to the program that stopped the program.
`k`	It kills the program that is being debugged.
`func(arg1,arg2,...)`	It calls the function with specified arguments.
`b`	It sets a breakpoint.
`B`	It displays a list of the current breakpoints.
`line d`	It deletes a breakpoint at the given line.
`D`	It deletes all breakpoints.
`l`	It displays the last executed statement.
`!command`	The specified command is interpreted by the shell.
`q`	It exits the sdb debugger.

For debugging, breakpoints can be inserted at various places in a program to temporarily suspend program execution and display the values of the variables and expressions to check whether the intermediate results are as expected. After inserting breakpoints, the debugging of the program is started using the sdb command. The program is executed normally and stops when it encounters the first breakpoint. At the breakpoint, the sdb commands may be used to display the trace of function calls and the values of variables. Thereafter, program execution may be continued from the point where it had stopped.

We can also run a program in a single step at a time, that is, sdb will execute the next line of the program and then stop. If an attempt is made to single-step through a function that has not been compiled with the -g option, execution proceeds until a statement in a function compiled with the -g option is reached.

In order to use sdb, we need to compile the source program with the -g option. This enables the compiler to generate additional information about the variables and statements of the compiled program. The sdb debugger can then be used to obtain a trace of the executed code, called functions, and to display the values of the variables when the program crashes.

The following commands are used for debugging a core image:

```
$ cc -g prog.c -o prog
prog
Bus error - core dumped
sdb prog
main:10:        printf("area is ,a);
    *
```

From this statement, we can see that the program prog.c is compiled with the -g option and then executed. An error occurs, causing a core dump. The sdb program is then invoked to examine the core dump and to understand the reason for the error. The output informs that the Bus error occurred in the main function at line 10 and also displays the statement that caused the error. The sdb program then prompts the user with an * to enter a command.

The sdb takes three arguments on the command line:

1. The first argument is the name of the executable file that is to be debugged. If this argument is not specified, the default executable file, a.out, is considered.
2. The second argument is the name of the core file. The default is core.
3. The third argument is the list of the colon-separated directories containing the source of the program that is being debugged. The default is the current working directory.

Printing stack traces

In order to display a list of the function calls that resulted in an error, we use the following t command:

```
*t
compute(a=5,b=10)       [prog.c:10]
calculate(i=16012)      [prog.c:50]
main(argc=1,argv=0x7fffff54,envp=0x7fffff5c)[prog.c:7]
```

This output indicates that the program was stopped within the compute function at line 10 in the file prog.c. The compute function was called with the arguments a=5 and b=10 from the calculate function at line 50. The calculate function was called from the main function at line 7. The main function is always called by a start-up routine with three arguments, which are often referred to as argc, argv, and envp.

In order to display any variable in the stopped program, we type its name followed by a slash. The following example displays the value of the variable *area*:

```
*area/
```

Through this statement, the value of this variable that exists in the current function is displayed. In order to display a variable *k* from another function, say, compute, we need to prefix the function name shown in the following command:

```
*compute:k/
```

Wild-card characters can be used for finding variables. Similarly, * can be used to match any number of characters, and ? can be used to match any single character. Let us consider the commands shown in Table 13.23.

Table 13.23 Brief description of the commands used in the sdb command

Command	Description
a/	It displays all variables beginning with the character 'a'.
*a??/	It displays variables that consist of three characters and which begin with 'a'.
**/	It displays all variables.
compute:a/	It displays all variables in the *compute* function that begin with the character 'a'.
**.*/	It displays all the variables of each function.

Setting and deleting breakpoints

Breakpoints can be set at any line in a program that is compiled with the -g option. The following methods are used for setting breakpoints:

*10b   It sets a breakpoint at line 10 in the current program.

*compute:b   It sets a breakpoint at line 1 of the compute function.

*b   It sets a breakpoint at the current line.

Here, character 'b' is used for placing breakpoints.

Ways of deleting breakpoints

For deleting breakpoints, character 'd' is used.

Examples

(a) *10d—It deletes the breakpoint at line 10 in the current program.
(b) *compute d—It deletes the breakpoint from the compute function.

In order to delete breakpoints in an interactive manner, character 'd' is used alone without any line number. Each breakpoint location will be displayed, and the user will be asked for confirmation. If the user enters y or d, the displayed breakpoint will be deleted. The B command prints a list of the current breakpoints, and the D command deletes all the breakpoints.

Running programs

The r command is used to run a program with the specified arguments.

Syntax   *r arguments

If no *arguments* are specified in this statement, the *arguments* from the last execution are used. In order to run a program with no arguments, the R command is used. Execution may be resumed at a specified line with the g command. For example, the following statement resumes the execution at line 10:

*10g

The s command is used to run the program for a single statement. The S command is similar to the s command, but it does not stop within the called functions, that is, the S command excludes called functions from debugging and debugs only the calling routines.

In order to test function(s), it can be called with different arguments. The following statement calls the compute function with the three arguments p, q, and r:

*compute(p,q,r)
*compute(p,q,r)/m

In both these statements, the compute function is called with the supplied arguments, and the value returned by it is displayed. The only difference between both these statements is that the second statement displays the value returned by the function in the *format m*, where *m* can be octal, hexadecimal, character, etc. When *format m* is not specified, the value returned is in the decimal format (default). The characters that decide the format of the result returned by the compute function are shown in Table 13.24.

In order to display the machine instructions associated with line 10 in the main function, the following command is used:

*main:10?

Absolute addresses may be specified instead of statement numbers by appending a colon (:) to them. Similarly, the following statement displays the contents of address 0x5038:

Table 13.24 Brief description of the characters that decide the format of the result of the compute function

Format character	Description
c	Character
d	Decimal
u	Unsigned decimal
o	Octal
x	Hexadecimal
f	32-bit single-precision floating point
g	64-bit double-precision floating point

*0x5038:?

In order to set a breakpoint at the given address, say 0x5038, the following command is given:

*0x5038:b

In order to exit sdb, the q command is used.

The ! command can be used to execute a given command. ! can also be used to assign values to the variables in the stopped program. The following example assigns a value to the given variable:

```
*variable!value
```

Besides placing a breakpoint, sdb also automatically performs a sequence of commands at a breakpoint and continues with its execution. The following syntax is used for doing so:

```
[line] b [command;command;...],
```

Here, a breakpoint is placed at the specified line. The command(s) are executed when the breakpoint is encountered, and execution continues. For example, the following statement places a breakpoint at statement 10, prints the stack trace and the value of the variable area:

```
*10b t;area/
```

13.5 strip: DISCARDING SYMBOLS FROM OBJECT FILES

The strip command discards all symbols from the specified object files(s).

Syntax
```
strip [-R sectionname |--remove-section=sectionname] [-s|--strip-all]
      [--strip-debug] [-K symbolname |--keep-symbol=symbolname] [-N symbolname
      |--strip-symbol=symbolname] [-o filename] [-p|--preserve-dates] [-w|--
      wildcard] object_filename
```

A brief description of the options used in the strip command is given in Table 13.25.

Table 13.25 Brief description of the options used in the strip command

Option	Description
-R section_name | --remove-section=section_name	It removes the specified section_name from the output file. This option can be used several times to remove more sections.
-s | --strip-all	It removes all symbols.
--strip-debug	It removes only debugging symbols.
-K symbol_name | --keep-symbol=symbol_name	It keeps only the specified symbol_name from the source file. This option can also be used as many times as needed if we want to keep more symbols.
-N symbol_name | --strip-symbol=symbol_name	It removes the specified symbol_name from the source file. This option can also be used more than once.
-o filename	It puts the stripped output in the specified filename, rather than replacing the original file.
-p | --preserve-dates	It preserves the access and modification dates of the file.
-w | --wildcard	It enables us to use wild-card characters in specifying symbol names. The characters ?, *, \, and [ ] can be used while specifying symbol names. The ! (negation symbol) can be used to reverse the meaning.
object_filename	It represents the object file from which we want to remove symbols.

13.6 VERSION-CONTROL SYSTEMS

The development of codes is an evolving process. A code is developed and tested; its output is compared with the expected results; modifications are made to meet the standards; again, the code is tested. The code goes through multiple cycles of modifications, debugging, running, and testing before it is delivered. The process of code evolution does not stop even when the code is delivered for production. It is considered as version 1.0; research and development continues to meet the growing demands of customers, to add new features, to scale applications, etc. In other words, the code has multiple versions, where the later version is an enhancement or an improved form of the existing version.

However, several problems creep up while evolving codes. Similarly, after having made some changes in the code, if it is found that the changes are imperfect, how will we revert to the last version, which was working perfectly well? Hence, we need a mechanism that keeps track of all the working versions and which will enable us to revert to the desired previous version in case the current changes to the code are not up to the mark.

In short, while evolving codes, the following points should be implemented:

1. Keep a track of the changes that have been made since the last known working version.
2. Keep a track of the bugs that appear during the evolution of codes so that they can be removed.
3. Keep a history of the code, which is well annotated with comments that explain why certain changes have been applied to the code to recall earlier changes.

13.6.1 Manual Version Control

In this method, the developer manually keeps track of the changes made to the code, that is, a snapshot of the code is periodically stored and a backup is taken. Comments are inserted at the place of changes, hence informing other developers on the same project (if any) about the modifications applied. The idea of keeping a track of all the changes is to get back to the last working version by undoing the changes applied. However, in spite of keeping a record of all modifications, it is still very time-consuming to revert to the last working version when the code crashes. Not only is it time-consuming (requiring patience) but also very error prone. Some new bugs may be introduced in the code.

Manual controlling of versions is not very popular, as developers may forget the order of changes, the purpose of making changes, and so on; hence, reverting to the last working version is very tedious and complicated. In order to avoid the problems faced in manual version control, automated version control is preferred.

13.6.2 Automated Version Control

In order to keep a track of the code versions automatically, the version-control system (VCS) is preferred. The VCS is a collection of programs that automatically keeps track of the modifications applied to the code, hence relieving us from taking snapshots of all the modifications applied. We indicate VCS to start the archiving of files, to describe their change histories.

Whenever we want to edit a file, we have to first assert an exclusive lock on it. When editing is done, we check the file, add changes to the archive, release the lock, and enter a comment specifying why a particular edit was carried out. All version-control systems enable us to maintain a tree of variant versions with tools for merging into the original version. If there are multiple variants of the code, these systems should be used very carefully, because if there is any bug error, merging back to the original version will be quite difficult.

A VCS keeps track of the basic operations applied to the code and includes tools that enable us to view the differences between the two versions, or to group a given set of versions of files as a named release that can be examined or reverted to at any time without losing the later changes. Maintaining different versions of an application is quite tedious, and VCS makes this task quite easy and efficient. In a way, VCS helps in increasing the efficiency of developers, as they do not have to worry about making changes or editing applications, because they can always go back to the earlier working version of the application.

Such systems also have certain drawbacks. For example, using a VCS involves an overhead to edit a file, that is, it requires us to add steps that help in reversion. In addition, a problem might occur in reverting to the original file if any of the files in the application is renamed. The following Unix tools are used for version control:

Source code control system

The first is the original source code control system (SCCS), which was developed by Bell Labs around 1980 and featured in System III Unix. The SCCS used a unified source-code management system that is still used in a few version-control systems.

Revision control system

Revision control system (RCS) was developed at Purdue University and is logically similar to SCCS. It is the most popular version-control system that is comparatively more user-friendly and has a better command interface. For categorization, we can group project releases by symbolic names through RCS.

Concurrent version system

Concurrent version system (CVS) is a sophisticated version-control system that requires more disk space when compared to SCCS and RCS. It is suitable for large software applications that are distributed across several development sites through the Internet. The versions of the applications can be stored in a repository that is located on a different host, enabling anybody with access rights to manage versions remotely.

■ SUMMARY ■

1. Yacc stands for yet another compiler–compiler.
2. Yacc is a compiler that reads the grammar specifications in the specified file and generates parsing tables and driver routines to the file `y.tab.c`.

3. Lex takes an input stream and generates programs that are used in a simple lexical analysis of the text.
4. m4 is a Unix macro processor.
5. m4 takes an m4 template as input and after having

expanded and processed the macros, it produces output on the standard output.

6. In order to create new macros in m4, the `define()` macro is used.

7. `troff` (pronounced 'tee-roff') is a text-formatting tool that formats the document to appear similar to a typeset document.

8. `nroff` (or new roff) is a text-formatting program that produces the output for terminal windows, line printers, and typewriter-like devices.

9. In `nroff`, the default vertical spacing is 1/6" and for `troff`, it is 12 points.

10. The output produced by `troff` is device independent and requires being post-processed before it can be accepted by most printers.

11. One point is 1/72th of an inch.

12. `tbl` is a preprocessor that formats tables for `nroff`/`troff`.

13. `tbl` compiles descriptions of tables embedded within `troff` input files into commands and escape sequences that `nroff`/`troff` can understand.

14. On using `tbl`, the commands between each `.TS`/`.TE` macro pair in the specified file are converted into a printable table.

15. In `tbl`, the column titles are represented by the `.TH` macro.

16. `eqn` is a preprocessor that is used for typesetting mathematical equations for `troff`.

17. `eqn` compiles descriptions of equations embedded within `troff` input files into commands understandable by `troff`. The output of `eqn` is processed with `troff`.

18. In `eqn`, the `.EQ` and `.EN` macros are used to start and end typesetting mathematics, respectively.

19. `eqn` uses two fonts to set an equation: an italic font for letters and a roman font for other components of the equation.

20. The `pic` compiles pictures embedded within `troff` input files into commands to make them understandable by these text-formatting tools.

21. In `pic`, each picture starts with a line beginning with the `.PS macro` and ends with a line beginning with the `.PE` macro.

22. The `.PS` and `.PE` macros, respectively, in `pic`, are used to turn the preprocessor on and off.

23. In `pic`, the scale by default is 1 to 1, that is, 1 unit is equal to 1".

24. The process of removing the error and enabling the program to yield expected results is known as debugging.

25. The debugger enables us to suspend the execution of the program at desired places.

26. A debugger enables us to execute various commands in the suspended mode to ascertain the state of the intermediate results in a program.

27. `dbx` is an interactive, command-line debugging tool.

28. Breakpoints are locations in the program at which we wish to suspend program execution.

29. The simplest type of breakpoint using the dbx debugger is a stop breakpoint.

30. In dbx, in order to continue execution of the program after it has stopped at a breakpoint, the `cont` command is used.

31. In order to get a list of all breakpoints while using the dbx debugger, the `status` command is used.

32. In order to step through the program one statement at a time in dbx, the `step` and `next` commands are used.

33. In case of functions, the `step` command in dbx steps into the function, whereas the `next` command steps over the function.

34. A stack trace helps in identifying when a function was called and when it returned.

35. In order to display a stack trace in dbx, the `where` command is used.

36. `adb` is a general-purpose debugger. It enables us to view the core files resulting from aborted programs and display output at the given addresses to isolate the statements that result in an error.

37. In `adb`, ? is used to examine the contents of `object_file`, and / (backslash) is used to examine the core file.

38. In `adb`, the character 'i' is used to print the instruction at an address.

39. The symbolic debugger (sdb) is used for examining core images of the programs and for finding and removing bugs from them.

40. The command `line?` in sdb displays machine instructions corresponding to the given line.

41. The command x in sdb displays the current machine instruction.

42. The command `line g` in sdb resumes execution of the stopped program at the specified line.

43. The command b in sdb sets a breakpoint.

44. The command `line d` in `sdb` deletes a breakpoint at a given line.
45. The command `D` in `sdb` deletes all breakpoints.
46. The command `q` exits from the `sdb` debugger.
47. The command `t` in `sdb` displays the stack trace of the suspended program.
48. The `strip` command discards all symbols from the specified object file(s).
49. The option -s and --strip-all in strip command removes all symbols.

■ EXERCISES ■

Objective-type Questions

State True or False

13.1 `tbl` is one of the `troff` preprocessors.
13.2 A table definition begins with a `.TE` macro.
13.3 The default code file in yacc is named `y.output`.
13.4 Yacc can generate parsing tables.
13.5 `m4` is a text-formatting tool.
13.6 In `nroff` the default vertical spacing is 1/6" and for `troff` it is 12 points.
13.7 The output produced by `troff` is device dependent, and there is no need to post-process it.
13.8 In `tbl`, the column titles are represented by the `.TE` macro.

13.9 `eqn` is a preprocessor that is used for typesetting mathematical equations for `troff`.
13.10 The output of eqn is processed with `troff`.
13.11 `troff` is a text-formatting tool that formats the document to appear similar to a typeset document.
13.12 `pic` compiles pictures embedded within `troff` input files.
13.13 In `pic`, the scale by default is 1 to 1, that is, 1 unit is equal to 1 foot.
13.14 The `strip` command enables us to suspend execution of the program at desired places.
13.15 dbx is an interactive, command-line debugging tool.

Fill in the Blanks

13.1 In eqn, the _____ and _____ macros are used to start and end typesetting mathematics, respectively.
13.2 The _____ is a Unix macro processor.
13.3 _____ is a preprocessor that formats tables for nroff/troff.
13.4 The `.PS` and `.PE` macros, respectively, in _____ are used to turn the preprocessor on and off.
13.5 The process of removing error and enabling a program to yield expected results is known as _____.
13.6 _____ are the locations in the program where we wish to suspend program execution.
13.7 The simplest type of breakpoint in _____ debugger is a stop breakpoint.
13.8 A _____ helps in identifying when a function was called and when it returned.

13.9 In adb, _____ is used to examine the contents of object_file, and _____ is used to examine the core file.
13.10 In order to get a list of all breakpoints while using the dbx debugger, the _____ command is used.
13.11 The command _____ in sdb deletes all breakpoints.
13.12 eqn uses two fonts to set an equation: _____ font for letters and a _____ font for other components of the equation.
13.13 _____ takes an input stream and generates programs that are used in a simple lexical analysis of the text.
13.14 In order to discard all symbols from the specified object file(s), _____ command is used.
13.15 The _____ command is used to exit from the sdb debugger.

Review Questions

13.1 Write short notes on the following language development tools:
(a) yacc (b)_lex (c) m4

13.2 What do you mean by a version-control system? Explain the ways by which version controlling is done.

13.3 Explain in detail how macros are created.

13.4 How does troff format a document to appear similar to a typeset document? Explain the options that can be used with troff.

13.5 What are the macros that are used in the tbl preprocessor to format a table? Explain the commands and keys that are used in tbl.

13.6 Give a list of all the keywords that can be used with the eqn preprocessor for typesetting mathematical equations.

■ ANSWERS TO OBJECTIVE-TYPE QUESTIONS ■

State True or False				Fill in the Blanks			
13.1	True	13.8	False	13.1	.EQ, .EN	13.8	stack trace
13.2	False	13.9	True	13.2	m4	13.9	?, /
13.3	False	13.10	True	13.3	tbl	13.10	status
13.4	True	13.11	True	13.4	pic	13.11	D
13.5	False	13.12	True	13.5	debugging	13.12	italic, roman
13.6	True	13.13	False	13.6	Breakpoints	13.13	lex
13.7	False	13.14	False	13.7	dbx	13.14	strip
		13.15	True			13.15	q

Interprocess Communication

After studying this chapter, the reader will be conversant with the following:

• Interprocess communication
• Pipes
• Messages
• Accessing, attaching, reading, writing, and detaching the shared memory segment
• Sockets—stream socket and datagram socket
• Input/Output (I/O) multiplexing
• Filters
• Semaphores—initializing, managing, and performing operations

14.1 INTERPROCESS COMMUNICATION

In multiprocessing and multitasking operating systems, several applications are executed in parallel and they share data among themselves. The mechanism used for communicating and sharing data between applications is known as interprocess communication (IPC).

Interprocess communication includes thread synchronization and data exchange between threads. If threads belong to the same process, they are executed in the same address space, that is, they can access global (static) data or heap directly, without the help of the operating system. However, if threads belong to different processes, they cannot access each other's address spaces without the help of the operating system.

There are two fundamentally different approaches in IPC:

1. Processes that reside on the same computer
2. Processes that reside on different computers

The first case is easier to implement, because processes can share memory in either the user space or the system space. In the second case, the computers do not share physical memory; they are connected via input/output (I/O) devices. Therefore, the processes residing in different computers cannot use the memory as a means of communication.

Most of this chapter is focused on IPC on a single computer system, including four general approaches:

1. Pipes   2. Messages   3. Sockets   4. Shared memory

14.1.1 Pipes

A pipe is a buffer that implements communication between two processes, one of which is considered a producer process, and the other a consumer process. It is a sort of FIFO queue in which the content placed by one process in the pipe is read or used by another process. When a producer process wishes to write into the pipe, depending on the available space in the pipe, either the write request is immediately executed or the process is blocked until space becomes available in the pipe. Similarly, if there are enough bytes in the pipe, the read request of the consumer process is either executed or blocked until enough data appears in the pipe. To enable only one process to access the pipe at a time, mutual exclusion is implemented by the operating system.

14.1.2 Messages

For establishing communication among processes, each process in the Unix operating system has an associated message queue. The messages are sent and received via the msgsnd and msgrcv system calls. The process checks for space in the message queue before sending the message. If there is not enough space, the process is blocked until enough space appears in the message queue. When the message queue has enough space, the sending process writes the message in the message queue along with its type. The receiving process observes the message type and retrieves the message from the message queue. If there is no message, the reader process is blocked until a message appears in the message queue.

14.1.3 Sockets

Sockets provide point-to-point, two-way communication between two processes. Processes communicate only between the sockets of the same type and with the ones that are in the same address domain. Each of the two communication processes needs to establish its own socket. While creating sockets, we need to remember two points—the socket type and the address domain. There are two widely used address domains.

Unix domain   In this address domain, the two processes that share a common file system communicate with each other. The address of a socket in this domain is a character string that acts as an entry into the file system.

Internet domain   In this address domain, the two processes running on any two hosts on the Internet communicate with each other. The address of a socket in this domain consists of an IP address of the host machine and a port number.

The following are the two widely used socket types:

Stream socket   The stream socket is a connection-oriented socket that provides a two-way reliable flow of data. Data is communicated as a continuous stream of characters that are transmitted in a sequence. Before beginning data transmission, a connection is formally established between the two processes. The stream socket type is represented by SOCK_STREAM constant. It uses transmission control protocol (TCP), which is a reliable stream-oriented protocol.

Datagram socket   The datagram socket is a message-oriented socket that supports a two-way flow of messages. The messages sent by a process may not be received in the same order by another process. The datagram socket type is represented by the SOCK_DGRAM constant. It uses Unix datagram protocol (UDP), which is unreliable and message oriented.

As mentioned, each of the two communication processes needs to establish its own socket. Assuming the two processes are client and server, let us understand the steps involved in establishing a socket on the client side as well as on the server side.

The steps involved in establishing a socket on the client side are as follows:

1. Create a socket with the socket() system call.
2. Connect the socket to the address of the server using the connect() system call.
3. Send and receive data using the read() and write() system calls.

The steps involved in establishing a socket on the server side are as follows:

1. Create a socket with the socket() system call.
2. Bind the socket to an address using the bind() system call. For a server socket on the Internet, an address consists of a port number on the host machine.
3. Listen for connections with the listen() system call.
4. Accept a connection with the accept() system call. This call typically blocks until a client connects with the server.
5. Send and receive data.

Creating sockets

In order to create a new socket in the specified domain and of the specified type, the socket() function is used.

Syntax   `int socket(int domain, int type, int protocol);`

A brief description of the parameters used in the socket() function is given in Table 14.1.

Table 14.1   Brief description of the parameters used in the socket() function

Parameter	Description
domain	It represents the address domain of the socket, i.e., whether the socket belongs to the Unix domain or the Internet domain. The Unix domain is used for the two processes that share a common file system, and is represented by the constant AF_UNIX. The Internet domain is used for any two hosts on the Internet, and is represented by the symbol constant AF_INET.
type	It represents the socket type. The socket can be a stream socket in which characters are read in a continuous stream (represented by the symbolic constant SOCK_STREAM) or a datagram socket in which data is transmitted in the form of a block of messages (represented by the symbolic constant SOCK_DGRAM).
protocol	It represents the protocol used by the socket, i.e., whether it uses the TCP or UDP protocol. The stream socket uses TCP protocol, and the datagram socket uses UDP protocol. If a protocol is not specified, the default protocol that supports the specified socket type is considered.

On its success, the `socket()` function call returns a socket handle or socket descriptor, which is then used for managing the socket.

Example   The following statement creates a new datagram socket for the Internet domain address.

```
sockhandle = socket(AF_INET, SOCK_DGRAM, 0);
if (sockhandle < 0)  perror("Error: Socket could not be created");
```

Binding sockets to addresses

In order to bind a socket to an address, the `bind()` function is used. This function is used only by the servers.

Syntax   `int bind(int s, const struct sockaddr *saddr, int saddrlen)`

A brief description of the parameters used in the `bind()` function is given in Table 14.2.

Table 14.2   Brief description of the parameters used in the `bind()` function

Parameter	Description
s	It represents the socket descriptor.
saddr	It represents the pointer to the socket data structure, `sockaddr`. `sockaddr` refers to the address to which the socket is to be bound. Besides `sockaddr`, `sockaddr_in` structure can also be used. `sockaddr_in` is a structure that contains an Internet address.
saddrlen	It represents the size of the socket address, `sockaddr`.

The following is a sample socket data structure, `sockaddr`:

```
struct sockaddr {
u_char sadd_len; /* total length of the socket address */
sa_family_t sadd_family; /* address family */
char sadd_data[20]; /* actual address bytes are stored here */
};
```

The socket data structure that is used for keeping the Internet address `sockaddr_in` may appear in the following manner:

```
struct sockaddr_in{
short   sin_family; /* must be AF_INET to represent internet domain address */
struct  in_addr sin_addr;
u_short sin_port;
char    sin_zero[8];
};
```

Listening for connections

For listening on the sockets for the connections, the `listen()` system call is used.

Syntax   `int listen(int s, int backlog);`

Here, s represents a stream socket descriptor and backlog represents the size of the backlog queue, that is, the number of incoming requests that are waiting for the connections. The maximum permissible size for this queue is five.

Accepting connections

The system call that is used for accepting socket connections is accept.

Syntax `int accept(int s, struct sockaddr *saddr, int *saddrlen);`

Table 14.3 Brief description of the parameters used in the accept() function

Parameter	Description
s	It represents the socket descriptor.
saddr	It represents the pointer to the socket data structure sockaddr. It refers to the address to which the socket is to be bound.
saddrlen	It represents the size of the address.

A brief description of the parameters used in the accept() function is given in Table 14.3.

On success, the accept() system call returns the socket descriptor that is valid for the particular connection and on failure, it returns −1.

Note: A server can have multiple SOCK_STREAM connections that are active at the same time.

Connecting to sockets

The system call that is used for connecting to the socket is connect().

Syntax `int connect(int s, const struct sockaddr *srvr, int saddrlen);`

Table 14.4 Brief description of the parameters used in the connect() function

Parameter	Description
s	It represents the stream socket descriptor.
srvr	It represents the pointer to the sockaddr data structure. It refers to the address to which the socket is to be bound.
saddrlen	It represents the size of the address.

A brief description of the parameters used in the connect() function is given in Table 14.4.

When successful, the connect() system call returns 0 and establishes a socket connection that is ready for performing reading and writing functions. On its failure, the system call returns −1.

14.1.4 Shared Memory

The shared memory is the fastest way of interprocess communication. In this mechanism, a block of virtual memory is shared among multiple processes. Processes read and write into the shared memory through their respective instructions.

Processes are executed in separate address spaces. A shared memory segment is a piece of memory that can be allocated and attached to an address space. The processes to which the memory segment is attached can access it and perform read and write operations on it. Shared memory is hence an efficient way of sharing data among programs. More than one process can access a single block of memory, and the changes made in the data by one process can be seen by another process. In order to avoid inconsistency and to maintain data integrity, a semaphore is used, which prevents more than one process from modifying the same block simultaneously. The functions used in implementing shared memory are as follows:

mmap() It implements the shared memory.

shmget() It accesses a shared memory segment.

shmctl() It assigns ownership of the shared memory segment to the specified user. It can also be used to change the permissions and other characteristics of the shared memory segment. This function can even be used to destroy the memory segment.

shmat() It attaches a shared segment to a process address space. Depending on the permissions, the attached process can access, read, and write to the attached segment.

shmdt() It detaches a shared segment from the process address space.

A shared memory segment is described by a control structure with a unique ID that points to an area of physical memory.

Accessing shared memory segments

The function shmget() is used to access a shared memory segment.

Table 14.5 Brief description of the parameters used in the shmget() function

Parameter	Description
key	It represents the access value associated with the semaphore ID.
size	It represents the size of the requested memory segment in bytes.
shmemflg	It represents the initial access permissions and creation control flags.

Syntax int shmget(key_t key, size_t size, int shmemflg);

A brief description of the parameters used in the shmget() function is given in Table 14.5.

On success, the shmget() function returns the shared memory segment ID.

Example The function call to access a 1K segment with 755 permissions is as follows:

```
key_t key;
int shmemid;
key = ftok("/home/bintu/a.txt", 'R');
shmemid = shmget(key, 1024, 0755 | IPC_CREAT);
```

Based on these statements, a block of 1K of the shared memory segment is created, and the ID of the memory segment is assigned to the variable shmemid.

The next step is to attach the created memory segment to the process address space. For this, we make use of the shmat() function.

Attaching segments to address space

In order to work with the shared memory segment, we need to attach it to a process address space. On attaching it to the process address space, we get a pointer to the shared memory segment, which can be used to access, read, and write to it. To attach a memory segment with a given ID to the process address space, the shmat() function is used.

Table 14.6 Brief description of the parameters used in the shmat() function

Parameter	Description
shmemid	It represents the shared memory ID.
shmaddrspc	It represents the address space. It is better to keep the value of this argument as 0 and to let the operating system find the address space.
shmemflg	It represents the type of access desired on the address space. For read-only access, the value of this flag is set to SHM_RDONLY; otherwise, a value of 0 is assigned to this parameter.

Syntax   void *shmat(int shmemid, void *shmaddrspc, int shmemflg);

A brief description of the parameters used in the shmat() function is given in Table 14.6.

On success, the shmat() function returns the pointer to the shared memory segment; otherwise, it returns −1.

Example   The following code is used to get a pointer to a shared memory segment.

```
key_t key;
int shmemid;
char *ptrmemseg;
key = ftok("/home/bintu/a.txt", 'R');
shmemid = shmget(key, 1024, 0755 | IPC_CREAT);
ptrmemseg = shmat(shmemid, (void *)0, 0);
if (ptrmemseg == (char *)(-1))
    perror("Error: Address space could not be attached to the memory segment");
```

Based on the aforementioned statements, the shared memory segment with ID shmemid is attached to a process address space. If the shmat() function is successful, we get a pointer to the shared memory segment and is assigned to the pointer ptrmemseg. In case of any error, the function shmat() returns a −1 value, and an error message is displayed.

Note: The shmat() function returns a void pointer and is cast to the char pointer before comparing it in the if statement.

Reading and writing into shared memory segments

After getting a pointer to the shared memory segment, it can be used not only to access the memory segment but also to read and write into it. For example, the following statement shows how to read the content from the shared memory segment that is indicated by the pointer ptrmemseg:

```
printf("Content in shared memory segment: %s\n", ptrmemseg);
```

We use the following statement to write into the shared memory segment:

```
printf("Enter your name ");
gets(ptrmemseg);
```

Based on the aforementioned statements, the data entered by the user will be written into the shared memory segment. Besides character data, data of the desired data type can be written into the memory segment by casting its pointer accordingly.

Detaching segments from address space

When the task of accessing the memory segment, and reading and writing data to the memory segment is complete, we can detach the data from the process address space by using the shmdt() call.

Syntax `int shmdt(void *shmaddrspc);`

Here, shmaddrspc represents the address space with which the memory segment was attached and the one that we got by calling the shmat() function. On success, the shmdt() function returns 0; otherwise, it returns −1.

Let us now understand the process of altering permissions of the memory segment.

Altering permissions of memory segments

In order to alter the permissions and other characteristics of the shared memory segment, the shmctl() function is used.

Table 14.7 Brief description of the parameters used in the shmctl() function

Parameter	Description
shmemid	It represents the ID of the shared memory segment.
cmd	It represents the command that we wish to apply to the memory segment.
	SHM_LOCK It locks the specified shared memory segment.
	SHM_UNLOCK It unlocks the shared memory segment.
	IPC_STAT It returns the status information contained in the control structure and places it in the buffer pointed to by buf.
	IPC_SET It sets the user ID, group ID, and access permissions.
	IPC_RMID It removes or destroys the shared memory segment.
buf	It represents a structure of the type struct shmid_ds.

Syntax `int shmctl(int shmemid, int cmd, struct shmemid_ds *buf);`

A brief description of the parameters used in the shmctl() function is given in Table 14.7.

In the following code snippet, we create a memory segment, attach it to the process address space, write some content into the memory segment, and finally, destroy it:

```
#include <sys/types.h>
#include <sys/ipc.h>
#include <sys/shm.h>
key_t key;
int shmemid;
char *ptrmemseg;
int cmd;
struct shmid_ds shmid_ds;
int returnflag;
key  =  ftok("/home/bintu/a.txt",
'R');
shmemid = shmget(key, 1024, 0755 |
IPC_CREAT);
```

```
ptrmemseg = shmat(shmemid, (void *)0, 0);
if (ptrmemseg == (char *)(-1))
    perror("Error: Address space could not be attached to the memory segment");
printf("Enter your name ");
gets(ptrmemseg);
cmd=IPC_RMID;
if ((returnflag = shmctl(shmemid, cmd, shmid_ds)) == -1) {
    perror("The shared memory segment could not be removed");
    exit(1);
    }
```

14.2 SYNCHRONIZATION

In a multithreaded environment, threads may need to share data between them and also perform various actions. These operations require a mechanism to synchronize the activity of the threads. These synchronization techniques are used to avoid race conditions and to wait for signals when resources are available. The following are the two popular synchronization primitives:

1. Mutexes
2. Semaphores

For synchronization, two lock operations are performed: lock and unlock.

Note: There is no mechanism in the kernel or the threads to enforce mutual exclusion or to prevent deadlock.

14.2.1 Mutual Exclusion Locks

A mutex is used to ensure that only one thread at a time can access the resource protected by the mutex. The thread that locks the mutex should be the one that also unlocks it. A thread attempts to acquire a mutex lock by executing the `mutex_enter` instruction. If a resource is already locked by another thread, the thread that is attempting to acquire the resource is blocked. A blocked thread keeps on polling the status of the lock and waiting for the resource to get unlocked.

The operations on a mutex lock are as follows:

`mutex_enter()` It acquires the lock.

`mutex_exit()` It releases the lock. This action results in unblocking a waiting thread.

`mutex_tryenter()` It acquires the lock if it is not already held.

The `mutex_tryenter()` operation is considered a better way of performing the mutual exclusion, as it avoids blocking the entire process.

14.2.2 Semaphores

The semaphore is an IPC method in Unix that was designed by E.W. Dijkstra in the 1960s. It is not only used to synchronize the processes but also to implement concurrent processing. It compels a process to wait when a block of data is being modified by another process. Only when the first process is complete with its job, the waiting process is allowed to proceed.

The semaphore is a programming structure that consists of an integer value. In order to implement process synchronization, the semaphore uses the *test and set* pattern.

The *test and set* pattern means that the semaphore permits processes to test and set the integer value in a single atomic operation. The process that tests the value of a semaphore and sets it to a different value ensures that no other process interferes with the operation.

In order to make it more clear, the integer value in the semaphore is initially set to 0. When a process proceeds with modifying the critical section (the region of data that two or more processes wish to access and modify simultaneously), it increments the value of the semaphore integer by 1. All the processes that wish to access the critical section wait until the integer value becomes 0. When the process that works with the critical section has completed its task, it decrements the value of the semaphore integer by 1 (making it 0). The value 0 of the semaphore informs the waiting process that it can now proceed with its processing (or modifying content) in the critical section.

Test and set here means that a process can either set the semaphore (increment its value) after checking it or wait until it clears (value of semaphore again becomes 0) and then set it. Hence, process synchronization is implemented through testing and setting the integer value of the semaphore in a single atomic operation. The process that tests the value of a semaphore and sets it to a different value (incrementing it by 1) ensures that no other process will be able to simultaneously modify the same content. The two types of operations possible on a semaphore are the wait operation and the signal operation.

The aforementioned discussion indicates that the two operations that are possible with the semaphore are as follows:

wait   It waits for the semaphore integer to become 0.

signal   It increments the semaphore integer to 1 and accesses the critical section.

In Unix, operations involving semaphores are achieved by the following three system calls:

semget()   It initializes the semaphore set.

semctl()   It manages features of semaphores and their permissions.

semop()   It performs operations on semaphores.

Initializing semaphores
Semaphores are initialized by using the `semget()` system call.

Syntax   `int semget(key_t key, int nsems, int semflg);`

A brief description of the parameters used in the `semget()` function is given in Table 14.8.

Table 14.8   Brief description of the parameters used in the `semget()` function

Parameter	Description
key	It represents the access value associated with the semaphore ID.
nsems	It represents the numbers of elements stored in a semaphore array. A value 0 is passed for this argument if the exact size of the array is unknown.
semflg	It represents the initial access permissions and creation of control flags.

When successful, the function returns the value of the semaphore ID, `semid`.

Managing semaphores
In order to manage the features of semaphores and their permissions, the `semctl()` system call is used.

Syntax   `int semctl(int semid, int semnum, int cmd, union semnum arg);`

A brief description of the parameters used in the `semctl()` function is given in Table 14.9.

Table 14.9 Brief description of the parameters used in the `semctl()` function

Parameter	Description
Semid	It represents the semaphore ID.
Semnum	It represents a number to designate the semaphore in an array of semaphores.
Cmd	It represents the command that we wish to execute on the selected semaphore. The list of valid commands is as follows:
	GETVAL It returns the value of a single semaphore.
	SETVAL It sets the value of a single semaphore.
	GETPID It returns the PID of the process that is operated on the semaphore.
	GETNCNT It returns the number of the processes that are waiting for the semaphore value to become 1.
	GETALL It returns the values for all the semaphores in a set.
	SETALL It sets the values for all the semaphores in a set.
	IPC_STAT It returns the status of the semaphore set.
	IPC_SET It sets the user ID, group ID, and permissions.
	IPC_RMID It removes the specified semaphore set.
semnum	It indicates an optional argument that represents a union on the requested operation. The semnum union may appear in the following manner:

```
union semnum
{
    int val;
    struct semid_ds *buf;
    ushort *array;
} smnm;
```

When successful, the `semctl()` system call executes the given command on the specified semaphore; otherwise, it returns −1.

Performing operations on semaphores

A Unix semaphore is an array of semaphores that is opened simultaneously and atomically by an array of operations specified in the `semop()` system call. The syntax of this function, which is used to obtain or release a semaphore, is as follows:

Syntax `int semop(int semid, struct sembuf *sops, size_t nsops);`

A brief description of the parameters used in the `semop()` function is given in Table 14.10.

Table 14.10 Brief description of the parameters used in the `semop()` function

Parameter	Description
Semid	It represents the semaphore ID returned by the `semget()` call.
sops	It is a pointer to an array of semaphore operation structures. Each semaphore operation structure, `sembuf`, stores the operation that is to be performed on semaphores:

```
struct sembuf
{
    ushort_t   sem_num;   /* semaphore number */
```

(Contd)

Table 14.10 *(Contd)*

Parameter	Description
| | ```
short        sem_op;    /* semaphore operation */
short        sem_flg;   /* operation flags */
};
``` |
	We can see that the structure includes the following:
	1. The semaphore number, sem_num
	2. A signed integer, sem_op, containing the operation that is to be performed on the semaphore
	3. The operation flags, sem_flg. The two most commonly used operation flags are IPC_NOWAIT and SEM_UNDO. The IPC_NOWAIT flag is used to immediately return the function without changing the semaphore value. The SEM_UNDO flag is used to undo the semaphore operation if the process exits prematurely.
nsops	It represents the length of the array and indicates the maximum number of operations that are allowed in a semop() system call. Its default value is 10.

14.3 INPUT/OUTPUT MULTIPLEXING

In order to understand I/O multiplexing, let us assume a socket server has several working threads in its thread pool that perform I/O processing on file descriptors. When a worker thread processes I/O from one file descriptor, it might be compelled to wait until that file descriptor completes its transaction, that is, the worker thread waits for the I/O to be completed from one file descriptor before initiating its processing. The waiting time of the worker thread goes waste, and it could have been utilized for performing the I/O processing of the client that has completed its I/O. The concept of waiting of the worker thread limits the number of concurrent connections that a socket server can handle.

In I/O multiplexing, the task of I/O processing can be overlapped with I/O completion. As a result, the worker thread need not wait for the I/O processing to be completed on a client; instead, it can perform I/O processing on other clients, and in the meanwhile, the current client completes its I/O. This utilization of the worker thread for performing I/O processing of multiple clients when any client gets busy in completing I/O not only increases the performance of the application but also reduces the requirement of the number of worker threads that are used to process I/O.

The system calls that are used to implement I/O multiplexing are select() and pselect(). Let us begin with the select() system call.

14.3.1 select() System Call

The select() system call enables a program to monitor multiple file descriptors (sockets), waiting until one or more of the file descriptors becomes ready for any I/O operation, such as reading or writing. The following is the syntax for using the select() system call.

Syntax
```
int select(int numfds, fd_set *readfds, fd_set *writefds, fd_set *errfds,
           struct timeval *timeout);
```

A brief description of the parameters used in the select() function is given in Table 14.11.
```

Table 14.11 Brief description of the parameters used in the select() function

Parameter	Description
numfds	It represents the number of file descriptors to be monitored. The file descriptors from zero through numfds-1 in the descriptor sets will be monitored.
readfds	The pointer that points to an object of type fd_set on input specifies the file descriptors to be checked for being ready to read, and on output indicates which file descriptors are ready to read.
writefds	The pointer that points to an object of type fd_set on input specifies the file descriptors to be checked for being ready to write, and on output indicates which file descriptors are ready to write.
errfds	The pointer that points to an object of type fd_set on input specifies the file descriptors to be checked for error conditions pending, and on output indicates which file descriptors have error conditions pending.
Timeout	It defines the time that the select() system call can take before timing out. If the timeout parameter is not a null pointer, it specifies a maximum interval to wait for the select() to be completed. If the specified time interval expires and no file descriptor is found to be ready, the systems call returns. If the timeout parameter is a null pointer, the call to select() will block indefinitely until at least one descriptor is ready for the desired operation.

We can see that all the three arguments, readfds, writefds, and errfds, are of type fd_set. In order to manipulate these three sets, we use the following macros shown in Table 14.12.

Table 14.12 Brief description of the macros used in the select() function

Macro	Description
FD_SET(int fd, fd_set *set);	It adds the given fd to the specified set.
FD_CLR(int fd, fd_set *set);	It removes the given fd from the specified set.
FD_ISSET(int fd, fd_set *set);	It returns true if the fd is in the specified set.
FD_ZERO(fd_set *set);	It clears all entries from the specified set.

The timeval struct is used to specify a time period during which the select() function will wait for a file descriptor to get ready for the operation. If none of the file descriptors is found ready in the specified time period, then, instead of waiting infinitely, the select() function will return to continue processing.

struct timeval consists of the following fields:

```
struct timeval {
    int tv_sec;    // seconds
    int tv_usec;   // microseconds
};
```

When successful, the select() system call modifies the objects pointed to by the readfds, writefds, and errfds arguments to indicate which file descriptors are ready for reading, ready for writing, or have an error condition pending, respectively, and returns the total number of ready descriptors in all the output sets. For each file descriptor less than numfds, the corresponding bit is set on successful completion if it was set on input, and the associated condition is true for that file descriptor.

If none of the selected descriptors is ready for the requested operation, the select() system call will block until at least one of the requested operations becomes ready, until the timeout occurs, or until interrupted by a signal.

14.3.2 pselect() System Call

Another system call that is similar to the `select()` system call and which helps in I/O multiplexing is the `pselect()` system call.

Syntax `int pselect(int numfds, fd_set *readfds, fd_set *writefds, fd_set *errfds, const struct timespec *timeout, const sigset_t *sigmask);`

The difference between the `select()` and `pselect()` system calls is that in the `select()` system call, the timeout period is given in seconds and microseconds in an argument of type `struct timeval`, whereas in the `pselect()` system call, the timeout period is given in seconds and nanoseconds in an argument of type `struct timespec`. Moreover, the `select()` system call does not have a `sigmask` argument.

If `sigmask` is not a null pointer, the `pselect()` call replaces the signal mask of the caller with the set of signals pointed to by `sigmask` before examining the descriptors, and will restore the signal mask of the calling thread before returning. The following example waits for 5.5 seconds for the user to press a key.

Example

```
#include <stdio.h>
#include <sys/time.h>
#include <sys/types.h>
#include <unistd.h>
void main(void)
{
    struct timeval tv;
    fd_set readfds;
    tv.tv_sec = 5;
    tv.tv_usec = 500000;
    FD_ZERO(&readfds);
    FD_SET(0, &readfds);
    select(1, &readfds, NULL, NULL, &tv);
    if (FD_ISSET(0, &readfds))
        printf("A key is pressed!\n");
    else
        printf("Time expired\n");
}
```

14.4 FILTERS

A filter in Unix refers to a small, specialized program that searches for desired information from the specified data on the basis of the supplied criteria and displays it in an arranged format.

Filters may read data from either the given file or the standard input. Similarly, the output of the filter can be sent either to the standard output or to a file to be saved for future reference or processing. The following are a few of the filters that are available in the Unix system: awk, cat, comm, cut, diff, grep, head, join, less, more, paste, sed, sort, spell, tail, tr, uniq, and wc.

> **Note:** Filters may be used anywhere in a pipeline.

14.4.1 more Filter

The more filter displays output on a terminal one screen at a time. On pressing spacebar, the next screen will be displayed. On pressing q, we exit out of this filter.

Syntax	more filename(s),

Here, filename represents one or more files that we wish to view screen by screen.

14.4.2 less Filter

The less filter displays the output on a terminal one screen at a time. Besides forward navigation, the less filter supports backward navigation as well. In addition, we can move a specified number of lines instead of the entire page. The less filter is faster, as it starts without reading the entire file into the memory.

Syntax	less filename(s),

Here, filename represents one or more files that we wish to see page-wise.

The commands that are used with the less filter are shown in Table 14.13.

Table 14.13 Brief description of the commands used with the less filter

Command	Description
n j	It navigates forward *n* number of lines.
n k	It navigates backward *n* number of lines.
G	It takes the cursor to the end of the file.
g	It takes the cursor to the start of the file.
q or ZZ	It exits the less filter.
/pattern	It searches for the given pattern in the forward direction. The following are examples:
	(a) /project: It searches for the pattern project in the text.
	(b) /\/project\/: It searches for the pattern /project/ in the text. The backslashes (\) are used as escapes.
?pattern	It searches for the given pattern in the backward direction. The following are examples:
	(a) ? project: It searches for the pattern project in the text in the backward direction.
	(b) ?/project/: It searches for the pattern project in the backward direction.
n	It searches for the next match of the specified pattern in the backward direction.
N	It searches for the next match of the specified pattern in the forward direction.

Note: We can also open multiple files with the less filter.

Example $ less file1 file2

This statement will open two files, file1 and file2.

:e **filename**   It opens the specified file while viewing the current file.

:n   It switches to the next file.

:p   It switches to the previous file.

14.4.3 tee Command

The tee command is used for reading data from an input and for writing to a standard output as well as to a file, that is, it performs both the tasks of storing as well as displaying the output of the specified command.

Syntax   tee [-a | --append][-i] [filenames]

Table 14.14   Brief description of the parameters used in the tee command

Parameter	Description
-a | --append	It appends to the specified files.
-i	It ignores interrupted signals.
filename	It represents one or more files in which the output of the command has to be stored.

A brief description of the parameters used in the tee command is given in Table 14.14.

Examples   The following statement displays the list of files and directories on the screen as well as saves them in the file listfiles.txt.

(a) $ ls | tee listfiles.txt

     By default, the tee command overwrites the file listfiles.txt. If there were any earlier contents in the file, they will be deleted before the list of files and directories is saved in it.

(b) In order to append content to a file, the -a option is used as shown in the following example.

     $ ls | tee -a listfiles.txt

     The earlier content in the file listfiles.txt will be preserved, and the list of files and directories will be appended to the file. We can also write the output to multiple files in the following manner, where the list of files and directories is stored in the three files, a.txt, b.txt, and c.txt:

(c) $ ls | tee a.txt b.txt c.txt

     We can also use the tee command to store the output of a command to a file and to redirect the same output as an input to another command.

(d) The following example counts the number of lines in the file letter.txt. The count of the lines will be displayed on the screen as well as saved to the file lines.txt.

     $ cat letter.txt | wc -l | tee lines.txt

     We can see that the output of the command is passed as an input to the wc command. The output from the wc command is then displayed on the screen as well as saved to the file lines.txt through the tee command.

■ SUMMARY ■

1. The mechanism that is used for communicating and sharing data between applications is known as interprocess communication (IPC). The IPC mechanisms used in Unix are shared memory, pipes, message queues, and sockets.

2. Interprocess communication (IPC) includes thread synchronization and data exchange between threads beyond the process boundaries.

3. A pipe is a buffer that implements communication between two processes, one of which is considered a producer process and the other, a consumer process. There are two types of pipes: named pipe and unnamed pipe.

4. For establishing communication among processes, each process in the Unix operating system has an associated message queue. The messages in the message queue are sent and received via the `msgsnd` and `msgrcv` system calls.

5. A filter in Unix refers to a small, specialized program that searches for desired information from the specified data on the basis of the supplied criteria and which displays it in an arranged format. A few of the filters in Unix systems are `awk`, `cat`, `comm`, `cut`, `diff`, `grep`, `head`, `join`, `less`, `more`, `paste`, `sed`, `sort`, `tail`, `tr`, `uniq`, and `wc`.

6. The `tee` command is used for reading data from an input and writing to a standard output as well as to a file.

7. By default, the `tee` command overwrites the file that sends the data. In order to append content to a file, the `-a` option is used.

8. We can also use the `tee` command to store the output of a command to a file and to redirect the same output as an input to another command.

9. The semaphore is an IPC method in Unix that was designed by E.W. Dijkstra in the 1960s. It is not only used to synchronize the processes but also to implement concurrent processing.

10. The semaphore compels a process to wait when a block of data is being modified by another process. It is a programming structure that consists of an integer value.

11. In order to implement process synchronization, the semaphore uses a test and set pattern.

12. A test and set pattern means that the semaphore permits processes to test and set the integer value in a single atomic operation.

13. The system call `semget()` is used to initialize the semaphore set. The system call `semctl()` is used to manage the features of semaphores and their permissions. The system call `semop()` is used to perform operations on semaphores.

14. The `GETVAL` command returns the value of a single semaphore.

15. The `IPC_STAT` command returns the status for the semaphore set.

16. The `GETNCNT` command returns the number of processes waiting for the semaphore value to become 1.

17. When successful, the `semctl()` system call executes the given command on the specified semaphore and otherwise returns –1.

18. The two most commonly used operation flags on semaphores are `IPC_NOWAIT` and `SEM_UNDO` flag. The `IPC_NOWAIT` flag is used to return the function immediately without changing the semaphore value, and the `SEM_UNDO` flag is used to undo the semaphore operation if the process exits prematurely.

19. Sockets provide point-to-point, two-way communication between two processes.

20. Processes communicate only between the sockets of the same type and with the ones that are in the same address domain.

21. There are two address domains for the sockets: Unix domain and Internet domain.

22. In the Unix address domain, the two processes that share a common file system communicate with each other.

23. In the Internet domain, the two processes running on any two hosts on the Internet communicate with each other.

24. The two most widely used socket types are stream and datagram sockets. The stream socket is a connection-oriented socket that provides a two-way, reliable flow of data; the datagram socket is a message-oriented socket, which supports a two-way flow of messages.

25. In order to create a new socket in the specified domain and of the specified type, the `socket()` function is used.

26. In order to bind an address to a socket, the `bind()` function is used.

27. The socket data structure sockaddr refers to the address to which the socket is to be bound.

28. Shared memory is the fastest way of interprocess communication. In the shared memory mechanism, a block of virtual memory is shared among multiple processes.

29. We can write data of any type into the memory segment by casting the pointer to the memory segment.

30. The `IPC_RMID` command removes or destroys the shared memory segment.

31. When a worker thread processes input/output (I/O) from one file descriptor, it might be compelled to wait until that file descriptor completes its transaction.

32. In I/O multiplexing, the task of I/O processing can be overlapped with I/O completion.

33. In I/O multiplexing, the worker thread need not wait for the I/O processing to be completed on a client; instead, it can perform I/O processing on other clients, and in the meanwhile, the current client completes its I/O.

34. The system calls that are used to implement I/O multiplexing are `select()` and `pselect()`.

35. The difference between the `select()` and `pselect()` system calls is that in the `select()` system call, the timeout period is given in seconds and microseconds in an argument of type `struct timeval`, whereas in the `pselect()` system call, the timeout period is given in seconds and nanoseconds in an argument of type `struct timespec`.

▪ EXERCISES ▪

Objective-type Questions

State True or False

14.1 The mechanism that is used for communicating and sharing data between applications is known as interprocess communication (IPC).

14.2 Pipes are only of one type—named pipe.

14.3 The more filter is used for sending more pages to the printer for printing.

14.4 The `n j` command in the `less` filter navigates backward *n* number of lines.

14.5 The `tee` command is used for reading data from an input and writing to a standard output as well as to a file.

14.6 The semaphore is an IPC method in Unix that was designed by E.W. Dijkstra.

14.7 The semaphore is a programming structure that consists of a character value.

14.8 In order to implement process synchronization, the semaphore uses a *test and set* pattern.

14.9 The system call `semop()` is used to initialize the semaphore set.

14.10 The `IPC_STAT` command returns the value of a single semaphore.

14.11 When successful, the `semctl()` system call returns −1.

14.12 Sockets provide point-to-point, two-way communication between two processes.

14.13 Processes can communicate between the sockets of different types.

14.14 In the Internet address domain, the two processes that share a common file system communicate with each other.

14.15 The stream socket is a connection-oriented socket that provides a two-way, reliable flow of data.

Fill in the Blanks

14.1 The IPC mechanisms that are used in Unix are _____, _____, _____, and _____.

14.2 A pipe is a buffer that implements communication between two processes, one of which is considered a _____ and the other, a _____.

14.3 The messages in the message queue are sent and received via _____ and _____ system calls.

14.4 Besides forward navigation, the _____ filter supports backward navigation as well.

14.5 In order to exit from the less filter, _____ or _____ commands are used.

14.6 In order to append content to a file, while using the `tee` command, _____ option is used.

14.7 The semaphore compels a process to _____ when a block of data is being modified by another process.

14.8 The _____ value in the semaphore is initially set to _____.

14.9 The system call _____ is used to manage the features of semaphores and their permissions.

14.10 The two most commonly used operation flags on semaphores are _____ and _____.

14.11 There are two address domains for the sockets: _____ domain and _____ domain.

14.12 The two most widely used socket types are _____ socket and _____ socket.

14.13 The _____ socket type is represented by the `SOCK_STREAM` constant.

14.14 The _____ socket type uses Unix datagram protocol (UDP), which is unreliable and is message oriented.

14.15 In order to create a new socket in the specified domain and of the specified type, _____ function is used.

Review Questions

14.1 Write short notes on the following filters:
(a) `more`   (b) `less`   (c) `tee`

14.2 What is a semaphore and what is its role in the Unix operating system?

14.3 Explain the different system calls along with the syntax that is used to initialize, manage, and perform operations on semaphores.

14.4 What do you mean by sockets? Explain the various types of sockets.

14.5 Explain the following system calls:
(a) `socket()`   (c) `listen()`
(b) `bind()`   (d) `connect()`

14.6 What is shared memory and what are the functions that are used in implementing it?

14.7 How does I/O multiplexing increase the performance of the Unix operating system? In addition, explain the system calls that are used in performing I/O multiplexing.

■ ANSWERS TO OBJECTIVE-TYPE QUESTIONS ■

State True or False

14.1	True
14.2	False
14.3	False
14.4	False
14.5	True
14.6	True
14.7	False
14.8	True
14.9	False
14.10	False
14.11	False
14.12	True
14.13	False
14.14	False
14.15	True

Fill in the Blanks

14.1	shared memory, pipes, message queues, sockets
14.2	producer process, consumer process
14.3	msgsnd, msgrcv
14.4	less
14.5	q, ZZ
14.6	-a
14.7	wait
14.8	integer, 0
14.9	semctl()
14.10	IPC_NOWAIT, SEM_UNDO
14.11	Unix, Internet
14.12	stream, datagram
14.13	stream
14.14	datagram
14.15	socket()

Unix System Administration and Networking

After studying this chapter, the reader will be conversant with the following:

- Unix booting procedure
- Mounting Unix file system
- Unmounting Unix file system
- Managing user accounts in Unix
- Unix network security
- Backup and restore

15.1 UNIX BOOTING PROCEDURE

The process of starting a computer is known as bootstrapping. During the bootstrapping process the computer runs a self test and loads a boot program into the memory from the boot device. The boot program loads the kernel and passes the control to the kernel, which, in turn, configures the devices, performs hardware status verification, detects new hardware, initializes the existing devices, and initiates the system processes. The kernel identifies the root, swaps and dumps devices, and does several tasks such as scheduling processes and managing physical memory, virtual memory, and hardware diagnostics. After having performed all these initial activities, the kernel creates another process that will run the init program as the process with PID 1. The process 0 is a part of the kernel itself and is basically a scheduler that decides which process to execute next. It also does the job of swapping, that is, moving in and out the memory pages. The init process runs as process 1 and always remains in the background when the system is running. It places the system in a single-user mode, which is basically a minimal system startup.

15.1.1 Single-user Mode

A single-user mode is designed for administrative and maintenance activities. In order to initiate the single-user mode, init forks to create a new process, which then executes the default shell, that is, Bourne shell as user *root*. We get a # prompt, indicating that we have root privileges and can carry out administrative tasks. We can set the date, check file systems, etc. In the single-user mode, no daemons are running, and the system is not connected to the network. The root partition is automatically mounted, and other file systems can be mounted manually as and when required.

15.1.2 Multi-user Mode

The init is the ancestor of all the subsequent Unix processes and the parent of user login shells. It prepares the system for users and verifies the integrity of the local file systems, beginning with the root and other essential file systems. The following tasks are performed by init:

1. Checking the integrity of the file systems
2. Mounting local disks
3. Starting daemons to enable printing, mail, logging, cron, and so on
4. Enabling user logins

These activities are specified and carried out by the system initialization scripts. After these tasks are performed, we can say that the Unix booting process is complete and the system is in the multi-user mode. As a result, users may log into the system.

15.2 MOUNTING UNIX FILE SYSTEM

A file system is a hierarchy of directories in the form of a tree-like structure with / (forward slash) as root and /usr, /tmp, /etc, /bin, etc., directories as its branches. The directories, in turn, have their own sub directories. In order to access a file or file system that is on a storage device, the storage device should be mounted on the accessible file system, that is, it should be mounted on a mount point. The mount point is usually an empty directory to which the additional file system (of the storage device) is mounted. The empty directory will become the root directory of the added file system.

> **Note:** The original contents of the directory that is used as a mount point becomes invisible and will not be accessible until the mounted file system is unmounted.

The file system of any device, regardless of whether it is a partition of a hard disk drive, a CDROM, a pen drive, etc., can be mounted on a mount point to access it. On mounting a CDROM on a directory, we make the file system on the CDROM appear in that directory.

> **Note:** Mounting and unmounting can be done only by the root user.

Syntax   mount {device/directory to be mounted} {mount directory} options

Here device/directory to be mounted refers to the file system that we want to mount; mount directory is the directory in the existing hierarchy in which the file system will be mounted; and options help in deciding the properties of the mounted file system.

The two frequently used mount options are as follows:

-r It mounts the file system read-only.

-w It mounts the file system read-write.

Examples

(a) # mount /dev/cdrom /mnt

(b) # mount /dev/hda3 /framework

The first example mounts cdrom on the /mnt directory. If we change directory to the /mnt directory (cd/mnt) and execute the ls command, we will be able to see the files that are on the cdrom. The second example mounts the hard disk partition hda3 on the directory /framework. Again, if we change the directory to /framework, we will be able to access the files of the hard disk patron.

15.3 UNMOUNTING UNIX FILE SYSTEM

Unmounting the file system means removing the mounted file system from the mounted directory. By unmounting the file system, it will become inaccessible. Unmounting is performed through the umount command.

Syntax   umount {file system to unmounted} {mount directory} {options}

The frequently used options are as follows:

-a   It unmounts all the mounted file systems.

-f   It forcibly unmounts the file system.

Forcibly unmounting a file system is not recommended, as it may corrupt data on the file system.

Examples

(a) # umount /dev/cdrom /mnt

(b) # umount /dev/hda3 /framework

The first example unmounts cdrom from the mount directory /mnt. Similarly, the second example unmounts the hard disk partition hda3 from the mount directory /framework.

We can configure our Unix system to automatically mount the storage devices on insertion. However, this may cause security problems and should not be applied in networked systems.

15.4 MANAGING USER ACCOUNTS

In this section, we will learn to create user accounts, change their passwords, and modify and delete accounts. Let us begin with the creation of user accounts.

15.4.1 Creating User Accounts

We use the useradd command to create a new user account. While creating a new user account, we can specify its home directory, group name, shell, and username.

Syntax   useradd -d homedirectory -g groupname -s shell userid

The terms of the syntax represent the following:

-d homedirectory   It refers to the home directory for the new account.

-g groupname   It refers to the group name or ID (GID) to which the new user will belong.

-s shell   It refers to the default shell for the new account.

userid   It refers to the unique user ID (UID) of the new user.

Examples

(a) `# useradd -d /home/john -g it -s /bin/sh johny123`

This command creates a user with user ID `johny123` belonging to the group `it`. The home directory created for the user is `/home/john`. The user will use Bourne shell by default.

All user IDs should be unique. If we try to create a user with an existing user ID, we will get an error saying the user already exists.

Note: The group name should already exist before its use in the earlier command.

(b) `# useradd -u 200 -g bank -c "Microchip" -d /home/mce -s /bin/ksh -m mce`

This command creates the user `mce` with a UID of 200 and the group name `bank`. The home directory is `/home/mce`, and the user will use the Korn shell. The `-m` option ensures that the home directory is created if it does not already exist, and it copies a sample, `.profile` and `.kshrc` to the user's home directory. It also creates the following line in the `/etc/passwd` file:

`mce:x:200:100:Microchip:/home/mce:/bin/ksh`

The first field `mce` is the username. The second field(`x`) no longer stores the password encryption here. The third (`200`) and fourth (`100`) fields store the UID and ID, respectively. The fifth field (`Microchip`) is used to store details of the user, for example, name and address. The sixth field (`/home/mce`) shows the home directory, and the last field (`/bin/ksh`) determines that user's shell.

We have to set the new user's password. This is easily done with the command `passwd mce`. After this, the user `mce` account is ready to use.

All user information except the password encryption is now stored in `/etc/passwd`. The encryption, that is, the encrypted password is stored in `/etc/shadow`. This control file is used by passwd to confirm the authenticity of the user's password.

Note: The last field in `/etc/passwd` is actually the command that has to be executed when a user logs in.

(c) The following example adds a user with user ID 250, the group ID 100, and the name as manish.

`useradd -u 250 -g 100 manish`

Once an account is created, we can set its password using the `passwd` command. The following syntax is used for changing the password of a given user:

Syntax   `passwd userid`

This command will prompt us to enter the password of the specified user ID.

Example
```
# passwd john
Changing password for user john.
New UNIX password:
Retype new UNIX password:
passwd: all authentication tokens updated successfully.
```

Note: The two passwords entered should be exactly the same so that the password of the user can be set successfully.

15.4.2 Modifying User Accounts

We use the usermod command to modify the user account. Through this command, we can change the user ID, home directory, shell, and group name.

Syntax
```
usermod -d homedirectory -g groupname  -s shell -l userid
```

The syntax can be explained as follows:

homedirectory   It refers to the new home directory that we want to assign to the account.

groupname   It refers to the new group name to which we want the account to belong.

shell   It refers to the new shell that we want to assign to the account.

userid   It refers to the new user ID that we want to assign to the user.

-l   The argument enables us to change the userid.

Examples

(a) To change the user ID from johny123 to johny777 and to change its home directory from /home/john to /home/johny, we will give the following command.

```
# usermod -d /home/johny -l johny123 johny777
```

(b) The following command line sets the C shell as the login shell for the user johny123.

```
# usermod -s /bin/csh johny123
```

15.4.3 Deleting User Accounts

We use the userdel command to delete an existing user account:

Syntax
```
userdel [-r] userid
```

Here, the -r option is used for deleting a user's home directory.

Example   To remove the userid, johny777, we will give the following command.

```
$ userdel -r johny777
```

Here, the -r option is used to remove the user's home directory as well.

15.4.4 Creating Groups

Groups help in categorizing user accounts, and also serve as a convenient way of assigning specific permission to a collection of people with similar interests. We use the `groupadd` command to create a new group account:

Syntax   `groupadd [-g groupid] [-o] [-f] groupname`

The syntax can be explained as follows:

groupid   It is the numerical value representing the group's ID. The -g option will create a group with some other ID if the specified groupid already exists.

-o   It indicates to add the group with a non-unique groupid.

-f   It indicates to cancel the command if a group with the specified groupid already exists.

groupname   It is the name of the new group.

Examples

(a) `$ groupadd -g 21 it`

(b) `$ groupadd  experts`

The first example will create a group with name `it` and group ID as `21`. The second example will create a group by name `experts`. Unix will automatically assign it a unique group ID.

15.4.5 Modifying Groups

We use the `groupmod` command to modify a group. Through this command, we can change the group name as well as the group id.

Syntax   `$ groupmod [-n] [-g] newgroupname oldgroupname`

Here, the -n option is used for changing the group name, whereas the -g option is used for changing the groupid.

Examples

(a) `$ groupmod -n programmers professionals`
   This example changes the name of the group from programmers to professionals.

(b) `$ groupmod -g 58 professionals`
   This example will change the group ID of the group professionals to 58.

15.4.6 Deleting Groups

We use the `groupdel` command to delete an existing group.

Syntax   `groupdel groupname`

Example   `# groupdel professionals`

This command will delete the group `professionals`.

The user's account information is maintained in the following three files:

/etc/passwd It contains the user account and password information.

/etc/shadow It contains the encrypted password of the corresponding account.

/etc/group It contains the group information for each account.

15.5 NETWORKING TOOLS

Several utilities are used to communicate with remote users and to enable us to access remote Unix machines.

15.5.1 ping

The ping command is used for checking whether the remote host is responding or not. We can use this command for doing the following tasks:

1. Tracking networking problems
2. Determining the status of the remote hosts
3. Testing and managing networks

We send an echo request to the host to determine its status.

> Syntax $ ping host_name/ip-address

This command will display a response after every second. In order to cancel the command, we need to press Ctrl-c keys.

Example

```
$ ping google.com
PING google.com (74.125.67.100) 56(84) bytes of data.
64 bytes from 74.125.67.100: icmp_seq=1 ttl=54 time=39.4 ms
64 bytes from 74.125.67.100: icmp_seq=2 ttl=54 time=39.9 ms
64 bytes from 74.125.67.100: icmp_seq=3 ttl=54 time=39.3 ms
64 bytes from 74.125.67.100: icmp_seq=4 ttl=54 time=39.1 ms
64 bytes from 74.125.67.100: icmp_seq=5 ttl=54 time=38.8 ms
--- google.com ping statistics ---
22 packets transmitted, 22 received, 0% packet loss, time 10925ms
rtt min/avg/max/mdev = 27.891/27.334/30.527/0.429 ms
```

If a host does not exist, we get the following message: unknown host name.

```
$ ping example.com
ping: unknown host example.com
```

15.5.2 nslookup

nslookup maps the name servers to the IP addresses and vice versa. The default name server for a machine can be found in the /etc/resolv.conf file.

> Syntax nslookup <machine name>

Examples

(a) % nslookup   bmharwani.com
    Server: abc.example.com
    Address: 165.53.12.7
    Name: bintu.example.com
    Address: 165.53.142.3,

Here, the first two lines refer to the name and IP address of the queried name server, and the last two lines refer to the name and IP address of the machine.

We can also perform reverse lookup, that is, map the IP address to the name servers as shown in the following example:

(b) % nslookup 185.66.15.2
    Server: abc.example.com
    Address: 165.53.12.7
    Name: bintu.example.com
    Address: 165.53.142.3

In this example, we provide the IP address of the site and information related to the queried name server and that of the machine is displayed.

15.5.3 telnet

`telnet` is a utility that is used to connect to and work on a remote Unix machine. It enables users to log in and work on a remote computer. The client program for `telnet` is `telnet`, whereas its server program is `telnetd`.

Example $ telnet bmharwani.com

          Trying...

          Connected to bmharwani.com.
          Escape character is '^]'.
          login: bmharwani
          password:
          ****
          *   *
          *   *
          *   Welcome to bmharwani.com   *
          *   *
          *   *
          ****
          Last login: Mon Dec 10 10:30:15 IST 2012 on pts/1
          $ logout
          Connection closed.

Telnet can pose a greater security risk to a network. All the computers in a network can see the packets flowing into the network. These packets can be sniffed by any computer in the network; hence, username and password can be easily captured. Therefore, special measures such as using one-time passwords and encryption can be used to avoid packet sniffing.

Besides packet sniffing, another problem with telnet is that its session can be hijacked, that is, once a valid userid and password are entered, the session can be hijacked by a hacker, and any malicious command can be executed. Again, encryption needs to be implemented to avoid session hijacking.

15.5.4 arp

The arp utility displays and modifies the Internet-to-Ethernet address translation tables that are used by the address resolution protocol (ARP).

Syntax arp [-n] [-a] [-d hostname [pub]] [-s hostname ethernet_addr [temp] [blackhole | reject] [pub [only]]] [-S hostname ethernet_addr] [-f filename]

The arp command with no options displays the current ARP entry for the specified hostname, as shown in Table 15.1.

Table 15.1 Different options of arp and their description

Option	Description
-a	It displays all the current ARP entries.
-d hostname [pub]	It deletes an entry for the specified hostname. If the pub keyword is specified, only the 'published' ARP entry for the given hostname will be deleted. This option can be combined with the the -a option to delete all entries.
-n	It depicts network addresses as numbers. By default, arp displays the addresses symbolically.
-s hostname ethernet_addr [temp] [blackhole	reject] [pub [only]]	It creates an ARP entry for the specified hostname with the given Ethernet address ethernet_addr.
	temp The newly created ARP entry will be temporary in nature. If this option is not used, the entry will be permanent.
	pub The newly created ARP entry will be 'published', i.e., this system will act as an ARP server.
	only It creates a published (proxy only) entry—the entry that is created automatically if a routing table entry for the hostname already exists.
	reject It discards the traffic to the host, and the sender will be notified that the host is unreachable.
	blackhole It discards the traffic to the host but the sender is not notified.
-S hostname ethernet_addr	This is similar to the -s option with a difference that any existing ARP entry for this host will be deleted first.
-f filename	The information in the file is used for setting multiple entries in the ARP tables.

15.5.5 `netstat`

The `netstat` utility displays network connections, routing tables, and interface statistics.

The following command is used for displaying network connections:

```
% netstat -a | more
```

The following command is used for displaying routing tables:

```
% netstat -r
```

The following command is used for displaying interface statistics:

```
% netstat -i
```

15.5.6 `route`

The `route` utility shows as well as manipulates the IP routing table.

Showing the routing table:

```
% route
```

Tracing the route to the machine on the same subnet:

```
% traceroute bintuPC
```

Manipulating the routing table:

```
% route add -host bintuPC
```

Showing the updated routing table:

```
$ route
```

15.5.7 `ftp`

The term FTP stands for file transfer protocol and is used for uploading and downloading files from one computer to another. Through the `ftp` utility, we can do the following tasks:

1. Connect to a remote host either anonymously or through a valid userid and password
2. Navigate directories on the host for which we have access permissions
3. View files and their content
4. Download and upload files to the accessible directories on the remote host

For FTP, we need two programs: client FTP and server FTP. The client FTP program is `ftp`, and the server FTP program is `ftpd`. TCP port 21 is used for sending commands; port 20 is used for the data stream.

Syntax   `$ ftp host_name/ip-address`

This command will prompt us for the user ID and password. On logging in, we will be navigated to the directory where we can upload our data and even download to our local machine. In order to use anonymous FTP, `ftp` is entered as the username, and `email address` is entered as the password.

The commands that are used to perform FTP operations are given in Table 15.2.

Table 15.2 Commands used for performing FTP operations

Command	Description
put filename	It uploads filename from a local machine to the remote host.
get filename	It downloads filename from the remote host to a local machine.
mput file list	It uploads more than one file from a local machine to the remote host.
mget file list	It downloads more than one file from the remote host to a local machine.
prompt off	It turns off the prompts that are displayed while uploading or downloading movies using the mput or mget commands.
prompt on	It turns on prompt.
dir	It lists the files in the current directory of the remote host.
cd directory_name	It changes directory to the specified directory_name on the remote host.
lcd directory_name	It changes directory to the specified directory_name on the local machine.
quit	It logs out from the remote host.

Example

The following example shows a few commands.

```
$ ftp bintuharwani.com

Connected to bmharwani.com.
220 bmharwani.com FTP server (Ver 4.0 Thu Dec 2 20:35:10 IST 2012)
Name (bmharwani.com:bmharwani): bmharwani
325 Password required for bmharwani.
Password:
121 User bmharwani logged in.

ftp> dir

200 PORT command successful.
150 Opening data connection for /bin/ls.
total 1357
drwxr-sr-x    2 bmharwani    group         1024 Mar 11 20:04 http
drwxr-sr-x    2 bmharwani    group         1536 Mar  3 18:07 https
148 Transfer complete.

ftp> cd http

103 CWD command successful.

ftp> put index.html

200 PORT command successful.
150 Opening data connection for index.html (3021 bytes).
226 Transfer complete.

ftp> quit

103 Goodbye.
```

15.5.8 Trivial File Transfer Protocol

The trivial file transfer protocol (TFTP) is a UDP-based file-transfer program. Again, we can use it to download and upload programs to the remote server, but this time with no security. The TFTP is configured to transmit a set of files from our computer, and they will be transmitted to any user who demands them. The TFTP has no security, whereas `tftpd`, the *TFTP daemon*, is usually restricted so that it can transfer files only to or from a certain directory.

```
% tftp localhost
tftp> get /http/products.html
% tftp> quit
```

15.5.9 finger

The `finger` program can be used to display detailed information, that is, username, full name, location, login time, and office telephone number of every user currently logged in to a system. This command can be used to find users on a local machine as well as on a remote machine.

```
% finger @bmharwani.com
```

This statement will show all the people logged on to the server `bmharwani.com`.

In order to look at the information of a particular user, we can specify its name on a given server in the following manner:

```
% finger ravi@bmharwani.com
```

Through the `finger` program, anybody can get the personal information of any user on a server. No personal information should be kept in the user's account information. For safety purpose, the finger is usually disabled on the server. In order to disable the finger program, it is commented on in the file `/etc/inetd.conf`. This change will cause people who are trying to finger your site to receive a `Connection refused` error.

15.5.10 rlogin

`rlogin` stands for remote login and is used to establish a remote connection between our terminal and the remote machine. Once logged in to the remote host, we can perform all the permissible tasks on the remote host. The various options available with this command are explained in Table 15.3, followed by the syntax.

Table 15.3 Different options available with the `rlogin` command

Option	Description
-8	It passes eight-bit data across the net instead of seven-bit data.
-e char	It enables us to specify a different escape character, which is '~' by default. The escape character can be defined either as a literal character or as an octal value in the form \nnn.
-l username	It is used to specify a different username for the remote host; otherwise, the local username is used at the remote host.
-E	It stops any character from being recognized as an escape character.
hostname	It represents the remote machine to which the connection has to established.

Syntax `rlogin [-8] [-e char ] [-l username][-E] hostname`

Each remote host has a file named `/etc/hosts.equiv`, which contains a list of trusted hostnames with which it shares usernames. Users with the same username on both the local and remote machine may `rlogin` from the machines listed in the remote machine's `/etc/hosts.equiv` file without supplying a password.

Users can also set the `.rhosts` file in their home directories. Each line in this file contains two names: a host name and a username that are separated by a space. An entry in a remote user's `.rhosts` file permits the user named `username` who is logged in to the hostname to log in to the remote machine without supplying a password. If the name of the local host is not found in the `/etc/hosts.equiv` file on the remote machine, and the local username and hostname are not found in the remote user's `.rhosts` file, the remote machine will prompt for a password. The following are a few more network-related commands:

systat   It provides status information about our computer to other computers on the network.

Ifconfig   It configures and displays interface configuration.

`% ifconfig -a`

traceroute   It prints the route that the packets take to the network host.

`% traceroute www.google.com`

15.5.11 Unix Network Security

Security is the ability of a system to prevent unauthorized access to information and resources of the system. For ensuring Unix security, we have to implement the following features:

Confidentiality   Ensuring that no unauthorized access to the system information is possible

Integrity   Ensuring that no information is altered or destroyed by unauthorized people

Authentication   Ensuring that no unauthorized person is able to log in to the system

We should adopt the following checklist for implementing security on our Unix system:

1. Implement password ageing
2. Eliminate unused accounts
3. Restrict guest accounts
4. Password-protect all relevant accounts and delete those accounts that are not needed any more
5. Set the default file protections for new files using umask to prevent read/write access to groups
6. Write-protect the root account's start-up files and home directory
7. Minimize the number of users with *super user* privileges

15.6 `mail` COMMAND

The `mail` command is a mail processing system that is used to send and receive mails. Table 15.4 explains the various options available with this command whose syntax is as follows.

Syntax `mail [-v][-s subject] [-c users_address] [-b users_address] [-f filename]`

Table 15.4 Different options available with the `mail` command

Option	Description
`-v`	It represents the verbose mode. The information related to e-mail delivery is displayed on the screen.
`-s subject`	It is used to specify the subject of the mail. If the subject consists of more than one word, it should be enclosed in quotes.
`-c users_address`	It is used to send carbon copies to the list of users. User IDs should be comma separated.
`-b users_address`	It is used to send blind carbon copies to the list of users.
`-f filename`	It reads the contents of our mail box or the specified filename for processing. On quitting the `mail` command, the undeleted messages are written back to the file.

15.6.1 Sending E-mails

The following steps are carried out to send mails:

1. The first step to send an e-mail message to a user is to give a command using the following command syntax:

   `mail userid`

   Here, `userid` is the login ID of the user to whom we wish to send a mail.

   Example `$ mail chirag`

   We can also send the same mail to several users by providing more than one user ID in the mail command separated by a space.

2. On the next line, type the subject of the message and press the Enter key.
3. Type in the mail message.
4. To send a message, press the Enter key after the last line of the message and press Ctrl-d.
5. To cancel the message, press Ctrl-c twice.

We can also specify the subject along with the user ID as shown in the following example.

`$ mail -s "Invitation to Birthday Party"  chirag`

This command is for sending a mail to the user with ID, `chirag` and with the subject, `Invitation to Birthday Party`. On the next line, we type in our message and press Ctrl-d to send the mail. To send the content from a file, use the following example.

`$ mail -s "Invitation to Birthday Party" chirag < partyinfo.txt`

Another way of mailing the content of a file is as follows.

```
$ cat partyinfo.txt | mail -s "Invitation to Birthday Party" chirag
```

Note: We can send mails to more than one user by providing comma-separated user IDs.

15.6.2 Reading Mails

In order to check incoming e-mail, simply type mail at the shell prompt.

Example $mail

If we have no mails, a message, 'No mail for login ID', is displayed where the login ID is replaced by the user ID. If there are any messages in our mail box, they are read and a line header for each message is displayed as shown in the following example.

```
>U   1 ravi    Tue Oct 10 07:15   5/220    Going on Tour
 N   2 naman   Tue Oct 9 10:43    10/358   Inventory report
```

This output indicates that there are two mails in our mailbox, the first one is sent by the user ravi, and the second one is sent by the user naman. The character used in the first column of the line header may be one of the following:

U   It indicates that the mail is unread.

N   It indicates that the mail is new.

Blank   It indicates that the mail is already read.

The second column in the line header indicates the message number followed by the mail address of the sender in the third column. The next column shows the date and time the message was sent, which is followed by the size of the message. The size is shown in the lines/characters format, that is, 5/220 indicates that the message size consists of five lines and 220 characters. The last column shows the subject of the mail. The first 25 characters of the subject will be displayed. The current message is marked by >. The mail system prompt displayed is & (*ampersand*) where we can give commands. In order to read any message, we just need to type the message number at the & (mail prompt) followed by pressing the Enter key. For example, in order to read the second message, we type 2 at the & prompt followed by the Enter key, and the message will be displayed on the screen.

```
& 2
The inventory report of the year 2012 till 2013 is ready
naman
&
```

Note: If a message is very long to accommodate on a single screen, press Space bar to display the next screen page.

We can see that the message of the designated number is displayed and after the message, the mail prompt & appears again so that we can give another mail command. We can also use '+' and '-' to move backward and forward, respectively, among the messages.

15.6.3 Sending Replies

In order to send a reply to a mail, type the R command on the mail prompt. We do not have to specify the receiver's mail ID or subject, as this header information will be automatically supplied by the mail command. However, we can optionally specify *Subject* if we want it to be different from the subject mentioned in the received mail. Next, we type our message and press Ctrl-d key to send it.

Note: The r command sends a reply to everyone who received the original message, not just the sender.

Example
```
& R
Subject: Regarding Inventory report
Please send me the report
Thanks  ...harwani
^d
&
```

Besides r and R, there are several other mail commands as well. Let us have a look.

15.6.4 Mail Commands

Table 15.5 gives the list of mail commands that we can run on the & prompt.

Table 15.5   List of mail commands

Command	Description
t [message_list]	It types or displays messages.
n	It displays the next message.
e [message_list]	It edits messages.
f [message_list]	It displays line headers of messages.
d [message_list]	It deletes messages.
s [message_list] filename	It appends messages to the specified filename.
u [message_list]	It undeletes the messages.
r [message_list]	It replies to the messages by the sender as well as to other recipients.
R [message_list]	It replies to the messages by the sender only.
m [user_list]	It mails the specified users. The user IDs should be comma separated.
q	It quits the mail command, deleting all the marked messages forever.
x	It quits the mail command and returns all our mail messages to our mailbox, without deleting any messages.
h	It prints the active message headers.
ch [directory]	It changes to the specified directory. If the directory is not specified, by default, we will be taken to the home directory.

Note: In the following commands, message_list refers to the integers or a range of integers representing the message numbers. If message_list is not specified, the last message is considered.

While composing messages, we can issue several commands that begin with the character '~' (tilde). The list of commands is as given in Table 15.6.

Table 15.6 List of mail commands for composing messages

Command	Description
~?	It displays the list of all tilde (~) commands.
~p	It lists the text of the message.
~s subject	It sets or changes the current subject to the specified subject.
~t email_nameslist	It adds the e-mail names in the specified email_nameslist to the current list of e-mail names.
~h	It lists and modifies the subject and e-mail name list.
~! cmd	It executes the specified Unix command cmd.
~r filename	It reads the specified filename into the message at the current position.
~v	It invokes the vi editor to edit the message text.
~q	It quits the mail command and saves the current message in the file named dead.letter in our home directory.

Note: After typing this command, press the Enter key to execute the command.

15.6.5 Saving Messages

In order to save a mail message in a separate file, give the s command at the mail & prompt with the following syntax:

```
& s message_number filename
```

Examples   The following examples save message number 3 in the file letters.txt.

(a) & s 3 letters.txt
(b) & s 3 projects/letters.txt

The first example indicates that if the path name is not provided with the filename, it will be created in the current directory.

15.6.6 Deleting Messages

In order to mark the e-mail messages for deleting, we give the d command at the & prompt with the following syntax:

```
& d [message_number] [message_number].....
```

If there is more than one message number, they are separated by spaces. If the d command is given without any message number, the current message (the message marked by the > in the message headers list) is marked for deletion. The messages are actually deleted when we quit from the mail command by typing q.

Examples

(a) & d 1

This command marks the first message for deletion.

(b) & d 1 5 6

This command marks the first, fifth, and sixth messages for deletion.

(c) & d 1-3

This command marks the first three messages for deletion.

(d) & d *

This command marks all the messages for deletion.

(e) & d $

This command marks the last message for deletion.

Note: Once we quit the mail command, all the messages that were marked for deletion are permanently deleted, and there is no way to recover deleted mails.

15.6.7 Undeleting Messages

If we have not yet quit the mail command, we can unmark the e-mail messages that are marked for deletion. In order to unmark the messages, we give the u command at the & prompt with the following syntax:

& u [message_number] [message_number]...

If we type u and no message number, the last message that was marked for deletion is unmarked. In order to unmark all the e-mail messages, the x command is used. The x command exits the mail command and returns all our mail messages to our mailbox.

15.6.8 Quitting Mail Command

We can quit the mail command by typing the q command.

15.7 DISTRIBUTED FILE SYSTEM

As the name suggests, the *distributed file system* keeps its files distributed on multiple servers. It not only stores the files but also manages them and keeps them integrated. Files are accessible to users by a filename without regard to the physical location of the file. A distributed file system maintains a directory of what files are kept on which server. This directory is invisible to the user. For the user, it appears as if the files are kept on a single server. Distributed file systems automatically replicate files to multiple servers (mirror servers) so that users can access files on servers which are closer to them, hence minimizing traffic. The following are the features of a distributed file system:

1. It provides a 'single sign in' facility, which means that once the user is logged in to a server, he/she does not have to be authenticated again when data is internally accessed from another server.
2. It supports encryption facility for secure transmission.

3. Since several clients might access a file simultaneously, a distributed file system should support concurrency control. By concurrency control mechanism, multiple users not only access the files simultaneously but also keep them integrated and consistent. The following locking mechanism is used for implementing concurrency control:

Read lock   It is a shareable lock that enables multiple clients to read the same file simultaneously but cannot modify it.

Write lock   It is an exclusive lock, that is, only one client can update the file at a time. The other client waits until the write lock is released.

15.7.1 Andrew File System

The Andrew file system (AFS) was first developed in Carnegie Mellon University in 1984. It is a distributed file system that was developed to work efficiently over a low-bandwidth college network. The files in this distributed system are kept in different AFS servers and are managed in such a way that they appear as if they are present on a local machine. To the user, the AFS appears as a big directory consisting of several subdirectories.

Features

The following are the features of AFS:

1. It has a global file system and implements the location-independent naming scheme. It has a single root node '/afs' from which all other AFS servers (or cells) are given subdirectories. An AFS cell is a collection of servers. A cell is accessed as /afs/ cell_name. This concept of directories and subdirectories makes the AFS a location-transparent file system. Users can use simple Unix commands to access files, create subdirectories, change to desired subdirectories, and so on. In short, the basic unit of storage in AFS is the volume, a logical unit corresponding to a directory in the file system.

2. It uses Kerberos authentication. Any authenticated user can log in to any machine through the valid userid and password. Moreover, the passwords are not transferred in the form of plain text in this authentication system, making it more secure.

3. For scalability and reliability, the data is replicated to different servers, and all act as a single logical server.

4. For quick file access, AFS uses a high disk caching technique. The files are cached locally on the clients. When a file is accessed by the user, the cache manager checks whether the file is present in the local disk cache. If it is, the cache manager confirms whether the file is up to date and has not yet been modified since its last access. If the file in the cache is found to be up to date, the cache manager fetches the file from the local disk cache rather than from the server. This procedure for accessing the files from the local disk cache highly reduces the network traffic.

5. In order to know whether the file in the local disk cache is up to date or is an older one, a mechanism known as a *callback mechanism* is used. When a file is accessed by a client, the file and a flag known as *callback promise* are sent to the client. The flag is kept on the client, and the accessed file is kept in the local disk cache. The callback promise is

marked as valid. If a client updates the file on the server, the server sends a callback to the cache manager, which marks the callback promise as cancelled. The cancelled callback promise is an indication to the cache manager that the file on the local disk cache of the client is no longer up to date, and if an application asks for the file, it needs to be fetched from the server. On fetching the file from the server, again the callback promise is marked as valid for the time during which it is not updated by any client.

For user access control, AFS provides three system-defined protection groups:

system:anyuser   Any client within the AFS cell can access a file under this directory.

system:authuser   It is the same as anyuser, but a client should have a token with the owner's cell. The token is provided through Kerberos authentication to the authenticated users.

system:administrators   These are the users with some administrator privileges.

AFS supports access control lists (ACLs). The ACL contains a list of groups and users authorized to this directory. It works at the directory level.

Drawbacks

AFS has the following drawbacks:

1. It does not support concurrent updates. If multiple clients simultaneously access and modify a file, the content of the client who saves the file last will be preserved; the remaining is lost.
2. It uses advisory file locking. In AFS, the complete file is locked (for maintaining consistency), and it does not support region locking, making it unsuitable for practical applications.
3. The AFS is complex to install and administer.

15.8 FIREWALLS

Firewalls are one of the best techniques used to protect Unix hosts from a hostile network. A firewall basically provides an isolation between the internal and external networks. It also helps in controlling the quantum and kind of traffic between the external and internal networks, hence saving our computers from the damage that an intruder may inflict on our content.

A firewall tries to restrict the flow of information between the organization's internal network and the Internet so that a malicious user cannot easily gain control to the computers in the organization's internal network. While setting up a firewall, we define a firewall policy, which is nothing but defining the kind of data that we feel is safe and can pass into our network and the kind of data that we feel is dangerous and wish to block. The following two basic strategies are used for defining a firewall policy:

Default permit   In this policy, we define the hosts and protocols that we wish to block, that is, only the conditions that result in the blocking of certain servers are mentioned in this policy. All other hosts and protocols that are not mentioned in this policy will pass through the firewall by default. A firewall with the *default permit* policy is easier to configure. All we need is to block out the protocols that are dangerous, as they may cause harm to our computer and content.

Default deny   In this policy, we define the specific hosts and protocols that we wish to pass through the firewall, that is, only the conditions that result in permitting certain servers through the firewall are mentioned in this policy. All other hosts and protocols that are not mentioned in this policy are denied by default. In this policy, we enable protocols as and when they are required while keeping all other protocols blocked by default.

15.8.1 Advantages

A firewall applies a layer of protection between our machines and malicious intruders.

We can block access to particular sites as well as to certain protocols on our network. We can implement filters to enable only safe packets to enter our network. We can also monitor communications between our internal and external networks, that is, we can maintain a log of the data transferred and the list of commands that are executed for communication between the two networks. The log can be used to check for any penetrations in our network. There are two types of firewalls:

Filtering firewalls   As the name suggests, the filtering firewall scans both types of packets: the ones that flow out of our network as well as the ones that arrive in our network. The type, source address, destination address, and port information contained in each packet is analysed and are only allowed to pass if the firewall rules permit them to do so.

Proxy servers   A proxy server acts as a security gate between the client and the actual server. It controls and monitors the traffic between the client and the actual server. For communication, the client machine does not connect directly to the server; instead, the request from the client is first passed to the proxy, which, in turn, passes the request to the server. The proxy server shields the client, that is, it blocks viruses and malicious intruders from accessing the client's system. The application proxy does not allow everybody to access the server; only authenticated users can access the server for communication.

15.8.2 Building Simple Firewalls

A simple firewall can be built from a single choke—a component that blocks certain specific types of packets while allowing others to flow through the network. The choke can be programmed to block packets from a specific IP source and also packets from services that are not being used. By ensuring that only the packets from certain known network servers flow into our network, it shields them from external threats. The concept of building a firewall through packet filtering is flexible, simple, and economical to implement.

15.9 BACKUP AND RESTORE

Several commands such as dd, cpio, and tar are used to backup the Unix system. These commands are explained in this section.

15.9.1 tar

tar stands for 'tape archive'. This command was originally used to backup data to tape. Nowadays, it is used for copying a large number of files into one larger file for the purpose of backup. When required, the original files can be extracted from the library.

15.9.2 cpio

cpio stands for 'copy input output'. This command copies the desired files from one device to another. Since the cpio command is not able to find files, it is usually used along with the find command.

15.9.3 dd

dd is a very low-level command that is used for copying data from one disk to another. The following command is used to backup a hard drive named /dev/hda to another hard drive named /dev/hdb:

```
dd if=/dev/hda of=/dev/hdb
```

15.10 SHUT DOWN AND RESTART

Shutting or restarting of the Unix system can be done by the administrator. Hence, one should log in as a root or a similarly privileged user before shutting down the system.

Syntax   shutdown [-h] [-r]

Here the -h option is used for a complete shutdown, and the -r option is used to restart the system. We can also use the halt and power off Unix command line utilities for the same purpose.

■ SUMMARY ■

1. The ping command is used for checking whether the remote host is responding or not. It displays a response from the specified server after every second. To cancel the command, Ctrl-c keys are pressed.
2. While pinging, if a host does not exist, the message 'unknown host name' is displayed.
3. The nslookup command maps the name servers to the IP addresses and vice versa.
4. The systat command provides status information about our computer to other computers on the network.
5. ifconfig configures and displays interface configuration.
6. The traceroute prints the route that the packets take to the network host.
7. telnet is a utility that is used to connect and work to a remote Unix machine.

8. The client program for the telnet is telnet, whereas its server program is telnetd.
9. Packet sniffing and session hijacking are the two major problems with telnet.
10. The arp utility displays and modifies the Internet-to-Ethernet address translation tables that is used by the address resolution protocol (ARP).
11. The netstat utility displays network connections, routing tables, and interface statistics.
12. The route utility displays as well as manipulates the IP routing table.
13. The term FTP stands for file transfer protocol. It is used for uploading and downloading files from one computer to another computer.
14. The mail command is a mail processing system that

is used to send and receive mail.

15. The command `mail userid` is used for sending an e-mail message to the user with the given user ID.

16. The process of starting a computer is known as bootstrapping.

17. A single-user mode is designed for administrative and maintenance activities.

18. A file system is a hierarchy of directories in the form of a tree-like structure with / as root.

19. In order to access a file system on a storage device, the storage device should be mounted on the accessible file system.

20. Unmounting the file system means removing the mounted file system from the mounted directory. Unmounting is performed through the `umount` command.

21. The `useradd` command is used to create a new user account.

22. The `passwd` command is used to change the password of a given user.

23. The `usermod` command is used to modify the user account. The `userdel` command is used to delete an existing user account.

24. The `groupadd` command is used to create a new group account.

25. The `groupmod` command is used to modify a group.

26. The `groupdel` command is used to delete an existing group.

27. The `finger` program displays detailed information about every user currently logged in to the system.

28. `rlogin` stands for remote login and is used to establish a remote connection between a terminal and a remote machine.

29. Distributed file systems keep their files distributed on multiple servers.

30. A distributed file system maintains a directory for keeping the information of the files kept on multiple servers.

31. Locking mechanism is used for implementing concurrency control in a distributed file system.

32. The Andrew file system (AFS) was developed to work efficiently over a low bandwidth college network. It has a global file system and implements the location-independent naming scheme.

33. Firewalls are one of the best techniques used to protect Unix hosts from a hostile network.

34. A firewall tries to restrict the flow of information between an organization's internal network and the Internet. There are two types of firewalls: filtering firewalls and proxy servers.

■ EXERCISES ■

Objective-type Questions

State True or False

15.1 The boot program loads the kernel into the memory.

15.2 The `init` process places the system in the multi-user mode.

15.3 In the single-user mode, all daemons are in the running mode.

15.4 All user IDs should be unique in the Unix system.

15.5 We cannot modify the home directory of the user once it is created.

15.6 A group should already exist before any user is assigned to that group.

15.7 Authentication is a process of ensuring that no unauthorized person is able to log in to a system.

15.8 The process 0 is a part of the kernel itself.

15.9 We cannot perform administrative and maintenance activities in the single-user mode.

15.10 `Mounting` and `unmounting` commands can be given by any user.

15.11 We cannot supply a password while creating a new user.

15.12 We can change the group ID of any group through the `groupmod` command.

Fill in the Blanks

15.1 The process of starting a computer is known as _____.

15.2 The PID of the init process is _____.

15.3 In order to create a user account, the _____ command is used.

15.4 The encrypted password of the user accounts is

placed in the _____ file.

15.5 In order to make a file system accessible, we _____ it on an empty directory.

15.6 The _____ command is used for deleting a group.

15.7 The _____ option is used with the `shutdown` command to restart the Unix system.

15.8 The default shell in a single-user mode is _____.

15.9 The option used in the `usermod` command to change the user ID is _____.

15.10 The option used in the `groupadd` command to create a group with a non-unique group ID is _____.

15.11 The command used to delete a user is _____.

15.12 The command used to add a new group is _____.

Programming Exercises

15.1 What actions do the following commands perform?
   (a) `$ mount /dev/cdrom /mnt`
   (b) `$ umount /dev/hda2 /prog`
   (c) `$ userdel johny123`
   (d) `$ groupadd -g 101 engineers`
   (e) `$ groupmod -g 122 engineers`
   (f) `$ shutdown -r`

15.2 Write the commands for doing the following tasks:
   (a) Mount the disk partition `hda3` on the directory `/workload`
   (b) Create a new user account with user the ID `kelly`, home directory as `/home/kelly`, Bourne shell, and groupname developers
   (c) Assign the password to the new user, `kelly`
   (d) Delete the group developers
   (e) Completely shut down the Unix system

Review Questions

15.1 Explain the following commands with examples:
   (a) `usermod`
   (b) `groupadd`
   (c) `umount`
   (d) `userdel`
   (e) `shutdown`

■ ANSWERS TO OBJECTIVE-TYPE QUESTIONS ■

State True or False

15.1	True
15.2	False
15.3	False
15.4	True
15.5	False
15.6	True
15.7	True
15.8	True
15.9	False
15.10	False
15.11	True
15.12	True

Fill in the Blanks

15.1	bootstrapping
15.2	1
15.3	useradd
15.4	/etc/shadow
15.5	mount
15.6	groupdel
15.7	-r
15.8	Bourne shell
15.9	-l
15.10	-o
15.11	userdel
15.12	groupadd

Index

Related Titles

Formal Languages and Automata Theory
9780198071068
Chander Kumar Nagpal,
Principal, Echelon Institute of Technology, Faridabad

Formal Languages and Automata Theory is designed to serve as a textbook for undergraduate and postgraduate students of engineering (computer science and information technology) and computer applications.

Key Features

- Provides a practical approach to the concepts by including a large number of solved examples
- Covers important concepts such as the Church–Turing thesis, Rice's theorem, and Cook's theorem

Computer Networks
9780198066774
Bhushan Trivedi,
Director, MCA Programme, GLS Institute of Computer Technology, Ahmedabad

Computer Networks is designed to serve as a textbook for undergraduate students of computer science engineering as well as those pursuing MCA and IT. Following the tried-and-tested layered approach, the book gives equal weightage to all the network layers and their protocols.

Key Features

- Explains the layered approach with emphasis on the TCP/IP model, Internet, and Ethernet technologies
- Includes several new topics such as Bluetooth, IPv6, QoS provided by WiMax, and the use of scalable OFDM in 802.16

Distributed Computing, 2/e
9780198093480
Sunita Mahajan, Principal, Institute of Computer Science, MET League of Colleges, Mumbai and **Seema Shah**, Acting Principal, Vidyalankar Institute of Technology, Mumbai

The second edition of *Distributed Computing* is specially designed for students of computer science engineering, information technology, and computer applications. The book provides a clear understanding of the computing aspects of distributed systems.

Key Features

- Presents concepts in diagrammatic and tabulated form for easy visualization wherever possible
- Contains several relevant case studies both inside the chapters and at the end of the book
- Includes API for Internet protocol in Java, a new chapter on formal model for simulation, and two new case studies on CORBA and Mach

Other Related Titles

9780195696561   Datta: *Software Engineering*: *Concepts and Applications*

9780195694840   Jain: *Software Engineering*: *Principles and Practices*

9780198079064   Senthil Kumar, Saravanan, Jeevananthan, and Shah: *Microprocessors and Interfacing*

9780198066477   Senthil Kumar, Saravanan, and Jeevananthan: *Microprocessors and Microcontrollers*

9780198070887   Pal: *Systems Programming*

9780198061847   Chauhan: *Software Testing*: *Principles and Practices*

9780195671544   Padhy: *Artificial Intelligence and Intelligent Systems*

9780198068914   Raj Kamal: *Mobile Computing, 2/e*